The Microsoft® Data Warehouse Toolkit

Second Edition

The Microsoft® Data Warehouse Toolkit

With SQL Server 2008 R2 and the Microsoft® Business Intelligence Toolset

Second Edition

Joy Mundy and
Warren Thornthwaite
with Ralph Kimball

Wiley Publishing, Inc.

The Microsoft® Data Warehouse Toolkit: With SQL Server 2008 R2
and the Microsoft® Business Intelligence Toolset, Second Edition

Published by
Wiley Publishing, Inc.
10475 Crosspoint Boulevard
Indianapolis, IN 46256
www.wiley.com

Copyright © 2011 by Joy Mundy and Warren Thornthwaite with Ralph Kimball
Published by Wiley Publishing, Inc., Indianapolis, Indiana

Published simultaneously in Canada

ISBN: 978-0-470-64038-8
ISBN: 978-1-118-06793-2 (ebk)
ISBN: 978-1-118-06795-6 (ebk)
ISBN: 978-1-118-06794-9 (ebk)

Manufactured in the United States of America

10 9 8 7 6 5 4 3 2

For general information on our other products and services please contact our Customer Care Department within the United States at (877) 762-2974, outside the United States at (317) 572-3993 or fax (317) 572-4002.

Wiley also publishes its books in a variety of electronic formats. Some content that appears in print may not be available in electronic books.

Library of Congress Control Number: 2011920894

About the Authors

Joy Mundy has focused on DW/BI systems since 1992 with stints at Stanford, WebTV, and Microsoft's SQL Server product development organization. Joy graduated from Tufts University with a BA in Economics, and from Stanford University with an MS in Engineering Economic Systems.

Warren Thornthwaite began his DW/BI career in 1980. After managing Metaphor's consulting organization, he worked for Stanford University and WebTV. Warren holds a BA in Communications Studies from the University of Michigan and an MBA from the University of Pennsylvania's Wharton School.

Ralph Kimball founded the Kimball Group. Since the mid 1980s, he has been the DW/BI industry's thought leader on the dimensional approach and has trained more than 10,000 IT professionals. Prior to working at Metaphor and founding Red Brick Systems, Ralph co-invented the Star workstation at Xerox's Palo Alto Research Center (PARC). Ralph has a Ph.D. in Electrical Engineering from Stanford University.

Credits

Executive Editor
Robert Elliott

Project Editors
Sara Shlaer
Ginny Munroe

Technical Editor
Ralph Kimball

Senior Production Editor
Debra Banninger

Copy Editor
Kim Cofer

Editorial Director
Robyn B. Siesky

Editorial Manager
Mary Beth Wakefield

Freelancer Editorial Manager
Rosemarie Graham

Marketing Manager
Ashley Zurcher

Production Manager
Tim Tate

**Vice President and
Executive Group Publisher**
Richard Swadley

**Vice President and
Executive Publisher**
Barry Pruett

Associate Publisher
Jim Minatel

Project Coordinator, Cover
Katie Crocker

Compositor
Craig Johnson,
Happenstance Type-O-Rama

Proofreader
Jen Larsen, Word One

Indexer
Robert Swanson

Cover Image
© Getty Images

Cover Designer
Ryan Sneed

Acknowledgments

First, we want to thank the thousands of you who have read the Kimball Group's *Toolkit* books, attended our courses, and engaged us in consulting projects. We always learn from you, and you've had a profound impact on our thinking and the business intelligence industry.

This book would not have been written without the assistance of many people on the SQL Server product development team. Dave Wickert reviewed the PowerPivot and SharePoint chapters and provided many excellent suggestions for improving the content. Bryan Smith was kind enough to read the chapters on Integration Services and Analysis Services, and those chapters are the better for his assistance. Carolyn Chau reviewed the Reporting Services chapter, Eric Hanson read the relational database chapter, Pej Javaheri commented on the SharePoint chapter, and Raman Iyer read the data mining chapter. Our sincere gratitude to all of them.

Other members of the SQL Server team provided significant assistance reviewing the SQL Server 2005 version of this book, and we were too embarrassed to impose on them a second time. These include Bill Baker, Stuart Ozer, Grant Dickinson, Donald Farmer, Siva Harinath, Jamie MacLennan, John Miller, Ashvini Sharma, Stephen Quinn, and Rob Zare.

Our colleagues at the Kimball Group were invaluable. Their encouragement kept us going while we were writing the book, and their reviews helped us polish and prune material. Ralph Kimball, of course, had a huge impact on the book, not just from his writing and thinking in the business intelligence arena but more directly by helping us improve the book's overall structure and flow.

Sara Shlaer, Ginny Munroe, and Bob Elliott, our editors at Wiley, have been very helpful and encouraging. It's been a pleasure to work with them.

To our life partners, thanks for being there when we needed you, for giving us the time we needed, and for occasionally reminding us that it was time to take a break. Tony Navarrete and Elizabeth Wright, the book wouldn't exist without you.

Contents at a Glance

Contents

Foreword

In the five years since the first edition was published, Microsoft has made impressive progress in building out its data warehousing and business intelligence tools suite. It is gratifying to those of us who work in this space to see the steady commitment that Microsoft has made to provide usable, professional quality tools. During these five years, Warren and Joy have consulted with dozens of clients, taught scores of classes, answered hundreds if not thousands of questions, had many "schema lunches" where the schema diagrams competed with the food, and have pounded on every module in Microsoft's DW/BI toolset. This current edition remains a unique reference, combining overall perspectives on what the tools do with accurate assessments of how well they do it. This book teaches judgment, not button clicks!

—Ralph Kimball

Introduction

The goal of this book is to guide the reader down the best path toward designing and building a successful business intelligence system and its underlying data warehouse databases using the Microsoft SQL Server product set.

The Data Warehouse and Business Intelligence System

Data warehousing and business intelligence are techniques to provide business people with the information and tools they need to make both operational and strategic business decisions. We'll break this down a bit so you can really understand the nature and magnitude of what you're about to take on.

First, your customers are the business people in the organization. Not all business people carry the same importance to you — you should be especially concerned with those who make strategic business decisions. One well-made business decision can translate to millions of dollars in many organizations. Your main customers are executives, managers, and analysts throughout the organization. The data warehouse and business intelligence (DW/BI) system is high impact and high profile.

Strategic also means important. These are decisions that can make or break the organization. Therefore, the DW/BI system is a high-risk endeavor. When strategic decisions are made, someone often wins or loses. The DW/BI system is a highly political effort.

Increasingly, the DW/BI system also supports operational decisions, especially where the decision maker needs to see historical data or integrated data from multiple sources. Many analytic applications have this operational focus.

Whether the decision making is strategic or operational, the DW/BI team needs to provide the information necessary to make decisions.

Any given decision will likely require a unique subset of information that generally cannot be predetermined. You'll need to build an information infrastructure that integrates data from across the organization, and potentially from outside the organization, and then cleans, aligns, and restructures the data to make it as flexible and usable as possible. Whereas most transaction system modules work with one type of information, such as billings, orders, or accounts receivable, the DW/BI system must eventually integrate them all. The DW/BI system requires technically sophisticated data gathering and management.

Finally, you need to provide the business decision makers with the tools they need to make use of the data. In this context, "tools" means much more than just software. It means everything the business users need to understand what information is available, find the subsets they need, and structure the data to illuminate the underlying business dynamics. "Tools" includes training, documentation, and support, along with ad hoc query tools, reports, and analytic applications.

Let's review. The DW/BI system:

- Is high profile and high impact
- Is high risk
- Is highly political
- Requires technically sophisticated and complex data gathering and management
- Requires intensive user access, training, and support

Creating and managing the DW/BI system is an extremely challenging task. We want you to take on this task with full knowledge of what you're getting into. In our experience, it's easier to deal with all of the challenges if you're at least somewhat forewarned.

We don't mean this to discourage you, but rather to warn you before you jump in that the waters are swift and deep. All the reasons that make the data warehouse challenging are also what make it a fun and exciting project.

The Kimball Group

While it's true that building and managing a successful DW/BI system is a challenge, it's also true that there are ways to approach it that will increase your likelihood of success. That's what the Kimball Group is all about. We've been working in the DW/BI area for more than 25 years. The authors of this book, who are members of the Kimball Group, have spent their careers working on data warehousing and business intelligence systems as vendors, consultants, implementers, and users. Our motto is "Practical techniques — proven results." We share a common drive to figure out the best way to build and manage a successful DW/BI system. We are also teachers at heart, with a strong desire to help you succeed and avoid the mistakes we and others have made.

Why We Wrote This Book

Data warehousing and business intelligence have been around in much the same form since at least the 1970s, and continue to enjoy an incredibly long technology lifecycle. In 1995, when the primary authors formed our first consulting organization, one of us voiced the opinion that data warehousing was finished, that the wave had crested and we'd be lucky to get a few more projects before we had to go find real jobs again. Years later, data warehousing and business intelligence are still going strong.

As the DW/BI industry has matured, it's become dominated by single-source providers — a safe choice for risk-averse organizations. The DW/BI technology stack covers everything from esoteric source system knowledge to user interface design and best-practice BI applications. Database vendors are best positioned to provide end-to-end solutions. Since SQL Server 2000 and especially SQL Server 2005, Microsoft has been forcing the concept of a viable, single-source data warehouse system provider into reality, and at an attractive price.

The book you're currently holding is a substantial revision of *The Microsoft Data Warehouse Toolkit with SQL Server 2005*. In addition to updating the content for new features and functionality such as PowerPivot and Master Data Services, the new version updates our previous recommendations with all that we've learned in recent years about building a DW/BI system with the Microsoft tools. The current book is based on the SQL Server 2008 R2 release, but the vast majority of its recommendations are valid for SQL Server 2008 as well. Any technology or recommendation that's new for SQL Server 2008 R2 is clearly identified in the text.

Who Should Read This Book

This book covers the entire DW/BI system lifecycle. As a result, it offers useful guidance to every member of the DW/BI team, from the project manager to the business analyst, data modeler, ETL developer, DBA, BI application developer, and even to the business user. We believe the book will be valuable to anyone working on a Microsoft SQL Server DW/BI program.

The primary audience for this book is the new DW/BI team that's launching a project on the Microsoft SQL Server platform. We don't assume you already have experience in building a DW/BI system. We do assume you have a basic familiarity with the Microsoft world: operating systems, infrastructure components, and resources. We also assume a basic understanding of relational databases (tables, columns, simple SQL) and some familiarity with the SQL Server relational database, although that's not a requirement. Throughout the book we provide many references to other books and resources.

A second audience is the experienced Kimball Method DW/BI practitioner who's new to the Microsoft SQL Server toolset. We'll point out which sections and chapters will be review for anyone who's read our other *Toolkit* books and practiced our methodology. But we've found that it doesn't hurt to read this material one more time!

Whatever your background, you'll benefit most if you're just starting on a new project. While we do provide suggestions on working with existing data warehouses, in the ideal case you won't have to contend with any existing data warehouse or data marts — at least none that will remain in place after the new system is deployed.

The Kimball Lifecycle

We've all felt the empty pit of panic in our stomach when, deep into a project, we realize the scope and scale of the effort before us will take much more work than we imagined at the outset. Many DW/BI projects begin with the notion that you'll just move some data to a new machine, clean it up a little, and develop some reports. That doesn't sound so bad — six weeks of effort, two months at the most. You charge into the forest and soon realize it's a lot darker and denser than you thought. In fact, you can't even see the road out.

The best way to avoid this sense of panic — and the resulting disaster — is to figure out where you're going before you jump in. It helps to have a roadmap and directions to lead you safely through unfamiliar territory — one that will tell you the places you have to visit and point out the danger zones on the trip ahead. This book is that roadmap for the Microsoft SQL Server DW/BI system project. This book follows the basic flow of the Kimball Lifecycle described in the book *The Data Warehouse Lifecycle Toolkit, Second Edition* (Wiley, 2008). The steps, tasks, and dependencies of the Lifecycle were crafted based on our collective experience of what works. The Lifecycle is an iterative approach based on four primary principles:

- *Focus on the business:* Concentrate on identifying business requirements and their associated value. Use these efforts to develop solid relationships with the business side and sharpen your business sense and consultative skills.

- *Build an information infrastructure:* Design a single, integrated, easy-to-use, high-performing information foundation that will meet the broad range of business requirements you've identified across the enterprise.

- *Deliver in meaningful increments:* Build the data warehouse in increments that can be delivered in 6 to 12 month timeframes. Use clearly identified business value to determine the implementation order of the increments.

- *Deliver the entire solution:* Provide all the elements necessary to deliver value to the business users. This means a solid, well designed, quality tested, accessible data warehouse database is only the start. You must also deliver ad hoc query tools, reporting applications and advanced analytics, training, support, website, and documentation.

This book helps you follow these four principles by using the Kimball Lifecycle to build your DW/BI system. These four principles are woven into the fabric of the Lifecycle. The secret to understanding the Kimball Lifecycle is that it's business-based, it takes a dimensional approach to designing data models for end user presentation, and it is a true lifecycle.

Lifecycle Tracks and Task Areas

The DW/BI system is a complex entity, and the methodology to build that system must help simplify that complexity. Figure 1 outlines the Kimball Lifecycle. The 13 boxes show the major task areas involved in building a successful data warehouse and the primary dependencies among those tasks.

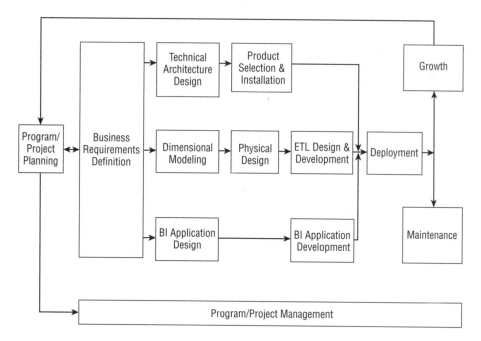

Figure 1: The Business Dimensional Lifecycle

There are several observations to make about the Lifecycle at this level. First, notice the central role of the Business Requirements Definition box. Business requirements provide the foundation for the three tracks that follow. They also influence the project plan, hence the arrow pointing back to the Project Planning box. You usually end up modifying the plan based on a more detailed understanding of the business requirements and priorities.

Second, the three tracks in the middle of the Lifecycle concentrate on three separate areas:

- *The top track is about technology.* These tasks are primarily about determining what functionality you will need, and planning which pieces of Microsoft technology you'll use, and how you'll install and configure them.

- *The middle track is about data.* In the data track you'll design and instantiate the dimensional model, and develop the Extract, Transformation, and Load (ETL) system to populate it. You could think of the data track as "building the data warehouse databases," although your data warehouse will not succeed unless you surround it with the rest of the Lifecycle tasks.

- *The bottom track is about business intelligence applications.* In these tasks you design and develop BI applications for the business users.

The tracks combine when it's time to deploy the system. This is a particularly delicate time because there's only one chance to make a good first impression. Although we've placed maintenance after deployment in the diagram, you need to design your system with the ability and tools for maintaining it. The growth phase of the project links to the arrow heading back to the beginning. This simple arrow has major implications. The Lifecycle's incremental approach is a fundamental element of delivering business value.

Underlying the entire Lifecycle is the Project Management box. The most important thing to remember here is that you need a leader, and that person needs access to senior management. The team leader is ideally one of those difficult-to-find people who can communicate effectively with both technologists and business people, including the most senior executives in the company.

Key Terminology and the Microsoft Toolset

The business intelligence industry is plagued with terminology that's used imprecisely, or in contradictory ways. Some of the most long-standing debates in the industry derive as much from misunderstandings about what others mean by a term, as from true differences in philosophy. Keeping that in mind, we'll try to be clear and consistent even if we don't settle all the historical debates. We highlight some of the key terms here.

As we define each term, we also relate it to the associated Microsoft technologies, most of which are components of SQL Server.

- The *data warehouse* is the "platform for business intelligence." In the Kimball Method, the data warehouse includes everything from the original data extracts to the software and applications that users see. We disagree with other authors who insist that the data warehouse is merely a centralized and highly normalized store of data in the back room, far from the end users. To reduce confusion, in this book we consistently use the phrase "data warehouse/business intelligence system" (DW/BI system) to mean the entire end-to-end system. When we're talking specifically and exclusively about the atomic level user queryable data store, we call it the *data warehouse database*.

- The *business process dimensional model* is a specific discipline for modeling data that is an alternative to normalized modeling. A dimensional model contains the same information as a normalized model but packages the data in a symmetrical format whose design goals are user understandability, business intelligence query performance, and resilience to change. Normalized models, sometimes called *third normal form* models, were designed to support the high-volume, single-row inserts and updates that define transaction systems, and generally fail at being understandable, fast, and resilient to change. We use the term "business process dimensional model" to refer both to the logical dimensional model that supports a business process and the corresponding physical tables in the database. In other words, dimensional models are both logical and physical.

- The *relational database* is a general purpose technology for storing, managing, and querying data. The SQL Server database engine is Microsoft's relational database engine. The business process dimensional model can be stored in a relational database. Normalized data models that support transaction processing can also be stored in a relational database.

- The *online analytic processing (OLAP) database* is a technology for storing, managing, and querying data specifically designed to support business intelligence uses. SQL Server Analysis Services is Microsoft's OLAP database engine. The business process dimensional model can be stored in an OLAP database, but a transactional database cannot, unless it first undergoes transformation to cast it in an explicitly dimensional form.

- An *Extract, Transformation, and Load (ETL)* system is a set of processes that clean, transform, combine, de-duplicate, household, archive, conform, and structure data for use in the data warehouse. These terms are described in this book. Early ETL systems were built using a combination of SQL and other scripts. While this is still true for some smaller ETL systems, larger and more serious systems use a specialized ETL tool. Moving forward, almost every DW/BI system will use an ETL tool such as SQL Server Integration Services because the benefits are significant and the incremental dollar cost is low or zero.

■ *Business intelligence (BI) applications* are predefined applications that query, analyze, and present information to support a business need. There is a spectrum of BI applications, ranging in complexity from a set of predefined static reports, all the way to an analytic application that directly affects transaction systems and the day-to-day operation of the organization. You can use SQL Server Reporting Services to build a reporting application, and a wide range of Microsoft and third-party technologies to build complex analytic applications.

■ A *data mining model* is a statistical model, often used to predict future behavior based on data about past behavior or identify closely related subsets of a population called clusters. Data mining is a term for a loose (and ever-changing) collection of statistical techniques or algorithms that serve different purposes. The major categories are clustering, decision trees, neural networks, and prediction. Analysis Services Data Mining is an example of a data mining tool.

■ *Ad hoc queries* are formulated by the user on the spur of the moment. The dimensional modeling approach is widely recognized as the best technique to support ad hoc queries because the simple database structure is easy to understand. Microsoft Office, through Excel pivot tables and PowerPivot, is the most popular ad hoc query tool on the market. You can use Reporting Services Report Builder to perform ad hoc querying and report definition. Nonetheless, many systems supplement Excel and Report Builder with a third-party ad hoc query tool for their power users.

■ Once again, the *data warehouse/business intelligence (DW/BI) system* is the whole thing: source system extracts, ETL, dimensional database in both relational and OLAP, BI applications, and an ad hoc query tool. The DW/BI system also includes management tools and practices, user-oriented documentation and training, a security system, and all the other components that we discuss in this book.

Roles and Responsibilities

The DW/BI system requires a number of different roles and skills, from both the business and technical communities, during its lifecycle. In this section, we review the major roles involved in creating a DW/BI system. There is seldom a one-to-one relationship between roles and people. We've worked with teams as small as one person, and as large as forty (and know of much larger teams). The vast majority of DW/BI teams fall between three and ten full-time members, with access to others as required.

It's common for a single DW/BI team to take on both development and operational duties. This is different from most technology project teams, and is related to the highly iterative nature of the DW/BI project development cycle. The following roles are associated with design and development activities:

- The *DW/BI manager* is responsible for overall leadership and direction of the project. The DW/BI manager must be able to communicate effectively with both senior business and IT management. The manager must also be able to work with the team to formulate the overall architecture of the DW/BI system.

- The *project manager* is responsible for day-to-day management of project tasks and activities during system development.

- The *business project lead* is a member of the business community and works closely with the project manager.

- The *business systems analyst* (or business analyst) is responsible for leading the business requirements definition activities, and often participates in the development of the business process dimensional model. The business systems analyst needs to be able to bridge the gap between business and technology.

- The *data modeler* is responsible for performing detailed data analysis including data profiling, and developing the detailed dimensional model.

- The *system architect(s)* design the various components of the DW/BI system. These include the ETL system, security system, auditing system, and maintenance systems.

- The *development database administrator (DBA)* creates the relational data warehouse database(s) and is responsible for the overall physical design including disk layout, partitioning, and initial indexing plan.

- The *OLAP database designer* creates the OLAP databases.

- The *ETL system developer* creates Integration Services packages, scripts, and other elements to move data from the source databases into the data warehouse.

- The *test lead* sets up the test environment, writes scripts to automate test execution, develops and distributes reports on the test log database, reaches out to the business user community to get user input into data quality tests, manages the ongoing process of automated data quality testing once the system is in production, and publishes data quality reports to the user community.

- The *DW/BI management tools developer* writes any custom tools that are necessary for the ongoing management of the DW/BI system. Examples of such tools include a simple UI for entering metadata, scripts or Integration Services packages to perform system backups and restores, and a simple UI for maintaining dimension hierarchies.

- The *BI application developer* is responsible for building the BI applications, including the standard reports and any advanced analytic applications required by the business. This role is also responsible for developing any custom components in the BI portal and integrating data mining models into business operations.

Most of the rest of the roles play a part in the latter stages of the DW/BI project development cycle, as the team moves toward deploying and operating the system. A few of the roles are strictly operational.

- The *data steward* is responsible for ensuring the data in the data warehouse is accurate. The data stewardship role is often best filled by someone in the business user community, who has a deep understanding of the data and can well judge its accuracy.

- The *security manager* specifies new user access roles that the business users need, and adds users to existing roles. The security manager also determines the security procedures in the ETL "back room" of the DW/BI system.

- The *relational database administrator (DBA)* is responsible for managing the performance and operations of the relational data warehouse database.

- The *OLAP DBA* is responsible for managing the performance and operations of the OLAP data warehouse database.

- The *compliance manager* ensures that the DW/BI policies and operations comply with corporate and regulatory directives such as privacy policies, HIPAA, and Sarbanes-Oxley. The compliance manager works closely with the security manager and internal audit.

- The *metadata manager* has the final word on what metadata is collected, where it is kept, and how it's published to the business community. As we discuss in Chapter 15, metadata tends not to be managed unless there's a person identified to lead the charge.

- The *data mining analyst* is deeply familiar with the business and usually has some background in statistics. The data mining analyst develops data mining models and works with the BI application developers to design operational applications that use the data mining models.

- The *BI portal content manager* manages the BI portal. She determines the content that's on the portal and how it's laid out, and keeps it fresh.

- The *DW/BI educator* creates and delivers the training materials for the DW/BI system.

- *User support* personnel within the DW/BI team must be available to help business users, especially with ad hoc access. Corporate-wide help desks tend not to have the specialized expertise necessary to do more than assist with minor connectivity issues.

How This Book Is Organized

We've divided the book into four parts:

1. Requirements, Realities, and Architecture
2. Building and Populating the Databases
3. Developing the BI Applications
4. Deploying and Managing the DW/BI System

Part 1: Requirements, Realities, and Architecture

Part 1 sets the stage for the rest of the book. Most of you are eager to get your hands on the Microsoft toolset. That's fine while you're experimenting and learning about the technology, but it's the kiss of death for a project. Stop, back away from the keyboard, and think about what you're setting out to do.

Chapter 1: Defining Business Requirements

Part 1 begins with a brief summary of the Kimball Lifecycle. We drill down on the most important step, gathering the business requirements, and briefly present the business requirements for the Adventure Works Cycles case study used throughout the book. Chapter 1 refers to the Business Requirements Definition box in Figure 1.

Readers who are very familiar with the Kimball Method can skip the first part of the chapter but should read the case study.

Chapter 2: Designing the Business Process Dimensional Model

We present a brief primer on how to develop a dimensional model. This chapter presents terminology and concepts used throughout the book, so it's vital that you understand this material. This chapter refers to the Dimensional Modeling box in Figure 1.

Readers who are very familiar with the Kimball Method can skim most of this material and review the Adventure Works overview at the end of the chapter.

Chapter 3: The Toolset

The Architecture and Product Selection tasks are straightforward for a Microsoft DW/BI system. In this short chapter we talk in more detail about how and where to use the various components of SQL Server, other Microsoft products, and even where you're most likely to use third-party software in your system. This chapter provides a brief overview of the Technical Architecture Design and Product Selection & Installation boxes in Figure 1.

Even readers who are very familiar with SQL Server 2005 should review this chapter, as it contains information about the new features of SQL Server 2008 R2, some of which are significantly different.

Chapter 4: System Setup

Chapter 4 is focused on the Product Selection & Installation box in Figure 1, and describes how to install and configure the various components of SQL Server 2008 R2. We talk about system sizing and configuration, and how — and why — you might choose to distribute your DW/BI system across multiple servers.

Part 2: Building and Populating the Databases

The second part of the book presents the steps required to effectively build and populate the data warehouse databases. Most Microsoft DW/BI systems will implement the dimensional data warehouse in both the relational database and the Analysis Services database.

Chapter 5: Creating the Relational Data Warehouse

Chapter 5 talks about creating the database structures for the relational data warehouse. We're not moving data yet, but we're getting closer. We begin by talking about the minor differences between the Kimball logical design and the physical data models, including issues such as the initial indexing plan, key structures, and storage decisions.

One of your key decisions for the relational data warehouse is whether or not to partition the fact data. As we discuss, partitioning provides many advantages, and is a necessity for large data warehouses.

Chapter 6: Master Data Management

Master data is reference data that is managed centrally for an organization. New with SQL Server 2008 R2, Master Data Services provides a toolset for building a master data management system. Chapter 6 describes master data management and the Master Data Services tools, then discusses some quick and easy uses of this new technology to improve the data warehouse. Over time, some organizations may shift the management of their dimensions from a classic ETL system implemented in SQL Server Integration Services, toward more active data stewardship via Master Data Services.

Chapter 7: Designing and Developing the ETL System

Finally it's time to start moving data. This chapter talks about the basic design for your ETL system. We begin by introducing SQL Server Integration Services (SSIS), then walk through how to use SSIS to build the 34 subsystems of any ETL system. The 34 subsystems have four major groups: data extraction, data cleaning and conforming, data presentation, and system management. Each of these areas is discussed within the context of SSIS.

Chapter 8: The Core Analysis Services OLAP Database

We recommend that your Microsoft DW/BI system use Analysis Services OLAP as the main database for users to query. The more closely the relational database and ETL process are designed to meet your business requirements, the easier it is to design the Analysis Services database. The Analysis Services wizards are easy to use, and with a small system, you don't need to worry very much about advanced settings. However, if you have large data volumes or a lot of users, you need to develop a deep understanding of the OLAP engine. Much of this chapter is focused on helping you learn enough to implement Analysis Services across your enterprise.

Analysis Services contains three major pieces of functionality: the core OLAP database, the data mining platform, and the PowerPivot user-driven Excel analytics. Data mining is addressed in Chapter 13, and PowerPivot in Chapter 11.

Chapter 8 revisits the Physical Design and ETL boxes of Figure 1, this time from the perspective of the OLAP database engine.

Chapter 9: Design Requirements for Real-Time BI

Chapter 9 takes on the topic of real-time business intelligence, discussing how to bring real-time data — loosely defined as data refreshed more frequently than daily — into the DW/BI system. SQL Server contains many features to enable real-time business intelligence. We talk about how to use these features, and the inevitable tradeoffs you face when implementing real-time BI.

Part 3: Developing the BI Applications

The third part of the book presents the steps required to present the data to the business users. BI applications are a key component of the complete DW/BI system. To most business users, BI applications are synonymous with the data warehouse. BI applications range from simple static reports to complex data mining applications, user-driven ad hoc analyses using PowerPivot and Excel, and the BI portal that provides a single point of entry into the business intelligence system.

Chapter 10: Building BI Applications in Reporting Services

Chapter 10 provides the basic information you need to understand the range of BI applications available to you. We start with an introduction to BI applications in general. We then offer a BI applications development process in the context of the Kimball Lifecycle. The rest of the chapter drills into Reporting Services as a platform for creating and distributing standard reports.

Chapter 11: PowerPivot and Excel

The core component of PowerPivot is an in-memory database add-in for Excel 2010. It allows Excel users to work with millions of rows of data at memory speeds. Business users can join data from multiple, disparate sources in the PowerPivot database, and create complex calculations and measures.

Chapter 11 begins with a look at Excel as an analysis and reporting tool. The rest of the chapter is dedicated to PowerPivot, starting with a brief description of PowerPivot and its product architecture. The bulk of the chapter is dedicated to working through an example. We'll finish up with a brief discussion of PowerPivot in the SharePoint environment and its role in the overall DW/BI system.

Chapter 12: The BI Portal and SharePoint

The BI portal is the primary starting point in the information quest for a large part of the business community. It needs to be structured in a way that allows people to find what they are looking for within an ever increasing number of reports and analyses. SharePoint is Microsoft's offering in the portal platform category.

The first part of Chapter 12 is a discussion of the BI portal including design guidelines and a simple example. In the second part, we take a high level look at SharePoint as a BI portal platform and discuss the process of getting SharePoint going with a set of BI-related functionality including Reporting Services and PowerPivot for SharePoint.

Chapter 13: Incorporating Data Mining

Data mining is perhaps the most powerful — and certainly the least understood — technology in the BI toolkit. This chapter defines data mining, and provides examples of how it can be used. We talk about Microsoft's data mining technology, including the algorithms that are included with SQL Server Analysis Services. We provide practical guidance on how to build a data mining model and how to incorporate the results of data mining into your systems. To make this theoretical discussion more concrete, we work through two case studies.

Part 4: Deploying and Managing the DW/BI System

The final section of the book includes information about how to deploy and operate your DW/BI system. It is one of the most exciting sections of the entire book.

Chapter 14: Designing and Implementing Security

We start our discussion of the DW/BI system's security by encouraging you to develop an open access policy for information. Sensitive data must of course be protected, but we think most contents of the data warehouse should be available to most authenticated users.

Even with an open security policy, some data must be protected. We describe how to control access in the various components of SQL Server: Reporting Services, the relational database, and Analysis Services. We also discuss the separate issues of security in the back room development area of the data warehouse.

The discussion of security is most closely related to the Deployment and Maintenance boxes of Figure 1.

Chapter 15: Metadata Plan

Lots of people talk about metadata, but we've seen few examples of it being implemented thoroughly and successfully. We'd like to have seen an integrated metadata service in SQL Server, which we could simply describe to you, but that's not the case. Instead, we spend most of this chapter detailing the metadata that we think is most important, and describing the steps to maintain and publish that information.

Metadata is related to the Deployment and Maintenance boxes of Figure 1.

Chapter 16: Deployment

Deploying the DW/BI system consists of two major sets of tasks. First, you need to deploy the system. This effort consists primarily of testing: testing of data, processes, performance, and the deployment scripts themselves. The deployment scripts should include a playbook, with step-by-step instructions for how to deploy the system changes.

The other major set of deployment activities is focused more on the business users than on the technology. You need to develop and deliver training and documentation materials. You need to pull together the BI portal that we describe in Chapter 12. And you need to develop a plan for supporting the business users, who will inevitably have questions.

Chapter 17: Operations and Maintenance

As business people begin to use the warehouse to answer their questions on a regular basis, they'll come to rely on it. If users don't believe the warehouse is reliable, they'll go back to their old ways of getting information. This reliance is a kind of trust, and you must do everything you can to build and keep that trust. You need to monitor usage and performance — both for data loads and user queries. Track system resources and make sure you don't run out of disk space. In short, maintain the warehouse as the production system it now is. You must be meticulous in your attention to the quality of the data that's loaded into the data warehouse. Once a business user loses trust in the accuracy of the data, that trust is nearly impossible to regain.

Chapter 18: Present Imperatives and Future Outlook

Chapter 18 reviews the major phases of the DW/BI project and highlights where the most significant risks are to the overall success of the project. We finish the book with a wish list of features and functionality that we hope to see in the Microsoft BI toolset in the years to come.

Additional Information

This book includes most of the information you need to successfully build and deploy a basic DW/BI system using SQL Server 2008 Release 2. In an effort to keep the book small enough to fit into a large backpack, we chose not to replicate tool instructions that could be easily found in SQL Server Books Online. Where appropriate, we provide search topics to assist in finding related materials. In several places, we recommend that you work through the tutorials provided by the SQL Server team before you can expect to fully understand some technical material.

This book doesn't attempt to re-teach the fundamentals of data warehousing. We summarize many of the concepts and techniques found in the other volumes in the *Kimball Data Warehouse Toolkit* series rather than including all the details found in those books. We also provide references to key sections of those books as needed. Table 1 shows the core books in the *Toolkit* series, their major focus, and their primary audiences.

These books encapsulate the collective wisdom of the Kimball Group about data warehousing and business intelligence. We recommend that you add these books to your team's library.

We've laced this book with tips, key concepts, sidebars, and chapter pointers to make it more usable and easily referenced. We draw attention to some of these with the following formats:

REFERENCE Look for reference pointers to find other materials you can use to supplement your DW/BI library. This includes references to SQL Server Books Online, other books and articles, and online reference materials.

RESOURCES Resources provide references to other Kimball Group material, such as the *Toolkit* books, articles, or design tips.

NOTE Notes provide some extra information on the topic under discussion, adding explanation or details to clarify the material.

WARNING Warnings help you avoid potential dangers that might cost you time, data, or sanity.

DOWNLOADS Resources that you can download.

Table 1: The core *Kimball Data Warehouse Toolkit* titles

TITLE	SUBJECT	PRIMARY AUDIENCE
The Data Warehouse Lifecycle Toolkit, Second Edition	Implementation guide	Good overview for all project partici-pants; key tool for project managers, business analysts, and data modelers
The Data Warehouse Toolkit, Second Edition	Dimensional data modeling	Data modelers, business analysts, DBAs, ETL developers
The Data Warehouse ETL Toolkit	ETL system architecture	ETL architects and developers
The Kimball Group Reader	DW/BI system design and development	A topical reference book for all project participants

On the Website

We've collected most of the listings and examples and made them available on the book's website along with additional links and references: `http://www`
`.kimballgroup.com/html/booksMDWT.html`

Part 1

Requirements, Realities, and Architecture

This first part of the lifecycle is where you lay the foundation for your success. Working with the business folks to understand and prioritize their requirements for analytics as we describe in Chapter 1 helps you set specific goals for your first pass through the lifecycle that are both valuable to the organization and achievable in a reasonable timeframe. Your understanding of the business requirements becomes the basis for designing a flexible, usable, high-performing dimensional model in Chapter 2.

What you learn in the first two chapters helps you tackle the architecture and technology track at the top of the Lifecycle. Your business understanding helps you determine what architectural components are important for your DW/BI system. Once you know the problem, you can identify the specific functionality you need, and where that functionality will come from in the Microsoft SQL Server toolset. This, in turn, allows you to make decisions on the server configurations and disk subsystems that will form the basic infrastructure of your DW/BI system.

Part 1 is about getting the lay of the land before you decide what you are going to build and where you will build it. Your primary focus here is on identifying the most promising business opportunities and designing the data structures and system architectures needed to deliver them. By the end of this section, you should have all the pieces in place for you to dig into the development work of creating the DW/BI system database. Skip this section at your peril.

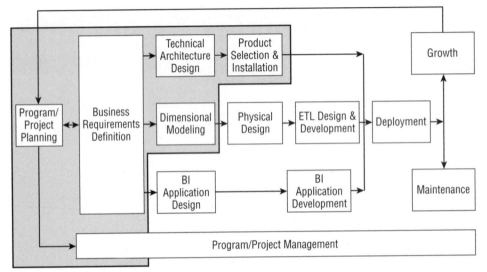

The Kimball Lifecycle steps covered in Part 1

Defining Business Requirements

Building the foundation.

Business requirements are the bedrock of the successful data warehouse/business intelligence (DW/BI) system. Business requirements guide the development team in making the biggest strategic choices, such as prioritizing subject areas for implementation, and in making the smallest tactical design decisions, such as how to present key performance indicators on the users' screens. In this chapter, we cover the process of gathering business requirements and converting them into a DW/BI system strategy. We describe the process of interviewing business and IT representatives and mapping their analytic requirements back to the core business processes (such as orders, page views, or account transactions) that generate the needed data. These business processes are the building blocks of the DW/BI system. After the requirements are documented, we offer a technique for working with senior management to prioritize the implementation of those business-process–based projects. We also illustrate these tasks with an example based on Microsoft's sample database business, Adventure Works Cycles.

As Figure 1-1 illustrates, the Business Requirements Definition step is the foundation of the Kimball Lifecycle methodology. Business requirements and their associated business value give you the guidance you need to make decisions in all three downstream tracks. As you'll see, they influence the project scope and plan, too.

RESOURCES If you skipped the Introduction to this book, you should at least go back and read the overview of the Kimball Lifecycle because it is the organizing framework for this book and for implementing a successful DW/BI system.

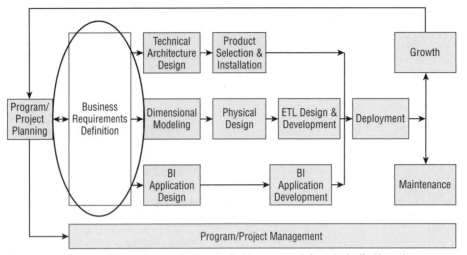

Figure 1-1: The Business Requirements Definition step of the Kimball Lifecycle

This chapter is primarily about resisting temptation. Gathering business requirements is often outside a technical person's comfort zone. The overall success of the project is largely determined by your understanding of the business requirements and your relationships with the business people. Resist the temptation to just start loading data.

In this chapter you learn the following:

■ The importance of understanding business requirements and securing solid business sponsorship

■ The steps used to define enterprise-level business requirements, including the interview process, synthesizing requirements into their underlying business processes, developing the enterprise analytic data framework called the data warehouse bus matrix, and prioritizing business processes with senior management

■ How to plan the initial business process dimensional model implementation and gather project-level business requirements

■ What goes into a typical requirements summary document and how it links to business requirements for analytics and business process implementations

RESOURCES Throughout the book, we provide specific references to the various titles in the *Kimball Toolkit* library to help you find more details on the concept or technique described. Each book in the *Toolkit* series is described in the Introduction to this book.

The Most Important Determinant of Long-Term Success

There is one common factor in successful business intelligence projects: delivering business value. Your DW/BI team must embrace the goal of enhancing business value as its primary purpose. This seems like an obvious statement, but most DW/BI folks are technologists at heart. We like the certainty of computers and programming and shy away from the vague uncertainties of the business side.

You can't deliver business value unless you work closely with business people. You need to understand their language and learn to see the world from their points of view. You'll be working in a non-technical, highly ambiguous, politically sensitive environment. Are you feeling queasy yet? This unsettled environment is what the DW/BI system is all about. You must develop the business knowledge and people skills right along with your technical skills to meet the needs of your business users. We realize the entire team will not become smooth-talking MBAs. However, someone on the team must have strong business and communications skills, and everyone will be more effective if they learn more about the business.

NOTE Perhaps your organization uses the "agile" development methodology. If so, then you have heard this story already! In the agile approach, projects are owned and driven by the business users. To learn more about this approach, see "agile software development" on www.wikipedia.org. For guidance relating agile to DW/BI system development, see *The Kimball Group Reader*, pp. 109–112.

So, while many DW/BI teams and consultants pay lip service to business value, the reality of their day-to-day behavior is that technology rules. Do not let this happen to you. Technology is important; business value is mandatory. We understand you bought this book to learn about the SQL Server DW/BI toolset, but SQL Server is just a tool. Your success in using that tool in your organization depends on your understanding of the organization's unique requirements and priorities for business intelligence.

As you read this book, you'll encounter recommendations that may seem unnecessarily complicated or just plain unnecessary. Every time you're tempted to dismiss the authors as overly fond of their design methodology or just overzealous, consider whether your reactions are driven by your technical convenience or by the business users' needs. Never lose sight of the business.

Adventure Works Cycles Introduction

It always helps to see new concepts in the context of a specific example. Since everyone's organization is different, we'll use some of the business requirements for Microsoft's demo database company to illustrate the process of defining business requirements described in this chapter.

The current SQL Server sample business intelligence databases are based on a fictitious company called Adventure Works Cycles, a multinational manufacturer and seller of bicycles and accessories. The database and associated samples are not part of the software distribution set. Instead, you download them from the Microsoft code-sharing site called Codeplex (Search for "SQL Server Samples Database" at `http://www.codeplex.com`) or download the database from the Wiley web site at `www.wiley.com/go/MsftDWToolkit2E`. You will need to download and install the SQL Server 2008R2 version of the sample databases to follow the examples later in this book.

DOWNLOADS You can find several detailed documents illustrating what the business requirements-gathering process might look like at a company such as Adventure Works Cycles on the book's web site (`http://kimballgroup.com/html/booksMDWTtools.html`). These include interview summaries and additional background information.

Uncovering Business Value

If you're going to be driven by business value, you need to go out and identify, understand, and prioritize the needs of the business. This is easier said than done if your focus has historically been on technology. Fortunately, the Kimball Lifecycle provides the tools to work through an entire development iteration of a data warehouse, beginning with business requirements.

Where do you start with your business intelligence system? What is the first step? Well, it depends on a host of factors, such as how your organization works, what you already know about the business, who is involved in the project at this point, what kinds of DW/BI efforts came before, and many other factors.

Let's talk about the most common scenario first, and then we'll address a few exceptions. More often than not, the DW/BI system starts as a project hosted by the Information Technology (IT) department of the organization. The IT-driven DW/BI project gets cranked up because the CIO decides the company needs a data warehouse, so people and resources are assigned to build one. This is a dangerous situation. Please refer to the first point in this chapter: Focusing on business value is the most important determinant of long-term success. The problem with the IT-driven DW/BI system is that it almost always centers on technology. The team has been assigned the task of building a "warehouse," so that's exactly what they do. They get some hardware and some software and start extracting data.

We know some of you are thinking, "Oops, I already bought the ETL server and the user reporting tools." That's probably okay, but put those tools aside for the moment. Step away from the keyboard. If you get sucked into the technology, you're missing the whole point. You can build a technically great DW/BI system that provides very little business value. As a result, your project will fail. You have to start with business value, and identifying business value involves several major steps:

- Recruiting strong business sponsorship
- Defining enterprise-level business requirements
- Prioritizing business requirements
- Planning the project
- Defining project-level business requirements

We'll run through each of these steps in the following sections.

Obtaining Sponsorship

Developing solid business sponsorship is the best place to start the DW/BI project. Your business sponsors (it is generally good to have more than one) will take a lead role in determining the purpose, content, and priorities of the DW/BI system. You will call on them to secure resources and to evangelize the DW/BI system to the rest of the organization. This includes activities such as arranging for a planning meeting with senior staff, speaking to a room full of business users at the project kick-off, and getting spending approval for your new server. You need to find at least one person in the organization who scores well in each of the following areas:

- *Visionary:* Someone who has a sense for the value and potential of information and some clear, specific ideas on how to apply it.
- *Resourceful:* Someone who is able to obtain the necessary resources and facilitate the organizational change the data warehouse will bring about.
- *Reasonable:* Someone who can temper his or her enthusiasm with the understanding that it takes time and resources to build a major information system.

If you've been with your company for a while, you already know who these people are. In this case, your task is to recruit them onto the project. However, if you're new to the company, or you don't get out of the IT group much, you'll need to investigate and find your business sponsors. In either case, the best way to find and recruit these people is by conducting an enterprise business requirements gathering project. Obtaining business sponsorship is fairly easy and well worth the effort. Good business sponsorship can provide the resources and support you need to deliver real business value.

RESOURCES Learn more about developing sponsorship in *The Data Warehouse Lifecycle Toolkit, Second Edition*, pages 16–21.

Defining Enterprise-Level Business Requirements

The successful DW/BI effort is an ongoing program guiding the multiple, iterative projects that build out the DW/BI system. Before you concentrate your efforts on specific projects within the larger data warehouse endeavor, you need a broad enterprise perspective that will help you set priorities and make better, more flexible implementation decisions. One long-term goal of the DW/BI team is to build an enterprise information infrastructure. Clearly, you can't do this unless you understand business requirements from an enterprise level.

We almost always preface the first iteration of the Lifecycle with an enterprise business requirements definition project. This project is essentially a set of interviews, documentation, and a prioritization session with senior management. It provides a clear implementation plan for the DW/BI system, and it can be done in three to six weeks for most organizations.

Every DW/BI program has to keep the enterprise requirements context in mind. Larger organizations need to begin by establishing this broad understanding because it is rare for the DW/BI team to have such an enterprise-level perspective. Even in a smaller company or a departmental effort, the enterprise perspective will help build in flexibility and resilience. It is also particularly important for organizations that are just starting their first DW/BI system (or starting over) because getting the enterprise perspective built into the initial project helps you avoid painful and costly redesign down the road. By the same token, DW/BI systems that are well into their implementation will gain by taking a little time to validate their understanding of the enterprise business requirements. This usually results in significant changes to the DW/BI system strategy. Better late than too late.

Given this need for an enterprise perspective, it's best to preface your first Lifecycle iteration with a narrow-scoped enterprise requirements definition project as shown in Figure 1-2.

In this subsection of the Lifecycle, defining the business requirements happens in several distinct steps. The rest of this section describes each of these steps in more detail.

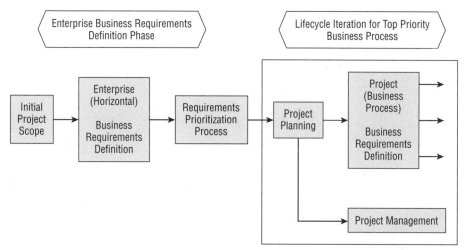

Figure 1-2: Prefacing the core Lifecycle with an Enterprise Requirements phase

---

BUSINESS PROCESS: THE DW/BI SYSTEM UNIT OF WORK

We use the term *business process* to mean an operational activity the organization engages in to accomplish its primary goals. You can think of business processes as the links in the organization's value chain. Each business process typically has its own operational system or module that enables it, such as the order entry system, or the call tracking system, or the inventory management system. The information generated by these business processes measures only the business process itself, but that information usually has value well beyond the boundaries of the individual business process. Information from a single business process, such as orders information, could be of great interest to sales, marketing, customer service, and other groups across the organization.

Each business process is a unique, coherent measurement system implemented as an operational system. If you need data from a given business process, you need to extract that data in its business context. In other words, you need to pull the measures and all of the associated descriptors in a careful, systematic fashion. This makes the business process the fundamental unit of work for the DW/BI system. Unless you have unlimited resources, your DW/BI team will concentrate on designing and loading data from one business process at a time.

Establishing Initial Enterprise Requirements Project Scope

The initial scope usually covers only the enterprise-level requirements definition and requirements prioritization steps, leaving the detailed project implementation plan for later when you have a much better idea of what the project needs to accomplish from a business perspective. The requirements and prioritization usually involve user interviews, interview write-ups, a few meetings, and the creation of the final requirements document. It typically takes three to six weeks (or more) depending on how many interviews you do.

COMBINING ENTERPRISE AND PROJECT REQUIREMENTS GATHERING

Some organizations we've worked with have a clear understanding of which business process is their top priority right from the start. In these cases, we often combine the enterprise requirements definition step and the project requirements definition step into a single effort.

This does not lessen the importance of understanding the full range of enterprise requirements for information. In fact, we almost always go through the enterprise prioritization process with senior management. However, because the top priority is clear early on, we make sure we gather enough detailed information about that business process and the data it generates in the same interview set so we can create the design for the first business process in one pass instead of two.

RESOURCES Learn more about DW/BI project planning and management in Chapter 2 of *The Data Warehouse Lifecycle Toolkit, Second Edition.*

Gathering and Documenting Enterprise-Level Business Requirements

The enterprise requirements definition step is designed to gather a broad, horizontal view of the organization from a business point of view. The process flow chart in Figure 1-3 breaks the Enterprise requirements definition box from Figure 1-2 down into its subtasks. As you see in Figure 1-3, the bulk of the work involves gathering and documenting those requirements.

While the four steps that are circled on the left side of the figure are shown as separate subtasks, we usually do them in a pipeline fashion, conducting and documenting an interview, and extracting its analytic requirements. As the interviews progress, we begin synthesizing what we've learned, identifying the business processes that support the users' analytic needs. At the same time, it's important to conduct initial data profiling to match analytic needs with data realities. At the end of the interview process, we build an initial bus matrix to summarize the business processes we've heard about during the interviews. We describe the bus matrix and each of the core subtasks in Figure 1-3 in this section, leaving the senior management prioritization session for its own section.

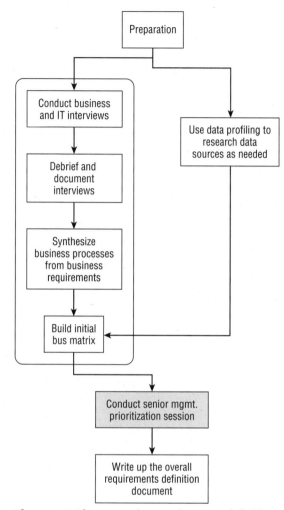

Figure 1-3: The enterprise requirements definition process flow chart

Preparation

Requirements definition is largely a process of interviewing business and technical people, but before you get started, you need to do a little preparation. Learn as much as you can about your business, your competitors, your industry, and your customers. Read your organization's annual report; track down any internal strategy documents; go online and see what's said about your organization, the competition, and the industry in the press. Find out what the big challenges are. Learn the terms and terminology the business people use to describe what they do. In short, do your homework.

Part of the preparation process is figuring out whom you should actually interview. This usually involves carefully examining an org chart with your sponsor and other key supporters. For the enterprise requirements pass, start the interview list with the CEO and senior staff. Add the analysts and managers who are known as leaders in the business intelligence area — folks whom senior management and co-workers turn to when they need information. They are also usually the folks who bug IT the most. If you've been at your company more than 12 months, you know who these people are. They have their own Access databases, they write SQL against the transaction system, and they create reports and charts with whatever tools they have available (mostly Excel and Access). Finally, add on a couple of the key IT folks who can educate you about the nature of the source systems and the quality of the data they collect.

NOTE You are just making the list of whom to interview at this point, not the interview schedule. When you do start the schedule, begin with a few people you know and trust before you turn to senior management. At the same time, make sure you get the elusive executives on the calendar as early as possible. Some of these folks can be tough to pin down.

A major goal during the interviews is to build positive working relationships with the business folks. These relationships will hinge on your understanding of the business issues your organization faces. In short, be prepared. Fortunately, gathering this information is not as difficult as it used to be, thanks to the internet. However, you still have to read it.

RESOURCES You can find additional information about preparing for interviews in *The Data Warehouse Lifecycle Toolkit, Second Edition*, pages 68–80.

Adventure Works Example: Preparation

Much of preparation is about knowing your business. Not being a real business, Adventure Works does not have much strategic or market information available. However, you can get a good sense for the nature of any business with SQL Management Studio and a basic knowledge of SQL, or even better, a query tool like Report Builder 3.0. You also need permission to query the source system (or a copy of it, so you don't cause any transaction problems).

A few simple SELECTs and SUMs can tell you what products are selling well, where they are selling, who is selling them, and how this has all changed over time. At Adventure Works, you could quickly find out that over 80 percent of their business is bicycles, versus clothing or accessories, and almost half their business is overseas. From a time series perspective, the company has been growing rapidly and the internet sales channel is a major contributor to this growth. Figure 1-4 shows a pivot table of the results of a query against the AdventureWorks2008R2 transaction database.

Sales Amount Row Labels	Column Labels FY 2006	FY 2007	FY 2008	% of 2008 Total
Bikes	$22,091	$28,180	$44,350	84.1%
Components	$1,167	$4,629	$6,003	11.4%
Clothing	$66	$751	$1,283	2.4%
Accessories	$37	$124	$1,077	2.0%
Grand Total	$23,361	$33,684	$52,714	100.0%
Sales in US dollars net of taxes and shipping				

Figure 1-4: Adventure Works sales by category by year

If you have a couple of hours, you can dig into other parts of the business, such as customer support, manufacturing, and finance.

DOWNLOADS See the web content for more examples of these kinds of queries and results for the Adventure Works business.

Conduct Business and IT Interviews

The key to success in requirements interviews is to remember your overall mission. You are designing a system to add significant long-term business value. The most common mistake in these interviews is to ask the business person what they want (or need). Asking this question is the equivalent of abdicating your design responsibility. You are saying, "Tell me what you want and I'll build it." At best, you will get a limited description of what the person wants to solve today's problem. For example, you may get a request to have all the data provided for a given report in an Excel format. This may sound great to you because it is easy to understand and execute. So, you go off to extract, clean, and load that data into a data warehouse, then set up a distribution system to put it into Excel and email it to the analyst every night. Once you are finished, you show it to the analyst, and they say, "It's nice, but what I really want is this other report in an Excel format." This is when we hear statements like "The business people don't know what they want!" Or, "The business people don't understand business intelligence!"

This lack of understanding is not their fault, and it's an easy mistake to avoid by changing the questions you ask in the interview. Remember, it's your job to design the system. In order to do that, you have to understand the business; you need to know what your users do and how they use information to do it. Once you know this, the required system designs, data models, and BI applications all become clear.

The easy way to find this out is to start out with the simple question: "What do you do? Tell me about your roles and responsibilities." Explore each of the areas they describe in terms of the information they need, and the value they provide to the organization (or could provide with better, more accessible information). Be flexible and follow the leads provided by the interviewee. Avoid sticking to a predetermined script planned in too much detail. Interviewing is a very valuable skill.

RESOURCES For more in-depth interviewing tips and techniques, see the articles in the *Kimball Group Reader* on pages 113 and 117.

In this first pass at gathering requirements, you will interview more senior level folks across the different departments and get a comprehensive list of the major challenges and opportunities your organization faces. These challenges and opportunities often (but not always) line up with the strategic goals and initiatives of the organization.

You will also interview some of the source systems experts to understand the structure and content of the source systems and the nature of any data problems that might be lurking out there. You must also perform data profiling on all candidate data sources. (Data profiling is described in an upcoming section.)

Debrief and Document Interviews

At the end of each interview the interview team must take a few minutes to debrief. Review your notes, fill in the blanks, make sure you understand the terms you heard, and capture the key issues. The longer you wait to do this, the less you will remember. We've found ourselves staring at a sentence that reads, "The most important factor in our business is . . ." with no idea what came next. Debrief as soon as possible. As you go through your notes, highlight and add comments to fully describe the following items:

- Common, repetitive business requirements themes
- Business processes (data sources) needed
- Business requirements for specific reports and analyses
- Misunderstandings or incomplete notes (the lead interviewer should keep a list of open issues)
- Data or other feasibility issues known to the team
- Success criteria

The individual interviews will yield a wealth of information including descriptions of the analytic requirements and their associated business processes, a starting point for the organization's overall information architecture, and a list of any feasibility issues such as poor data quality.

Identifying the business requirements for analytics is the hardest part. Depending on who you are talking to, similar analytic opportunities may be described broadly or specifically. As the interviews progress, you'll see common requirements repeated over time. For example, the marketing person responsible for internet promotions might describe an opportunity to improve promotion response and conversion rates by better targeting certain geographic and demographic subsets of the population. The person responsible for product promotions might describe an opportunity to improve conversions by offering product recommendations based on customer behaviors. Both of these opportunities could be grouped together under a broader heading called Improve Customer Acquisition.

Each of these broader analytic themes should have brief descriptions of the kinds of reports or analyses you heard in the interview. It should also include some sense of the business value of meeting the requirements. In other words, how much is improving customer conversion rates, or negotiating better prices and terms worth? Look for action words to identify these opportunities. Words like *improve*, *reduce*, *increase*, and *enhance* all lead to a business requirement we'd like to know about.

Do not put this review off. After a day of interviews, you will have a hard time remembering who you spoke with, let alone the details of what they said. Be cautious about scheduling too many interviews in one day. Our rule of thumb is four interviews and four debriefing periods per day.

It's a good idea to write up a summary document of each interview based on the annotated set of interview notes as soon as you can. This is more work because you need to summarize the various analytic areas covered in the interview, but it is a good communication and relationship-building tool with the business folks. Share this summary with the interviewee and ask for feedback; it shows that you listened to what they had to say and have an interest in helping. It also gives them a chance to clarify any misunderstandings and add any relevant items they overlooked.

RESOURCES You can find additional information about conducting the interviews and debriefing on pages 80–85 of *The Data Warehouse Lifecycle Toolkit, Second Edition.*

Adventure Works Example: Interview Documentation

Adventure Works has close to 300 employees. The CEO has seven direct reports, and the vast majority of employees are manufacturing workers. In most small-to medium-sized organizations like this, you could build a solid set of business requirements for analytics by speaking to most of the senior staff and a subset of managers and analysts; maybe 15 people, plus or minus five.

The primary content of each interview summary write up will be a list of business analysis requirements. Each analytic requirement should also include a list of the business processes that generate the data needed to support the analysis, and any associated issues or concerns, such as data quality or availability problems. Figure 1-5 shows a summary of the business requirements identified by the VP of Sales.

DOWNLOADS   You can find an Adventure Works organizational chart and an example interview summary from the Adventure Works VP of Sales in the web content downloads.

It should come as no surprise that most of the VP of Sales' business requirements for analysis are based on data from the orders business process. However, there are several other business processes that inform decision making for the sales department. Note that the VP has described a requirement for a customer satisfaction dashboard. By decomposing it to its underlying data sources, it becomes clear that you will need data from three major source systems: orders, call tracking, and returns. This means three iterations of the Lifecycle with three sets of ETL code, BI applications, testing, and deployment. Now is a good time to start educating and setting expectations.

Data Auditing/Data Profiling

At the same time you are interviewing people and creating the summaries, you will also need to do some queries against the source system data to get a firsthand understanding of the data issues. This kind of querying has come to be known as *data profiling* or *data auditing*, and there are several tools on the market designed to support it. There are three major points in the Lifecycle where data profiling is helpful. The first is here, during the requirements definition process where you should do a simple red light/green light assessment of your organization's data assets. You aren't looking for nuances at this point, but if a data source needs to be disqualified, now is the time. The second place to do data profiling is during the design of the dimensional model, and the third is during the design and implementation of the ETL process. You will want to do more in-depth data profiling once you select a specific business process and begin defining project-level business requirements. We describe data profiling in more detail when we discuss the dimensional modeling process in Chapter 2.

Business Requirements Category	Inferred or Requested Analyses	Supporting Business Process	Comments
Sales Planning	Reseller historical orders analyses	Orders	By customer, by territory, by sales region (from state)
	Sales forecast	Orders	Forecast is a business process that uses orders data as an input
Sales Performance	Orders by current territory	Orders	
	Orders by original territory	Orders	
	Sales rep performance report	Orders, Orders forecast	Orders and forecast by sales rep
Sales Reporting	Resellers ranked by orders in a given territory	Orders	
	Churned customer list	Orders	Customers who have not ordered in X months
Price Lists	Current price list	Orders	This is a connectivity issue, not a data warehouse issue
Special Offers	Relevant customers by territory based on orders history	Orders	
	Inventory status (out of stock)	Inventory	
Customer (Reseller) Satisfaction	Customer Satisfaction Dashboard	Multiple	This is a compound requirement based on several underlying business processes
	Calls by complaint type, product, and customer attributes	Call tracking	
	Order metrics of satisfaction	Orders	e.g., due date versus ship date
	Returns by reseller by return reason	Returns	
International Support	Local language translations of product descriptions	n/a (product dimension)	This is a transaction system problem. We need to make sure we can handle multiple languages in the DW/BI system, but the source system has to capture them when new products are created.

Figure 1-5: Business requirements and supporting business processes from the interview summary

Creating the Program Requirements Findings Document

The overall findings document for the enterprise-level requirements includes the business process summaries, the bus matrix, and the prioritized results. You might want to include the interview summaries as an appendix for those readers who want all the detail.

The bulk of the requirements document will be a list of the business processes and the business requirements they support. Each business process section should include some sense for the business value it would generate, the data quality and other feasibility issues associated with it, and the parts of the organization that will benefit from it. Some of the requirements on the list may represent new ways of doing business and will require new transaction systems, or at least significant changes to existing transaction systems. But even a quick review of the simple list provided begins to bring out ideas about how the DW/BI system can address some of these needs in the short term.

Synthesize Around Business Processes

The goal here is to tie the business requirements back to the underlying data needed to make them happen. This is the primary factor in determining the level of effort required to deliver a solution to a given business requirement.

As you extract the business requirements from the interview summaries, you need to dig into each opportunity to identify the business process (or processes) that generate the data needed to perform the desired analyses. For example, the requirement to reduce purchasing costs through better contract negotiations can be supported by historical data from the purchasing transaction system. You convert from requirements to business processes because business processes are the units of work in building the DW/BI system. Each business process is usually measured by a single source system module, which translates into a single pass through the Kimball Lifecycle process. (Refer back to the related sidebar, "Business Process: the DW/BI System Unit of Work," for more information.)

Although many business requirements need information only from a single business process, one challenge you will face is that some requirements need data from multiple business processes to meet the overall analytic needs. Customer and product profitability analyses are good examples. The "customer scorecard" may sound like a single analysis, but it actually requires data from many separate business processes. We call these *consolidated requirements* (or, occasionally, *second level business processes*) because they cannot be completely built until data from all prerequisite business processes have been loaded into the data warehouse.

Tying business requirements to the underlying business processes helps determine the level of effort needed to support a given requirement. If a requirement must have data from more than one business process, it will take more than one iteration of the Lifecycle. While these passes can happen in parallel with additional resources, there is no way around doing the work.

Converting from business requirements to business processes involves thinking about which business processes are required to support each requirement. For example, you can get a start at improving promotion response rates with data from a single business process: orders. As long as the order data captures a promotion code, you can calculate response rates and purchase amounts associated with each promotion. Better analysis would need to include data from the promotions business process; specifically, what was the total population of prospects who received a promotion. Now you can see who responded from orders, and who didn't from promotions. In the best case, you may want to bring in demographic data for prospects and use a data mining model to help identify the characteristics of prospects that are more likely to respond to a given promotion. Ultimately, complete promotions analysis would need data from at least three business processes (at least one, demographic data, comes from an external source). If improving promotion response rates is a top business priority, this decomposition process will help you show why it will take three iterations to complete the required data set. It will also show that basic analysis can begin once the first business process (orders) is loaded.

The most demanding type of business requirement is often called a *scorecard* or *executive dashboard*. This deceptively simple application draws on data from almost all business processes in the organization. You can't create the entire dashboard until you've built the whole data warehouse foundation. Or worse, you end up building the dashboard by hand every day, manually extracting, copying, and pasting data from all those sources to make it work. It can be difficult to get business folks to understand the magnitude of the effort involved in creating this "simple" report.

Adventure Works Example: Enterprise Requirements Documentation

This section walks you through the steps to create a requirements findings document for the Adventure Works example. The easiest way to create the requirements summary is to start with the requirements from one interview, such as those shown in Figure 1-5, and add in requirements from subsequent interviews. Often requirements from different interviews will fall into existing business requirements categories.

To understand what analyses will be enabled by each iteration of the Lifecycle, you need to re-sort the requirements by business process. Table 1-1 shows a subset of the analyses enabled by each individual business process. The Letter column is meant to serve as a shorthand reference you may use later in the prioritization process.

This table includes analytic requirements from across the Adventure Works enterprise. The VP of Sales' requirements are underlined. You should keep track of where the individual requirement for analysis came from within the organization. This will help you track back to the originator later on, after you re-sort the requirements by underlying business process.

Table 1-1: A subset of business processes derived from the requirements interviews

LETTER	BUSINESS PROCESS	SUPPORTED BUSINESS ANALYSES
A	Orders	Orders reporting and analysis, orders forecasting, advertising effectiveness, customer satisfaction, production forecasting, product profitability, customer profitability
B	Orders forecast	Sales performance, business planning, production forecasting
C	Call tracking	Call center performance, customer satisfaction, product quality, call center resource planning, customer profitability, product profitability
D	Returns	Customer satisfaction, product quality, customer profitability, product profitability, net sales

Building the Initial Data Warehouse Bus Matrix

As you identify the business processes needed to support each analytic requirement, you will also add those business processes to an enterprise data framework called the *Data Warehouse Bus Matrix*. This matrix maps your organizational business processes to the entities or objects that participate in those processes.

Each row in the matrix is a business process. Figure 1-6 shows a simplified example bus matrix for a retail company. Notice how the business processes down the left side of the matrix follow the organization's value chain. In this case, the company buys goods from their vendors and stores them in distribution centers. Then, as goods are demanded by consumers, they are moved out to the retail stores where they're held on shelves until the customer buys them and the goods leave the company's value chain. These business processes generally correspond to individual source systems or modules in the overall Enterprise Resource Planning (ERP) system.

The columns in the bus matrix are the descriptive objects that participate in the various business processes, such as store, product, and date. They contrast with the measurement-driven business processes that label the rows of the matrix. We call these objects *dimensions* in the dimensional model. Each dimension participates in one or more business processes — we indicate this by placing an X in the intersecting cell in the matrix. For example, the Vendor dimension is involved in both the purchasing and delivery processes. The store sale business process, on the other hand, does not involve the vendor or distribution center.

Business Processes	Dimensions						
	Date	Product	Vendor	Shipper	Dist Ctr	Store	Promo
Purchase Orders	X	X	X		X		
Dist Ctr Deliveries	X	X	X	X	X		
Dist Ctr Inventory	X	X			X		
Store Deliveries	X	X		X	X	X	
Store Inventory	X	X				X	
Store Sales	X	X				X	X

(Value Chain)

Figure 1-6: Example enterprise bus matrix for a retail company

The bus matrix is essentially your enterprise dimensional data architecture. For each business process (row), you can see exactly which dimensions (columns) you need to implement. And for each dimension, you can see which business processes it must support. This dimension-oriented view is the visual representation of *conformed dimensions* — a concept we define in the next chapter.

The business processes in the bus matrix, and the analytic requirements they support (and the value those requirements represent) become the major inputs to the next step in the requirements definition process: a prioritization session with senior management.

Adventure Works Example: Bus Matrix

As you go through the interview process, you may be surprised to discover a many-to-many relationship between people and data. That is, people need access to data from multiple business processes, and many people often want to look at data from the same business process, but from their own business perspective. For instance, people in marketing might be interested in orders data by product over time, while folks in sales might be interested in the same orders data, only by sales rep and region. As a reminder, this means you would design the orders data model at the atomic level so the same data set could be used to support both sales and marketing. It does NOT mean you should have two separate data marts, one for each department.

Figure 1-7 shows the start of a bus matrix for Adventure Works based on the interview with the VP of Sales that is included on the book's web site.

Adventure Works Cycles: Enterprise Data Warehouse Bus Matrix Entries for Sales Department											
	Dimensions										
Business Process	Date	Product	Employee	Customer (Reseller)	Customer (Internet)	Sales Territory	Currency	Channel	Promotion	Call Reason	Facility
Orders Forecasting	X	X	X	X	X	X	X	X			
Orders	X	X	X	X	X	X	X	X	X		
Inventory	X	X	X								X
Call tracking	X	X	X	X	X	X				X	
Returns	X	X		X	X	X	X		X		X

Figure 1-7: Bus Matrix business processes referred to in the VP of Sales interview

Here you see that one person, the VP of Sales, is interested in data from five different business processes.

Once you've got the requirements documented, it will become clear that you can't deliver them all at once. The prioritization process will help you and your organization figure out the appropriate order of events.

Prioritizing the Business Requirements

If you're a technical person, it's safe to say the prioritization process we describe here is one of the most powerful business tools you'll ever use. This is a bold statement, but we have used this tool many times and have been repeatedly successful. We've conducted a few prioritization sessions where the client decided not to move forward with the DW/BI project right away. This decision is usually reached because the prioritization process helped senior management better understand the nature of the commitment or the size of the data problems. This is also a success because it means they will work to fix the problems rather than try to build a DW/BI system on shaky ground.

The prioritization process is a planning meeting involving the DW/BI team, the DW/BI project business sponsors, and other key senior managers from across the organization.

In this meeting, you describe the business processes you identified in the enterprise requirements gathering process so everyone has an understanding of the full list of possibilities. Go into this session armed with a PowerPoint presentation that describes each business process, gives a few examples of the associated analyses it will support along with a feel for the business value of those analyses, and includes an initial sense of level of effort needed to implement the business process (its feasibility). Be as crisp and clear as possible. Try to keep this presentation under 90 minutes. As you describe each business process, you also describe the relative effort involved in supplying the needed data. Once everyone has an understanding of the business processes and terminology, take a break.

The second half of the session involves prioritizing the business processes. Lead the group in placing a sticky note for each business process onto a large version of a two-by-two grid like the Adventure Works example shown in Figure 1-8. This is an interesting exercise in negotiation and education and can easily take another hour and a half or more.

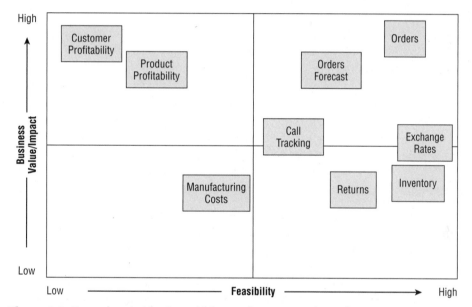

Figure 1-8: Example prioritization grid from Adventure Works Cycles

The prioritization grid is deceptively simple: Study it carefully. The Y axis is about relative business value. The group needs to reach consensus on the relative impact of implementing each business process. The participants need to remember to take an organizational approach to assigning business value. There will always be someone who thinks any given business process is the absolute top priority. Gently remind them that there's more to the business than their little slice.

The X axis represents the level of effort each business process will take to implement. It is stated in terms of relative feasibility so the easier business processes go to the right (high feasibility) and the harder business processes go to the left (low feasibility). The DW/BI team leads the assignment of feasibility because team members have a better sense about the technical difficulties involved in each business process (although feasibility is not just technical — there are often organizational and political difficulties as well).

The true feasibility is not fully understood at this point. If you have someone on the team who's been in the organization long enough, she should have a good sense for the level of effort required to implement each business process. One obvious factor is when business processes must be implemented together to support a high value, consolidated theme, such as customer or product profitability.

The prioritization session is a good opportunity to educate the business folks about how bad things really are. You don't want to sound negative, but it's important to explain the level of effort it takes to gather the data and make it useful. For example, integrating customer IDs from two different source systems is a grind.

When reviewing Figure 1-8, note that there are two items on the grid that are not actually business processes. Customer profitability and product profitability are consolidated themes that senior management has expressed significant interest in analyzing. These have been included on the grid to show their importance, but they are far over to the left to indicate the difficulty involved in building all the needed business processes. Given the number of analyses supported by data from the orders business process, it should come as no surprise that orders is the top priority. The team should get to work on this right away!

A CREDIBILITY BOOSTER

The prioritization process uses a common business school tool called the two-by-two matrix. This matrix was popularized in the early 1970s by the Boston Consulting Group. BCG used a "Growth-Share Matrix" to compare different business units in a portfolio by comparing relative market share with industry sales growth rates. A business unit with high market share in an industry with high growth rate was called a "Star." By contrast, a business unit with low market share in a low-growth industry was a "Pet" (later referred to as a "Dog").

The great thing about the matrix is the positive impression the DW/BI team makes by cleverly adapting a classic MBA tool.

Sources: The Boston Consulting Group, Perspectives on Experience, and The Product Portfolio (Boston, MA: The Boston Consulting Group, 1968).

Once all the business processes have been placed and everyone agrees on their relative locations, convert the matrix to a prioritized list of projects. One way to do this is to start in the upper-right corner of the prioritization grid and move to the lower-left corner, numbering the business processes as you encounter them. The two-dimensional nature of the matrix makes this a little difficult. Use the concept of concentric circles to establish a priority order, like ripples on a pond, centered in the upper-right corner.

The output of the prioritization process is a list of business processes in priority order. This list is your DW/BI roadmap; it tells you which row on the matrix, and which dimensions, to implement first. Less tangible, but equally important outcomes of the prioritization process are senior management consensus around the DW/BI roadmap, and a general improvement in the relationships between IT and the business.

In most cases, you will make only one pass at the enterprise requirements. Once the priorities are in place, the next pass and all subsequent passes will be at the level of the individual row on the bus matrix, the business process. Each row essentially becomes a project in the overall DW/BI program. From here on out, you will update enterprise business requirements and revisit priorities as the business changes, but most requirements definition efforts will be at the business process project level.

RESOURCES Learn more about the requirements prioritization process on pages 91–93 of *The Data Warehouse Lifecycle Toolkit, Second Edition.*

Once you've completed the prioritization session you can finalize the overall requirements document by including the resulting list of prioritized business processes. At this point the conceptual foundation of the DW/BI system is in place. The rest of the Lifecycle depends on what you learned in these initial steps to make decisions and set priorities for all three tracks that follow, and on into the deployment, maintenance, and growth phases.

RESOURCES You can find additional information about creating the requirements deliverables on pages 85–91 of *The Data Warehouse Lifecycle Toolkit, Second Edition.*

Revisiting the Project Planning

Now that you have a clear idea of your top priority business process, the data it generates, and the business requirements it supports, you can lay out a more detailed and precise project plan. This process is not much different from project planning for any major information technology project.

The plan will continue to evolve as you get more detail about the business requirements in the next step. There is a two-way arrow between the project planning and business requirements definition steps in Figure 1-1, but the backward flow is not as large because you gained significant understanding of the nature of the opportunity in the enterprise requirements gathering and narrowed your scope in the prioritization process.

Gathering Project-Level Requirements

Gathering project requirements follows the same basic process as the enterprise requirements gathering process described earlier. The difference is that now you have selected a particular business process on the bus matrix to implement. The enterprise requirements definition process provides a solid foundation for the project requirements. You now will deepen your understanding of the chosen business process.

The project requirements gathering step is about pulling together the information you need to be successful in the three tracks that follow. Specifically, you need enough detail to create real, practical, flexible data models that will support a broad range of analytic needs. You need a solid understanding of the technical issues around data volumes, data cleaning, data movement, user access, and a host of other issues so you can create a capable, flexible technical architecture to support the warehouse now and in the future. Finally, you need a clear understanding of the business analysis requirements to build the initial set of business intelligence applications to demonstrate value from the very start.

The same three steps you followed in the enterprise requirements process apply to the project requirements process: preparation, interviews, and documentation.

As we described in the enterprise requirements section, preparation is the critical first step. If you haven't already, do your homework. Study the particular business process in detail. Figure out as much as you can about how it works before you begin the interviews. Learn the business terminology, the steps in the business process, and how it is measured.

The goal with this round of interviews is to drill down on the selected business process in detail to understand the analyses, data models, and technologies required to make it work. This time you may take a more vertical slice of the organization, depending on the business process (some business processes have broader organizational appeal than others). Talk to the analysts, managers, report developers, and source systems people who can help you understand the intricacies of the business process in question. The actual interview process itself is generally the same as before.

Applying this interview approach to the Adventure Works example, the team will need to hold an additional set of interviews to drill down on orders-related analyses before it can start working designing the Orders business process dimensional model. The team needs to understand several issues that were raised in the enterprise requirements process. We'll look at the impact of a detailed understanding of questions like, "What is a customer?" and, "How do we determine the Sales Territory?" in the next chapter, which is on dimensional modeling. The team should also get more specific about the kinds of new reports and analyses people want to see as input to the BI Application track.

In fact, all of the information gathered in this second pass becomes the grist for the Adventure Works Cycles business dimensional modeling process case study in Chapter 2.

ALTERNATIVES TO INDIVIDUAL INTERVIEWS

If interviews won't work in your situation, we have had success with group requirements gathering sessions, but they are more risky. If you must do group sessions, here are a few tips:

- **Preparation is even more important. You have to know the business, and you also have to know what you want to accomplish and how you are going to go about it.**

- **Have a clear agenda with times listed for each section, breaks, and food and drink. Reserve a good room with plenty of space and comfortable chairs. Make sure you have all the tools you need — flip charts, markers, white boards, computers, and a projector — whatever makes sense for your plan.**

- **Get a strong, experienced design meeting leader to run the meetings. You have only a short time. If someone takes the meeting off course, you won't get what you need.**

Depending on the business process selected, consider whether to interview your customers and suppliers. They are, or could be, business users of information in the DW/BI system. In fact, the need to offer information outside the organization is common enough that many of the BI tool vendors include extranet access functionality as part of their product line. Listen carefully during the interviews to see if this is a likely source of significant business value for your organization.

Interviews with key source system people and data profiling play a bigger role in the project requirements gathering process. Strive to learn as much as possible about both the business requirements and the data realities.

The documentation process for the project requirements is similar to that of the enterprise definition process, except it is more detailed. Where the analytic requirements at the enterprise level ranged across all the business processes, at the project level, they should all be focused on the initial business process.

Although the project requirements definition task sounds a bit abbreviated here, it is actually the definition task you will repeat over and over, every time you iterate through the Lifecycle to bring the next priority business process into the DW/BI system. Let's hope you need to do the enterprise-level task only once, and then keep it updated.

RESOURCES To learn more about defining project level requirements, see pages 93–101 of *The Data Warehouse Lifecycle Toolkit, Second Edition.* Search kimballgroup.com for the topics "Business Requirements" and "Business Acceptance" for several related articles.

Summary

This chapter concentrated on the early tasks in the Lifecycle involving business requirements gathering, prioritization, and project planning. We gave special emphasis to the importance of understanding and documenting the business requirements.

We described a process for gaining sponsorship, defining and documenting the enterprise-level business requirements, prioritizing the opportunities with senior business people, and gathering project requirements related to the top priority business process. This process also included the challenging task of tying the analytic requirements down to the business processes that provide the underlying information.

The chapter also summarized some of the business requirements that might be found at a company like Adventure Works Cycles. The VP of Sales provided a set of analytic business requirements that tied to the business processes that fed into the bus matrix and the prioritization process.

These upfront business-related phases of each DW/BI project iteration are the most important. Unfortunately, they can be intimidating for technologists. Do not resist or avoid the requirements gathering phase of the project. The resulting understanding of the business issues, their priorities, and the data that supports their solution is priceless for the DW/BI team. The requirements document will be your reference point for all major decisions from here on out. You get huge value just from the content of the document alone.

But wait, there's more! The requirements gathering process also helps you build positive working relationships with the business people. As the business people participate in the requirements process, they see that you've done your homework. You understand them, you speak their language, you want to help solve the problem — in short, you get it.

If that's not enough to convince you, there are even more benefits to this process. Not only do you get documented requirements and better relationships, you gain active user support. As the business folks begin to understand your vision for an information solution, they see how your success ultimately leads to their success. They begin to see how their involvement will improve the chances of success for the DW/BI system and for the business itself.

CHAPTER 2

Designing the Business Process Dimensional Model

"To arrive at the simple is difficult."
— Rashid Elisha

This chapter is about the basic concepts of dimensional modeling and the process of designing a business process dimensional model. Designing the dimensional model falls within the central section of the Kimball Lifecycle, as shown in Figure 2-1. This middle row of the Lifecycle's central section focuses on data, hence the clever name: *the data track*. The main objective of the data track is to make sure users get the data they need to meet ongoing business requirements. The key word in this objective is *ongoing*: Your goal in this step is to create a usable, flexible, extensible data model. This model needs to support the full range of analyses, both now and for the foreseeable future.

The dimensional model is the true heart of the DW/BI system. It is the target for the ETL system, the structure of the database, and the model behind the user query and reporting experience. Clearly, the model must be well designed. The first part of this chapter is a brief primer on dimensional modeling, including an overview of facts, dimensions, the data warehouse bus matrix, and other core concepts. The second major section of the chapter delves into more detail on several important design techniques, such as slowly changing dimensions, hierarchies, and bridge tables. Once the basic concepts are in place, the third section presents a process for building dimensional models.

The fourth part of the chapter describes a dimensional model for the Adventure Works Cycles orders business process, providing an opportunity to explore several common dimensional modeling issues and their solutions.

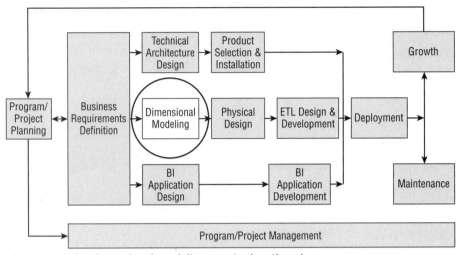

Figure 2-1: The dimensional modeling step in the Lifecycle context

RESOURCES This chapter describes what a dimensional model is, why it's a useful design technique for a DW/BI system, and how to go about designing a strong data foundation. You cannot possibly learn everything you need to know about dimensional modeling in a single chapter — even a long one like this. For additional detailed guidance on the techniques, including industry case studies, we refer you to *The Data Warehouse Toolkit, Second Edition*, Ralph Kimball and Margy Ross (Wiley, 2002). We provide page references for more information on specific concepts and techniques throughout this chapter.

Dimensional Modeling Concepts and Terminology

We approach the modeling process with three primary design goals in mind. We want our models to accomplish the following:

- Present the needed information to users as simply as possible
- Return query results to the users as quickly as possible
- Provide relevant information that accurately tracks the underlying business processes

Albert Einstein captured the main reason we use the dimensional model when he said, "Make everything as simple as possible, but not simpler." As it turns out, simplicity is relative. There is broad agreement in data warehousing and business intelligence that the dimensional model is the preferred structure for presenting information to users. The dimensional model is much easier for users to understand than the typical source system normalized model even though a dimensional model typically contains exactly the same content as a normalized model. It has far fewer tables, and information is grouped into coherent business categories that make sense to users. These categories, which we call dimensions, help users navigate the model because entire categories can be disregarded if they aren't relevant to a particular analysis.

Unfortunately, *as simple as possible* doesn't mean the model is necessarily simple. The model must reflect the business, and businesses are complex. If you simplify too much, typically by presenting only aggregated data, the model loses information that's critical to understanding the business. No matter how you model data, the intrinsic complexity of the data content is ultimately why most people will use structured reports and analytic applications to access the DW/BI system.

Achieving our second goal of good performance is a bit more platform-specific. In the relational environment, the dimensional model helps query performance because of the denormalization involved in creating the dimensions. By pre-joining the various hierarchies and lookup tables, the optimizer considers fewer join paths and creates fewer intermediate temporary tables. Analytic queries against the SQL Server relational database generally perform better — often far better — against a dimensional structure than against a fully normalized structure. At a more fundamental level, the optimizer can recognize the dimensional model and leverage its structure to dramatically reduce the number of rows it returns. This is known as *star join optimization*, and is, of course, an Enterprise Edition feature.

In the Analysis Services OLAP environment, the engine is specifically designed to support dimensional models. Performance is achieved in large part by pre-aggregating within and across dimensions.

Achieving the third goal requires a full range of design patterns that allow us to create models that accurately capture and track the business. Let's start with the basic patterns first. A *dimensional model* is made up of a central fact table (or tables) and its associated dimensions. The dimensional model is also called a *star schema* because it looks like a star with the fact table in the middle and the dimensions serving as the points on the star. We stick to the term dimensional model in this book to avoid confusion.

From a relational data modeling perspective, the dimensional model consists of a normalized fact table with denormalized dimension tables. This section defines the basic components of the dimensional model, facts and dimensions, along with some of the key concepts involved in handling changes over time.

Facts

Each fact table contains the measurements associated with a specific business process, like taking an order, displaying a web page, admitting a patient, or handling a customer support request. A record in a fact table is a measurement event. These events usually have numeric values that quantify the magnitude of the event, such as quantity ordered, sale amount, or call duration. These numbers are called *facts* (or *measures* in Analysis Services).

The primary key to the fact table is usually a multi-part key made up of a subset of the foreign keys from each dimension table involved in the business event.

Just the Facts

Most facts are numeric and additive (such as sales amount or unit sales), meaning they can be summed up across all dimensions. Additivity is important because DW/BI applications seldom retrieve a single fact table record. User queries generally select hundreds or thousands of records at a time and add them up. A simple query for sales by month for the last year returns only 12 rows in the answer set, but it may sum up across hundreds of thousands of rows (or more!). Other facts are semi-additive (such as market share or account balance), and still others are non-additive (such as unit price).

Not all numeric data are facts. Exceptions include discrete descriptive information like package size or weight (describes a product) or store square footage (describes a store). Generally, these less volatile numeric values end up as descriptive attributes in dimension tables. Such descriptive information is more naturally used for constraining a query, rather than being summed in a computation. This distinction is helpful when deciding whether a data element is part of a dimension or fact.

Some business processes track events without any real measures. If the event happens, we get an entry in the source system; if not, there is no row. Common examples of this kind of event include employment activities, such as hiring and firing, and event attendance, such as when a student attends a class. The fact tables that track these events typically do not have any actual fact measurements, so they're called *factless fact tables*. We usually add a column called something like event count that contains the number 1. This provides users with an easy way to count the number of events by summing the event count fact.

Some facts are *derived* or computed from other facts, just as a net sale number might be calculated from gross sales minus sales tax. Some semi-additive facts can be handled using a derived column that is based on the context of the query. Month end balance would add up across accounts, but not across date, for example. The non-additive unit price example could be addressed by defining it as an average unit price, which is total amount divided by total quantity. There are several options for dealing with these derived or computed facts. You can calculate them as part of the ETL process and store them in the fact table, you can put them in the fact table view definition, or you can include them in the definition of the Analysis Services database. The only way we find unacceptable is to leave the calculation to the user.

NOTE Using Analysis Services to calculate computed measures has a significant benefit in that you can define complex MDX calculations for semi-additive
facts that will automatically calculate correctly based on the context of each
query request.

The Grain

The level of detail contained in the fact table is called the *grain*. We strongly
urge you to build your fact tables with the lowest level of detail that is possible
from the original source — generally this is known as the *atomic level*. Atomic
fact tables provide complete flexibility to roll up the data to any level of summary needed across any dimension, now or in the future. You must keep each
fact table at a single grain. For example, it would be confusing and dangerous
to have individual sales order line items in the same fact table as the monthly
forecast.

NOTE Designing your fact tables at the lowest practical level of detail, the
atomic level, is a major contributor to the flexibility of the design.

Fact tables are very efficient. They are highly normalized, storing little redundant data. For most transaction-driven organizations, fact tables are also the
largest tables in the data warehouse database, often making up 95 percent or
more of the total relational database size. The relational fact table corresponds
to a *measure group* in Analysis Services.

Dimensions

Dimensions are the nouns of the dimensional model, describing the objects
that participate in the business, such as employee, subscriber, publication, customer, physician, vehicle, product, service, author, and store. Each dimension
table joins to all the business processes in which it participates. For example,
the product dimension participates in supplier orders, inventory, shipments,
and returns business processes. A single dimension that is shared across all
these processes is called a *conformed dimension*. We talk more about conformed
dimensions in a bit.

Think about dimensions as tables in a database because that's how you'll
implement them. Each table contains a list of homogeneous entities — products
in a manufacturing company, patients in a hospital, vehicles on auto insurance
policies, or customers in just about every organization. Usually, a dimension
includes all occurrences of its entity — all the products the company sells, for
example. There is only one active row for each particular occurrence in the table
at any time, and each row has a set of attributes that identify, describe, define,

and classify the occurrence. A product will have a certain size and a standard weight, and belong to a product group. These sizes and groups have descriptions, like a food product might come in "Mini-Pak" or "Jumbo size." A vehicle is painted a certain color, like "White," and has a certain option package, such as the "Jungle Jim sports utility" package (which includes side impact air bags, six-disc CD player, DVD system, and simulated leopard skin seats).

Some descriptive attributes in a dimension relate to each other in a *hierarchical* or one-to-many fashion. A vehicle has a manufacturer, brand, and model (such as GM Chevrolet Silverado, or Toyota Lexus RX Hybrid). Dimensions often have more than one such embedded hierarchy.

The underlying data structures for most relational transaction systems are designed using a technique known as *normalization*. This approach removes redundancies in the data by moving repeating attributes into their own tables. The physical process of recombining all the attributes of a business object, including its hierarchies, into a single dimension table is known as *denormalization*. As we described earlier, this simplifies the model from a user perspective. It also makes the join paths much simpler for the database query optimizer than a fully normalized model. The denormalized dimension still presents exactly the same information and relationships found in the normalized model — nothing is lost from an analytic perspective except complexity.

You can spot dimensions or their attributes in conversation with the business folks because they are often the "by" words in a query or report request. For example, a user wants to see sales *by* month *by* product. The natural ways users describe their business should be included in the dimensional model as dimensions or dimension attributes. This is important because many of the ways users analyze the business are often not captured in the transaction system. Including these attributes in the warehouse is part of the added value you can provide.

THE POWER OF DIMENSIONS

Dimensions provide the entry points into the data. Dimensional attributes are used in two primary ways: as the target for constraints and as the labels on the rows and columns of a report. If the dimensional attribute exists, you can constrain and label. If it doesn't exist, you simply can't.

Bringing Facts and Dimensions Together

The completed dimensional model has a characteristic appearance, with the fact table in the middle surrounded by the dimensions. Figure 2-2 shows a simple dimensional model for the classic example: the retail grocery sales business process. Note that this is one of the business process rows from the retail bus matrix shown in Figure 1-6 back in Chapter 1. It all ties together if you do it right.

This model allows users across the business to analyze retail sales activity from various perspectives. Category managers can look at sales by product for different stores and different dates. Store planners can look at sales by store format or location. Store managers can look at sales by date or cashier. There is something for everyone in the organization in this dimensional model. While this model is reasonably robust, a large retail grocer would have a few more dimensions, notably customer, and many more attributes.

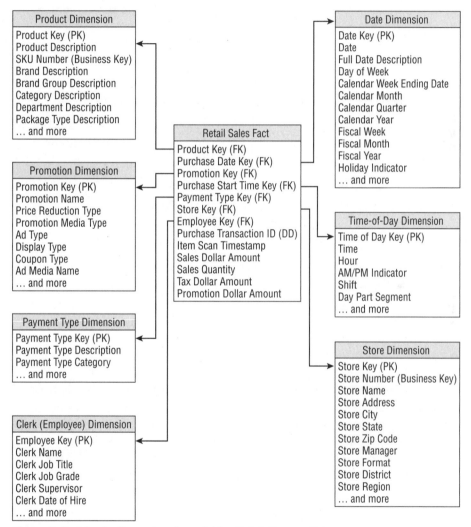

Figure 2-2: A basic dimensional model for Retail Grocery Sales

In Figure 2-2, fields labeled PK are primary keys. In other words, these fields are the basis of uniqueness for their tables. In a dimensional model, the primary keys of dimensions are always implemented physically as single columns. The fields labeled FK are foreign keys, and must always match the corresponding PKs in the dimensions in order to ensure referential integrity. The field labeled DD is a special degenerate dimension, which is described later.

RESOURCES To grasp the concept of dimensions and facts, it's helpful to see examples of dimensional models from a variety of industries and business processes. *The Data Warehouse Toolkit, Second Edition* has example dimensional models from many different industries and business processes, including retail sales, inventory, procurement, order management, CRM, accounting, HR, financial services, telecommunications and utilities, transportation, education, health care, e-commerce, and insurance.

The Bus Matrix, Conformed Dimensions, and Drill Across

The idea of re-using dimensions across multiple business processes is the foundation of the enterprise DW/BI system and the heart of the Kimball Bus Matrix. In the retail grocery example, a dimension such as product will be used in both the retail sales and the store inventory dimensional models. Because they are exactly the same products, both models must use the same dimension with the same keys to reliably support true, cross-business process analysis. If the logistics folks at the grocer's headquarters want to calculate inventory turns, they need to combine data from retail sales and inventory at the product level. This works only if the two business processes use the exact same product dimension with the same keys; that is, they use a *conformed* dimension. Conformed dimensions are the cornerstone of the enterprise-enabled DW/BI system. This kind of analysis involving data from more than one business process is called *drill across*.

NOTE The precise technical definition of conformed dimensions is that two dimensions are conformed if they contain one or more fields with the same names and contents. These "conformed fields" must then be used as the basis for the drill-across operation.
  Note that this idea of drilling across multiple fact tables and combining the answer sets requires a front-end tool capable of supporting this function. A powerful reason to use Analysis Services is that conformed dimensions are part of the basic architecture of the cube, so its calculation engine smoothly supports drill across.

Examine the Adventure Works Cycles high-level bus matrix shown in Figure 2-3. Each row of the bus matrix represents a business process and defines at least one fact table and its associated dimensions. Often, a row in the matrix will result in several related fact tables that help track the business process from different perspectives. The orders business process might have an orders transaction fact table at the line-item level and an orders snapshot fact table at the order level. Both of these orders-based dimensional models belong to the orders business process. We call this grouping a *business process dimensional model*. The fully populated enterprise DW/BI system contains sets of dimensional models that describe all the business processes in an organization's value chain. As you create the business process dimensional models for each row in the bus matrix, you end up with a much more detailed version of the matrix. Each dimensional model has its own row grouped by business process. Order transactions and order snapshot would be separate rows under the orders business process.

Adventure Works Data Warehouse Bus Matrix — Business Process	Business Priority	Date (Order, Start, Ship)	Product	Promotion	End Customer	Employee	Reseller	Page	Internet Registered User	Part	Vendor	Shipper	Problem	Account	Department	Currency (Source, Dest.)	Benefits Plan
Advertising																	
TV		X	X	X													
Print		X	X	X													
Online		X	X	X	X												
Promotions		X	X	X	X		X										
Co-op Programs		X	X	X		X	X										
Web Site Marketing		X	X	X	X			X	X								
PR		X	X	X													
Orders																	
Reseller Orders	1	X	X	X		X	X										
Internet Orders	1	X	X	X	X			X	X								
Orders Forecasting	2	X	X	X		X	X										
Purchasing		X	X		X	X				X	X	X					
Parts Inventory		X	X	X						X	X						
Manufacturing	6	X	X							X							
Finished Goods Inv.		X	X	X													
Shipping		X	X	X	X	X	X					X					
Returns	5	X	X		X	X	X					X					
Registration Cards		X	X		X												
Customer Calls	4	X	X	X	X	X	X				X		X				
Web Support		X	X		X	X	X	X	X				X				
Financial Forecasting		X	X	X	X	X	X					X			X	X	
Exchange Rate Mgmt.	3	X														X	
GL-Revenue and Expense		X												X	X		
Cost Accounting		X	X											X	X		
Payroll		X			X										X		
Benefits Enrollment		X			X												X

Figure 2-3: Adventure Works Cycles high-level enterprise bus matrix

The bus matrix is the enterprise business intelligence data roadmap. Creating the bus matrix is mandatory for any enterprise-wide DW/BI effort. Getting enterprise agreement on conformed dimensions is an organizational challenge for the data modeler and data steward. Having a single dimension table to describe the company's products, customers, or facilities means the organization has to agree on how each dimension table is defined. This includes the list of attributes, attribute names, hierarchies, and the business rules needed to define and derive each attribute in the table. This is politically hard work, and the effort grows as a function of the number of employees and divisions. But it is not optional. Conformed dimensions ensure that you are comparing apples to apples (assuming you are selling apples).

Additional Design Concepts and Techniques

Even though the dimensional modeling concepts we've described are fairly simple, they are applicable to a wide range of business scenarios. However, there are a few additional dimensional modeling concepts and techniques that are critical to implementing viable dimensional models. We start this section with a couple of key concepts: surrogate keys and slowly changing dimensions. Then we look at several techniques for modeling more complex business situations. Finally, we review the different types of fact tables. We briefly describe each concept or technique and provide references so you can find more detailed information if you need it.

Surrogate Keys

You will need to create a whole new set of keys in the data warehouse database, separate from the keys in the transaction source systems. We call these keys *surrogate keys*, although they are also known as meaningless keys, substitute keys, non-natural keys, or artificial keys. A surrogate key is a unique value, usually an integer, assigned to each row in the dimension. This surrogate key becomes the primary key of the dimension table and is used to join the dimension to the associated foreign key field in the fact table. Using surrogate keys in all dimension tables reaps the following benefits (and more):

- Surrogate keys help protect the DW/BI system from unexpected administrative changes in the keys coming from the source system.

- Surrogate keys allow the DW/BI system to integrate the same data, such as customer, from multiple source systems where they have different keys.

- Surrogate keys enable you to add rows to dimensions that do not exist in the source system. For example, the `date` table might have a "Date not known" row.

- Surrogate keys provide the means for tracking changes in dimension attributes over time.

- Integer surrogate keys can improve query and processing performance compared to larger character or GUID keys.

The ability to track changes in dimension attributes over time is reason enough to implement surrogate keys that are managed by the data warehouse. We've regretted it more than once when we decided not to track changes in attribute values over time, and later found out the historical values were important to support certain business analyses. We had to go back and add surrogate keys and re-create the dimension's change history. This is not a fun project; we encourage you to do it right the first time. If you use surrogate keys for all dimensions at the outset, it's easier to change a dimension later so that it tracks history.

The biggest cost of using surrogate keys is the burden it places on the ETL system. Assigning the surrogate keys to the dimension rows is easy. The real effort lies in mapping those keys into the fact table rows. A fact row comes to the DW/BI system with its source transaction keys in place. We call the transaction system key the *business key* (or *natural key*), although it is usually not business-like. In order to join these fact rows to the dimension tables, the ETL system must take each business key in each fact row and look up its corresponding surrogate key in the appropriate dimension. We call this lookup process the *surrogate key pipeline*. Integration Services, used to build the ETL system, provides functionality to support this lookup, as we describe in Chapter 7.

RESOURCES The following resources offer additional information about surrogate keys:

- *The Data Warehouse Toolkit, Second Edition*, pages 58–62.

- Search `http://msdn.microsoft.com` using the search string "surrogate key."

Slowly Changing Dimensions

Although we like to think of the attribute values in a dimension as fixed, any attribute can change over time. In an employee dimension, the date of birth should not change over time (other than error corrections, which your ETL system should expect). However, other fields, such as the employee's department, might change several times over the length of a person's employment. Many of these changes are critical to understanding the dynamics of the business. The ability to track these changes over time is one of the fundamental reasons for the existence of the DW/BI system.

Almost all dimensions have attributes whose values will change over time. Therefore, you need to be prepared to deal with a change to the value of any attribute. The techniques we use to manage attribute change in a dimension are part of what we call *slowly changing dimensions* (SCDs). However, just because something changes, it doesn't mean that change has significance to the business. The choice of which dimension attributes you need to track and how you track them is a business decision. The main technique used to deal with changes the business doesn't care about is called type 1, and the main technique used to handle changes the business wants to track is called type 2.

HOW SLOW IS SLOW?

We call this concept a *slowly changing dimension attribute* because the attributes that describe a business entity generally don't change very often. Take customer address, for example. The US Census Bureau did an in-depth study of migration patterns (`www.census.gov/population/www/pop-profile/geomob.html`), and found that 16.8 percent of Americans move in a given year, and 62 percent of these moves are within the same county. If a change in zip code is considered to be a significant business event, a simple customer dimension with name and address information should generate less than 16.8 percent change rows per year. If an attribute changes rapidly, causing the dimension to grow at a dramatic rate, this usually indicates the presence of a business process that should be tracked separately, either as a separate dimension, called a *mini-dimension*, or as a fact table rather than as a dimension attribute.

Handling changes using the type 1 technique overwrites the existing attribute value with the new value. Use this method if the business users don't care about keeping track of historical values when the value of an attribute changes. The type 1 change does not preserve the attribute value that was in place at the time a historical transaction occurred. For example, the Adventure Works customer dimension has an attribute for commute distance. Using type 1, when a customer moves, their old commute distance is overwritten with the new value. The old value is gone. All purchases, including purchases made prior to the change, will be associated with the new value for commute distance.

If you need to track the history of attribute changes, use the type 2 technique. Type 2 change tracking is a powerful method for capturing the attribute values that were in effect at a point in time and relating them to the business events in which they participated. When a change to a type 2 attribute occurs, the ETL process creates a new row in the dimension table to capture the new values of the changed dimension attribute. The attributes in the new row are in effect as of the time of the change moving forward. The previously existing row is marked to show that its attributes were in effect right up until the appearance of the new row.

Using the type 2 technique to track changes to the example commute distance attribute will preserve history. The ETL system writes a new row to the customer dimension, with a new surrogate key and date stamps to show when the row came into effect and when it expires. (The system also updates the expiration date stamp for the old row.) All fact rows moving forward will be assigned the surrogate key for this new row. All the existing fact rows keep their old customer surrogate key, which joins to the old row. Purchases made prior to the change will be associated with the commute distance that was in effect when the purchase was made.

Type 2 change tracking is more work to manage in the ETL system, although it's transparent to the user queries. Most of the popular ETL tools, including Integration Services, have these techniques built in. The commute distance example is a good one in terms of its business impact. If a marketing analyst does a study to understand the relationship between commute distance and bicycle purchasing, type 1 tracking will yield very different results than type 2. In fact, type 1 will yield incorrect results, but that may not be apparent to the analyst.

Here's a good guide for deciding if it's worth the effort to use type 2 change tracking for an attribute: Ask yourself if the data has to be right.

NOTE A third change tracking technique, called type 3, keeps separate columns for both the old and new attribute values — sometimes called "alternate realities." In our experience, type 3 is less common because it involves changing the physical tables and is not very extensible. If you choose to use type 3 tracking, you will need to add a new type 3 column for every major change, which can lead to a wide table. The technique is most often used for an organization hierarchy that changes seldom, perhaps annually. Often, only two versions are kept (current and prior).

RESOURCES The following resources offer additional information about slowly changing dimensions:

- *The Data Warehouse Toolkit, Second Edition*, pages 95–105.
- Books Online: A search for "slowly changing dimension support" will return several related topics.

DOWNLOADS You can find a more detailed version of the commute distance example with example data on the book's web site (`kimballgroup.com/html/booksMDWTtools.html`).

Dates

Date is the fundamental business dimension across all organizations and industries, although many times a date table doesn't exist in the operational environment. Analyses that trend across dates or make comparisons between periods (that is, nearly all business analyses) are best supported by creating and maintaining a robust date dimension.

Every dimensional DW/BI system has a date (or calendar) dimension, typically with one row for every day for which you expect to have data in a fact table. Calling it the date dimension emphasizes that its grain is at the day level rather than time of day. In other words, the Date table will have 365 or 366 rows in it per year.

> **NOTE** The date dimension is a good example of a *role-playing* dimension. It is common for a date dimension to be used to represent different dates, such as order date, due date, and ship date. To support users who will be directly accessing the relational database, you can either define a view for each role named appropriately (e.g., Order_Date), or define synonyms on the base view of the date dimension. The synonym approach is simple, but it only allows you to rename the entire table, not the columns within the table. Reports that can't distinguish between order date and due date can be confusing.
>
> If your users will access the data through Analysis Services only, you don't need to bother with views or synonyms to handle multiple roles. Analysis Services has built-in support for the concept of role-playing dimensions. As we discuss in Chapter 8, however, the Analysis Services role-playing dimensions are akin to creating relational synonyms: You can name the overall dimension role, but not each column within the dimension role.

We strongly recommend using a surrogate key for date because of the classic problem often faced by technical people: Sometimes you don't have a date. While we can't help the technical people here, we can say that transactions often arrive at the data warehouse database without a date because the value in the source system is missing, unknowable, or the event hasn't happened yet. Surrogate keys on the date dimension help manage the problem of missing dates. Create a few rows in the date dimension that describe such events, and assign the appropriate surrogate date key to the fact rows with the missing dates.

In the absence of a surrogate date key, you'll create date dimension members with strange dates such as 1-Jan-1900 to mean *Unknown* and 31-Dec-9999 to mean *Hasn't happened yet*. Overloading the fact dates in this way isn't the end of the world, but it can confuse users and cause erroneous results.

The date dimension surrogate key has one slight deviation from the rule. Where other surrogate keys are usually a meaningless sequence of integers, it's a good idea to use a meaningful value for the date surrogate key. Specifically, use an integer that corresponds to the date in year-month-day order, so September 22, 2010 would be 20100922. This can lead to more efficient queries against the relational database. It also makes implementing date-based partitioning much easier, and the partition management function will be more understandable.

Just to prove that we're not entirely dogmatic and inflexible, we don't always use surrogate keys for dates that appear as dimension attributes. Generally, if a particular date attribute has business meaning, we use the date surrogate key. Otherwise we use a `date` or `smalldatetime` data type. One way to spot a good candidate for a date surrogate key is if the attribute's date values fall within the date range of the organizational calendar, and therefore are all in the `Date` table.

RESOURCES The following resources offer additional information about the date dimension:

- *The Data Warehouse Toolkit, Second Edition*, pages 38–41.
- Books Online: Search for the topic "Time Dimensions (SSAS)" and related topics.

Degenerate Dimensions

Transaction identifiers often end up as degenerate dimensions without joining to an actual dimension table. In the retail grocery example, all the individual items you purchase in a trip through the checkout line are assigned a transaction ID. The transaction ID is not a dimension — it doesn't exist outside the transaction and it has no descriptive attributes of its own because they've already been handled in separate dimensions. It's not a fact — it doesn't measure the event in any way, and is not additive. We call attributes such as transaction ID a *degenerate dimension* because it's like a dimension without attributes. And because there are no associated attributes, there is no dimension table. We include it in the fact table because it serves a purpose from an analytic perspective. You can use it to tie together all the line items in a market basket to do some interesting data mining, as we discuss in Chapter 13. You can also use it to tie back to the transaction system if additional orders-related data is needed. The degenerate dimension is known as a *fact dimension* in Analysis Services.

Snowflaking

In simple terms, snowflaking is the practice of connecting lookup tables to fields in the dimension tables. At the extreme, snowflaking involves re-normalizing the dimensions to the third normal form level, usually under the misguided belief that this will improve maintainability, increase flexibility, or save space. We discourage snowflaking. It makes the model more complex and therefore less usable, and it actually makes it more difficult to maintain, especially for type 2 slowly changing dimensions.

In a few cases we support the idea of connecting lookup or grouping tables to the dimensions. One of these cases involves rarely used lookups, as in the example of joining the `Date` table to the date of birth field in the customer dimension so we can count customers grouped by their month of birth. We call this purpose-specific snowflake table an *outrigger* table. When you're building your Analysis Services database, you'll see this same concept referred to as a *reference dimension*.

Sometimes it's easier to maintain a dimension in the ETL process when it's been partially normalized or snowflaked. This is especially true if the source data is a mess and you're trying to ensure the dimension hierarchy is correctly structured. In this case, there's nothing wrong with using the normalized structure in the ETL application. Just make sure the business users never have to deal with it.

NOTE Analysis Services can handle snowflaked dimensions and hides the added complexity from the business users. In the interest of simplicity, we encourage you to fully populate the base dimensions rather than snowflaking. The one exception is that the Analysis Services build process can go faster for large dimensions, say more than 1 million rows, when the source is snowflaked or fully denormalized in the ETL staging database. Test it first before you do all the extra work.

RESOURCES The following resources offer additional information about snowflaking:

- *The Data Warehouse Toolkit, Second Edition*, pages 55–57.
- Books Online: Search for the topic "Dimension Structure" and other Books Online topics on dimensions.

Many-to-Many or Multivalued Dimensions

The standard relationship between a dimension table and fact table is called *one-to-many*. This means one row in the dimension table will join to many rows in the fact table, but one row on the fact table will join to only one row in the dimension table. This relationship is important because it keeps us from double counting. Fortunately, in most cases this relationship holds true.

There are two common instances where the real world is more complex than one-to-many:

- Many-to-many between the fact table and a dimension
- Many-to-many between dimensions

These two instances are essentially the same, except the fact-to-dimension version is missing an intermediate dimension that uniquely describes the group. In both cases, we introduce an intermediate table called a *bridge table* that supports the more complex many-to-many relationship.

The Many-to-Many Relationship Between a Fact and Dimension

A many-to-many relationship between a fact table and a dimension occurs when multiple dimension values can be assigned to a single fact transaction. A common example is when multiple sales people can be assigned to a given sale. This often happens in complex, big-ticket sales such as computer systems. Accurately handling this situation requires creating a bridge table that assembles the sales rep combinations into groups. Figure 2-4 shows an example of the SalesRepGroup bridge table.

The ETL process needs to look up the appropriate sales rep group key in the bridge table for the combination of sales reps in each incoming fact table record, and add a new group if it doesn't exist. Note that the bridge table in Figure 2-4 introduces a risk of double counting. If we sum dollar sales by sales rep, every sales rep will get credit for the total sale. For some analyses, this is the right answer, but for others you don't want any double counting. It's possible to handle this risk by adding a weighting factor column in the bridge table. The weighting factor is a fractional value that sums to one for each sales rep group. Multiply the weighting factor and the additive facts to allocate the facts according to the contribution of each individual in the group.

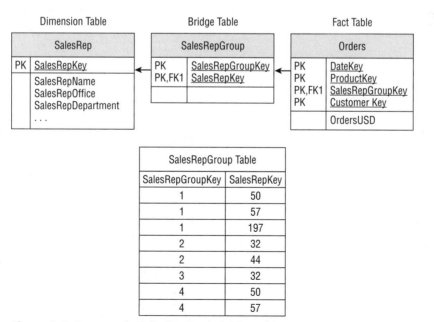

Figure 2-4: An example SalesRepGroup bridge table

Note that you might need to add a `SalesRepGroupKey` table between `Orders` and `SalesRepGroup` to support a true primary key - foreign key relationship. This turns this fact-to-dimension instance into a dimension-to-dimension instance.

Many-to-Many Between Dimensions

The many-to-many relationship between dimensions is an important concept from an analytic point of view. Most dimensions are not entirely independent of one another. Dimension independence is more of a continuum than a binary state. At one end of the continuum, the store and product dimensions in a retail grocery chain are relatively independent, but not entirely. Some store formats don't carry certain products. Other dimensions are much more closely related, but are difficult to combine into a single dimension because of their many-to-many relationship. In banking, for example, there is a direct relationship between account and customer, but it's not one-to-one. Any given account can have one or more customers as signatories, and any given customer can have one or more accounts. Banks often view their data from an account perspective; the `MonthAccountSnapshot` is a common fact table in financial institutions. The account focus makes it difficult to view accounts by customer because of the many-to-many relationship. One approach would be to create a `CustomerGroup` bridge table that joins to the fact table, such as the `SalesRepGroup` table in the previous many-to-many example. A better approach takes advantage of the relationship between account and customer, as shown in Figure 2-5.

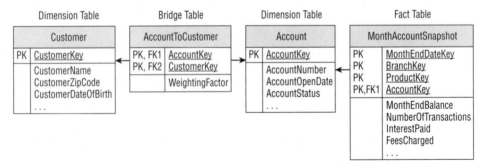

Figure 2-5: An example many-to-many bridge table between dimensions

An `AccountToCustomer` bridge table between the account and customer dimensions can capture the many-to-many relationship with a couple of significant benefits. First, the relationship is already known in the source system, so creating the bridge table will be easier than the manual build process required for the `SalesRepGroup` table. Second, the account-customer relationship is interesting in its own right. The `AccountToCustomer` bridge table allows users to answer questions such as "What is the average number of accounts per customer?" without joining to any fact table.

Bridge tables are often an indicator of an underlying business process. This is especially true if you must keep track of changes to bridge tables over time (that is, the relationship itself is type 2). For customers and accounts, the business process might be called account maintenance, and one of the transactions might be called "Add a signatory." If three customers were associated with an account, there would be three Add transactions for that account in the source system. Usually these transactions and the business processes they represent are not important enough to track in the DW/BI system with their own fact tables. However, the relationships and changes they produce are important to analyzing the business. We include them in the dimensional model as slowly changing dimensions, and in some cases as bridge tables.

NOTE Analysis Services has functionality to support many-to-many dimensions. Analysis Services expects the same kind of structure that we described in this section. They call the bridge table an *intermediate fact* table, which is exactly what it is.

RESOURCES The following resources offer additional information about many-to-many relationships:

- *The Data Warehouse Toolkit, Second Edition*, pages 262–265 for many-to-many between fact and dimension and pages 205–206 for many-to-many between dimensions.

- Books Online: Enter the search string "Defining a Many-to-Many Relationship" for a list of related Books Online topics.

Hierarchies

Hierarchies are meaningful, standard ways to group the data within a dimension so you can begin with the big picture and drill down to lower levels to investigate anomalies. Hierarchies are the main paths for summarizing the data. Common hierarchies include organizational hierarchies, often starting from the individual person level; geographic hierarchies based on physical location, such as a customer address; product hierarchies that often correspond to merchandise rollups such as brand and category; and responsibility hierarchies such as sales territory that assign customers to sales reps (or vice versa). There are many industry-related hierarchies, such as the North American Industrial Classification System (replacement for the Standard Industrial Classification [SIC] code) or the World Health Organization's International Classification of Diseases — Tenth Modification (ICD-10).

Simple hierarchies involving a standard one-to-many rollup with only a few fixed levels should be denormalized right into the granular dimension. A four-level product hierarchy might start with product, which rolls up to brand, then to subcategory, and finally to category. Each of these levels would simply be columns in the product dimension table. In fact, this flattening of hierarchies is one of the main design tasks of creating a dimension table. Many organizations will have several different simple hierarchies in a given dimension to support different analytic requirements.

Of course, not all hierarchies are simple. The challenge for the dimensional modeler is to determine how to balance the tradeoff between ease of use and flexibility in representing the more difficult hierarchies. There are at least two common hierarchy challenges: variable-depth (or ragged hierarchies) and frequently changing hierarchies. Both of these problems require more complex solutions than simple denormalization. We briefly describe these solutions here, and refer you to more detailed information in the other *Toolkit* books if you should need it.

Variable-Depth Hierarchies

A good example of the variable-depth hierarchy is the manufacturing bill of materials that provides the information needed to build a particular product. In this case, parts can go into products or into intermediate layers, called subassemblies, which then go into products, also called *top assemblies*. This layering can go dozens of levels deep, or more, in a complex product (think about a Boeing 787).

Those of you who were computer science majors may recall writing recursive subroutines and appreciate the efficiency of recursion for parsing a parent-child or self-referencing table. In SQL, this recursive structure is implemented by simply including a parent key field in the child record that points back to the parent record in the same table. For example, one of the fields in an `Employee` table could be the `Parent Employee Key` (or `Manager Key`).

RECURSIVE CAPABILITIES

SQL 99 introduced recursion into the "official" SQL language using the `WITH` Common Table Expression syntax. All the major relational database products provide this functionality in some form, including SQL Server. Unfortunately, recursion isn't a great solution in the relational environment because it requires more complex SQL than most front-end tools can handle. Even if the tool can recursively unpack the self-referencing dimension relationship, it then must be able to join the resulting dataset to the fact table. Very few of the query tools are able to generate the SQL required to navigate a parent-child relationship together with a dimension-fact join.

On the other hand, this kind of recursive relationship is easy to build and manage in the Analysis Services dimensional database. Analysis Services uses different terminology: *parent-child* rather than *variable-depth* hierarchies.

The Data Warehouse Toolkit, Second Edition describes a navigation bridge table in Chapter 6 that solves this problem in the relational world. But this solution is relatively unwieldy to manage and query. Fortunately, we have some powerful alternatives in SQL Server. Analysis Services has a built-in understanding of the parent-child data structure, and Reporting Services can navigate the parent-child hierarchy using some of the advanced properties of the tablix control. If you have variable-depth hierarchies and expect to use the relational database for reporting and analysis, it makes sense to include both the parent-child fields and the navigation bridge table to meet the needs of various environments.

Frequently Changing Hierarchies

If you need to track changes in the variable-depth hierarchy over time, your problem becomes more complex, especially with the parent-child data structure. Tracking changes, as you recall, requires using a surrogate key. If someone is promoted, they will get a new row in the table with a new surrogate key. At that point, everyone who reports to that person will have to have their manager key updated. If manager key is a type 2 attribute, new rows with new surrogate keys will now need to be generated for these rows. If there are any folks who report to these people, the changes must ripple down until we reach the bottom of the org chart. In the worst case, a change to one of the CEO's attributes, such as marital status, causes the CEO to get a new surrogate key. This means the people who report to the CEO will get new surrogate keys, and so on down the entire hierarchy.

Ultimately, this problem is really about tracking the Human Resources business process. That is, if keeping track of all the changes that take place in your employee database is a high priority from an analytic point of view, you need to create a fact table, or a set of fact tables that track these events. Trying to cram all this event-based information into a type 2 dimension just doesn't work very well.

RESOURCES The following resources offer additional information about hierarchies:

- The *Data Warehouse Toolkit, Second Edition,* pages 161–168.
- The *Data Warehouse Lifecycle Toolkit, Second Edition*, pages 268–270.
- SQL Server Books Online: Enter the search string "Attributes and Attribute Hierarchies" as a starting point.

Aggregate Dimensions

You will often have data in the DW/BI system at different levels of granularity. Sometimes it comes to you that way, as with forecast data that is created at a level higher than the individual product. Other times you create it yourself to give the users better query performance. There are two ways to aggregate data in the warehouse, one by entirely removing a dimension, the other by rolling up in a dimension's hierarchy. When you aggregate using a hierarchy rollup in the relational database, you need to provide a new, shrunken dimension at this aggregate level. Figure 2-6 shows how the Adventure Works Cycles `Product` table can be shrunken to the subcategory level to allow it to join to forecast data that is created at the subcategory level.

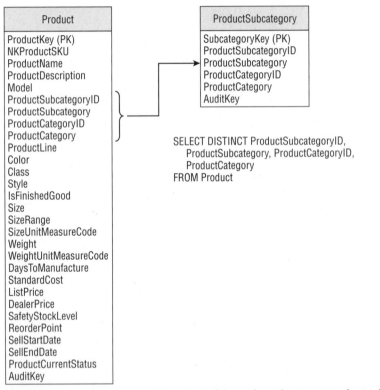

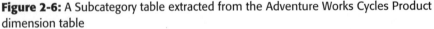

Figure 2-6: A Subcategory table extracted from the Adventure Works Cycles Product dimension table

Each subcategory includes a mix of color, size, and weight attributes, for example. Therefore, most of the columns in the `Product` table do not make sense at the Subcategory level. This results in a much shorter dimension, hence the common term *shrunken dimension*.

The keys for aggregate dimensions need to be generated in the ETL process and are not derived from the base table keys. Records can be added or subtracted from the base table over time and thus there is no guarantee that a key from the base table can be used in the aggregate dimension.

NOTE The Analysis Services OLAP engine automatically manages all this behind the scenes.

You can easily hook in a fact table at any level of a dimension. Of course you may still need aggregate dimensions to support business process metrics (such as forecast), which live at the aggregate level only.

RESOURCES The following resource offers additional information about aggregate dimensions:

- Kimballgroup.com: Search for the string "Shrunken Dimensions" for an article on aggregate dimensions. This article also appears on page 539 of the *Kimball Group Reader*.

Junk Dimensions

Many business processes involve several flags or status indicators or types. In a pure dimensional model, these would each be placed in their own dimension table, which often is just the surrogate key and the descriptive column, usually with only a few rows. For example, an order transaction might have a payment type dimension with only three allowed values: "Credit," "Cash," or "Account." Another small order dimension could be transaction type with only two allowed values: "Order," or "Refund." In practice, using a single table for each small dimension can make the model confusing because there are too many tables. Worse, it makes the fact table much larger because each small dimension table adds a key column to the fact table.

The design pattern we apply to this situation is called a *junk dimension*. A junk dimension is a combination of the columns of the separate small dimensions into a single table. Transaction type and payment type could be combined into a single table with two attribute columns: `Transaction_Type` and `Payment_Type`. The resulting `TransactionInfo` table would only need six rows to hold all possible combinations of payment type and transaction type. Each fact row would contain a single transaction info key that would join to the dimension row that holds the correct combination for that fact row.

NOTE In Analysis Services, each of the different attributes included in the junk dimension becomes a separate attribute hierarchy. As in the relational data model, the disparate attribute hierarchies would be grouped together under one dimension, `TransactionInfo` in our example. You'd hide the bottom level of the dimension that has the surrogate key representing the intersection of the codes.

RESOURCES The following resources offer additional information about junk dimensions:

- ▪ *The Data Warehouse Toolkit, Second Edition*, pages 117–119.
- ▪ *The Data Warehouse Lifecycle Toolkit, Second Edition*, pages 263–265.
- ▪ Kimballgroup.com: Search for the topic "Junk Dimensions" for a relevant article.

The Three Fact Table Types

There are three fundamental types of fact tables in the DW/BI system: transaction, periodic snapshot, and accumulating snapshot. Most of what we have described thus far falls into the transaction category. *Transaction* fact tables track each transaction as it occurs at a discrete point in time — when the transaction event occurred. The *periodic snapshot* fact table captures cumulative performance over specific time intervals. It aggregates many of the facts across the time period, providing users with a fast way to get totals. Where periodic snapshots are taken at specific points in time, after the month-end close, for example, the *accumulating snapshot* is constantly updated over time. Accumulating snapshots is particularly valuable for combining data across several business processes in the value chain. Generally, the design of the accumulating snapshot includes several date fields to capture the dates when the item in question passes through each of the business processes or milestones in the value chain. For an orders accumulating snapshot that captures metrics about the complete life of an order, these dates might include the following:

- ▪ Order date
- ▪ Requested ship date
- ▪ Manufactured date
- ▪ Actual ship date
- ▪ Arrival date
- ▪ Invoice date
- ▪ Payment received date

The accumulating snapshot provides the status of open orders at any point in time and a history of completed orders just waiting to be scrutinized for interesting metrics.

NOTE Transaction fact tables are clearly what Analysis Services was designed for. Your Analysis Services database can accommodate periodic and accumulating snapshots, but you do need to be careful. The problem is not the model, but the process for updating the data. Snapshot fact tables — particularly accumulating snapshots — tend to be updated a lot in the ETL process. This is expensive but not intolerable in the relational database. It's far more expensive for Analysis Services, which doesn't really support fact table updates at all.

For snapshot facts to work in Analysis Services for even moderate-sized data sets, you'll need the Enterprise Edition feature that allows cube partitioning or you'll need to reprocess the entire cube on every load.

RESOURCES The following resources offer additional information about the three fact table types:

- ▪ *The Data Warehouse Toolkit, Second Edition,* pages 128–130 and 132–135.

- ▪ *The Data Warehouse Lifecycle Toolkit, Second Edition*, pages 273–276.

- ▪ Kimballgroup.com: Enter the search string "Snapshot Fact Table" for articles on the different fact table types.

Aggregates

Aggregates are precalculated summary tables that serve the primary purpose of improving performance. If the database engine could instantly roll the data up to the highest level, you wouldn't need aggregate tables. In fact, precalculating aggregates is one of the two reasons for the existence of OLAP engines such as Analysis Services (the other reason being more advanced analytic capabilities). SQL Server Analysis Services can create and manage aggregate tables in the relational platform (called relational OLAP or ROLAP) or in the OLAP engine. The decision to create aggregate tables in the relational versus OLAP engines is a tradeoff. If the aggregates are stored in Analysis Services' format, access to the data is limited to tools that generate MDX. If the aggregates are stored in the relational database, they can be accessed by tools that generate SQL. If your front-end tool is adept at generating MDX, using Analysis Services to manage aggregates has significant advantages. If you must support relational access, especially ad hoc access, you need to create and manage any aggregate tables needed for performance (using indexed views if possible), along with the associated aggregate dimensions described earlier.

NOTE Kimball Group refers to the summary tables as aggregates and the summarization process as aggregation. SQL Server Analysis Services uses essentially the opposite terminology; in that environment, an aggregation is the summary table, and aggregates are the rules that define how the data is rolled up.

In this section, we have covered several of the common design challenges you will typically run up against in developing a dimensional model. This is not an exhaustive list, but it should be enough to help you understand the modeling process. If you are charged with the role of data modeler and this is your first dimensional modeling effort, we again strongly encourage you to continue your education by reading *The Data Warehouse Toolkit, Second Edition*.

The Dimensional Modeling Process

With a basic understanding of dimensional modeling and the core techniques under your belt, this section shifts focus to describe the process of building a dimensional model. Creating a dimensional model is a highly iterative and dynamic process. After a few preparation steps and some exploratory data profiling, the design process begins with an initial graphical model pulled from the bus matrix and presented at the entity level. This model is critically scrutinized in a high-level design session that also yields an initial list of attributes for each table and a list of issues requiring additional investigation. Once the high-level model is in place, the detailed modeling process takes the model table by table and drills down into the definitions, sources, relationships, data quality problems, and transformations required to populate the model. The last phase of the modeling process involves reviewing and validating the model with several interested parties. The primary goals of this process are to create a model that meets the business requirements, provides the ETL team with a solid starting point and clear direction, and verifies that the data is available to fill out the model.

Designing a dimensional model is a series of successive approximations, where you create more detailed and robust models based on your growing understanding of the source systems, the business needs, and the associated transformations. Often we've made changes that sounded clever at the time, but ended up changing them back in a later pass because they didn't work, either from the user or technical perspective, or both! This series of iterations usually stops once the model clearly meets the business needs in a flexible and extensible way. This iterative process typically takes a few weeks for a single business process dimensional model, but can take longer depending on the complexity of the business process, availability of knowledgeable participants, existence of well-documented detailed business requirements, and the number of pre-existing reusable dimension tables.

RESOURCES We dedicated an entire chapter to the dimensional modeling process in the *Lifecycle Toolkit*. This is required reading for the lead dimensional modeler: *The Data Warehouse Lifecycle Toolkit, Second Edition*, Chapter 7 (pages 287–325).

NOTE Creating the dimensional model is where an expert can help. If your team is new to the dimensional modeling process, bringing in someone who has extensive experience creating dimensional models can save you weeks of time, pain, and suffering. However, do not let the consultant take over the process — make them lead the team and facilitate the effort so everyone can participate in the design process and learn why various design decisions were made. Don't let the consultant disappear for a few days or a week or two and bring you back a completed model. The goal is to learn what goes into a dimensional model and why, so you know how to maintain and improve your model over time. More important, you need to know how to do the next one, so you don't have to pay someone to do this for you forever.

Preparation

It's a good idea to do a little preparation before you pull everyone into a conference room to create the dimensional model. First, you need to figure out who is going to be involved and what they are supposed to do. Next, the core participants should revisit the business requirements and the data architecture strategy. Meanwhile, the lead modeler needs to get the modeling tools in place and prepare a set of naming conventions. Let's discuss each of these preparation steps in a bit more detail.

Identify Roles and Participants

As Table 2-1 shows, several roles are involved in the modeling step, but a core modeling team of two or three people usually does most of the work. The core modeling team includes a data modeler with a strong technical background and solid experience with the source systems, and a business analyst who brings a solid understanding of how the data is used in the analysis process and how it could be made more useful or accessible. The core modeling team often includes someone from the ETL team with extensive source systems development experience and an interest in learning. The *data modeler* has overall responsibility for creating the dimensional model.

Table 2-1: Major participants in creating the dimensional model

PARTICIPANT	PURPOSE/ROLE IN MODELING PROCESS
Data modeler	Primary responsibility
Business analyst	Analysis and source expert, business definitions
Data steward	Drive agreement on enterprise names, definitions, rules, and data quality

Continued

Table 2-1 *(continued)*

PARTICIPANT	PURPOSE/ROLE IN MODELING PROCESS
Business power user	Describe and refine data sources and business rules from a user perspective
Source system developer	Source expert, business rules and data quality
DBA	Design guidance, early learning
ETL designer	Early learning
ETL developer	Early learning
Steering/Governance Committee	Naming, business definitions, model validation

The core modeling team works closely with source system developers who can explain the contents, meaning, business rules, timing, and other intricacies of the particular source system involved in the dimensional model.

We also suggest you include the DBA who will be implementing the physical database and the ETL designer and developer in the modeling process. These folks do so much better if they understand the business rationale for the model. This is especially true of the DBA who may have a transaction system background and does not understand the purpose of dimensional modeling.

There are generally a few additional participants as well. Although you risk slowing down the design process a bit by including more people, the benefits of a more robust design and engaged partners are almost always worth the price.

Revisit the Requirements

After the modeling team and the data strategy are in place, the team's first step will be to pull out the detailed requirements documentation and carefully comb through it. If you skipped to this chapter with the idea that you could avoid all that business stuff, sorry, but you need to go back and do the work. The modeling team must understand the business problems the users are trying to solve and the kinds of analyses they perform to solve them. It's the team's job to translate those requirements into flexible dimensional model that can support broad classes of analysis, not just re-create specific reports. This isn't an easy job. The data modeler must be able to function at an advanced level in both the business and technical areas. In fact, much of the initial dimensional modeling effort actually begins as part of the requirements definition process.

The detailed business requirements document discussed in Chapter 1 has several sections that describe the high-priority business processes in detail. That document identifies analytic requirements supported by each high-priority business process. It describes the broad classes of questions and problems that management and business analysts have been trying (or would like to try) to answer. The requirements document should include a list of data elements, example questions, and even a list of desired reports that would help answer the analytic questions. These all play a central role when it comes time to defining the dimensional model. Your dimensional model must not only be able to answer these specific questions easily when it is finished, but also allow business users to explore new opportunities.

DATA-DRIVEN MODELS VERSUS BUSINESS REQUIREMENTS–DRIVEN MODELS

An experienced dimensional modeler can build a reasonable dimensional model based on the source system data structures. However, this model will inevitably fall short of meeting the business needs in many small but substantive ways. These little shortcomings add up to a weak dimensional model. We recently worked with a client whose requirements gathering had revealed a need for a field called `PricingCategory`. It turns out there is no such thing as `PricingCategory` in the source system. However, there was a `Rate_Code` field that in combination with some other status flags was the basis of what the business users called `PricingCategory`. A dimensional model based literally on the source system would have included `Rate_Code` (maybe) and left the users to re-create the business rules for determining `PricingCategory` every time they built a query that needed the field.

In short, you must understand the business requirements in detail before you dive into the task of designing the dimensional model. Your designs will start with the source content but typically need to be augmented with additional fields defined by your organization's business rules.

NOTE It is too easy for technical folks to build a data model that meets specific report requirements and only those requirements: to build a reporting system, not a DW/BI system. For that reason, we prefer to merely glance at the report specifications in the early phases of the design process. Once the data model is largely developed, look at the report specifications in depth to ensure the design can easily support those reports.

Understand the Data Architecture Strategy

One of the big DW/BI architecture discussions centers on the issue of how you structure and manage your data. The questions are: What data do you keep, where do you keep it within your technical architecture, and how is it structured. Our standard approach is to build a set of dimensional models in the relational database platform that hold the lowest level of detail. This atomic-level relational database enables consistent data definitions, business rules, and tracking of history. It supports the integration of data from multiple sources across the enterprise and from external sources such as vendors, customers, and third-party data providers. This atomic level also provides a means for including value-added data that is important to the analytic process but that currently exists only in spreadsheets on users' desktops, or embedded deep within a report definition. The atomic-level dimensional data warehouse is designed to be queried by users and built to meet their analytic needs and performance expectations. As we describe in Chapter 3, this is generally true even though we encourage you to build atomic-level Analysis Services databases from the atomic-level relational warehouse and use Analysis Services as the primary query platform.

We believe both the relational and Analysis Services databases are key components of a successful enterprise Microsoft DW/BI system. The goal of this chapter, and of all the chapters that focus on the data track of the Lifecycle, is to make sure we build the system in a way that leverages the strengths of both tools. The good news is that a solid, well-designed dimensional model is the best foundation for both platforms.

Set Up the Modeling Environment

It helps to get a few tools in place before you dive into the modeling process. We often start the modeling process using a spreadsheet as our initial tool because it allows us to make changes easily. This spreadsheet captures the key elements of the logical model plus many of the physical attributes you'll need later. It also gives you a place to begin capturing some of the ETL information, such as source system table and column(s), and a brief description of the extract and transformation rules. Finally, it includes the initial set of business metadata in the form of the names, descriptions, example values, data quality issues, and comments. In our *ETL Toolkit* book, we call this the "logical data map." Regardless of the name, the central idea is to describe each attribute in the final target and associate them all with their original sources and required transformations.

DOWNLOADS You can get a copy of the modeling spreadsheet we use at the book's web site. It includes a simple macro to generate the DDL to create the target tables in SQL Server. You can then use the reverse-engineering capabilities of your modeling tool to pull the model out of the database. Our spreadsheet also writes the metadata info, such as the column descriptions, transformations, and comments columns, into extended properties fields in the database system tables. Afterward, you can move this information into the metadata schema.

Once the model gets fairly firm, typically after a few weeks, you can convert to your standard modeling tool. Most of the popular modeling tools (such as ERwin, PowerDesigner, and E/R Studio) allow you to lay out the logical model and capture physical and logical names, descriptions, and relationships.

Once the design is considered complete (for the first round, anyway), the modeling tools can help the DBA forward engineer the model into the database, including creating the tables, indexes, partitioning, views, and other physical elements of the database. Chapter 4 discusses these physical design issues. If you start using your modeling tool early on, things will be easier later.

Establish Naming Conventions

Naming conventions are the rules you use to consistently name the objects in your dimensional model, and ultimately in the physical database. Spending time determining your naming conventions is one of those irritating tasks that feels like make-work. But it is definitely worth it in the long run.

Fortunately, it doesn't have to become your life's work. There are ways to abbreviate the process. First, don't start from scratch. Use whatever naming conventions your organization has in place. Almost all large organizations have a group of data modelers and/or DBAs somewhere — they might be called data administration, or data management. Somewhere in that group is the holder of the organization's official naming conventions. Given that you are reading the dimensional modeling chapter, you are likely either one of the folks in this group, or very close to them. Find the document and see if you can make the existing conventions work for the DW/BI system. Existing naming conventions don't always work because sometimes they are not oriented toward user-friendly, descriptive names.

As you develop the DW/BI naming conventions, remember that table and column names will be visible to the user community. They're an important component of the ad hoc user experience, and they show up in report titles and headers. Names must be descriptive, but not so long that users and report developers will be tempted to rename them every time they use the data element.

DOWNLOADS If you're in a smaller organization, don't despair. The web site for this book has an example of naming conventions along with links to a few other examples on the internet. The point is, you don't need to start from scratch.

Data Profiling and Research

Once you've done your prep work, you can get started on the model. Throughout the modeling process, the modeler needs to dig into the underlayers of the data to learn about its structure, content, relationships, and derivation rules. You need to verify that the data exists (or can be created), that it's in a usable state, or at least its flaws are manageable, and that you understand what it will take to convert it into the dimensional model form. You don't have to find every piece of bad data or completely document every transformation at this point. Leave a little bit for the ETL folks to do.

This is not your first trip into data exploration. The requirements definition process in Chapter 1 included initial data profiling and data audit tasks to aid in the assessment of feasibility. The findings from those tasks are the starting point for this one.

Although data profiling is listed here as part of the preparation step, it's an ongoing process. As you work through the model table by table, filling in the list of attributes, you'll return to these data profiling and research tasks many times to resolve issues and clearly define each attribute.

There are several useful sources for detailed information about an organization's data, including the source system, data experts, and existing reporting systems.

Data Profiling and Source System Exploration

The data modeler usually has the benefit of both first-hand observation and documentation from the source system under investigation. Unfortunately, these two don't always line up. Gather and carefully review whatever documentation is available for the source systems. This might include data models, file definitions, record layouts, written documentation, and source system programs. More advanced source systems may have their own metadata repositories with all this information already integrated for your convenience. Don't count on this.

Perusing the source system data itself usually provides a quick jolt of reality. First, what you see typically does not match the documentation you carefully gathered and reviewed. Second, it usually is more difficult to unravel than you would hope. The older the system, the more time it's had to evolve. This evolution, usually driven by short-term business needs, often takes the form of one or more of these standard fixes: substituted fields where data is stored in a field with a different name; overloaded fields where multiple values are stored in a single field; variable definition fields where the meaning of the content changes depending on its context; and freeform entry fields where there are no controls on the values being entered.

This is only a short list — there are plenty of other problems to be discovered. You can discover many of the content, relationship, and quality problems first-hand through a process known as *data profiling* or *data auditing*. Data profiling is about using query and reporting tools to get a sense for the content of the system under investigation. Data profiling can be as simple as writing some SQL SELECT statements with COUNTs and DISTINCTs. An experienced modeler with a decent query tool and a source system data model can quickly develop a good understanding of the nature of the source system data required for a given business process dimensional model.

There are also tools to help with the data profiling process. Integration Services has a data profiling task that can be configured to write out an XML file of profiling statistics including counts, length and value distributions, candidate keys, and column patterns. To use the data profiling task, you must create an SSIS package, include the task, and configure it to generate the statistics you would like to view against the tables you are profiling, and execute the task. You then open the Data Profile Viewer and navigate to the resulting XML output file.

If your source data is in SQL Server, we have created a set of reports that serve as a simple data profiling tool. Figure 2-7 shows a data profile report for the Production.Product table from the Adventure Works Cycles transaction database. It gives a good sense for what the data in the Product table looks like. Starting at the top of the report, we see that there are 504 rows in the table. There are 504 distinct ProductIDs, Names, and ProductNumbers. It's interesting to note the ProductNumber isn't really a number at all. Moving down the list, only about half the products have a Color, the rest are NULL, and there are only nine distinct values for Color. A commercial tool would give you more information at the table level, and more sophisticated results at the detail level. But even this simple report gives you a good start on understanding the contents of the table.

DOWNLOADS The Reporting Services project that was used to create the data profiling report shown in Figure 2-7 is available at the book's web site. They work on SQL Server tables only, but they do give you an easy place to start.

Your goal is to make sure the data exists to support the dimensional model and identify business rules and relationships that will have an impact on the model. Write down any interesting complexities you uncover so the ETL folks won't have to re-discover them. You may not understand the exact business rules and derivation formulas as part of the modeling phase, but the modeling team should all agree that what you are proposing is reasonable, or at least possible.

Target schema and table name: [Production].[Product]
Table row count: 504

Server Name: VM2008R2 | Database Name: AdventureWorks2008R2

Column Name	Col #	Data Type	Max Length	Min Value (1st 100 chars)	Max Value (1st 100 chars)	Distinct Values	Null Count	Pct Null	Avg Length/ Value	Max Char Length
[ProductID]	1	int(10)	10	1	999	504	0	0.0 %	673	
[Name]	2	nvarchar(50)	50	Adjustable Race	Women's Tights, S	504	0	0.0 %	18	32
[ProductNumber]	3	nvarchar(25)	25	AR-5381	WB-H098	504	0	0.0 %	8	10
[MakeFlag]	4	bit	1	n/a	n/a	0	0	0.0 %		
[FinishedGoodsFlag]	5	bit	1	n/a	n/a	0	0	0.0 %		
[Color]	6	nvarchar(15)	15	Black	Yellow	9	248	49.2 %	5	12
[SafetyStockLevel]	7	smallint(5)	5	4	1000	6	0	0.0 %	535	
[ReorderPoint]	8	smallint(5)	5	3	750	6	0	0.0 %	401	
[StandardCost]	9	money(19)	19	0.00	2171.29	114	0	0.0 %	258	
[ListPrice]	10	money(19)	19	0.00	3578.27	103	0	0.0 %	438	
[Size]	11	nvarchar(5)	5	38	XL	18	293	58.1 %	1	2
[SizeUnitMeasureCode]	12	nchar(3)	3	CM	CM	1	328	65.1 %	2	2
[WeightUnitMeasureCode]	13	nchar(3)	3	G	LB	2	299	59.3 %	1	2
[Weight]	14	decimal(8)	8	2.12	1050.00	127	299	59.3 %	73	
[DaystoManufacture]	15	int(10)	10	0	4	4	0	0.0 %	1	
[ProductLine]	16	nchar(2)	2	M	T	4	226	44.8 %	1	1
[Class]	17	nchar(2)	2	H	M	3	257	51.0 %	1	1
[Style]	18	nchar(2)	2	M	W	3	293	58.1 %	1	1
[ProductSubcategoryID]	19	int(10)	10	1	37	37	209	41.5 %	12	
[ProductModelID]	20	int(10)	10	1	128	119	209	41.5 %	37	
[SellStartDate]	21	datetime(8)	8	Jun 1 2002 12:00AM	Jul 1 2007 12:00AM	4	0	0.0 %		
[SellEndDate]	22	datetime(8)	8	Jun 30 2006 12:00AM	Jun 30 2007 12:00AM	2	406	80.6 %		

Select a Column Name above to view additional details

Report Description: The Data Profiler Column List report lists all the columns in a given table and retrieves basic descriptive information about the contents of each column. This can take a while for large tables. This report is a sub-report called from the Table List report.

Report Name: 2 ColumnList
Report Folder: /Data Profiler v2

Figure 2-7: A simple data profile report for the Adventure Works OLTP Product table

Data profiling helps you understand the complexities of the source system data, but it should not be your only source of source information, so to speak. You need to develop good working relationships with the source system developers and DBAs. These folks often know the business rules and quality problems you could never find with a tool, such as the fact that a middle initial of $ means the customer is difficult to work with. Some of the expert business users will also be able to shed additional light on the data. They have often worked with it for years and know what transformations are needed to make it line up with the official reports. The official reports themselves are also a good source of understanding. Look through the queries and report calculations to see what business rules they include. Even better, find the main developer of the existing reporting system and get him or her involved in the modeling process.

Building Dimensional Models

After a round of data exploration, the process of building dimensional models typically moves through three phases. The first is a high-level dimensional model design session that defines the boundaries of the business process dimensional model. The second phase is detailed model development that involves filling in the attributes table by table and resolving any issues or uncertainties. The third phase is a series of model review, redesign, and validation steps.

High-Level Dimensional Model Design Session

The first dimensional modeling design session is meant to put several major stakes in the ground in terms of the basic structure and content of the dimensional model. This session is facilitated by the lead data modeler, and involves the core modeling team and any interested participants from the source system group and the ETL group. It can take a day or more to work through the initial model, so set expectations accordingly.

NOTE It is extremely valuable to learn from the experience of those in your organization who developed earlier versions of reporting systems or data warehouses, but be very careful not to frighten or offend them. They may be threatened by the possibility that they will no longer be needed. They might be angry or offended that you, not they, are building the DW/BI system. This is where your interpersonal skills will save you. Work to include them as part of the team early on. Keep them informed as the project moves forward. Involve them in the design of the database. Teach them how to use the reporting tools and include them in the development of new reports and applications from the DW/BI system. Let them (and their boss) know how much you appreciate their help.

The first part of this session involves creating the high-level dimensional model — a graphical representation of the dimension, fact, and utility tables involved in representing the business process. As we describe in the next section, you should follow a four-step process for creating this high-level dimensional model. The second part of the session is creating the initial list of attributes for each dimension. The three deliverables are: 1) the high-level graphical model; 2) the initial attribute list; and 3) the initial issues list.

Creating the High-Level Dimensional Model: The Four-Step Modeling Process

The initial task in the design session is to create a high-level dimensional model for the top priority business process. The high-level dimensional model is a data model at the entity level. Draft your starting point model straight from the bus matrix. You may also include any utility tables, such as lookup tables or user hierarchies, but usually these don't surface until later in the process. The design process generally flows through four steps:

- *Step 1: Identify the business process.* In other words, what row on the bus matrix should you start with? In most cases, you will already know the business process as the outcome of the prioritization process. It's the row on the bus matrix associated with the top priority opportunity.

- *Step 2: Declare the grain.* The grain is the level of detail captured in the fact table. Your goal is to describe the meaning of a single fact row. Filling in the statement, "The fact table has one row per X" where "X" is the business event, is a good way to get started. The answer might be one row per order line item, one row per customer call, or one row per employee status change. This is a subtle, but important step. If you aren't clear on the grain, you may end up with a fact table that does not capture data at the atomic level, and is therefore less flexible. Make sure that the grain declaration is not a list of dimensions. That comes in the next step. Grain is a business event.

- *Step 3: Choose the dimensions.* Now ask yourself the question, what objects participate in the target business process at the declared grain? Most of these will come directly from your understanding of the business process and the bus matrix should give you a starting point. As you list dimensions, you will also begin listing all the individual attributes associated with each dimension. It helps to refer to user information requests and source system models to verify your choice of dimensions and their attributes.

- *Step 4: Choose the facts.* The facts are the measures of the business process in question. There are usually a set of facts that are directly measured by the source system that supports the business process, and a set of facts that are derived from the base facts. Make sure the facts are true to the grain.

The High-Level Graphical Model

Graphically summarize the initial design session in a deliverable called the high-level graphical model (or the *bubble chart*, for short). The model shown in Figure 2-8 is an example of a starting point dimensional model for Adventure Works Cycles' orders business process based on the bus matrix from Chapter 1. We improve on this model in the next section.

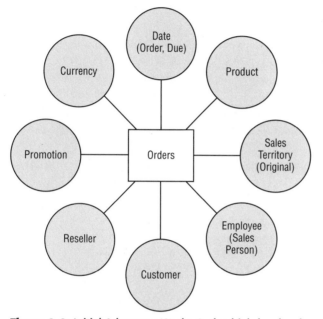

Figure 2-8: Initial Adventure Works Cycles high-level orders dimensional model

Identifying Dimension Attributes and Fact Measures

The second part of the initial design session involves filling in each table with a robust *attribute list*. List all the relevant attributes needed by the business, grouped according to the dimension or fact table to which they belong. If you're using the dimensional modeling spreadsheet from the book's web site to keep track of your attribute lists, create one worksheet per table in the model and fill in its attribute list.

The team will identify a large number of attributes for each dimension coming from a wide range of sources and a list of base level and computed measures for the fact tables. List them out brainstorm-style, grouping them by the dimension or fact table to which they belong. Don't get caught up in naming or derivation yet; just pick a name and make a note of the alternative names and the controversy on the *issues list,* one of the deliverables from the high level modeling session. The issues list comes to life in the high level model design session, but it's constantly updated throughout the detailed modeling process. It's the best way we've found to remember all the little details about the problems we encountered and how we decided to resolve them.

Assign someone the role of list keeper in every meeting. This person notes every data-related issue that comes up during the meeting and marks off previous issues that have been resolved. It helps to save time at the end of each meeting to review and validate the new entries and their assignments. The data modeler can be the keeper of the issues list, but we've often seen it fall into the hands of the project manager. This is in large part because keeping the list updated and encouraging progress on resolving issues are usually strengths of a good project manager.

The results of this initial design session, the high level dimensional model, the attributes list, and the issues list, are the foundation for the logical and physical business process dimensional models. At this point, you've identified the dimension and fact tables, each with a list of its associated attributes or measures. This model, along with the issues list, gives the data modeling team enough guidelines to carry the process into the next level of detail.

Developing the Detailed Dimensional Model

Once this high level dimensional model is completed, the hard work of filling in the dimension attributes and hierarchies, identifying and validating data sources, and defining names begins. At this point, the process gets specific to each individual organization. The last part of this chapter explores the process of identifying dimension attributes and facts, and validating the model in the context of the Adventure Works Cycles business.

Detailed dimensional model development is primarily about filling in all the missing information in the dimensional model and testing it against the business requirements. This process is ultimately about *defining the contents of the DW/BI system,* table by table and column by column. Because the DW/BI system is an enterprise resource, these definitions must work for the entire enterprise. The data definition task is a business data governance task — the BI team and the data steward usually drive the process, but the business folks must determine and approve the standard names and definitions. This will take some time, but it's an investment that will provide huge returns in terms of users' ability to understand and willingness to accept the dimensional model. This is another one of those organizational processes that can be uncomfortable for the technically minded.

One of the most important decisions from this detailed modeling process is the assignment of the type 1 or type 2 change tracking technique to each column in each dimension. This is a business decision and relates to the need for accurate historical analysis. If there is now, or may someday be, a need for predictive analytics using a given attribute, you must use type 2 change tracking. In a similar vein, if there is any need to report historical data as it was when it occurred, for example, sales by sales region as of December 31st last year, you must use type 2 change tracking.

The team should meet on a regular basis, perhaps daily or every other day, to discuss the proposed alternatives and make decisions on open issues. Use these meetings to critically explore the progress, review any recommendations, and update the issues list. Focus these meetings on one or two tables at a time — too many and the meeting starts to get bogged down.

Address all the data quality issues you find in a separate meeting (or two) with key business and source systems people. The quality experts tell us the only way to truly solve a quality problem is to fix it at its source. If you "fix" these data quality problems in the ETL system, you will reduce the incentive for the organization to fix them in the source systems. The reality is, the source systems team usually does not have resources or even the necessary information to fix all of the problems, or even just the most important ones. Therefore, you will end up taking on the task of fixing some of these problems in the ETL system until the business recognizes the importance of data quality and allocates resources to correct the source system. The earlier you discuss data quality issues, the better, because many data quality problems end up being roadblocks, or at least add unexpected work to the ETL process.

DOWNLOADS If you aren't already using it, try the modeling spreadsheet mentioned in the "Preparation" section of this chapter. It provides a place to capture most of the important descriptive information about each table and attribute. It allows the modeler to quickly move or copy attributes around the model as needed. It is a spreadsheet, after all.

The model will go through some major shifts during this phase. You'll identify additional attributes, along with new dimensions and facts. If this is the primary focus of the dimensional modeling team, the model should begin to settle down with a week or two of intensive work.

RESOURCES See the following resources for additional information about developing the detailed model:

- *The Data Warehouse Lifecycle Toolkit, Second Edition*, Chapter 7, "Designing the Dimensional Model."

- Kimballgroup.com: Search for the topic "Naming Game" for an article on the process of driving organizational agreement on attribute names. It can also be found in the *Kimball Reader* on page 220.

Testing and Refining the Model

Once the model is fairly stable, step back and test it against the business require-ments. The requirements are an integral part of the model development process, but a separate test step helps you think at a more practical level. Approach the test by asking the question "How would I actually get this information out of the model?"

The requirements document should have a bundle of test materials, includ-ing a candidate list of structured reports, example user reports, and ad hoc or future-oriented questions people would like to investigate. Pull these out and go through them one by one. For each request, decide how it could be answered (we often think up the SQL it would take) and assign it an effort score: low, medium, or high. A low effort query would be a simple SQL SELECT statement — no sub-selects or case statements or unions — that would be easy to construct in any desktop query tool. At the end of the test, most of the questions should fall into the low effort category — shoot for 75 percent.

Invariably, this testing process leads to several refinements in the model. You may identify missing attributes or hierarchies. Occasionally, you'll make major structural changes to the model based on a deeper understanding than you had before you created the detailed model.

Reviewing and Validating the Model

Once you're confident in the model's stability, the process moves into the review and validation phase. This phase involves reviewing the model with succes-sive audiences, each with different levels of technical expertise and business understanding. At a minimum, plan on talking to three groups. Start with the core DW/BI team and involved expert users. Next, review the model with key folks in the IT organization; the source system developers and DBAs can often spot errors in the model very quickly. (You may need to teach these folks about dimensional modeling before they start normalizing your dimensions.) Finally, get feedback from any core business users who were not directly involved in the model development process. After each meeting, incorporate the feedback into the dimensional model.

You may want to end by reviewing the model with the broader user com-munity. Do this more in the form of a presentation and tie the model back to the business requirements. A series of statements that show how a user might get answers to a range of questions pulled right from the requirements document can be very powerful.

The modeling team will get valuable feedback from the review and valida-tion process. The DW/BI team also gets value from these reviews in the form of a more informed and engaged user community.

Case Study: The Adventure Works Cycles Orders Dimensional Model

This fourth major section of this chapter is meant to impart a sense of how business requirements drive the dimensional model. We draw our example from the Adventure Works Cycles business and source system data in the AdventureWorks transaction database. We use the initial orders dimensional model from Figure 2-8 as our starting point and discuss the major design changes that were driven by business requirements, including the facts and the employee, customer, and currency dimensions.

The Orders Fact Table

The grain of the fact table is at the order line item level. This is the atomic level, and the only point in the transaction where the product is specified. However, there are some facts, such as taxes and shipping, which appear at the order header level. Our goal would be to allocate those down to the individual line item level if at all possible. This would give us one atomic level fact table that can be rolled up to any level across any dimension for any order-related analytic purpose. This is how we create a flexible model with long-term viability.

There could be some confusion about what goes into the `Orders` fact table at Adventure Works because there are two distribution channels: internet and resellers. Since the sales organization is generally only interested in sales for which they receive compensation, giving them a reseller sales fact table removes the risk of accidentally including internet sales in their analyses. However, separate fact tables would require more complex cross-table queries to generate reports at the total company level. It makes more sense to combine all orders into a single fact table and use dimension constraints, (e.g., `Customer_Type = 'Reseller'`), to help the sales people get what they need.

The Dimensions

Using the dimensional model shown in Figure 2-8 as our starting point, we'll summarize how the Adventure Works Cycles DW/BI team resolved major design issues with several dimensions. At the end of this section, we show the resulting updated high-level orders dimensional model.

Employee

Several business requirements had been voiced about tracking the impact of organizational changes, and about basic employee counts. (Note that these are questions about the Human Resources business process.) Without a type 2 dimension, it would be impossible to relate the employee attributes that were in effect at the time a transaction occurred with the actual transaction itself. Only current attribute values could be used to analyze history.

Based on this discussion, the team decided to treat the employee dimension as a hybrid slowly changing dimension, with most of the attributes tracked as type 2 attributes. This decision had a significant ripple effect on the model. First, it revealed a weakness in the sales territory dimension. Having a type 2 attribute called historical sales territory in the employee dimension tracks the same information as the `Sales Territory` table, only better: It locks in both the sales territory and the sales rep that got credit at the time of the sale.

As a result, the sales territory dimension can be removed from the model. Second, there is still a need to apply the currently assigned sales territory to all of history, which means keeping the current sales territory attribute in the employee dimension as a type 1 attribute. The ETL process will have to change all historical rows in the employee dimension for the current sales territory when the sales territory changes for a given employee.

> **NOTE** The decision to include type 2 attributes in the employee dimension really means expanding the scope to include a second business process: Human Resources transactions. In a large organization, the ETL process will essentially create an employee transaction fact table that can then be used to build the employee dimension. For Adventure Works Cycles, with fewer than 300 employees, this decision is probably not too onerous. For a larger organization with thousands of employees, this could be a lot of work.

The team also noted that the issue of finding reliable historical information for employee changes will have to be researched, but lack of historical data is a bad reason to avoid implementing type 2 tracking. The sooner you get started, the more history you will have.

Customer and Reseller

The initial design identified two customer-related dimensions, customer and reseller, based on the two major distribution channels. While these do share some attributes, like an address, the company has certain information about each that it doesn't have about the other. The sense when the bus matrix was created was that the two customer types are different enough to be split into separate dimensions.

Business requirements can help the team decide whether they need one or two versions of the customer dimension. First, there is a clear need to report total sales across both customer types in the same report, so the model must include an integrated master customer dimension of some kind. Second, there are fewer than 20,000 customers in total, and the distribution is highly imbalanced: Less than 4 percent are resellers. Third, only 10 or so attributes are unique to reseller customers (items such as store annual sales and number of employees).

Based on these requirements, the design team decided to combine all the attributes of the two customer types into a single, master customer dimension. This decision allows much greater reporting and analysis flexibility and simplifies the dimensional model. However, it means the users need to understand and be able to work with the idea that both customer types are in the same table. When they want a count of internet customers, they will need to limit the customer type field to "Internet." (It's also possible to create views on the combined customer dimension that would look exactly like the separate dimensions, for those folks who can't handle two customer types in one table!)

Currency

Every sale in the source system is captured in its original, local currency. The source system relies on a currency conversion table for translating currencies and reporting in U.S. dollars. This table tracks the conversion rate between the local currency and U.S. dollars both at the end of each day and as an average for each day. Getting standardized reports in U.S. dollars to compare across countries requires a fairly complicated query and has long been a sore point for most of the folks in headquarters. At the same time, sales people in the field want to create reports in local currency to show their customers. Finance, of course, wants both, along with the conversion table so they can assess the impact of exchange rates on budget variances.

Based on these requirements, the design team decided to include both local currency and U.S. dollar fields in the fact table, with a currency dimension to indicate the currency of the local data. This means the ETL process would have to bring in the `Exchange Rates` table to convert non-U.S. sales into U.S. dollars.

Although it was out of scope for the initial phase 1 project, the design team also decided to include the exchange rates as a separate business process dimensional model. The exchange rates model is essentially the `Exchange Rates` fact table combined with the currency dimension and the date dimension. Making this available to the users was an easy political decision because it is incrementally very little work. The `Exchange Rates` table must already be brought into the ETL staging area in order to support the currency conversion in the `Orders` table. Besides, the Director of Finance is particularly interested in getting access to this data.

NOTE This is already the second piece of scope creep in the design, the first being treating employee as a type 2 dimension. We don't encourage this kind of scope creep in real life. In our experience, almost all DW/BI teams are overly ambitious in their first iteration. We're constantly coaching our clients not to over-commit — your mantra should be under-promise and over-deliver.

Those are the major changes that came out of the high-level modeling discussion. Before we show the updated model, let's complete the second part of the design session because there still might be a few changes.

Identifying Dimension Attributes and Facts for the Orders Business Process

The second half of the initial design session involves creating an initial data element list. This is an attribute list for each dimension and a list of fact-related data elements. The starting point for this list is the detailed requirements document — one of its appendices should be a list of key data elements (attributes) that people specifically identified as important.

Figure 2-9 shows what a portion of the attributes list might look like for the Adventure Works Cycles orders business process dimensional model. The Sample Values column is helpful in identifying attributes.

NOTE Creating a stand-alone attribute list can be helpful, but if you are using the modeling spreadsheet we described earlier in the chapter, you already have a place to keep your attribute lists.

The process of creating the attribute list can trigger changes to the initial high-level dimensional model. The Adventure Works Cycles modeling team came across two attributes that did not have an obvious home: sales reason and channel. The business expert on the design team explained how sales reason comes from a list on the internet order form where customers could select one or more reasons for their purchase. This is an example of a many-to-many relationship, and a good candidate for a bridge table. However, discussions with the business users revealed that they were interested in the primary reason only, which can be identified in the ETL process. In an effort to avoid additional scope creep, the team decided to include only the primary sales reason. (This will probably be a decision they regret in the long run.)

Users also mentioned sales channel several times in the business requirements document — usually referring to resellers or the internet. If sales channel refers only to reseller and internet, the Customer Type field can handle this distinction. However, it was clear during the requirements interviews that there is a drive to open up new sales channels, including opening Adventure Works Cycles retail stores and providing private label bikes for large retailers.

Promotion

Attribute Name	Description	Alternate Names	Sample Values
Special Offer ID	Source system key		
Special Offer Name	Name / description of the Special Offer	Promotion name, Special Offer description	Volume Discount 11 to 14; Mountain-100 Clearance Sale
Discount Percent	Percent item is discounted		
Special Offer Type	Description of the type of promotion, special offer or discount	Promotion Type	Volume Discount; Discontinued Product
Special Offer Category	Channel to which the Promotion applies	Promotion Category	Reseller; Customer
Start Date	First day the promotion is available		2005-07-01
End Date	Last day the promotion is available		2008-12-31
Minimum Quantity	Minimum quantity required to qualify for the promotion		0
Maximum Quantity	Maximum quantity allowed under the promotion		NULL

Notes: The main table that Promotion information comes from is called SpecialOffer in the source system, but the business users refer to the general class as promotions.

Attributes Not Elsewhere Classified

Attribute Name	Description	Alternate Names	Sample Values
SalesReasonID	Sales reason ID from source system		
SalesReason	Reason the customer bought the product, as reported by the customer (Internet only)		Demo Event; On Promotion; Price; Review; Sponsorship
SalesReason Type	Grouping for Sales Reason		Marketing; Promotion; Other
Channel	Channel through which the item was sold	OnlineOrderFlag	Customer; Reseller

Notes: This attribute list is a good candidate to be a junk dimension.

Figure 2-9: Promotion dimension portion of the Adventure Works Cycles initial Orders attribute list

A quick query of the source system revealed there are only ten sales reasons and two sales channels so creating two separate dimensions seemed inefficient to the design team. They opted to create a junk dimension called `Order Info` that would contain both concepts. The ETL process will have to manage the assignment of surrogate keys and watch for new entries in the source systems.

Revisit the source system tables at this point, as a final check to make sure you haven't left anything useful behind. This is meant to be a validation step, not a starting point.

Not all of the data elements on the attribute list will necessarily be attributes of the final dimensional model. Some of them are not really attributes; rather they're aggregates or constraints. Others are the same attribute masquerading under a different name. Still other attributes are missing altogether, either because they were so obvious people didn't think to mention them, or they were so little used, people didn't know to mention them. As you build the lists, keep an eye out for these kinds of redundancies and omissions. Start to boil down all this information to create the master attribute list for each table.

The Final Draft of the Initial Orders Model

At the end of the initial design session, the team has created a good high-level dimensional model for the orders business process. The high-level model shown in Figure 2-10 is the result of merging the changes identified in the process of creating the attributes list (adding the order info dimension) along with the changes from the model design session itself (merging reseller and customer, removing the sales territory dimension, and adding the exchange rates business process). This dimensional model contains all the elements needed to meet Adventure Works Cycles' orders related business requirements in a simple, powerful, flexible form — at least as far as the team understands them at this point. This model will change, but it is a strong first pass.

We encourage you to compare this model with the initial model in Figure 2-8 to see how it evolved during the initial design session. Review the business requirements described in Chapter 1 and available from the book's web site to get a sense for how well the model will meet the needs.

The last deliverable from the initial modeling session is the issues list. This list will evolve as you work through the details of each table, solving some issues and adding others.

DOWNLOADS You can see an example of the issues list from the Adventure Works Cycles Orders business process design session on the book's web site.

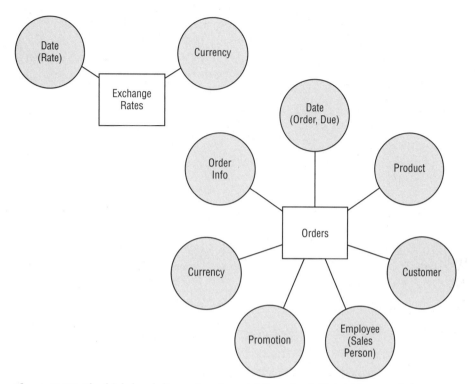

Figure 2-10: The high-level dimensional model from the initial design session

Detailed Orders Dimensional Model Development

Develop the detailed dimensional model one dimension at a time. Begin with the attribute information you captured in your modeling spreadsheet in the initial design session. Start with an easy dimension such as date, and fill in as much of the spreadsheet as possible based on current information. Source tables and columns are often fairly clear for most of the attributes. Transformations for most of the attributes are direct copies from the source. Target data types can be inferred based on the source system as well, although the data warehouse DBA will have the final say in determining the data types.

Once the known information is filled in, the open issues are more obvious. At this point, it's time to continue with the data exploration/data profiling process described earlier in this chapter.

Identifying SCD Change Types

One of the columns in the modeling spreadsheet is the SCD Change Type. The data modeler will use this to identify how each attribute needs to be tracked over time and flag it appropriately. Remember, this is a business question. It's okay to make a first pass and flag all the attributes whose changes obviously must be tracked over time, or whose changes have no impact on the business whatsoever. All of the less obvious attributes should be discussed with the modeling team. Review all of these change-tracking decisions with the core business users before you make a final decision.

The ETL process must re-create the historical changes for every type 2 SCD attribute in each dimension, at least as far back in time as the oldest fact table rows the dimension will support. This is because the ETL process will need to load historical fact rows with the dimension surrogate keys that were in effect when the fact row occurred. Therefore the ETL developer has to go back into the transaction system to find all relevant historical changes that apply to the dimension in question. While this is not the data modeler's task, it's helpful to look for indicators as to whether or not re-creating historical dimension data will be difficult or even possible.

Reviewing the Issues

Even though you may have filled in most of the spreadsheet, there will still be several issues that require a second or third opinion. In some cases, you can resolve these issues using the research tools described earlier in the chapter. In other cases, you need a sounding board to explore alternative solutions. Bring up open issues in the next data modeling team meeting and work them through. Then move on to the next dimension.

Identifying the Facts

Filling in the detailed fact table description is much like filling in the dimensions. Start by copying in the list of measures and filling in all the easy items. Then use the research tools to address as many of the open items as possible. Finally, work with the data modeling team to resolve the remaining issues.

There are several issues that are specific to fact tables. These include:

- *Derived columns:* Identify the formula and indicate whether the derivation is additive or semi-additive, as in a month-end account balance.
- *Allocations:* In the case of the Adventure Works Cycles orders dimensional model, the grain is at the order line item level. The team must decide how to handle the handful of facts that are collected at the order level. Sales tax can easily be allocated to each line item. Other facts, such as shipping costs, might need to be allocated based on weight or size.

NOTE Don't avoid the allocations! If you leave shipping costs in a fact table at the order (not line item) level, all your product related financial rollups will omit the shipping costs. Grit your teeth and allocate!

- *Conformed facts:* The dollar sales field is a good example of creating a conformed fact. As the team discussed in the design session, there's a need to have all transactions stated in a single currency (U.S. dollars), as well as the original local currency from the source system.

- *Degenerate dimensions:* While no transformations need to be applied to any degenerate dimensions in the dimensional model, you do need to indicate which fields in the fact table are degenerate dimensions. In the orders dimensional model, there are several degenerate dimensions.

Final Dimensional Model

When all the design reviews are finished, the user meetings over, the source systems carefully scrutinized, and the requirements reviewed, it's time to physically instantiate the dimensional model. This is a job for the DBAs, but we usually set up a test database and run the script from the spreadsheet. (You will probably already have done this several times by now so you could reverse engineer the model into your modeling tool to create a presentable data model.)

DOWNLOADS You can find the completed modeling spreadsheet we used to create the MDWT_AdventureWorks database at the book's web site: kimballuniversity.com/html/booksMDWTtools.html.

At this point, you're ready to take on the real database physical design process and start thinking about designing the ETL system.

Summary

Designing dimensional models for business intelligence is no simple trick. The first part of this chapter concentrated on defining and describing the basic concepts of dimensional modeling: facts, dimensions, the bus matrix, and conformed dimensions. The next section expanded the description of dimensional modeling with key concepts such as surrogate keys and tracking changes with slowly changing dimensions. We described several techniques to model a broad range of common (and uncommon) business processes and relationships like many-to-many relationships, hierarchies, and junk dimensions.

The third part of this chapter covered the process of dimensional modeling. Begin with a preparation step to identify the team, set up the modeling environment, and determine naming conventions. Begin the modeling process by using our four step approach to create a high level business dimensional model, along with attributes and issues lists. The next step is to develop the detailed model, table by table and column by column, filling in all the needed information and addressing all the issues. The last step in the process of creating the dimensional model involves reviewing the proposed model with several interested parties, including other IT people and core business users.

The last part of the chapter applied the dimensional modeling concepts and process to the Adventure Works Cycles case study, resulting in a dimensional model for the orders business process. This dimensional model will be the target for the physical database creation and the ETL system described over the next several chapters.

CHAPTER 3

The Toolset

"But lo! Men have become the tools of their tools."
— Henry David Thoreau, Walden

In this chapter, we describe the architecture and product selection for the Microsoft data warehouse/business intelligence (DW/BI) system. It may seem pointless to talk about architecture alternatives and product selection for a Microsoft system, but Microsoft offers enough software components that there's a significant element of product selection.

Figure 3-1 repeats the familiar Kimball Lifecycle diagram, highlighting the Architecture and Product Selection boxes that are the focus of this chapter. In this version of the diagram, we've included a mapping between the Lifecycle boxes and the Microsoft products and components you may use during your development and management processes.

The first part of this chapter walks through the overall architecture of a Microsoft-based DW/BI system and the rationale behind the major components. We next discuss the specific product editions and components that make up Microsoft's DW/BI related offerings.

This chapter continues with a description of the two main tools that you'll use to develop and operate your DW/BI system. You'll use a single integrated environment called the Business Intelligence Development Studio (BIDS) to develop most of your DW/BI system, and a second environment called the SQL Server Management Studio to manage it. We introduce the two tools here and provide an overview of the elements that are the same no matter what part of the DW/BI project you're working on.

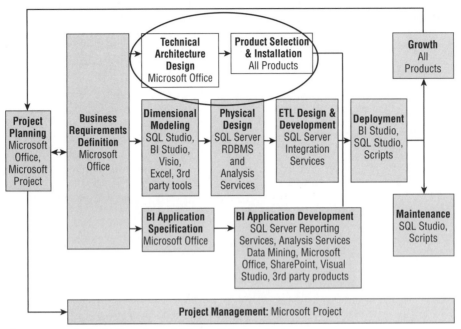

Figure 3-1: Kimball Lifecycle and Microsoft technologies

The Microsoft DW/BI Toolset

The core set of DW/BI tools that Microsoft Corporation sells is Microsoft SQL Server. SQL Server includes several major components of primary interest for DW/BI projects:

- The *relational engine (RDBMS)* to manage and store the dimensional data warehouse database.

- *SQL Server Integration Services (SSIS)* to build the extract, transformation, and load (ETL) system.

- *SQL Server Analysis Services (SSAS)* analytic database to support users' queries, particularly ad hoc use.

- *SQL Server Analysis Services data mining* to develop statistical data mining models, and also to include those models in advanced analytic applications.

- *SQL Server Reporting Services (SSRS)* to build predefined reports. The majority of the Reporting Services features are most appropriate for the DW/BI team, but you may provide some ad hoc query and report building functionality with *Report Builder*.

- *Master Data Services (MDS)* to create a range of master data management applications to feed the data warehouse, and possibly integrate that data management with the source transaction systems.

- *Development and management tools, especially SQL Server BI Development Studio (BIDS) and SQL Server Management Studio* to build and manage your DW/BI system.

The SQL Server product contains the software necessary to build, deploy, populate, and manage your DW/BI system. Microsoft also offers a second significant set of tools beyond the SQL Server product designed for the business user, including:

- *Excel* is the most common tool for ad hoc users to access Analysis Services databases. The Excel pivot table controls connect directly into SSAS cubes, in an environment that most users are already familiar with. Pivot tables can also connect directly to a relational data warehouse.

- *PowerPivot* functionality is new in SQL Server 2008 R2. It combines the power of Analysis Services and Excel in an in-memory desktop experience. It's very popular with power analytic users and provides a strong BI application platform in conjunction with SharePoint.

- *SharePoint* has several roles within the DW/BI system. Many organizations develop their BI portals in SharePoint, providing an integrated place to host reports, ad hoc query tools, online training, user support, and documentation.

- *PowerPivot for SharePoint* expands the usefulness and manageability of PowerPivot, by enabling power users to share their PowerPivot workbooks via SharePoint.

- *Master Data Services* can also be configured to integrate with SharePoint, in order to provide workflow functionality in the master data management system.

Some organizations supplement their Microsoft end-user tools with third-party query, reporting, and analytic software.

Microsoft Visual Studio is a fundamental tool for the DW/BI development team. The SQL Server DW/BI development tools are hosted in Visual Studio. The necessary Visual Studio components are installed for you, and you may not even realize that you are using the standard Microsoft development environment.

You can use Visual Studio to build a custom application, such as an analytic application that connects your DW/BI system back to transaction systems. The heavy lifting of such an application may occur within your Analysis Services data mining model, but you'd still need to develop a bit of plumbing to connect the two systems.

Why Use the Microsoft Toolset?

Before we go on to describe how to build a DW/BI system using Microsoft technologies, it's worth asking the question: What is interesting about the Microsoft toolset? As it turns out, there are several compelling answers to this question:

- *Completeness:* From the operating system, database engines, and development environment, to a SharePoint portal and the Office and Excel desktop, you can build a complete DW/BI system using only Microsoft software. You have an extra margin of confidence that all the components work together effectively.

- *Lower cost of ownership:* The licensing cost of SQL Server has been less than comparable product suites from other vendors, but total cost of ownership depends as much on ongoing support, training, and operations costs as on licensing costs. Microsoft asserts that SQL Server systems need fewer administrative resources than competitive products. Your organization may already have .NET programming skills. If so, it may be possible for you to customize and extend your DW/BI system.

- *Openness:* Although you can build a complete DW/BI system with Microsoft software — and this book describes how to do it — you don't have to. Any component of the Microsoft DW/BI framework can be swapped out for a third-party product, and many customers build DW/BI systems in heterogeneous environments.

- *High performance and scale:* At the time of this writing, Microsoft-based DW/BI systems with data volumes of 10 terabytes are fairly common and 50 TB is not rare. As DW/BI systems are built on sub-transactional data like clickstreams and RFID data streams, even moderate-sized organizations may find themselves in the "terabyte club." Microsoft recognizes this trend, and has engineered and tested its products, especially the SQL Server components, to perform well at high data volumes. Microsoft has also extended its SQL Server product line with the Parallel Data Warehouse system that uses a massively parallel processing architecture to scale up to hundreds of terabytes.

- *Microsoft investment in business intelligence:* The SQL Server business intelligence suite consists of real tools that work together, if not seamlessly, then at least with seams that have been professionally sewn. Some of the tools — notably Analysis Services — are best of breed. All of the tools are competitive on their own merits with standalone products. Microsoft is clearly committed to building tools to enable you to build great business intelligence applications. And you can be reasonably confident that Microsoft will remain in business for a long time.

Architecture of a Microsoft DW/BI System

All DW/BI systems consist of several major components, as pictured in Figure 3-2: sources of data, an ETL system, data warehouse databases, and a wide variety of uses. Metadata is the glue that binds together the complete DW/BI system.

As we explained in Chapter 2, the data warehouse databases should be in a dimensional form, consisting of fact tables and their associated dimension tables. Dimensions should be conformed across the enterprise. For example, all business processes that are described by the customer dimension should use the same customer dimension with the same keys.

Some enterprises take advantage of SQL Server Master Data Services (MDS) to build a master data management system. As we explain in Chapter 6, simple MDS deployments fall squarely within the purview of DW/BI, supplementing the ETL system. But complex, enterprise master data management systems are more closely aligned with the source systems. That's why the Master Data Services box straddles the source systems and ETL in Figure 3-2.

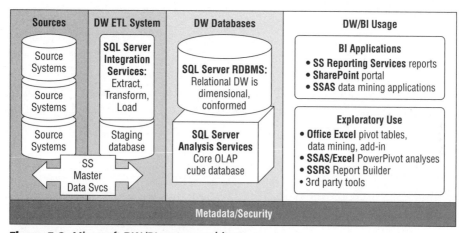

Figure 3-2: Microsoft DW/BI system architecture

The primary place to store and manage the dimensional model is in the relational data warehouse database. In Microsoft terms, this is the SQL Server database engine. You'll use Integration Services to develop an ETL system that populates that database, performs inserts and updates, and also manages system resources such as disk space, partitions, and indexes.

The second place to store and manage the dimensional model is in the core online analytic processing (OLAP) data warehouse database. In Microsoft terms, this is the Analysis Services OLAP engine. You'll write a small ETL module to incrementally populate the core SSAS database from the clean, conformed relational data warehouse database.

There are two major categories of DW/BI system usage: BI applications and exploratory use. There are many kinds of BI applications, ranging from standard predefined reports to complex analytic applications that use data mining technology to affect business operations. Microsoft offers many technologies here, from Reporting Services for predefined reports, to Analysis Services data mining and the Visual Studio development environment to build custom applications.

The other kind of usage is exploratory or ad hoc. Here, Office Excel continues to be popular, although many organizations struggle with the data anarchy that comes with extensive use of Excel in the enterprise. New to SQL Server 2008 R2, the PowerPivot analytic tool that combines Excel and Analysis Services may help with the data anarchy problem. Or it may make it worse! Many organizations use non-Microsoft tools to deliver more structured, yet still highly flexible, ad hoc query functionality. As we discuss in Chapter 10, the Report Builder component of Reporting Services is designed to provide some ad hoc functionality. Data mining is another kind of exploratory use, delivered by the Analysis Services data mining features. Most business users will access SSAS data mining via the Excel add-in.

All these tools use metadata for development and operations, but there's no specific metadata feature or central metadata management capability that we can point to. That doesn't mean the metadata is missing or even that it's unavailable; it's just not as easy to get to, nor as integrated as we'd like.

Most readers understand why the relational data warehouse database is important. Let's talk first about why your architecture should include Analysis Services.

Why Analysis Services?

What functionality is addressed by the OLAP database engine? Why would you want an OLAP engine — an Analysis Services implementation — in addition to the dimensional model stored in the relational database?

All DW/BI systems need a user-oriented layer on top of the dimensional data stored in the relational database. This layer can simply be a set of predefined reports. But for successful ad hoc access by business users, you need a layer that performs the following basic functions:

- *Easy user navigation:* User-oriented names for database objects, and transparent join paths between dimensions and facts and between multiple fact tables

- *Complex calculations:* Centralized storage of calculation logic and execution of calculations

- *Fast user query performance:* Usually accomplished through aggregate navigation and aggregate management

- *Data security definition and enforcement:* Preferably managed on a server rather than on users' desktops

For many years, people have used relational techniques such as views and client-side query tools to deliver this functionality. An OLAP engine such as Analysis Services provides a better way. Analysis Services supports the basic user-oriented functions already described, with two key additional features:

- *Query language:* OLAP engines use a different — and better — query language than SQL to express complex calculations.

- *Computational performance:* The OLAP engine has been designed as a high-performance server — its enterprise functionality, data capacity, and capability to resolve the most complex calculations far outstrips any client-based tool.

The concepts introduced here are discussed more thoroughly in Chapter 8, which describes how to design the core Analysis Services database.

Although Analysis Services is an extremely popular component of SQL Server, there are still several common objections to using it:

- *Scalability:* Relational data warehouses can scale higher than Analysis Services. We wouldn't hesitate to implement systems with several terabytes of data in Analysis Services, but we'd be cautious at scales approaching 10 TB. We've seen implementations larger than 5 TB, but they are rare.

- *Duplication of data:* Many users dislike the notion of duplicating all the relational data warehouse data into a second database management system.

- *Changes to the user applications:* Your business users are accustomed to using a SQL-based query and reporting tool, which might not work the same way (or at all) against an Analysis Services database. There is significant cost in purchasing new tools and retraining your users.

Of the three common arguments against using Analysis Services, we find only the third to be broadly compelling. Worries about scalability and data duplication shouldn't prevent the vast majority of SQL Server implementations from reaping the very real benefits of a DW/BI system that's built on Analysis Services.

Why a Relational Store?

Perhaps you're convinced that Analysis Services is a vital part of your DW/ BI system architecture. Your next question may be: why do you need to store the dimensional data in the relational database? You aren't required to do so: Microsoft provides several mechanisms for populating cubes directly from non-dimensional source systems. Why go to the trouble and expense of implementing a relational data warehouse database? Here's why:

- *Manageability:* As discussed in Chapter 17, it's much easier to handle changes in structure and content in the relational database than in Analysis Services.

- *Conforming dimensions and facts:* In a hypothetical, simple example, you can conform data on the way into the Analysis Services database. In the real world, you'll have to update and delete some data in the ETL pipeline, and you really want to do this in a relational database.

- *Comfort:* DBAs and power users are familiar with SQL and relational databases and will violently resist the elimination of the relational layer.

- *Future flexibility:* The notion of eliminating the relational data warehouse database and populating the Analysis Services database directly from transaction systems may sound appealing. But if you choose this approach, you're committing to an architecture that's difficult to transfer to another database platform, not that you would ever want to do that.

There are scenarios, particularly around the real-time delivery of analytic data, where it may make sense to skip the relational storage of the dimensional data and populate the Analysis Services database directly from transaction systems. But these are edge cases. Most of us, most of the time, should plan to store and manage the dimensional data in the relational database, and use that store to feed Analysis Services. Think of the Analysis Services layer as metadata for the dimensional database, which possibly includes a data cache for enhanced performance.

ETL Is Not Optional

We expect that most of the readers of this book are interested in building a data warehouse system. We will only briefly review the reasons that most in the information management industry agree that a data warehouse is a good idea. In short, the data warehouse:

- Separates analytic workloads from transaction processing
- Integrates multiple transaction data sources

- Reduces the complexity of data models for easier reporting and ad hoc analysis

- Improves query performance for reporting and ad hoc analysis by redesigning the data models

- Enhances analytics by supporting the addition of information that's not managed in the transaction systems

- Maintains a longer time series of data for facts and selective dimension attributes than is typically found in the transaction systems

- Presents a single version of the truth to the business user community

More to the point, the data warehouse adds significant value to the data. A well designed and built data warehouse provides data capture, searching, extracting, staging, archiving, cleaning, conforming, duplicating, allocating, transforming, computing, arranging, packaging, aggregating, presenting, analyzing, modeling, estimating, projecting, recommending, and connecting the decision to operations!

From time to time, observers argue that a data warehouse is too expensive. Instead, they propose a virtual data warehouse to provide many of the advantages of a real data warehouse, with presumably less cost. The ETL system is particularly expensive; isn't it possible to provide a user navigation layer on top of the transaction systems, and skip ETL altogether? In fact, Microsoft provides tools that could do that. It's theoretically possible to build an Analysis Services database, a PowerPivot workbook, or a Report Builder model directly on top of a transaction database or even multiple databases.

In all but the most trivial cases, this approach is so deeply flawed as to be unworkable. You'll be shifting the burden of ETL onto the business users, who will do the same thing multiple times, with inefficient tools (usually Excel), and in inconsistent ways. Attempting to implement a virtual warehouse technique on even a simple and clean sample database such as AdventureWorks is an exercise in frustration.

ETL is a job for IT professionals, not the user community. Build it once, build it right, and the downstream uses such as cubes, reports, and PowerPivot snap into place much more easily. It's easy to create a cube or PowerPivot workbook from very clean, well structured, and integrated data, such as the data in a dimensional data warehouse. With PowerPivot, it's not terribly difficult to integrate one or two additional data sources, such as demographic information or custom groupings.

Even if your user community is saying they just want tools such as PowerPivot without an underlying infrastructure, they most assuredly will not enjoy doing IT's job in the long term.

The Role of Master Data Services

SQL Server Master Data Services has an unusual position in the data warehouse architecture, as pictured in Figure 3-2. It straddles the source transaction systems and the data warehouse ETL system.

Although most information architectures do not yet include a formal master data management system, almost every existing data warehouse does perform some master data management. Functionality to integrate customer names or product lists from multiple source systems and applets to manage reporting hierarchies or custom attributes are required by most data warehouse environments.

We're advocating several changes from the status quo:

- Manage this master data externally and explicitly, rather than folding it into the batch ETL operations. One of the key advantages of explicit management is the opportunity to leverage experts' judgment as entities are created, rather than during the nightly batch ETL process.

- Consider using Master Data Services to replace most of the complex logic for dimension table ETL. Master Data Services can process changes during the day, and then submit the new and changed rows to the batch ETL system for processing into the dimension tables.

- Set the stage for your organization to implement "real" master data management, which integrates tightly with the source transaction systems and eliminates the need for downstream data integration. Data is integrated at the source. As we discuss in Chapter 6, this admirable goal is out of immediate reach for many organizations, which haven't even begun to take a serious view of data stewardship.

Delivering BI Applications

Reporting Services is the primary platform in the SQL Server toolset for delivering BI applications. It is essentially a standalone enterprise report definition, storage, execution, and delivery service. It offers a reasonable set of report creation and distribution tools, primarily targeted at the developer community.

Reporting Services includes Report Builder, a desktop tool that offers almost the same report design experience as the BIDS-based report designer without the need for BIDS or Visual Studio. This makes it more accessible to power users, and it has an optional metadata model to help simplify the data set definitions even further. However, it is still a fairly complex tool and does not find broad use in most organizations. We explore Reporting Services and Report Builder in greater detail in Chapter 10.

If you want to deliver more flexible data interaction to your users, you need to include tools outside the SQL Server toolset. The obvious candidate under the Microsoft umbrella is Excel. Its PivotTable control connects directly to Analysis Services cubes and shows the available facts and dimensions based on the cube's metadata. This makes it easy for business users to create their own simple queries and reports against Analysis Services cubes. PivotTables can also access relational data sources, but it is difficult to present the dimensional model because there is no associated metadata in the relational environment to define it.

The PowerPivot add-in for Excel 2010 takes PivotTables to a new level. It is a desktop-based Analysis Services cube that uses an in-memory column store technology to support fast access to millions of rows of data in combination with an enhanced PivotTable control called the PowerPivot Field List. The big leap forward of the PowerPivot Field List is its capability to allow the user to define new columns that are computed in the PowerPivot database. This enables users to embed computed columns in their reports that are completely context-aware, a critical function for creating flexible, modifiable reports.

PowerPivot has a SharePoint component that allows you to share access to PowerPivot reports across your organization. In order to reach this level of reporting, you need Microsoft Office 2010 or higher on every user desktop and a SharePoint server. We will explore the implications of these additional tools in Chapter 11 on PowerPivot and Chapter 12 on the BI Portal and SharePoint.

Overview of the Microsoft Tools

Many readers will start to work with SQL Server by experimenting with its functionality in a single machine sandbox. If you have the time and bandwidth to do so, this is a great way to determine which product features are important to your business and users. In this environment, we recommend that you acquire a true sandbox machine: a new or rebuilt machine with a clean operating system and no other applications. You can use virtual machine technology to simulate a clean machine and run SQL Server well enough to evaluate functionality.

Other readers are launching real projects and need to be more rigorous and thoughtful in setting up their environments. As we discuss in Chapter 16, plan from the outset for the standard three-tier system, with separate servers for development, test, and production. Your test system should be as similar to the production system as you can possibly make it. The more different your test and production systems are, the more difficult it is for your database administrators to evaluate alternative approaches to tuning and configuration before rolling those changes into production.

Most teams set up their development environment with a central server or two to hold relational and Analysis Services databases. Developers install the development tools — the studio workbenches described in the next section — on their own machines, and point those tools to the development database server. Early in the development cycle, developers may have personal databases, either on the shared server or on their own machines.

Which Products Do You Need?

There are four editions available that are interesting for DW/BI projects, starting at the high end:

- Data Center Edition
- Enterprise Edition
- Standard Edition
- Developer Edition

You will need to purchase and run either Data Center, Enterprise, or Standard Edition on your production servers. Enterprise Edition contains almost the entire product feature set, and — unsurprisingly — costs several times as much as Standard Edition. Enterprise Edition lacks a few features that are available in Data Center Edition, having to do with managing multiple instances. But the main difference between Enterprise and Data Center is the hardware: Enterprise Edition is limited to 8 CPU sockets and 2 TB of memory.

RESOURCES You can find detailed information on each edition at www
.microsoft.com/sql, and in Books Online. See the Books Online topic
"Features Supported by the Editions of SQL Server."

There is no hard and fast rule for which edition you should purchase. A simple rule of thumb suggests that Standard Edition is probably sufficient for most small and some medium implementations. If your data volume, measured as data only without indexes, is 50 gigabytes (GB) or less, then you can do without the scalability features in Enterprise Edition. Depending on incremental load volumes, frequency, and uptime requirements, a medium-sized implementation of up to 250 GB can also work on Standard Edition. Any large, real-time, or otherwise challenging implementation should plan to use Enterprise Edition. Extremely large deployments, which plan to use more than 8 CPU sockets for a component of the DW/BI system, should use Data Center Edition.

Whichever edition you use in production, your developers should use Developer Edition. Developer Edition is extremely inexpensive, it will run on desktop operating systems such as Windows 7, and it contains all the functionalities of the Enterprise and Data Center Editions.

EDITIONS AND FEATURES OF SQL SERVER 2008 R2

The features that are excluded from Standard Edition support scalability in the enterprise. Mostly, scalability refers to data volumes, and often has more to do with maintaining and operating very large systems than actually storing and querying them. Another aspect of scalability is complexity; some of the excluded features would help your business users navigate a complex enterprise-level system more easily.

Here, we list and comment on our favorite Enterprise Edition features:

- **Relational database engine**

  Relational database partitioned tables are a key feature for fast loading and improved maintainability of large tables. We talk about partitioning in Chapter 4.

  Relational database maintenance functionality, including online index operations and parallel index operations, is particularly important for loading new data into large tables in a short time frame and performing periodic maintenance.

  Resource Governor lets you define groups of users and types of usage, and define ceilings for their use of the relational database. The Resource Governor can help prevent one or two killer queries from taking over the server. Resource Governor is described in Chapter 17.

  Change Data Capture is defined on the source transaction database. It will generate tables with images for rows that have been added, updated, or deleted.

  Star join query optimization can dramatically improve the performance of queries on the dimensional or star schema structures in the relational data warehouse.

  Data compression can reduce storage and have a significant improvement on query performance from the relational data warehouse.

- **Integration Services**

  Integration with Analysis Services dimensions, cubes, and data mining models is a really nice feature, but not absolutely necessary. You could have SSIS launch a script that updates the cube or data mining model.

  Advanced transforms such as fuzzy lookup and text mining are very cool, but they may be too complicated for most small projects to deal with anyway.

Continued

Continued

- **Analysis Services OLAP engine**

  Scalability and performance features, such as automatic parallel processing and partitioned cubes, are very important for delivering great performance with medium and large data volumes.

  Features such as Account Intelligence, Writeback Dimensions, and particularly Perspectives, Semi-additive Measures, and Translations let you build more usable and complex OLAP databases.

- **Analysis Services data mining**

  Parallelism for processing and prediction is important for large data volumes and heavy usage scenarios.

  The statisticians in your organization will appreciate the advanced tuning and configuration options for the algorithms.

  The integration with Integration Services, as we've already described, is useful but not absolutely necessary.

- **Reporting Services**

  Scale-out report servers are an important feature for large-scale deployments. This is basically creating a web farm for the report servers.

  Data-driven subscriptions may be useful for a large enterprise. With this feature, you can email a personalized budget variance report to a dynamic list of managers, run from a single report definition.

- **PowerPivot for SharePoint**

  PowerPivot for SharePoint is not available in Standard Edition.

- **Master Data Services**

  Master Data Services is not available in Standard Edition.

SQL Server Development and Management Tools

Two toolsets are installed as part of the client tools installation. The SQL Server Management Studio (Management Studio) is used to *operate* and *manage* your DW/BI system. The Business Intelligence Development Studio (BIDS) is used to *design* and *develop* your business intelligence system.

SQL Server Management Studio

Management Studio is the primary tool for database administrators. In most cases, the Management Studio client tools are the only component of SQL Server that is installed on database administrators' workstations. The Management Studio screen is pictured in Figure 3-3.

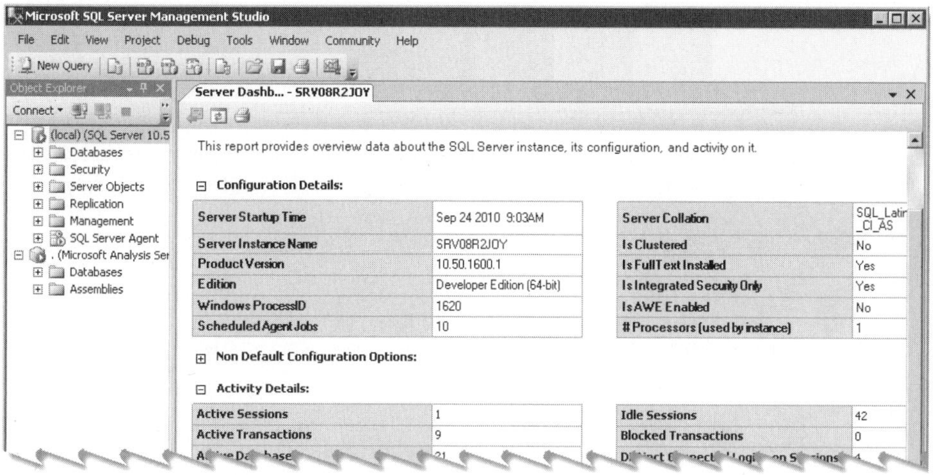

Figure 3-3: SQL Server Management Studio

Relational Database Management Operations

Within Management Studio, you perform most development and management activities for the relational database. There are point-and-click user interfaces to:

- Create, delete, back up, and restore databases.
- Create tables.
- View the data in tables.
- Create database diagrams.
- Create and manage stored procedures, views, security, and other database objects.
- Generate a T-SQL script to create any database object.

Alternatively, from within Management Studio, you can open a SQL window to perform all of these functions through T-SQL.

Management Studio includes many predefined server management reports. The server dashboard report is illustrated in Figure 3-3. There are additional reports available for the server, each database, and other objects such as security.

Analysis Services Management Operations

When you connect to an existing Analysis Services database in Management Studio, you can perform management operations including:

- Delete the SSAS database.
- Back up and restore SSAS databases.

- Define storage characteristics for cube partitions.
- Create and process partitions.
- Manage security.
- Run aggregation design wizards, and create and process performance aggregations.

You can also open three types of query windows for an Analysis Services database:

- *Multidimensional Expressions (MDX):* MDX is the query language for Analysis Services. Use a simple control to browse the cube, or type your own MDX.
- *Data Mining Extensions (DMX):* Using a syntax similar to SQL, issue queries on the data management views for Analysis Services. Alternatively, from within this same query window, use SQL syntax or a simple UI to issue queries into an existing data mining model.
- *XML for Analysis (XMLA):* Issue a query to browse the structure of the SSAS structure, modify that structure, or process the cube. As you might guess from the name, XMLA uses XML syntax.

It is technically possible to edit and re-issue the Analysis Services object creation XMLA. In fact, it is technically possible to write a complete cube definition or Integration Services package by typing an XML file. Just because something is possible doesn't mean it's a good idea. Use BIDS to design and debug BI objects (except for the relational database). In the rare cases when you need to automatically generate an object, you should use the appropriate programming object model rather than attempt to manipulate the XML directly.

Reporting Services Management Operations

When you connect Management Studio to a Reporting Services instance, you can manage security and shared schedules. Many organizations use the Reporting Services default web application to perform these activities, rather than Management Studio.

Integration Services Management Operations

When you connect Management Studio to an Integration Services instance, you see the packages that are currently executing. You can also see all packages that have been installed in the SQL Server database or package store. As we discuss in Chapter 7, many organizations simply leave their packages in the file system, in which case they do not show up here in Management Studio.

Business Intelligence Development Studio (BIDS)

BIDS is designed for all BI system designers and developers, with user interfaces for designing and debugging Analysis Services databases, data mining
models, Integration Services packages, and Reporting Services reports. The
obvious omission from this list is the design and development of the relational
data warehouse database. Use Management Studio for the relational part of the
project and BIDS for the rest.

Like Management Studio, BIDS is integrated with Visual Studio. This is great
news for developers who already use Visual Studio because the interface will
be somewhat familiar. Even though the Visual Studio environment appears
complex at first, everyone benefits from this integration. Your team can use
integrated source control to manage project files; you can set breakpoints and
debug Integration Services packages and MDX scripts; any code you may need
to develop is integrated in the same environment; and all projects benefit from
a unified approach to separating development from deployment.

BIDS uses the same kind of hierarchical grouping as Visual Studio. You will
create one or more solutions; each solution has one or more projects; each project
has one or more associated files. Each project is associated with a technology
such as Integration Services or Reporting Services. In theory, you can have one
BI solution that spans your DW/BI system, with multiple projects inside it for
each component of that system (SSIS, SSAS, and SSRS). Practically speaking,
most teams keep a one-to-one correspondence between projects and solutions,
or at most a handful of projects for each solution. That's because the solution
takes a long time to open up if there are hundreds of files in it.

DW/BI development teams should manage their files under source control,
and BIDS makes that very easy to do. You won't see this functionality unless
you've integrated your source control product into Visual Studio.

The files in the project folder completely define the project: They are the source
code for the project. During the development process (especially if you're not
using source control!), you may want to share your project definition with a col-
league so she can view your work. You can simply send her a copy of the project
folder, ensure she has appropriate database permissions, and she is set.

BIDS shows different windows depending on whether you're working on an
Analysis Services, Integration Services, or Reporting Services project. Figure 3-4
illustrates the BIDS window for an Integration Services project. This is a new
project that doesn't have much content yet.

All the different types of projects use a similar layout, imposed by Visual
Studio. The Solution Explorer window, located by default in the upper right, lists
the files in the project and lets you navigate between them. The Properties pane,
located by default in the lower right, shows all the properties associated with

an object; read-only properties are gray. As you'll see in subsequent chapters, BIDS contains extensive wizards whose job, in effect, is to help you set these properties.

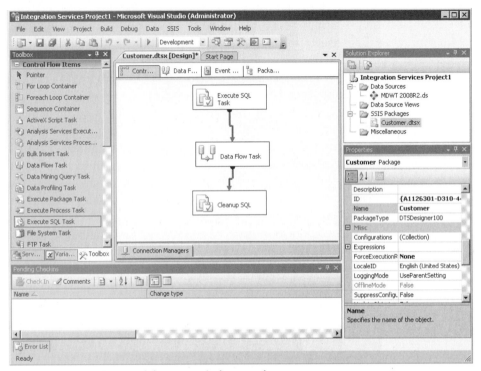

Figure 3-4: Basic layout of the BIDS windows and panes

BIDS gobbles up screen real estate, and is a good excuse to get an upgraded monitor and video card. You can maximize screen real estate by setting windows such as the Solution Explorer and Properties pane to "auto-hide."

Many of the BIDS components use the Toolbox pane on the left-hand side. The big section in the middle, which currently displays the control flow for a new SSIS package, is used as a design surface. In here you'll design Integration Services packages, Analysis Services dimensions, cubes, and data mining models, Reporting Services reports, and so on. You generally want this central area to be as big as possible.

Finally, the BIDS tools use Visual Studio's build, deploy, and debugging features such as watch windows. Sometimes it feels like there are dozens of extra little windows, located by default at the bottom of the screen.

The other chapters in this book focus on the specific BI features such as Analysis Services and Integration Services. In those chapters, we spend more time describing how to use BIDS, although this book is not intended to be a product tutorial. The tutorials that ship with SQL Server do a very good job of explaining how to use the product.

Summary

In this chapter, we described how the Microsoft BI toolset maps to industry standard terminology. We made a compelling argument that you can build your entire business intelligence system using software only from Microsoft. You're not tied to Microsoft for your entire project, however: the components are "open," in the sense that they are linked together by published interfaces. If you wish, you can use a non-Microsoft product for any component of your DW/BI system.

We described the basic recommended architecture of a Microsoft DW/BI system and introduced the studio tools — SQL Server Management Studio and BI Development Studio. We will provide much more information about these tools in upcoming chapters.

CHAPTER 4

System Setup

Let's get physical.

Up to this point, we've been talking about project management, business requirements, logical data models, and system architectures. Until now, you haven't needed any technology more sophisticated than a laptop with Office. That changes in this chapter, as we discuss issues surrounding the setup of your development, test, and production systems, and get you ready to start the development process.

As you can see in Figure 4-1, the product installation and setup issues addressed in this chapter come toward the end of the technology track of the Kimball Lifecycle, once you've created your system architecture, and selected any additional products you might need, and worked through the dimensional model design.

We begin by helping you get a handle on the size of your business intelligence system, so you can make decisions about its basic physical configuration. Will you install all the server software components for your DW/BI system on a single machine or several? Will you use clustering or web farms? Do you need to budget for server hardware or expensive storage networks? We can't answer these questions for you, but we've provided some guidance that should help you answer them for yourself.

The decisions you make about your production hardware and software configuration should be reflected, as much as economically feasible, in your test or quality assurance system. It may seem wasteful to spend money on test systems, but if you're serious about delivering good-quality service to your existing business users, you need to be serious about testing before you roll system changes into production.

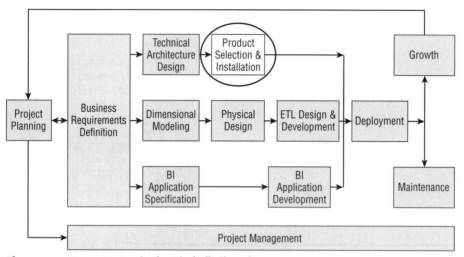

Figure 4-1: System setup in the Kimball Lifecycle

We suspect many readers will be tempted to skip this chapter. At least one person on your project team should read it, even if you have a separate server management group who will do all the work for you.

In this chapter, we address the following specific questions:

- Early in the design process, how can you determine how large your DW/BI system will be? What are the usage factors that will push you to a larger and more complex configuration?

- How should you configure your system? How much memory do you need, how many servers, what kind of storage and processors?

- How do you install the SQL Server software on the development, test, and production servers? What do different members of the DW/BI team need to install on their workstations?

System Sizing Considerations

We're sure that all readers of this chapter are hoping for a simple chart that will specify what kind of server machine they should buy. Sorry, it's not going to happen: The problem is too difficult to reduce to a simple matrix or tool. The best we can do is describe the different options and parameters, and the kinds of operations that require bigger and more expensive hardware.

There are four main factors that will push your project to more expensive hardware: data volumes, usage complexity, number of simultaneous users, and system availability requirements. These factors are illustrated in Figure 4-2 and discussed in the following sections.

Calculating Data Volumes

The first and most obvious characteristic of your DW/BI system that will affect your hardware purchases is data volumes. By the time you've finished your logical model and initial data profiling, you should have enough information to estimate how big your DW/BI system is going to be. Later, during the database setup, your DBAs will calculate database sizes in great detail, but for now you can just think about fact table row counts. Unless you have a monster dimension of 50–100 million rows, dimension sizes are insignificant.

For starters, just figure out what order of magnitude number of rows you'll have for your initial historical load of fact data. Multiply that number by 100 bytes, which is our generous rule-of-thumb for fact row sizes. You can get more precise if you like, but we like arithmetic that we can do on our fingers. One hundred million fact rows require about 10GB as stored in the relational database, measured as uncompressed atomic data only, no indexes. It might be 7GB; it might be 12GB; it won't be 100MB or 100GB. When you add relational indices and Analysis Services indices and MOLAP storage, multiply that base number by 2 to 4. In the early stages, before we have a specific design, we use a factor of 3. The requirements for the ETL staging area could conceivably add another factor, although the staging area may be relatively small.

	Small	Medium	Large
Data Volumes	< 500 M fact rows < 50 GB atomic fact data	< 5 B fact rows < 500 GB atomic fact data	Billions and billions
Usage Complexity	> 60% Simple use 30% Medium complexity < 10% Demanding use	50% Simple use 35% Medium 15% Demanding	35% Simple 40% Medium 25% Demanding
Number of Users	< a dozen simultaneous users	< 200 simultaneous users	Thousands
Availability	Several hours of downtime each night acceptable	< 1 hour downtime or query slowdown each night	24x7 with excellent query performance
Configuration Options	One "Commodity" 2 CPU, 4 core 32 GB memory	One high-end system w/max memory OR distribute components to multiple commodity servers	Distributed system on high-end servers, some clusters

Figure 4-2: DW/BI system sizing considerations and configuration options

The incremental daily or monthly load volume is important, too. From the incremental volumes, you can compute expected data volumes for each fact table one, three, and five years out, which will help you decide what class of storage system to buy today.

Although we've talked in this section about counting all the fact rows in your system, not all fact tables are created equal. A single billion-row fact table is going to be more demanding of system resources than ten 100 million–row fact tables would be. We don't have a scientific way to quantify this difference, but you should list the fact table sizes by fact table, in addition to an overall count.

In Figure 4-2, a small system is characterized by less than 500 million rows of fact data, or 50GB using our simple multiplier. A large system is more than 5 billion fact rows, into the terabyte range and above.

Determining Usage Complexity

The next key factor in deciding how big your hardware needs to be is to consider how your business users are going to use the data. There are two main questions: how many users will be working simultaneously, and what will they be doing? The usage patterns of a business intelligence system are quite different from the familiar workload of a transaction system. Even the simplest DW/BI query — for example, a query browsing a dimension — is more complex than most transactional queries. And the most complex DW/BI query is several orders of magnitude more complex, and touches more data, than any operational transaction.

You can't expect to already have a great understanding of system usage during the design phase of the DW/BI system; however, you do need to think about different kinds of usage and the approximate volume of use in each category. The data model tests we described in Chapter 2 are a good place to start. Your business requirements document should also contain information about the kinds of usage you will need to support.

Simple or Controlled Access

The more simple or predictable the users' queries, the more simultaneous users can be supported on the same size system. Examples of simple use include:

- *Predefined queries and reports based on highly selective sets of relational or Analysis Services data:* Because these queries are relatively simple and predefined, a relational system can easily be tuned to support them. On the other hand, it's particularly hard to understand what's simple and what's challenging to Analysis Services OLAP databases. Please refer to the related discussion in the following two subsections.

■ *Reporting Services scheduled and cached reports:* As described in Chapter 10, scheduled reports may be extremely complex. But because they are run and cached at night, the load placed by users of these reports during business hours is relatively light.

■ *Data mining forecasting queries:* Data mining represents another kind of predefined query. As we discuss later, training a data mining model is most definitely *not* simple access. But performing a forecasting query on new information about a customer is highly selective.

Moderate Complexity

Examples of moderately complex use include:

■ *Predefined reports based on a broad set of relational data not supported by aggregates,* such as specific constraints on all sales for the past year. On the positive side, the report is predefined and so it can be tuned. On the negative side, the underlying query touches a lot of data and so is expensive. Consider using Analysis Services as the report's data source, scheduling and caching these reports in Reporting Services, or experimenting with aggregated indexed views.

■ *Ad hoc query and analysis using Analysis Services,* where the analysis does *not* need to look at a large portion of the atomic data. If a lot of business users are performing ad hoc queries, the odds are good that they're hitting different parts of the OLAP database. In this case, the server's data cache will be of limited use (unless you have a *lot* of memory). Contrast this moderately complex ad hoc use of Analysis Services with the highly complex situation described next.

Highly Demanding Use

Examples of highly complex use include:

■ *Ad hoc query and analysis using the relational data warehouse database:* These queries typically join many tables and often access large volumes of data. The business users aren't experts, so they may make mistakes. It's not feasible for them to use query hints.

■ *Advanced ad hoc query and analysis on Analysis Services:* The analysis requires wide queries that access a large portion of the atomic data. There is a class of analytic problems that by definition must touch very detailed data. For example, a query that counts the unique values in a large set is unavoidably expensive because it must touch detailed rows. Similarly, a query that returns a median or top *N* percent must also touch many more rows than are handed back in the result set.

▪ *Training of a data mining model:* As we discuss in Chapter 13, creating the case sets for a data mining model often involves several full table scans of the fact tables.

Most DW/BI systems will be used in all these ways. The mix on a typical DW/BI system will lean toward the simple end, with about 60 percent simple, 30 percent moderately complex, and 10 percent demanding usage, as illustrated in Figure 4-2. At the other end, a challenging usage profile has 35 percent simple, 40 percent moderate, and 25 percent demanding usage.

Estimating Simultaneous Users

The number of potential users of the DW/BI system provides only the roughest possible estimate of how many people are using the system at the same time. One analyst doing very complex work, or a manager opening a multi-report dashboard, can use as many resources as dozens of users who are accessing simple reports. It's as important to know the system usage characteristics as it is to know how many people access the system.

If you currently have no DW/BI system in place, it will be difficult for you to forecast usage frequency and timing. Even our old standby recommendation, that you interview the business users, will be of little value. During the design and development phase, business users are not able to guess how much they'll use the system, and during what times of day.

A few broad patterns are easy to predict. There is usually a surge of demand in the morning, when people arrive at work and check the reports run on yesterday's data. Other cycles may be based on obvious work patterns, like month-end, quarterly, or year-end financial reporting calendars. It's a good idea to plan your system capacity to meet these peak times, even if your system is underutilized the rest of the year. These peaks are when people need the data most urgently and will be most frustrated with delays.

Even with these patterns, however, remember that a DW/BI workload is quite different from the fairly constant stream associated with a transaction system. In most cases, a business user executes a query or report, and then examines and thinks about the information before executing a follow up query. You should be careful to incorporate this think time into your understanding of simultaneous usage. If you buy or develop a performance testing suite, make sure it uses randomly generated think times of between 30 seconds and several minutes.

If you have a DW/BI system already in production, the current usage statistics will provide a more certain estimate of future use. But if the current DW/BI system performs poorly, expect increased use with a new higher performance system than with the old. A lot of DW/BI queries and reports are somewhat optional for business users. If the current system is painful to use, they won't use it; they'll get the data some other way, or do without.

A small system may have only a dozen simultaneous users — people who are issuing queries and reports at more or less the same time. A large system, by contrast, will have hundreds or even thousands.

Assessing System Availability Requirements

The final factor affecting system size and configuration is the business requirements for system availability. These requirements can range from an 8-hour load window (midnight to 8 a.m.) during which the DW/BI system can be offline, to the opposite extreme of providing system availability 24 hours a day, 7 days a week. If your business users require high availability, you may need to purchase a substantially larger and more complex system than you'd otherwise need.

The stronger the business need for a high availability system, the more likely you will be to cluster some of the components, notably the relational database and Analysis Services database, and to set up a web farm for Reporting Services. You may also need parallel server resources allowing you to run ETL jobs against one version of the data while users query yesterday's version at the same time. We'll see one version of using parallel structures when we explore partition switching in Chapter 5.

How Big Will It Be?

With a little thought and research, you should be able to determine where you fall on the spectrum in each of the four sizing factors in Figure 4-2. This leads to a general sense for the size of the system and your high level scaling options. A small system can work with a single server; in the mid-range, consider a single large server, or multiple good sized commodity servers; and at the high end, you may need to look at multiple large servers. We'll look at how all these servers might be configured in the next section.

System Configuration Considerations

At this point, you might be wondering how you can possibly determine what configuration is the most appropriate for your workload. It helps to break the question down into the major system components and configuration options. These include memory, monolithic or distributed systems, storage, and high availability systems.

Memory

All of the SQL Server DW/BI components love physical memory. The relational database uses memory at query time to resolve the DW/BI style of query, and during ETL processing for index restructuring. Analysis Services uses memory for resolving queries and performing calculations, for caching result sets, and for managing user session information. During processing, Analysis Services uses memory to compute aggregations, data mining models, and any stored calculations. The whole point of Integration Services' data flow pipeline is to avoid temporarily writing data to disk during the ETL process. Depending on your package design, you may need several times as much memory as your largest incremental processing set. Reporting Services is probably the least memory-intensive of the four major components, but rendering large or complex reports will also place a strain on memory resources.

Because all the DW/BI system components are memory intensive, the obvious solution is to buy hardware that supports a lot of memory. When we wrote this, you could purchase a two processor, four or six-core 64-bit server with 32GB of memory for around $5,000. A commodity 64-bit eight or twelve-way machine like this can be an all-in-one server for smaller systems, and the basic workhorse system for more complex configurations. The largest and most complex DW/BI systems will need one or more high-performance systems sold directly by the major hardware vendors. As a general guide, we try to outfit our servers with at least four GB of memory per CPU core. More is better. Remember, SQL Server 2008 R2 Standard Edition is limited to four CPU sockets and 64 GB total, but Windows Server 2008 R2 Standard Edition is limited to 32 GB.

Monolithic or Distributed?

There are two primary strategies for applying more horsepower to your DW/BI system: using fewer, larger machines or using more, smaller machines. The monolithic approach is also known as scaling up; the distributed approach is also known as scaling out.

For smaller systems, an all-in-one configuration is appealing: You'll minimize operating system and SQL Server licensing costs, and one server is easiest to manage. If you need a larger system and decide to use the scale out approach with several distributed servers, the first way to do so is by putting one or more SQL Server components onto separate machines. This architecture is easier to manage than distributing the workload by splitting up the data sets and hosting them on separate servers, each with its own set of SQL Server components. You need a high-bandwidth network between the DW/BI system servers, and between the ETL server and the source systems, as significant volumes of data are shipped back and forth between the components.

The all-in-one configuration illustrated in Figure 4-3 has all server components, including possibly SharePoint Server as a reporting portal, running on a single machine. Note that SharePoint is resource intensive, and will do better on its own server. Most users (clients) will access the DW/BI system by connecting to Reporting Services, either directly or through SharePoint. Some analytic business users will connect directly to Analysis Services or the relational database for ad hoc and complex analyses.

Figure 4-4 illustrates a common step up from the all-in-one configuration by creating a reporting server. Consider this configuration if your business users make heavy use of standardized reports built primarily from Analysis Services, and your DW/BI system processing occurs at night when users are not on the system. In this configuration, the Reporting Services catalog database will probably work best on the SQL Server Data Store server, although it could be placed on the reporting server. In the reporting server configuration, some business users access the SQL Server data store directly.

REFERENCE The Microsoft SQL-CAT team has a white paper at SQLCAT.com called "Report Server Catalog Best Practices" that describes how to manage and tune the report server catalog in detail.

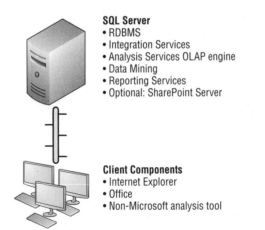

SQL Server
• RDBMS
• Integration Services
• Analysis Services OLAP engine
• Data Mining
• Reporting Services
• Optional: SharePoint Server

Client Components
• Internet Explorer
• Office
• Non-Microsoft analysis tool

Figure 4-3: All-in-one business intelligence system

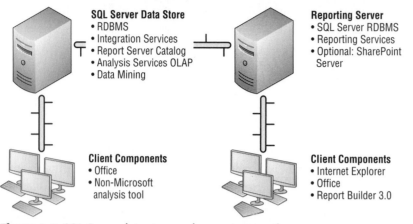

Figure 4-4: SQL Server data store and separate reporting server

If your system is allowed only a relatively short downtime, you should separate Analysis Services from the relational database, as pictured in Figure 4-5. In this configuration, the ETL process and relational database load will not compete with Analysis Services queries, most of which will use the data cache on the reporting and analysis server. The Reporting Services catalog, located on the data store server, will compete with the ETL process for resources, but this is almost certainly better than having it compete with the reporting and analysis services. This configuration is not appropriate for a very high availability operation, which requires the use of clusters as discussed later in this chapter.

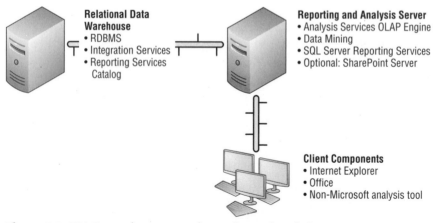

Figure 4-5: SQL Server data store and reporting and analysis server

As your system grows larger and places more demands on the hardware, you may end up at the logical end point of the scale out approach: with each SQL Server component on its own server. Each of the chapters about the different components discusses some of the issues around distributing the system. But in general there is no built-in assumption that any two of the components are co-located on a single physical server.

You can even push the SQL Server architecture past the point of one server per component. Analysis Services can distribute the partitions of an OLAP database across multiple servers. Reporting Services can run on a web farm, which can greatly enhance scalability. Your network of Integration Services packages can also be distributed across multiple servers, although we expect only the most extreme ETL problems would need to use this architecture.

After you've reached the limit of distributing the SQL Server components to multiple machines, you can think about partitioning along the lines of business process dimensional models. Usually, when a DW/BI system is distributed throughout the organization, it's for political rather than performance reasons. Only for really large systems is it technically necessary to partition the DW/BI system along dimensional model boundaries. Also, various components may employ varying approaches to achieve uptime guarantees. We discuss how to make a horizontally distributed system work, but we prefer and recommend a more centralized architecture.

In the development environment, a common configuration is for developers to use a shared instance of the relational database and Analysis Services database on a two- or four-socket server. Some developers may also choose to run local instances of the database servers, in order to experiment in isolation from their colleagues.

SERVER ARCHITECTURE OPTIONS

All of the server machines discussed thus far are known as symmetric multi-processing (SMP) machines. The CPUs on SMP machines generally have shared access to all the available system memory and disk. As the machine gets bigger, the system bus becomes a bottleneck as all these CPUs try to process different threads in parallel, accessing memory and disk through the same system bus. Larger machines use a non-uniform memory architecture (NUMA) to mitigate this by grouping subsets of memory and CPUs together on local busses, called nodes, and tying the nodes together with a cross-node bus. If you are facing the prospect of a multi-terabyte data warehouse, you have another system architecture option called massively parallel processing (MPP). MPP systems use a network of smaller SMP nodes, each with its own memory and disk. Microsoft's Parallel Data Warehouse product allows you to implement an MPP SQL Server data warehouse on commodity hardware from most of the major vendors.

Storage System Considerations

Reading and writing data to and from disk is by far the slowest point in the system. There are several issues to consider when it comes to data storage. Regardless of what kind of storage system you use, you must make sure the data pipeline from the CPUs down to the disk drives is properly balanced. You also need to make sure your storage system provides some level of fault tolerance to protect against data loss, and you need to determine whether you will use a storage area network, or attach storage directly to your server.

Balancing the Data Pipeline

Every data bit processed in the data warehouse has to travel from the source system through a CPU and out to a disk for long-term safekeeping. The data is then retrieved from disk, often many times, to answer user queries. There are several components along the way that may act as bottlenecks if they do not have sufficient capacity. Figure 4-6 shows the major components in this pipeline, any one of which could choke off your throughput if it does not have sufficient capacity.

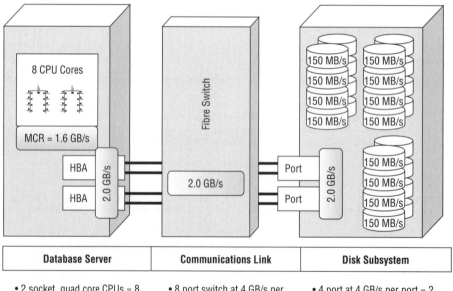

Database Server	Communications Link	Disk Subsystem
• 2 socket, quad core CPUs = 8 CPU cores • Data consumption per CPU = 200 MB/s • 2x dual port host bus adapter at 4 GB/s per port = 2.0 GB/s	• 8 port switch at 4 GB/s per port = 2 GB/s throughput (port-to-port)	• 4 port at 4 GB/s per port = 2 GB/s • 3 arrays of 4 300 GB disks each, configured as RAID 1+0 (24 disks total = 3.6 TB) = 1.8 GB/s

Figure 4-6: The data pipeline

There are six major potential bottlenecks in Figure 4-6: CPUs, host bus adapters, the fibre channel switch ports, the storage subsystem ports, the array controllers, and the disk drives. This system is reasonably balanced, with the 1.6 gigabytes per second maximum consumption rate of the CPUs being the overall limiting factor. A system like this should be able to scan a 1 billion row fact table in about 60 seconds.

Microsoft has created reference hardware architectures with each of the major hardware vendors called SQL Server Fast Track Data Warehouse architecture. The system architecture concentrates on balancing the data pipeline and storing data for sequential access, where disk drives perform best.

REFERENCE You can find a detailed white paper describing the fast track architecture, including throughput calculations, in a document titled "Fast Track Data Warehouse 2.0 Architecture" on MSDN. This is a very helpful document if you are responsible for architecting your server environment.

Disk Performance

The disk drives are the slowest component in the DW/BI system; as much as 100 times slower than memory. Disk drive system designers have worked to overcome this problem for decades. One major technique has been to put memory in the disk drive and at the disk controller level. Recently requested data is cached in this memory in the hopes that it may be needed again soon. SQL Server uses system memory to do the same thing on a much larger scale, caching whole tables and results sets for future use.

The basic disk strategy in the data warehouse is to use more, smaller disks rather than fewer large disks. When configured in an array with data spread across multiple disks, several disks can be used to read or write a data set in parallel. This is the reason for the 12 disks in Figure 4-6.

SILICON STORAGE DEVICES

Silicon Storage Devices (SSDs) are basically non-volatile memory packaged to look like a disk drive. They perform much faster than standard hard disk drives for certain operations. In particular, random access reads can be an order of magnitude faster or more. However, they have some limitations in other areas, such as sequential writes, which might be a major part of the ETL process. They also have some technical limitations in terms of the number of times a particular cell can be written to (called the program-erase cycle). As these technologies improve, they will fundamentally change our disk subsystem strategies. Meanwhile, SSDs may be a relatively cheap and easy way to boost performance for certain parts of the DW/BI system. The Analysis Services database is an ideal candidate because of its heavy random access read patterns.

Fault Tolerance and RAID

Almost all DW/BI system servers use a Redundant Array of Independent Disks (RAID) storage infrastructure. RAID-1, also known as mirroring, makes a complete copy of the disk. RAID 1+0 (or RAID 10) is an array of at least two mirrored disk sets with the data striped across the mirrors. RAID-1 and RAID-1+0 are used for replicating and sharing data among disks. They are the configurations of choice for performance-critical, fault-tolerant environments, but require 100 percent duplication of disks. RAID-1 has the same write performance as single disks, and twice the read performance. RAID-5's read performance is good, but its write performance suffers in comparison to RAID-1. All of these RAID configurations, including RAID-5, are vulnerable to a kind of second-order disaster that occurs when a failed drive is being restored and simultaneously a disk read error occurs. In this case the entire data set is lost. An enhanced version of RAID-5, known as "RAID-6 with hot spare" avoids this situation.

The RAID array needs to be managed, either by hardware or by software. A wide variety of hardware RAID-controlling technologies are available, including the Fibre Channel used by many SAN solutions. Use hardware to control the RAID. If you let the operating system control the RAID, those activities will compete with the operation and performance of the DW/BI system.

Don't skimp on the quality and quantity of the hardware controllers. To maximize performance you may need multiple controllers; work with your storage vendor to develop your requirements and specifications.

Storage Area Networks

The most flexible, although most expensive, approach for disk storage is to use a storage area network (SAN). A storage area network is defined as a set of interconnected *servers* and *devices* such as disks and tapes, which are connected to a common high speed communication and data transfer infrastructure such as Fibre Channel. SANs allow multiple servers access to a shared pool of storage. The SAN management software coordinates security and access. Storage area networks are designed to be low-latency and high-bandwidth storage that is easier to manage than non-shared storage.

A SAN environment provides the following benefits:

- *Centralization of storage into a single pool:* Storage is dynamically assigned from the pool as and when it is required, without complex reconfiguring.

- *Simplified management infrastructure*: Adding capacity, setting up RAID configurations, allocating data across multiple disks, and providing access to the shared storage to multiple machines can all be easily accomplished with the SAN's management tools.

- *Data can be transferred at fibre channel speeds directly from device to device without server intervention:* For example, data can be moved from a disk to a tape without first being read into the memory of a backup server.

- *The SAN can be physically implemented on a campus several kilometers in size:* For example, backup staging copies of all data sets can be physically located in a separate building from the primary DW/BI servers, thereby supporting disaster recovery scenarios. The remote staging copies can be updated and refreshed at disk channel speeds over the SAN.

These benefits are valuable to a DW/BI system environment. As the DW/BI system grows, it's much easier to allocate storage as required. For very large systems, a direct copy of the database files at the SAN level is the most effective backup technique. Finally, SANs play an important role in a DW/BI system with high availability requirements.

NOTE Directly attached RAID disks can offer better performance at a much lower price than SANs, particularly for sequential I/O. However, the advantages of the SAN technology usually, although not always, outweigh the difference in performance for DW/BI applications.

One common problem with SANs is they are often considered a shared resource. This means they are managed by a separate group and a single SAN often hosts multiple applications. If you use a SAN, insist on a dedicated SAN and make sure it is configured properly for data warehousing.

Processors

To make a gross generalization, DW/BI systems are more likely to be limited by memory or I/O than processing power. However, all of the SQL Server components individually are designed for parallelism, so systems will benefit — often significantly — from additional processors. It's hard to imagine anyone taking the time to build a DW/BI system that wouldn't at least benefit from a dual processor box, and most systems use four or more processors. Multi-core CPUs are an easy way to add processing capacity without increasing your SQL Server license costs.

The additional memory address space and processing capacity that comes from the 64-bit platform is mandatory for the DW/BI system. Given that Windows Server stopped offering 32-bit versions with Windows Server 2008, the option for 32-bit servers is almost a thing of the past.

Setting Up for High Availability

What does high availability mean for a DW/BI system? The answer, as you might expect, lies with the business users' requirements. The job of the DW/BI team is to gather requirements, evaluate and price technical options, and present the business sponsor with a recommendation and cost justification.

Because the DW/BI system is most often focused on longer term decisions and inquiries, the business users may be satisfied with access to the system from approximately 7 or 8 a.m. to 10 p.m. local time. A DW/BI system that's used primarily for strategic and non-operational decision making can tolerate an occasional downtime during the day. As a result, relatively few DW/BI teams deliver 24x7 availability for the entire DW/BI system.

Very high availability for the entire system is most common for multinational companies with business users spread throughout the globe. Even so, extremely high availability is seldom a mandate. If you add real-time data to your DW/BI system, you'll need to design more rigorously for high availability. Typically, although not always, real time affects a relatively small subset of the data, and the high availability requirements might not affect the bulk of data and operations.

It may be necessary to cluster your Analysis Services and relational database servers in order to deliver the highest availability. A properly configured cluster can provide failover in the event of an emergency. A cluster can also provide scalability under normal circumstances. You can run Reporting Services in a web farm configuration, which provides similar advantages for both scalability and availability for that portion of your DW/BI system. SQL Server Books Online provides clear instructions for clustering databases and installing Reporting Services on a web farm. But if high availability is mission critical, you should contact your Microsoft sales team for references to highly qualified consultants who can help with the system design and configuration.

RESOURCES The following references help when scaling out the individual components across multiple servers:

- **SQL Server Books Online topic "How to: Configure a Report Server Scale-Out Deployment (Reporting Services Configuration)."**
- **White paper titled "Scale-Out Querying for Analysis Services with Read-Only Databases" can be found at SQLCAT.com.**

For the vast gray area between needing 24x7 availability and having an 8-hour load window, there are a lot of things that you can do to minimize the system's downtime. The easiest thing to do is to use Analysis Services as the primary or only presentation server. The heavy lifting of the ETL processing occurs in

Integration Services and in the relational database. Once the data is cleaned and conformed, the process of performing an incremental OLAP database update is generally quite fast. And even better, Analysis Services performs updates into a shadow partition so the database remains open for querying during processing. You can't expect query performance to remain at the same level while the database is being processed, but in most cases you can schedule the update at a time when the system is lightly used.

Even if you use the relational data warehouse database to support queries and reports, you can minimize the amount of downtime. Dimension updates are seldom the problem; it's the fact table inserts and especially updates, for example for a rolling snapshot fact table, which are most problematic. As we discuss in Chapter 5, you can use partitioned fact tables to load current data without affecting the availability of yesterday's fact table. If your fact table is small and you're not using partitioning, you can use a similar technique to perform inserts and updates on a copy of yesterday's fact table, and then quickly switch it into production with an extremely short downtime. See the "Partitioned Tables" section in Chapter 5 for a more detailed description of this technique.

NOTE Partitioning for Analysis Services and relational databases are features of SQL Server Enterprise Edition. These features are not available in the Standard Edition.

If you need very high availability for the relational data warehouse database, you may need to use the database snapshot feature. Users would query the snapshot while the underlying database is being loaded. This approach is most useful for those delivering 24-hour access to a global enterprise.

Software Installation and Configuration

The basic installation of the SQL Server and other Microsoft components is straightforward and well documented in Books Online. We won't discuss the installation experience here. Instead, we'll describe which pieces of software need to be installed on different developers' workstations, depending on what part of the DW/BI project they're working on. Next, we'll describe some best practices for the initial configuration of the various SQL Server components, including the relational database, Analysis Services, Integration Services, and Reporting Services.

Most multi-person development teams share one or two database servers and install only the development tools on their personal machines. A common development team configuration is illustrated in Figure 4-7.

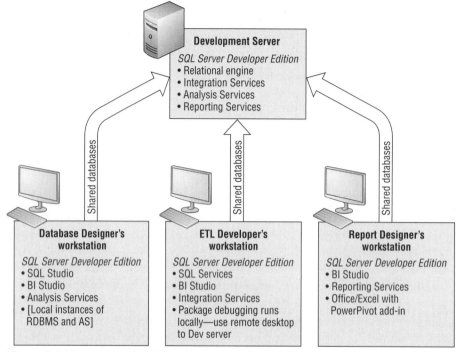

Figure 4-7: A common development team configuration

Depending on their roles, different members of the development team will need to install different components of SQL Server, and some will need to install other Microsoft and third-party software. These requirements are outlined in the next section.

Development Environment Software Requirements

The following section outlines the software to be installed on the development database server, and the workstations for different common development roles.

HOW POWERFUL SHOULD DEVELOPMENT AND TEST SYSTEMS BE?

In a perfect world, the test system will be physically identical to the production system. The test system plays two key roles. First, it's the system on which modifications are tested. In this first role, it's as important to test the scripts that deploy the system changes as it is to test the changes themselves. For testing the deployment process, the test system doesn't need to be identical to the production system. It's not uncommon to use a virtual machine in this functional test role.

The second major role of the test system is to serve as a place to experiment with performance optimizations, such as indexes and aggregates. For performance tests to be valid, the test system should have similar physical characteristics as production. Virtual machines are not yet as effective as performance test environments, although they are getting better. Many hardware vendors have Technology Centers, and may make those resources available to help validate system sizing prior to purchasing your production servers.

Development often takes place on a subset of data. If so, the developers' systems, including shared development database servers, can be much less powerful than the test and production servers. Memory is important. Install at least 8GB of RAM on any computer that's running one of the database services.

The ETL system developer may need to work on the development server by way of a Remote Desktop session because Integration Services packages run in debugging mode on the machine where BI Studio is running. With significant data volumes, package execution can overwhelm a typical developer's desktop.

Finally, the screenshots in this book should convince you that team members who use BI Studio will need big monitors. The screenshots in this book were taken at 1024 × 768, and that's really not big enough.

Development Database Server

As we described in the previous sidebar, most DW/BI teams share a database server for development purposes. The SQL Server components to install on the development database server are:

- Relational engine
- Integration Services
- Analysis Services
- Reporting Services
- BI Studio for remote use by ETL developers

Most development occurs with small data volumes, so co-hosting all the server components on a single machine is usually fine from a technical point of view. If you have access to plenty of servers, distribute the components in the same way for development as is planned for production.

Database Designer

BI Development Studio (BIDS) is the main design tool for Analysis Services databases. The relational data warehouse database is primarily developed in

Management Studio. Relational database designers may choose to install the relational database server on their local workstation. The SQL Server components to install on the database designer's workstation are:

- SQL Server Management Studio
- BI Development Studio
- Analysis Services
- Relational database engine (optional)

In addition, the database designer should install Visual Studio Team System, or any other source control product that can be integrated with Visual Studio.

The relational database designer may want a data-modeling tool such as ERwin, ER/Studio, or PowerDesigner. These tools support visual modeling of the database, with excellent forward engineering capabilities.

Development Database Administrator

Development databases are usually not managed very well — they are for development, after all. However, someone needs to perform some basic DBA tasks like ensuring the database has enough space. Backups are a really good idea, too. Management Studio is the tool for operating and maintaining databases (relational and OLAP), and managing the operation of Integration Services packages. The only SQL Server component required on the development DBA's workstation is Management Studio.

The development DBA should install and use the team's source control system for the management of any database maintenance scripts.

ETL System Developer

The ETL system developer will create Integration Services packages. BIDS is the tool for developing and debugging Integration Services, and the Integration Services components also need to be installed on the developer's workstation. The SQL Server components to install on the ETL developer's workstation are:

- SQL Server Management Studio
- BI Development Studio
- Integration Services

In addition, the ETL system developer should install the source control client. Depending on how complex and unusual your ETL problems are, the ETL system developer may need to install the full Visual Studio product in order to develop custom objects in C# or VB. This is relatively unusual; the vast majority of ETL systems can be developed without any need for custom coding in a Visual Studio .NET language.

The ETL system developer often uses the development server to work on packages because packages run in debug mode on the same machine where BI Studio is running. Some teams start developing packages on the development server from the outset. Others may start on the developer's workstation but move packages to the development server when it's time to test with a reasonable volume of data. Still other teams find that it's easiest to simply buy bigger workstations for the ETL developers.

Report Designer

The DW/BI team members who develop reports need the following software on their workstations:

- BI Development Studio.
- Source control software.
- Microsoft Office, especially Excel with the PowerPivot for Excel add-in. Excel is often the final delivery platform for more complex reports and dashboards.
- Optional: A non-Microsoft relational ad hoc query tool. It's a matter of taste, but some folks prefer to use a third-party tool to formulate the query and then paste the SQL into the report designer.
- Optional: A non-Microsoft Analysis Services query tool. As we have discussed elsewhere in this book, many Microsoft-based DW/BI systems use a third-party Analysis Services query tool to circumvent the limitations of the Office suite. The PowerPivot pivot table controls help address some of the limitations, but they can't be used directly against standard relational or Analysis Services sources.

Reporting Portal Developer

As we discuss in Chapter 12, many DW/BI systems embed Reporting Services into a reporting portal built using SharePoint Server or some other portal software. The reporting portal developer needs the following software:

- BI Development Studio
- Source control software
- Microsoft Office Excel and the PowerPivot for Excel add-in
- Microsoft SharePoint Designer
- Access to a server running Microsoft SharePoint Server with PowerPivot for SharePoint

It would be unusual for the reporting portal developer to need Visual Studio .NET to implement functionality not included with SharePoint.

Data Mining Model Developer

As we discuss in Chapter 13, the first major step in building a data mining application is to develop and train data mining models. This is an activity that requires knowledge of statistics, of the business problems, and of the data, but it does not require actual coding skills. The software required includes:

- BI Development Studio for developing the data mining models
- Write access to Analysis Services
- Relational and Analysis Services query tools for building the input data sets and investigating the data
- Source control software

Analytic Application Developer

Analytic applications embed domain expertise and best practices into a guided analytic activity. Although some analytic applications are just a collection of predefined reports, sometimes they're more structured than that. The more structured the application, the more likely the developer is to write code, and perhaps to integrate the data mining model described previously with the operational systems. The analytic application developer needs the following software:

- SQL Server client and developer tools. The application developers typically work with databases and data mining models that others have developed. You will need the SQL Server object models, which are installed by default with the client components.
- Source control software.
- Visual Studio, with one or more .NET languages such as C# or VB.

Test and Production Software Requirements

In a perfect world, your test and production machines will have the same physical configuration. We recognize that's not always realistic, but it *is* realistic and mandatory that they have the same software configuration. They must have the same operating system and the same SQL Server components, with the same configurations and versions, including service packs.

If you're using your test system only for testing, and not for any production use, you can use Developer Edition on the test systems. This is extremely appealing for components that use Enterprise Edition in production, not only because Enterprise Edition is expensive but also because the feature set of Developer Edition is the same as that of Enterprise Edition. But it's problematic to use Developer Edition on test machines where the production machines are running Standard Edition. That's because the Developer Edition feature set is richer, and you might not discover a dependency on an Enterprise Edition feature until too late. This issue is discussed at greater length in Chapter 16.

If the test system is for functional testing only, it may be a virtual machine candidate. Make sure you have someone with extensive VM experience to set this up.

Earlier in this chapter we discussed how a small system might build an all-in-one server, with all SQL Server DW/BI components on a single machine. A large system will require a larger server and/or distribute the components across multiple machines.

Database Server

The database servers, unsurprisingly, require the SQL Server components:

- Relational database and/or
- Integration Services and/or
- Analysis Services and/or
- Reporting Services

To manage the system effectively, you should install the following Windows Server components:

- Performance Monitor (also known as System Monitor) is installed automatically with Windows. It is the tool that exposes the performance counters that are published by the database servers, and is an invaluable tool for monitoring system performance.
- Microsoft Systems Center Operations Manager is a Systems Center product that provides system monitoring and management services. Large or complex systems should evaluate whether they should purchase Operations Manager or use alternative systems operations software.

Database Administrator

The DBAs for the test and production machines will use SQL Server Management Studio (Management Studio) to operate and maintain the DW/BI system, and manage the operation of Integration Services packages.

Operating Systems

SQL Server 2008 R2 requires a Windows Server operating system in production: Windows Server 2003 SP2, or later. In general, you will get more functionality from more current versions of Windows Server and from Enterprise versus Standard Edition. For example, the Hyper-V virtual machine role can dynamically allocate memory across virtual machines in Windows 2008 R2 SP1, and Windows Server 2008 R2 Standard Edition is limited to 32GB of memory, while Enterprise Edition can support up to 2TB. The SQL Server setup program will not let you install on a machine that is not configured appropriately.

Server operating systems and software are usually installed on a RAID-1 array, for data redundancy and failover.

SQL Server Relational Database Setup

Use the following guidelines when installing, configuring, and securing SQL Server.

Install the relational database component of SQL Server Enterprise Edition or Standard Edition. You may choose to install the Management Studio tools on a server; often the server is managed remotely from a DBA's workstation. Upgrade the instance to the latest service pack. You can install the relational database as either a default instance or a named instance. The only compelling reason we've come up with for installing multiple instances on a single server is to test multiple scenarios on a single machine.

NOTE Multiple SQL Server components can be installed on the same machine. Most organizations use per-processor licensing for DW/BI systems rather than licensing based on the number of users. Your licensing cost is the same if you install and use all SQL Server components on a machine, or only one component such as the relational engine.

The SQL Server relational database is resource intensive and you'd seldom choose to share the physical server that holds the data warehouse database with another data application. In production, you usually create the data warehouse databases in the default instance. In the development and test environments, multiple named instances may be very useful.

The SQL Server relational database is a Windows service just like any other Windows service. Use the Management Studio tool to start, stop, administer, and manage a SQL Server relational database instance. The SQL Server database engine service has no dependencies on any other component of SQL Server. If you already have other DW/BI products in place, you can choose to install and use the relational database as the only component from the SQL Server product suite.

Security Options During Installation

Install and run the SQL Server relational database using Windows Authentication mode only. The mixed authentication mode is inherently less secure and should be avoided if possible. During installation, you are asked to provide a Service Account to run each service. This gives you greater security control by granting each service account only the permissions required to do its job. On the other hand, it's easier to manage if you use the same account for all the services. You can modify this choice later by using the SQL Server Configuration Manager utility.

> **WARNING** Use the SQL Server Configuration Manager utility to change the characteristics of the service account, rather than the Administrative Tools ➢ Services tool from the Control Panel.

Restrict access to SQL Server data and log files to system administrators and the SQL Server and SQL Server Agent service accounts. The system databases are secured by default by the SQL Server setup program, but we still like to check.

After you've installed the SQL Server database engine, you may need to run the Configuration Manager to turn on or enable some features and services. If, for example, you'd like to access the database from another computer, you need to go to the Network Configuration directory in the Configuration Manager and enable a protocol, such as TCP/IP.

Security issues are discussed in detail in Chapter 14.

Files, Filegroups, and RAID

SQL Server data is stored in files, which can be grouped into *filegroups* at the database level. Each file in a filegroup is assigned a location on disk. Database objects are assigned to filegroups, so when data is written out to a table, for example, it will actually write to each file in the filegroup in proportion to the available space in the file. Filegroups make it easier to balance I/O across multiple disks from within SQL Server. If you place database files on RAID drives with striping, this I/O balancing is handled by the RAID controller.

Smaller systems can keep their filegroups simple. Start by creating a single filegroup for data with a single file on the RAID array, and set it to be the default filegroup. If you have larger data volumes, you may consider creating a filegroup and file for all dimensions and a filegroup and file for each fact table. A single file should be adequate for the staging database and the metadata database, unless your DBAs have strong feelings about an alternative configuration. Partitioned tables often have their own filegroups. You can mark the older filegroups as read-only to reduce your backup workload.

We strongly recommend that all relational database files be placed on RAID arrays, either RAID-1+0 or RAID-5, preferably with hardware controllers rather than managed by the operating system. RAID-1+0 is significantly better than RAID-5, although predictably more expensive, because it's faster both for writes and for recovery after a disk failure.

The SQL Server system master, model, and msdb databases can be placed on the RAID-1+0 array that holds the operating system. These databases are typically very small, and there's usually plenty of room for them on that array. Alternatively, place them on their own small RAID-1 array. A third alternative is to place them on the same RAID array as user databases. It is vital that these databases, especially master, be placed on a fault-tolerant array.

The fourth system database, tempdb, could grow significantly as the data warehouse database is being used. You should pre-allocate tempdb to a large size to avoid auto-growth during query operations. Don't place tempdb on the system RAID-1+0 array, which is usually small. Use at least one file per CPU for high-performance tempdb operations. Be sure to spread tempdb out over many drives to maximize I/O performance. If the total number of drives on your system is limited, you can place tempdb on the same RAID array as the user databases, especially if you use RAID-1+0 for the user databases. However, if you set up the user databases on a RAID-5 array, you should consider separating out tempdb onto its own RAID-1+0 array to minimize potential bottlenecks.

You'll likely have at least three user databases: the data warehouse database, a staging database, and a metadata database. Reporting Services has two separate databases, which in some circumstances can grow to be quite large. You can put all these databases together on a single RAID-1+0 or RAID-5 array. Because of the size of the data warehouse database and possibly the Reporting Services catalog, the size of this array will dwarf the other databases' arrays.

Assuming you're using RAID, you could put all of the data warehouse's data into a single file and let the RAID array distribute the file across multiple drives. But long before you reach 2TB, the maximum drive size that SQL Server can address, you'll want to break the database into multiple files and filegroups in order to simplify management and backup.

REFERENCE The file layout discussion in this section was directed primarily at small- to medium-sized systems. If you have larger data volumes, in the terabyte range and above, you should work with your storage vendor to lay out your files and disks very carefully. Search for the "Fast Track Data Warehouse 2.0 Architecture" white paper on MSDN (`http://msdn.microsoft.com/`) for more information.

Database Recovery Model

SQL Server logs every change to the structures and contents of a database. These log files are used to return SQL Server to a consistent state in case of a system crash, and in conjunction with backups, to restore a database in case of a data loss event, such as the failure of a disk that was not part of a RAID array.

SQL Server provides three recovery modes: Full, Bulk Logged, and Simple. All changes are still logged in all three modes; the differences lie in the level of detail captured, and how the log file is managed. In Simple recovery mode, transactions are cleared from the log file once they complete and have been committed to the database. This keeps the log file relatively small, and reduces the maintenance effort. However, a database that is operated with Simple recovery mode can be recovered only to the point of the last backup.

> **NOTE** Even if you empty out the staging database at the beginning of each load, keep a copy of the extracted data somewhere. We often keep a copy of the extracts in the file system, in a file whose name includes the date and time of the extract. These extracts should be backed up, as should any permanent data in the staging database. More often than not, the kinds of backups you can do with the Simple recovery model meet the needs of backing up the staging database.

The Full recovery model keeps every change in the log file since the last backup, which enables you to do a full recovery after a crash, hence the name. The problem with the Full recovery model is the log files can grow to large sizes, and need to be actively managed.

The Bulk Logged recovery model logs individual transactions like the Full recovery model, but it treats bulk inserts like the Simple recovery model. This is useful for a database that supports both transactions and bulk loads. The log file is smaller because certain bulk loads are minimally logged, but non-bulk transactions are kept. Bulk Logged is meant as an adjunct to Full recovery mode and has the same log file management requirements. You would generally operate in Full recovery mode, switch to Bulk Logged when you load a large dataset, and then switch back once the load is completed.

In general, we don't do individual transactions in the data warehouse. If you back up your database immediately after the nightly ETL process is finished, there should be few if any changes until the next ETL run.

Given this, the Simple recovery model makes sense for most data warehouses. It requires less maintenance and supports bulk inserts when the conditions are met. You will probably set your staging and development databases to Simple recovery mode as well. Just make sure your DBAs are backing everything up on a regular basis, and that they test those backups and restores.

There are other implications of the recovery model choice. One of the ways to speed up data loading is to invoke minimal logging in a bulk load. Minimal logging requires either the Simple or Bulk Logged recovery model. On an ongoing basis, many of our incremental loads don't meet other conditions for minimal logging: we are not inserting into an empty table, or we have not dropped all the indexes. However, you may want to create the necessary conditions for a minimally logged load because it is so much faster. This is particularly true when you're using partitioned tables or other parallel structures, as we discuss in Chapter 5.

Initial Database Size

Set up your SQL Server database with an initial size adequate to hold the initial historical load plus anticipated growth for the next year or so. You might permit automatic growth up to a certain maximum to avoid a crisis, but you should monitor the database size carefully and manually increase the database's file size during a period of slow usage. That's because the initial allocation and subsequent increases are resource-intensive. It's better to pay this file initialization price at a time managed by the DBAs than during the DW/BI system's load processing window.

Windows Server 2003 and higher versions include a feature called Instant File Initialization that improves the performance of database allocation. However, "instant" is a bit of a misnomer; it's still a resource-intensive process. For best performance, especially for very large databases, don't rely on auto-grow. Instead, set up an automated process to check for needed file space, programmatically increase file sizes if necessary, and set an alert well before you run out of space.

As we discuss in Chapter 17, you should set up an automated process to check for disk space on a weekly, daily, or load-by-load basis.

RESOURCES See the Books Online topic "Database File Initialization" for more information.

After the database tables' physical design has been finalized, as we discuss in Chapter 5, you can accurately assess the storage requirements for the initial database setup and storage layout.

Analysis Services Setup

The Analysis Services server machine must have at least the Analysis Services component of SQL Server installed on it. Other components, including the relational database engine and the Studio tools, are not required on that server. Often, especially in locked down production environments, the server is always managed remotely from the DBA's workstation. Make sure you keep up to date with service packs.

You can run Analysis Services alone, if you wish, without using any other SQL Server technology because it keeps its metadata in XML files. It's not unusual to run Analysis Services as an intermediate data platform between the users and a large non-Microsoft relational data warehouse that has not been optimized to support ad hoc queries.

> **NOTE** Remember that if you install the relational database on one machine and Analysis Services on a second machine, you have to pay for two licenses.

Like the relational database, Analysis Services supports multiple instances on a single server machine. In a standard production environment, we don't see a compelling argument for using multiple instances rather than multiple databases within the same instance. Multiple instances may be useful during development and testing. If you're building a solution for external parties such as vendors, you may find that multiple instances provide an extra level of security or comfort to your customers.

Analysis Services File Locations and Storage Requirements

The main configuration choice to make at or soon after installation time is where the program, data, and log files are located. These choices are made for an instance; all cubes and databases within that instance use the same default location. A RAID array, either RAID-1, RAID-1+0, or RAID-5, is the best choice for all file locations. The program files for a production system should be installed on a RAID-1 array, often the operating system array.

The best place for the log files is their default location, near the SQL Server program files. We recommend using RAID-1 or RAID-1+0 for these files, as you would probably use for the program files.

Analysis Services data files are by far the largest kind of files. It is nearly impossible at design time to estimate with any degree of accuracy how big the Analysis Services data files will be. Let's start with a simple rule of thumb: an Analysis Services database that's built at the same grain as a relational fact table will take approximately 25 percent of the space of that fact table (non-compressed atomic data only, no indexes). This 25 percent rule includes Analysis Services data and indexes, before aggregations are added, and again it's worth emphasizing that this is at the same grain as the fact table. We have seen Analysis Services atomic data at 15–40 percent of its corresponding relational data, but 25 percent is a reasonable midpoint.

When you add well-designed aggregations, the total data size is usually 35–100 percent of the non-compressed relational data. You will be at the high end of that range if you use distinct count measures. In our experience, Analysis Services databases including indexes and aggregations typically take 35–50 percent of the data of the corresponding non-compressed relational table at the same grain, data only, no indexes. This factor was included in the very high-level storage space guesstimate that we discussed at the beginning of this chapter.

For small- and medium-sized installations, a 50 percent factor should suffice for disk planning. For larger installations, you should partition your Analysis Services database. Build a test database with several partitions, and then scale that storage requirement by the number of partitions.

We recommend that you use RAID-1+0 to store the data files. Use a SAN for large installations. To maximize processing speed, use a different RAID array, with a different physical controller, than the location of the relational data warehouse database that feeds the Analysis Services database.

If you're too cost conscious to use RAID-1+0 for the data files, but don't want to take the write performance hit of RAID-5, it's not as important to use redundant storage for the Analysis Services database as for the relational database. After all, you can always reprocess the Analysis Services database from the relational data warehouse database, or restore it from backup. Be warned, however, that it could take many hours to process an Analysis Services database that covers multiple terabytes of relational data. We strongly recommend using some level of fault tolerant storage.

When you create a partition for an Analysis Services cube, you can place that partition anywhere in your storage system. Assuming you're using RAID, we see no compelling reason for placing data files anywhere but in the default location.

Finally, you may want to avoid all this disk design work and just put the Analysis Services data on a silicon storage device (SSD). Ad hoc queries against an Analysis Services database are primarily random access reads; the sweet spot for SSDs. It may actually cost you less because you won't need as many high speed hard disk drives in a large array, and your users will be amazed at how well the system performs.

ANALYSIS SERVICES METADATA

There is no formal repository for Analysis Services beginning with SQL Server 2005. Instead, the metadata consists of the XML files throughout the OLAP Data directory, such as *DatabaseName.db.xml*, *CubeName.cub.xml*, *DimensionName.dim.xml*, and so on.

The main implication for Analysis Services administrators is improved manageability, particularly for backups and restores, as described in Chapter 17.

Analysis Services and Memory

Analysis Services loves memory. Analysis Services was redesigned with SQL Server 2005 to solve the most intractable memory problems associated with prior versions. Nonetheless, the more data you can cache in physical memory, the happier you and Analysis Services will be.

Analysis Services dimensions do not need to be memory resident. Information about dimension members will move in and out of memory cache as needed. This is great, for certainly a server should handle memory contention gracefully. Nonetheless, for excellent query performance you want plenty of memory for dimension members, a result set cache, the computation engine's cache, and other uses. Don't skimp on memory.

Integration Services Setup

Integration Services has two major components: a design environment, which is part of the BI Studio; and a runtime environment, which is what you install on your production servers. The design environment is where you create and edit packages. You can see a visual representation of the package's tasks, and run the package in debug mode on the development machine, and only on the development machine. The only way to remotely execute an Integration Services package in development/debugging mode is to use a remote desktop connection to the remote machine.

On the production server, install the Integration Services component of SQL Server Enterprise Edition or Standard Edition. You may install the Management Studio tools on your production server, although often production instances of SQL Server are managed remotely from an administrator's workstation.

You can use Management Studio to interactively execute a package that's been deployed to test or production. But for the ETL system, you will use SQL Agent to schedule the execution of the DTExecUI or DTExec utility. Using these utilities, you can run on one server a package that is stored on a second server. In production, Integration Services packages can be located anywhere, and can be run on any server that has the Integration Services runtime executables.

You can design your ETL system to run multiple packages on multiple servers. If you choose this architecture for your large scale ETL problem, install Integration Services executables (and pay SQL Server licenses) on all of the servers on which the packages are running.

Integration Services has no dependency on any other component of the SQL Server product suite. It could even be used as the ETL tool for an otherwise non-SQL Server DW/BI system.

Integration Services presents the option of storing package definitions in the SQL Server. This is not something you need to decide at installation time.

As we described earlier in this chapter, most DW/BI systems will run Integration Services on the same server as the relational data warehouse database. It is easy to change package locations as your warehouse matures and your requirements change.

Integration Services File Locations and Storage Requirements

You may use a relational database to stage data during ETL processing. As we describe in Chapter 7, you will probably use both a relational staging area and a file system staging area. You may use the file system staging area to rest data after it has been extracted from the source systems but before the heavy duty ETL processing begins; you may also use this staging area for intermediate storage and for a kind of backup of changed data before launching an update. Many people hold on to the source system extracts for days, weeks, or months before deleting them or moving them to offline storage. The volume of disk space you'll need for the file-based and relational staging areas depends completely on the design of your ETL system.

If you can extract the exact same data sets from the source system as needed, you may not need fault tolerant storage for the staging area. However, many source systems overwrite data and do not keep history. In these cases, the extract is the only record of the source system at that point in time. It's best not to lose it. RAID-1 or RAID-1+0, as always, is recommended.

Reporting Services Setup

Like all the other components of SQL Server, Reporting Services can be installed on a standalone reporting server, or it can share a server with one or more other components of SQL Server. However, Reporting Services does require access to a SQL Server relational database to store its metadata, known as the report server catalog.

When you install Reporting Services, you must supply several pieces of configuration information:

- *The location of the report server catalog database:* The report server catalog is where report definitions, metadata, histories, and snapshots are stored. The installation program will create the report server database for you. The report server database can be located on a different machine, but your service account must have appropriate database creation privileges on that machine. This catalog database must be a SQL Server relational database.

- *Configuration options for email delivery of reports:* You will probably want to run a subset of standard reports, and use email to deliver either the report or a link to the report. The email service account information and other configuration options are well documented in Books Online.

You may choose to install the client-side report authoring tool, Report Designer, on the server. Report Designer is integrated into BI Development Studio, and most developers use it on their workstations rather than on the server.

Reporting Services is a Windows service just like the SQL Server relational database or any other Windows service. It is also implemented as an ASP.NET Web service based on http.sys. Both the Windows service and the Web service are implemented on the report server. Use the Reporting Services Configuration Manager tool to configure, start, stop, administer, and manage a Reporting Services instance.

Reporting Services doesn't require any significant file storage other than the report catalog database. Issues around the potential size and placement of the report server catalog were discussed earlier in this chapter, in the section on the SQL Server relational database setup.

NOTE Like the other components of SQL Server, Reporting Services can be installed in isolation. However, it does need access to a SQL Server relational database server for the report catalog.

Summary

We began this chapter by discussing various options for configuring your DW/BI system. System sizing is challenging because it depends on so many factors — some of which you won't have much information on until your system is in production. The easy factors to predict are data volumes and system availability requirements. It's harder to guess how many simultaneous users you'll have, and how many of them will be performing challenging ad hoc queries. Nonetheless, we conclude that the vast majority of systems will use one or several commodity 2 to 4 socket, multi-core 64-bit servers. High-end systems will use one or more 8 or 16 socket, or even larger 64-bit servers. The 64-bit architecture is necessary because it allows so much more addressable memory. All the BI software components love memory.

We discussed storage architecture and the importance of creating a balanced data pipeline between the disks and CPUs. We also stressed the importance of using a fault tolerant disk subsystem to reduce the impact of the inevitable disk drive failures. These needs emphasize the value of a storage area network with some level of hardware-controlled redundant RAID.

We briefly described the SQL Server software installation issues for the development, test, and production servers. We also touched on standard workstation configurations for key roles on the DW/BI team. General installation and setup issues are well documented in SQL Server Books Online. This chapter is long enough that it makes no sense to repeat that information here. Instead, we focused on issues that are specific to data warehousing.

Part

2

Building and
Populating the Databases

The second part of the Lifecycle is where you create the back room infrastructure for the data warehouse, where you realize the designs described in Part 1. The first big step is creating the relational data warehouse database. The logical model you've already developed translates directly to the physical database, though there are still plenty of physical design decisions for the database administrator to make.

Once you've built the relational data warehouse, it's time to start populating it. The most successful data warehouse projects take place in organizations with strong data governance practices. You can use SQL Server Master Data Services to implement a wide range of master data management systems, including simple applications for those organizations new to data governance. Most of your DW/BI team's time and effort is spent using Integration Services to build the ETL system. The cost and quality of that system are greatly improved by thinking through the architectural issues before you start writing packages to move data.

The last chapter in Part 2 describes how to build and populate the core Analysis Services OLAP database, which is a recommended component of any Microsoft DW/BI system. The Analysis Services database includes rich metadata that helps business users navigate the data, which is so vital for successful ad-hoc use.

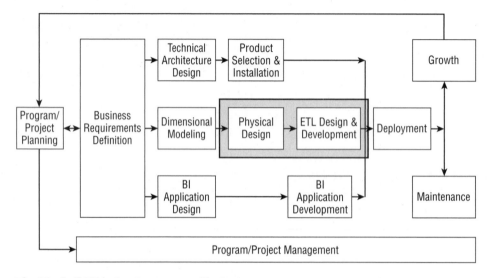

The Kimball Lifeycle steps covered in Part 2

CHAPTER 5

Creating the Relational Data Warehouse

Where the rubber starts to meet the road.

This chapter is about instantiating the target relational dimensional model in a SQL Server database. Now that you have your servers set up, software installed, development environment in place, dimensional model designed and well documented, and, of course, your business requirements and priorities clearly defined, you can actually start writing some code in this chapter, if T-SQL counts as code in your book. Figure 5-1 provides a graphical example of the lifecycle context just described for this chapter.

Our goal in this lifecycle step is to get the physical structures in place so they can be populated by the ETL process in the next step. Creating the database and building the tables is a task for the DBA role. Folks who have prior SQL Server DBA experience should have no problem with this chapter. Those of you who are not really DBAs, but ended up with this role because no one else volunteered shouldn't panic. Basic DBA work in SQL Server is generally straightforward. Although this chapter is not a tutorial, we will tell you the key tasks and provide some examples to point you in the right direction.

In this chapter, you will learn:

- How to deal with specific table and column implementation decisions such as surrogate keys, string data types, Unicode, NULLs, and default values
- How to use table and column extended properties to capture descriptive metadata

- About adding housekeeping columns that may not be in the logical dimensional model to support change tracking, process auditing, and sort orders

- What to do about declaring entity and integrity constraints

- A good starting point for indexes and an approach to creating relational aggregate tables

- The value and cost of data compression

- What table partitioning is and how to implement it in SQL Server

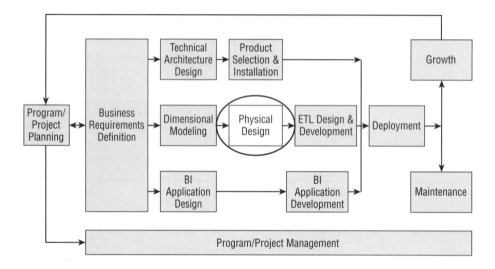

Figure 5-1: The Business Dimensional Lifecycle

Getting Started

Before you start the relational database physical design process, you should have completed the logical model. In fact, you should have very little design work to do in translating from the logical model to the physical model. Here are some of the key elements that should already be in place as deliverables from your dimensional modeling process:

- Object names should be clearly defined and agreed to by your data governance team. Your logical model should already be using good, clear, sensible names that conform to your naming conventions. You should already have defined naming conventions for database objects such as tables and columns.

■ All columns should have the correct data types. Start off with the column definitions from the modeling process, but you may need to modify data types later, after you've completed the data profiling discussed in Chapter 2. For example, you may learn that some customer surnames take more than the 35 characters called for in the logical model.

■ Primary keys and foreign key relationships should be identified.

The best tool for developing the physical model is a data modeling tool such as ERwin, PowerDesigner, or ER/Studio. These tools can generate the data definition language (DDL) needed to create your database, a feature known as forward engineering. Using a modeling tool makes it very easy to modify the database during the early, iterative design phases.

NOTE At this time, Microsoft is not selling an effective data modeling tool. Old versions of Visio were usable (though hardly best of class), but that functionality has been removed. There are various tools in the Microsoft world that offer modeling capabilities, but they are not as effective as the stand-alone database modeling tools. Visio 2010 can document models, but has no forward engineering capabilities. Visual Studio 2010 has a database project type that is meant more to support DBAs with ongoing database management and maintenance. You can add an ADO .NET Entity Data Model template to a Visual Studio project to get a graphical design environment, but you need the full Visual Studio product. Or, you can use the Database Diagram feature in SQL Management Studio, but it is tightly linked to the database objects.

The high-end data modeling tools can be expensive, and some small companies will balk at purchasing them. In Chapter 2, we introduced the Excel workbook and macro to support the logical modeling process. You can use the workbook and macro to generate the DDL to create the physical database if you don't have a data modeling tool. We provide this spreadsheet because not all readers will have a real data modeling tool.

Complete the Physical Design

There are always some decisions the DBA must make with regard to the makeup of the tables and columns. These include managing surrogate keys, working with string data types, handling NULLs, adding housekeeping columns, and creating extended property entries to capture basic metadata. We'll walk through each of these topics in this section.

Surrogate Keys

The primary key for dimension tables should be a surrogate key assigned and managed by the DW/BI system. The most common method for creating surrogate keys in SQL Server is to enable the IDENTITY property on the surrogate key column. Every time a row is inserted, the identity column populates itself by incrementing.

Check to ensure the surrogate key column is an integer data type. If you have Enterprise Edition and will use page compression, just use regular integers, unless you need the larger size. Be a little more thoughtful with Standard Edition. Choose the appropriate integer type given the anticipated size of the dimension:

- *Tinyint* takes values in the range 0 to 255 and requires 1 byte of storage. Note that tinyint does not support negative numbers.
- *Smallint* ranges from -2^{15} ($-32,768$) to $2^{15} - 1$ ($32,767$) and takes 2 bytes.
- *Int* ranges from -2^{31} to $2^{31} - 1$ and takes 4 bytes.
- *Bigint* ranges from -2^{63} to $2^{63} - 1$ and takes 8 bytes.

Choose the smallest integer type that will work for your dimension, keeping in mind how much the dimension will grow over time. This isn't important for the dimension table itself, but it makes a difference for the fact table's size and performance. These same surrogate keys show up as foreign keys in the fact table. Using the small data types is also important for minimizing memory use during data processing. Make sure you use the same integer types for the foreign key columns in the fact table as for the corresponding dimension tables.

We usually frown on using meaningful surrogate keys — which is something of an oxymoron — but we make an exception in every DW/BI system we build. The date dimension should use a surrogate key. That surrogate key should be a 32-bit integer. But it's awfully convenient for it to be a meaningful integer of the form year-month-day, such as 20110723. Developers are people, too.

String Columns

If you didn't pay close attention to string column lengths during the modeling process because you were focused on business meaning, you need to clean this up in the physical model. This is particularly true for columns in very large dimensions, and the occasional string column in fact tables. The relational database stores variable length string columns, type varchar and nvarchar, efficiently. It doesn't pad these columns with spaces. However, other parts of the SQL Server toolset will fill these columns out to their full width. Notably,

Integration Services and Analysis Services pad string columns with spaces as they are loaded into memory. Both Integration Services and Analysis Services love physical memory, so there's a cost to declaring string columns that are far wider than they need to be.

TIP **Start by making the string columns in the data warehouse database the same length as in the source database. We've seen source systems that routinely use varchar(100) for all string columns. In this case, investigate the actual lengths of string data. Make the data warehouse columns wider than any historical width, just for insurance. Add a data quality screen to your ETL application to catch especially long strings in the future.**

Don't get carried away by the varchar data type. Any column smaller than 5 (some people say 10) characters should just be a char data type, even if the data length varies somewhat. If the string length varies little, say from 10 to 13 characters, simply use the char type.

Char and varchar can be used to support text in many languages, including most European languages. The corresponding Unicode data types, nchar and nvarchar, can store any character including cursive and glyph languages such as Arabic or Korean. Unicode accomplishes this feat by assigning two bytes to store each character, instead of one byte used by char and varchar. Microsoft uses Unicode data types in AdventureWorks because the same sample database structure needs to work worldwide.

There are several good reasons to use the Unicode data types for strings, and one reason not to. On the plus side, using Unicode will ensure you can load any strings that get thrown at you in the future, even if you are storing only ASCII characters today. Unicode doesn't require any conversion or code page when you move data from one environment to another, and it is the standard encoding for web-based systems. Finally, SQL Server Integration Services is heavily biased toward working with Unicode data. On the minus side, all your strings will require twice as much space.

Our recommendation is to use Unicode data types wherever possible. Most dimensions are so small that the extra space hit won't matter. If you have large dimensions with lots of strings, you should still consider Unicode if you are using SQL Server 2008 R2 Enterprise Edition or higher because you can apply row or page compression, which will recover most of the space. In the worst case, go ahead and use char and varchar if you will never need to support non-Latin character sets, and you don't have Enterprise Edition.

If the character column is in a fact table, for example to hold a degenerate dimension such as an invoice number, you should use a char data type. Unless, of course, your invoice numbers require Unicode.

To Null, or Not to Null?

At this point in creating the tables, you need to decide whether you want the database to allow null values or not. When you define columns, you can tell the database engine to not allow NULLs. In general, you should avoid null values in the data warehouse dimension tables. They are confusing to business users, especially when constructing queries that filter or report on a dimension attribute that's sometimes null. If you decide to let a column be null, document your rationale in your system documentation.

Numeric fields in fact tables, on the other hand, generally act more gracefully with null values. All of the aggregate operators (SUM, MIN, MAX, COUNT, and AVG) do the "right thing" when a null is encountered. Generally the null value is ignored by all these operators as if the record didn't exist. In almost all situations, a zero value (instead of a null value) would produce undesirable and misleading results.

It's not strictly necessary to enforce nullability in the database. The data warehouse tables are loaded through an ETL process and only through the ETL process. Your ETL process should look for nulls and substitute an appropriate value, so no nulls should sneak through. One easy way to do this is to define a default value constraint on any column that might have a null. Something simple, such as "Missing Region" will usually do the trick. As long as you don't actually load any null values, you should be okay.

But let's be professional here. If a column isn't supposed to be null, it should be declared NOT NULL in the database.

Housekeeping Columns

There are several columns that should be added to the physical model, if they're not already included in the logical model. Any dimension that includes an attribute that's tracked as type 2 needs columns to track the date range for which each dimension row is valid.

NOTE You don't have to add these columns to a dimension table that has no type 2 (track history) slowly changing dimension attributes in it. Although, you should have a only few dimensions that don't have type 2 attributes.

The RowStartDate and RowEndDate columns indicate the date range for which the dimension row is valid. Make these dates be inclusive, so that a SQL statement that includes a BETWEEN clause works as expected. If these columns are at the grain of a calendar day, make sure that the RowEndDate is one day less than the RowStartDate of the succeeding record for that dimension member so that the BETWEEN syntax fetches back only a single dimension record. If these

columns must be at the grain of minute or second, then the RowStartDateTime
and RowEndDateTime fields have to be administered more carefully. In this case
the RowEndDateTime of a record must be set exactly equal to the RowStartDateTime
of the succeeding record, and you must replace the BETWEEN constraint with
RowStartDateTime <= YOURDATETIME < RowEndDateTime.

For the current row, you can leave RowEndDate as a NULL, but it works better if
you make it the maximum date for your data type. These maximum dates are
12/31/2079 for *smalldatetime*, and 12/31/9999 for *datetime, datetime2,* or *date* data
types. Populate a third column, RowIsCurrent, with the value yes or no (Y/N).
Although this column can be inferred from the row's end date, sometimes it's
easier to use the current indicator. In the MDWT_2008R2 case study data model,
the customer and employee dimensions include type 2 attributes. Therefore,
their table definitions include these tracking columns.

Occasionally it's interesting to the business users to be able to easily tell which
of several columns propagated a type 2 change in the dimension. A simple way
to do this is to add a column to track the RowChangeReason: the columns that
changed on the date this row was added. The customer and employee dimensions in our case study database include this column.

RESOURCES　For more information on how to populate the RowChangeReason
column, search for Design Tip #80 Adding a Row Change Reason Attribute at
www.kimballgroup.com.

The audit dimension keeps track of when and how a row was added to the
DW/BI system. It is closely tied to the ETL system, and keeps track of the package and step that loaded the data. Using an audit dimension for both fact and
dimension rows is becoming more important, as increasingly strict compliance
regulations mean we must track the lineage of the data in our warehouse. In
Chapter 7, we provide examples of how to populate a simple audit dimension.
All dimension and fact tables in our case study database include a key to the
audit dimension. In fact, we add two audit dimension key columns to each table:
one for the process that initially loaded a row, and one for the latest update to
that row.

REFERENCE　*The Data Warehouse ETL Toolkit* (Wiley, 2004) outlines more
complex auditing procedures. You need to evaluate your business and auditing requirements against the cost and complexity of maintaining a richer data
auditing system.

Consider adding one or more sorting columns to your dimension tables.
There may be some sort order other than alphabetical that makes sense to your
business users. This is especially true of chart of accounts dimensions.

Table and Column Extended Properties

When your team developed the DW/BI system's logical model, you specified several metadata elements including sources, descriptions, and how each dimension tracks history. We like to capture this information in the physical database using column extended properties. For tables and views, we recommend storing a business description and possibly a second technical description as table extended properties at a minimum.

- For each table, create a table extended property called *Table Description* to hold the business description of the table.

- For each column in each dimension table, create a column extended property called *Description* to hold the business description of the column. Create a column extended property called *Source System* to hold a business-oriented summary of the source system.

- For each non-key column in each dimension table, create a column extended property called *SCD Type*. The value of the *SCD Type* extended property should be 1-Overwrite History or 2-Track History.

REFERENCE The Excel spreadsheet that we've already talked about, and which is posted on the book's website at `http://www.kimballgroup.com/html/booksMDWTtools.html` automatically creates these and other extended properties for you.

Define Storage and Create Constraints and Supporting Objects

The core definition of the tables and columns are enough to get started, and for a small data warehouse, they are probably all you need. DBAs building larger data warehouses will need to spend some time working on creating files and filegroups for storage, determining a data compression strategy, declaring primary and foreign keys, building indexes and aggregates for performance, creating views to support user access, and adding data rows to support missing values.

Create Files and Filegroups

Before you can create your tables and indexes, you have to know where you are going to put them. Where data gets stored in the file system can dramatically impact performance. Files and filegroups are the mechanisms for determining where SQL Server stores the data. Files are the physical operating system files where data and transaction logs are stored. Filegroups are sets of files that SQL Server manages together. There are more layers in the file subsystem that determine where the data actually gets written, but they are determined outside of SQL Server by the file system and the disk subsystem. You need to deal with files and filegroups when you create your tables because the CREATE TABLE statement includes a filegroup assignment.

SQL Server creates two default files when you create a database: the main datafile with a suffix of .mdf and the transaction log file with a suffix of .ldf. It puts these files in the default location, which is in the /MSSQL/DATA/ directory in SQL Server directory in Program Files. SQL Server also creates the default filegroup called PRIMARY, which contains the main datafile. Log files can be located wherever you like, but they cannot be assigned to filegroups. By default, all data will be written to the PRIMARY filegroup and into the default datafile it contains.

You will need to determine where your files should live and how many you should have per filegroup. This is based on how many disk drives you have and how they are configured in the disk subsystem, along with the nature and usage of your data and indexes. Here are a few guidelines:

- Create at least one additional filegroup and make it the default.

- Create files on all available local disks and add them to the filegroup.

- Pre-allocate a generous amount of space evenly across all files; enough for all the history you are loading, plus at least an additional year. Three years of additional space would be even better if you can see that far into the future.

- Put the transaction log file on a separate disk from your data files.

If a filegroup has multiple files, SQL Server writes data to them in a round robin fashion, but prorated based on the space available in each file. Keep the file sizes the same so the data will be distributed evenly across the disks.

Much of what you do with files and filegroups will depend on the nature of your disk subsystem. You can achieve the goal of distributing data across multiple disks using files and filegroups, or by how you define your disk subsystem or SAN. If you create one file on a logical disk on the SAN, that logical disk can be designed to stripe the data across an array of physical disks. In other words, the SAN can accomplish the same data distribution you get with multiple files and filegroups within SQL Server.

Our recommendation is to get help from someone who is an expert at configuring disk subsystems for SQL Server data warehousing on your hardware.

REFERENCE   Search msdn.microsoft.com for the MSDN page titled "Using Files and Filegroups" and search TechNet.Microsoft.com for the white paper titled "Fast Track Data Warehouse 2.0 Architecture" for two good starting points on files and filegroups.

Data Compression

Data compression came to SQL Server with the 2008 release. Data compression offers several benefits and a few costs. The benefits are space related: Compressed data takes up less disk space. Often the compressed table is less than half the original table size and it can be as small as 10 percent of the original size depending on the table definition and data distribution. Compression uses less memory because table rows are kept in a compressed form in the buffer cache until the contents of a row are needed by the relational engine. More rows on each page and more rows in memory also mean less I/O needed to resolve any given query. As a result, you will typically see both a space savings and query speed improvement with data compression.

There are two major costs to data compression. The first is a true dollar cost: Data compression is an Enterprise Edition feature. The second is a CPU cost. All this compression and uncompression requires additional CPU cycles, so if your system is already CPU bound, data compression will actually reduce performance.

SQL Server offers two major types of compression: row and page. Row compression essentially applies the concept of variable-width encoding to all columns in the table. Row compression may not make a huge difference because most data warehouse dimensions are relatively small, and they already use varchar for the character attributes. Large dimensions with many Unicode fields will benefit from a special Unicode compression added to row and page compression in SQL 2008 R2. Row compression is generally not recommended for the data warehouse.

Page compression applies three different algorithms to compress all the data on a given page. First it applies row level compression. Next it applies what is known as prefix compression, where a value is stored in the compression information section after the page header for each column with a commonly used prefix. Some columns can take better advantage of this than others. Donald Farmer uses the example of the page in the Scottish phone book with all the last names that start with 'Mac'. By storing 'Mac' in the page header, you can save significant space.

The third step in page compression, called dictionary compression, looks for repeating values within a page and stores a single copy of frequent values in a dictionary section of the page. In individual rows that contain these values, an index is stored that points back to the value in the page dictionary. In the phone book example, dictionary compression might store "MacDonald" in the dictionary with pointers to that entry from all fields in the page that contain "MacDonald."

Page compression can make a big difference on fact tables and large dimensions. You can explore the impact of compression using a stored procedure called `sp_estimate_data_compression_savings` that estimates compression results by sampling rows from the target table. For example, the stored procedure predicted a data size reduction of the Adventure Works `FactInternetSales` table and its associated indexes as follows:

Compression Type	Size (KB)	% Reduction in Size
None	19,272	0%
Row	11,000	43%
Page	7,104	63%

You'll want to experiment with data compression in terms of table size and query performance, but in general, you should expect a size reduction from page compression of 50% or more.

> **REFERENCE** For more information on data compression, search Technet (`www.technet.com`) for the topic titled *Creating Compressed Tables and Indexes.*

Backup compression is separate from table compression. Most DBAs who deal with larger datasets have used third party backup utilities, which have included compression for years. Backup compression was introduced in the core SQL Server product with the SQL Server 2008 release, as an Enterprise Edition feature.

Entity and Referential Integrity Constraints

In the data warehouse, most of the tables have certain rules and relationships they must follow. All tables have a primary key, which is that column or set of columns that will identify a single row when constrained to a single value. This is known as entity integrity. For the dimension tables, the primary key is obviously the surrogate key. For the fact tables, the primary key is usually a combination of all of the foreign keys from each dimension.

Foreign keys define the relationships between the fact and dimension tables. It says every value for a given foreign key found in the fact table is guaranteed to have an entry in the associated dimension table. This is known as referential integrity.

Declaring the primary key on a table means the database will not allow the insertion of duplicate rows. The database will look up each new row to make sure it doesn't already exist before it is inserted. With foreign key constraints in place, every time a row is added to the fact table the SQL Server engine will check that each dimension key exists in its corresponding dimension table.

The issue before you at this point is deciding whether you want the database to enforce these constraints for you. Declaring the primary key on the dimensions makes sense, but what about the primary key on the fact table? And what about the foreign key constraints between the fact table and the dimension tables? The textbook DBA answer is that of course you should declare the fact table keys, both primary and foreign. Even though you should do so, a few paragraphs from now we'll talk about why you often don't.

Let's start with the technically right, but practically wrong approach. Declaring primary and foreign keys in the database is technically the right thing to do. Database administrators without data warehouse experience will look at you funny if you suggest anything different. In the case of a fact table, there is usually little value in defining a surrogate (integer) primary key on the fact table. Instead, you can enforce uniqueness by creating a unique index over the set of columns, usually dimension keys, that makes a fact row unique. In Figure 5-2 it's all three dimensions, but that's not always the case.

NOTE The unique, primary key index on a fact table should never be a clustered index. The primary key index is a big, multicolumn index. If it's a clustered index, all other indexes on the fact table will be huge and inefficient because they will use the clustered index as their row identifier.

In the indexing section coming up, you will create single-column indexes on some of the individual foreign key columns in the fact table, and their primary key reference columns in the corresponding dimension tables. If you are doing things by the book you should add a foreign key constraint between the fact table and its dimensions. You need to let SQL Server check referential integrity, usually when you add the constraints, but you can schedule this task for later. If SQL Server doesn't check referential integrity, the constraints are just window dressing and don't do anything.

In practice, data warehouse DBAs often do not create the primary key and foreign key constraints on the fact table. Maintaining these structures is extremely expensive and slows down the data loads. As we describe in Chapter 7, one of the most important jobs of your ETL system is to prevent referential integrity violations — and substituting surrogate keys in the fact table is a nearly foolproof way to do that. Having the database look up foreign keys in every dimension for every incoming fact row is a very expensive check for something that you did just moments before when you looked up the fact table's surrogate keys. Along the same lines, for SQL Server to maintain a multiple-column unique index is obviously expensive. Since SQL Server resolves most queries by using the single-column indexes that you've created on the more selective dimension keys in the fact table, this unique index provides very little value for its cost of maintenance.

NOTE Generally, you won't declare referential integrity constraints. If you feel it's important, test the options in your environment to understand the cost. Build your fact tables the right way, with key constraints defined and enforced in the database. For the initial historical load, disable the constraints, load all the data, and then re-enable and check the constraints. Test your incremental load process. If it's too slow, and you're positive the slowness is occurring during the insert step, test the performance gains that result from removing the primary key index and foreign key constraints. If you decide to run without these constraints, check periodically (weekly or daily) for referential integrity violations, which can creep in no matter how beautifully you've designed your ETL system.

Initial Indexing and Database Statistics

Indexes are one of two major performance tools available in the data warehouse database platforms, the other being aggregates. In this section we provide a simple starting point indexing plan for your relational data warehouse database. You will need to evaluate your query workload against your data on your test system, in order to optimize your indexing plan. We'll talk more about performance tuning in Chapter 17 on maintenance.

Dimension Indexes

Dimension tables with a single column integer surrogate primary key should have a clustered primary key index. The clustered part defines the physical order of the rows. In this case, the clustered index actually becomes the physical table itself. The primary key part is that column (or columns) that uniquely identify a single row in the table: the surrogate key. When you define a primary key on a table in SQL Server it also creates a clustered index by default. Unless the dimension is small, you should also create an index on the business key to support the ETL fact table key substitution process.

For small dimensions, the only other index you might want to define at the outset is a single column index on any foreign keys. In the case study database, all dimensions have two foreign keys to DimAudit, so we created indexes on those columns. All of the dimensions in our sample database are small enough that it's unlikely to be worthwhile creating any additional indexes.

For larger dimensions, your indexing plan depends on how the relational data warehouse database will be used. The hardest case to tune for is if the relational data warehouse will support significant reporting and ad hoc queries. Insofar as you know what that query and reporting load will be, you can tune the index plan for the expected use. Any attribute commonly used in query constraints or select lists is a candidate for a single-column index. Often, columns in a hierarchy are such candidates. You should already have identified the hierarchical relationships in your dimension. For a large dimension supporting direct queries, these hierarchical attributes are probably the first non-key attributes that you'll want to index. A very simple dimensional model is illustrated in Figure 5-2. If `DimProduct` is large and heavily used, consider single-column indexes on `ProductCategory`, `ProductSubcategory`, and `ProductName`.

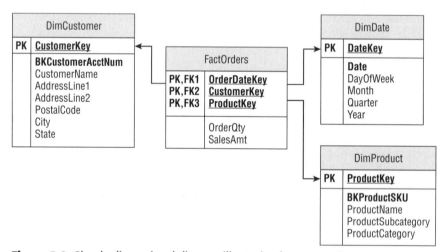

Figure 5-2: Simple dimensional diagram illustrating key constraints

---

INDEXING VERY LARGE DIMENSIONS

A very large dimension that contains some type 2 slowly changing dimension attributes should have a four-column index on the business key, row begin date, row end date, and the surrogate key. The row end date and surrogate key can be created as `INCLUDE` columns in the index. This index will speed the performance of surrogate key management during the ETL process, especially for loading historical fact rows.

See the Books Online topic "Indexes with Included Columns."

Microsoft SQL Server's query engine will use multiple indexes on a single table when resolving a query. With a specific workload of predefined queries, you can probably define multicolumn indexes that are very useful. However, if you know very little about how users will access the data, the single-column index approach is the most sensible starting point.

Fact Table Indexes

For fact tables, the standard starting point is to create a single-column clustered index on the date key. If your fact table has multiple date foreign keys, start with the transaction date or, if your fact table is partitioned, start with the field that's used in the partitioning strategy. This will keep your fact table from getting too fragmented because new transactions will be added to the end of the table. However, business queries may not perform well if they refer to some other date, such as effective date. In this case, you may need to index the queried date and rebuild your index every so often.

Next, create a single-column index on most of the other foreign keys to the dimension tables. If you have a low cardinality dimension that won't limit the selected rowset, such as a transaction type with only five values, it's probably not worth creating an index.

In the simple database illustrated in Figure 5-2, you would create a clustered index on `OrderDateKey` and single-column indexes on `CustomerKey` and `ProductKey` in the `FactOrders` table. Most DW/BI systems do use the relational database for some queries and reports, so the simple fact table indexing described here is a good starting point. As with the dimensions, you should tune the fact table indexing plan with your data and query mix.

Statistics

The optimizer looks at indexes in conjunction with a set of statistics it keeps about the cardinality and distribution of column values across the tables in a query. In most cases, you can rely on the default settings for statistics which will autocreate and autoupdate statistics as the system sees fit. In larger data warehouse databases, especially when you are loading data into a date partition or your fact table is clustered by date, you should update statistics for that date column after every load. Otherwise, the optimizer won't realize the data is available. You may also want to consider creating multicolumn statistics on combinations of fact table foreign keys that are often used together. You will need to script these and update them on a regular basis because they will not be included in the autoupdate.

NOTE If your relational data warehouse is being used only to stage the Analysis Services database, you can get away with building fewer indexes. You'll certainly want to keep the primary key index on dimensions. Fact tables can be left largely unindexed. Because the queries Analysis Services uses to find data for processing are always the same, you can run the Database Tuning Advisor and tune the relational database exactly for that set of queries.

Aggregate Tables

Most BI reports and analyses start at a summary level, and then allow the users to drill down into greater detail. A time series report showing sales by month for the last two years returns only 24 rows, but if it is built on the atomic level detail, it may have to sum up hundreds of millions, or even billions of rows each time it is run. If you can preaggregate this data during the ETL process, any report that uses the aggregates will run dramatically faster. In fact, aggregate tables are the single most useful way to improve query performance on a dimensional DW/BI system. An aggregate table summarizes data at a higher level than the atomic data maintained in the detailed fact table. You create aggregate tables by either omitting one or more of the dimension foreign keys entirely, or by summing to a parent level in a dimension, say at category of product, country of geography, or month of date. Some or all of the other dimensions would remain at their leaf levels.

RESOURCES The process of designing and maintaining aggregate tables in the relational data warehouse database is discussed in the books *The Data Warehouse Toolkit* (Chapter 14), *The Data Warehouse ETL Toolkit* (Chapter 6*)*, and *Mastering Data Warehouse Aggregates* by Chris Adamson (Wiley, 2006), and in several articles in *The Kimball Group Reader*.

Most Microsoft DW/BI systems that would benefit from aggregates use Analysis Services to manage those aggregates. As we describe in Chapter 8, the Analysis Services OLAP functionality has a host of features for designing and maintaining aggregates. This is one of the core features of Analysis Services. Even if Analysis Services provided no other benefits, its usefulness as an aggregate manager and navigator makes implementing it worthwhile.

Microsoft has a few tools to help you maintain aggregate tables in the relational database. We've seen people use indexed views as a substitute for aggregate tables. You can define an indexed view on a fact table which will summarize the detailed data and physically store the summary in an indexed view. This approach is most appealing to people who have done a lot of data warehousing in Oracle, which has a similar feature. One big advantage of an indexed view over simply creating a summary table is the optimizer understands that the view is based on the atomic fact table. When a user submits a query against the atomic fact table, the optimizer will automatically try to use the summary level indexed view if it can resolve the query. The incoming query does not have to be aware of the existence of a separate indexed view. This query redirection is known as aggregate navigation and is a key component to making aggregates broadly usable.

There are a lot of little rules about creating indexed views. Most importantly, they work automatically only in Enterprise Edition. In Standard Edition, you need to refer to the indexed view by name and use the NOEXPAND hint to make the optimizer use it as if it was a stored table. At that point, you might as well simply create a stored table. Even in Enterprise Edition, you may need to use the NOEXPAND hint to get the optimizer to choose the indexed view.

NOTE Indexed views are not perfect in SQL Server. Most importantly, they work automatically only in Data Center, Enterprise, and Developer editions. Future releases beyond SQL Server 2008 R2 will likely turn to other technologies, such as column store indexes, to accelerate analytic queries against the relational database.

If you are running Standard Edition and just can't do OLAP, and really need to maintain relational aggregate tables for performance, we recommend that you don't use indexed views, since they don't provide automatic aggregate navigation. Instead, maintain separate aggregate tables the old-fashioned way: in your ETL process. You will have to update the aggregates by hand. If you only ever add new, incremental rows to your data warehouse database, and you only build aggregates on type 2 slowly changing dimensions, then maintaining aggregate tables isn't that difficult. In most cases, it's a bit more effort. Again, see the books referenced above for a more complete description of the issues and approaches.

REFERENCE For more details, search `msdn.microsoft.com` for the article titled "Improving Performance with SQL Server 2008 Indexed Views."

Create Table Views

All business user access to the relational data warehouse database should come through views. Similarly, Analysis Services databases should be defined on views, rather than the underlying tables. In both cases, the rationale is to provide a protective layer between the users and the underlying database. This layer can be very helpful when you need to modify the DW/BI system after it's in production. It is also a bit of a pain for the developers because some of the design tools in the BI studio rely on foreign key constraints to identify join paths between tables. These design tools are unable to pull these relationships up through the views, so you will need to draw them in yourself.

All user access should be through views rather than to the underlying tables. The table names shouldn't even show up in a user's list of database objects. In the simplest case, a table's view would select all the columns from the underlying table. You may want to omit some columns from the view, especially some of the housekeeping columns described previously.

If you have snowflaked a dimension, create a single view for the dimension that collapses the multiple tables into a single logical table. To improve performance, you may choose to make this an indexed view.

All of your database object names should be business user friendly. But the view definition is an opportunity to rename columns, especially when you use a dimension in multiple roles, such as `Order_Date` and `Ship_Date`.

Insert an Unknown Member Row

A corollary to forbidding nulls, especially for the fact table foreign keys, is how to handle a fact row that does have a null as one of its incoming business keys. For example, how would we load a fact row that has a missing customer ID? We talk about handling other referential integrity failures in Chapter 7, but a good solution to the missing source key problem is to add an unknown member row to each dimension table. We habitually do this as soon as we create the table, and we use –1 as the unknown member's surrogate key (unless the key is a tinyint).

If you enable the identity column property to generate dimension surrogate keys, you can add the unknown member row by using the following logic:

```
SET IDENTITY_INSERT Dim_MyDim ON
INSERT Dim_MyDim (MyDim_Surrogate_Key, MyDim_Business_Key, Attribute1,
Attribute2)
VALUES (-1, NULL, 'Unknown', 'Unknown')
SET IDENTITY_INSERT Dim_MyDim OFF
```

Example CREATE TABLE Statement

The following T-SQL creates the `DimProduct` table from Figure 5-2 with most of the constraints and associated items we've discussed thus far. You might not use all of these settings for every table, but we wanted to include the syntax.

```
-- Create the table with an IDENTITY generated surrogate key, default
-- values, a primary key and clustered index on the surrogate key, on a
-- specific filegroup with page level data compression

CREATE TABLE [dbo].[DimProduct](
        [ProductKey] [int] IDENTITY(1,1) NOT NULL,
```

```
        [BKProductSKU] [nvarchar] (25) NOT NULL DEFAULT N'ZZ-000-ZZ',
        [ProductName] [nvarchar](50) NOT NULL
            DEFAULT N'Product unknown or not provided',
        [ProductSubCategory] [nvarchar](50) NOT NULL
            DEFAULT N'Product Subcategory unknown or not provided',
        [ProductCategory] [nvarchar](50) NOT NULL
            DEFAULT N'Product Category unknown or not provided',
    CONSTRAINT [PK_dbo.DimProduct] PRIMARY KEY CLUSTERED ([ProductKey]
ASC)
) ON [DimFileGroup]
WITH ( DATA_COMPRESSION = PAGE );  -- only if this is a very big
dimension

-- Create the extended property entry for the table description
exec sys.sp_addextendedproperty @name=N'Table Description',
@value=N'Information about products', @level0type=N'SCHEMA',
        @level0name='dbo', level1type=N'TABLE', @level1name=DimProduct;
GO;

-- Create the user access view of the table
CREATE VIEW [Product] AS SELECT [ProductKey], [BKProductSKU],
        [ProductName], [ProductSubCategory], [ProductCategory]
FROM [DimProduct];
GO;
```

You may want to separate the table creation DDL from the index DDL for tables with multiple indexes, and especially for fact tables. This will allow you to drop and recreate the indexes separate from the table itself. Also, note that if you create a default value such as 'ZZ-000-ZZ' for BKProductSKU, you must make sure that value will never be used to describe a different entry in the table.

Partitioned Tables

A partitioned table is essentially a large table split out into smaller tables under the covers. Each of these smaller tables, called partitions, can be accessed, indexed, and managed independently. Meanwhile, the set of partitions still looks and behaves like a single table to any incoming query. Partitioned tables are important for the scalability of the relational data warehouse database. The big win comes from greatly increased manageability of very large tables. With a very large partitioned table, everything from loading data, to indexing, and especially to backing up the data, can be much easier and faster than with a single monolithic table.

Because large is the operative word, you would typically partition only the fact tables in a relational data warehouse database. The definition of large depends on the size and strength of your server and disk system, but as a rule of thumb, tables with around 100 million rows, and/or ten gigabytes of data are low end partition candidates. Dimension tables, even very large dimension tables, seldom benefit from partitioning.

Analysis Services databases can also be partitioned. Most people use the same partitioning scheme for Analysis Services as for the relational database, and create, merge, and delete partitions from the two data stores on the same schedule. This is just a convenience; there is no requirement that Analysis Services partitions be synchronized with relational partitions.

Relational and Analysis Services partitioning are both features of SQL Server Enterprise Edition only. Like many SQL Server features, there are wizards to help you create and maintain partitioned tables. These can be helpful learning tools, but in most cases you will want to create scripts and use tools you can programmatically invoke from your ETL system.

How Does Table Partitioning Work?

The classic partitioning scheme is to partition by month. Each month of fact data goes into a separate physical table, which is tied together with the other months' identically structured tables. There are some specific requirements, discussed shortly, for how the partitions are physically structured.

DOWNLOADS   **In this section, we illustrate an extremely simple partitioned table that is loaded monthly. These scripts, along with example data, are available under the Tools and Utilities tab on the book's website:**
http://www.kimballgroup.com/html/booksMDWT.html

There are four basic steps to creating a partitioned table:

1. Create files and filegroups if needed
2. Define the partition function
3. Define the partition scheme
4. Create the partitioned table on the partition scheme

We'll use a simple example of creating a partitioned table to hold the first three months of data for 2012 to demonstrate each of these steps.

Create Files and Filegroups

You can map the partitions in your partitioned table to one or more filegroups. The single filegroup approach allows for simpler management, and can make it easier to set up the underlying storage for faster sequential access. However, because backup and restore occur at the filegroup level, you must backup and restore the entire table. By creating partitions on separate filegroups, you can set older filegroups that no longer receive data or updates to Read Only. You can create a backup process that will recognize these filegroups as unchanged and back them up only once, thus greatly speeding the differential backup and reducing its size. You can also do a partial restore of a single partition if need be.

In our example, we will create a filegroup for each partition. Create files and filegroups with simple ALTER DATABASE commands. This code creates a new filegroup, MDWT_FG1, and a new file, MDWT_Data1.ndf on the G: drive, adding it to the filegroup:

```
ALTER DATABASE MDWT_2008R2 ADD FILEGROUP MDWT_FG1;

ALTER DATABASE MDWT_2008R2
ADD FILE ( NAME = MDWT_2008R2_Data1, FILENAME = 'G:\MDWT_Data1.ndf',
  SIZE = 1GB, MAXSIZE = 1200MB, FILEGROWTH = 100MB )
TO FILEGROUP MDWT_FG1;
```

It's a good idea to define the initial file sizes large enough to accommodate your initial historical load plus data for some time out into the future. Having files autogrow can cause unexpected slowdowns and file fragmentation.

Since our example involves three months of data, we would copy the filegroup and file creation code to create a total of five files and filegroups. This will make more sense in the next step.

Create the Partition Function

Once the filegroups are in place, the first step in defining a partitioned table is to define a partition function, using the CREATE PARTITION FUNCTION syntax that's well defined in Books Online. If you're creating monthly partitions for a DateKey surrogate key, you would use syntax like:

```
CREATE PARTITION FUNCTION PFMonthly (int)
AS RANGE RIGHT
FOR VALUES (20120101, 20120201, 20120301, 20120401);
```

In this very simple example, we have four breakpoints, which results in five partitions. The first partition holds all data before January 2012, the second partition holds January data, the third holds February data, the fourth holds March data, and the fifth holds all data for April onward. Note that a partition function automatically creates partitions to hold all possible values. Four boundary points, as in the preceding example, create five partitions, hence the five filegroups.

At this point, the alert reader is wondering why we created five partitions since our goal is to create a partitioned table to hold three months of data. Look carefully at the preceding paragraph and you will see we have created an empty partition on either side of the partitions that will have data in them. This allows us to add new data at either end of the table without having to split a populated partition. Splitting a populated partition is a slow process because SQL Server has to examine each row to see which of the new partitions it belongs to.

If you're using meaningless surrogate date keys, you need to create an integer function that uses the appropriate key ranges. You can create complex partition functions, but most people will just create simple functions like the one illustrated here. (This is the main reason to use a meaningful surrogate key for Date.)

TIP Always leave yourself at least one empty partition that covers the date range that you plan to split later. Create new partitions and filegroups well before you need them, so that you are always splitting an empty partition. In most cases, you want the first and last partitions always to be empty.

Create the Partition Scheme

The next step is to define a partition scheme, which maps each partition in a partition function to a specific physical location. A simple example is illustrated here:

```
CREATE PARTITION SCHEME PSMonthly
AS PARTITION PFMonthly
TO (MDWT_FG1, MDWT_FG2, MDWT_FG3, MDWT_FG4, MDWT_FG5);
```

This is where the filegroups we created in the first step come into play. It is possible to map more than one partition to a filegroup. This makes managing partitions easier, but reduces flexibility.

Create the Partitioned Table

Finally, create your partitioned table on the partition scheme. The syntax is really simple: Basically you're replacing the standard ON <filegroups> syntax with an ON <PartitionScheme> clause. Here is example DDL for the FactOrders table from Figure 5-2:

```
CREATE TABLE FactOrders
(    OrderDateKey int NOT NULL,
     CustomerKey int NOT NULL,
     ProductKey int NOT NULL,
     OrderQty int,
     SalesAmt money
)
     -- The ON clause refers to the partition scheme
ON PSMonthly(OrderDateKey);
```

NOTE The partition key (OrderDateKey in our example) must be NOT NULL.

The end result of all this is a single table called `FactOrders` with the characteristics shown in Figure 5-3.

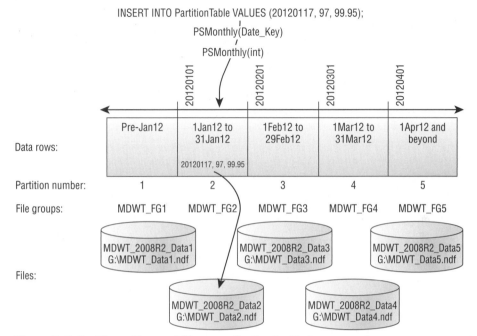

Figure 5-3: Partitions, files, and filegroups for the FactOrders example

Inserting a row into `FactOrders` invokes the partition scheme, `PSMonthly` with `OrderDateKey` as its argument. This passes through the partition function to determine the partition to which the row belongs. The row is then inserted into the proper partition, which lives in a filegroup on a particular disk (or set of disks if you are designing for high performance).

RESOURCES To examine data and partition information within the specific partitions, see the Books Online topic "Querying Data and Metadata from Partitioned Tables and Indexes."

At this point, you can insert the three months of data directly into your partitioned table just like any other table. However, it shouldn't surprise you to learn that this is not a fast loading process: At best it's as fast as an insert into a normal table because every row has to go through the partition function to determine the partition to which it belongs. Especially for your initial load, you'll want to know how to load the partitioned fact table as fast as possible. There's an elegant trick that works great, which we'll describe in the next section.

Managing Partitioned Tables

Once your partitioned table is defined, you will need to manage it on an ongoing basis. This section covers the major repeating tasks including adding new partitions, loading data quickly, using mixed grain partitions, and dropping old data.

Adding a New Partition

This very simple example can keep going until the end of March, but then what happens? How do you add a new partition for April? Remember, you want to keep an empty partition out in front of the data, so split the existing empty partition at the May 1 breakpoint to create an empty April partition and an empty partition starting at May 1. Assuming you have already created files and a filegroup for the new, split partition, you can use the following ALTER PARTITION commands:

```
-- Alter the Partition Scheme to use a new filegroup for the next
partition
ALTER PARTITION SCHEME PSMonthly
    NEXT USED MDWT_FG6;  -- this filegroup must already exist

-- Split the partition function range at May 1
ALTER PARTITION FUNCTION PFMonthly ()
    SPLIT RANGE (20120501);
```

Just like INSERTING, splitting a partition would be very slow if it contained data because SQL Server runs each row through the partition function to determine the partition to which it belonged. Splitting an empty partition is clearly the way to go.

A second syntax for the ALTER PARTITION FUNCTION command will merge two partitions. As with splitting partitions, you'd prefer to merge empty partitions. We'll discuss how to do so most effectively.

Use Table Partitions for Fast Data Loads and Minimal Downtime

Now that there's an empty partition in place for April data, we will unveil our fast data load trick. The trick is to create a separate table structured exactly like the target partition, load data into it, add indexes and constraints, and then swap it with the actual partition. We'll call this separate table a pseudo-partition. It has to structurally match the target partition before we can swap it — same columns, data types, indexes, filegroups, and so on. Note the CREATE TABLE script that follows is exactly the same as we used for the partitioned table, excluding the ON <PartitionScheme> clause:

```
-- Create an empty table nearly identical to the partitioned table
CREATE TABLE PseudoPartition_201204
```

```
(OrderDateKey int NOT NULL,
    CustomerKey int NOT NULL,
    ProductKey int NOT NULL,
    OrderQty int,
    SalesAmt money,
CONSTRAINT CKPseudoPartition_201204 CHECK
    (OrderDateKey >= 20120401 and OrderDateKey <= 20120431)
)
ON MDWT_FG5; -- The same filegroup as the April partition
```

PSEUDO-PARTITION CHARACTERISTICS

The pseudo-partition table must be defined on the same filegroup as the partition it's destined to replace. At the point where you switch the partitions, everything about the pseudo-partition table must be exactly the same as the target partitioned table, with one exception. You must define a check constraint for the partition key (OrderDateKey in our example), to ensure that the pseudo-partition table contains only data appropriate for the partition.

If you have indexes on keys other than the partitioning key, you must INCLUDE the partitioning key in the indexes of the pseudo-partition. SQL Server automatically adds the partitioning key as an INCLUDE column to any partitioned index that doesn't already have it included, but it's better to do it in advance so the partition switch can be very fast.

See the Books Online topic "Index with Included Columns."

Use standard fast load techniques to load the data into that pseudo-partition:

- Set the database to Bulk-Logged or Simple recovery mode if it's not already.
- Confirm the pseudo-partition is empty and/or disable all indexes and constraints.
- Bulk Insert or BCP from a file, or develop an Integration Services package using a SQL Server Destination task in the data flow.
- Enable (or create) indexes and constraints.
- Return the database to the desired recovery mode.
- Perform appropriate backups.

Once the data is loaded into the pseudo-partition, the indexes rebuilt, and the constraints re-enabled, switch the pseudo-partition into the partitioned fact table. This switch is a metadata operation and executes very quickly, although it requires a schema-modification lock and can be blocked while other DML locks complete.

```
-- The magic switch - very fast even with large data volumes
ALTER TABLE PseudoPartition_201204 SWITCH TO FactOrders PARTITION 5;
```

`FactOrders` now contains data through April, 2012, and the table `PseudoPartition_201204` is empty. When we executed the `ALTER TABLE ... SWITCH TO` command, no data actually moved. Instead, the system's metadata logically swapped the places of the empty partition and the populated pseudo-partition. This is why they have to be structured identically and located on the same filegroup.

> **NOTE** For populating the initial historical data, it's usually fastest to create all indexes after the entire partitioned table is populated and stitched together. SQL Server will build the indexes in parallel.

This partition switching technique minimizes overall load time and system resources because you can perform a fast, non-logged load of large volumes of data. At the same time, you're minimizing the impact on the database's users. The data is loaded into a table that's invisible to users; during that load the partitioned table remains available for query, and the switch step executes extremely fast. In addition, the pseudo partition can be backed up as a separate table, improving system manageability.

THE BROADER PARALLEL STRUCTURE DESIGN PATTERN

Partition switching is an example of using parallel structures to enable high availability. You can use the same basic technique at the table, database, disk subsystem, or virtual machine level. At the table level, for example, you can load incremental data into `Fact_Sales_Load`, manage its indexes, indexed views, and any other dependencies, and then, when all is ready, change the table names like so:

```
EXEC sp_rename  'Fact_Sales', 'Fact_Sales_Temp';
EXEC sp_rename  'Fact_Sale_Load', 'Fact_Sales';
EXEC sp_rename  'Fact_Sales_Temp', 'Fact_Sale_Load';
```

Users would be able to query `Fact_Sales` while `Fact_Sales_Load` is being loaded without blocking the load process.

The first step of the load process would be to bring `Fact_Sales_Load` up to date. The easiest way to do this might be to insert the last two incremental loads because `Fact_Sales_Load` will start out two days behind.

All you need to provide this high availability is enough disk space to copy your tables, and enough CPU and memory to process user queries and data loads at the same time.

Using Mixed Grain Partitions

Most systems with partitioned fact tables will partition monthly by date. Most will implement the fast load and partition switching technique for the historical load, but not bother to do so for the daily incremental loads. If your DW/BI system has extreme data volumes, on the order of 10 million new fact rows a day or more, you may need to play this game on your daily loads.

If you're in this situation, the easiest thing to do is to partition by day instead of by month. However, you want to keep the total number of partitions for any one table to several hundred. There's a default limit of 1,000 partitions per table.

Clearly daily partitioning is in conflict with the 1,000 partition limit; keeping even one year of data, or 365 daily partitions, is a bit worrisome. If you need daily partitions to support the load process, you should consolidate the daily partitions into weekly or monthly partitions as they age. Obviously you want to do this the fast way, using partition switching, rather than by merging populated partitions. The recommended approach is to build a monthly merge Integration Services package that would automate the following steps:

1. SELECT INTO the new monthly pseudo-partition from all the daily partitions (you can do this right from the partitioned table).

2. Switch the empty daily partitions into the partitioned table.

3. Change the partition function and partition scheme so the breakpoints fall on the new boundaries — a whole month instead of days for last month, and individual days for the next month.

4. Switch the merged month pseudo-partition into the partitioned table.

5. Clean up the leftover daily pseudo-partitions that are still lying around.

Have fun.

Dropping Old Data from a Partitioned Table

One of the great advantages of a partitioned table is that it makes it so easy — and fast — to drop aged data. It's a common practice to keep a rolling window of data in the fact table, usually in multiples of a year plus one month (for instance, 61 months). Without table partitioning, dropping the oldest month of data requires a resource intensive DELETE FROM statement.

The best way to drop an old partition is to create an empty pseudo-partition, and swap it into the partitioned table for the old partition. As before, the pseudo-partition table must be structured identically to the partition it replaces, although in this case you don't need to add a check constraint on the partition key.

After you execute the ALTER TABLE ... SWITCH PARTITION command, the pseudo-partition will contain the aged data and can be backed up, truncated, and dropped from the database if you wish.

Using Partitioned Tables in the Data Warehouse Database

If you've read this whole section on partitioned tables, you've already figured out that partitioned tables are too complicated to use unless you really need them. So when do you need them? As we said earlier, 100 million rows is a reasonable point. If you have a fact table that contains a billion rows, you certainly want it to be partitioned. You should seriously consider partitioning for smaller fact tables if you can't find a better way to reduce your backup window or load window to an acceptable target. At the low end, it's hard to imagine that a 10 million row fact table would truly need to be partitioned.

If you decide to partition your fact table, you must automate the process of loading and managing the table and partitions. Your ETL system should be partition-aware, and automatically add new partitions as needed to accommodate new data.

> **DOWNLOADS** Books Online provides examples of best practices for how to manage partitions. You can also download a utility from Microsoft's Codeplex site that automates the creation of new partitions and the roll out of aged partitions at `http://sqlpartitionmgmt.codeplex.com/`.

PARTITIONED TABLE LIMITATIONS

We really like the partitioned table feature. But there are some limitations that it's important to know about.

- There's a limit of 1,000 partitions per table in most SQL Server editions. (SQL Server 2008 SP2 can support 15,000 partitions, but this is not part of SQL Server 2008 R2, and is expected to be a Data Center Edition feature in the future.)

- Partitioned tables can have indexed views defined on them, but they add a layer of management overhead when you use partition switching to load data.

- Either the target or source partition/table needs to be empty to use the partition switch technique.

- Issue the ALTER PARTITION FUNCTION ... MERGE RANGE and SPLIT RANGE commands only against empty partitions. SQL Server will let you issue the command against a populated partition, and it will move the data around, but it will do it very slowly. If you have enough data that you're using partitions, you need to move the data yourself, most likely with an Integration Services package.

- For simplicity, the examples in this section did not include indexes on the partitioned table. Indexes can — and should — be partitioned!

RESOURCES There are two useful white papers on TechNet.Microsoft. com with additional information on partitioned tables: The "Fast Track Data Warehouse 2.0 Architecture" paper previously mentioned, and "Partitioned Table and Index Strategies Using SQL Server 2008".

Finishing Up

With all the tables, indexes, aggregates, storage, partitions, and related items created, there are still a few more items to get in place before the initial physical setup is complete. You need to set up the staging tables that will be used in the ETL system, and you need to set up your business and process metadata structures.

▪ Staging Tables

One of the last steps in your physical design process is to develop staging tables. Staging tables are relational tables that are used to hold data during the ETL process. Use staging tables for data that you want to use as a lookup for other processing. You may create a staging table based on each dimension that contains today's version of the key lookups, for use during the fact table surrogate key assignment process. You may create a staging table to tie together similar members such as people from multiple source systems.

Because staging tables are intimately tied to the ETL process, the ETL developer is usually the person who specifies the requisite structure. A defining characteristic of a staging table is that it is not available to business users for querying. Best practice puts staging tables in a separate database from the relational data warehouse, though usually on the same server.

During your staging area design process, it's particularly important to stage in relational tables any data that is used for lookups, and to index it appropriately to speed those lookups. You can use the file system, and especially the Integration Services raw file format, to stage data that's not used for lookups.

Metadata Setup

At this point in the process, when you are setting up your other databases and file system, you should also define your metadata database. We have an entire chapter devoted to metadata, in which we suggest some structures that integrate with the way we like to build Microsoft DW/BI systems. See Chapter 15 for details.

Aside from the data model for metadata that you define, the other issue with metadata is where it is stored. We like to store user-defined metadata in its own relational database. Usually this database is on the same server as the data warehouse database. The reason you want it in a separate database is that the metadata database is more transactional than the data warehouse or staging databases. You should back it up frequently — which is easy to do because it's small.

Summary

This chapter discussed setup and design issues for physically instantiating the target dimensional model in the relational data warehouse database. We described how to convert the logical data model into a physical data model, including surrogate keys, string data types, and NULLs. We also discussed the initial index recommendations, statistics, creating aggregates with indexed views or separate summary tables, data compression, and primary key/foreign key enforcement. We described relational table partitioning, which can greatly improve the manageability of large fact tables. We finished up with a brief mention of staging tables and metadata structures.

Once you have completed the initial database setup and table creation, you should be ready to start the ETL process.

CHAPTER 6

Master Data Management

"The truth will set you free, but first it will make you miserable."
— Attributed to James A. Garfield

If you are reading this book from start to finish, you should now have the target dimensional model built in the relational database and be ready to start working on the ETL system. One of the big issues you may have struggled with in designing the dimensional model was figuring out where all the attributes in a given conformed dimension were going to come from. In many organizations, there are multiple sources for the same attribute, and multiple versions of the same entity. In addition, you probably identified attributes the business users need in the dimension that only exist in an Excel spreadsheet.

If this describes your source environment, you would do well to deal with these data integration issues before you pull the dimensions into the warehouse. In the broader IT world, this is called master data management. Master data is reference data that is managed centrally for an organization. Master data describes the business entities that participate in the transaction systems. These business entities include people such as customers and employees; places such as warehouses, sales offices, and manufacturing plants; physical entities such as products and assets; and logical entities such as organizational structures and charts of accounts.

Master data sounds a lot like dimensions. Dimension data and master data are closely related, but they are not exactly the same thing. Ideally, master data is much closer to the transaction systems. A master data management system can be an excellent source for the dimension data in the data warehouse. A data warehouse architect would love to have a robust master data management system in place in the transaction environment, because such a system would solve the hardest problems in the dimension table ETL process.

In this chapter, we describe master data and master data management. We introduce a wide range of potential master data management implementations, and discuss how such implementations can benefit the downstream DW/BI system. In SQL Server 2008 R2, Microsoft introduced a new component of SQL Server, called Master Data Services. As you can infer from its name, you can use Master Data Services, or MDS, to build a master data management solution. We provide an overview of the new MDS, and describe how to implement a simple MDS deployment.

In this chapter, you will learn:

- What master data management is, and how it may fit into your enterprise.

- What are the scenarios in which it makes sense to manage master data before the ETL process.

- What is Microsoft's Master Data Services product.

- How to get started with simple applications in Master Data Services.

Managing Master Reference Data

Master data should more properly be called *master reference data*. Master data is the centrally managed reference data for your organization. Few organizations have a clear system in place to manage the master reference data in the transaction environment. This has led to multiple versions of the same data entities being created and maintained in different transaction subsystems. Data warehouses have long managed the process of reintegrating these entities for the purposes of reporting and analysis. This is sometimes called *downstream master data management*. Only a few organizations have leveraged this downstream master data management to improve the transactional data because rarely are there effective pipelines for the reverse flow of data from the data warehouse back to the transaction systems. Practically speaking, the best place for managing your organization's master reference data is *before* the data warehouse, in a separate though related management system.

RESOURCES For more information on master data management system architectural approaches, see The Kimball Group Reader, pp. 515–520, or search `KimballGroup.com` for "MDM."

Master data management is also related to data governance: the processes and rules for managing data in your organization. These rules include required fields, standard values, data retention policies, and so on. Some organizations have mature data governance policies in place; others have scarcely given it a thought. Most organizations are a patchwork, with some areas strongly managed, such as definition of a chart of accounts. Within the same organization, other data is managed in a more ad hoc fashion. The more rigorous your organization is about data governance, the easier it will be to implement a master data management system. Indeed, it's impossible to be truly serious about data governance without some kind of master data management system in place. But even organizations with little rigorous data governance can benefit from a new master data management solution, as we'll describe.

An effective master data management solution must enable effective data governance, while providing the technical infrastructure to solve a wide range of data problems. The most common master data management problems include incomplete attributes, data integration, and systems integration.

Incomplete Attributes

Few transaction systems include all the descriptive attributes needed for rich reporting and analytics. After all, transaction systems are built to process transactions, for which a rich set of descriptive attributes is seldom necessary. Most organizations use purchased ERP systems for some or all of their key operations, and these packaged systems can be difficult to extend.

As you gather the business requirements for the data warehouse, the business users often voice complaints about incomplete attributes. Most often the missing attributes are alternate rollups or hierarchies. Business users maintain additional product rollups or organizational hierarchies in various unmanaged applications, typically Excel or Access.

NOTE One recent client, a large multinational corporation, was limited by its accounting software to a 5-level organizational hierarchy. The top three levels were Global Area (Americas, EMEA, Asia), Region (such as Western Europe and SE Asia), and Country. This left just two levels to describe the organization inside a country, which worked fine for Switzerland or Columbia but not so well for the U.S. or China where this company did most of its business.

As crazy as this sounds, the organizational structure enabled transactions to be processed, and senior management to get the top line reports they needed. But as you'd expect, middle managers throughout the world had created all sorts of rollups to help them analyze their operations in sufficient detail. Consolidating those rollups into a single hierarchy — or at worst two or three hierarchies — presents challenges both technical and managerial.

The data warehouse team attempts to address the problem of incomplete attributes. Often, the team begins by importing the missing attributes from an Excel file on a business user's desktop. There are two advantages to the Excel solution: it puts the business people in charge of defining the analytic attributes, and it's quick and easy (until it breaks). But Excel is a fragile building block for systems, and we all know where this will lead. Eventually, either the process breaks causing a failed load, or the data is incorrectly attributed causing data quality problems and retroactive updates.

A better solution is to build a custom applet for business users to maintain the attributes. Many data warehouse teams have done so, building a handful of custom applications for the most important attributes that need to be maintained outside of the transaction system. As we describe later in this chapter, you can use SQL Server's Master Data Services as the platform for business users to maintain dimensional attributes and hierarchies.

There are plenty of data governance issues to consider even in such a simple master data management project as adding attributes to existing members. These include:

- Which user or users are responsible for maintaining the attributes?
- As new members, or rows, are added to the master data, such as new products or new customers, what are the procedures for ensuring new attributes are assigned and confirmed?
- How will the organization manage changes to the attributes?
- What is the process for managing a structural change to the attributes or hierarchies, for example adding a new attribute or a new level to a hierarchy?
- Even if the master data management application exists solely to create new attributes for the data warehouse, other legitimate uses of the same information may arise. How will you manage those external dependencies?

Data Integration

One of the goals of a data warehouse is to integrate information from multiple source systems. It's all too common for an entity such as customer to be sourced from multiple transaction systems. This is certainly true if your organization has grown by acquisition. Even within a unified company, the sales system and the customer care system may both maintain their own copies of customer attributes. The business wants a single master source for customer data, combining information from all transaction systems and subsidiaries.

Data integration is often attempted as part of a data warehouse project. The initial project to map and combine data is bad enough, and often takes two to three times as long as anticipated. Nonetheless, there are tools to help uniquely identify persons and organizations from one or more sources. As long as you can tolerate some level of unresolved noise, the initial cleanup and mapping is generally doable.

In the dimensional modeling world, we often talk about conformed dimensions as the key enablers of enterprise integration. A conformed dimension is a dimension, or part of a dimension, that's common to many different business processes. The conformed attributes in such a dimension have the same names, values, and keys wherever they appear. Using these conformed attributes, business users can drill across multiple business processes and assemble integrated reports. But we must be careful to not make the process of deploying conformed dimensions be too ambitious. These integration projects can easily take too long, and raise political resistance if the content of the conformed dimension appears to override the favorite dimensional attributes of each separate business process.

The best approach for achieving data integration through conformed dimensions is to start modestly and proceed incrementally, ideally with techniques drawn from the agile development community. Start by proposing a small number of "enterprise attributes" that will be added non-destructively to a key dimension, such as customer. Introduce these attributes into the local copies of dimension tables maintained by separate business processes. Expand the coverage of business processes one at a time, perhaps as agile "sprints." In each sprint, show the business users how to build BI reports drilling across the supported subject areas, constraining and grouping on the conformed attributes. Once the business users understand the value of analyses that leverage conformed dimensions and integrated drill across, they will eagerly await each sprint!

The biggest problem with data integration is the process of maintaining it over time. So often we've seen massive data integration efforts generate a lovely mapping, which begins to be polluted the day it goes live.

It's extraordinarily difficult to maintain data integration over time within a "lights-out" (fully automated) data warehouse ETL process. The lights-out ETL process requires that data integration be algorithmic and deterministic. No matter how good your algorithms, there's an inevitable trickle of transactions that a person will need to eyeball. You need these integration decisions to be made before the ETL load — before the fact data is associated with the wrong dimension key, and before performance aggregations are computed or updated. For the majority of data warehouses on a nightly ETL process, it makes sense to manage mapping changes during the day, before the nightly load begins. And the technical solution to the mapping maintenance problem must include a loop for some or all mapping decisions to be evaluated by a person before being finalized and passed downstream.

Data integration is a second kind of master data management system, more complex than merely adding missing attributes and hierarchies. You can use SQL Server MDS to host the entities, attributes, and mapping tables, and use its workflow features to interact with the decision maker.

A data integration master data management system must address all the data governance issues we've already discussed, and many new ones, including:

- What level of confidence from a matching algorithm is accepted without triggering a review by a person? The decision depends on the cost of incorrect matches relative to the cost of the review.

- Some attributes will be maintained in multiple systems. If these attribute values are inconsistent, what are the rules for determining a winner?

- What is the process for undoing an incorrect match?

Systems Integration

A master data management system that performs data integration is always going to be a struggle to maintain. The system and business users must continually react to data entered in a variety of source systems, with a broad range of data quality. Of course, as you build a data integration master data management system you will (hopefully) improve your data governance. Nonetheless, data integration is a stopgap measure — though in most cases it's a necessary step along the road to a more complete solution.

The real solution should be obvious: in a perfect world the various source transaction systems are integrated with each other. Entities are managed centrally, and various systems subscribe to the master data. How can you reach that utopia?

Most organizations have a mixture of transaction systems from various vendors, including some systems developed internally. In such a heterogeneous environment, it makes sense to have a separate master data management system as the communications hub — the system of record connecting the various transaction systems. You may resist the notion of yet another major system in your IT environment. But the more heterogeneous your environment, the more attractive a separate master data management solution becomes.

Implementing a systems integration master data management solution is not for the faint of heart. Most existing transaction systems are designed as if they're the center of the universe. You need to coerce these systems into accepting new entities such as products or customers from an external source — the master data management system — rather than always creating new entities themselves.

Often, one transaction system is identified as the source for new entities; other systems cannot create a new entity but can modify the attributes of an existing entity. Your organization may decide that only the ERP system can create a new customer; the CRM system — even if it has functionality to create an account — is configured only to update customer attributes. The master data management system must communicate in both directions. As with the data integration scenario, it receives feeds of new entities and updated attributes. It also distributes the updated attributes to the various systems, though not all attributes must be consumed by all systems.

An even stronger form of systems integration master data management is where all of the transaction systems turn over control of entity creation and updates to the master data management system. Any request to create a new customer account is passed to the master data management system, which creates the basic structure and hands back the new customer account key.

Master Data Management Systems and the Data Warehouse

The master data management system straddles the line between the data warehouse and the operational systems. The data warehouse team can certainly develop an entry level master data management system to manage attributes and hierarchies that are not collected in the operational systems.

More complete systems integration implementations feel much closer to the operational systems than to the data warehouse. The data warehouse will subscribe to the integrated information, but the architecture of the solution belongs on the transactional side of the IT organization. In our experience, the role of the data warehouse team is usually to set the stage for robust master data management and data governance. The early efforts of the data warehouse team will prove the value of integrated information to the organization.

The remainder of this chapter focuses on the simplest master data management applications, and does not address the issues of bi-directional communication, latency, and systems modification that are characteristic of the systems integration master data management implementations.

Introducing SQL Server Master Data Services

People have been managing master data for decades without the benefit of a class of software called master data management. Yet this class of software has been growing, and now Microsoft has entered the game with its Master Data Services (MDS). What features does MDS offer?

- User interface to define the master data structures, called models
- Database structure to hold the master data
- Security for both model definition and data management
- Hierarchy management, including security that can limit a user to a portion of the tree

- Programmability
- Full versioning of models
- User interface to manage the master data, including workflow
- Mechanisms to import and update elements
- Mechanisms to export data
- Full versioning of all attributes

SQL Server Master Data Services is an Enterprise Edition feature, and can be installed only on 64-bit hardware.

Model Definition Features

The first set of MDS features support the creation of new models, and the improvement of existing models. These features work at the metadata level, manipulating the structure of the data rather than its contents.

User Interface: Defining the Master Data Model

Somewhat surprisingly, the user interface to define and manipulate the MDS data models is not part of SQL Server BI Development Studio. Instead, it's a web application. The same web application can be accessed by business users to maintain data in an existing MDS model, though of course business users will have fewer permissions than the developer of a model.

Figure 6-1 illustrates the home screen of the Master Data Manager web application, which is included in the MDS installation and configuration. As an administrator, a user can define models, manage security, import and export data, enter or update data through the Master Data Manager user interface, or browse the structure of the models.

A Master Data Services model corresponds roughly to a dimension in the data warehouse. It's the base level entity that you'll be managing in MDS. A complete deployment will have many models, one for each conformed dimension you're managing through the system.

The initial tasks involved in defining the model are:

- Create the model; for example, the Product model. This step creates the basic structure of the master data management system.
- Create attributes whose values are limited to a specific set, called a domain, such as product type. MDS refers to these as entities.
- Create attributes that do not have a domain, such as product description. MDS refers to these as attributes.

- Create hierarchical relationships.
- Define business rules for data validation. A simple rule would check that a numeric field called percent ownership is less than or equal to 100. Rules can also send email to notify a user of violations.

Later in this chapter we provide additional detail on how to define models.

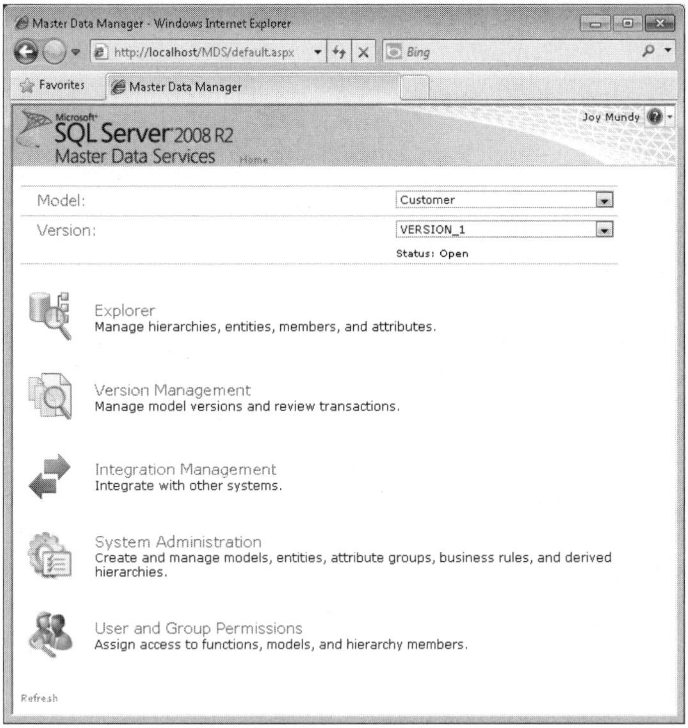

Figure 6-1: Master Data Manager home screen

Creating Database Structures

There is no explicit data modeling task to create database objects that will hold the master data. All of the database work is handled by the Master Data Services application.

Security

As we've already discussed, one of the key advantages of a master data management solution is that it provides an opportunity for users, even business users, to participate in the management of the data. This is particularly important for adding attributes and managing hierarchies that are not sourced from existing transaction systems. Clearly, this access must be secured.

You can assign permissions to modify the structure of a model, or to add or modify the data within a model. You can even specify which users are permitted to modify a branch of a hierarchy definition.

The security definition tasks can be accomplished from within the Master Data Manager web application.

Programmability of Model Definition

Every task that you undertake in the Master Data Manager web application can be accomplished instead by programming to the MDS API. You can completely replace the Master Data Manager web application with custom code, if you wish. Most organizations that build master data management applications will use the Master Data Manager to define the model structure. Programmability will be very important for the ongoing data governance, especially for systems integration applications.

Full Versioning of Models

Master Data Services contains features for you to easily archive the structure of a model, explore the ancestry of a model, and validate a model.

Data Management Features

Once an MDS model has been defined, efforts turn to populating it with data. Most of the Master Data Manager's features are focused on managing data contents.

User Interface: Exploring and Managing the Master Data

The administrator of an MDS model will grant browsing and editing privileges to a handful of users. Those users can use the Master Data Manager web application to maintain the data. Although users can create new members, such as a new product, their main tasks will be to resolve data conflicts and add or change attributes that are not sourced from the transaction systems.

It's easy for users to find data that fails business rules, in order to resolve those issues. In addition, the system can be set up to email notifications to users.

NOTE "Easy" is probably not the right word. We find the Master Data Manager user interface a bit confusing. As a web application, it doesn't have all the navigational richness that we'd like. However, when you use Master Data Manager with user privileges (rather than full administrative or developer privileges), it's a lot less confusing.

As we've already described, reporting and analysis hierarchies are a common initial master data management application. The Master Data Manager web application contains hierarchy maintenance functionality, including the ability to move a branch of a hierarchy from one node to another — and helps prevent the inevitable mistakes that arise when this activity is managed in Excel.

You can see the structure of a sample customer model and hierarchy in Figure 6-2. If the user browsing the hierarchy has editing privileges, she can browse the data elements and restructure the hierarchy by dragging and dropping a hierarchy branch from one parent to another.

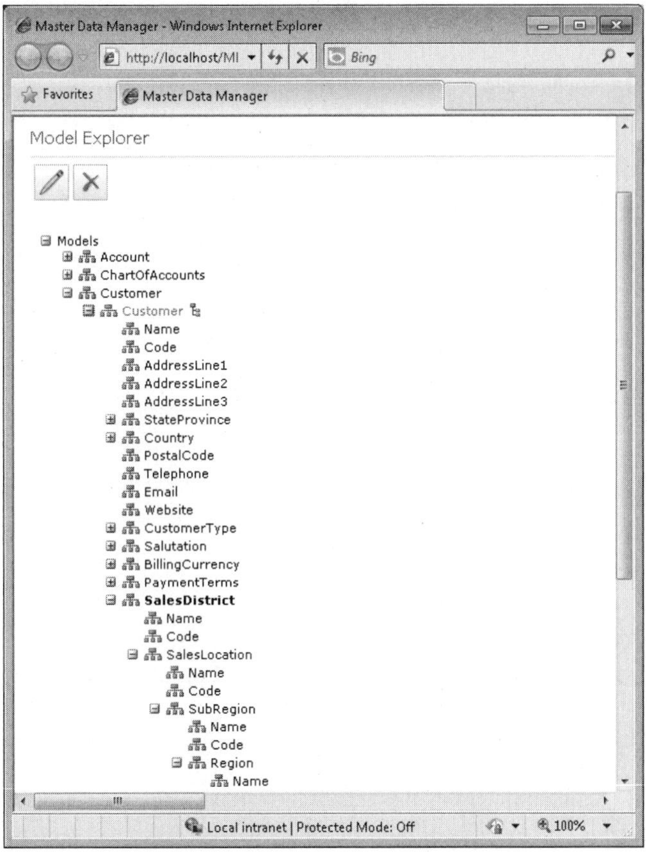

Figure 6-2: Master Data Manager Model Explorer

As we will describe subsequently, all MDS transactions, including those entered directly into the UI, can and should be logged.

Importing and Updating Data

Although you can use the Master Data Manager web application to type in the contents of a model, that's not a scalable method to add or update members. MDS relies on several staging tables to populate and maintain a model. Staging tables are a comfortable interface for the DW team, which certainly has the skills to load data into a table.

There are three staging tables. The tables are in the canonical form of attribute/value pairs. In other words, the same three tables work for all master data models, no matter their structure.

- `tblStgMember` is used to stage new members, such as a new product or customer. You provide only the member name and identifying code or source system key in this table, plus a little metadata to describe the target model, entity, data owner, and so on.

- `tblStgMemberAttribute` is used to stage attribute values for each member. Stage the data with one row per attribute: a product model with 100 attributes will use 100 rows in this staging table for each product. The column in the staging table that contains the attribute value is `nvarchar(2000)`, so you may need to explicitly cast numeric or date attributes. You must also supply identifying metadata, including the member code to map the attribute to the applicable member. If the attribute exists already, it will be updated and the prior value logged. Use a system attribute called `MDMMemberStatus` to "delete" a member by turning its status to inactive.

- `tblSTGRelationship` is used to add or maintain parent-child or explicit hierarchies.

You can use any method you wish to populate these staging tables. The obvious candidates include:

- Write a SQL `INSERT ... SELECT` statement. This is a good choice for demo and experimentation purposes, where the source database is on the same server as Master Data Services.

- Use SQL Server Integration Services.

- Export to a text file and bulk load.

Once you have candidate rows in the staging tables, you can use the Master Data Manager to launch the process to bring them into MDS. Navigate to Data Integration and choose Import, as illustrated in Figure 6-3. Batches are logged, and each staged row is updated with the batch that loaded it, the current status, and any error code. You can keep appending data into the staging tables; MDS is smart enough to grab only unprocessed rows. However, you should develop a process for periodically pruning the fully staged rows.

In most production scenarios, you should schedule an automated process to import the staged data, rather than relying on a person to click the button in the Master Data Manager. The easiest way to do this is to use the processing stored procedures in the MDS database, notably `updStagingSweep`.

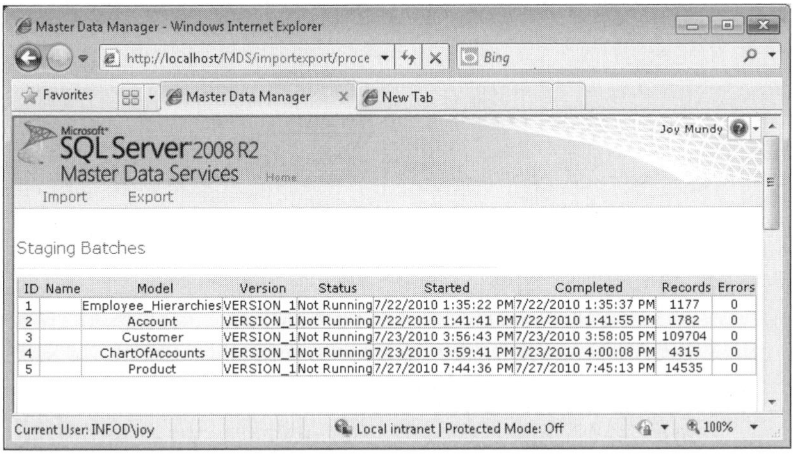

Figure 6-3: Master Data Manager Import Data screen

Once the data has been imported, validate it by processing it against the business rules embedded in the model. Within Master Data Manager, you can navigate to Version Management ➢ Validate Version to manually validate the data in the model. Once you've automated the import, you should automatically launch validation once the import batches have completed by executing the `updValidateModel` stored procedure.

RESOURCES None of these stored procedures nor the steps to automate and schedule processing is documented in the early releases of Books Online. Luckily the Microsoft MDS team is good about monitoring and responding to the official MDS forum, which you can find at `http://social.msdn.microsoft.com/Forums/en-US/sqlmds/threads`.

Exporting Data

Master Data Services is a back room, helper application. It's of no use to your organization unless you can easily extract the master data in a form that other applications can consume. Our discussion will of course focus on extracting the data for loading into the data warehouse. But other systems — even operational transaction systems — can extract information from MDS as well.

Master Data Services makes exporting data very easy, by providing a tool to create data export views. These views are simply relational database views that the UI creates for you in the database that's installed with MDS. Unlike the strange attribute/value pair format for the import tables, the export views look perfectly normal: one row for each member, with its attributes displayed as columns.

There is one slight oddity, which is that you need to create additional views for each hierarchy that's derived from attribute relationships. The main attribute view contains only the first level of the hierarchy; the second view contains the first level and continues up the tree. To get all the columns in your flattened star dimension table, you need to join the main attribute view with the hierarchy view. No doubt there's a good reason they didn't create one view that spans all the attributes (hierarchical or not), but it's so easy to combine them that it doesn't really matter.

The nicest feature of these export views is that they're created with interesting metadata like:

- **Version:** Filter on this to extract only the current model's data.

- **Member entered and last updated date and time, user, and model version:** Filter on these to extract only the rows that have been added or changed since your last data warehouse update.

- **Validation status:** Filter on this to extract only rows that meet all the model's business rules.

Figure 6-4 illustrates the output from an attribute view on the Product model.

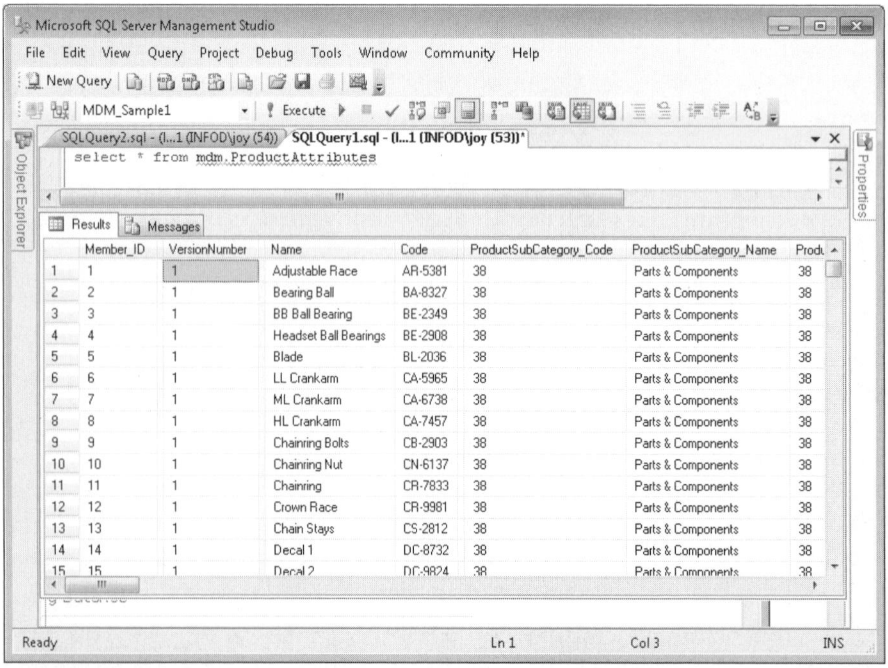

Figure 6-4: Sample rows from an export view for product attributes

Full Versioning of All Attributes

Master Data Services keeps a complete audit trail of each attribute: every value it's ever been assigned, where it came from, who changed the attribute's value, and when. This is a useful feature that can simplify the ETL application and associated staging area.

Part of the dimensional design process for the data warehouse is to determine, based on business user requirements, which dimension attributes are to be managed as type 1 (restate history) and which as type 2 (track history). The decisions should be made once and apply to all subject areas of the eventual complete conformed data warehouse, even those for business processes you've not yet analyzed during the iterative design process. Inevitably, some of the attributes you initially identify as type 1 are later determined to require type 2 tracking. Often we keep the history of all attributes, even type 1 attributes, in the data warehouse staging area. Being able to rely on Master Data Services for that history makes the ETL system that much simpler.

Creating a Simple Application

Now that we have described master data, master data management, and Master Data Services, we will walk through the development process for an extremely simple MDS application. Our goal is not to present a tutorial, but rather to provide a picture of what it's like to create the simplest possible application.

The Business Scenario

The business problem that we're illustrating in this scenario is the common problem of business users wanting to see attributes that don't have a systematic source. The data warehouse currently has a product dimension, and a development project is under way to improve that dimension by adding a few attributes, as illustrated in Figure 6-5.

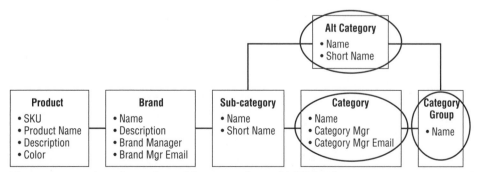

Figure 6-5: Product dimension, with new attributes highlighted

The data warehouse team is going to become familiar with Master Data Services by maintaining these new attributes in MDS. There will be several new attributes: product category manager name and email, product category group, and alternate category.

> **NOTE** You should always create a logical model of your dimension before you get started building the MDS model, as illustrated in Figure 6-5. The model highlights the attribute relationships that imply hierarchies (product, brand, subcategory, and so on). You must clarify your thinking about which entities an attribute is associated with. You should develop a taxonomy for which attributes are freeform, and which belong to a domain.
>
> If you don't have access to modeling software, simply draw a picture as illustrated in Figure 6-5.

Keep It Simple

The data warehouse team doesn't want to have to sell MDS and data governance throughout their organization. That's an eventual goal, but for this little project they just want to kick the tires of MDS while solving a real problem. The team recognizes it will take a long time and many small steps to get from where they are — near-zero data governance — to their desired goal of integrated master data.

With that goal in mind, the team decides to keep the MDS model as small as possible. They initially assumed they'd model the entire product dimension, and add these new attributes to that model. But management decided that was too risky, and asked the team to modify the current dimension ETL process rather than replace it entirely. If this little test is successful, that will be the next step.

The MDM model will encompass only a piece of the product dimension. If you look back at Figure 6-5 you can see that all the new attributes are based on hierarchy levels above subcategory. So the MDM model will start at subcategory and include category, category group, and alt category (and all their attributes).

Create the MDS Model

Installing Master Data Services from the SQL Server Developer Edition media took a little time because it wasn't immediately obvious that they needed to run a separate install process. This is such a small project that the team initially decided to use an old 32-bit server. Once the team read the documentation and switched to a 64-bit machine, things went more smoothly.

NOTE MDS has its own installation process that's not integrated with the main SQL Server installation. You need to browse the install DVD and navigate to the MasterDataServices directory. MDS only runs on 64-bit hardware. Search MSDN for "Install Master Data Services." You can download sample MDS models from MSDN that are useful for exploring the product.

The team downloaded the sample master data services models and explored their contents. After a few hours of poking around, they felt ready to move ahead to create their own application.

The first piece of work was to create a new model: Product Subcategory. That work took two seconds, and is illustrated in Figure 6-6.

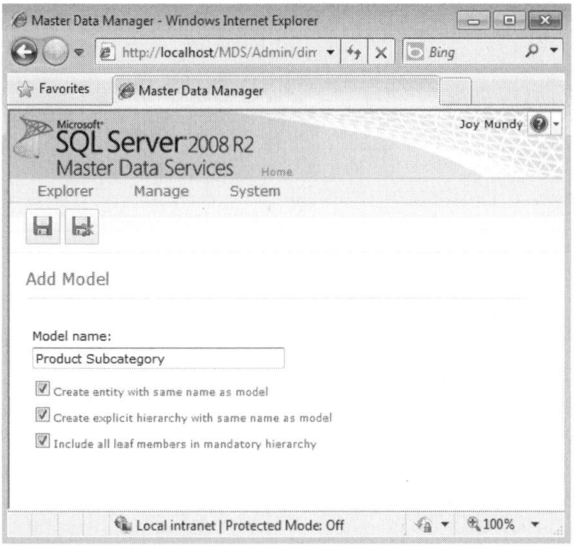

Figure 6-6: Creating the Product Subcategory model

REFERENCE The simple model described here is available for download from the book's website.

Looking at Figure 6-5, you can see that the model needed to have additional entities for category, category group, and alt category. The basic structure for the subcategory entity was automatically created with the model itself. If you want to declare referential integrity between the levels of these hierarchies, the level attributes must be created as separate entities. Creating those entities was equally easy, as illustrated in Figure 6-7.

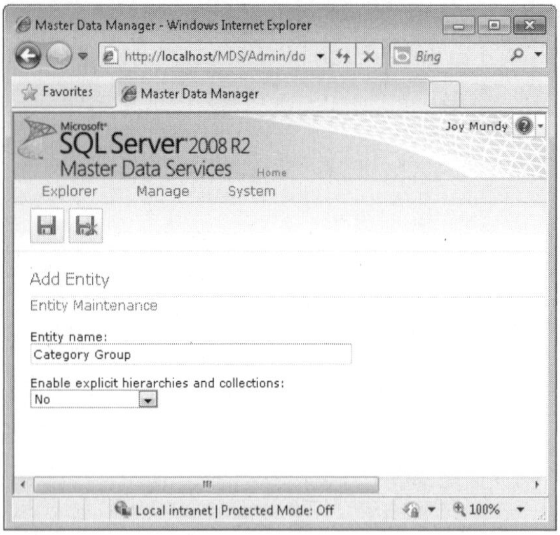

Figure 6-7: Creating an entity for a hierarchical level

The next step was to hook these entities together, declaring referential integrity between the levels of the hierarchy. To do so, the team edited the Product Subcategory entity to add a leaf attribute, told MDS that it's constrained to a domain, and pointed it to the category entity created earlier. Figure 6-8 illustrates the screen for creating a domain attribute.

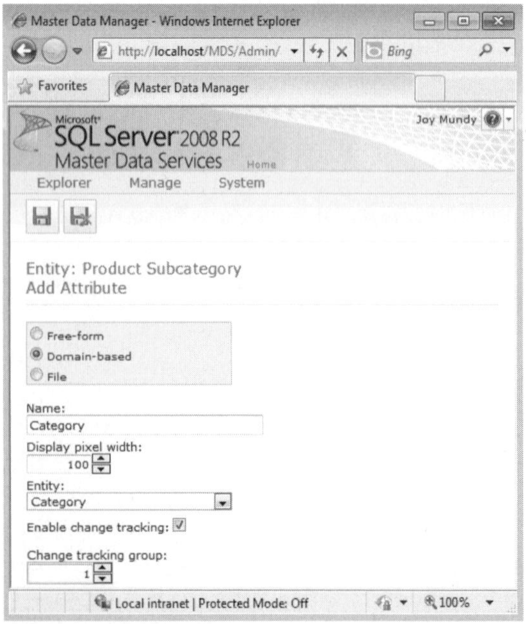

Figure 6-8: Creating an attribute that's associated with a domain

The team finished up the subcategory entity by creating a freeform attribute for short name, as illustrated in Figure 6-9.

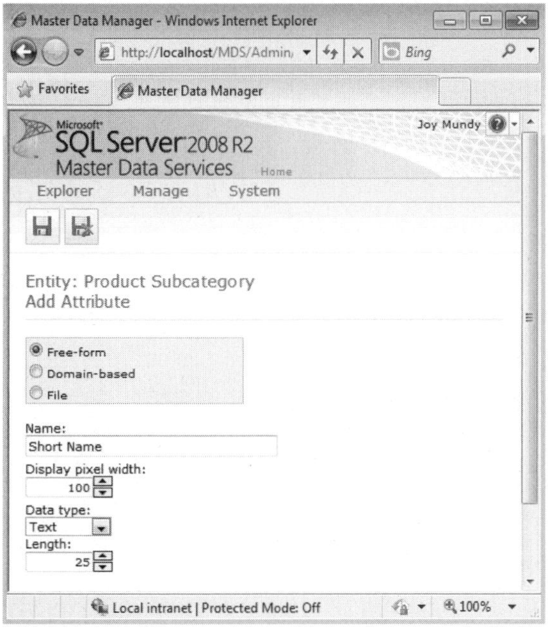

Figure 6-9: Creating a freeform attribute

With similar steps they created links between category and category group, between subcategory and alt category, and between alt category and category group. Finally, they defined freeform attributes for category manager, category manager email, and the short name for the alt category.

Load the Subcategory Members

There are 37 subcategories in the transaction database, which the team deems far too many to type by hand. They choose to populate the staging tables with a SQL script (assuming the source database is on the same server as MDS):

```sql
-- insert 37 Subcategory members into the staging table
INSERT INTO mdm.tblStgMember
    (
            ModelName
        , EntityName
        , MemberType_ID
        , MemberName
        , MemberCode
```

```
    )
    SELECT
          'Product Subcategory'
        , 'Product Subcategory'
        , 1
        , Name
        , ProductSubcategoryID
    FROM    AdventureWorks2008R2.Production.ProductSubcategory
```

By navigating to the Integration Management ➢ Import page from the Master Data Manager home page, the team quickly figured out how to load the subcategories into the model. Loading only took a few seconds, and the newly imported members can be viewed by navigating to Explorer ➢ Entities ➢ Product Subcategory, as illustrated in Figure 6-10.

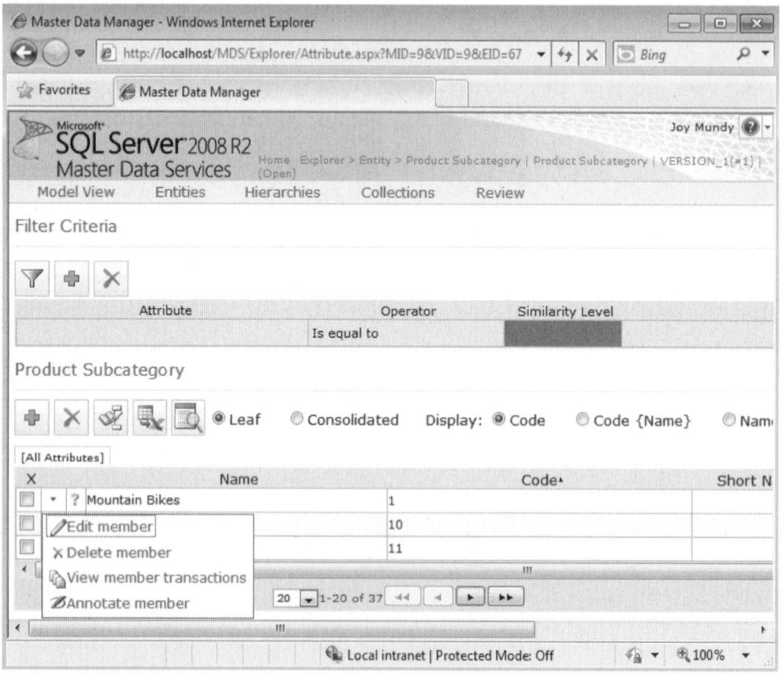

Figure 6-10: Exploring the newly added members

The initial data import process added only the new members; none of the attributes is populated yet. There are categories in the source database, but the other attributes don't exist anywhere else and must be added by hand. Remember that loading the categories uses the `mdm.tblStgMemberAttributes` staging table.

Polish the Model

The basic structure of this model was very simple to create, but there are some additional steps to make the model production-ready. Most important, the team needs to add business rules to ensure the data is correct. This is particularly important in the current business scenario, where some of the attributes must be added by hand. The team has the following wish list for business rules:

- Null or empty values are not allowed.

- Referential integrity between levels is maintained at all times. The team lead notes that linking together the hierarchy levels as domain-driven entities ensures this will always be the case.

- The category manager name should look like a person's name, containing 2–4 capitalized words. Similarly, the category manager email should look like an email.

- The names and emails should be validated in Active Directory.

- If the short name attributes aren't supplied in an import, the business rule should copy the standard name.

- An email should be sent to team members when any data element violates these business rules.

The team should define named hierarchies for subcategory, category, category group and subcategory, alt category, category group. Even though the attribute relationships exist, the hierarchies must be defined in order for Master Data Manager to create the export view for the hierarchical levels.

Export to the Data Warehouse

The team created three export views: one for the base level attributes for subcategory, one for the main hierarchy, and one for the alternative hierarchy.

The data warehouse load process for the product dimension is a straightforward SSIS package. That package must be modified to pick up the category, category group, and alt category information from the MDS export views. This is a minor change, and is expected to take only a few days to code and thoroughly test.

Even though the data in this model is fairly static, it's possible that new subcategories will be added in the future. The team hasn't done a good job of thinking through how they will learn about new subcategories, other than a failure in the ETL processing. They will probably begin by querying the subcategory table in the transaction database on a daily basis. Longer term, they need to better understand the business process that leads to the creation of new products, subcategories, and other product-related entities. They need a clear notification that something has been added or changed, and default strategies for dealing with those changes.

Summary

The information stored in Master Data Services can be the perfect input for the periodic — usually nightly — data warehouse ETL process. Many of the cleaning steps of the ETL process that we perform on dimension data can be accomplished by Master Data Services.

What MDS does particularly well is provide a mechanism for people to augment data and fix data problems. ETL, by contrast, is typically a batch process. There's certainly no built-in mechanism in SSIS for someone to review, correct, and validate data. Some of the problems that are most intractable for the data warehouse ETL system, especially data integration problems, are well suited for a master data management system.

For MDS to work well in a data warehouse environment, the MDS model for a dimension must be updated in advance of the data warehouse ETL cycle. There must be time for users to react to data validity issues before the new or updated information is used in the data warehouse. For this to really work, management and business users must commit to data governance. They may have to change their workflows in order to ensure there's enough lead time for the data to be well managed.

This is a hard sell for the data warehouse team to make. The carrot is improved data quality, and a mechanism by which user-driven attributes can be maintained and included in the data warehouse. As ever, the impetus must come from the user community, because in the long run they are the ones who must maintain the data.

As we described at the beginning of this chapter, a full master data management system falls outside the purview of the data warehouse team. For most organizations, such a system is simply infeasible at the moment. We need to solve simpler problems, and nurture the organization's commitment to data governance, a little bit at a time. Successful MDS implementations, however small, will move us toward that goal.

CHAPTER 7

Designing and Developing the ETL System

Measure twice; cut once.

Some people like to plan, specify, and document systems; most don't. We've observed that Extract, Transformation, and Load (ETL) system development draws folks in the latter category. We've found so few people who write adequate design specifications for their ETL systems that we've practically stopped asking to see our clients' planning documents. Either they're unaware of the impending complexity, or they don't have the planning tools.

In this chapter, we begin by discussing the steps you need to take before you start development of your ETL system: Round up your requirements and write an ETL plan. Next, we briefly introduce SQL Server Integration Services (SSIS) and present some of the basic concepts and vocabulary of that product.

Most of this chapter is structured around the 34 subsystems of a well designed ETL system. We describe each of the 34 subsystems and recommend alternative approaches for implementing them within SSIS. Throughout, we will refer to the Adventure Works Cycles case study.

As Figure 7-1 illustrates and common sense dictates, the ETL portion of the project is part of the data track. Remember, however, that these boxes aren't to scale. The ETL effort is the most time-consuming step in the data track and often in the entire project.

In this chapter, you learn:

- How to plan for the ETL system, including the components of a solid ETL design specification, and how to create this document.

- What SQL Server Integration Services is and its role in the DW/BI system. You'll receive an overview of its most important features for ETL system design.

- The components and functionality of a well designed ETL system, grouped into 34 subsystems.

- How to implement those subsystems in the SSIS environment.

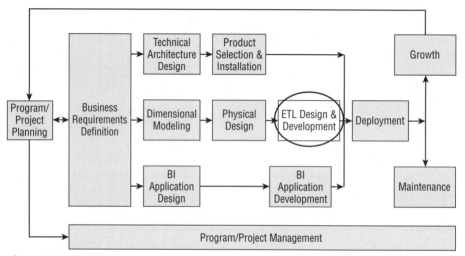

Figure 7-1: The Business Dimensional Lifecycle

RESOURCES This chapter describes the basic components of an ETL system and how to go about implementing a production quality system in SSIS. For additional detailed guidance about the ETL subsystems, we refer you to *The Data Warehouse Lifecycle Toolkit, Second Edition*. We will provide page references for more information on specific concepts and techniques throughout this chapter.

Round Up the Requirements

Establishing the architecture of your ETL system begins with one of the toughest challenges: rounding up the requirements. By this we mean gathering and understanding all the known requirements, realities, and constraints affecting the ETL system. The list of requirements can be overwhelming, but it's essential to lay them on the table before launching into the development of your system.

The ETL system requirements are mostly constraints you must live with and adapt to. ETL system requirements should not drive or even affect the target dimensional model. And the ETL developers seldom have any ability to substantially affect the design or operation of the source transaction systems. The job of the ETL system is to bridge those two immovable objects. Within the framework of these requirements, there are opportunities to exercise your judgment and leverage your creativity, but the requirements dictate the core elements that your ETL system must deliver. These elements include:

- *Business needs:* Wise ETL designers maintain a dialogue with the business community. Often, we learn during development that the source data doesn't match our expectations. The business requirements, rather than the whim of the developer, should dictate how these issues are resolved. Make sure the ETL designers and developers have good lines of communication with the team members who best understand the users' requirements.

- *Compliance:* Changing legal and reporting requirements have forced many organizations to tighten their reporting and provide proof of report accuracy. Of course, DW/BI systems in regulated industries have complied with regulatory requirements for years. But the tenor of financial reporting has become more rigorous for everyone. Typical due diligence requirements for the ETL system include:

  - Saving archived copies of source data.

  - Providing proof of the complete ETL flow.

  - Fully documenting algorithms for allocations, adjustments, and derivations.

  - Supplying proof of security of the data copies over time.

- *Data quality:* Business users demand quality data. They are increasingly using data rather than intuition to run their businesses. Regulation and compliance issues also heighten the demand for good data. Unfortunately most business users have no idea what data problems exist, where they originate, or how hard it is to identify and fix them. The ETL team needs to be agile and proactive:

  - Push back hard on the transaction systems to clean data at the source.

  - Implement a master data management system to fix data before it enters the ETL stream.

  - Decide what can and should be fixed in ETL based on business requirements, not on developer convenience.

  - Enlist the user community as partners to identify and prioritize data faults. Ideally, this would be part of an overall data governance/data stewardship program.

- *Data latency:* Data latency describes how quickly the source system data must be delivered to the business users via the DW/BI system. As we discuss in Chapter 9, most DW/BI systems process data on a daily basis; we expect this to continue to be true for the near future. As far as ETL is concerned, the basic system architecture can remain unchanged for populating data several times a day. If you are planning to deliver DW/BI data with very low latency (seconds or minutes), your ETL system and data warehouse database architectures may profoundly change.

- *Archiving:* Archiving requirements are driven by auditing and compliance demands. Depending on your architecture, other reasons to store copies of extracted and staged data include:

  - Maintain extracted data for restarting the ETL process after a failure.

  - Determine historical changed rows in the absence of a reliable source of changed data from the transaction system.

- *Lineage:* Lineage requirements, like archiving requirements, are driven by auditing and compliance demands. But business users are also interested in lineage. They'd like to look at a number in a report and be able to learn exactly how and when it entered the data warehouse, and what transformations occurred to it along the way. Delivering lineage information to business users in the context of a report is a bit impractical today because Microsoft doesn't provide a tool to make it easy. Nonetheless, the ETL system design should strive to make lineage as transparent as possible.

- *Cube processing:* If your DW/BI system architecture includes Analysis Services cubes, the ETL job flow includes cube processing. If you're not using Analysis Services, your architecture probably includes summary tables (also called *aggregates*) in the relational database. In this case, the ETL job flow includes updating the summary tables. In sum, the ETL job flow includes all the processing steps necessary to present a complete, consistent set of data to the business user community.

- *Available skills:* The most important experience for the ETL team on the SQL Server platform is to have good system development skills, knowing how to develop as part of a team, being able to write and execute comprehensive unit tests, and to build resiliency and redundancy into the ETL system. Of course, good SQL skills are required. And every production quality SSIS ETL system will need a little bit of scripting in a scripting language (VB or C#). Most ETL systems do not use any coding beyond SQL and some simple scripting; the rest is provided by SSIS. It is helpful to have at least one team member who already has experience with SSIS 2005 or later, but many teams learn as they go.

Develop the ETL Plan

Before you begin the ETL system design for populating a dimensional model, you should have completed the logical dimensional model, drafted your high-level architecture plan, and drafted the source to target mapping for all data elements. The physical design and implementation work described in Chapters 4 and 5 should be well under way.

The ETL system design process is critical. You should make some key architectural design decisions up front, and design all the components of your system in a consistent way. Any deviations from the standard pattern should be briefly justified and fully documented.

Start the design process with a simple schematic of the pieces of the plan that you know: sources and targets. Keep it high level, highlighting in one or two pages the data sources and annotating the major challenges that you already know about.

Next, develop a schematic for each table in the target dimensional model, graphically diagramming the complex restructurings. Where the high level plan graphics can fit all the target tables in a business process onto a single page (more or less), the detailed plan graphics may devote a page or more to each complex target table. This detailed schematic is backed up with a few pages of discussion and pseudo-code for any truly complex derivations.

Figure 7-2 illustrates what we mean. This schematic describes the ETL flow for part of the customer dimension of the Adventure Works data warehouse. The SSIS package for this part of the customer dimension will follow the flow of this schematic very closely.

NOTE We use some shorthand notation in our detailed schematics. These include:

■ *(+)* indicates we can't rely on the source system for referential integrity, and must use some kind of outer join technique with defaults for the missing values.

■ *SCD(2)* indicates the business users have told us these attributes should be managed as type 2.

■ *Hist* indicates the question or issue is related to the one-time historical load.

■ *Incr* indicates the question or issue is related to the ongoing incremental load.

RESOURCES See *The Data Warehouse Lifecycle Toolkit, Second Edition*, pages 428–436 for more information about developing the ETL plan.

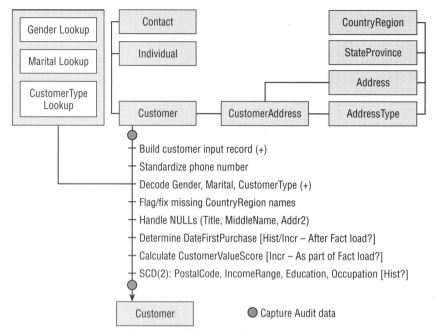

Figure 7-2: Example draft of detailed load schematic for the customer dimension

The ETL specification document should include:

- Default strategies for the major subsystems, including data extract, archiving, data quality tracking, and dimension attribute change management
- High level schematics
- Table design, detailed source to target mappings, and data profile reports
- Detailed table-level schematics

DOWNLOAD The book's web site at `http://kimballgroup.com/html/booksMDWTtools.html` contains a sample outline ETL specification document.

Introducing SQL Server Integration Services

Before we dive into the details of ETL system design on the Microsoft platform, we present an overview of SQL Server 2008 R2 Integration Services. The goal of the introduction is to familiarize you with SSIS so that you can understand its features and grow comfortable with its vocabulary. This overview is not a tutorial on Integration Services; we're focusing more on the "what and why" of the tool than on the "how."

SQL SERVER 2008 RELEASE 2 CHANGES

SQL Server 7.0 and SQL Server 2000 included a product called Data Transformation Services, DTS for short. SQL Server 2005 introduced Integration Services (SSIS), which was effectively a new product. When you move from the old DTS to SSIS you should completely redesign your ETL system. Moving from SSIS 2005 to SSIS 2008 requires a simple, relatively painless upgrade process. Moving from SSIS 2008 to SSIS 2008 R2 requires no change.

Your ETL team will develop SSIS packages to populate your DW/BI system. A package is analogous to a computer program or a script. You can execute a package to perform a database maintenance task, to load a table, or to populate an entire business process dimensional model.

An Integration Services package contains a single control flow which contains one or more tasks. In the ETL application you'll use a handful of control flow tasks, like manipulating files, sending email to an operator, or executing a SQL statement. By far the most interesting control flow task is called the data flow task, in which most of the real ETL work is done. We'll talk a lot more about the data flow task later in this chapter.

PREPARE THE DEVELOPMENT ENVIRONMENT

There are a few characteristics of the development environment, discussed in Chapter 4, which we'll briefly repeat here.

- Install SSIS and SQL Server BI Development Studio on a shared machine. Plan for developers to remote desktop into that shared server for their ETL development. If developers use BI Studio locally, then during their development and testing the packages will run on their local machines. If your development database is large, you may be moving a lot of data to the developer's desktop.

- Install the BIDSHelper add on, which is available for free download from CodePlex (www.codeplex.com). It includes many features to help you develop SSIS packages. BIDSHelper affects only the development environment; it contains no code that runs in production.

- Most development teams store packages in the file system during development, and use source control to check packages in and out.

- For initial package development, especially for the packages for the one-time historic load, it's useful to work from a static copy of the source database(s).

Control Flow and Data Flow

There are two major *design surfaces* in SSIS: control flow and data flow. They look similar — rectangles connected by arrows on a pale yellow background — but they are quite different. Control flow is where the basic logic of the package is defined, and a package has only one control flow. Most ETL packages consist of the following components, as illustrated in Figure 7-3.

- A few control flow tasks to define variables, setup auditing metadata, and so on. Usually these tasks consist of Execute SQL statements and scripts.

- One or more data flow tasks to perform the heavy lifting of the ETL.

- A few control flow tasks to clean up the package.

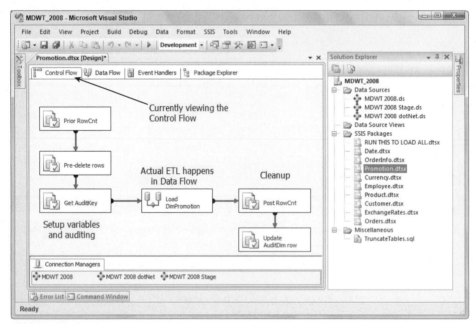

Figure 7-3: Viewing a control flow

There are dozens of control flow tasks available. Of these, you will heavily use:

- Execute SQL
- Execute package
- Data flow
- Script

You will undoubtedly use some of the other types of tasks as well.

NOTE The Execute SQL task, like many other tasks and objects in Integration Services, uses an interface such as OLE DB or ADO.NET to execute SQL even against SQL Server. You may find that a statement that you develop and test in Management Studio will generate an error inside the Execute SQL task. Errors are most common if your T-SQL scripts include parameters.

Data Flow

The data flow task is a pipeline in which data is picked up, processed, and written to a destination. The key characteristic of the pipeline is defined by the task's name: The data *flows* through the pipeline in memory. An implication of the data flow pipeline architecture is that avoiding I/O provides excellent performance, subject to the memory characteristics of the physical system.

In the control flow design surface, the data flow task looks like any other task. It's unique in that if you double-click on the data flow task, you switch tabs to the data flow design surface where you can view and edit the many steps of the data flow, as illustrated in Figure 7-4.

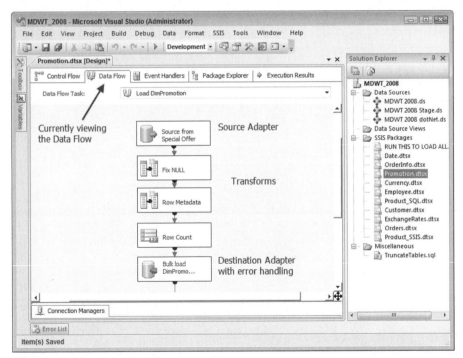

Figure 7-4: Viewing a data flow

The appearance and content of data flow tasks varies widely, depending on the work that they need to perform. Most data flow tasks will include:

- *One or more data sources:* Think of a data source as a query that brings a set of data into the data flow. Data flows out of a data flow source.

- *Multiple transformation steps:* Common transformations derive new columns, perform lookups to database tables, combine multiple data flow sources, and split one data flow into multiple streams. Data flows into and out of a data flow transform.

- *One or more data destinations:* The data destination is typically the data warehouse relational table or staging table that the data is being written to. Data flows into a data flow destination; it's the end of the line.

Error Flows

Most of the data flow sources, targets, and transformations support two kinds of output flows: normal flows (which appear in green on the design surface) and error flows (in red). The error flow from a flat file source would include any rows with a type mismatch, for example string data in a numeric field. The error flow from an OLE DB destination would include any rows that violate table constraints. The error flow is a data flow just like the normal flow. You can transform the data to fix the error, and hook it back up with the normal flow. You can write the error flow to a table or file.

The most important characteristic of the error flow construct is that an error in some data rows does not halt the entire data flow step unless you design the flow to do so. And, you can perform arbitrarily complex transformations to the error flow, to correct the data or to log the bad rows for a person to examine and fix.

Error flows are arguably the single most valuable feature of SSIS.

WARNING By default, all steps in the data flow are set up to fail (and therefore halt the process) if an error is encountered. To make use of error flows, you'll need to modify this default behavior by setting up an error flow and changing the error flow characteristics of the transform.

DATABASE ENGINE VERSUS DATA FLOW PIPELINE

The data flow pipeline is a distinct execution engine from the relational database engine. When a data flow task executes, SSIS picks up a batch of data, buffers it, and operates on that batch. If you watch a package execute in BI Development Studio, you may notice SSIS picking up a second batch at the top while the bottom of the flow is still working on the first batch.

At design time it feels like you're designing something that operates row by row, which sets off warning bells to experienced ETL developers. Experienced ETL developers know that for good processing performance, you need to operate on data in batch. The data flow pipeline does operate on batches of data, and is designed to be intelligent and perform well.

We've reviewed many SSIS implementations that do most of the ETL in the query embedded in the data flow source. At its extreme, this approach performs all the work in SQL, and uses SSIS only as a framework to glue scripts together. At this extreme, the data flow tasks consist only of a source and a target, with no transformation steps between. Some vendors call this architecture "ELT," meaning that the data is extracted (E), immediately loaded (L) into a relational table, and then all the heavy transforming (T) is done by complex SQL commands.

We prefer to use SSIS as it has been designed. We recommend keeping source queries simple, and using data flow transforms to do most of the transformation work. The advantages of this approach include:

- **Error flows:** Leverage the power of the error flow architecture to handle errors elegantly, within a single pass over the data.

- **Readability and maintainability:** A recent client had source queries that combined 30 tables. Pity the future developer who is charged with maintaining that SQL query!

- **Transparency of lineage:** Recall our desire for a user to click on a number in Excel and see a report describing exactly how that data got into the data warehouse. If all the transformation logic is embedded in a SQL statement, we'll never be able to track the detailed lineage in any useful or readable way.

- **Comparable performance:** It's impossible to make a blanket statement that SSIS data flow pipeline is faster or that SQL is faster. It depends on too many variables. We have observed roughly comparable performance from well designed packages using the two approaches.

This preference for transforming within SSIS rather than SQL does not mean blind adherence. The SQL Server relational engine is a powerful tool. Throughout this chapter we'll highlight several places where you can save yourself a lot of pain — and greatly improve performance — by staging data to a table and using the power of the relational engine.

SSIS Package Architecture

The standard ETL system design approach in SSIS is to develop a separate package to load each table, and a master package that calls each of these table-specific packages. The master package contains one Execute Package task for each child package. Many of the dimension packages can execute in parallel, but some dimension tables may have a dependency on another table. Use control flow precedence arrows to define these dependencies.

A master package can use package configurations to pass variables to the child package. Variables you might want to coordinate between all packages include auditing information and the date range for which the current set of packages is to be run.

When the child package finishes, it returns control to the master package, along with an indicator of whether the package succeeded or failed. You must design the logic for whether the master package should continue loading other tables or stop all work when it receives notification of child package failure.

WARNING Other than success or failure, there is no direct mechanism for a child package to communicate to the master package. It can be useful for the child package to communicate an error reason (if any), count of rows loaded, and so on. The only way to do this is to have the child package write the information — usually to a table — and have the master package read that same information.

The Major Subsystems of ETL

Now that you have an understanding of the existing requirements, realities, and constraints; a commitment to design before you develop; and a basic understanding of SSIS; it's time to introduce the critical subsystems that form the architecture for every ETL system. Although we've adopted the industry ETL acronym to describe these steps, the process really has four major components:

- *Extracting:* Gathering raw data from the source systems and usually writing it to disk in the ETL environment before any significant restructuring of the data takes place. Subsystems 1 through 3 support the extracting process.

- *Cleaning and conforming:* Sending source data through a series of processing steps in the ETL system to improve the quality of the data received from the source, and merging data from two or more sources to create and enforce conformed dimensions and conformed metrics. Subsystems 4 through 8 describe the architecture required to support the cleaning and conforming processes.

- *Delivering:* Applying the standard dimensional constructs such as surrogate keys, attribute change tracking, and fact table key substitution. Physically structuring and loading the data into the presentation server's target dimensional models. Subsystems 9 through 21 provide the capabilities for delivering the data to the presentation server.

- *Managing:* Managing the related systems and processes of the ETL environment in a coherent manner. Subsystems 22 through 34 describe the components needed to support the ongoing management of the ETL system.

Our descriptions of these four major components, and the 34 subsystems they encompass, may be familiar to readers of other Kimball Group books such as *The Data Warehouse Lifecycle Toolkit* and *The Kimball Group Reader*. In this chapter, we've provided just enough description of the subsystems to provide context for the descriptions of how to implement those subsystems in the Microsoft toolset.

Extracting Data

To no surprise, the initial subsystems of the ETL architecture address the issues of understanding your source data, extracting the data, and transferring it to the data warehouse environment where SSIS can work on it independent of the operational systems.

Subsystem 1: Data Profiling

Data profiling is the technical analysis of data to describe its content, consistency, and structure. In some sense, any time you perform a `SELECT DISTINCT` investigative query on a database field, you're doing data profiling.

As we've already discussed in Chapter 2, data profiling must begin as soon as you identify a possible data source. Serious profiling occurs during the dimensional model design process, as you develop the source to target map that describes exactly how each data warehouse column is populated. Any holes in your early data profiling must be plugged now.

SSIS contains a Data Profiling task and viewer that you can run against your source databases. That feature, combined with the interactive reports described in Chapter 2, inexpensively meets most data profiling requirements. In addition, many teams are finding the PowerPivot feature of Excel described in Chapter 11 to be an effective ad-hoc data profiling tool. This certainly isn't the main use for which PowerPivot was developed, but it's a great way to poke around and get a feel for the structure of the data in the source systems.

WARNING ETL development is too late to start profiling! If you've waited to begin profiling your source system data until you're starting ETL development, you are virtually guaranteed to uncover roadblocks that you cannot maneuver around. If you're not already deeply familiar with the source systems and data, drop everything else until you are comfortable that you actually can populate your dimensional database with the data available today.

Subsystem 2: Change Data Capture System

During the data warehouse's initial historic load, capturing incremental source data content changes is not important because you're loading all data from a point in time forward. However, many data warehouse tables are so large they cannot be refreshed during every ETL cycle. You must have a capability to transfer only the relevant changes to the source data since the last update. Isolating the latest source data is called *change data capture.*

There is no one-size-fits-all solution to change data capture: the best solution varies from source to source. The most common approaches include:

- *Audit columns:* Many source systems include audit columns that store the date and time a record was added or most recently modified. For daily processing, a new row is identified as where the date part of the inserted timestamp equals the date part of the modified timestamp.

> **WARNING** If you're using source system audit columns, make sure they are reliable. Often these columns are maintained by application logic, and a batch operation by a database administrator might not maintain the audit columns. Even if the columns are correctly maintained by database constraints or triggers, we've seen the DBAs turn off those constraints before performing a batch operation. There's no perfect solution; the best is to have detailed written procedures for DBAs to follow whenever they touch the transaction database.

- *Triggers:* A trigger is an obvious solution to the problem of identifying changed rows in the source database. It's not a perfect solution, however — it suffers the same fragility as the audit column technique. We've seen triggers used most often to capture deletes from transaction systems that perform hard deletes, but use audit columns for inserts and updates. A hard delete is when a data row is physically deleted, as opposed to being marked as inactive. In most systems, deletes are relatively unusual, so you can overcome DBAs' resistance to triggers by confining them to deletes.

- *Replication:* Replication is a time honored technique for capturing the change data stream. Set up replication on the source database to see changes flow to the replicated database. Replication alone doesn't solve the problem, as it creates a copy of the replicated elements. But sometimes you can create triggers on the replica, when those same triggers are forbidden on the transaction system.

- *Change Data Capture:* If your source transaction system is implemented in SQL Server 2008, the new change data capture (CDC) feature is the obvious solution. Like replication, CDC works from the SQL Server logs. When you set up CDC on a source system table, it will accumulate an image of all new or deleted rows, and the before and after image of any changed rows. You can track a subset of the table's columns. In most cases with daily processing you'll want only the end of day image of the updates, which is easy to find. Be aware that you will need to prune the CDC tables periodically, and that pruning should be synchronized with your ETL job stream.

■ *Change Tracking:* The Change Tracking feature is very similar to CDC, but it identifies only the keys for changed rows, not the full text of the changes. For that reason, it uses fewer system resources at the time the transaction is entered, at the cost of a more expensive query during the ETL process.

RESOURCES There is a Books Online topic that clearly describes how to access CDC data from SSIS. Look for the topic "Improving Incremental Loads with Change Data Capture."

CHANGE DATA CAPTURE VERSUS REPLICATION

If you're trying to decide whether to use SQL Server Replication or Change Data Capture to identify changed rows in your source system, the answer is CDC. Replication is a great feature with many uses, and it may still have a place in your overall architecture. But if CDC is available to you, it's the right choice for capturing changed data.

Using replication to identify changed rows is a trick to overcome poorly designed transaction systems that don't have modified date audit columns. You add that column to the replication target and add a trigger to maintain it. Replication lets you circumvent a proscription against modifying the transaction database itself.

CDC by contrast delivers exactly what you want: an image of new, deleted, and changed rows; accurate timestamps of the event; and an indicator of what the event was (insert, update, delete).

Both replication and CDC work from the SQL Server logs. You can have replication and CDC active on the same table.

■ *Non SQL Server techniques:* If your source database is not SQL Server, there may still be non-Microsoft tools available to help you identify the change data stream. Other relational database engines have their own versions of replication and CDC. And there are third party "log scraper" tools that may meet your requirements.

■ *Full "diff compare":* A full diff compare keeps a snapshot of yesterday's data and compares it, record by record, against today's data to find what changed. This technique is very resource intensive. Investigate using cyclic redundancy checksum (CRC) or hash algorithms to quickly tell if a complex record has changed. Full diff compare is the solution of last resort, especially for fact tables and very large dimension tables. The only sensible place to identify new and changed rows is in the source system itself.

Subsystem 3: Extract System

Extracting data from the source systems is a fundamental component of the ETL architecture. If you're lucky, all your source data is in a single system that can be readily extracted using SSIS. More commonly, each source is in a different system, environment, and/or DBMS.

For each source system, identify the best way to implement the extract. Except in the simplest cases, you're unlikely to come up with a single solution for all sources. Organizations that need to extract data from mainframe environments often run into issues involving COBOL copybooks, EBCDIC to ASCII conversions, packed decimals, and multiple and variable record types. Older legacy systems may require the use of different procedural languages. Although you might be able to write or purchase an SSIS task or transform to read an idiosyncratic source, it's usually easiest to have older source systems push the data for you into a flat file.

Most source data is stored in databases, usually relational databases. Integration Services can access a wide variety of databases through its OLE DB and .NET providers, including the .NET provider for ODBC. SQL Server ships with providers for all sorts of Microsoft formats, including Excel, Access, and even Analysis Services. It includes providers for Oracle. Other providers are available from database vendors or third party vendors.

> **NOTE** Providers are not created equal. If you're accessing data from a non-Microsoft database, you should evaluate a variety of providers. If you do a web search on "oracle ole db providers" you'll see conflicting anecdotes about which provider is faster. As far as we can tell, there is no clear winner. As ever, "it depends."
>
> If you're having trouble getting good performance between SSIS and a non-Microsoft data source, consider pushing the data from the source system into flat files. Let SSIS begin its work with the flat files rather than touching the source database directly.

The extract system should be separate from the transformation and delivery systems. In other words, you should create separate SSIS packages for the extract that simply pull the appropriate data from the source systems and stage it, untransformed, in a staging database or flat files. If you're using a push technique, you already have those extracts as flat files.

WARNING Many SSIS demos and examples work directly from transaction databases rather than use the separate extract-to-stage design pattern that we advocate. That's fine for demos, but there are excellent reasons to decouple the extract from the transformation and load:

- **Reduce the connection time into the source database. This can be a very important issue for large data volumes, creating significant pressure on the source database logs while the package is running.**

- **Provide a consistent restart point in the event of a failure. Not only do you avoid touching the source database again, but also you have the consistent image as of the extract date and time.**

- **Maintain the untransformed data for auditing purposes. Your internal auditors will love you.**

It may seem that decoupling extract from transformation and load is a lot of busy work. As with much of the Kimball Group's advice, it's a recommendation based on experience: any time we've skipped this step, we've come to regret it.

Figure 7-5 illustrates the data flow for the extract of a single table. The source query is trivial, performing no joins, transformations, or even column name changes. The staging table is structured the same as in the source database.

The untransformed extracts should be archived for at least a week. Many organizations archive the extracts for a month or even forever.

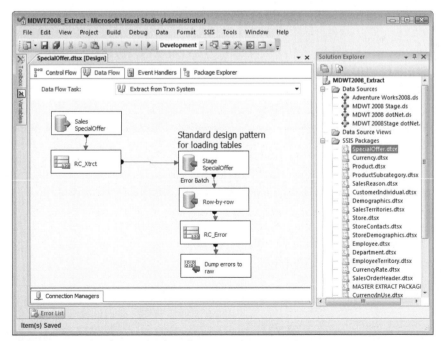

Figure 7-5: A simple extract data flow

Loading Data

The point at which you load data into a database table — whether a staging table as in Figure 7-5, or a real data warehouse target table — is a potential bottleneck for the performance of the ETL application. You want to load data as fast as possible, but you also don't want the load to fail because of one bad row in a billion.

As we discuss in Chapter 5, SQL Server can load data quite fast, but certain conditions must be in place for the fastest possible loads:

- *Slow:* Row-by-row or very small batches
- *Medium:* Reasonable sized batches (1000, 10k, 100k), depending on your system
- *Fast:* Large batches plus the target table either has no data or no indexes (or both)

We can meet the conditions for fast bulk load during the initial extract to staging tables, and for the one-time historical load into the data warehouse tables. But medium bulk load is still pretty good, and a lot faster than row by row. The problem with medium bulk load is that if we encounter a bad row — violating a constraint in the target table — the entire batch is rejected.

Our recommended design pattern for loading data is illustrated in Figure 7-5. First, always build and test your packages so that you test and fix data before inserting. In other words, a design goal is to create an insert stream into the target table that will insert without errors. That said, one of our mantras is Bad Things Happen, so design a failsafe.

With SSIS, our favorite feature of error flows provides that failsafe. Build in an error flow from all of your destination adaptors. The first destination (labeled Stage SpecialOffer in Figure 7-5) uses large batches. If there are no bad rows in a batch, all the data is inserted with good performance. However, any batch that contains an error row has all its rows flow into the error flow (labeled Error Batch). We immediately attempt to insert those rows again, this time one-by-one. The first and second destination transforms are identical, except the first one uses a batch (in this case, 1,000 rows), and the second inserts row by row.

Finally, we must do something with the true error rows. There might be only one error, or perhaps many. In this case, we're writing the error rows into a raw file.

NOTE A raw file is a data file stored in a format unique to SSIS. It's effectively the memory image of the data flow written down onto disk. There are several advantages and disadvantages of raw files:

- **Good: It is a fast write, because there is no conversion between the memory data stream and the disk file.**

- **Good: It won't throw a data type error, because there's no conversion.**

- **Bad: It can only be written onto the server where SSIS is running.**

- **Bad: It can only be read by an SSIS package. However, there are inexpensive third-party utilities that will read raw files for you.**

Our sample packages make ample use of raw files, but that's merely to make it easy to install the sample packages. Most organizations write data to structured flat files instead of using raw files, but raw files are a good choice in the real world if you are strongly constrained by performance.

If you're working with large data volumes, you may create larger batches, say of 100,000 rows. In that case, you can design a cascade of successively smaller batches on the error flows before you implement the row by row insert as the final error step.

Figure 7-6 illustrates how to configure a data flow destination with batches, whose controls are revealed by selecting Table or view - fast load in the Data access mode box. Figure 7-7 shows a data flow destination that will load row by row when the Data access mode is set to Table or view.

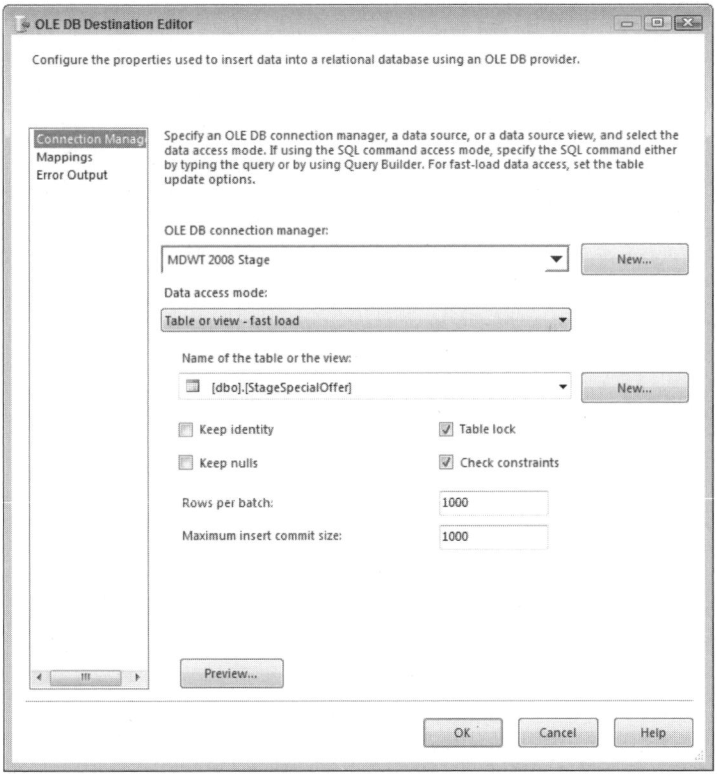

Figure 7-6: SSIS Destination Editor, batches

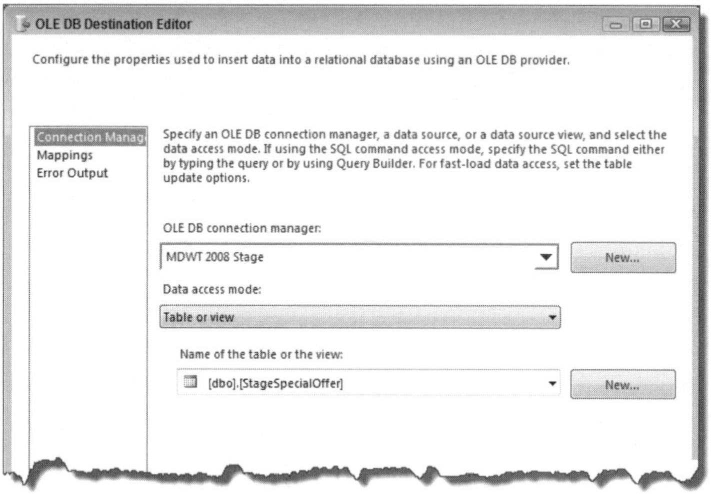

Figure 7-7: SSIS Destination Editor, row by row

Cleaning and Conforming Data

Cleaning and conforming data are critical ETL system tasks. These are the steps where the ETL system adds value to the data. The other activities, extracting and delivering data, are obviously necessary, but they simply move and load the data. The cleaning and conforming subsystems actually change data and enhance its value to the organization. In addition, these subsystems can be designed to create metadata used to diagnose problems with the source systems. Such diagnoses should eventually lead to business process reengineering initiatives to address the root causes of dirty data and improve data quality over time.

Subsystem 4: Data Cleaning System

The ETL data cleaning process is often expected to fix dirty data, yet provide an accurate picture of the data as it was captured by the organization's production systems. Striking the proper balance between these conflicting goals is essential.

The heart of the ETL architecture is a set of quality screens that act as diagnostic filters in the data flow pipelines. Each quality screen is a test. If the test against the data is successful, nothing happens and the screen has no effect. But if the test fails, the package must either attempt to fix the data, tag the data, or halt the process. The SSIS error flow is well suited for this architecture.

There are three categories of quality screens:

- *Column screens:* Test the data within a single column, for example for nulls, data type, or range violations.

- *Structure screens:* Test data relationships, for example lookup failures.

■ *Business rule screens:* Test complex business logic, for example requiring that a Platinum customer has a high lifetime value and has made a purchase in the last two years. Business rule screens often require a historical time series or comparison to aggregate data, and as such may be run on a periodic (perhaps monthly) basis on data already in the data warehouse.

RESOURCES You can learn more about data quality and data screens by reading:

- ■ *The Data Warehouse ETL Toolkit*, pages 131–147
- ■ *The Data Warehouse Lifecycle Toolkit, Second Edition*, pages 381–383.
- ■ *Data Quality: The Accuracy Dimension*, Jack Olson (Morgan Kaufmann, 2002).

In most cases you want to identify data problems and fix them as quickly and smoothly as possible. Only in the most extreme cases would you want to halt processing. Most of the "pull the plug" tests that we build into the ETL process are actually looking for incomplete or corrupted extracts.

Cleaning Data in the Data Flow

The data flow step is the logical place to perform data cleaning operations. Recall from earlier in this chapter that we advocate a separate package for the extract of each table. The data flow for the cleaning step will consist of a data source, several transformation steps, and then a load into the destination table.

The vast majority of the data cleaning screens and subsequent transformations are column screens. Of these, we see many examples of data type conversions and filling in null values. Checking for and fixing up range or domain violations is less common, as even the simplest transaction system data entry interfaces tend to do an adequate job of this task.

Within the SSIS framework, there are two main methods for fixing the column screen violations:

- ■ Make conversions within the source query, using for example the ISNULL or CAST function.

- ■ Implement conversions explicitly using SSIS data flow transforms such as the derived column transform.

We have a slight preference for the second approach, but in most cases either approach is just fine. Many ETL developers prefer to implement column screen transforms in SQL because they are comfortable with SQL. Our reasons for preferring the alternative approach include:

- *Readability:* Transforms are explicitly called out and graphically displayed.

- *Error event logging:* As we discuss in the next section, you may decide to log data quality screening errors in an error event schema. Usually you'd do this only if required for compliance purposes. If you're logging quality screen errors, it's more elegantly done by using SSIS transforms, because you can perform the test, log the error, and fix the data in a single pass over the row. Not only is the SSIS transform solution more elegant, but it also should perform better than the SQL approach when you're logging errors.

The second most common type of data quality screen and data cleaning are the structure screens, for example translating a code into a more readable text string. It's surprisingly common for decode tables to be missing values. It seems even with the best source systems, there's always some historical data floating around that violates the rules for full and complete text descriptions of all coded values.

As with the column screens, there are two methods for implementing structure screens and transformations: SQL and SSIS transforms. If you implement a structure screen and cleanup in SQL, you'd write your source SQL statement with an outer join to the decode table, and fill in any missing values with a default. Figure 7-8 illustrates a data flow task that uses the SQL-based approach. It has a relatively complex source query and a simple data flow structure. This is the clean and transform package for the product dimension, whose logical flow was outlined in Figure 7-2.

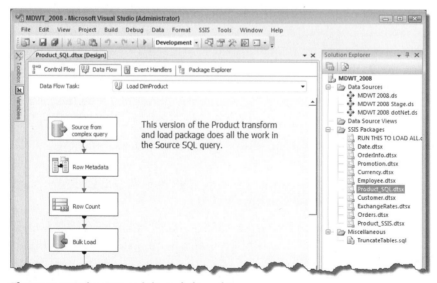

Figure 7-8: Using SQL to join and clean data

All the work in the package illustrated in Figure 7-8 occurs in the SQL query in the source adapter:

```sql
SELECT [ProductID] AS ProductSKU
      ,p.[Name] AS ProductName
      ,p.[Name] AS ProductDescr
      ,ISNULL(m.[ProductModelID],0) AS ProductModelID
      ,ISNULL(m.[Name], N'Unknown Model') AS ProductModel
      ,p.[ProductSubcategoryID]
      ,s.[Name] AS ProductSubcategory
      ,s.[ProductCategoryID]
      ,c.[Name] AS ProductCategory
      ,CASE p.ProductLine
             WHEN 'T' THEN N'Touring'
             WHEN 'M' THEN N'Mountain'
             WHEN 'R' THEN N'Road'
             WHEN 'S' THEN N'Accessory'
             ELSE N'Bike part'
          END AS ProductLine
      ,ISNULL(p.Color, N'None') AS [Color]
      ,CASE p.[Class]
             WHEN 'H' THEN N'High'
             WHEN 'M' THEN N'Medium'
             WHEN 'L' THEN N'Low'
             ELSE N'No product class'
             END AS [Class]
      ,CASE p.[Style]
             WHEN 'M' THEN N'Men'
             WHEN 'W' THEN N'Women'
             WHEN 'U' THEN N'Unisex'
             ELSE N'No product style'
             END AS [Style]
      ,CASE p.[FinishedGoodsFlag]
             WHEN 1 THEN N'Finished good'
             ELSE N'Unfinished good'
             END AS IsFinishedGood
      ,CASE p.[Size]
             WHEN 'L' THEN N'Large'
             WHEN 'M' THEN N'Medium'
             WHEN 'S' THEN N'Small'
             ELSE ISNULL(p.[Size], N'N/A')
             END AS [Size]
       ,cast(ISNULL(p.[SizeUnitMeasureCode], N'N/A') AS NCHAR(5))
    AS SizeUnitMeasureCode
      ,p.[Weight]
      ,CASE p.[WeightUnitMeasureCode]
             WHEN 'LB' THEN N'pound'
             WHEN 'G' then N'gram'
             ELSE ISNULL(p.[WeightUnitMeasureCode], N'N/A')
             END AS WeightUnitMeasureCode
```

```
        ,p.[DaysToManufacture]
        ,p.[StandardCost]
        ,p.[ListPrice]
        ,p.[SafetyStockLevel]
        ,p.[ReorderPoint]
        ,p.[SellStartDate]
        ,p.[SellEndDate]
        ,CASE
                WHEN SellEndDate IS NULL THEN N'Current'
                ELSE N'Discontinued'
                END AS ProductCurrentStatus
    FROM [StageProduct] p
    LEFT OUTER JOIN StageProductSubcategory s ON
(p.ProductSubcategoryID=s.ProductSubcategoryID)
    LEFT OUTER JOIN StageProductCategory c ON
(s.ProductCategoryID=c.ProductCategoryID)
    LEFT OUTER JOIN StageProductModel m ON
(p.ProductModelID=m.ProductModelID)
```

The data flow displayed in Figure 7-8 is simple, but the mess is swept under the rug and hidden in the SQL query embedded in the source adapter.

The alternative approach is to use a lot of SSIS data flow transforms. Begin with a source query that simply pulls the StageProduct table, without performing any joins or transformations. Set up a Lookup transform for each code lookup. Transform the stream of lookup failures, logging to the error event schema if required. Then union the error flow back into the main stream and implement the next lookup. Figure 7-9 illustrates the same ETL process as Figure 7-8, but uses the SSIS transform approach. As you can see, the data flow design surface is filled with transforms as each error screen is handled separately.

Comparing Figures 7-8 and 7-9, the first method is probably more appealing. But recognize that we've chosen a very simple example for the purposes of exposition. We do not like to see 300-line SQL statements joining 30 tables as the source query of a data flow step. No one wants to maintain such a thing. Also, recognize that your ability to perform complex actions, such as logging the error to an error schema, is very limited within a single SQL statement.

As part of your ETL design process, you should decide on a general approach to data quality screening and transformation. An example policy would be:

- Use the source SQL statement to:
  - Replace a null with a single default value.
  - Cast data types.
  - Rename columns.
  - Use simple (non-outer) joins to decode lookups where referential integrity is strictly enforced in the source systems.
  - Use outer joins to decode lookups where all lookup failures are assigned a simple text such as "Unknown: <code>".

- Join fewer than six tables. Queries that join six or more tables must be reviewed and justified in the system documentation.

- Pull data only from the extract tables in the staging database.

■ Use SSIS transform logic to:

- Log data quality violations to an error event schema.

- Perform complex transformations (other than `isnull` or `cast`).

- Handle lookup violation errors in a more complex way than can be handled in SQL.

In most cases, performance is not the deciding factor in determining whether to use SQL or SSIS transforms to test and clean the data. Both approaches should have similar performance characteristics.

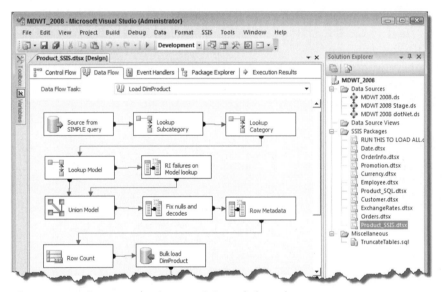

Figure 7-9: Using SSIS transforms to join and clean data

Halting Package Execution

When you're finished with the data quality screening and subsequent transformation, you're still not quite ready to write the data into the destination data warehouse table. After all, data cleaning is only subsystem 4 of the 34 subsystems. Even the simplest ETL system still needs to add audit information, manage changes to dimension attributes, and manage fact table surrogate key substitution.

Post-cleaning is a good checkpoint for staging the data a second time. Staging data at this point can improve restartability. Also, if you're processing data in small batches during the day, you may accumulate the cleaned data and perform the final delivery steps at midnight.

That said, we often don't bother to stage the data after cleaning. Instead the data flow goes on to perform the delivery steps and write directly into the target data warehouse tables. In many implementations, we'll stage the data once on extract, and write it again only when it goes into the data warehouse tables.

However, at the beginning of this section on data cleaning, we described data quality screens that might cause you to halt processing or at least to notify an operator. A simple example would be a huge drop in data volume in today's load, indicating a potential problem with an extract or transfer. If you need to halt processing because of a data quality screen violation, you *must* stage the data to a table and exit the data flow task. In SSIS, the only place you can gracefully halt execution is in the control flow. The data flow task will halt only if it triggers a fatal error, which is not the same as a data quality screen violation.

Figure 7-10 illustrates the control flow for a package that conditionally halts after data quality screening. It contains two data flow steps; the first for the data quality screening and the second for the delivery into the target fact table. Between the two data flow tasks is a simple script that evaluates whether or not processing should continue. If all is good, the second data flow is launched. If not, page the operator and return to the master package with an error condition.

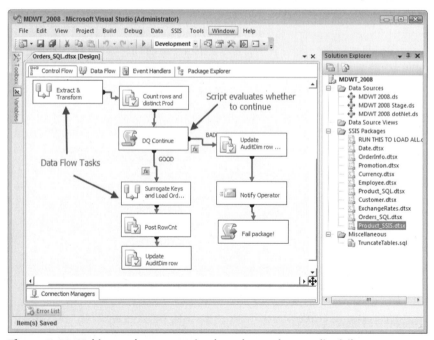

Figure 7-10: Halting package execution based on a data quality failure

FUN WITH SCRIPTS

You can't develop a production-ready ETL system in SSIS without writing a few scripts. It's really not hard. Let's take a closer look at the two scripts in Figure 7-10.

The first script, DQ Continue, performs a few basic checks on the data after the data flow task. Table 7-1 shows the SSIS variables used in the script.

Table 7-1: SSIS variables used in sample script

VARIABLE	USE OF THE VARIABLE
ProdLowLimit	Default value for variable
ProdCount	Count of distinct products loaded into the staging table in the first data flow step (populated in an Execute SQL task)
XtrctLowLimit	Default value for variable
RC_Xtrct	Count of rows loaded into the staging table in the first data flow step (populated in an Execute SQL task)
bXtrctOK	Set by the script

All the script does is evaluate whether the number of rows extracted today is above some minimum threshold, and the same for the number of product types in the extract. If so, continue with processing, and set the value of bXtrctOK to TRUE; otherwise bXtrctOK remains FALSE.

When you create a script task or transform, SSIS creates the outline of the script for you. The quantity of code that you need to write is often quite small: in this case, the seven lines shown here:

```
Dim ProdCount As Integer =
    CType(Dts.Variables("ProdCount").Value, Integer)
Dim ProdLowLimit As Integer =
    CType(Dts.Variables("ProdLowLimit").Value, Integer)
Dim RC_Xtrct As Integer =
    CType(Dts.Variables("RC_Xtrct").Value, Integer)
Dim XtrctLowLimit As Integer =
    CType(Dts.Variables("XtrctLowLimit").Value, Integer)

If ProdCount > ProdLowLimit AndAlso RC_Xtrct > XtrctLowLimit Then
    Dts.Variables("bXtrctOK").Value = True
End If
```

Looking back at Figure 7-10 you can see two precedence constraints labeled GOOD and BAD. The expression for the "good" path is @bXtrctOK==True. This example is simple enough that we could have eliminated the script and conducted our test in the precedence expression. But we recommend using a script, because it is much easier to read, understand, and edit.

Continued

(continued)

The second script in Figure 7-10 is absolutely trivial. On the BAD path, after we notify the operator of the error, we want to pass an error condition up to the master package. We need to translate the business logic that identified our extract as a bad one into a message to SSIS so the master package can stop processing of other packages. This script contains one line of code:

```
Dts.TaskResult = ScriptResults.Failure
```

The package ends at this point and reports failure to the master package.

Subsystem 5: Error Event Schema

The error event schema is a centralized dimensional schema whose purpose is to record every error event thrown by a quality screen. The error event schema consists of a fact table at the grain of an error event — at the grain of a failure of any quality screen. For each row that fails, for example, a referential integrity check would add a row to the error event schema. The error event schema holds error events from across the ETL pipeline, and as such is a great place to evaluate overall data quality.

RESOURCES You can find more information about logging error events in *The Data Warehouse Lifecycle Toolkit, Second Edition*, pages 383–385.

In addition to the integrated error event schema, it is often very useful to create error tables for each target table. The error table is designed to hold rows that have failed a critical data screening, and will hold the image of the row at the time of the failure. Error tables don't have to be SQL Server tables — a raw file or flat file can be good choices for error tables.

Note that error tables are usually limited to critical data screening errors, such as a lookup failure. We seldom log an error image row for something as simple as a null violation. There are several characteristics of error tables that you need to include in your design:

- *Table layout:* Columns and data types.
- *Table location:* Database, table name, and/or file name.
- *Error type:* You should develop a taxonomy for the types of errors to track. Possible error types include, but aren't limited to:
  - RI violation (specify which foreign key).
  - Numeric value out of bounds (specify which column).
  - Business rule violation (specify which rule).

- *Error level:* Usually critical or moderate. Critical error tables contain data rows that were not inserted into the target table. Moderate error tables contain data rows that were inserted into the target table, but we want to hold the image of the row at the time of data screening.

- *Resolution information:* For critical error tables, was the row eventually "fixed" and added to the data warehouse? When and how?

The error tables are part of the back room — we don't expect the business user community to use them. One possible exception is an auditing user or a data steward.

DOWNLOAD Several of the sample packages on the book's web site, including ExchangeRates, Orders_SQL, and Orders_SSIS, use error tables.

Subsystem 6: Audit Dimension Assembler

The audit dimension is a special dimension that's assembled in the back room by the ETL system. The audit dimension in Figure 7-11 contains the metadata context at the moment a specific row is created. Every data warehouse table contains two keys to the audit dimension: the key for the batch in which the row was originally inserted, and the key for the batch where the row was most recently updated.

The audit dimension receives one row each time an SSIS package is executed. The audit dimension is a small table. You might notice that the sample packages on the web site also use the audit dimension for loads into staging and error tables.

The mechanics of implementing the audit dimension in SSIS are very straightforward. Each package begins with a few steps that insert a new row into the audit dimension table. Those steps update an SSIS variable with the key for the new audit dimension row. The work of the ETL occurs in the data flow task, and any inserts or update are flagged with today's audit key for this table. Finally, after the data flow, end the package with a few steps that update the audit table with information such as the number of rows processed and the time processing finished.

The audit dimension contains a foreign key to itself: the audit key points to the parent audit key. When a master package begins, it creates a row in the audit table, and generates its own audit key. It passes that audit key down to any child package. You can use the parent audit key to tie together all the packages that ran in a single batch, called from a single parent.

DOWNLOAD Every package on the book's web site contains the same design pattern for using the audit dimension.

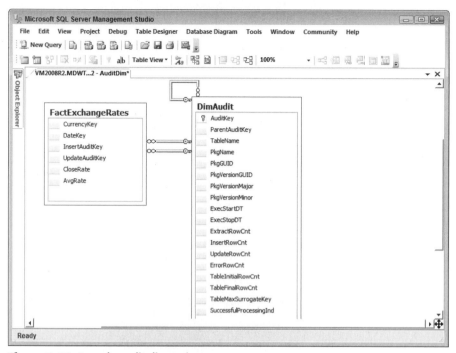

Figure 7-11: Sample audit dimension

Subsystem 7: Deduplication System

Often dimensions are derived from several sources. This is a common situation for organizations that have many customer-facing source systems that create and manage separate customer master tables. Customer information may need to be integrated from several lines of business and outside sources. Sometimes the data can be matched through identical values in important columns. However, even when a definitive match occurs, other columns in the data might contradict one another, requiring a decision on which data should survive.

Unfortunately, there is seldom a universal column that makes the merge operation easy. Sometimes the only clues available are the similarity of several columns. SSIS contains data flow transforms that can help develop a solution to this problem — the Fuzzy Lookup and Fuzzy Grouping transforms.

As we discussed in Chapter 6, it is extraordinarily difficult to build deduplication into the standard automated ETL stream. The ETL jobs must run without human intervention, but some deduplication problems cannot be resolved without human eyes. We strongly advocate that the deduplication system be initiated *before* the nightly ETL process runs. Within the Microsoft SQL Server product, we suggest that you implement a deduplication system in Master Data Services.

Subsystem 8: Conforming System

Conforming consists of all the steps required to align the content of some or all of the columns in a dimension with the columns in similar or identical dimensions in other parts of the data warehouse. For instance, in a large organization you may have fact tables capturing invoices and customer service calls that both use the customer dimension. The source systems for invoices and customer service often have separate customer databases, with little consistency between the two sources of customer information. The data from these two customer sources needs to be conformed to make some or all of the columns describing customers share the same domains.

The conforming subsystem is responsible for creating and maintaining conformed dimensions and conformed facts. Incoming data from multiple systems need to be combined and integrated so that it is structurally identical, deduplicated, filtered, and standardized in terms of content rows in a conformed image. A large part of the conforming process is the deduplicating, matching, and survivorship processes described previously. In the SQL Server data warehouse, this work is best implemented in a master data management system that serves as a source to the ETL process.

The hardest effort of the conforming system is political — wresting agreement across the enterprise about entity and attribute names and business rules. These political problems fall under the umbrella of data governance, and they need to be solved during the design phase of your DW/BI project.

The conformed dimension should be managed in one place and distributed to "subscribers" of the dimension. The easiest way to distribute copies of conformed dimensions is to set up a simple SSIS package to copy the updated dimension tables to the other servers in a distributed environment. The packages can end with a notification to the subscribers that the dimensions have been successfully published. Alternatively, you can set up SQL Server replication to publish the centrally managed dimension to other databases.

NOTE The Kimball Approach supports a distributed data warehouse, with separate databases for, say, accounting and customer care. Where separate business process dimensional models have dimensions that are completely identical — such as customer — those copies of the dimension should have the same keys. Each can be a subset of the master dimension — each subset can filter rows and/or columns — but they should use the same warehouse surrogate keys.

The payoff for building conformed dimensions is the ability to drill across separate business processes, assembling an integrated final result. The bare minimum requirement for drilling across is that the separate conformed dimensions have at least one common field with the same contents. When such a common field is used in the SELECT list of each of the SQL or MDX queries in the drill across report, the results can then be merged to produce the integrated final result. This simple recipe has a profound result. It is the core of enterprise data warehouse integration.

Delivering Data for Presentation

The primary mission of the ETL system is the handoff of the dimension and fact tables in the delivery step. For this reason, the delivery subsystems are the most pivotal subsystems in your ETL architecture. Though there is considerable variation in source data structures and cleaning and conforming logic, the delivery processing techniques for preparing the dimensional table structures are more defined and disciplined. Use of these techniques is critical to building a successful dimensional data warehouse that is reliable, scalable, and maintainable.

Many of these subsystems focus on dimension table processing. Dimension tables are the heart of the DW/BI system. They provide context for the fact tables. Although dimension tables are usually smaller than the fact tables, they are critical to the success of the DW/BI system because they provide the entry points into the fact tables, through constraints and grouping specifications.

The delivery process begins with the cleaned and conformed data resulting from the subsystems just described. For many dimensions, the delivery plan is simple. Perform basic transformations to the data to build dimension rows for loading into the target presentation table. This typically includes surrogate key assignment, splitting or combining columns to present the appropriate data values, and joining underlying third normal form table structures into denormalized flat dimensions. Dimension tables are usually small, and subject to many transformations.

Preparing fact tables is important because fact tables hold the key measurements of the business. Fact tables can be very large and time consuming to load. However, preparing fact tables for presentation is typically straightforward.

Subsystem 9: Slowly Changing Dimension Manager

One of the more important elements of the ETL architecture is the capability to implement slowly changing dimension (SCD) logic. The ETL system must determine how to handle a dimension attribute value that has changed from the value already stored in the data warehouse.

In Chapter 2, we talked about the two main techniques for handling changes in dimension attributes:

▪ *Type 1:* Restate history by updating the dimension row when attributes change.

- *Type 2:* Track history by propagating a new dimension row when attributes change.

Standard Handling for Slowly Changing Dimensions

Any dimension that contains a type 2 attribute should track the date range for which each dimension row is valid. For any dimension with a type 2 attribute, add three columns: `RowStartDate`, `RowEndDate`, and `IsRowCurrent`. For every dimension member like customer, there should be one and only one current row at any one time. Older rows have their `RowStartDate` and `RowEndDate` set appropriately. Figure 7-12 illustrates the logic for handling updates to a dimension with both type 1 and type 2 attributes during the daily incremental load.

We've seen companies get so intimidated by this complexity that they decide to manage all dimensions as type 1, even if that's not what the users want. The SSIS Slowly Changing Dimension transform is a useful feature. It does most of this work for you.

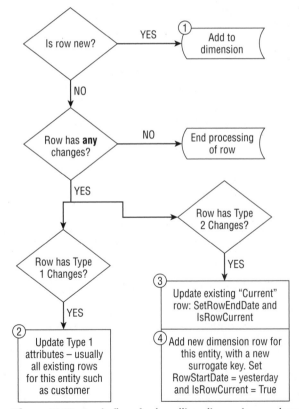

Figure 7-12: Logic flow for handling dimension updates

USING THE SLOWLY CHANGING DIMENSION TRANSFORM

The SSIS Slowly Changing Dimension (SCD) transform is available in the data flow. Typically, your dimension's data flow begins by sourcing data from the extracted data in the staging database, and performs any necessary cleaning and transformation steps. The final section of the data flow is where you insert and update this flow into the target dimension table.

When you drag the SCD transform into the data flow design palette, it consists of a single rectangle like all the other transforms. When you edit it, it launches a wizard with several pages of questions. And when you finally click Finish, the wizard generates a bunch of transforms and flows for you. The generated transforms and flows do the work that's outlined in Figure 7-12.

The wizard starts by asking you to specify the dimension table you'll be loading. Next, identify the business key, used to tie together all the instances of a particular entity. In a customer dimension the business key is usually the account number or customer ID. Map the other columns in the input flow to the attributes in the target dimension.

The wizard next has you identify how to manage the changes in each attribute. In addition to the types 1 and 2 (restate and track history) described previously, Integration Services includes a Fixed attribute, which should never be updated. Set the attribute change type for all the columns in your target table.

On the next screen you're asked several housekeeping questions. Do you want the processing to fail when you encounter a change to a Fixed attribute? Answer No (you rarely want processing to fail outright). Do you want the bad row to go into an error flow? Answer Yes. You're also asked if a type 1 change, when encountered, should update all the historical rows for the dimension entity, or just the current row. The textbook definition of a type 1 attribute indicates you should update all the rows, and this is the recommended setting.

If you have any type 2 attributes in your dimension, you're next asked how to identify the current row. Do you use row start and end dates, or an indicator like `IsRowCurrent`?

You can't have the SCD Wizard maintain both the row start and end date and the row current indicator. It's one or the other. As we discuss in the next section, you can edit the results of the wizard, and you can generally make it do what you want. We find it easier to generate the SCD Wizard using the row current indicator technique, and then edit the resulting transforms to add the row date handling.

Perhaps you're exasperated with the complexity of the SCD wizard, although we'll point out that it's a complex problem. Your reward comes when you click Finish and see all the transforms that have been created for you. These objects insert new rows, update rows that have a type 1 change, and perform the update and insert steps for existing rows that have a type 2 change.

The Slowly Changing Dimension transform will meet many projects' requirements without any further changes. However, there are circumstances where you need to do something tricky, or circumvent the wizard altogether. The next few sections discuss some advanced topics around handling dimension changes.

Custom Handling for Slowly Changing Dimensions

You will probably want to customize the output from the SCD Wizard. It may even make sense for you to develop custom handling for dimension changes.

The SCD Wizard will identify the current row for an entity like customer in one of two ways: with a True/False (or Yes/No) indicator, or with a range of dates for which the row is valid. If you choose the date range approach, the SCD transform will look for the single row for each natural key that has a null end date.

We recommend that you use both the row current indicator technique and the valid date range technique. Also, set the end date to a date far in the future, rather than leave it null. Can you still use the SCD Wizard? Yes you can, but you need to modify the generated objects in order to populate your dimension the way you want. This is easy to do, but be warned: If you need to go through the wizard again, perhaps to switch an attribute from type 1 to type 2 handling, you'll lose any customizations you've made to the generated objects.

> **NOTE** The objects generated by the SCD Wizard are standard Integration SSIS transforms. You can edit them to do whatever you like.

The only logic that you can't modify is the comparison logic that's hidden in the SCD transform itself. Under the covers, this transform takes a row in the pipeline and compares it to the current row in the dimension table; determines if the pipeline row is new or an update; and sends the row to the correct downstream path or paths. You can't change any of the logic in this transform without going through the wizard again.

Alternatives to the Slowly Changing Dimension Transform

We like the SCD transform because it's well thought out and reasonably flexible. However, it's not perfect. The two main issues are:

- *Performance:* The SCD transform, particularly the comparison logic, does not perform as fast as some alternative approaches. The slow performance is a cost you pay every time the package executes.

■ *Resilience:* If you need to change the dimension table, for example to add a column or change a column from type 1 to type 2, you will have to reapply any edits you've made to the objects generated by the transform. As we have already described, you're very likely to want to edit the objects generated by the transform. This problem doesn't affect the execution of the package in production, but it can be quite frustrating for the developers. This is particularly true if you rushed into ETL development before your data model design was finalized.

There are many alternatives to using the SSIS SCD transform. You can develop the logic yourself, or there are a variety of free and moderate cost transforms that you can download.

DOWNLOADS The two most popular third-party tools for replacing the Microsoft SCD transform are:

■ **Kimball Method SCD Transform, available for free download from `www.codeplex.com/kimballscd/` and developed by Todd McDermid. This transform offers more functionality than the Microsoft SCD transform, and performs much better. Edits are not destructive to downstream elements. This transform is not associated with the Kimball Group, though the developer followed Kimball published best practices in his design.**

■ **TableDifference, available for purchase from `www.cozyroc.com` and designed by the folks at SQLBI.eu. This component does only the "comparison" step of the SCD problem. You need to build out the updates, inserts, and so on. The comparison step is notably faster than the Microsoft SCD transform, and edits are not destructive to downstream elements.**

The good news is that the problem of managing SCDs has been solved many times by many people. Our advice is to use the Microsoft component unless you find its faults intolerable. If you choose an alternative approach, you'll assume the risk of incorporating a third-party object into your solution. Are you better off with a very functional, free solution with limited support? Or a low cost solution backed by a company that — we can safely say — does not have the financial resources of Microsoft? No solution is free of risk.

Another approach to handling SCDs is to perform the work not in the SSIS data flow, but in the database. To implement this technique, the final step of the clean and transform data flow would write the dimension data to a staging table. Out in the control flow, write an Execute SQL task that uses the MERGE statement to perform the SCD processing.

RESOURCES You can find a discussion of how to use the MERGE statement for slowly changing dimensions in the Kimball Group design tip #107, available at `www.kimballgroup.com/html/designtips.html`.

Subsystem 10: Surrogate Key Generator

As you recall from Chapter 2, we strongly recommend the use of surrogate keys for all dimension tables. This implies that you use a robust mechanism for producing surrogate keys in your ETL system. The goal of the surrogate key generator is to create a meaningless integer key to serve as the primary key of the dimension row.

In SQL Server, we implement the surrogate key generator in the database, by defining the table's primary key with the keyword IDENTITY. Inserts into the table exclude the primary key column, and each new row generates a new surrogate key. We have implemented this technique with very large dimensions, and have not experienced problems with performance or logic.

Subsystem 11: Hierarchy Manager

It's normal for a dimension to have multiple, simultaneous, embedded hierarchical structures. These multiple hierarchies coexist as dimension attributes within the denormalized dimension table. The hierarchy manager ensures that each attribute be a single value in the presence of the dimension's primary key. For example, a product rolls up to one and only one brand; a brand to one and only one product subcategory; and a subcategory to one and only one product category.

Hierarchies are either fixed or ragged. A fixed hierarchy has a consistent number of levels and is modeled and populated as a separate dimension attribute for each of the levels. Slightly ragged hierarchies like postal addresses are most often modeled as a fixed hierarchy, with placeholders for the "missing" levels. Profoundly ragged hierarchies are typically used for organization structures that are unbalanced and of indeterminate depth. The data model and ETL solution required to support ragged hierarchies in relational databases require the use of a bridge table containing the organization map. Ragged hierarchies in Analysis Services are supported more directly, not requiring a bridge table. Please see Chapter 8.

Snowflakes or normalized data structures are not recommended for the presentation level. However, the use of a normalized design may be appropriate in the ETL staging area to assist in the maintenance of the ETL data flow for populating and maintaining the hierarchy attributes. The ETL system is responsible for enforcing the business rules to assure the hierarchy is populated appropriately in the dimension table.

One of the biggest challenges with hierarchies is that transaction systems typically contain stripped down hierarchies that contain only the groupings needed to enter transactions. Business users often have alternative ways of viewing and analyzing the data, and there is no official source for these alternate hierarchies. They are often sourced from Excel.

The main problem with sourcing from Excel is that it's an unstructured source. Referential integrity violations are common. And the solutions usually require a person's intervention — it's not a problem that is well solved by the overnight ETL loading process.

The new SQL Server 2008 R2 feature Master Data Services, discussed in Chapter 6, is the best place to manage the integration of this kind of user information. Redefine your business processes so that Master Data Services maintains good clean hierarchies, and have your ETL job stream subscribe to those hierarchies.

Subsystem 12: Special Dimensions Manager

The special dimensions manager is a catch-all subsystem: a placeholder in the ETL architecture for supporting an organization's specific dimensional design characteristics. These design techniques were introduced in Chapter 2. Some organizations' ETL systems will require all of the capabilities discussed here, whereas others will be concerned with few of these design techniques:

■ *Date and time dimensions:* Date and time are unique in that they are completely specified at the beginning of the data warehouse project and they don't have a conventional source. Most often, these dimensions are built in a spreadsheet.

DOWNLOADS The book's web site contains a sample date dimension in Excel, and a package for loading that dimension into the MDWT_2008R2 database.

■ *Junk dimensions:* Junk dimensions are made up from text and miscellaneous flags left over in the fact table after you've removed all the fields related to the other dimensions. As we describe in Chapter 2, you sometimes combine unrelated flags and text into a junk dimension to avoid creating dozens of tiny dimensions. If the theoretical number of rows in the dimension is fixed and a relatively small number, you can populate the junk dimension in advance. In other cases, you must load the junk dimension as you load the fact table, inserting dimension rows as you observe new combinations of flags and text. As illustrated in Figure 7-13, this process requires assembling the junk dimension attributes and comparing them to the existing junk dimension rows to see if the row already exists. If not, a new dimension row must be assembled, and the row loaded into the junk dimension on the fly during the fact table load process. In SSIS, this design pattern is easily implemented as part of the fact table surrogate key pipeline. There is a more thorough discussion of this design solution later in the chapter, in the section on the surrogate key pipeline.

- *Shrunken dimensions:* Shrunken dimensions are conformed dimensions that contain a subset of rows or columns of one of your base dimensions. Shrunken dimensions are used to support data at different levels of granularity, for example monthly budgets. The ETL data flow should build conformed shrunken dimensions from the base dimension to assure consistency.

- *Small static dimensions:* A few dimensions are created entirely by the ETL system without a real outside source. These are usually small lookup dimensions where an operational code is translated into words. In these cases, there is no real ETL processing. The lookup dimension is simply created by the ETL team as a relational table in its final form.

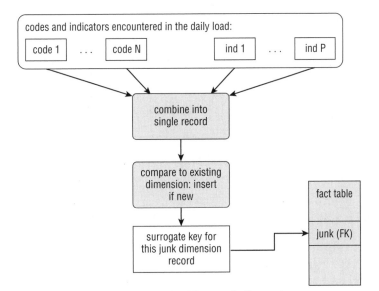

Figure 7-13: Architecture for building junk dimension rows

Subsystem 13: Fact Table Builders

The fact table builder subsystem focuses on the ETL architectural requirements to effectively build the three primary types of fact tables: transaction grain, periodic snapshot, and accumulating snapshot fact tables. Your fact table load packages *must* maintain referential integrity with the associated dimensions. The surrogate key pipeline (subsystem 14) is designed to support this need.

You will almost certainly need two sets of fact table builder packages: one for the one-time historical load and a second set for the ongoing incremental loads. First, it's common for transaction systems to evolve over time, so the historical load packages need to track the changes to the data structures and meanings. In addition, the historical fact table surrogate key pipeline must associate each fact row with the type 2 dimension member in effect when the fact event occurred. The problem is discussed in greater detail in the late-arriving fact problem (subsystem 16). As far as the surrogate key pipeline is concerned, the historical load is one huge set of late arriving fact data!

NOTE As you design your fact table packages, you need to remember the demands of SQL Server Analysis Services (SSAS) processing. As we describe in Chapter 8, SSAS can be a very effective database engine for the presentation area. But the ETL team needs to be aware that during processing of the SSAS database, Analysis Services cannot easily handle fact table updates or deletes. The only way to process a fact row update or delete is to fully process the SSAS partition that contains that fact row.

The easiest approach is to fully process the fact table into SSAS every day. This is a fine idea for modest data volumes (in the tens of gigabytes), but doesn't scale well.

For larger data volumes, you need to:

- Partition the SSAS fact data by date.

- In the fact table ETL, keep track of the dates that are receiving updates.

- Fully process the SSAS partitions with updates (or deletes, though we usually don't design hard deletes into the data warehouse).

Transaction Grain Fact Table Loader

The transaction grain represents a measurement event defined at a particular instant. A line item on an invoice is an example of a transaction event. A scanner event at a cash register is another. Transaction grain fact tables are the largest and most detailed of the three types of fact tables. The transaction grain fact table loader receives data from the changed data capture system and loads it with the proper dimensional foreign keys. Most rows are inserted. In the SSIS data flow, use the bulk load options of the destination, as we described in subsystem 3.

LOADING INTO A PARTITIONED TABLE

Large fact tables are often partitioned, usually by date. Monthly partitions are the most common. For most fact tables, it is perfectly fine to use the partitioned table in the data flow's destination. SSIS performs the load into the destination table, and SQL Server determines to which physical partition each row belongs. It's not the fastest possible load performance, but in many cases it's just fine.

However, transaction grain fact tables may be very large, and loading the data into the target table may become a bottleneck. We have worked with some organizations that are loading a billion rows a day into a single fact table. Obviously, such implementations need to be careful to optimize load performance.

To get the very fastest load performance, you need to load into an empty table. For daily loads, partition the fact table on a daily basis, load into an empty pseudo-partition, and then swap that partition into the fact table. Refer back to Chapter 5 for a discussion of partitioning.

Implementing this load-and-swap technique in SSIS requires some steps in both the control flow and the data flow. First, in the control flow, you need to perform the following steps:

- Modify the partitioning scheme, creating an empty partition for "yesterday's" data by splitting the last empty partition.

- Create new standalone tables (and indexes) as pseudo-partitions that correspond to the real partitions.

- Define a view on the standalone pseudo-partition table with a static name. Each pseudo-partition table usually includes the date in the table name; you need an unchanging view name to use inside the data flow step, as you cannot change the target table name in SSIS at runtime.

The data flow task is completely normal, except you set up the destination adapter to load into the view rather than either the partitioned fact table or one of the pseudo-partitions. The data will flow into the view, which points to the newly created empty pseudo-partition.

Once the data flow task is complete and the new pseudo-partition is populated, return to the control flow. There, you need to complete a few more steps:

- Index the pseudo-partition, if you didn't load it with indexes in place.

- Switch the new pseudo-partition into the partitioned table. The pseudo-partition table now has zero rows in it; all those rows are in the partitioned table.

- Periodically, consolidate the daily partitions into weekly or monthly partitions. This is usually a separate process.

All the partition management activities in the control flow are straightforward to set up. You can write scripts to handle the logic, but a much better choice is to use the partition management utility designed and built by the SQL Server customer advisory team. It's available for download from `CodePlex.com` (search for Partition Management). The Partition Management utility does not have an SSIS task wrapper. It's a command line tool, so to call it from SSIS you need to use the Execute Process task. Write a simple script to construct the list of arguments.

The addition of late arriving records is more difficult, requiring processing capabilities described in subsystem 16.

As much as we like to think of a transaction grain fact table as only receiving new rows, updates are necessary. In some cases, updates are relatively unusual, driven from fixing an earlier error. But in other cases there are systematic business rules that call for updating a fact. If you have a small volume of fact table updates, you may implement them in SSIS within the data flow, by using the OLE DB Command transform.

The OLE DB Command transform is the only way to perform database updates and deletes within the data flow. The advantage of the OLE DB Command transform is the availability of the error flow discussed previously. Any row for which the attempted update fails will go into the error flow and can be handled or at the very least captured.

There is one huge disadvantage of the OLE DB Command transform: it operates row by row and hence is very slow. If you need to update many rows, you should instead flow the entire image of the row to be updated into yet another staging table. Once you exit the data flow, use an Execute SQL task to execute a bulk UPDATE or MERGE statement.

WARNING The OLE DB Command transform is one of the first things we look for when reviewing the design of SSIS packages that have performance problems. It's great for small data volumes because of the error flow. But it is several orders of magnitude slower than the SQL-based bulk update technique.

Periodic Snapshot Fact Table Loader

The periodic snapshot grain represents a regular repeating set of measurements, such as financial account balances. Periodic snapshots are a common fact table type and are frequently used for monthly account balances, standard financial reporting, and inventory balances. The periodicity of a periodic snapshot is typically daily, weekly, or monthly. Periodic snapshots are often paired with a transaction fact table that details the movements into and out of the snapshot.

Periodic snapshots have similar loading characteristics to those of the transaction grain fact tables, especially if you load the latest snapshot at the end of the period. A common design for periodic snapshots is to maintain the current period daily, then freeze that snapshot at the end of the period. This design creates a twist for the ETL processing, because you need to completely replace (update!) the current period's set of data.

Luckily, this problem is rendered very simple by the use of table partitions. If the periodic snapshot is monthly, design monthly partitions with the usual pseudo-partition staging tables. Load into the pseudo-partition and swap it into the partitioned tables. For each month you only need one pseudo-partition table, which you truncate, load, and swap every day.

If you're not using table partitions, you can either bulk delete the current month's rows before entering the data flow, or you can use the bulk update technique described previously.

Accumulating Snapshot Fact Table Loader

The accumulating snapshot grain represents the current evolving status of a process that has a finite beginning and end. Order processing is the classic example of an accumulating snapshot. The order is placed, shipped, and paid for at different points in time. The transaction grain provides too much detail separated into individual records in multiple fact tables. Business users want to see all the events related to a given order in a single record so they can easily explore bottlenecks in processes.

The design and administration of the accumulating snapshot is different from the first two fact table types. All accumulating snapshot fact tables have many roles of the date dimension, usually four to ten. These are the dates that the snapshot tracks, such as order date, order fulfilled date, ship date, payment date, and delivery date. At the time the fact row for the new order is created, only the order date is known. The other date keys point to a row in the date dimension that indicates "Hasn't happened yet." Each time a significant event occurs, the same row in the accumulating snapshot fact table is updated.

The ETL design must account for the heavy updates. If you're using Enterprise Edition or Data Center Edition, you can partition the accumulating snapshot fact, say by order month. In many implementations, it is faster to completely reload the most recent month or two (into an empty pseudo-partition) than to perform even a bulk update.

There's inevitably a trickle of data from months ago. The older updates are best handled through the bulk update technique described previously.

Accumulating snapshot fact tables present a particular challenge for Analysis Services cubes. Even if you get just one fact row update for an order opened six months ago, you need to fully process its entire SSAS partition. You can increase the granularity of your SSAS partitions, but accumulating snapshot fact tables in SSAS are often faced with fully processing a large chunk of the cube.

Subsystem 14: Surrogate Key Pipeline

Every ETL system must include a step for replacing the operational natural keys in the incoming fact table record with the appropriate dimension surrogate keys. Referential integrity (RI) means that for each foreign key in the fact table, one and only one entry exists in the corresponding dimension table.

WARNING Maintain referential integrity! Of all the rules and advice included in the Kimball Method, this is the one we feel most strongly about: Never build a system that does not maintain referential integrity between facts and dimensions. You should never have a null foreign key in the fact table. You should never have a fact key that does not correspond to a row in the dimension table. Never. Not ever.

> A dimensional model without RI is unusable for ad hoc business users, and is highly dangerous even for expert users like IT staff. It is too easy to construct a query that unintentionally drops rows.
>
> As we discuss in Chapter 5, you might choose not to have the SQL Server database enforce the foreign key constraints. But the underlying data absolutely must not violate RI, and the surrogate key pipeline is the ETL subsystem where you do that work.

After the fact data has been cleaned and transformed, just before loading into the presentation layer, a surrogate key lookup needs to occur to substitute the source system keys in the incoming fact table record with the proper current surrogate key. To preserve referential integrity, complete dimension processing before starting the surrogate key pipeline. The dimension tables are the legitimate source of primary keys to be replaced in the fact table.

There are several methods of handling an RI failure. Your choice depends on the business requirements. This is seldom a requirement that you collect during the initial design, but the ETL team needs to discuss the design issues and decisions with a representative of the user community. The possible approaches include:

- *Throw away the fact rows.* This is rarely a good solution.

- *Write the bad rows to an error table.* This is the most common solution, but it should not be implemented unless you have procedures (both human and technical) to get the bad rows out of prison and into the fact table.

- *Insert a placeholder row into the dimension.* The placeholder dimension row contains the only information you have at the moment: the natural key. It receives a surrogate key, which is inserted in the fact table. All other attributes are set to appropriate defaults agreed to by the business users. This is an excellent solution if you can identify a legitimate business process or technical reason why you can receive a fact row before its corresponding dimension member. Keeping such "early arriving facts" in the fact table preserves overall totals and measures of activity even while you are waiting for the dimension detail to arrive. Once you do receive the dimension row, simply update the default labels with the correct ones. No changes need to be made to the fact table.

- *Fail the package and abort processing.* This seems a bit draconian.

WARNING In our consulting practice we review existing DW/BI implementations. We've often seen another technique for handling RI failures, which we cannot recommend. That solution is to map all the bad fact rows to a single Unknown member (such as -1). The single unknown member solution is popular because it gets the bad rows into the fact table so amounts add up, and it's incredibly easy to implement. But it makes no business sense.

Most often in normal daily batch processing designs, we write the bad rows to an error table. For a minority of the dimensions, and in aggressive low latency situations where early arriving facts are more common, we use the placeholder dimension row technique. We almost never throw away the bad rows, and failing the package just seems silly.

The surrogate key pipeline is one of the heaviest processing activities of the ETL system. With large data volumes, it's important to implement it as efficiently as possible. As with most of the ETL subsystems, there are two main approaches to implementing the surrogate key pipeline in SSIS: use SSIS lookups, or use database joins.

Surrogate Key Pipeline Technique #1: Cascading Lookups

The Cascading Lookups technique can be implemented in the same fact table data flow where cleaning and transforming occurs. Alternatively, if you chose to stage the fact data after cleaning and transforming, the OLE DB source query would pull in the entire staging table.

Figure 7-14 illustrates a sample package for populating the FactOrders table. Displayed here is a portion of the data flow, including the surrogate key pipeline for six keys. All of the lookups illustrated here use the technique of flowing error rows to an error table.

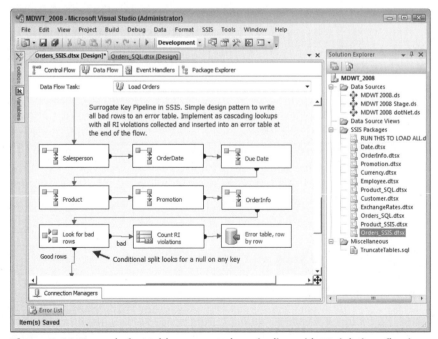

Figure 7-14: Example fact table surrogate key pipeline with RI violations flowing to an error table

The main work of the surrogate key pipeline occurs in the Lookup transform, which looks up the source system key from the fact table flow into a database table, in this case, the dimension table. The lookup adds the surrogate key to the flow. The Lookup transform does the same thing as a simple SQL join, but performs that operation on the data in the flow, rather than having to stage the data to write SQL. The lookup can be cached, and in most cases you want to fully cache the lookup.

> **WARNING** Always specify a SQL query for the lookup data source. In most cases you need just two or three columns. For example, the source query for a lookup to the date dimension for the surrogate key pipeline is
>
> ```
> SELECT DateKey, FullDate FROM DimDate
> ```
>
> The default behavior is to bring in the entire dimension table. The lookup table is cached in memory, so you want it to be as small and efficient as possible.

There are two misleading characteristics of this cascade of lookups:

- It appears that the lookups will operate in series, one after the other. Actually, SSIS is smart enough to perform the work in parallel.

- It appears that the referential integrity failures are not handled. Each lookup is set to ignore failures, with missing surrogate keys set to null. However, the failures *are* being handled. They are collected near the end of the data flow and placed in an error table. The conditional split labeled "Look for bad rows" strips out rows with a null value in any surrogate key column. This design lets you collect an error row only once, even if it has problems with RI to multiple dimensions. The target error table looks just like the real fact table, but it also includes columns for the source system keys.

The sample package Orders_SSIS also includes a sample of the design pattern for creating a placeholder row in the dimension table. Figure 7-15 illustrates this design pattern. The data flow splits the unmatched data: the rows for which there was no corresponding entry in the currency dimension. The OLE DB Command transform adds a placeholder row to DimCurrency, followed by an uncached lookup to pick up the key for that new row. (You can do this in the OLE DB Command transform. It's the same work either way.) Finally, the Union transform combines the main flow with the error flow.

> **WARNING** The Union transform can be troublesome during development. If you change the shape of the data flow above the transform, for example by adding a column, the Union transform often doesn't adjust properly. We've found a measure of peace by always deleting and replacing the Union transform, rather than trying to fix it. Most other transforms can be fixed up, often as easily as opening the object. But you occasionally have to delete and replace more complicated objects than the Union transform as well.

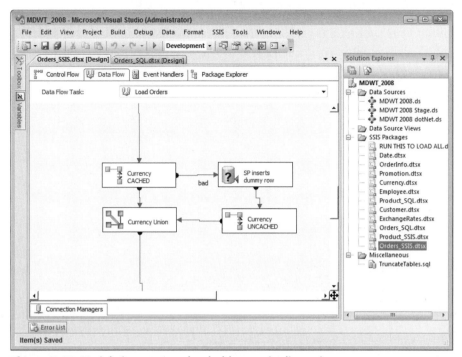

Figure 7-15: RI violations create placeholder row in dimension

Surrogate Key Pipeline Technique #2: Database Joins

The database intensive technique requires that you stage the data before the surrogate key pipeline. As we discussed in subsystem 4, you may already have chosen to stage the data after cleaning and transformation, for auditing or restarting the ETL process.

The design pattern starts with a big query, joining the clean staged data to each of the dimensions. In the case of the `Orders` fact table, this query joins the fact table to eight dimension tables (date is used twice), using outer joins to pick up the RI violations. The output flow from the source adapter contains columns for all eight surrogate keys, all eight natural keys, and all the other columns in the fact table.

Stage the clean, transformed data to a table, then write a SQL query joining the staged data to the dimension tables. This approach is illustrated in Figure 7-16. Note that the surrogate key lookups that are handled in the standard way — by flowing into an error table — do not explicitly show up in the data flow. Their design pattern here is the same as in Figure 7-15, using the conditional split near the bottom of the flow.

The SQL-based design pattern for adding a placeholder row to the dimension, as we saw in the currency lookup, is very similar to before. But here we use a conditional split to identify unmatched rows (where the CurrencyKey is null).

The OLE DB Command, Lookup, and Union All transforms are the same as previously. You would add a conditional split branch for each dimension that may need a placeholder entry.

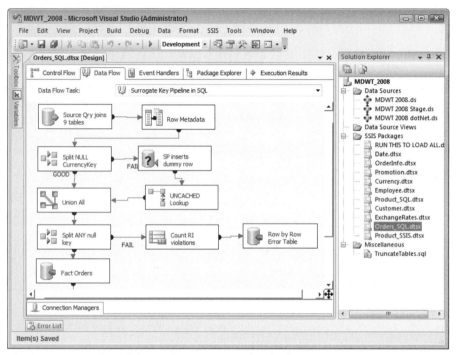

Figure 7-16: Database joins perform surrogate key lookups

Which Technique Is Best?

We don't have a strong opinion about which is the best technique for incremental loads. Both techniques use the data flow task, and so you still have an opportunity to perform complex manipulations on error flows. As a rule of thumb, if you're already staging the cleaned and transformed fact data for other reasons, the database join technique probably performs better. If not, you need to count the cost of staging and indexing the fact data in your assessment of relative performance.

When you're designing the packages for the one-time historic load, the database join technique is likely to be your best choice. The historic load requires a complex join to each dimension with type 2 attributes, in order to pick up the surrogate key associated with the dimension member at the time the fact event occurred. As we discuss in subsystem 16, the data volumes associated with the historic load push you toward using the database join technique.

Subsystem 15: Multi-Valued Dimension Bridge Table Builder

Sometimes a fact table must support a dimension that takes on multiple values at the lowest granularity of the fact table, as described in Chapter 2. If the grain of the fact table cannot be changed to directly support this dimension, the multi-valued dimension must be linked to the fact table via a bridge table. Bridge tables are common in the healthcare industry, financial services, insurance, and for supporting variable depth hierarchies (see subsystem 11).

The challenge for the ETL team is building and maintaining the bridge table. As multi-valued relationships to the fact row are encountered, the ETL system has the choice of either making each set of observations a unique group, or reusing groups when an identical set of observations occurs. Reusing groups is more work for the ETL process, but results in a much faster user query experience. In the event the multi-valued dimension has type 2 attributes, the bridge table must also be time-varying, such as a patient's time-varying set of diagnoses.

Within SSIS, the bridge table row can be constructed on the fly during fact table loading. If a row does not already exist in the bridge table for the current set of observations, construct it, add it to the bridge table, and return the key to the fact table flow. The design is almost identical to the "placeholder row" technique detailed in subsystem 14.

Subsystem 16: Late Arriving Data Handler

Data warehouses are built around the ideal assumption that fact rows arrive around the same time the activity occurs. When the fact rows and dimension rows both refer to "yesterday," the ETL design for the incremental load is straightforward and performs well. However, there may be cases where either fact or dimension rows trickle in long after the event occurs.

Late Arriving Dimension Members

We've already described the design pattern for late arriving dimension data. If your business processes or technical environment are such that you can reasonably expect to see fact rows arrive before their corresponding dimension rows, the best approach is to insert the placeholder row in the dimension table, as detailed in subsystem 14. When the dimension information eventually shows up, all you need to do is update the attributes in the dimension row. The fact row doesn't have to change.

> **NOTE** There's a nuance here around how you treat the first update to the dimension row, in the case where the dimension has any type 2 attributes. You should be able to make the initial update to the dimension attributes as a type 1 change. The best way to handle this is to add a metadata column to the dimension table that tracks whether the row was added by the fact table processing, and flips a bit when you update the attributes the first time. The SSIS slowly changing dimension transform can handle this situation, with the feature called Inferred Member Support.

Late Arriving Dimension Updates

What if you have a dimension member already, but you receive a late notification of a change to a type 2 attribute? This happened with a recent client who was building a schema around employees' projects and activities. The human resources business process queued up changes until the end of the month and then made those changes en masse. But the employee might have had new responsibilities for a full month by the time the systems received the information! The monthly update included a retroactive effective date.

Although it's easy to say the business process is stupid and should change (you can rest assured we did say that, but a little more diplomatically), the reality is that a change to the underlying business process is unlikely in the necessary timeframe. In this scenario, the ETL system needs to monitor for retroactive type 2 changes to dimension rows. The unfortunate cascading implication is that the existing fact rows for events after the late arriving change may need to update their surrogate key to point to the dimension member in effect at the time the fact event occurred.

The ripples of the late arriving update continues into Analysis Services. The fact table updates imply that you'll usually be fully processing the most recent month or two of partitions in SSAS (or the entire cube if you're not using cube partitions).

Note that late arriving dimension members and updates are far more likely to occur the closer to real time you're pushing your data warehouse. There can be a significant performance issue associated with frequent updates of the fact table keys.

Late Arriving Facts

At first glance, late arriving facts don't appear to be a problem. It seems the only difference is that the surrogate key for the date dimension isn't yesterday, but some other date in the past. The wrinkle comes with a dimension that has type 2 attributes. You need to assign the late arriving fact row the dimension surrogate key that was in effect at the time the fact event occurred, not the surrogate key that's in effect today.

It turns out this problem is not a difficult one to solve in SSIS. The solution depends on which surrogate key pipeline technique you're using (subsystem 14):

■ *Database joins:* If you're using a large outer join query to perform the work of the surrogate key pipeline, you need to make that query a bit more complex. The join to any type 2 dimensions for fact tables that may experience late arriving data needs to use a BETWEEN clause. Join on the source system key, where the event date on the fact table is BETWEEN RowStartDate and RowEndDate: the dates for which this is the active row for this dimension member.

DOWNLOADS You can see the database joins design pattern in the Orders_SQL package on the book's web site. The cascading lookups design pattern is illustrated in the Orders_Lookups package.

■ *Cascading lookups:* The situation is a little trickier if you're using cascading lookups to implement your surrogate key pipeline. The reason is that the Lookup transform doesn't have an easy way to set up a BETWEEN clause on the implicit join. But you can trick the Lookup transform into doing what you want. An overview of the steps are to:

■ Use a conditional split to divide the data flow into current and late arriving fact data streams.

■ Use the standard cached lookup on the current stream, as described in subsystem 14.

■ Use a derived column transform to add a copy of the event date to the late-arriving stream.

■ Use an *uncached* lookup on the late arriving stream. On the mappings tab, map one event date to RowStartDate and the second derived event date to RowEndDate. Finally, on the Advanced tab, you can modify the query to be parameterized.

■ Use the Union All transform to combine the current and late-arriving data streams, and continue processing.

In most cases of late arriving facts, the late arriving stream is less than 3% of the incremental load. The cascading lookups technique works surprisingly well for incremental loads where a small minority of fact data is late arriving. Make sure there's an index on the natural key in the dimension table.

Don't use the cascading lookups technique to perform the surrogate key pipeline work for the one time historic load, unless you have no history of type 2 dimension changes. For the historic load, the vast majority of data is not current, and hence would go through the uncached lookup. Use the database join technique to implement the surrogate key pipeline for the historic load.

Subsystem 17: Dimension Manager

The dimension manager is a centralized authority who prepares and publishes conformed dimensions to the data warehouse community. A conformed dimension is by necessity a centrally managed resource; each conformed dimension must have a single, consistent source. The dimension manager's responsibilities include the following ETL processing tasks:

- Implement the common descriptive labels agreed to by the data stewards and stakeholders during the dimensional design.
- Add new rows to the conformed dimension for new source data, generating new surrogate keys.
- Manage attribute changes, generating new surrogate keys or updating in place, as appropriate.
- Distribute the revised dimension simultaneously to all fact table providers.

If you have a single centralized data warehouse, perhaps feeding downstream Analysis Services cubes, the dimension manager's job is easy: there's only one copy of the dimension table. The job is harder in a distributed environment. As described in subsystem 8, many of the challenges are political as much as technical.

RESOURCES For a longer discussion of the Dimension Manager system, see *The Data Warehouse Lifecycle Toolkit, Second Edition*, page 402.

Subsystem 18: Fact Provider System

The fact provider owns the administration of one or more fact tables, and is responsible for their creation, maintenance, and use. If fact tables are used in any drill-across applications, then by definition the fact provider must be using conformed dimensions provided by the dimension manager. The fact provider's responsibilities include:

- Receive duplicated dimensions from the dimension manager.
- Add new records to fact tables after replacing their source system keys with surrogate keys.
- Modify records in all fact tables for error correction, accumulating snapshots, and late arriving dimension changes.
- Remove and recalculate prestored aggregates that have become invalidated (see subsystem 19).

- Assure the quality of all base and aggregate fact tables.

- Bring updated fact and dimension tables online.

- Inform users that the database has been updated. Notify them of any major changes or issues.

Subsystem 19: Aggregate Builder

Aggregates are the single most dramatic way to affect performance in a large data warehouse environment. Aggregates are like indexes: they are specific data structures created to improve performance.

In SQL Server implementations, most organizations that need performance aggregates implement them in Analysis Services. As we describe in Chapter 8, SSAS has a wealth of features for designing, defining, and updating performance aggregates.

RESOURCES For a longer discussion of building aggregates when you are deploying to a relational database, see *The Data Warehouse Lifecycle Toolkit, Second Edition*, page 134–137, and also detailed articles in *The Kimball Group Reader*, pages 536–546.

Subsystem 20: OLAP Cube Builder

OLAP cubes present dimensional data in an intuitive way, enabling analytic users to slice and dice data. SQL Server Analysis Services is a sibling of dimensional models in the relational database, with intelligence about relationships and calculations defined on the server that enable faster query performance and more interesting analytics from a broad range of query tools. You shouldn't think of SSAS as a competitor to a relational data warehouse, but rather an extension. Let the relational database do what it does best: provide storage and management.

The relational dimensional schema is the foundation for the Analysis Services cubes. It is easy to design cubes on top of clean, conformed, well maintained dimensional models. If you try to perform ETL and data cleaning during cube design and processing, you're asking for trouble.

You can launch Analysis Services processing from within your SSIS packages. Most often, the master package launches dimension table processing, then fact table processing, and then ends with a package or packages that perform SSAS processing. An alternative approach is to integrate SSAS processing with each object: end the customer dimension package with a task to process the customer dimension in SSAS. We'll return to this question in Chapter 8.

Subsystem 21: Data Propagation Manager

The data propagation manager is responsible for the ETL processes required to transfer conformed, integrated enterprise data from the data warehouse presentation server to other environments for special purposes. Many organizations need to extract data from the presentation layer to share with business partners, customers, vendors, data mining applications, or government organizations.

These situations require extraction from the data warehouse, possibly some light transformation, and loading into a target format: ETL. The big difference between data propagation projects and normal data warehouse projects is usually that the target format is completely non-negotiable. Consider data propagation as part of your ETL system and leverage SSIS to provide this capability. The SSIS packages to deliver data warehouse data to downstream BI applications are usually much simpler than the "real" ETL packages.

Managing the ETL Environment

A DW/BI system can have a great dimensional model, compelling BI applications, and strong sponsorship. But it will not be a success until it can be relied upon as a dependable source for business decision making. One of the goals for the data warehouse is to build a reputation for delivering timely, consistent, and reliable information to the user community. The ETL system must strive for reliability, availability, and manageability.

The remaining thirteen ETL subsystems have to do with managing your ETL environment. We briefly introduce them here, and talk about many of these issues in more depth in Chapter 17.

- *Subsystem 22 — Job Scheduler:* Every enterprise data warehouse needs a robust ETL scheduler. The ETL process should be managed through a metadata-driven job control environment. In production, many organizations launch the SSIS master package from SQL Agent. SQL Agent supports simple job scheduling and dependency, and the master package itself provides more complex control. There is nothing special about using SQL Agent to launch the master package. An alternative approach is to use command line utility dtexec to start the package; use a script or other enterprise scheduling software to call dtexec.

- *Subsystem 23 — Backup System:* The data warehouse is subject to the same risks as any other computer system. Disk drives fail and power supplies go out. Though typically not managed by the ETL team, the backup and recovery process is often designed as part of the ETL system. We discuss backup and recovery at greater length in Chapter 17.

- *Subsystem 24 — Recovery and Restart System:* After your ETL system is in production, failures can occur for countless reasons beyond the control of your ETL process. Common causes of ETL process failures include network, database, disk, and memory failures. As we have discussed throughout this chapter, you need staged data sets as a basis for restarting the system. Without staged data, you'll have to redo all the hard ETL work, and may be in a situation where you do not have a consistent starting point. SSIS contains features for checkpoints and binding multiple tasks into transactions. These features are useful, but you need to design your packages for restartability; there's no magic. One of the easiest recovery and restart systems to implement is simply to snapshot the data warehouse database as the first step in the ETL process. If there is a failure in ETL, the database can simply roll back to the snapshot. The snapshot adds a bit of overhead to the system, but remarkably little for such a convenient technique.

- *Subsystem 25 — Version Control System:* The version control system is a "snapshotting" capability for archiving and recovering your SSIS packages. As we discuss at the beginning of this chapter, the BI Development Studio integrates with a wide variety of source control applications including Microsoft's Team Foundation Server.

- *Subsystem 26 — Version Migration System:* After the ETL team gets past the difficult process of designing and developing the ETL process and manages to complete the creation of the jobs required to load the data warehouse, the jobs must be bundled and migrated to the next environment — from development to test and on to production. Migrating SSIS packages between environments is quite straightforward. These issues, and the use of package configurations to modify variables and connection information at runtime, are discussed in Chapter 16.

- *Subsystem 27 — Workflow Monitor:* The ETL system must be constantly monitored to ensure the ETL processes are operating efficiently and the warehouse is being loaded on a timely basis. The audit system, ETL logs, and database monitoring information are your key tools. In Chapter 17 we provide an overview of the kind of monitors to place on your system, and some items to keep an eye out for.

- *Subsystem 28 — Sorting System:* Certain common ETL processes call for data to be sorted in a particular order. Because sorting is such a fundamental ETL processing capability, it's called out as a separate subsystem. SSIS contains a Sort transform within the data flow. This transform works well for small to medium data volumes, but should be avoided for very large data sets. The Sort transform functions well when the entire data set fits in memory; its performance degrades significantly when data must be paged to disk. You have two alternatives to the built-in Sort transform. If the data is in a staging table, use an ORDER BY clause on the source query to pre-sort the data. You need to go into the Source Editor and tell SSIS that the data is sorted. This is easy to do; you just need to remember to do it. Alternatively, there are third-party sort utilities available, including SyncSort, CoSort and NSort. These utilities constitute the "high end" for extreme high performance sorting applications. In some cases, it makes sense to drop data out of a relational format just in order to use these packages. As ever, you'll need to evaluate your specific problem to reach a conclusion as to the best course for you.

- *Subsystem 29 — Lineage and Dependency Analyzer:* Two increasingly important elements requested of enterprise-class ETL systems are lineage and dependency. Lineage is the ability to look at a data element — for example a number in a report — and see exactly how it was populated. Dependency is the other direction: look at a source table or column, and identify all the packages, data warehouse tables, cubes, and reports that might be affected by a change. Although you can lay the groundwork for a lineage and dependency analyzer by following the practices outlined in this chapter, Microsoft does not provide such an analyzer. The good news is that all SQL Server components rely on well structured metadata, so the problem is theoretically solvable. Someday.

- *Subsystem 30 — Problem Escalation System:* The execution of the ETL system should be a hands-off operation, running like clockwork without human intervention. If a problem occurs, the ETL process should handle it gracefully: logging minor errors, and notifying the operator of major errors. In subsystem 4 we discussed the design pattern for halting package execution in the event of a major error. Before you go to production, you should have processes in place for examining the error logs, and rehabilitating bad data.

- *Subsystem 31 — Parallelizing/Pipelining System:* The goal of the ETL system, in addition to providing high quality data, is to load the data warehouse within the allocated processing window. For many organizations this can be a challenge, and you should always look for opportunities to parallelize your process flows. SSIS is good at doing this on your behalf. There are several properties of the Data Flow task that you can adjust for each task to improve performance. These are DefaultBufferMaxRows, DefaultBufferSize, and EngineThreads. In addition, since each target table has its own package, you can experiment with the layout of dependencies in the master package, executing different packages at the same time. Of course, dimensions must be processed before facts, but different fact tables can start at different times. Also consider that if you're staging the data at multiple points in the process, you'll be creating varying loads on the database server and SSIS.

- *Subsystem 32 — Security System:* The ETL system and staging tables should be off limits to all business users, with the possible exception of an auditing organization. Administer role-based security on the servers and databases and backup media. Security is discussed in greater detail in Chapter 14.

- *Subsystem 33 — Compliance Manager:* In highly regulated environments, supporting compliance requirements is a significant new requirement for the ETL team. Compliance in the data warehouse boils down to maintaining the chain of custody of the data. The data warehouse must carefully guard the compliance-sensitive data entrusted to it from the moment it arrives. The foundation of your compliance system is the interaction of several subsystems already described: lineage and dependency analysis, version control, backup and restore, security, the audit dimension, and logging and monitoring.

- *Subsystem 34 — Metadata Repository Manager:* We continue to hope that Microsoft will deliver a Metadata Repository Manager someday. Metadata is discussed in greater detail in Chapter 15.

Summary

Developing the ETL system is one of the greatest challenges of the DW/BI project. No matter how thorough your interviews and analyses, you'll uncover data quality problems when you start building the ETL system. Some of those data quality problems may be bad enough to force a redesign of the schema.

One of the key early steps in the ETL system development is to write the ETL plan. Ideally, we like to see a specification document that describes your standard approaches for the subsystems presented in this chapter and that documents nonstandard techniques for specific challenges. All of these issues need to be addressed before you go into production, and it's best to give some thought before you start writing your first SSIS package. At the very least, you need to finish the logical and physical data models, complete the source to target maps, and write a brief overview of your planned approach.

The extract logic is a challenging step. You need to work closely with the source system programmers to develop an extract process that generates quality data, does not place an unbearable burden on the transaction system, and can be incorporated into the flow of your automated ETL system.

The ETL system may seem mysterious, but hopefully at this point you realize it's fairly straightforward. We've tried to demystify the jargon around implementing dimensional designs, emphasizing the importance of using surrogate keys and maintaining referential integrity.

We hope that the many ideas presented in this chapter have sparked your creativity for designing your ETL systems. More than anything else, we want to leave you with the notion that there are many ways to solve any problem. The most difficult problems require patience and perseverance.

CHAPTER 8

The Core Analysis Services OLAP Database

The tip of the iceberg.

Once you've designed, built, and loaded the relational data warehouse, it's time for the fun part: delivering information to the business user community. In order for users to be able to consume that information — especially for ad-hoc use — you need to make sure they can formulate queries and get responses quickly. The Analysis Services OLAP database is a popular and effective tool for meeting these goals, and should be a core part of your strategy to enable self-service business intelligence. *OLAP* stands for On Line Analytic Processing, to distinguish this analytic database from the more familiar OLTP transaction processing database.

Designing and developing the Analysis Services database straddles the data track of the Kimball Lifecycle, as illustrated in Figure 8-1. The OLAP design process begins with modeling. If you've followed the Kimball Method to implement the dimensional model in the relational database, the OLAP design step is a straightforward translation from that existing design. There are some physical design decisions to be made later in the development process, and a modest extension of the ETL system for populating the OLAP database.

Start the process of building the OLAP database by sourcing it from a robust, cleanly populated, relational dimensional model, as described in the previous chapters. From a solid starting point, you can develop a decent prototype in a few days.

It'll take more than a few days to polish that prototype, adding complex calculations and other decorations, making the physical design decisions, and setting up and testing the process to keep the Analysis Services database up-to-date. But you're starting from a clean and conformed dimensional model, so it's really not that hard. The investment in building and populating the OLAP database is typically measured in person-weeks, not person-months.

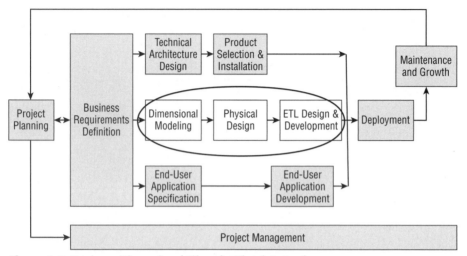

Figure 8-1: Business Dimensional Lifecycle: The data track

This chapter starts with an overview of SQL Server Analysis Services (SSAS) OLAP. We discuss why you should include an SSAS database in your DW/BI system. What it comes down to is this: It's substantially easier, and lots more fun, to deliver fast query performance and complex analytics in Analysis Services than in a relational database. Analysis Services works well. Especially when you consider its price, it's the obvious choice of OLAP technology on the Microsoft platform.

We spend most of the chapter discussing how to develop your SSAS dimensions and measures. We end with a discussion of physical design considerations, including precomputed aggregations and partitions, along with an overview of the approaches for keeping your Analysis Services database up-to-date.

This chapter describes how to use Analysis Services as a core presentation server in your DW/BI system. The core OLAP database is typically managed centrally, and is closely tied to the relational data warehouse and ETL systems. In Chapter 11 we describe the Power Pivot functionality of SSAS, new in SQL Server 2008 Release 2. Power Pivot is a standalone Excel add-in version of Analysis Services designed for business users. It can query data from a central OLAP cube for some or all of its data. In Chapter 13, we look at the other part of Analysis Services' functionality: data mining.

Overview of Analysis Services OLAP

The relational database is a great place to store and manage the data in your DW/BI system. But the relational database doesn't, by itself, have enough intelligence. There are several things missing from the relational data store:

- Rich metadata to help users navigate the data and create queries.
- Powerful analytic calculations and functions defined in a context-sensitive query language
- Excellent and consistent query performance for a broad range of ad hoc queries.

For non-Microsoft DW/BI systems, the most common approach to providing these missing elements is to use a full-featured reporting tool on the relational data warehouse. The reporting tool contains the metadata to help users navigate. And the reporting tools work closely with the database engine to construct well-formed SQL queries. Some reporting tools can also provide transparent aggregate navigation for performance and more advanced analytics.

This is a common architecture in Microsoft DW/BI systems as well. In the SQL Server environment, you can use Reporting Services Report Builder as the ad hoc query and reporting tool, accessing the relational data warehouse directly. This scenario is described in Chapter 10.

The preferred architecture in the Microsoft platform is to use SSAS as the primary presentation database. As you'll see in this chapter, when you define an Analysis Services database on top of your relational data warehouse, you're creating that rich metadata layer. At the same time, you can create a physical storage layer that includes aggregations and indexes to deliver excellent query performance. Analysis Services also brings a powerful, although complex, language that supports advanced, context sensitive analytics.

In the Microsoft SQL Server DW/BI system, we recommend building an Analysis Services database for ad hoc users, and possibly to serve as the database for most predefined reports as well. This chapter describes how to use SSAS as the presentation database — what we call the core OLAP database.

Why Use Analysis Services?

The obvious reason for using Analysis Services is that it plugs several gaps in the relational database's analytic functionality. We'll begin with a summary of why we generally recommend this architecture for SQL Server.

- *User-oriented metadata:* The definition of an OLAP cube highlights elements of the dimensional model that improve the user experience, especially for ad hoc queries. These metadata elements include the distinction between facts and dimensions, hierarchies and drilldown paths, groupings of attributes and facts, and the ability to easily combine facts from multiple business processes through conformed dimensions. These elements are defined once on the SSAS server, and are available to any client tool without further configuration.

▪ *Calculations:* You can define business calculations like profit, sales year to date, and sales same period last year. You can define sets like top 10 customers and a host of other calculations. Once these calculations are defined, all business users — no matter what tool they use to access Analysis Services — will use the same formula. Complex calculations can be challenging to define correctly, but the work is done once by the development team and shared by all. The cube calculations that you define using the MDX language can be orders of magnitude more complex than those supported by SQL.

▪ *Complex security rules:* One of the challenges of providing ad hoc access to the relational data warehouse is to secure detailed data but provide open access to summarized data. This is particularly true for ad hoc use. SSAS security enables complex security rules, as we discuss in Chapter 14.

▪ *Query performance:* Query performance is the first reason most people are attracted to OLAP. In general, Analysis Services offers excellent dimensional query performance, in a way that's usually cheaper and easier to manage than is possible from the relational database alone. You can get good query performance from a pure relational system, but it requires a lot of work that SSAS does for you. Best of all, achieving this performance is transparent to the user.

NOTE The SQL Server relational database has an indexed views feature, which performs some aggregate navigation. However, we've not found it to be particularly useful for dimensional schemas. Analysis Services works so well that almost no one uses SQL Server indexed views directly for aggregate navigation on dimensional schemas. There are some storage configurations, known as relational OLAP, in which SSAS uses indexed views to build performance aggregations in the relational database. In this scenario, Analysis Services manages the indexed views for you.

▪ *Aggregation management:* The single most important thing you can do to improve the query performance of any DW/BI system, regardless of platform, is to define aggregations. Aggregations are precomputed and stored summarizations of the detailed data in the fact table. They're nothing mysterious: They're simply summary tables at different grains, for example monthly, or by geographic region, or both. We called these aggregate tables in the relational database, but Analysis Services calls them aggregations, so that's what we call them here. Defining a good set of aggregations is more valuable to query performance than index-ing and cheaper than upgrading your hardware. SSAS helps you define and maintain these aggregations. And queries into your OLAP cube will seamlessly use the appropriate aggregations.

WHAT'S NEW IN ANALYSIS SERVICES 2008 R2 OLAP?

Not much. The core OLAP database tools and technology improved slightly between SQL Server 2005 and 2008, and even more slightly between SQL Server 2008 and 2008 Release 2. Look for the following improvements made in SQL Server 2008:

- Improved query performance.

- Improved aggregation design wizards. You can now manually specify which aggregations you want SSAS to build. Aggregations are discussed in greater detail later in this chapter.

- Attribute relationship designer. Attribute relationships are, unsurpris-ingly, how you specify that two attributes are related. Correctly setting attribute relationships is vital for query performance for medium and large cubes, as we discuss later in this chapter.

- Better design guidance. The wizards and editors do a better job of encouraging good dimension and cube design.

- Improved backup and restore.

Why Not Analysis Services?

We recommend that most DW/BI systems use Analysis Services as the primary query server. The relational version of the dimensional schema serves as the permanent store of the cleaned and conformed data, and feeds data to the OLAP database.

Some systems will close the relational data warehouse database to business users. This is an appealing architecture, for in this case the relational database can be lightly indexed. The Analysis Services database, including data, indexes, and a reasonable set of precomputed aggregations, is smaller than the relational indexes it replaces. Standard reports, KPIs, analytic reports, and ad hoc analyses can all be sourced from SSAS, using Reporting Services, Excel, and SharePoint.

Other systems will permit user access to both Analysis Services and the cor-responding relational database. And others don't use Analysis Services at all. What are some of the common reasons to commit less than fully to SSAS?

- The Analysis Services development market is immature. There are fewer tools, experts, and informational material about how to work with SSAS than there are for relational data warehouses.

- The query and reporting tool market is confusing and immature. Companies have a large investment in existing client tools and developer and user skills.

- Some kinds of analyses are intrinsically difficult in OLAP. This is particularly true for analyses that align data not by dimension attributes but by an event that's buried in the facts.

NOTE Most ad hoc analyses are easier to construct with MDX and OLAP than with SQL. A counter-example from a clickstream business process is to analyze how users behave after they first visit a certain page. First you need to go into the facts to find who visited the page (and when). Then you may want to align all the users' page clicks by time to see patterns in behavior. This is moderately difficult in SQL but extremely challenging in OLAP and MDX. In truth, this kind of analysis is best handled by data mining. But sometimes we just want to poke around, and for this kind of problem we prefer SQL.

Designing the OLAP Structure

If you've followed our instructions to build the relational layer of your DW/BI system with surrogate keys, conformed dimensions, and well-managed dimension changes, then building an Analysis Services OLAP database is straightforward. There are several major steps:

1. Develop your plan.
2. Set up the design and development environment.
3. Create a Data Source View.
4. Create and fine tune your dimensions.
5. Run the Cube Wizard and edit the resulting cube.
6. Create calculations and other decorations.
7. Iterate, iterate, iterate.

Later in the chapter, we discuss physical storage issues, which are largely independent of the database's logical design.

NOTE Analysis Services contains features to help you overcome flaws in the design of the source database, like referential integrity violations, but we're not going to talk about those features. Instead, build your DW/BI system correctly, as described in this book.

Planning

The first step in developing your SSAS database is to document its scope. If you're following the Kimball Method, your phase 1 project includes a single business process dimensional model. This is a reasonable sized chunk for the first phase of an Analysis Services cube: usually 3–5 related fact tables and their associated dimensions. You will need to consider the contents of each cube, the grain of the fact tables and their dimensions, and the nature of cube usage in your plan.

RESOURCES We reviewed the Kimball Method very briefly in the introduction to this book. For much more detail, see *The Data Warehouse Lifecycle Toolkit* — an entire book devoted to the subject of the Kimball Method.

Cube Content

A single cube can — and should — contain multiple fact tables. The most challenging aspect of cube planning is to decide how many fact tables to include in a single cube. There's no physical upper limit on the number of fact tables to include, and the best design for you depends on your data and usage patterns. When two fact tables are in the same cube, it's trivial for users to develop queries and analyses that include information from both. This is hugely valuable, and is the reason we create conformed dimensions in the first place. The payoff for building conformed dimensions is the ability to drill across separate business processes, assembling an integrated final result.

HOW MANY FACT TABLES IN A CUBE?

There is a hierarchy of sorts inherent in an Analysis Services installation. At the top is the server instance. Usually there is one server instance on a machine, just as with the relational database engine.

A server can have multiple databases, and a database can contain multiple cubes. Finally, each cube can contain multiple fact tables, which Analysis Services somewhat confusingly calls *Measure Groups*. All of the measure groups and cubes in a database share conformed dimensions.

Most organizations will have a handful of databases in production, each of which has 1–10 cubes. There's no technical limit on how many databases, cubes, or fact tables you have.

Rules of thumb: Five fact tables in a cube should be entirely comfortable in most situations. A cube that includes fifteen fact tables is often reasonable, though your experience will depend on your data volumes, the complexity of your calculations, and usage patterns. Fifty fact tables in a cube is almost certainly too many for broad use.

If you have resources to spare, consider creating an exploratory cube that contains many or all fact tables, but is open only to the DW team and a very small number of power users. The exploratory cube is used to inform the development of smaller subset cubes.

The fact table and dimensions in a single business process dimensional model equates comfortably to a single cube. It is certainly the place to begin for your first SSAS core cube development effort. But as you iterate through the Lifecycle and add new business process dimensional models, don't blindly spin up a new cube for each. There is so much analytic richness to be gained from including additional fact tables in a single cube. The problem is that as the cube grows in complexity, its performance degrades.

Cube Granularity

As you're deciding which fact tables are included in the cube, you should also determine which dimensions, and which grain of the dimensions, are included. Analysis Services scales very well, and in many cases it is reasonable — and best practice — to build cubes with the same grain as the underlying fact tables. Cubes that are built on and include a terabyte of relational data are not uncommon. Remember, SSAS manages and uses precomputed performance aggregations, so most user queries will not actually use the detailed data.

Our initial approach is to build the cubes at the same grain as the dimensional data in the relational database. The factors that might lead us to deviate from that approach include:

- Severe resource constraints.
- Potential usability problems, usually because of poorly structured natural hierarchies that lead to a huge number of children in a drilldown path. It's not a good idea to have 100,000 nodes open up when a user clicks a + sign in an Excel spreadsheet, as she will wait a long time for the data to return or Excel to crash.
- Clearly defined business cases for accessing the lowest grain of detail. In this case, it can be quite effective to reach back into the relational database for that lowest level of detail.

We usually exclude the audit dimension described in Chapter 7.

Cube Usage

The cube scope document should also detail how much of the overall ad hoc access will go through Analysis Services. Typically, the answer is between 90 percent and 100 percent. Document any scenarios where business users need to access the relational data warehouse directly for ad hoc use. Also, document how much of standard reporting will go through SSAS. This is a much broader range, typically between 50 percent and 100 percent.

Getting Started

There are several steps in the setup process. First, you need to install and configure one or more Analysis Services development servers. You need to ensure the correct software is installed on developers' desktops. You should have some clean data loaded into the data warehouse database, and you should have created a set of views on those database tables.

Setup

As the Analysis Services database developer, the only SQL Server components you must have on your desktop PC are the development tools, notably BI Development Studio (BIDS) and Management Studio. Many developers run the server components on their desktop PCs, but it's not required. You can point to a shared Analysis Services development server, just as you would share a development relational database server. Use BI Studio to design and develop the Analysis Services database, and Management Studio to operate and maintain that database.

Work through the tutorial that ships with SQL Server before trying to design and build your first OLAP database. It's a good tutorial, and not only teaches you which buttons to push but also provides information about why. This chapter is not a replacement for the tutorial. Instead we assume you'll learn the basics from the tutorial. Here, we focus more on process and design issues.

Create Relational Views

In Chapter 5, we recommended that you create a database view for each table in the dimensional model. End users' and Analysis Services' access to the relational database should come through these views. The views provide a layer of insulation, and can greatly simplify the process of making future changes to the DW/BI system. Give the views and columns user-friendly names: These names become SSAS object names like dimensions and attributes.

> **NOTE** Analysis Services does a pretty good job of turning the common styles of database object names into friendly names. It will parse CamelCase and Underscore_Case names, stripping underscores and inserting spaces as appropriate. It's not perfect; you do need to review the friendly names in the Data Source View.

The downside of using views is that you obscure any foreign key relationships defined in the data. Many tools automatically create join paths based on these relationships; these join paths must be added by hand when you use views.

> **NOTE** Creating the view layer sounds like make-work. But we've always regretted it when we've skipped this step.

Populate the Data Warehouse Database

You don't need to wait until the ETL system is finished, and the relational data warehouse is fully populated with historical and incremental data, before you start working on the Analysis Services database. Technically, you don't have to populate the database at all. But that's just a theoretical point: In practice, you want to look at the data as you're designing the OLAP database.

> **NOTE** There is nothing like designing, processing, and exploring an SSAS dimension to highlight data inconsistencies. We recommend that you experiment with building SSAS dimensions as soon as you have data available. You will be amazed by what you'll turn up in what you perhaps imagined was very solid and clean data.

We hate to see projects that finish the ETL work before anyone begins poking around the data in SSAS. Some organizations run projects in a very compartmentalized way and declare that once ETL is accepted, it cannot be changed. If your organization is that way, you will be well served to mock up your dimensions as soon as possible. It's helpful during the design process to work from a static copy of the warehouse database. It's much easier to design and debug the cube if the underlying data isn't changing from day to day. Most people fully populate the dimensions and several months of data in the large fact tables. Small fact tables, like the `Exchange Rates` fact table in the Adventure Works Cycles case study, can be fully populated.

Fully populate most of the dimensions because that's where most of the design work occurs. Dimensions are usually small enough that you can restructure and rebuild them many times, without an intolerable wait to see how the modified dimension looks. If you have a larger dimension, say 100,000 to 1 million members, you may want to work on a dimension subset for the early phases of the design cycle. Define your dimension table view with a `WHERE` clause so that it subsets the dimension to a reasonable size, iterate on the design until you're satisfied, and then redefine the view and rebuild the dimension at its full size. We can almost guarantee you'll still tweak the design a few more times, but you should be past the worst of the iterations.

We mentioned that most people use a few months of fact data. This works great for structural design tasks like setting the grain, dimension usage, and base measures for that fact data. But defining complex calculations is often easier to do with a longer time series. As a simple example, consider a measure that compares sales this month to the same month last year.

If you have really big dimensions and facts, you should take the time to build a physical subset of the relational database. Keep all small dimensions intact, but subset large dimensions to fewer than 100,000 members. Randomly choose leaf nodes rather than choose a specific branch of the dimension. In other words, if you have 5 million customers, randomly choose 100,000 of them rather than choose all of the customers from California (who may not be representative of your full customer base). Choose the subset of facts from the intersection of your dimensions. Be very careful to avoid grabbing facts for the dimension members you've excluded from the test database. In other words, load facts for the 100,000 selected customers only.

Create a Project and a Data Source View

Finally, you're ready to use the tools to get started on the design process. Create an Analysis Services project in BI Studio. By default, BI Studio points to the default instance on the local server — the developer's desktop. To specify a different Analysis Services instance or server, right-click the project name in the Solution Explorer, and choose Properties. As illustrated in Figure 8-2, you can specify several properties of the development and deployment servers.

NOTE Most DW/BI teams will use SQL Server Developer Edition, which contains all the functionality of the Data Center and Enterprise Editions. If you're using Standard Edition in production, change the Deployment Server Edition property of the project to Standard. That way, you'll get warnings if you attempt to use functionality that's not available in Standard Edition.

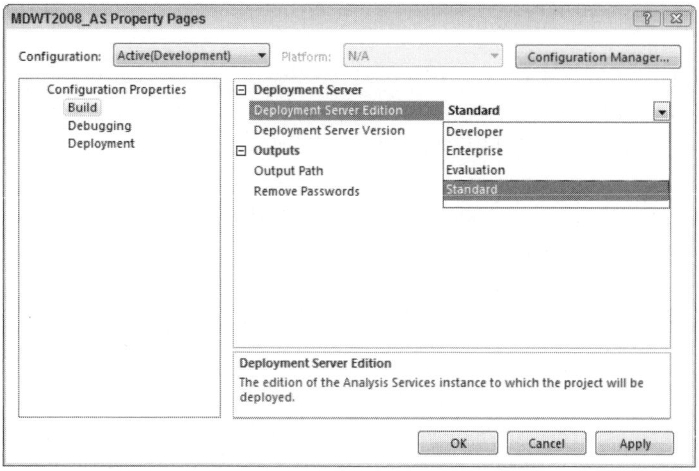

Figure 8-2: Choose the Deployment Server Edition

The next step in designing the Analysis Services database is to create a Data Source View (DSV) on the relational data warehouse database. The Analysis Services database is built from the Data Source View, so you must create a DSV before designing the database.

The DSV contains the tables that will be included in your cube. As its name implies, it is a view of your data source — in this case, the relational data warehouse database. The main activities that you will perform in the DSV are:

- Identify the subset of dimension and fact tables that will be included in the cube.

- Identify the primary key in dimension and fact tables.

- Specify foreign key relationships between fact and dimension tables, and between multiple dimension tables. These usually show up correctly if you build the DSV directly from tables, but you have to add them by hand if you build the DSV from views. This is a task that takes 20 seconds, so it's not a good enough reason to avoid using relational views.

- Rename the tables and columns, although the relational view definition is a better place to do this. Note that dimension and attribute naming should take place during the dimensional modeling step with the active involvement of key users. In general, those names should be used in the relational database and here in SSAS.

- Add computed columns, although the relational view definition is a better place to do this. The kinds of computed columns you can add in the DSV are exactly the same kinds of things you can do in the relational view definition. This is not the same thing as an Analysis Services computed measure, which we discuss later in this chapter.

NOTE There's an option on the first screen of the Data Source Wizard to create a data source based on another object. Use this option to pick up the data source from another project rather than creating a new one.

Figure 8-3 illustrates the DSV for the MDWT_2008R2 database in the DSV Designer. Use the list of tables on the left-hand side to quickly find a table.

You must construct the relationships correctly in the DSV because these relationships help define the Analysis Services database. A relationship between a fact and dimension table appears as an arrow, as you can see in Figure 8-3. Make sure you set the relationship in the correct direction.

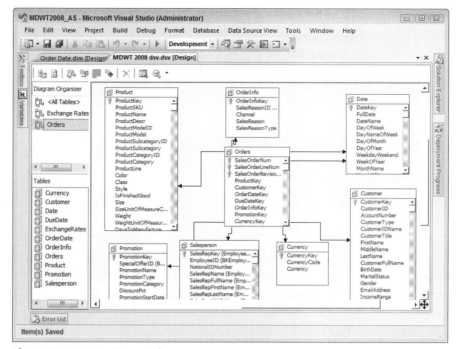

Figure 8-3: A Data Source View

WARNING Avoid using the DSV to cobble together an Analysis Services database from a variety of heterogeneous sources. First, unless you've scrubbed all the data, it's not going to join well at all. Second, there's a considerable performance cost to joining remotely. You're almost certainly better off cleaning and aligning the data and hosting it on a single physical server before building your cube. Yes: You're better off building a data warehouse.

However, if you're careful and judicious, you can use this distributed sources feature to solve some knotty problems, especially for a prototype. A distributed DSV uses the SQL Server engine under the covers to resolve the distributed query. At least one SQL Server data source must be defined in order to create a distributed DSV.

Dimension Designs

The database that you design and build in Analysis Services will be very similar to the relational data warehouse that you've built using the Kimball Method.

This section describes how Analysis Services handles dimensions in general, and how it handles several of the dimension design issues we discussed in Chapter 2.

After we've talked about how OLAP dimensions correspond to the dimension tables in your relational data warehouse, we describe the actual process of creating and editing those dimensions.

Standard Dimensions

A standard dimension contains a surrogate key, one or more attributes (columns), and usually one or more multilevel hierarchies. Analysis Services can build dimensions from dimension tables that:

- Are denormalized into a flat table structure, as the Kimball Method recommends
- Are normalized into a snowflake structure, with separate tables for each hierarchical level
- Include a mixture of normalized and denormalized structures
- Include a parent-child hierarchy
- Have all type 1 (update history) attributes, type 2 (track history) attributes, or a combination

Even though Analysis Services doesn't require a surrogate key, recall that surrogate keys are a cornerstone of the Kimball Method — build a permanent, enterprise Analysis Services database only from a dimensional relational source with surrogate keys.

Your business users will tell you whether dimension attributes should be tracked as type 1 or type 2. We've found that most dimension attributes are tracked as type 2. In Chapter 6 we talked extensively about how to set up your ETL process to manage the propagation and assignment of surrogate keys for type 2 dimension attributes. Although type 2 dimensions seem harder to manage in the ETL system, the payoff comes with your SSAS database. Analysis Services handles type 2 attribute changes gracefully. The larger your data volumes, the more you should be relying on type 2 changes, where they make sense for the business user.

Type 1 attributes can cause some problems for OLAP databases for the same reason they're troubling in the relational world: precomputed aggregations. When a dimension attribute is updated in place, any aggregations built on that attribute are invalidated. If you were managing aggregations in the relational database, you'd have to write logic to fix the historical summary tables when an attribute changes. Analysis Services faces the same problem. You don't have to perform any action to fix up the historical attributes — SSAS does that for you.

But this is an expensive operation. If you have a lot of type 1 changes in a very large database, you're going to be unpleasantly surprised by the incremental processing performance, as the system responds to your changes and rebuilds its aggregations.

Variable Depth or Parent-Child Hierarchies

Variable depth or parent-child hierarchies are a useful way of expressing organization hierarchies and bills of materials. However, these dimension structures are difficult to maintain in the relational data warehouse. This is especially true if the dimension has type 2 attributes.

If you can maintain your variable depth hierarchy in the relational database as either a type 1 or type 2 dimension, then Analysis Services can consume it. It's straightforward to set up a Parent-Child dimension in Analysis Services. It's straightforward to query that dimension — far more so in Analysis Services, by the way, than using standard SQL.

> **NOTE** Parent-Child hierarchies are a valuable feature in Analysis Services. However, it's not a trivial exercise to get them to perform well in a very large database or with many members in the Parent-Child dimension. If your system is large, you may want to bring in an expert or launch phase 1 using a standard dimension. Add the variable depth relationship when your team has developed more expertise.
>
> We usually try to avoid implementing a variable depth hierarchy in our dimensional models. Sometimes it's possible to shoehorn the variable depth hierarchy into a standard hierarchy of fixed levels, and that's our preferred approach. If that's just not possible, the SSAS Parent-Child hierarchy is the best way to store the information for consumption by the users.

When you build a Parent-Child hierarchy in Analysis Services, you don't need a bridge table, although it can improve performance for large hierarchies. You may have built a bridge table to facilitate relational queries, as described in Chapter 2. If so, you should eliminate that bridge table from the DSV for the SSAS database.

Multivalued or Many-to-Many Dimensions

A multivalued dimension has a many-to-many relationship between a dimension and the fact table, or between two dimension tables. Each row in the fact table connects to potentially many rows in the dimension table. Common examples are patient hospital visits and diagnoses (one patient visit can have multiple diagnoses), and purchase reasons (a customer can have multiple reasons for purchasing your product).

The relational design for a multivalued dimension includes a bridge table between the fact and dimension tables. This bridge table identifies a group of dimension values that occur together. The example in the Adventure Works Cycles case study is the sales reason. Adventure Works Cycles collects multiple possible reasons for a customer purchase, so each sale is associated with potentially many reasons. The bridge table lets you keep one row in the fact table for each sale, and relates that fact event to the multiple reasons.

This same structure serves to populate the Analysis Services database. The only nuance is that the bridge table is used as both a dimension table and a fact table, or as just a fact table, within Analysis Services. This seems odd at first, but it really is correct. The fact the bridge table tracks is the relationship between sales and sales reasons — you can think of it as the `Reasons Selected` fact table.

Keep the bridge table from your relational data warehouse in your DSV. The designer wizards correctly identify the structure as a multivalued dimension, which Analysis Services calls a *many-to-many dimension*.

Role-Playing Dimensions

Often a dimension plays multiple roles within the context of a fact table. For example, you may track several roles of an employee dimension, such as the sales executive and the salesperson for an account. It's quite common for the date dimension to play multiple roles in a fact table.

There are two ways to implement role-playing dimensions in Analysis Services, and neither is entirely satisfactory:

- Create one relational view corresponding to the physical dimension table, include that one view in the DSV, and create one physical dimension in Analysis Services. Use the Analysis Services role-playing dimension feature to use that single dimension many times.

  - *Advantage:* The resulting cube is more efficient, because only one physical dimension is created.

  - *Disadvantage:* Analysis Services does not let you rename columns for each role. You rename the entire dimension, but not each attribute. This may be acceptable when a user is constructing an analysis, because that user knows which dimension she's working with. But it presents serious challenges to other people looking at the same analysis or report, because the context of the dimension role is not always obvious. If you take this approach, you will need to train users to label their reports thoroughly (good luck with that).

- Create one relational view for each role, include those multiple views in the DSV, and create multiple Analysis Services dimensions.
  - *Advantage:* You can uniquely name each attribute in each role.
  - *Disadvantages:* This approach uses more system resources, which can be a significant performance drain in a complex system. Also, it substantially increases development complexity as there's no good way to keep the dimension definitions in sync.

Despite the disadvantages of the second approach, we are inclined to recommend it as the default strategy. Having two objects with the same name (such as currency name rather than local currency name and standard currency name) violates a fundamental principle of good dimensional design.

However, the Analysis Services role-playing feature should be used for the dimension that most often plays multiple roles: date. That's because you should define one and only one dimension of type Time. Having an officially designated Time dimension lets you use functions like `YearToDate` in calculations, and create measures that are semi-additive across time. Later in this chapter, we describe how to designate the date dimension as type Time.

It's a judgment call whether to treat the date dimension one way and other role-playing dimensions another, or to handle all dimensions consistently by using the SSAS role-playing feature. We dislike both alternatives.

Creating and Editing Dimensions

The process of creating a new dimension consists of two steps: run the Dimension Wizard and then edit the results. Create one dimension at a time, refining and improving it until you're satisfied. Remember, dimensions are the windows into the data. They are a key element of the user's experience, so you need to make them as clean and well formed as possible.

As you run through the Dimension Wizard, you're asked to identify the key of the dimension. You should identify the surrogate key as the key column, which SSAS does for you automatically. However, by definition the surrogate key is anonymous and is not at all useful to business users. In the Dimension Wizard, always change the surrogate key name column to something meaningful to business users, like the date as illustrated in Figure 8-4, or an account number (perhaps combined with customer name) for a customer dimension. The data warehouse surrogate key becomes the physical key in the SSAS dimension, but the user never sees it.

RUNNING THE CUBE WIZARD: THE ONE-CLICK CUBE

In most materials about Analysis Services, including Books Online and the tutorials, you're encouraged to start building your OLAP database by running the Cube Wizard after you've defined the DSV. The Cube Wizard reads the relationships you've defined in your Data Source View, and automatically generates the definition for the entire OLAP database, including all dimensions.

We've found that most people will take this route two or three times. It certainly makes a fun demo. But if you're trying to get work done, you'll probably find this alternative process more productive. Create dimensions one at a time, as we describe in the next section. Work on each dimension, setting its attributes and properties correctly, processing and browsing it until you like the way it looks. Move down the list of dimensions until you've defined all the dimensions associated with a fact table. Only then should you run the Cube Wizard.

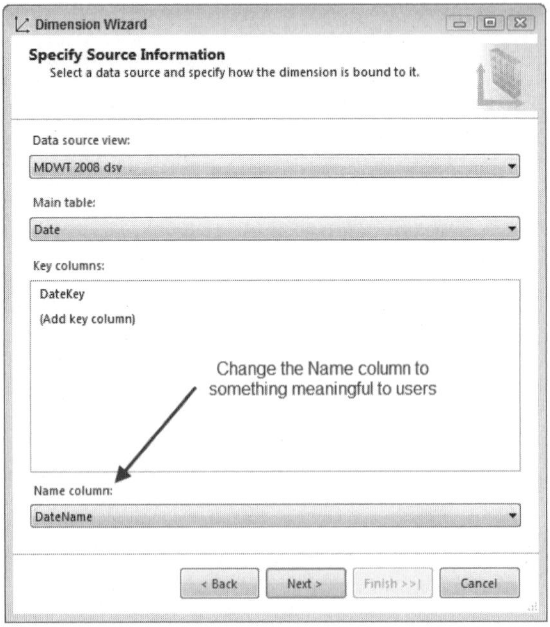

Figure 8-4: Defining the key in the Dimension Wizard

The next step of the Dimension Wizard is to identify the attributes that you want to include in the SSAS dimension. It's tempting to choose to include all attributes, but there are costs:

- Users have to locate the attributes they really want.
- Each attribute — especially those attributes that are available for users to slice and dice during analysis — uses valuable system resources.

WARNING Small databases, say less than 100 GB, can often be casual in their definition of the cube's dimensions and measures. The defaults are good enough for a wide range of scenarios. However, as the demands of your system increase — including more data, more complexity, and more users — you need to be increasingly careful of decisions that can impact performance. Pruning the list of browsable attributes is one of those decision points.

As you can see in Figure 8-5, for each column in the dimension table you have three choices in the Dimension Wizard:

- Make the column into a completely flexible attribute, which can be included in multilevel hierarchies, dragged, dropped, used in filters, and so on. Activate this option by checking "Enable browsing" for the column in the Dimension Wizard, as shown in Figure 8-5.

- Include the column as a non-drillable attribute. Users can display this non-browsable attribute in analyses, but it's not something they can use to pivot, slice, or dice. There are additional options for this type of attribute, which we discuss shortly.

- Exclude the column from the SSAS dimension.

Any of the choices you make in the Dimension Wizard can be changed later in the Dimension Designer.

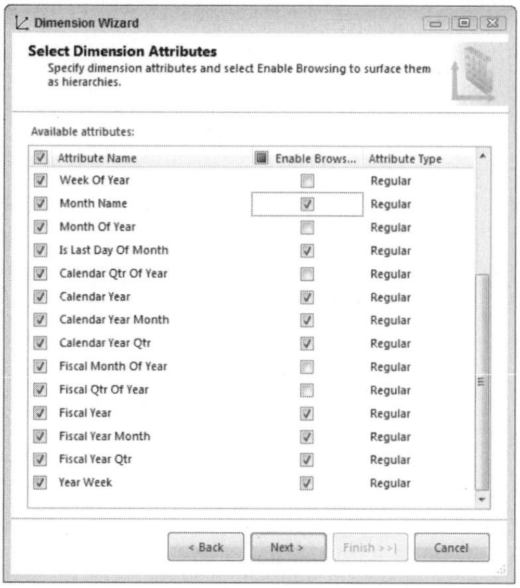

Figure 8-5: Choosing attributes in the Dimension Wizard

As you exit the Dimension Wizard, BI Studio generates the metadata for the dimension and leaves you looking at the basic dimension structure in the Dimension Designer. Next, edit your dimensions in the Dimension Designer, getting each dimension the way you like it before moving on to the next one. At this point in the process, you have only metadata — the definition of the dimension. Later we describe how you build, deploy, and process the dimension so you can actually look at the dimension's data.

Figure 8-6 shows the final version of the date dimension. In the rightmost pane of the Dimension Designer is a representation of the tables or views that underlie the dimension. This pane is linked to the Data Source View; if you try to edit the entities in this pane, you're flipped over to the DSV Editor. When you edit the DSV and return to the Dimension Designer, the changes follow.

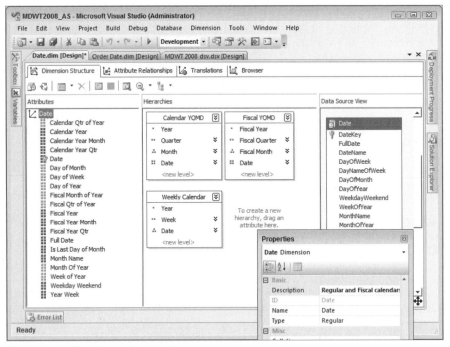

Figure 8-6: The Dimension Designer

The left-hand pane of the Dimension Designer is the Attributes pane, and shows the list of attributes within the dimension. Within the Attributes pane, you can rename and delete attributes, and change the properties of those attributes. To create a new attribute, drag a column from the data source in the DSV. You may need to create a calculated column in the DSV.

In the central pane of Figure 8-6 is the view of Hierarchies. Create a new hierarchy by dragging an attribute into the background area. Add levels to hierarchies by dragging and dropping.

The final pane in Figure 8-6 is the Properties pane, which is sometimes docked below the Solution Explorer. We set it to float in order to maximize screen real estate. Some of these properties are very important; others you might never change.

When you're editing a new dimension, take the following steps:

- Edit the name and other properties of the dimension.
- Edit the names and other properties of each attribute in the dimension.
- Create hierarchies.
- Create attribute relationships.
- If necessary, define dimension translations.
- Build, deploy, and process the dimension so you can look at the dimension's data.
- Iterate, iterate, iterate.

The order of these steps isn't very important, but it helps to have a checklist. As you can see by reviewing the preceding list, the process of editing the dimension is largely a process of editing object properties. There are only a few other design tasks, like creating attribute relationships and creating hierarchies.

In the next few sections, we'll run through the properties of dimensions, attributes, hierarchies, and levels. We'll talk only about the most important properties that you can change; see Books Online for the details. In all cases, the Properties pane shows the properties for the highlighted item. Properties that you've changed from the default values are highlighted in boldface.

Editing Dimension Properties

A dimension has several editable properties. The most important during your initial development phase are:

- *Name:* You've had many opportunities to get the dimension name right. This is your last chance.
- *Description:* Most query tools for Analysis Services have a way of showing the description to the user, usually as a tool tip. Populate the Description metadata from the information you captured as part of the dimensional modeling process step in Chapter 2.

DOWNLOADS There is no way to directly connect descriptions held in the relational database to the Description property in SSAS dimensions and attributes. SSAS orphans the descriptions collected in the Excel spreadsheet that we introduced in Chapter 2. However, there is an extremely useful tool called BIDS Helper than you can download from Codeplex (`http://bidshelper`
`.codeplex.com`). BIDS Helper extends the functionality of BI Studio (BIDS) with several dozen features. One of those features lets you copy descriptions held in SQL Server table and column extended properties, into dimension and attribute descriptions.

- *AttributeAllMemberName:* This label will show up to users when they start to drill down in the dimension and look at the highest level member of the dimension. The default name is "All."

- *ErrorConfiguration:* Analysis Services provides a lot of different options for handling problems with the dimension data, such as duplicate keys and referential integrity violations. You can see the options if you set ErrorConfiguration to (custom). If you're sourcing your dimension from a solid Kimball Method relational dimension table, as we've described in great detail in this book, you shouldn't have to worry about this property. You shouldn't have bad dimension data; shame on you if you do.

NOTE Though you shouldn't have duplicate surrogate keys — or bad data anywhere in your dimension — it's not unheard of between levels of a dimension hierarchy. For example, Postal Code should roll up to State, but in the source data there may be a handful of violations. If your ETL process doesn't catch and fix these violations, it should be modified to do so. If you change the ErrorConfiguration from its default to custom, and change the KeyDuplicate property from IgnoreError to ReportAndContinue or ReportAndStop, you'll enlist Analysis Services' help in figuring out where your data problems are. We usually turn on at least this level of error checking on dimensions.

RESOURCES See the Books Online topic "Database Dimension Properties" for a complete list and extremely brief descriptions of all the dimension properties.

Editing Attribute Properties

As with the dimension properties, most of the important properties of an attribute are set correctly by the Dimension Wizard. A few useful properties aren't set by the wizards. And if you add attributes within the Dimension Designer, you need to be aware of how to define these important attributes.

- *Name* and *Description:* Ensure these properties are set correctly, as we discussed earlier for the dimension.

- *Usage:* This property is usually set correctly by the Dimension Wizard. One attribute for the dimension can and should have its usage set as Key. This is, obviously, the surrogate key for the dimension. Almost always, the other attributes are correctly set as Regular. The exception is the parent key for a Parent-Child dimension (set to Parent).

- *NameColumn:* You have an opportunity to set the NameColumn for the Key attribute in the Dimension Wizard. If you forgot to set it there, set it here. Sometimes, you set the NameColumn for other attributes of a dimension, especially levels that you will make into a hierarchy. The Key for each attribute must be unique, but the NameColumn doesn't have to be. If you don't explicitly supply a different NameColumn, SSAS uses the Key as the name.

- *OrderBy:* You can set the default sort order for each attribute to its Key or its NameColumn. You can even define one attribute to be sorted by another attribute, as long as you've already defined an attribute relationship between the two attributes. Later in this chapter, we describe how to define relationships between attributes.

- *AttributeHierarchyEnabled:* This property can be set to True or False. If it's set to False, the user can include the attribute in a query or report, but usually cannot pivot, slice, or dice on it. You can substantially improve the performance of your cube by setting many attributes to False. Consider setting AttributeHierarchyEnabled to False for any attribute, such as an address line or product description, that's not constrained to a domain.

- *AttributeHierarchyDisplayFolder:* You can add a lot of value to your Analysis Services database by adding display folders for the Attribute Hierarchies. If you have more than 10 to 12 attributes in your dimension, you should create multiple display folders and assign attributes to them. Creating a display folder is as simple as typing a name into the attribute's AttributeHierarchyDisplayFolder property.

NOTE The usefulness of the display folder depends on the client tool you're using to access the Analysis Services database. The display folder shows up in a Report Builder Report Model that you build atop the SSAS database, and in Excel. Using display folders substantially improves the user experience.

RESOURCES See the Books Online topic "Defining Dimensional Attributes" for a complete list of attribute properties, and a terse description of each property. There are many more attribute properties than we've listed here.

Time and Account Dimensions

You may have noticed the Type property of a dimension or attribute. It's a frustratingly vague name for a property, but it's hard to think of a better name. Type is a classification of the dimension that's used by Analysis Services only in a few special cases (Time and Account). Most of the time, if you set the dimension type to anything other than Time or Account, nothing happens.

The best way to set the types correctly is to run the Add Business Intelligence Wizard. To set up Time intelligence, the wizard has you identify the core date dimension, and then specify which attribute refers to year, quarter, month, and so on. The advantage of going through this step is that you'll be able to use built-in MDX functions like `YearToDate` and `PriorPeriod`. If you have multiple physical date dimensions, run through the wizard for only one of them.

If your cube includes financial data, such as in a chart of accounts, the Add Business Intelligence Wizard will let you identify accounts as assets, liabilities, and so on.

There are about a dozen other kinds of dimension types that you can add, but Time and Account are the only ones that do anything within Analysis Services.

NOTE If you're a software developer building a packaged application on Analysis Services, you can use the dimension Type property to identify dimensions that are important to your application. You can't rely on the name because users can name the dimension whatever they want.

Creating Hierarchies

A hierarchy is a metadata relationship that defines standard drill paths in the data. Classic examples of hierarchies include calendar (day, month, year); geography (city, state, country, region); and product rollups. The dimension design should include hierarchies where appropriate, because a hierarchy will provide:

- *User navigation of the dimension.* A hierarchy is essentially a paved road for user navigation to drill up and down the data.

- *Complex calculations.* A hierarchy provides a framework for many interesting calculations and analyses, such as sales contribution to parent.

- *Improved query performance.* As we discuss in this section, SSAS leverages hierarchies to provide substantial query performance gains, by storing precomputed aggregations.

- *A framework for security.* It's common to define a security role that limits a user group to one branch of a hierarchy, such as the western region. Security is discussed in Chapter 14.

Creating multilevel hierarchies is incredibly easy. Just drag and drop attributes from the Attribute pane to the Hierarchies pane. You can create many hierarchies, or none at all.

When you first create a new hierarchy such as the standard Date-Month-Quarter-Year calendar hierarchy as shown back in Figure 8-6, you'll see a warning sign on the hierarchy. What this exclamation point is telling you is that you have not defined attribute relationships between the levels of this hierarchy.

We'll describe how to do that in the next section. Here we'll discuss when and why you need to worry about attribute relationships for hierarchies.

The hierarchy just defined, even with the exclamation point warning in place, is a valid hierarchy. Users can start at year and drill down to quarter, month, and day. Whether or not you define attribute relationships on the hierarchy doesn't affect the user experience of browsing the dimension.

What's missing is an assurance to Analysis Services that a month rolls up to one and only one quarter, and a quarter to one and only one year. That sounds kind of stupid when we're talking about the date dimension, but it's a very good example.

What if your quarter attribute took the values Q1, Q2, Q3 and month took the values Jan, Feb, Mar. This won't work! A month (Jan) always rolls up to Q1, but it rolls up to many years. You can't define the levels that way. Our sample date dimension includes attributes YearQtr (2010Q1) and YearMonth (2010-01). You have two options:

- Build key columns for hierarchical levels into your relational date dimension table or view definition. This is our recommended solution.

- Use concatenated keys for the hierarchical levels. In other words, the key of the quarter attribute is actually year and quarter. Set this up in the Key Columns property of the attribute.

If a hierarchy really does have referential integrity in place, you should declare the attribute relationships. Once you do so, that warning will go away. There are two reasons why it's important to declare attribute relationships (where they exist) between levels of a hierarchy:

- Analysis Services will build intermediate performance aggregations only within hierarchies with attribute relationships defined. Remember that performance aggregations are a cornerstone to good query performance.

- As your system grows to include fact tables at different levels of granularity, they connect correctly only if the attribute relationships are in place. For example, you have detailed transaction data at the daily level and want to hook it to planning data at the quarterly level. Analysis Services needs your guarantee that daily data rolls cleanly to monthly and quarterly.

The warning about not having attribute relationships in place is just that: a warning. You can process, browse, and deploy a hierarchy without attribute relationships defined. In some cases it makes sense to do so: if users for whatever reason want to drill down in a product dimension from color to size to manufacturing location, you can make that easy. Analysis Services still calls this a hierarchy, and no analytic tool's UI will distinguish between it and a clean, structured hierarchy.

There are a handful of little details to clean up in the new hierarchy:

- *Fix the name:* The default name generated by SSAS is quite long.

- *Add a description:* As usual.

- *Hide the non-hierarchical attributes:* When you create a multilevel hierarchy, the hierarchy's levels are still available as standalone attributes. In most cases you want to hide the standalone attribute, and force users to navigate through the hierarchy. Do this by setting the attribute's AttributeHierarchyVisible property to False.

- *Set the display order for multiple hierarchies:* A subtlety of the Dimension Designer interface is that the order in which the hierarchies are displayed in the hierarchy pane is the same order in which they'll appear in most query tools' user interfaces. You can drag and drop the hierarchies to re-order them. This isn't an official property that you can edit, except by re-ordering the hierarchies.

RESOURCES See the Books Online topic "User Hierarchy Properties" for a complete list of the properties of a multilevel hierarchy.

See the Books Online topic "Level Properties" for a complete list of the properties of hierarchy levels.

Set Up Attribute Relationships

We've already described the most important scenario for which you must set up attribute relationships: declaring referential integrity between levels of a multilevel hierarchy. Attribute relationships are also used to sort one column by another, for example month name by month number.

A careful dimension designer will think about attribute relationships for all attributes, not just those that define the level in a hierarchy or need a sort order. Think about shrunken subset dimensions — the piece of a dimension that's associated with fact tables at a higher grain, such as quarterly forecasts by brand. In Analysis Services, you don't need to create separate shrunken subset dimensions. They come "for free" when you bring in a fact table and associate it with a dimension at the appropriate grain. But you do need to tell SSAS which dimension attributes are available at a higher grain. For example, a product dimension has some attributes that are rightfully associated with the brand, such as brand manager. If you accept the default, which is to associate all attributes with the dimension key (the product SKU), then queries of quarterly sales forecasts by brand won't have access to the name of the brand manager.

All of these relationships should have been documented in your initial dimensional model design. Dig back through your documentation and spreadsheets, and take a few minutes to set up the attribute relationships correctly and completely.

It's easy to set up attribute relationships in Analysis Services 2008. Go to the Attribute Relationships tab of the Dimension Designer, as illustrated in Figure 8-7. The first time you go to the Attribute Relationships tab, Analysis Services provides a hint of where you need to fix relationships. All attributes that are used in multilevel hierarchies have been dragged up to the yellow design surface. Your job is to drag and drop (from left to right or detailed to summary), to fix up the relationships.

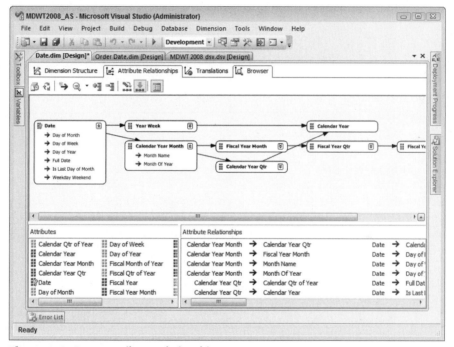

Figure 8-7: Create attribute relationships

Looking closely at 8-7, you can see that there are six attributes correctly associated with the date: if you know the date, you know the day of the month. There are three multilevel hierarchies: calendar year, quarter, month, day; calendar year, week, day; and fiscal year, quarter, month, day. The layout is a little messy, and there's nothing you can do to change it, but Figure 8-7 illustrates correctly defined attribute relationships for these three hierarchies. Several of the levels contain additional attribute relationships. The Calendar Year Month level is expanded to show the two attributes that apply to this level.

NOTE An observant reader may be surprised by the path of attribute relationships that goes day, month, fiscal month, fiscal quarter, fiscal year. Why did we put the calendar month between day and fiscal month? For Adventure Works Cycles, fiscal months directly map to calendar months; they're simply offset. If you know the calendar month, you know the fiscal month. The advantage of setting up the attribute relationships this way is that Analysis Services can create aggregations at the calendar month level, and use those same aggregations for queries along the fiscal calendar. Monthly aggregations are very common, and this one little trick substantially cuts down the number of aggregations that Analysis Services will need to build and maintain. Adding calendar month to the attribute relationships doesn't change the way the hierarchy works for the users.

By declaring attribute relationships correctly, you're informing SSAS that it can index and aggregate the data and rely on that relationship. Query performance will improve relative to a dimension whose attribute relationships are not set correctly. For medium and large data volumes, especially with very large dimensions, query performance improves substantially, largely because of improved design of aggregations that are based on the attribute relationships.

NOTE It can be tricky to define the attribute relationships correctly, but it's vital that you do so. If you've defined a relationship between two attributes, but the relationship is not truly many-to-one, problems will crop up when you process the dimension. You'll see error messages complaining about duplicate keys.
    Consider a U.S. geography hierarchy that rolls from zip code to city to state. If the city attribute is built on the city name, you'll get many duplicate key errors for the city named Riverside (46 U.S. states have a location named Riverside). You can solve this problem in several ways:

- Redesign the relational dimension to include a surrogate key for the city. The surrogate key would distinguish Riverside, CA from all the other Riversides. In SSAS, define the attribute so that the Key uses the surrogate key and the NameColumn property uses the city name. This approach is recommended if the hierarchy is defined as type 2 (tracking history).

- Redesign the dimension in Analysis Services to use state plus city as the key for the city attribute.

- Remove the attribute relationship from the hierarchy.

There is one vital property associated with a Related Attribute: RelationshipType, which can be Rigid or Flexible. RelationshipType affects how Analysis Services manages dimension changes. *Rigid* means the historical relationship is fixed. Usually this means that you're managing those attributes as type 2, and not updating history. *Flexible* means the historical relationship can change over time: Your ETL can perform updates on the hierarchical attributes. As you might expect, Flexible is the default, and this setting works well and is easy to manage for small- to medium-sized cubes.

The date dimension is an unusual example, because of course the relationship between a day, month, and year will not change over time. For the date dimension, define all attribute relationships as rigid.

If your cube is built on hundreds of gigabytes or terabytes of data, you need to pay careful attention to the settings for RelationshipType, and the aggregations that are built on attributes with flexible relationships. The issue, as we discuss later in the chapter, is about whether aggregations are dropped during incremental processing. Aggregations build really quickly, so this isn't a big deal for small cubes. But it's an important tuning consideration for large cubes.

RESOURCES See the Books Online topic "Attribute Relationships" for a description of attribute relationships.

See the Books Online topic "Attribute Relationship Properties" for a complete list of the properties of attribute relationships.

Browsing Dimension Data

The fourth tab across the top of the Dimension Designer is labeled Browser. This is where you can look at the dimension's data and hierarchies, as illustrated in Figure 8-8.

Before you browse the dimension's data, you need to process the dimension. Up to now we've been dealing at the logical level, refining the dimension's structure without reference to its data.

Later in this chapter, we talk more about building and deploying the Analysis Services database. But for the purposes of looking at a dimension whose attributes you've been editing, it's sufficient to know that you don't need to build, deploy, and process the entire database in order to look at the dimension. You can right-click the dimension in the Solution Explorer, and choose to build and deploy the changes to the project, then process the changed dimension.

Take time to look at the dimension in the browser. Look at the different hierarchies, available from the dropdown list as highlighted in Figure 8-8. Drill around the different levels and attributes in the dimension to ensure everything looks the way you want it to. It's a good bet that you'll need to adjust something. On the first time through, you're fairly likely to have to go back to your ETL team and talk about improving the cleaning of the dimension's data. You should get detailed feedback from a representative of the business user community before you decide that a dimension is correctly defined.

Keep working on your dimensions, hierarchies, and dimension data until you're pleased with them. At the very least, be sure to define the key level of each dimension correctly before moving on to the Cube Designer.

> **NOTE** It's hard to overemphasize the importance of ensuring that the dimension's data and structure are clean and make sense to the business users. The dimension attributes are used for drilling down in queries; they also show up as report column and row headers. Spend time now to get them right, or you'll be stuck with ugliness and confusion for years to come.

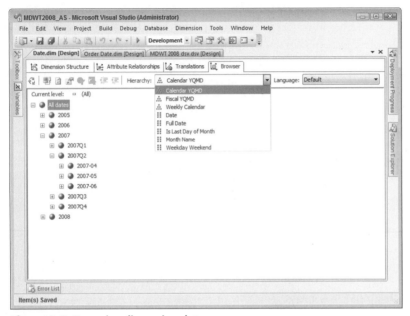

Figure 8-8: Browsing dimension data

Creating and Editing the Cube

After you've created and perfected your dimensions, it's time to run the Cube Wizard to bring in the facts and create the cube structure. As illustrated in Figure 8-9, the Cube Wizard asks you to identify the fact tables (which it, somewhat perplexingly, calls *measure group tables*). You can have it suggest fact tables for you, though you really should know which tables in your DSV are fact tables.

The Cube Wizard automatically creates a measure for each numeric non-key column in the fact table, plus a count measure. This is usually what you want. Next, the Cube Wizard identifies the existing dimensions that will be included in the new cube. Finally, it may suggest creating some new dimensions; as we discussed previously, you should have built out all your dimensions already.

Figure 8-9: Identifying fact tables in the Cube Wizard

When you finish with the Cube Wizard, you're dropped into the Cube Designer interface, illustrated in Figure 8-10. Anything you did in the Cube Wizard, you can do in the Cube Designer. You can — and will! — modify the objects that were created by the Cube Wizard. Use the Cube Designer to improve the cube, add new dimensions to a measure group, and add new measure groups.

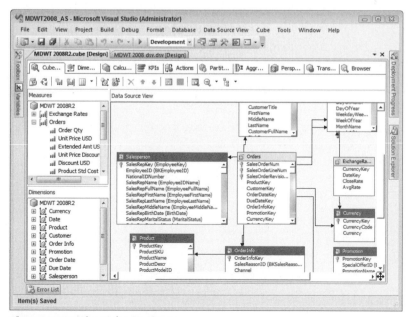

Figure 8-10: The Cube Designer

There's a lot going on in the Cube Designer, but it's organized logically. Note the tabs going across the top of the window of Figure 8-10, titled Cube Structure, Dimension Usage, and so on. We'll examine these tabs in greater depth, but first we'll quickly describe what each is for.

- *Cube Structure:* Use this tab to examine the physical layout of the cube's sources, and to modify the properties of measures. This is the active pane in Figure 8-10.

- *Dimension Usage:* Use this tab to refine the dimensionality of each measure group.

- *Calculations:* Use this tab to define, edit, and debug calculations for the cube.

- *KPIs:* Use this tab to create and edit the Key Performance Indicators (KPIs) in a cube.

- *Actions:* Use this tab to create and edit Drillthrough and other actions for the cube. Actions are a powerful mechanism for building an actionable business intelligence application that does more than just view data.

- *Partitions:* Use this tab to set up the physical storage of the measure groups. We usually accept defaults during initial development, and turn our attention to these issues later in the development cycle. Physical storage decisions are discussed later in this chapter.

- *Aggregations:* Do not use this tab during initial development. Defining and building performance aggregations are tasks for later in the development cycle.

- *Perspectives:* Use this Enterprise Edition tab to create and edit the perspectives in a cube, to provide a simplified logical view of the cube for a set of business users.

- *Translations:* Use this Enterprise Edition tab to create and edit the translated names for objects in a cube, like measures.

- *Browser:* Use this tab to look at the data in the cube, once the cube has been deployed and processed.

Edit the Cube Structure

Figure 8-10 illustrates the Cube Structure tab of the Cube Designer. In the center pane is a representation of the Data Source View of the relational tables or views on which the cube is built. This is similar to the source data pane in the Dimension Designer, but a lot more complicated because it includes all the tables used in the cube. As with the Dimension Designer, if you want to edit the Data

Source View you're flipped into the DSV Editor. Changes in the underlying DSV are reflected here immediately. In this view, fact tables are coded in yellow and dimensions in blue.

As with dimensions, the main activity in editing the cube structure consists of editing the properties of objects. In the case of the cube, edit the properties of measure groups, measures, and cube dimensions.

Edit Measure Groups and Measures

Measure group is the Analysis Services term for fact table. The small pane in the top left is where the cube's measure groups are listed. Open a measure group to see its measures. The most important properties for a measure group are the name and description. We discuss the other properties of the measure group later, in the discussion of physical design considerations. For the initial iterations of the design and development, these other settings are not very important.

The most important properties for a measure are:

- *Name*, *Description*, and *FormatString:* Ensure these are set correctly. Most Analysis Services client query tools automatically format data correctly, according to the FormatString (search Books Online for "FORMAT_STRING Contents" for more on format strings).

- *DisplayFolder:* Measures are grouped by measure group. Since each measure group can have many measures, DisplayFolders give you an extra grouping layer within a measure group. They don't exist anywhere else. You make them up by typing them in the property window.

- *AggregateFunction:* Most measures are defined to summarize by summing or counting; less frequently by distinct count, min, or max. You can also define options for semi-additive or non-additive measures: averaging, beginning of period, end of period, and so on.

> **NOTE** Perhaps you noticed that one obvious aggregate function is missing from the list: a simple average. There's an average of children, but not a simple average. The reason is that Analysis Services requires you to explicitly define how the average is computed: the numerator is a simple sum, and the denominator is some kind of count. You need to create a calculated measure to present a measure that aggregates by averaging. We usually change the name of the measure we want to average and set its visibility property to False. Then we create a new calculated measure with the correct name, as you'll see later in this chapter in the section "The Calculations Tab," with Unit Price USD.

- *Visible:* It's surprisingly common to hide a measure. Many measures are used for calculations but aren't very interesting on their own. Hiding them reduces clutter for the business users.

Edit Dimensions in the Cube

The small pane in the lower left is where the cube's dimensions are listed. You can launch the Dimension Editor from here or from the Solution Explorer as we discussed earlier.

The primary editing activity in the Dimensions pane of the Cube Structure tab is to add a new dimension or to re-order dimensions. The order of the dimensions in the cube, as they appear in this pane, is the same as they'll show up to the users. Put the obscure dimensions at the bottom!

> **NOTE** There is a second implication of the order of the dimensions in this list, which is vital if you have complex calculations. The order of dimensions in this list affects the application of dimension calculations, like unary operators. This is particularly important for a financial model, where you might allocate along one dimension before calculating along a second dimension (usually the account dimension). You can see this in the Adventure Works DW 2008 Analysis Services database. The organizations dimension in that database must be listed before the accounts dimension for the calculations to work properly. Try reordering the dimensions and recalculating the measure group to see how important the ordering is.

Dimensions are defined first at the database level, then optionally added to the cube. As we discussed earlier in this chapter, most cubes correspond roughly to a business process dimensional model, and contain between 5 and 15 fact tables or measure groups. If you add new dimensions to your database after your initial run through the Cube Wizard, you may need to add them to your cube as well. Do so here.

The properties of a cube dimension that you might edit are:

- *Name:* The dimension name as created in the database is usually the correct name. The only time you're likely to want to edit the name of the dimension in the cube is if the dimension has multiple roles. This is very common with the Date dimension: Order Date, Due Date, Ship Date, and so on are different roles of the Date dimension.

- *Description:* Similarly, adjust the Description property for dimension roles.

You can also edit the properties of the hierarchy of a cube dimension, and attributes of a cube dimension. It's unlikely that you'd want to do this.

Cube Properties

There are a few properties of the cube that you might want to adjust during development. You can see the list of these properties by clicking the cube in either the Measures or Dimensions panes of the Cube Structure tab.

- *Name* and *Description:* Edit the cube's name and description as appropriate.

■ *DefaultMeasure:* One measure will come up by default, if users don't specify a measure in a query. You should choose which measure that is, rather than letting Analysis Services choose it for you.

Most of the other options have to do with physical storage and processing, and are discussed later in the chapter. During the first part of the development cycle, the defaults are usually fine.

Edit Dimension Usage

You specify exactly how dimensions participate in measure groups on the next tab of the Cube Designer. Figure 8-11 illustrates the Dimension Usage tab for the MDWT_2008R2 sample cube. Our simplification of the Adventure Works schema presents a simple display. To see a more realistic display of dimension usage, check out the Adventure Works DW 2008 sample Analysis Services database that you can download from CodePlex.

The Dimension Usage tab's summarization is very similar to the Kimball Method bus matrix with the rows and columns flipped. At a glance you can identify which dimensions participate in which measure groups, and at which level of granularity.

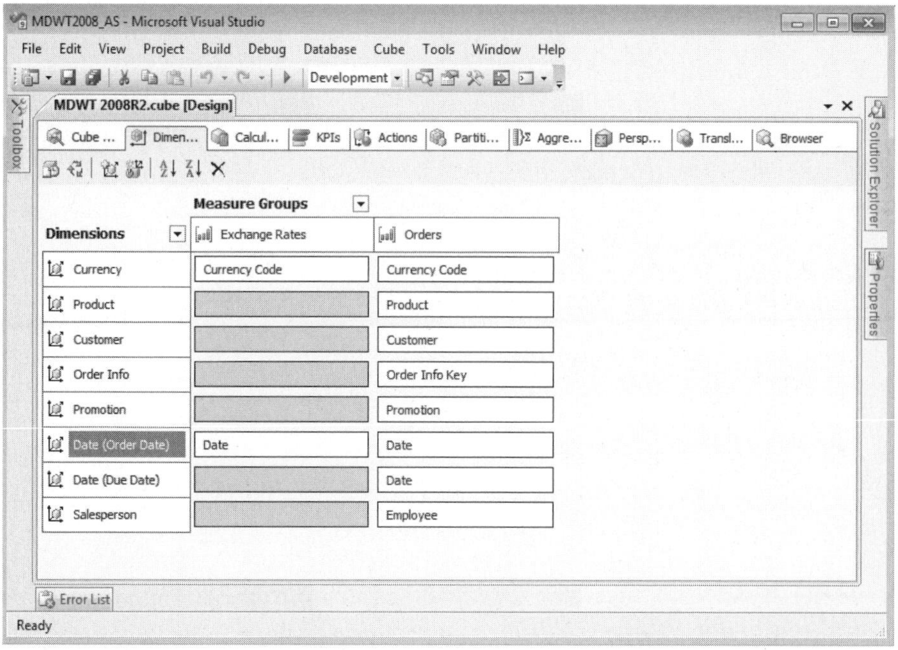

Figure 8-11: Dimension usage

The dimensionality of the Orders measure group displayed in Figure 8-11 has been modified from the defaults generated by the Cube Wizard. There are three date keys in the two fact tables, each with a different name. Originally, Analysis Services defined three roles for the date dimension: date from the Exchange Rates measure group, and order date and due date from the Orders measure group. However, the business users think of the order date as the main date key. Therefore, we deleted the order date role, and reassigned the OrderDateKey to the main date role, using the Define Relationship window shown in Figure 8-12.

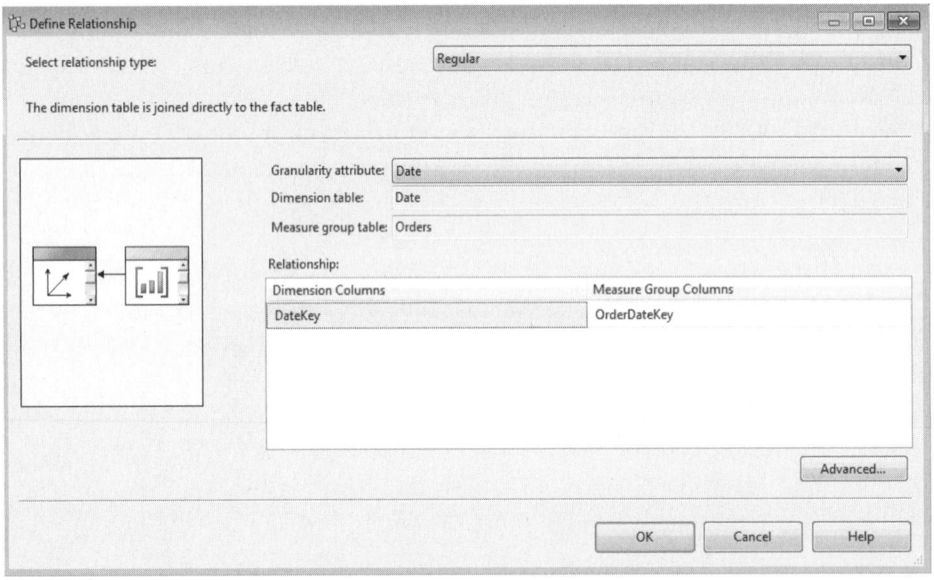

Figure 8-12: Define the relationship between a fact table and a dimension

Measure Groups at Different Granularity

Measure groups, and their underlying relational fact tables, may hook into a conformed dimension at a summary level. The most common scenario is for forecasts and quotas. Most businesses develop forecasts quarterly or monthly, even if they track sales on a daily basis. The fundamentals of dimensional modeling tell you to conform the date dimension across uses, even if those uses are at different grains. By re-using the dimension, you're making it easy to compare quarterly data from multiple measure groups.

Analysis Services makes this conformation easy for you. All you have to do is correctly define the granularity attribute in the Define Relationship dialog box. Make sure you set the attribute relationships properly in any dimension for which some measure groups join in at a coarser grain.

WARNING It's absolutely critical to set the attribute relationships properly in any dimension that's used at multiple granularities. You need to inform Analysis Services that it can expect referential integrity between various attributes in the dimension. If you aren't careful here, you can see inconsistent query results because aggregations are computed and stored incorrectly.

Complex Relationships Between Dimensions and Measure Groups

There are several kinds of relationships between dimensions and measure groups, which you can set in the Dimension Usage tab. Most dimension relationships are Regular, but you can also specify Fact, Reference, Data Mining, and Many-to-Many relationships here.

The Cube Wizard does a good job of setting up these relationships correctly, but you should always check them.

Build, Deploy, and Process the Project

At this point in the development cycle, you've worked on your dimensions, and you've built and processed them several times. You've defined the basic structure of your cube, including the relationships between measure groups and dimensions.

Now is a good time to perform the first processing of the OLAP database. The easiest way to do this is to right-click the project name in the Solution Explorer and choose Process. By choosing Process, you're doing three things:

- Building the project, looking for structural errors.
- Deploying that project to the target Analysis Services server, creating a new database structure (or updating an existing database structure).
- Processing that database, to fully or incrementally add data.

The last tab of the Cube Designer is where you browse the data in the SSAS database. You don't need to work through all the other tabs before you take a look at the data. After you've defined the basic cube structure and verified the relationships with the dimensions, you generally want to check your work.

As we described earlier when talking about browsing the dimensions, you need to build, deploy, and process the cube before you can browse the data. The browser tab will remind you to do that if necessary.

Earlier in this chapter, we talked about starting your Analysis Services development against a much reduced data set. As you process the cube for the umpteenth time to check the implications of an edit, you'll recognize why this was a good idea.

Create Calculations

The third tab of the Cube Designer is where you'll create calculations using the Multidimensional Expression language, or MDX. Most BI teams we've worked with have resisted learning MDX as long as they can. No one wants to learn a new language, but all eventually agree that at least one person on the team needs to step up to this challenge. The good news is that the BI Studio tools include wizards to help you define common calculations. And you can learn a lot about MDX by looking at how these calculations are defined for you.

You have opportunities to sprinkle MDX throughout the definition of the cube. The most obvious place is here, on the Calculations tab, where you can create calculated measures, other calculated members, sets, and calculated sub-cubes. You'll greatly improve the usefulness and user-friendliness of your Analysis Services database by defining common calculations that benefit all business users regardless of how they're accessing the cube.

- Calculated measures will show up under the Measures dimension. Many calculated measures are quite simple, like the sum or ratio of two other measures. To a business user browsing the cube, calculated measures are largely indistinguishable from physical measures. Some query tools, including the Cube Browser integrated with BI Studio, will show a different icon for calculated measures and physical measures. A calculated measure is really just a calculated member, assigned to the Measures dimension. A very complex calculated measure may perform less well than a physical measure because calculations are performed at runtime.

- Calculated members can be created on any dimension. Non-measure calculated members can be very powerful. They're a way to create a kind of calculation that applies for some or all measures. For example, you can create a calculated member Year To Date on the Date dimension, to automatically calculate multiple measures year-to-date.

> **NOTE**   The Add Business Intelligence Wizard will create a wide variety of calculations for you, including the Year To Date calculated member.

- Named sets are a set of dimension members. A really simple named set would specify the set explicitly, perhaps as a list of important products. More complicated set definitions locate the set of products with a high price, products that sold well this year, and so on.

- Calculated sub-cubes are a way to calculate an arbitrary portion of the cube's data and summarizations. A common use of calculated sub-cubes is to allocate summary data (like monthly quotas) down to more fine-grained data. Or, calculated sub-cubes can provide a complex summarization method, if your business rules are more complicated than can be supported by the standard aggregate functions.

NOTE How do you know whether you need a calculated member or a calculated sub-cube? A calculated member changes the visible structure of the cube; you can see the calculated member in the list of dimension members. A calculated sub-cube doesn't change the list of members or attributes in a dimension. Instead, it changes the way the numbers inside the cube are calculated.

The Calculations Tab

The Calculations tab of the Cube Designer is illustrated in Figure 8-13. As you can see, this is another complicated screen. But let's face it: Calculations are complicated.

In the upper left is the Script Organizer. This pane lists the calculations that have been defined for this cube. The selected calculation is a calculated measure called [Unit Price USD], which calculates unit price as an average. Recall from earlier in this chapter that there is no standard aggregation method for a simple average: if you want to display an average, you need to create a calculation. The main area of the Calculations tab shows a form where this calculation is defined. The lower-left pane contains three tabs that show a list of objects in the cube; a list of available functions, which you can drag into your calculation; or a set of templates, which can provide a starting point for some kinds of calculations.

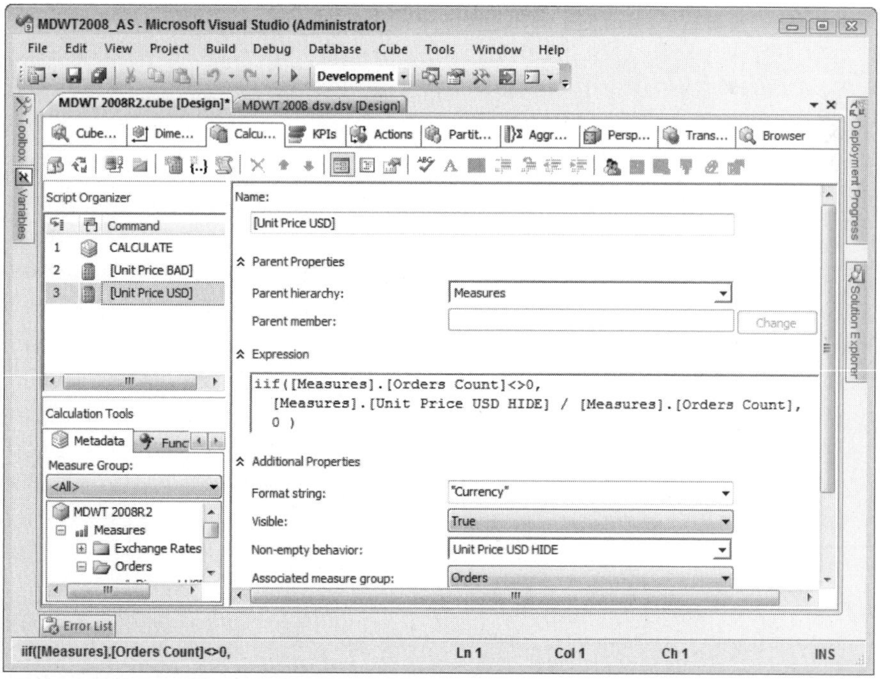

Figure 8-13: The Calculations tab

This calculated member is defined on the Measures dimension; it's a calculated measure. The next area contains the MDX for the calculation. Even if you don't know anything about MDX, you can probably parse this statement:

- If the denominator — [Orders Count] — is not zero, return [Unit Price USD HIDE], which aggregates as a sum, divided by [Orders Count], which aggregates as a count.

- Otherwise, the denominator — [Orders Count] — is zero, so return zero.

There are several important properties of a calculated member:

- *Description:* It's possible to set the description of a calculated member, but they sure don't make it easy to find. It's on a different screen entirely, called Calculation Properties, that you can launch from a toolbar icon.

- *Format string* and *Visible:* The same as for physical measures.

- *Non-empty behavior:* You should always set this to one or a few items in the calculation. What you're telling Analysis Services by setting this property is that if the base measure ([Unit Price USD HIDE] in this case) is empty, don't spend any time calculating the measure.

> **WARNING** Always set the non-empty behavior property. It can make a huge difference in the query performance of your calculated measures. In one case, we saw query performance drop from hours to seconds, simply by filling in the non-empty behavior property.

- *Associated measure group* and *Display folder:* These settings are largely cosmetic, but can make it much easier for users to find the measures you've so painstakingly created.

The calculation form view shown in the Calculation tab is a good way to create new measures and named sets. It is an item-by-item form that builds an underlying script. If you want to look at the entire script, switch to the script view by choosing Cube ➢ Show Calculations in Script (or click the Script toolbar icon).

Let's take a look at the MDX for a second calculation: [Contribution to Parent Product]. Wherever you are in the product hierarchy, whether at the category, subcategory, or product level, calculate the current member's contribution to the sales of the parent. If you're at the product category level it's your sales divided by all sales, at the subcategory level it's those sales divided by all sales for this category, and so on. The MDX for this calculation is:

```
Case
  When [Product].[Product Categories].CurrentMember IS
          [Product].[Product Categories].[All Products]
  Then 1

  Else [Measures].[Sales Amt USD] /
```

```
    ( [Product].[Product Categories].CurrentMember.Parent,
         [Measures].[Sales Amt USD] )
End
```

This may not be clear to someone new to MDX, but it's fairly straightforward:

- If you're at the "all" level of the product dimension, return 1.
- Otherwise, wherever you are in the product category hierarchy, return the ratio of your sales divided by your parent's sales.

You can get an idea of how the calculation works by viewing the browser output in Figure 8-14.

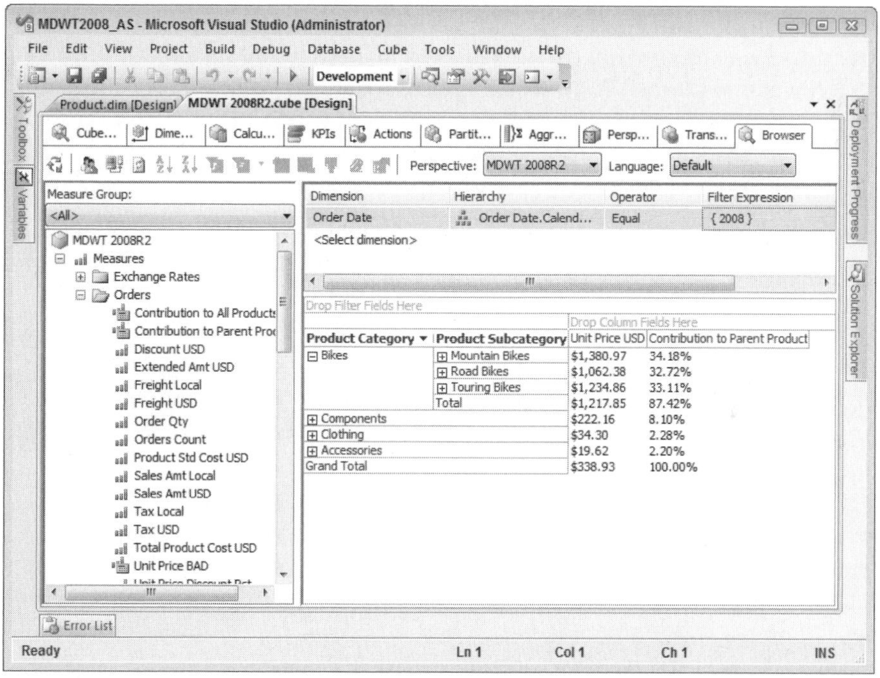

Figure 8-14: Browsing a cube to examine calculated members

NOTE If you find yourself defining lots of similar calculations, like [Product Contribution to Subcategory] and [Subcategory Contribution to Category], you should step back and figure out how to generalize. Probably you really need a single calculation that computes relative to the current position in the cube — a far more elegant solution.

RESOURCES Like so much we've introduced, Calculations and MDX are rich and complex topics about which entire books are written. We've barely scratched the surface here.

The first place to go for help is the excellent section on Calculations in the SQL Server Analysis Services tutorial. This tutorial walks you through the process of creating several calculated members, named sets, and calculated subcubes. The tutorial shows you how to debug your Calculation Script by setting breakpoints, stepping through calculations, and watching how each step modifies the cube's structure and data.

The debugger is a great feature. Learn how to use it, especially if you have any MDX scripts. The debugger is absolutely vital if you have multiple calculations that overlap one another.

The MDWT_2008R2 database is available on the book's website (`http://kimballgroup.com/html/booksMDWTtools.html`). It contains a handful of calculated members and sets, for the same simplified version of the Adventure Works case study that we've used throughout this book.

The Adventure Works DW 2008 SSAS database that's available on CodePlex is a good learning tool for MDX and calculating. It contains a lot of fairly complex calculations, especially for the finance module.

There are several books that the MDX expert on your team should own:

- *SQL Server 2008 MDX Step by Step* by Smith and Clay (Microsoft, 2009). This is probably the best place to start if you need to learn MDX. Like other books in the Step by Step series, it's practically an extended class or tutorial.

- *MDX Solutions* by Spofford, Harinath, Webb, Huang, and Civardi (Wiley, 2006). Make sure you get the edition for Analysis Services 2005 and Hyperion Essbase. MDX has not changed substantially since SQL Server 2005, and the reference is still up-to-date.

- *Professional SQL Server Analysis Services 2008 with MDX* by Harinath, Zare, Meenakshisundaram, and Quinn (Wrox, 2009). This book covers a lot more than MDX.

Adding Business Intelligence

Unless you're already an MDX expert, one of the best ways to get started in adding calculations to your cube is by using the Business Intelligence Wizard. This wizard will build for you the most common kinds of calculations. You can launch the Business Intelligence Wizard in several ways, including from the leftmost icon on the toolbar in the Calculations tab.

Most application developers will use the Business Intelligence Wizard to add "time intelligence" to their cube. This wizard option will automatically create for you calculations like [Year to Date], [12 Month Moving Average], and so on. These calculations appear on the Date dimension. They're non-measure calculated members. As such, they can apply to multiple underlying measures in one fell swoop.

A second advantage of the Business Intelligence Wizard is that you can pick apart the calculations to learn how they were done.

Define Key Performance Indicators

Key Performance Indicators (KPIs) are numbers or displays that are intended to measure the health of the organization. When KPIs are based on a clear understanding of the factors that drive the business, and a robust DW/BI platform, they can be an extremely powerful organizational management tool. Unfortunately, most KPIs are either brain-dead simple, divorced from the underlying data, or both. Really, who cares that sales are down 0.1 percent today unless we know that today is a Friday and Friday's sales are usually up 0.1 percent? And even if we did know the context, simply telling the executive that sales are down doesn't provide any understanding about why.

We hope that the definition and display of KPIs with Analysis Services will help address these shortcomings. The KPI implementation is well thought out. Because KPIs are defined in the cube, the supporting data can be made available in useful ways.

Any KPIs you create should be defined as part of the BI Applications track based on the business requirements and with business user involvement. Do not try and make them up here on the fly.

Analysis Services defines a KPI on the KPIs tab of the Cube Designer:

- *Name of the KPI:* And the measure group with which the KPI is associated.

- *Value to be measured:* The underlying measure for the KPI. Most often you'll use a calculated measure that you've already defined. You can enter an MDX expression here, but it usually makes more sense to create a calculated measure and use that. In the very simple example we used in this section, the value to be measured might be [Sales Revenue].

> **NOTE** Whenever you specify an MDX expression when you create a KPI, the server will create a hidden calculated measure.

- *Goal for the value:* An MDX expression that defines the target for the measure. A trivial goal would be a number: The sales target is $100,000. That would give a stupid KPI. More interesting would be a goal to increase sales 0.1 percent from the same day the previous week, or a goal that's based on sales quotas. Often, targets are defined and stored as their own measure group within the cube. The KPI goal is then a simple reference to the appropriate measure within the sales target measure group.

- *Status:* A graphic and an MDX expression that describe how the value to be measured is doing relative to its goal. Analysis Services provides several built-in graphic gauges, including thermometers, traffic lights, and happy faces. The MDX expression needs to evaluate to numbers between −1 (very bad) to +1 (very good). If you're clever about defining the status expression, you can do a good job of conveying important information about wide deviations from the goal, and keep minor deviations quiet.

- *Trend:* A graphic and an MDX expression that describe whether the value to be measured is moving toward or away from its goal. Is the situation getting better or worse? As with the status graphic, Analysis Services provides a few built-in trend graphics, notably a trend arrow. The MDX expression must evaluate to numbers between −1 (going south in a hurry) and +1 (getting better fast).

To display your KPIs, you need some client software that understands KPIs. Microsoft's current versions of Excel, Reporting Services, and SharePoint are able to work with Analysis Services KPIs. Software vendors who sell packaged analytics on Analysis Services often use KPIs extensively in their front ends.

NOTE Excel, Reporting Services, and SharePoint all do a very nice job of displaying KPIs that are defined in the cube. There is SharePoint functionality that lets power users define and modify KPIs while working in the BI portal. The functionality to play "what if" scenarios with SharePoint KPIs does not write those KPIs back to the Analysis Services database.

Create Actions

The next tab in the Cube Designer is the Action tab. An Analysis Services *Action* is a command that's stored on the server. Actions are defined using MDX, which means that the command is context-sensitive. In other words, you can define an Action that executes when the user right-clicks a cell in a report. The Action knows the values of each of the dimensions that make up the address of the cell and can execute a customized command for that address.

Like KPIs, the server-side definition of an Action is only half of the solution. You need a client tool that implements Actions. It's the job of the query tool to intercept the "right-click" on a report cell, and present (and execute) the appropriate list of Actions. Luckily the most common query tool, Excel, does implement Actions.

The most obvious use of an Action is to execute a relational query. As we've already described, Analysis Services databases are often built at the same grain as the underlying dimensional model. An interesting BI application can include an Action that drills back to enterprise data, perhaps even back to the original transaction system. This query Action can easily be implemented as an Action that launches a Reporting Services report.

Analysis Services provides for several kinds of Actions including:

- Execute a Reporting Services report.
- Execute a generic Action. Actions can bring up a URL, return a rowset or data set, or execute a command. An Action is defined as an MDX statement, and can be attached to specific parts of the cube. For example, you can have one Action that executes when someone right-clicks the Month label in the Date dimension, and a second Action that launches when someone right-clicks a data cell.

WARNING Two kinds of Actions — HTML scripts and Command Line Actions — pose security risks and should be avoided. Microsoft has moved these Action types out of the BI Studio interface. You'd have to create the Action by writing a script without the benefit of the UI.

Under the covers, the Drillthrough Action is simply a kind of rowset Action that's common enough that Microsoft built a simple user interface for defining it. Similarly, the Report Action is just an instance of a URL Action.

Drillthrough and Reporting Services Actions are very easy to set up. Generic Actions, like launching a parameterized web page, are pretty tricky. Start with something really simple, like launching a static web page (like Google or MSN). Add complexity a bit at a time. Process the cube and try out the Action in the browser window before adding another layer of complexity. If you change only an Action definition between processing, the processing step refreshes only metadata (not data), so processing occurs quickly.

Partitions and Aggregations

Partitioning allows you to break up a large cube into smaller subsets for easier management, much like relational partitioning. You can use the Partitions and Aggregations tabs of the Cube Designer to define the physical storage characteristics of your cube. During the first part of your development cycle, don't bother with these tabs. Use the default settings so you can focus on getting the cube structure and calculations correct.

In the next section of this chapter, we discuss physical design considerations. We talk at some length about what's going on under the covers, so you can make informed decisions about how to deploy your Analysis Services database in production.

Maintain Perspectives

An Analysis Services Perspective limits a user's view to a set of related measure groups and dimensions. A Perspective is analogous to a business process dimensional model in the Kimball Method vocabulary. It's a very nice approach because you're not replicating data into multiple cubes. You're simply providing different users with different views of the same data.

You'll almost certainly define a few Perspectives if you follow the best practice recommendation of creating a large Analysis Services cube that contains multiple measure groups. Unless your implementation is really simple, this single-cube approach will lead to a structure that's challenging for business users to navigate. Remember, though, the advantage of many measure groups (fact tables) in a cube is that it's easy for users to construct analyses that combine data from those fact tables — which is the whole point of conformed dimensions and the bus architecture.

Use the Perspectives tab of the Cube Designer to define your cube's Perspectives. You can create as many Perspectives as you like; it's a simple matter of choosing which portions of the overall cube to hide in each Perspective. You can also specify which measure is shown by default in each Perspective.

Most users will use only a few Perspectives, rather than the entire cube containing all measure groups. You can hide the cube itself by setting its `Visible` property to False, and reveal only the Perspectives that contain the information your user communities are interested in.

It may feel as though Perspectives are a security mechanism. Not so! As we discuss in Chapter 14, Analysis Services security is applied at the database object level.

NOTE Unfortunately, Perspectives are not available in SQL Server Standard Edition. Many organizations don't have the users or data volumes needed to justify Enterprise Edition or Data Center Edition, but almost all organizations can benefit from Perspectives.

Translations

Translations are a very nice feature of Analysis Services Enterprise and Data Center Editions. If your company is multinational, business users will probably prefer to view the cube in their native languages. A fully translated cube will have translations for its metadata (names and descriptions of dimensions, attributes, hierarchies, levels, and measures) as well as the dimension data itself (member names and attribute values). In other words, the dimension name Date needs to be translated, the attribute name Month, and the attribute values January, February, and so on.

The translations for the metadata occur in two places: in the Translations tab of the Dimension Designer and the Translations tab of the Cube Designer. You can create translations in multiple languages.

If you want to translate the dimension attribute values, your relational dimension table or view needs to have additional columns for the new languages. These don't become additional attributes in the Analysis Services dimension; instead you can set them up as the translation content in the dimension Translations tab.

NOTE Be very careful when you are setting up the translations, especially translations of the dimension attribute values. If you make a mistake in the translation, users of different languages will find it very difficult to construct comparable reports.

When you use the Browser tab to browse the data, you can view the data in different languages. This is fun to do, and if your organization is multilingual, it is certainly worth including in any demos you create for senior management. The Adventure Works DW 2008 sample database includes a rich set of translations.

The Translation feature works really well. It leverages the localization technology in all Microsoft products. It picks up the locale ID from the user's desktop and automatically displays either the appropriate translation, if it exists, or the default language. Most client tools don't need to do anything special.

Designing the Analysis Services cube is generally straightforward if you're starting from a clean, dimensionally structured relational data warehouse. In most cases, the only hard part is defining the calculations. Someone on the DW/BI team is going to have to learn MDX for that. But most concepts translate very smoothly from the relational dimensional database into Analysis Services. When we've seen people struggle with designing their cubes, it's usually because they're trying to build the cube from a faulty dimensional design.

Physical Design Considerations

Up to this point in this chapter, we have discussed the logical design process for the Analysis Services OLAP database. We recommend that you work with a small subset of data so that you can concentrate on the structure, calculations, and other cube decorations, without worrying about the physical design.

Now it's time to address the physical issues. Most of the time, physical implementation decisions are made independently of the logical design. That's not completely true, and in this section, we discuss how some design decisions can have a large impact on the manageability and performance of your cube.

CUBE PHYSICAL STORAGE TERMINOLOGY

Readers who are familiar with older versions of Analysis Services will already be familiar with the terminology for the physical storage and processing of the Analysis Services database. This sidebar merely defines these concepts. Recommendations and implications are discussed in detail elsewhere in the chapter.

- *Leaf data:* Leaf data is the finest grain of data that's defined in the cube's measure group. Usually, the leaf data corresponds exactly to the fact table from which a cube's measure group is sourced. Occasionally you'll define a measure group at a higher grain than the underlying fact table, for example by eliminating a dimension from the measure group.

- *Aggregations:* Precomputed aggregations are analogous to summary tables in the relational database. You can think of them as a big SELECT ... GROUP BY statement whose result set is stored for rapid access.

- *Data storage mode:* Analysis Services supports three kinds of storage for data:
  - *MOLAP (Multidimensional OLAP):* Leaf data and aggregations are stored in Analysis Services' MOLAP format.
  - *ROLAP (Relational OLAP):* Leaf data and aggregations are stored in the source relational database.
  - *HOLAP (Hybrid OLAP):* Leaf data is stored in the relational database, and aggregations are stored in MOLAP format.

- *Dimension storage mode:* Dimension data, corresponding to the relational dimension tables, can be stored in MOLAP format or left in the relational database (ROLAP mode).

- *Partition:* Fact data can be divided into partitions. Most systems that partition their data do so along the Date dimension; for example, one partition for each month or year. You can partition along any dimension, or along multiple dimensions. The partition is the unit of work for fact processing. Partitions are a feature of SQL Server Enterprise and Data Center Editions.

- *Fact processing:* Analysis Services supports several kinds of fact processing for a partition:
  - *Full processing:* All the data for the partition is pulled from the source system into the Analysis Services engine, and written in MOLAP format if requested. Aggregations are computed and stored in MOLAP format if requested, or back in the RDBMS (ROLAP mode).
  - *Incremental processing:* New data for the partition is pulled from the source system and stored in MOLAP if requested. Aggregations — either MOLAP or ROLAP — are updated. It's your job to tell Analysis Services how to identify new data.
  - *Proactive caching:* Proactive caching is a mechanism for automatically pushing data into a cube partition. When you set up proactive caching, you're asking SSAS to monitor the relational source for the measure group's partition and to automatically perform incremental processing when it sees changes.

Understanding Storage Modes

The first question to resolve in your physical design is the easiest one. Should you use MOLAP, HOLAP, or ROLAP mode to store your Analysis Services data? The answer is MOLAP.

We're not even being particularly facetious with this terse answer, but we will justify it a bit.

Analysis Services MOLAP format has been designed to hold dimensional data. It uses sophisticated compression and indexing technologies to deliver excellent query performance. All else being equal, query performance against a MOLAP store is significantly faster than against a HOLAP or ROLAP store.

Some people argue that MOLAP storage wastes disk space. You've already copied data at least once to store it in the relational data warehouse. Now you're talking about copying it again for the cube storage. To this argument we reply that a relational index also copies data. No one asserts you shouldn't index your relational database.

MOLAP storage is highly efficient. The 20 percent rule says that leaf data in MOLAP mode (data and indexes) tends to require about 20 percent of the storage of the uncompressed relational source (data only, no indexes). The MOLAP store of the leaf data is probably smaller than a single relational index on the fact table — and buys a lot more for you than any single relational index can possibly do.

Another common argument against MOLAP is that it slows processing. ROLAP is always the slowest to process because writing the aggregations to the relational database is expensive. HOLAP is slightly faster to process than MOLAP, but the difference is surprisingly small.

Dimensions also can be stored in MOLAP or ROLAP mode. Use MOLAP.

> **NOTE** Why does Microsoft offer these alternative storage modes, if they're inferior to MOLAP storage? The main answer is marketing: It's been an effective strategy to get Analysis Services into companies that would never countenance an instance of the SQL Server relational database in their data center. The multiple storage modes make the initial sale. Often, the DW/BI team figures out how much faster MOLAP is, and convinces management that it's okay. It's also a hedge against the future. It's possible that improvements to relational technology can make HOLAP or ROLAP storage more appealing. Certainly we'd love to see Analysis Services' indexing, aggregation, compression, and processing abilities integrated into the SQL Server RDBMS, as does appear to be happening.

In Chapter 9 we back off slightly from the strong recommendation to use MOLAP in situations where you have a compelling business need for near-zero data latency. In this case, you may set up a ROLAP partition for data for the current hour or day.

Developing the Partitioning Plan

You can define multiple partitions for a measure group. Multiple partitions are a feature of SQL Server Enterprise Edition, and are very important for good query and processing performance for large Analysis Services measure groups. If you have a measure group with more than 50 million rows, you probably should be using partitioning.

Partitioning is vital for large measure groups because partitions can greatly help query performance. The Analysis Services query engine can selectively query partitions: It's smart enough to access only the partitions that contain the data requested in a query. This difference can be substantial for a cube built on, say, a billion rows of data.

The second reason partitioning is valuable is for management of a large cube. It's faster to add a day's worth of fact data to a small partition than to incrementally process that same day of data into a huge partition that contains all of history. With a small partition for current data, you have many more options to easily support real-time data delivery.

Partitioning also makes it possible — even easy! — to set up your measure group to support a rolling window of data. For example, your users may want to keep only 90 days of detailed data live in the cube. With a partitioned measure group, you simply drop the dated partitions. With a single partition, you have no option for deleting data other than reprocessing the entire measure group.

If your ETL performs updates or deletes on fact table rows, partitioning is important for good processing performance. Recall from Chapter 7 that the only way to process an update or delete to a fact row is to fully process the partition that contains that row. This means that even if only one fact row in a measure group is updated, the entire partition that contains that fact must be fully processed. If you have a large fact table that requires many updates, SSAS partitions are a necessity.

Partitioning improves processing performance, especially for full processing of the measure group. Analysis Services automatically processes partitions in parallel.

The largest measure groups, containing hundreds of millions or even billions of rows, should be partitioned along multiple dimensions — say by month and product category. More partitions are better for both query and processing performance, but at the cost of making your maintenance application more complicated.

NOTE If you've defined a lot of partitions, say a thousand, Management Studio will be slow. It'll take a few minutes to populate the lists of database objects.

NOTE You can always set up partitioning on your development server because SQL Server Developer Edition contains all the functionality in Data Center Edition. But those partitions won't work on your production server if you use Standard Edition in production. As we described previously in this chapter, be sure to set the project's Deployment Server Edition property, so Analysis Services can help you avoid features that won't work in production.

There are two ways to define multiple partitions:

- Create multiple relational views, one for each partition. You can use multiple physical fact tables, but most people want an integrated relational fact table.

- Define a WHERE clause in the SSAS source query for each partition, limiting each partition to the appropriate range in the single fact table. This is our recommended approach, as the alternative leads to a large number of otherwise useless relational views.

Every measure group initially has one partition. To create additional partitions, you first need to explicitly change the scope of the original partition. Whether in BIDS or Management Studio, change the binding type on the original partition from Table Binding to Query Binding. Then you can add the WHERE clause. For a cube that's partitioned by date, we usually change the WHERE clause on the first partition to span the period before the data in the fact table begins. In effect, it becomes an empty partition, there as a safeguard in case you unexpectedly get old data.

WARNING When you convert the original partition from Table Binding to Query Binding, you break its connection to the table in the Data Source View. If you modify the fact table structure in the DSV, you will need to remember to come into each partition and adjust the source query appropriately. This is yet another reason you should wait until the logical cube development is very nearly complete, before implementing partitioning.

Once you've added a WHERE clause to the original partition, you can add new partitions. Although most partitioning plans are simple — the majority of them are monthly — partitioning plans can be complex. If you partition by multiple dimensions, say by product category and month, you can put each large category in its own monthly partition, and lump all the small product categories in a single monthly partition.

WARNING You need to be very careful to define the WHERE clauses correctly. Analysis Services isn't smart enough to see whether you've skipped data or, even worse, double-counted it.

When you're working with your database in development, you set up the partitions by hand in BIDS or Management Studio. In test and production, you need to automate the process of creating a new partition and setting its source. These issues are discussed in Chapter 17.

Designing Performance Aggregations

The design goal for aggregations is to minimize the number of aggregations while maximizing their effectiveness. Effective aggregations will greatly improve query performance, but they're not free. Each aggregation adds to the time it takes to process the cube, and the storage required. You don't have to define every possible aggregation. At query time, Analysis Services will automatically choose the most appropriate (smallest) aggregation that can be used to answer the query. Aggregation design is a difficult problem, and Analysis Services provides several tools to help you out.

Before we talk about designing aggregations, however, it's worth pointing out that small cubes don't really need aggregations at all. During your development cycle, you're probably working with a small enough data set that you don't need to worry about aggregations. Systems with small data volumes may not need to create any aggregations even in production. If you have only a hundred thousand rows in your measure group's partition, you don't need to worry about aggregations. Even large enterprises can find that many of their measure groups — for example for quotas and financial data — are so small that aggregations are unnecessary.

Large data volumes, of course, do require thoughtful aggregation design. You should be experimenting with different aggregation plans in the later part of your development cycle, when you start to work with realistic data volumes. During development, you can design aggregations within BIDS, by launching the Aggregation Design Wizard from the Partitions tab of the Cube Designer. Often, this task is deferred until the database has been deployed to the larger test server. Exactly the same functionality is available from SQL Server Management Studio.

The Aggregation Design Wizard will design aggregations based on the cardinality of your data. It looks at your dimensions and figures out where aggregations are going to do the most good. As a simplification of what it's doing, consider that aggregating data from a daily grain up to monthly creates an aggregation that's one-thirtieth the size of the original data. (This isn't strictly true, but suffices for explanatory purposes.) Summarizing from monthly to quarterly gives an aggregation that's only one-third the size. The Aggregation Design Wizard has sophisticated algorithms to look at the intersection of hierarchical levels to figure out where aggregations are best built.

NOTE One of the most common physical design mistakes is to build too many aggregations. The first several aggregations provide a lot of benefit. After that, the incremental benefit at query time is slight; and the cost during processing time can grow substantially.

Run the Aggregation Design Wizard only once you've loaded the full dimensions, usually in the test environment. The first time you run the Aggregation Wizard, it will connect to the relational database to count dimension attribute objects. Those counts are cached as metadata. If you ran the wizard against subset dimensions in the development database, you will need to flush the stored counts in order to gather new counts. Or, you can enter estimated counts manually. This is all very easy to do in the wizard.

We recommend running the Aggregation Design Wizard at 5–10% "performance improvement," rather than the default 30% that shows up in the wizard. We think 30% is too high, and the SQL CAT team agrees with us, as you can see in their technical note (search www.sqlcat.com for "aggregation design strategy").

As clever as the Aggregation Design Wizard is, and as good as its recommendations are, it's missing the most important information in aggregation design: usage. The aggregations that you really want are those based on the queries that business users issue. Once the system is in production you can monitor what queries are issued against the system. Even during the test phase, you can build aggregations for the queries underlying standard reports and ad hoc usage of the system. Rely primarily on the Usage-Based Optimization Wizard for the ongoing design of SSAS aggregations. The Usage-Based Optimization Wizard is available from Management Studio.

You have to perform a little bit of setup before you can use the Usage-Based Optimization Wizard. First, you need to turn on the query log, to collect information about which queries are being issued. Note that the query log used by the wizard is not the SQL Profiler query log that we will discuss in Chapter 17. Instead, this usage log is designed exclusively for use by this wizard. You can find the properties needed to turn on the usage log by right-clicking on the server name in Management Studio and choosing Properties. The *TechNet* article titled "Configuring the Analysis Services Query Log" provides detailed instructions.

Once you've turned on the query log, you should let it run for a few days. The log is stored in a relational table, configured when you turn on the query log. Maintain a script that contains all the known queries from predefined reports, so that it's easy to automatically run the known set. Delete from the query log any very fast queries, for example any query that takes less than a tenth of a second. There's no point in designing aggregations for those queries.

Finally, run the Usage-Based Optimization Wizard from Management Studio, to design an effective set of aggregations for your system. Continue re-running the wizard weekly during the test phase, and into the first month or two of production. Ongoing, plan to evaluate aggregation design monthly or even quarterly.

Planning for Deployment

After you've developed the logical structure of your Analysis Services database using a subset of data, you need to process the full historical data set. This is unlikely to take place on the development server, unless your data volumes are quite small. Instead, you'll probably perform full cube processing only on the test or production servers.

In Chapter 4, we discussed some of the issues around where the Analysis Services data should be placed. We discussed using RAID and SAN arrays; you should have your hardware vendor assist with the detailed configuration of these technologies. Note that Solid State Drives are a strong candidate for Analysis Services database storage.

One of the biggest questions, of course, is how to size the system. Earlier in this chapter, we mentioned the 20 percent rule: The leaf level MOLAP data tends to take 20 percent of the space required by the same data in the uncompressed relational database (data only, no indexes). Another equally broad rule of thumb is that aggregations double that figure, up to a total of 40 percent of the uncompressed relational data. This is still amazingly small.

> **NOTE** We've seen only one or two cubes whose leaf data plus aggregations take up more space than the uncompressed relational data (data only, no indexes). The uncompressed relational data size is a reasonable upper bound to consider during the early stages of planning for Analysis Services.

Your system administrators, reasonably enough, want a more accurate number than this 40 percent figure pulled from the air. We wish we could provide you with a sizing tool, but we don't know how to solve that problem. Exact cube size depends on your logical design, data volumes, and aggregation plan. In practice, the way people perform system sizing for large Analysis Services databases is to process the dimensions and one or two partitions using the initial aggregation plan. The full system data requirements scale up the partitions linearly (ignoring the dimension storage, which usually rounds to zero in comparison to the partitions).

When you're planning storage requirements, it's very important to understand that during processing, you'll need temporary access to significant extra storage. Analysis Services is designed to remain available for queries while processing is under way. It does so by keeping a shadow copy of the portion of the SSAS database being processed. If you plan to process the entire database as one transaction, you'll need double the disk space during processing. Most very large SSAS databases are processed in pieces (each dimension, each measure group), in order to save disk space during processing.

Processing the Full Cube

In an ideal world, you'll fully process a measure group only once, when you first move it into test and then production. But change is inevitable, and it's pretty likely that one or more necessary changes to the database's structure will require full reprocessing.

You can fully process a measure group from within Management Studio: right-click the measure group and choose Process. Once you're in production, this is not the best strategy for full processing. Instead, you should write a script or Integration Services package to perform the processing.

> **NOTE** Don't get in the habit of using Management Studio to launch pro-
> cessing. This isn't because of performance — exactly the same thing happens
> whether you use Management Studio, a script, or Integration Services. The
> difference is in a commitment to an automated and hands-off production
> environment. These issues are discussed in Chapter 17.

We recommend that you use Integration Services to perform measure group processing. This is especially true if you're using Integration Services for your ETL system, as you'll have a logging and auditing infrastructure in place. Integration Services includes a task to perform Analysis Services processing.

If you're not using SSIS as your ETL tool, you can still automate cube process-ing by writing a script. There are two approaches for writing a script: XMLA (XML for Analysis) or AMO (Analysis Management Objects). We find AMO easier to work with than XMLA, but exactly the same thing happens under the covers, no matter which interface you use.

Developing the Incremental Processing Plan

Long before you put your Analysis Services database into production, you need to develop a plan for keeping it up-to-date. There are several ways to do this. Scheduled processing will continue to be the most common method of processing.

> **NOTE** The alternative to scheduled processing is to use the SSAS feature
> called Proactive Caching. Proactive Caching is a feature that lets your cube
> monitor the source database — the relational data warehouse in this case —
> and automatically kick off processing when new data is detected. In the vast
> majority of cases, you know exactly when you added data to the data ware-
> house. It's more straightforward simply to tack on cube processing at the
> end of the ETL job, rather than use Proactive Caching. We discuss Proactive
> Caching in Chapter 9 when we describe low latency scenarios.

Scheduled Processing

Scheduled processing of Analysis Services objects is basically a pull method of getting data into the cube. On a schedule, or upon successful completion of an event like a successful relational data warehouse load, launch a job to pull the data into the cube. In this section we provide an overview of techniques. We go into greater detail in Chapter 17.

Full Reprocessing

The simplest strategy is to perform full processing every time you want to add data. We're surprised by how many people choose this strategy, which is akin to fully reloading the data warehouse on every load cycle. It's certainly the easiest strategy to implement. Analysis Services performs processing efficiently, so this approach can perform tolerably well for monthly or weekly load cycles — or even daily for small measure groups.

The same script or Integration Services package that you used for the initial population of the cube can be re-executed as needed. If full processing completes within the ETL load window, it's the simplest approach and there's no need to develop an incremental processing plan.

Incremental Processing

If your data volumes are large enough that full processing is not desirable, the next obvious choice is to schedule incremental processing.

Incremental dimension processing is straightforward and can be scripted in the same way as database, cube, or measure group full processing. In Chapter 7, we recommend that you create an Integration Services package for each dimension table. You can add the Analysis Services processing task to each dimension's package, to automatically start dimension processing when the corresponding relational dimension has successfully loaded. Alternatively, wait until the relational work is done and process all Analysis Services objects together in a single transaction.

Incremental measure group processing is more complicated than dimension processing because you must design your system so you process only new data. Analysis Services doesn't check to make sure you're not inadvertently adding data twice or skipping a set of data.

The best way to identify the incremental rows to be processed is to tag all fact table rows with an audit key, as we describe in Chapter 7. All rows that were added today (or this hour, or this month) are tied together by the audit key. Now, you just need to tell Analysis Services which batch to load. You can write a simple program that would redefine a view of the fact table that filters to the current batch. Or, define a static metadata-driven view definition that points Analysis Services to the fact rows that haven't been loaded yet.

NOTE It's tempting to use the transaction date as the filter condition for the view or query that finds the current rows. In the real world, we usually see data flowing in for multiple days, so we tend to prefer the audit key method. If you're sure that can't happen in your environment, you can use the transaction date.

As before, once your view of the fact table has been redefined (if necessary) to filter only the new rows, it's simple to launch measure group processing from a script or package.

NOTE Every time you incrementally process a partition, it gets a bit fragmented. If you rely primarily on incremental processing, you should fully process occasionally. For daily processing, monthly full reprocessing should be fine.

Incremental Processing with Multiple Partitions

If you're using SQL Server Data Center or Enterprise Edition and are partitioning your measure groups, your incremental processing job is even more challenging. First, you need to be sure that you create a new partition or partition set before you need it. In other words, if you're partitioning your measure group by month, then each month you need to create a new partition designed to hold the new month's data.

NOTE There's no harm in creating twelve monthly partitions in advance. But you still need to add some logic to your Integration Services package, to be sure you march through the partitions as each new month begins.

Make sure that the source query for the measure group's incremental processing has two filters:

- Grab only the rows that are new.
- Grab only the rows that belong in this partition.

This is particularly tedious if you have late-arriving facts — in other words, if today's load can include data for transactions that occurred a long time ago. If this is the case, you'll need to set up a more complicated Integration Services package. Query the data loaded today to find out which partitions you'll need to incrementally process; define a loop over those time periods.

REFERENCE SQL Server includes a sample Integration Services package that manages Analysis Services partitions. Explore and leverage this excellent sample. It's installed by default at `C:\Program Files\Microsoft SQL Server\100\Samples\Integration Services\Package Samples\ SyncAdvWorksPartitions Sample`.

Planning for Updates to Dimensions

Updates to dimensions generally happen gracefully and automatically in the dimension incremental processing. The easiest kind of dimension update is a type 2 dimension change. Analysis Services treats a type 2 change as a new dimension member: It has its own key, which the database has never seen before. From the point of view of dimension processing, there's no way to distinguish between a new set of attributes for an existing customer and a new row for a new customer.

Type 1 changes are picked up during dimension processing. Type 1 changes are potentially expensive because if any aggregation is defined on the type 1 attribute, that aggregation must be rebuilt. Analysis Services drops the entire affected aggregation, but it can re-compute it as a background process.

Specify whether or not to compute aggregations in the background by setting the ProcessingMode property of the dimension. The ProcessingMode can be:

- *Regular:* During processing, the leaf-level data plus any aggregations and indexes are computed before the processed cube is published to users.

- *LazyAggregations:* Aggregations and indexes are computed in the background, and new data is made available to the users as soon as the leaf-level data is processed. This sounds great, but it can be problematic for query performance, depending on the timing of the processing. You want to avoid a situation where many users are querying a large cube at a time when that cube has no indexes or aggregations in place because it's performing background processing.

Most dimensions should be defined to use lazy aggregations, combined with the processing option to Process Affected Objects. This processing option ensures that indexes and aggregations are rebuilt as part of the incremental processing transaction.

The place to worry about a type 1 change is if you have declared the attribute to have a rigid relationship with another attribute: in other words, if you have declared there will never be a type 1 change on the attribute. You do want to use rigid attribute relationships because they provide substantial processing performance benefits. But if you try to change the attribute, Analysis Services will raise an error.

Deleting a dimension member is impossible, short of fully reprocessing the dimension. Fully reprocessing a dimension requires that any cubes using this dimension also be fully reprocessed. If you must delete dimension members, the best approach is to create a type 1 attribute to flag whether the dimension member is currently active, and to filter those dimension members out of most reports and queries. Monthly or annually, fully reprocess the database.

Planning for Fact Updates and Deletes

The best source for an Analysis Services cube is a ledgered fact table. A *ledgered fact table* handles updates to facts by creating an offsetting transaction to zero out the original fact, then inserting a corrected fact row. This ledgering works smoothly for the associated Analysis Services measure group, because the ledger entries are treated as new facts.

Sometimes it's not that easy. How do you plan for the situation where you mess up and somehow incorrectly assign a bunch of facts to the wrong dimension member? The only solution — unless you want to ledger out the affected rows — is to fully reprocess the affected partition.

NOTE Multiple partitions are starting to sound like a really good idea.

There are several kinds of deleted data. The simplest, where you roll off the oldest month or year of fact data, is easily handled with a partitioned measure group. Just delete the partition by right-clicking it and choosing Delete in Management Studio or, more professionally, by scripting that action.

The only way to delete a fact row is to fully process the partition that contains that row. The scenario is fairly common: You inadvertently load the same data twice into the relational database. It's unpleasant but certainly possible to back out that load from the relational tables, especially if you use the auditing system described in Chapter 7. But within Analysis Services, you must fully reprocess the affected partition.

NOTE As we describe in Chapter 7, your ETL system should perform reasonableness checks to ensure you're not double-loading. If you have late-arriving facts, where you're writing data to multiple partitions during each day's load, you'll be especially motivated to develop a solid ETL system.

Summary

Analysis Services is one of the key components of the Microsoft Business Intelligence technologies. It's a solid, scalable OLAP server that you can use as the primary or only query engine for even the largest DW/BI system. In Chapter 11, we discuss the new PowerPivot functionality of Analysis Services, which enables power users to define their own cubes and powerful analyses. In Chapter 13, we discuss how to use Analysis Services to build a data mining application.

In this chapter, you learned:

- After you build a conformed dimensional relational data warehouse database, building the Analysis Services database is relatively easy.

- The tools and wizards in the BI Studio give you a good head start on the logical design of your cube database.

- There's still lots of editing to do when you've finished the wizards. The more challenging your application — in data volumes or complexity — the more careful you need to be in your logical and physical design choices.

- There's still more work to do to integrate cube processing with the ETL system.

- You must set attribute relationships correctly to get good query performance. The single most important Analysis Services feature of SQL Server Enterprise and Data Center Editions is measure group partitioning. Partitioning greatly improves the query and processing performance of your database, and provides greater flexibility in system management. These benefits come with the fairly substantial cost of increased system complexity.

- Some of the interesting features of Analysis Services, such as KPIs and Actions, require support from client software in order to be useful additions to your system. The Microsoft tools (Excel, ReportBuilder, and SharePoint) generally support these SSAS features.

- Most features, like calculations, storage mode, advanced processing techniques, and even translations, are available to even the simplest Analysis Services client software.

Analysis Services is a complex piece of software. In this chapter, we presented only the bare essentials of the information necessary for you to be successful. The Analysis Services expert on your team should plan to purchase a few additional books devoted to the subject of Analysis Services and MDX.

CHAPTER 9

Design Requirements
for Real-Time BI

"The only reason for time is so that everything doesn't happen at once."
— Albert Einstein

What does *real time* mean in the context of data warehousing and business intelligence? If you ask your business users what they mean when they ask for real-time data, you'll get such a range of answers that you may decide it simply means "faster than they get data today."

Throughout this book we've been assuming the DW/BI system is refreshed periodically, typically daily. All the techniques we've discussed are perfectly appropriate for a daily load cycle. In this chapter, we turn our attention to the problem of delivering data to business users throughout the day. This can be every 12 hours, hourly, or possibly even with a very low latency of seconds.

We'll begin the chapter by confessing that we're not huge fans of integrating real-time data into the data warehouse. This isn't to say we don't think real-time data is interesting — just that putting it in the data warehouse database can be very expensive and may be requested impulsively by end users who haven't made a solid case for real-time data. The best use cases we've heard for very low latency data come from mixed workload operational applications where a customer is on the phone or online.

Putting aside our doubts, and assuming your business users truly require intraday data, we turn our attention to the hard problem: getting low latency data to the business users. Depending on users' requirements, as well as the technologies you're sourcing data from, there are several ways to deliver real-time data. The first and easiest approach is to skip the data warehouse database entirely and write reports directly on the source systems.

Next, we talk about several approaches for bringing the real-time data into the DW/BI system. These techniques are most valuable for solving the data transformation and integration problems inherent in complex reporting. We recommend that you segregate the real-time data in its own relational database: the real-time partition. Set up a nightly process to consolidate the real-time partition into the historical data warehouse. Because most of the data cleaning and conforming tasks have taken place as the data flows into the partition during the day, this nightly processing is usually quick.

If your business users need to perform ad hoc analysis on the real-time data, you should set up Analysis Services to process the incoming data stream. There are several techniques for processing real-time data into the Analysis Services cube.

Real-Time Triage

If you ask your business users if they want "real-time" delivery of data, they're almost certain to answer yes. So don't ask that question. During business requirements interviews, ask the users if "having yesterday's data today" meets their analytic needs. In the cases where the answer is no, you may ask a few additional questions to determine if the problem can be solved by improvements to the transaction system (as it is a majority of the time). If the real-time need is complex, we suggest you make a note of it during your initial interviews, and plan to return later for a discussion exclusively around real time.

You need to understand several elements of the real-time requirements in order to craft an effective architecture with the resources you have available.

What Does Real-Time Mean?

What is meant by real-time delivery of data? Is it instantaneous, frequent, or daily? Many times we've spoken with users who've asked for real-time data, only to learn that they mean daily. As we've already discussed, daily loads are the most common business practice, and in most cases nothing to get alarmed about. When requirements call for a latency of less than 24 hours, there is a significant boundary that drives changes in your ETL architecture and data structures. This is the boundary between frequent and instantaneous updates.

Daily is the norm for business today. Whether your DW/BI system supports daily, weekly, or monthly loads, the design for that system is fundamentally the same.

NOTE A fairly common scenario related to timely data updates affects global companies, whose customers — and DW/BI users — span the globe. It's common for a global company to process data in a handful of regions, after local midnight. This isn't a true real-time scenario because each region's data is processed daily.

Frequent means that the data visible in a report or analysis is updated many times a day but is not guaranteed to be the absolute current truth. Most of us are familiar with stock market quote data that's current to within 15 minutes. Frequently delivered data is usually processed as micro-batches using a conventional ETL architecture: SQL Server Integration Services (SSIS). The data undergoes the full gamut of change data capture, extraction, staging, cleaning, error checking, surrogate key assignment, and conforming.

Very low latency means the data must be delivered to the business users faster than we can load it into the DW/BI system, but not truly instantaneously. The lower bound for very low latency is measured in seconds. The upper bound is measured in minutes, usually less than 5 minutes. A very low latency BI solution is usually implemented as an enterprise information integration (EII) application. Such a system must limit the complexity of query requests. BizTalk is a key Microsoft technology for EII solutions. BizTalk offers lightweight data cleaning and transformation services, but the underlying ETL cannot approach the complexity that SSIS can handle. Usually, the very low latency application has its own data store, and is an application that is related to the data warehouse, but not actually in the data warehouse database.

Instantaneous means that the data visible on the screen represents the true state of the transaction system(s) at every instant. When the source system status changes, the screen responds instantly and synchronously. An instantaneous BI solution is outside the scope of this chapter, and this book. It's a requirement that the transaction system itself must meet.

This chapter focuses on the "frequent" scenario: Latency of less than a day but not instantaneous. We touch on the "very low latency" scenario, as we discuss techniques to reduce the latency of "frequent" delivery of information.

Who Needs Real Time?

The requirements for your real-time BI system should include a specification of which business users need real-time access, and for what. Most often, the consumers of real-time information are those in operational roles. This makes perfect sense: your executives ought not to be worrying about how many orders were placed in the past 15 minutes. The operational focus of the information consumers is good news for the real-time system designer, because you can focus on delivering the required information without having to support ad hoc use of the current data.

NOTE We have seldom seen ad hoc requirements for real-time data. In the vast majority of cases, real-time needs are met by a handful of predefined reports and displays, usually parameterized along a very small set of attributes such as customer account number. You may have to do some work to extract crisp requirements from the users, because a demand for ad hoc access may be covering up uncertainty about what information is important. But delivering predefined reports on real-time data is an order of magnitude easier than supporting a wide range of random ad hoc queries.

As you consider the tradeoffs that must inevitably be made in order to accommodate real-time information, you need to keep the usage scenarios in mind. Don't weaken a powerful analytic system to deliver real-time data unless the rewards are great and the alternatives poor.

REAL-TIME SCENARIOS

My favorite example of a silly real-time data warehouse was a chain of dental clinics whose CEO wanted to know how many teeth have been filled as of right now. I can just picture the CEO pushing the refresh button on his BI dashboard while his ship is sailing onto the rocks. On the other hand, the IT guy who related this anecdote actually did deliver this report, though not integrated with the entire DW/BI system. The CEO was so impressed that he provided enough funds to build a real data warehouse.

The best examples we've seen of a strong need for real-time information is in the new economy. Consider an online services company that has a team of analysts who adjust the placement and pricing of advertisements based on usage not just for the last 30 days but also up to the moment. In the long term this task would have to be automated and hence not at all ad hoc. But in the short to medium term there's a clear need for analytic access to low latency data.

The most common scenario for real-time information is a call center support application. The help desk operator needs to know the caller's historical usage, including the current activity. Often this information is scattered across multiple transaction systems, so we can't solve the problem by improving the operational systems. Note, however, that this scenario does not require the call center operator to perform any ad hoc analysis. Rather, we must simply provide a report or screen that contains very low latency data. This is a requirement that we can fill in a variety of ways, without necessarily hosting the real-time data in the data warehouse database.

Real-Time Tradeoffs

Responding to real-time requirements means you'll need to change your DW/BI architecture to get data to the business users faster. The architectural choices you make will involve tradeoffs that affect data quality and administration.

We assume that your overall goals for your DW/BI system are unchanged by the move to real-time delivery. You remain just as committed to data quality, integration, conformance, usability, and security as you were before you started designing a real-time system. If you agree with this statement, you will have to juggle a number of tradeoffs as you implement a real-time architecture:

- *Delivering real-time data to people who want it, while insulating those who don't.* One of the biggest issues for the DW/BI team is to meet both the demands of those who want real-time data, and those who most decidedly do not. You may think that pushing latency closer to real time would be a win for everyone. Surely, in the absence of any cost of delivering data, we'd all prefer to have real-time data?

  Actually, no. Anyone who's trying to develop a non-trivial analysis knows that you need to work on a static dataset, where the numbers aren't changing from moment to moment and query to query. If you try to make these analysts work against a dynamic database, they'll copy a bunch of data to a personal computer — exactly the kind of behavior you're probably hoping to stem with your DW/BI project.

- *Managing a DW/BI team that has an operational focus.* If you add operational duties to your team's charter, you risk having the urgent overwhelm the important. In other words, the real-time operations will co-opt the strategic nature of the DW/BI system. Think about it: This is why strategic groups generally have no operational responsibility.

- *Replacing a batch file extract with reading from a message queue or transaction log file.* A batch file delivered from the source system should represent a clean and consistent view of the source data. The extract contains only those records resulting from completed transactions. Message queue data and frequent pulls of transaction log (change data capture or CDC) data, on the other hand, is raw instantaneous data that may not be subject to any corrective process or business rule enforcement in the source system. In the worst case, the incoming data is incorrect or incomplete. In this case we recommend a hybrid strategy where today's data residing in the "hot partition" is replaced during the quiet period at night with data that is extracted from the conventional batch source.

- *Restricting data quality screening only to column screens and simple decode lookups.* As the time available to process data moving through the ETL pipeline is reduced, it may be necessary to eliminate more costly data quality screening. Recall that column screens involve single field tests or lookups to replace or expand known values. Even in the most aggressive real-time applications, including instantaneous, most column screens should survive. But the more complex structural and business rule screens, which by definition require more fields, rows, and tables, may not be feasible to execute within the time and resources allowed. For example, you may not be able to perform a remote credit check through a web service. You may need to educate users about the provisional and potentially unreliable state of the real-time data.

▪ *Allowing current facts to be posted with old copies of dimensions.* In the real-time world, it's common to receive transaction events before the context (such as the attributes of the customer) of those transactions. In other words, you're very likely to get facts arriving before their dimension members. If the real-time system can't wait for the dimensions to be resolved, you can use the technique described in Chapter 7 of posting generic placeholder versions of the dimension members in order to maintain referential integrity between facts and dimensions. You are much more likely to need to design this logic in the real-time ETL than for a daily batch.

▪ *Eliminating data staging.* Some real-time architectures, especially very low latency EII systems, stream data directly from the production source system to the users' screens without writing the data to permanent storage in the ETL pipeline. If this kind of system is part of the DW/BI team's responsibility, you should have a serious talk with senior management about whether backup, recovery, archiving, and compliance responsibilities can be met, or whether those responsibilities are now the sole concern of the production source system. At the very least, the data stream going through the DW/BI system should be captured in its entirety.

▪ *Tracking misleadingly separate dimension attribute changes.* Depending on your source system architecture and your latency requirements, you run a real risk of tracking an unreasonable number of dimension attribute changes during the day when actually there is only one administrative event taking place that needs to change several attributes. Recall that a type 2 dimension adds a new row to the dimension table when a tracked attribute is updated. If you don't have a good way of pulling only fully committed changes from the source system, you can find yourself adding multiple rows to your customer dimension, dated seconds or minutes apart, for what is really one address change. Remember that this conformed dimension table is used throughout the DW/BI system, not just the portion of it being updated in real time.

▪ *Recalculating performance aggregations.* Perhaps the greatest design challenge in integrating real-time data into your DW/BI system has to do with type 1 updates to dimension attributes. The update to the dimension table itself isn't so problematic. The challenging operation is to keep all performance aggregations or summary tables updated. Let's say you're managing customer address as type 1, and some of your fact tables have performance aggregations on levels of the geography hierarchy (region, country, state, and city). When you update a customer's address as type 1, updating the attribute in place, you also need to adjust the pre-computed aggregations. You need to move that customer's historical fact rows from the old geography to the new one. This problem ripples to every fact table that subscribes to the dimension, whether or not that fact table itself is being updated in real time.

WARNING If you're updating a dimension in real time, and an important attribute is managed as type 1 (update in place), you are placing a huge constraint on all fact tables that subscribe to that dimension. Every performance aggregation that's built on the type 1 attribute, for each fact table in your DW/BI system, for all of history, must be adjusted. As your latency drops and you get closer to instantaneous, there are only a few practical alternatives:

- Forbid the processing of type 1 attributes during the day. You can add new dimension members and process type 2 attributes, but type 1 updates must be deferred to nightly processing. Depending on your requirements, this approach may be unacceptable to the business users.

- Forbid the use of performance aggregations on type 1 attributes that will be updated in real time. This proscription applies to all fact tables whether or not that fact table is updated in real time. You may see a large negative impact on query performance if the performance aggregation was frequently used.

- Use a different version of the customer dimension for the real-time data than for the rest of the data warehouse. You'll need to educate users about the potential data inconsistencies. As mentioned above, it's common to reprocess the real-time data on a nightly basis, at which point the inconsistencies would be resolved.

If you're using Analysis Services as your presentation server, as described in Chapter 8, it will identify these type 1 attribute changes during incremental processing, and will rebuild the affected performance aggregations for you. The problem is that as you get closer to real time, SSAS will be spending all of its time dropping and re-creating the aggregations. It will not be pretty.

In general, we've found that real-time DW/BI systems are harder, more costly, and more time consuming to build. Adding a real-time element to your project will greatly increase its risk of failure. We certainly don't recommend pushing toward zero latency data delivery in a phase 1 project.

Scenarios and Solutions

The business has a problem: It needs better, more flexible access to real-time data. Business users often look at the DW/BI tools, and ask for that same level of functionality and flexibility on operational systems.

Often, the best solution is to improve the operational systems. If your operational system is purchased — as most are — your company can extend the set of reports that are shipped with the product. If those reports can't be modified, you should think about whether you made a great product selection. But in the meantime, you can certainly replace or extend the packaged reports with a Reporting Services portal. That portal may even be integrated with the DW/BI portal.

The problem is more interesting if the need for real-time data spans several operational data sources. In this case, you must perform some data transformation and integration steps. For really simple scenarios, where the data is perfectly clean (what alternate universe would that be?), both Analysis Services and Reporting Services can span multiple data sources. But realistically, any integration that's not trivial will require that the data flow through Integration Services. From there it can populate a relational database, or even flow directly into a cube. The most common and effective scenario is to create a real-time partition rather than to flow real-time data directly into the historical data warehouse tables.

The remainder of this chapter describes the technical features in the SQL Server toolset that you can use to create an architecture that supports access to real-time data. Always strive to keep your solution as simple as possible. The different technological approaches usually require a compromise between latency and integration. The closer to instantaneous you need the data, the less opportunity and ability you have to integrate and transform that data. Table 9-1 below summarizes the options discussed in this section.

Table 9-1: Alternative architectural solutions to delivering real-time business intelligence

SOLUTION	LATENCY	INTEGRATION
Execute reports in real time	Very low latency; instantaneous at the moment the report is executed	None
Serve reports from a cache	Frequent	None
Create an ODS using database mirror and snapshot	Frequent	None
Create an ODS using replication	Very low latency	Very little
Build a BizTalk application	Very low latency	Moderate
Build a real-time partition	Frequent	Substantial

Executing Reports in Real Time

The most common way to use SQL Server technology to access real-time data is to use Reporting Services. A report written against the transaction system will, by default, be executed on demand using live data. If your system is small, your usage is light, you have few cross-system integration requirements, and no one needs ad hoc access to the real-time data, you can serve real-time data from standard reports.

The main drawback of this approach is that it stresses the transaction system. Many companies decided to build a DW/BI system in part to move reporting off of the transaction systems. A popular report that queries a large section of the relational tables is going to be very expensive to run in real time. You shouldn't abandon Reporting Services immediately, however. As we describe in the next section, Reporting Services provides several caching features that will help you address this performance problem.

Executing reports directly from the transaction systems provides very low latency information. It delivers instantaneous access at the moment the report is executed, but changes in the data are not automatically pushed into the report. The closest you can get to instantaneous is to have the user hit the refresh button repeatedly (which we are not recommending!).

Reporting directly from the transaction database provides no opportunity to integrate or improve the data, beyond that which can be done in the report definition.

Serving Reports from a Cache

Reporting Services offers two ways to cache reports to improve user query performance, but at the cost of an increase in latency. The first technique is to cache reports on a schedule. A user can't tell the difference between a cached report and a normal on-demand report, except for the date and time the report ran. The first user to run the report has to wait for the query to execute and the report to render. Subsequent users simply pull the report from the cache. You specify a schedule for each report, detailing how long the report can be cached before it expires. Once the cached report expires, the next query will result in a new, refreshed report being created and cached. Users may be surprised to see uneven query performance from one time the report is run to the next.

The second very easy technique for improving performance of reports against live data is to create a snapshot report. A snapshot report is a feature of Reporting Services Enterprise and Data Center Editions. A snapshot report saves the report's body, *including the dataset*, in the report catalog database. A snapshot report addresses the problem of cached reports' uneven performance. Someone — we can't predict who — is going to pay the price of executing a cached report after the old cache has expired. With a snapshot report you can instead schedule the execution of the report to run on a schedule and store its results. You'd probably choose this approach if you're worried that the CEO would be the one who might execute the expired cached report and have to wait for the refresh.

Cached and snapshot reports can be parameterized, but you need to define and cache the parameter values that will be used. Realistically, most parameterized reports are not served from a cache but instead execute directly against the underlying database. Cached and snapshot reports are very easy to implement. You should certainly consider whether they meet your needs, before turning to more complex architectures.

Creating an ODS with Mirrors and Snapshots

The phrase Operational Data Store (ODS) has been used to mean so many things that we hesitate to use it. By ODS, we mean a low latency copy of the transaction systems. The ODS may be part of the overall DW/BI system, but is definitely not the data warehouse database itself.

The simplest ODS is a copy of a transaction database with little or no integration. If the transaction database is in SQL Server 2005 (or later), the easiest way to set up the ODS is to create a database snapshot of a mirror of the transaction system.

Mirroring is a feature of SQL Server that's used primarily to increase the availability of a transaction database. Typically, the transaction database is mirrored to a separate server in a different location. Depending on how you configure and run the mirror, it can act as either a hot or warm standby.

Mirroring by itself doesn't help the ODS, because a characteristic of a mirror is that it cannot be queried. Create a database *snapshot* on top of the mirror, and serve low latency reports from the snapshot. A database snapshot is a read-only, static view of the source database. Snapshots always reside on the same server instance as the source database, which is why it's better to snapshot a mirror rather than the transaction database directly.

Mirroring and Snapshots are enterprise features of SQL Server.

REFERENCE Books Online has a lot of information on mirroring and snapshots, and more is available on MDSN. To get started, read these Books Online topics:

- ▪ *How Database Snapshots Work*
- ▪ *Database Mirroring and Database Snapshots*
- ▪ *Database Mirroring Overview*

Creating an ODS with Replication

An alternative approach for creating an ODS is to use SQL Server replication. Most people use database mirrors and snapshots to create an ODS, but replication continues to be a popular technique. It has several advantages over the mirror + snapshot approach, including:

- Replication is available on older versions of SQL Server, prior to SQL Server 2005.

- Replication can be defined on a subset of the source database. If the real-time requirements are focused in a specific area of the database, replication may be faster and use fewer resources.

- Slight transformations are possible as the data is moved into the replication target. This feature doesn't come close to providing the functionality available in Integration Services, and should be used with caution. Any significant transformations can affect performance on the source system. This will not make you popular with the DBAs.

Building a BizTalk Application

BizTalk Server is a Microsoft development environment for enterprise application integration, business process automation, and inter-business communication. BizTalk is a rich and robust environment for building integration applications, but it's not a general-purpose replacement for Integration Services. SSIS can do far more complex transformations, on a much higher volume of data, than BizTalk.

However, you may want to consider using BizTalk to build an application to meet your real-time information requirements. The scenarios in which BizTalk is particularly appealing to include in the DW/BI system architecture are:

- Well-defined, such as a report or dashboard.

- Integrating data from multiple sources. Otherwise, the reporting solutions are more appealing.

- Very low latency. Otherwise, the DW/BI team will use the more familiar Integration Services.

We view a BizTalk application as ancillary to the core DW/BI system. We would consider using it to solve a specific problem, to populate a table that feeds a specific report or dashboard object, or feed data into a data mining application. Depending on the circumstances, its target data structures may be nearby, but not exactly inside, the main data warehouse database.

Building a Real-Time Relational Partition

It's time to discuss how to load the DW/BI system in real time. The problems with loading the relational data warehouse database are design issues, not technology issues. There's no technical reason that you could not trickle-feed your relational data warehouse database every hour, even every minute. The problem, as we've already discussed, is meeting a diverse set of requirements with a single integrated system.

The design solution for responding to the business users' demands is to build a real-time partition as an extension of the conventional daily data warehouse. To achieve real-time reporting, build a special partition that is physically and administratively separated from the conventional data warehouse tables.

The real-time partition should meet the following tough set of requirements. It must:

- Contain all the activity that has occurred since the last update of the historical data warehouse, for the fact tables that have a low latency requirement.
- Link as seamlessly as possible to the grain and content of the historical data warehouse fact tables.
- Be indexed so lightly that incoming data can continuously be trickled in.
- Support highly responsive queries.

The real-time partition is usually not a true table partition. Instead, it's a separate physical table, usually in a different database that uses transactional database options. Most implementations will use Integration Services to populate this real-time partition intraday. If you need very low latency, and have (or can obtain) BizTalk expertise in-house, you may consider using BizTalk instead of SSIS. The real-time partition should store data for the current day only.

NOTE It's usually best to put the real-time partition database on the same server as the historical data warehouse database. Presumably, your users will need to combine current and historical data. Although distributed queries are feasible, it's easier and works better if all the data is on the same server.

The real-time partition should contain tables that are structured similarly to the relational data warehouse database. Start with the fact tables that you plan to track in real time. These fact tables should look just like the corresponding fact table in the data warehouse database, with the same columns in the same order. There is one vital difference: these fact tables contain the transaction system keys, not the surrogate keys that are managed by the data warehouse. You will want to add the date and time of the transaction, and any other information necessary to identify the transaction, like a transaction number. We generally recommend that you include such information in the main fact table, but be sure to include it here.

Dimension tables are a little trickier, because conformed dimensions are used throughout the enterprise data warehouse, not just in the portion being updated in real time. Most often, you'd copy dimensions to the real-time partition each morning, and make inserts and updates into those versions of the dimension. Create a nightly process to consolidate those changes into the permanent dimensions at the same time the real-time fact data is moved over.

There are several reasons for implementing the real-time partition with transaction system keys rather than surrogate keys.

- The surrogate key pipeline is usually the most expensive piece of processing in the ETL system, by a substantial margin.

- All of the type 2 (track history) dimension attribute changes for a dimension member can be compressed to the end-of-day state. Most DW/BI environments choose to track attribute changes daily.

- The main data warehouse database is insulated from the type 1 (restate history) dimension attribute changes. Recall from earlier in this chapter that any performance aggregations in the entire data warehouse which are built on a type 1 attribute will have to be adjusted whenever that attribute is updated.

If you have decided not to process dimension attribute changes during the day, then evaluate whether you can support the fact table surrogate key pipeline in real time. If so, you can integrate the real-time partition into the main data warehouse as part of the normal fact table.

NOTE Even if you don't have a compelling need to query integrated data in real time, you may still develop a real-time partition. By populating it in real time, you can spread much of the ETL burden over 24 hours, and reduce the time required to perform the DW/BI system's daily update.

Querying Real-Time Data in the Relational Database

A purely relational implementation of real-time data is appealing, because it minimizes the processing steps. However, the drawback of a pure relational implementation is that we don't have a way to break apart a query into the portion that needs to be sent to the historical data warehouse tables, and the portion to be resolved from the real-time partition.

In a scenario where there is no ad hoc use of the real-time partition, this isn't a deal-breaker. Report builders in IT should not find it difficult to construct a report that combines identically structured data from the historical data warehouse with the real-time partition. The data can be combined into a single consolidated chart or report. This may be as simple as a query that UNIONs today with history, or you may need to join the result sets in Reporting Services. Today's data is always queried with the current set of attributes. Depending on the report's business requirements, the historical data will include either the current attributes from the real-time partition or the historical attributes from the data warehouse. Given the nature of operational information needs, it's more likely that you'll use the current image of the dimension for the entire report.

Alternatively, a very useful display might show the most recent activity as a heartbeat-style graph, with a different format such as a table for older data. This scenario can be implemented as two separate but similar queries presented together in a linked report or dashboard.

Using Analysis Services to Query Real-Time Data

If your users absolutely, positively, have to have ad hoc access to real-time data, the best way to provide this access is to use Analysis Services. SSAS can provide the service to redirect the historical part of a query to one storage location, and the low latency part of the same query to a different data store.

WARNING Build a separate Analysis Services database exclusively for the business users who need real-time information. Don't attempt to modify your core SSAS database to be updated in real time. Strip down this real-time cube to be as small as possible while still meeting users' needs.

Build a real-time cube much the same as described in Chapter 8, in an SSAS database devoted to delivering real-time data. You should be using Enterprise Edition, because you'll need multiple partitions.

The dimensions should be structured identically to the corresponding dimension in the core SSAS database, but they will be built from the real-time versions of the dimension tables located in the relational real-time partition.

The cube's measure groups must be partitioned by date, with the majority of the data coming from the historical fact table in the main data warehouse, and the current day from the real-time partition. Make sure your aggregation plan for this real-time cube does not contain any pre-computed performance aggregations for dimension attributes managed as type 1, as we described earlier in this chapter.

Often, you can get perfectly acceptable query performance by leaving the real-time partition in the relational database (using ROLAP storage mode). For best processing performance, the real-time partition should have no performance aggregations defined on it. The dimensions and the historical fact data should use MOLAP storage mode as usual, with plenty of performance aggregations. If query performance is not good enough with this approach, use MOLAP storage on the real-time partition.

There are several ways to get the real-time data into Analysis Services. All of these methods allow background processing while users are connected to, and actively querying, the cube.

- *Schedule frequent processing.* You can set up scheduled processing of the real-time dimensions and partition. Have SSIS perform its ETL into the relational database at the latency you need, such as hourly. When the ETL is done, kick off dimension processing and then incremental processing of the real-time partition. If the real-time partition is stored as ROLAP with no aggregations, processing will be extremely fast. The design of the ETL is fundamentally the same as for the common daily processing scenario described in Chapter 7. As always, the Analysis Services cube remains available for user queries while processing is under way.

- *Use SSIS to process data directly.* Similar to the processing scenario just described, you can use the SSAS destination adapter of the SSIS data flow to reduce latency a little bit. The difference between this scenario and the scheduled processing just described is that SSIS flows the data directly into SSAS instead of into a relational table first, and from there, into SSAS. If you implement this approach, you should multicast the flow just before the insert, and flow it into the relational real-time partition at the same time it's processed into Analysis Services. This approach is unlikely to shave more than a few seconds from the data delivery time, as SSAS processing is quite fast, especially if the Analysis Services partition is in ROLAP with no aggregations.

- *Use proactive caching.* Proactive caching is a feature of SSAS that transparently maintains a dimension or partition. Proactive caching consists of two components:

    - A mechanism for watching the relational database from which the cube is sourced, to identify new data.

    - Sophisticated caching that enables uninterrupted high-performance querying while the new data is being processed and added to the cube.

    Proactive caching itself does not provide real-time capability; it's a feature that helps you manage your real-time business needs.

Summary

We've spent a lot of time in this chapter talking about the challenges of real-time BI. These challenges are even greater if you're trying to deliver real-time data that's consistent across the enterprise with the well managed data warehouse database.

Our goal in this chapter is to present you with a realistic description of the challenges, the alternatives and their pros and cons, and practical advice for implementing each significant alternative.

These alternatives start with encouraging you to keep the real-time data out of the data warehouse database, and away from the DW/BI team. We've seen strategic-thinking DW/BI teams get sucked into delivering real-time data, never to be heard from again. A lot of the business requirements for real-time data can be met by the transaction system owners using the very nice functionality in SQL Server, especially Reporting Services, directly against the transaction systems.

If you need to present data in real time that integrates information from multiple sources, you'll need to use Integration Services. Store the results of these expensive integration and transformation operations in the real-time partition of the relational data warehouse. We described several designs and techniques for populating the DW/BI system in real time.

We believe that the greatest benefit to the real-time functionality offered in SQL Server 2008 will be to software vendors who are building and improving operational systems, and the future customers of those systems. Ideally, the operational systems will present information in a useful, timely, flexible way. We hope software developers will use these features to deliver products that delight rather than frustrate their users.

Developing the
BI Applications

We've reached the point in the DW/BI Lifecycle where we can actually start delivering value to the business community. It turns out this delivery step is more important than you might think. We believe the business folks should be wildly enthusiastic about getting at their data and understanding it better.

The problem with this belief is that most business people do not seem to agree. In fact, based on our experience, you will be lucky to get 10 percent of your user base to actually build their own reports from scratch. We suspect this is because learning the tools and the data is just too far outside the comfort zone of most business people. Therefore, a critical part of every DW/BI project is providing the other 90 percent of the user community with a more structured, and easier, way to access the data warehouse.

This section is about the components in the SQL Server platform, and in the broader Microsoft product line, which you will use to close the last gap between the DW/BI system and the business users. These components include Reporting Services and Report Builder, Excel and PowerPivot, SharePoint, and SQL Server data mining.

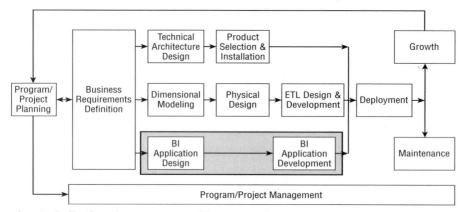

The Kimball Lifecycle steps covered in Part 3

chapter 10

Building BI Applications in Reporting Services

Building a bridge for those who don't want to swim.

We refer to all the tools, reports, and applications used to access the DW/BI system for business purposes as *BI applications*. This covers a range of concepts and technologies, which we will describe in the first part of this chapter.

One of the BI application categories is called *standard or enterprise reports*. These are the core DW/BI system reports, usually created and maintained by the DW/BI team, that provide the business with official numbers for a given business process. Reporting Services is SQL Server's standard report delivery platform. Therefore, most of this chapter is focused on creating and delivering standard reports on the Reporting Services platform.

Every user of your DW/BI system will access it through BI applications and especially standard reports. The vast majority of those users — typically between 70 and 90 percent — will use *only* standard reports. To them, the standard reports and the portal they live in *are* the DW/BI system. After working through the relational and OLAP database designs and the ETL system to populate them, creating reports seems easy. If you've built a solid, dimensional information infrastructure, creating reports is the fun part where all that work finally pays off.

Reporting Services has been well received by the Microsoft customer base and has been successfully implemented in many large organizations. Given its reasonable level of functionality and its more than reasonable incremental cost, we expect that a large percentage of folks reading this book will choose Reporting Services as the delivery vehicle for their standard reports and analytic applications.

This chapter provides the basic information you need to understand the range of BI applications available to you and to build your core set of BI applications. We start with an introduction to BI applications in general. We then offer an overview of Reporting Services as a platform for creating and distributing standard reports. Moving down to the practical level, we provide a development process for creating standard reports in the context of the Kimball Lifecycle. This development process applies equally to the creation of other kinds of BI applications. The last section walks through the creation of a standard report in Reporting Services.

By the end of this chapter, you should be able to answer the following questions:

- What are the various types of BI applications and why are they important?

- What is Reporting Services? How does it work, and where does it fit in the overall DW/BI system?

- What process and techniques should one employ to design and develop standard reports or other BI applications?

- What tools does Reporting Services provide for report development?

- What does it take to create a standard report in the Reporting Services environment?

- What does it take to manage and maintain the standard report set?

- What are the additional components of Report Builder 3.0 that help make it a reasonable ad hoc query and reporting tool?

LEARNING REPORTING SERVICES

This chapter is not a tutorial on Reporting Services. If you've been charged with the task of building the initial set of reports, you should first install Reporting Services and the samples on your development machine. Then review the documentation in Microsoft's Books Online and work through the tutorials. You may also want to get one of the many Reporting Services books available, or even take one of the many classes offered on Reporting Services. Visit the book's website for references to a few current books.

A Brief Overview of BI Applications

Before we describe how to build a set of BI applications, we should be clear about what they are and why they are important. This section defines several types of BI applications and covers why BI applications are important.

Types of BI Applications

There are many tools and report types that pull data from the data warehouse, from canned, pre-run reports to custom coded applications. In an effort to bring some structure to this confusion, Figure 10-1 lists several categories of BI applications along with the roles they play, the consumer types who typically use them, and the Microsoft tools used to build them. These categories include:

■ *Direct access query and reporting tools:* These applications allow users to query the dimensional model directly and allow users to define a results set. Simple ad hoc tools deliver only tabular results sets, while more advanced tools allow the creation of fully realized, complex reports. These more sophisticated ad hoc tools also serve as the development tools for standard reports that other users can run themselves.

■ *Data mining:* Data mining applications are included in the direct access box in Figure 10-1 because the process of developing a data mining model involves a highly iterative direct access data exploration process. The models that are the outcome of the data mining process are often embedded in other BI applications. We've dedicated a chapter (Chapter 13) to data mining because it is such a powerful component of the SQL Server platform.

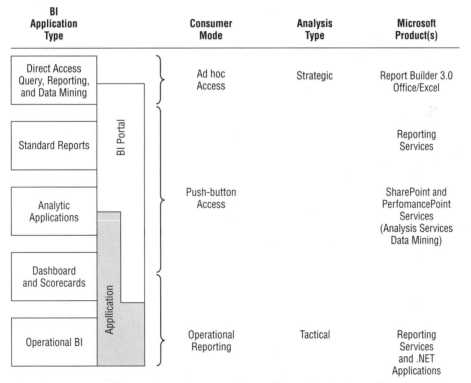

Figure 10-1: BI applications, consumer modes, and associated Microsoft tools

- *Standard reports:* These are predefined, preformatted reports that generally provide some level of user interaction, like the ability to enter a parameter, drill down to a lower level of detail, and link to related reports.

- *Analytic applications:* These applications are managed sets of reports that usually embed domain expertise about how to analyze a particular business process. Most analytic applications require an interface layer for user access. Analytic applications that include forecasting or prediction, such as a promotion analysis system or a sales rep dashboard, often take advantage of data mining models.

- *Dashboards and scorecards:* These applications generally involve a combination of multiple reports and charts in a seamless interface that use exception highlighting and drill-down capabilities to analyze data from multiple business processes.

- *Operational BI and closed loop applications:* These include the use of applications that are more sophisticated than typical operational reports. These applications leverage the rich historical context across multiple business processes available in the data warehouse to guide operational decision making. Operational BI applications often include data mining models to help identify patterns and opportunities, and make recommendations, at the operational level.

- *The BI portal*: The portal is the business's primary interface to the BI applications. It provides an organizing framework to help people find the information they need. We describe the BI portal in Chapter 12.

There is a significant overlap across these categories. For example, a dashboard may be essentially a collection of standard reports integrated into a single interface with a common set of parameters. Or, you may use dashboard tools to build an analytic application. We recommend you concentrate on doing whatever you need to do to deliver business value, and don't get too caught up on the terms.

The Value of Business Intelligence Applications

Before we dive into the details of creating these applications, it's worth reviewing the value you get from them to help justify the effort. As it turns out, they add significant value in several ways.

- *Business value:* The process of identifying and creating BI applications based on business requirements almost guarantees that you will provide something of significant value to the business.

- *Broad access:* The BI applications provide data warehouse access for a broad, important user community. Remember, 80 percent or more of your knowledge workers will not develop the technical skills and data acumen needed to build their own reports. You must provide them with a means to get the information they need to make informed decisions.

- *Early impact:* BI applications built in the development phase of the Lifecycle demonstrate the value of the DW/BI system from day one. Business users across the organization can take advantage of the initial business process dimensional model as soon as you deploy it.

- *Data validation:* BI applications help validate the data warehouse content because they represent real-world analyses that bring together dimensions and facts in a way that hasn't happened prior to this point. Typically, you will uncover some data irregularities, in spite of your rigorous data quality and design efforts.

- *Query performance:* Similar to data validation, the BI applications generate more complex queries than the basic testing that has taken place prior to this point. So much so, you should capture the SQL and MDX queries from the BI applications and use them to generate some of the ongoing performance metrics.

- *Tool functionality:* Because the BI applications are real business analyses, it is important that your front-end tool be able to handle them easily. Building BI applications during development provides an opportunity to test the ability of the tools to meet the business needs. You can bring in a development expert from the vendor's consulting organization (surely, you negotiated this as part of your purchase) to show you how to work around some of the rough edges of the product.

- *Relationship building:* Including your power users in the BI application development process is a great way to keep them excited about the DW/BI system and motivated to climb the learning curve. The users get early, supervised training on the reporting tool and the data, and the team gets extra help building the applications. (So maybe it isn't so helpful in terms of actually getting reports built, but the relationship part is worth the extra effort.) Make this process more fun by setting up a development lab where users and team members can all work and learn together. Bring donuts.

- *Feedback:* Finally, building BI applications helps the DW/BI team experience the impact of their design decisions. Many of the tradeoffs that were made during the design phase surface at this point. For example, it is now possible to estimate the full cost of decisions about pre-calculating a value versus letting the users calculate it in their reports. Consider having your data modelers and ETL developers participate in creating some of the BI applications. Experience is the best teacher.

We hope you were already planning to include BI applications as part of your DW/BI system development effort and this section has served only to highlight the wisdom of your plans. Now that you are appropriately motivated, let's dig into the process of designing and developing the standard reports set of BI applications on the Reporting Services platform, starting with the product's overall architecture.

A High-Level Architecture for Reporting

With an understanding of BI applications in place, we now turn our attention to the technology in SQL Server used to create and deliver them. Remember, the initial step in any development effort is to understand the business requirements. The Lifecycle shows that business requirements determine the architecture, and the architecture defines product requirements. Standard report users' business requirements should determine the capabilities your BI applications need to provide, and the specific functionality of the tool you use.

Following the Lifecycle flow, this section begins with a list of high-level business requirements for standard reporting and the architectural or functional implications of each of these requirements. Next we present an architectural overview of Reporting Services, Microsoft's enterprise reporting platform. Then, we examine Reporting Services to see how well it maps back to the general reporting requirements.

This is a good time for you to pause and consider your organization's reporting and analysis requirements because it may turn out that Reporting Services doesn't provide all the functionality your users need. You will need to gather detailed requirements for reporting and analysis as part of the requirements definition process. The functional list we provide here is not enough for you to do a rigorous product evaluation.

Reviewing Business Requirements for Reporting

The real, detailed business requirements will come from the requirements-gathering process. The steps outlined in this section are not a substitute for that process. However, it's possible to identify some common, high-level business requirements for reporting. Create a mental image of your user community. The group includes people at all levels of the organization, with a broad range of technical skills. The common element is that they're business focused. As a result, they're generally not that excited by technology and will rarely build their own queries from scratch. They're more interested in getting a quick answer to a specific business question than in working through an analysis process or figuring out the correct SQL or MDX syntax for a query.

Table 10-1 summarizes the major, high-level requirements of this group related to standard reports. A few of the major functional implications are listed for each requirement. Look at the second row of the table for example: In order to meet the business need to find reports, the DW/BI team will need to provide navigation, metadata, and search functions. Table 10-1 serves as a roadmap for describing the basic requirements for reporting and their architectural implications.

Table 10-1: User requirements and functional implications

BUSINESS REQUIREMENT	FUNCTIONAL IMPLICATIONS
Create reports	• Powerful, easy, fast report development tool
	• Variety of presentation formats (tables, charts, matrices, interactive pivots, maps, and so on)
	• Compound reports with shared controls and parameters
Find reports	• Navigation framework
	• Metadata
	• Search
	• Personalization ("My Reports")
View reports	• Access through a variety of methods and devices
	• User-initiated (for example, browser-based)
	• System-initiated (for example, auto email)
Receive results in most useful way	• Output to a variety of file types, formats, and locations
Change report as needed	• Parameters
	• Drill down/additional attributes
	• Linking
Solid, reliable system	• Performance
	• Scalability
	• Management

In practice, you need to back up each functional implication with a more detailed description of the required functionality. For example, if you ask any tool vendor a question like "Do you provide a variety of presentation formats?" the answer, spoken in a loud, confident manner, will be "Absolutely!" Instead, you need to list several detailed examples of how people need to see information in your organization. Make them tough, real-world examples and use them to test out the tool's functionality and to give you a chance to see how difficult it is to work with the tool.

Examining the Reporting Services Architecture

The primary intent of Reporting Services is to provide a solid, scalable, extensible enterprise reporting infrastructure. This helps us understand the pieces of the architecture and how they fit together to become Reporting Services. Figure 10-2 shows the high-level architecture of Reporting Services and its operating environment.

Reporting Services is a Windows service that contains three applications: Report Manager, Reporting Services Web service, and a background processing application. Each of these applications call on a set of shared processing extensions that provide specific functionality. Reporting Services uses HTTP.SYS to provide web functionality, which means the service is accessible either through a browser pointed to the Report Server URL, or through an application using the SOAP API. The SOAP API allows developers to integrate reports seamlessly into other applications. It also means Reporting Services no longer has a dependency on Microsoft's web server, IIS.

The Report Server communicates with its metadata store hosted in a SQL Server database called ReportServer. The ReportServer database stores all the information needed to define and manage the reports and the report server. It also is used to cache data to improve performance. It is not the source for report data.

At the core of the report server is a processing engine that supports functions like sorting, filtering, aggregations, and conditional formatting. It has several components that are designed to be extensible: Data, Rendering, Security, and Delivery.

- *Data:* A data extension allows the server to connect to a data source. Reporting Services ships with several data extensions, including SQL Server, Analysis Services, Oracle, SAP NetWeaver BI, Teradata, Hyperion Essbase, and ADO.NET. ADO.NET indirectly provides access to a wide range of data sources that have OLE DB or ODBC drivers. Microsoft provides a set of APIs in the data extension space if you need to add a data extension of your own. If you have invested in an ADO.NET data extension, you can plug it into the Report Server.

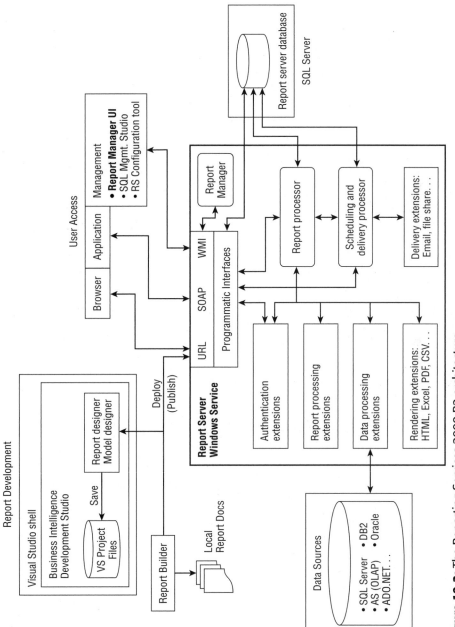

Figure 10-2: The Reporting Services 2008 R2 architecture

▪ *Rendering:* Rendering extensions allow the processing engine to take a report defined in the Report Definition Language (RDL) and output it to any number of formats including HTML, Excel, PDF, CSV, images, and others. There is also a rendering extension that generates Atom-compliant data feeds that can be read by an application. For example, an easy way to get a chunk of data to PowerPivot might be via a Reporting Services Atom data feed. Beyond this, you can write your own rendering extension and add it to the list, but it is non-trivial because of the complexity of the formatting options in RDL.

▪ *Security:* The standard edition of Reporting Services relies on existing Windows authentication for security. If you have an application that is not using Windows Integrated security, you can support it through an extensible security component included in SQL Server Enterprise Edition.

▪ *Delivery:* Reporting Services supports several ways to distribute reports in addition to direct access to the web server. The delivery function allows you to send reports through file shares and email. This, too, is extensible, and partners have built other delivery options like fax and networked printers.

From a user access perspective, the upper-right corner of Figure 10-2 shows how Reporting Services provides three major methods for directly interacting with the server. Most users access the server through the web browser using a URL that points to the reporting service. As we described earlier, it is also possible to access the server through an application using SOAP APIs. The management functions are accessible through the Windows Management Instrumentation (WMI) provider objects. This is what the Report Manager uses from the browser or from the Management Studio to manage Reporting Services.

Overall, the Reporting Services architecture accomplishes its primary intent — it is an extensible, scalable reporting infrastructure designed to meet the technical needs of a broad range of organizations, from small companies to large enterprises. While good technology is important, technical products succeed only if they meet business users' needs. The next section compares this architecture to see how it maps to the business requirements for reporting.

Using Reporting Services as a Standard Reporting Tool

The goal here is to make sure Reporting Services provides the necessary functionality to meet a general set of business requirements for reporting. We compare Reporting Services to the list of general requirements from Table 10-1 to see how it does.

Creating Reports

Reporting Services has two primary tools for authoring reports: the Report Designer in BI Development Studio, and Report Builder 3.0. As we discussed in Chapter 3, BIDS lives in, and leverages the power of, the Visual Studio development environment. This means the person creating the reports in Report Designer is working in a software development environment. The report creator needs to know about words like debug, build, and deploy. He'll need to be able to create a data connection and write SQL. It's not a place for the faint of heart, and certainly not a place for the vast majority of end users. Report Designer allows developers to create reports, manage them in source control, and publish them up to the report server.

Report Builder 3.0 is a stand-alone report authoring tool. You can access it by selecting the Report Builder button on the menu bar in the Report Manager, or you can download and install it as a stand-alone reporting tool. It has a more Office-like Ribbon interface, and offers essentially the same report components and design experience as the Report Designer in BIDS. In addition, Report Builder can use shared datasets and pre-defined report parts that it draws from a library on the report server. Report Builder can read and write reports directly to the report server, or save them locally.

After the report is defined in Report Designer or Report Builder, the definition is saved in Report Definition Language (RDL), which is an open XML schema for defining all the components of the report. This includes the definition of the datasets; calculations, expressions, conditional formatting, sorts, and filters; and layout of information including tables, pivots, charts, text, and formatting. When you publish, or deploy, a report to the Report Server, it writes the RDL out to the Reporting Services database in an XML data type field in one of the metadata tables. Any tool that creates RDL files can leverage Reporting Services as their enterprise report distribution and execution engine.

REPORT DEFINITION LANGUAGE

You can see what the Report Definition Language looks like by opening up a report in a browser (look for files ending in .rdl). If you want to see the full XML schema, go to the beginning of the .rdl file and look for the URL of the namespace. It should be right after "xmlns=". Copy the URL you see into the address box of another browser window. You can see the entire XML schema of the Report Definition Language.

Report Designer and Report Builder include tools to create complex cross-tab reports, charts, maps, sparklines, data bars, and various indicators. Because Report Designer is oriented more toward programmers, the solution to many problems is to write code rather than use the GUI to make a selection, drag and drop, or check a box, as with some of the third party tools used for creating reports. Report Builder can also be fairly complex to use. Of course, this is the universal tradeoff: power and flexibility versus ease of use. The nature of this tradeoff will become clearer later in this chapter when we create an example report. It will become obvious when you begin working with the tool firsthand to create real reports.

Finding Reports

After the developers have created and deployed a set of standard reports, users need to be able to find a report they want when they want it. This begins when you organize the reports into categories that make sense to users, as we described in the section on creating the navigation framework earlier.

Microsoft has included a basic navigation framework system as part of the Reporting Services product called Report Manager. The Report Manager plays two roles. It allows the developer to set some of the parameters and properties of the report server environment and the reports themselves. It can also serve as a simple vehicle to organize standard reports and deliver them to the users.

Figure 10-3 shows the top level of a simple Report Manager home page. The interface is essentially a list of directories that follow the basic file system tree structure of the projects that have been deployed to the report server. This simple three-level hierarchy (Home/Project/Report) serves as the rough navigation framework for the user. You can add levels to this hierarchy by adding folders in the Report Manager or in the TargetReportFolder property of the Project Properties under the View menu of the Report Designer. When the report is deployed to the server, the default target folder is based on the BIDS project name. To view a report, the user navigates the folders starting with the Report Manager home and then selects the desired report name.

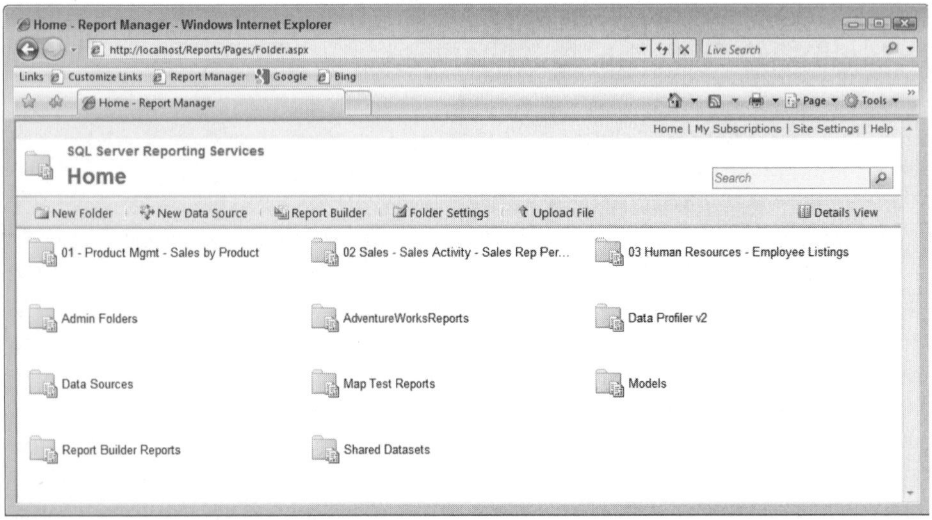

Figure 10-3: Report Manager home page

Figure 10-4 shows the three Sales by Product reports available when the user clicks on the 01 - Product Mgmt - Sales by Product directory shown in Figure 10-3.

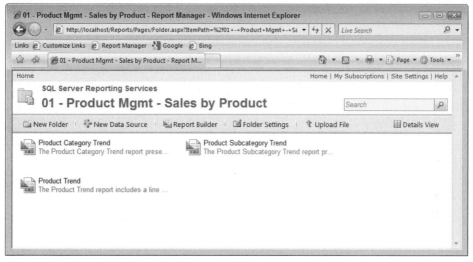

Figure 10-4: Reports in the Sales by Product directory

Under the covers, Report Manager is a web application that uses the SOAP and WMI protocols to access to the Report Server and its contents. SQL Server Management Studio also provides some operational report management functionality. This primarily includes defining security roles and shared schedules, and monitoring of report execution. Management Studio does not display the contents of the reports or provide the other user-oriented functions that Report Manager in the browser does.

Report Manager does provide many useful functions. Because it's based on the file system directory structure, users can view reports as soon as they've been deployed. It also provides some means for users to subscribe to reports and publish their own reports if they have appropriate permission. There is a search capability within the report site, which searches both the file names and description metadata in the Reporting Services catalog. Report Manager displays parameter entry boxes and dropdown choice lists in the Report Manager header area, enabling users to enter their own choices and rerun the report. There is a Find function to search within the body of a report, which can be particularly helpful in large reports. Finally, users have the ability to export the report to a file in any of several formats.

In spite of all this useful stuff, Report Manager is a limited report delivery solution. You can customize its appearance by changing the color scheme and displaying your own logo. But at the end of the day the reports are still grouped by project and ordered by name. If Report Manager doesn't offer the functionality you need, you can build your own portal. The sample set includes a sample called RSExplorer that shows you how.

On the other hand, this is why SharePoint is often part of the overall BI delivery solution, in spite of the extra effort. You can completely customize the look and feel of the BI portal in SharePoint. We begin to explore this option in Chapter 12. All of the report management capabilities are available when you run Reporting Services in SharePoint integrated mode.

While it is not a full-featured information portal, Report Manager does provide enough functionality to be considered a viable delivery solution. Even in the face of these (and other) limitations, many companies have successfully employed Report Manager as their standard report delivery vehicle. In any case, it does give you an out-of-the-box starting point you can use to get going quickly and verify your business users' needs before building a custom portal.

Viewing Reports

After a user has found a report that seems like it might contain the needed information, he has to have a way to view its contents. This is known as a "pull" model, where the user finds the reports and interactively pulls the data from the server.

Users can view reports through any application that can access the report server, either through a URL with an Internet browser or through an application that uses the SOAP methods, like the Report Manager interface. Both allow easy integration of Reporting Services reports into existing portals or into custom-built or third-party applications.

The browser is the most popular tool for viewing reports. Using a browser means users don't need additional software installed on their machines and IT doesn't need to manage the software distribution and upgrade process. (Unless, of course, your users have browsers other than Internet Explorer, or they have a version of Internet Explorer not supported by Reporting Services.)

Figure 10-5 shows what the user would see in the browser as a result of clicking on the Product Subcategory Trend link shown in Figure 10-4.

This example shows the report in the Report Manager interface. You can view the report directly in the browser without the Report Manager's organizing structure. You'll see this direct access when we include a report in a simple portal structure later in this chapter.

The custom application approach to accessing reports might be something like an ASP.NET application built to integrate reports into a larger system that provides additional functionality. For example, a customer care system might use Reporting Services to display a customer's purchasing and returns history to the customer care agent. On the same screen, there can be a button to allow the agent to select a recent order and submit it to the transaction system to generate a Returned Merchandise Authorization.

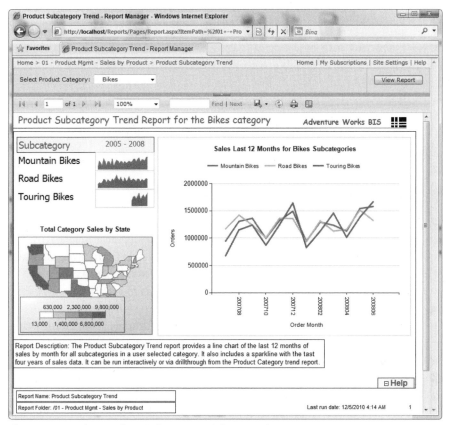

Figure 10-5: The Product Subcategory Sales Trend report

Receiving Results

Reporting Services offers several delivery methods and file formats other than the pull approach described in the Viewing Reports section. It's helpful to look at these options in two separate categories: first in terms of delivery methods, and then in terms of formats.

The idea of the push model is to deliver the report to the user based on a predefined schedule. Selecting "Subscribe…" from a given report's drop-down menu in the Report Manger takes the user to a page for defining the nature and timing of the subscription. The reports data sources must use the proper credential settings to allow it to be executed in a batch fashion. The subscription includes a schedule based on a time event or a data event. In the case of a time event, the report is distributed at a certain time on a periodic basis (at 8:00 a.m. every weekday, for example). In the case of a data event, the report is distributed whenever the underlying report snapshot is updated. Users can create their own subscriptions to reports they'd like pushed to them, or the report administrator can create shared schedules that send reports to a list of users. Reporting Services supports pushing reports out through email or to a file share. However, because this function is extensible, several companies are offering more push-style delivery options, like faxing and printing.

Reporting Services provides several output formats for exporting or subscribing to a report. These formats include Excel, XML, TIFF, PDF, CSV, images, and various HTML versions. Like the delivery mode, the format choices are extensible.

Changing Reports

Static reports based on carefully identified business requirements often provide enough information to answer commonly asked questions. In most organizations, standard report users want the ability to make changes to a report without having to ask someone else to do it, or having to learn the complexities of the data model and the ad hoc tool. In these cases, it makes sense to provide users with the ability to customize the standard reports to meet their individual needs. Reporting Services includes several common functions that provide users with the ability to change a report, including parameters, report linking, drill-down, and content modification.

The report in Figure 10-5 includes a parameter in the control section above the body of the report section labeled Select Product Category. The parameter has been set to the value Bikes using a pull-down menu. A user can select a particular product category and then click the View Report button to re-execute the report. We discuss some of the other functions for allowing users to interact with reports in the second half of this chapter when we step through the process of building a report.

THE LIMITS OF SECURITY

Once someone removes a report from the Reporting Services environment, either through email or by directly exporting the report, access to the data is no longer managed by Reporting Services. Once users have the information in a file format, there's very little the DW/BI team can do to control what they do with it. This is one of the reasons the DW/BI system must have a clear security and privacy policy, and compliance with that policy must be monitored. See Chapter 14 for more details.

Solid, Reliable System

Having a solid, reliable system is not the kind of business requirement you like to hear from your users. The only time they specifically mention this requirement is when previous efforts haven't performed well or have been unreliable. Regardless of the history, you want your DW/BI system to meet expectations. This involves setting up the standard reporting process infrastructure, securing access to reports, and managing performance.

The process infrastructure is a combination of Reporting Services functions like shared schedules, and process-oriented metadata connections with the rest of the DW/BI system. You need to create a mechanism for initiating the execution of a set of standard reports when a particular ETL process completes. The process should implement simple logic like, "When the nightly orders update is finished, start these reports."

Security is also part of a solid, reliable reporting system. After you've designed the report, you need to control who has access to the report, when they can view it, and how they can interact with it. This can be accomplished using role-based security. These roles can be managed through SQL Server Management Studio and assigned to users in Report Manager.

Performance is part of the system reliability job. If the report server is too slow, users will get frustrated. Reporting Services has several options for managing performance, including scaling out to multiple report servers, and scheduling reports to be executed during low demand windows like early in the morning. You can set up a large report to execute on a regular schedule, and save its results in an intermediate snapshot structure. Users have fast access to the snapshot rather than re-executing the report itself. This option works well for the daily load cycle of the standard DW/BI system. In Chapter 17, we discuss ways to monitor performance over time to find opportunities for improvement.

Reporting Services Assessment

Overall, Reporting Services provides the basic functionality needed to create and deliver standard reports that will meet a majority of the business requirements. Because it's oriented toward developers, it's more difficult to use than other reporting tools. Creating reports will take a bit longer. This is balanced by the flexibility of the programming paradigm. You can generally create a work-around to solve most any problem.

In a way, Reporting Services is a "nobody ever got fired" choice. The incremental cost and reasonable functionality make it an easy decision. Reporting Services' Report Builder component offers acceptable ad hoc query functionality to those advanced business users who are capable of and interested in developing their own queries. When you add in the reporting and analysis capabilities of Office/Excel, and the collaboration and structure of SharePoint, you should be able to solve most of the significant reporting and analysis related business problems.

Of course, there are third party tools for query and reporting, and many organizations already have licenses for one or more of these tools. You will need to decide how these tools will fit into your overall DW/BI system strategy. Remember, selecting end-user tools is more than just a technical process. It is also highly political and personal. You need to get the end users deeply involved in making these decisions.

The Reporting System Design and Development Process

With an understanding of the Reporting Services architecture in place, you can now start working on your standard reports. This section uses the Lifecycle approach to outline a process for defining and building your standard reports. This same process can be easily adapted to other BI applications types as well.

The BI application track highlighted in Figure 10-6 includes two major steps: design and development. The design step begins soon after the business requirements are complete. Most of the design effort is about identifying and documenting the set of reports and analyses you will deliver as part of the current Lifecycle iteration.

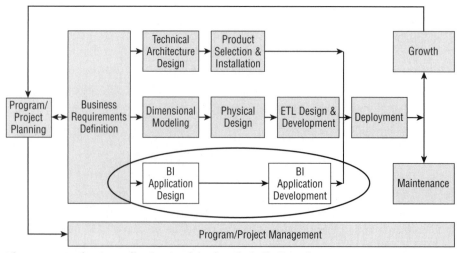

Figure 10-6: The BI application track in the Kimball Lifecycle

The development step is about building the target set of reports and analyses and the portal environment where they can be found. Of course, you can't really get started on the development step until you have data available in the target dimensional model and the BI tools are installed. Let's examine these two steps in more detail.

Reporting System Design

The goal of the design step is to capture what you learned about reporting needs during the requirements definition process in a way that can be quickly turned into real applications once the pieces are in place. Create these specifications as soon after gathering requirements as possible. The longer you wait, the harder it will be to remember the details. It's a good idea to include some of your key end users in this process of defining the applications, assigning priorities, and generally making sure you get it right. Report specification typically includes the following tasks:

- Determining the initial report set
- Creating a standard look-and-feel template
- Creating a mock-up and documentation for each target report
- Designing the navigation framework
- Conducting the user review

Let's go through each of these tasks in a bit more detail.

RESOURCES *The Data Warehouse Lifecycle Toolkit, Second Edition* **(Wiley, 2008) pp. 505–521 offers additional details and tools on the BI application design process.**

Determining the Initial Report Set

The first step in creating the target BI application or report set is to go back through the user interview documentation and pull out every reporting/analysis request, desire, fantasy, or hope that anyone expressed. As you make this list of candidate reports, give each report its own name and description. Capture your best sense of its business value and the effort it will take to build. Group related reports that draw on the same data sources to speed the prioritization process. It also helps to make note of who asked for it, (there may be several people), and any other parties you think might benefit from it. These are the folks who will help you further define the report should it make it on to the target list.

It's easiest to capture this list in a spreadsheet, like the example shown in Figure 10-7, or perhaps in SharePoint. The list shown here is a bit simplified in order to fit on the page. Your list will likely have additional descriptive information.

Doc Title:	Project:			Prepared by:		Date Prepared:		
Candidate Report List	AWBI System: Orders business process			J. DeLisio		2011-07-09		
#	Report Name	Short Description	Report Category	Primary Owner	Business Value	Level of Effort	Report Type	Comment
1	Sales Rep Performance Ranking	Total orders by Sales Rep for target year and prior year, with rank for each year and the change in rank.	Sales Performance	Brian Welker	9	3	Table	Add a drill down to sales details for a select Rep.
2	Product Performance	Product Orders and Market Share by Current Period vs Prior by Geography	Marketing Results	Mary Gibson	8	4	Matrix/ Bar Chart	List of Measures calcs, drill downs, etc.
3	Territory Orders Time Series	Last 13 months Actual Orders vs Forecast by Territory	Orders Analysis	Amy Alberts	7	3	Line Chart	
4	Product Orders Time Series	Last 13 months Actual Orders vs Forecast by Product level	Marketing Results/ Orders Analysis	Mary Gibson	8	3	Line Chart	
5	Product Cross-sell	. . .						

Figure 10-7: Example candidate report list

Work with some of the key business users to make sure you have a complete list of candidate reports and that they are ranked in priority order. Review the list and the business value scores with the group, making sure everyone understands the reports. Some reports, like actual orders versus quota, might be particularly interesting to the VP of Sales, but they may get a lower priority than the reports that include only orders data because quota information may not be in the DW/BI system yet. If everyone agrees on the business value score, the rest is relatively easy.

NOTE You may find yourself in a scenario where you have a requirement to replace an existing reporting system so it can be phased out. This is unfortunate because it means you will do a lot of work and end up with the same set of reports everyone already had. You may be saving some money when you turn off the old system, but the perceived value of your efforts will be close to zero.

In this case, see if you can improve the reports in the migration process. Perhaps combine several similar reports by using parameters or sub-reports. You may even get agreement on removing some reports that are no longer used, and adding some new reports that people would like to have.

After the whole list has been reviewed, re-sort the rows and set a cutoff point at about 10 to 15 reports down the list. This is your initial target list. Eyeball the results with the group to make sure all the reports on the target list deserve their success. Also, make sure all the reports that didn't make the target list deserved to be cut. Remember, this decision is often as political as it is logical, and just because a report doesn't make the initial list doesn't mean it won't get done. Many of these may be handed off to the experts from the departments (the power users) who were most interested in the reports in the first place.

Creating the Report Template

People can find information more quickly if it's presented to them in a consistent fashion. If you read the newspaper at all, you are well aware of this (or at least you benefit from it). The information is grouped in categories: sports, business, lifestyle, and world news. Even though different newspapers generally carry much of the same information, each has its own standard structures and formats.

The BI applications team is in the publishing business. You need to have your own format and content standards and use them consistently. You'll need standards at the portal level and at the individual document level. (We deal with the portal level in the section on navigation structure.) Create a template to identify the standard elements that will appear on every report, including their locations and styles.

It's helpful to define the standard report template before you begin documenting the individual reports because the template will give you some context for defining the reports. The following standard elements need to be defined and in most cases included on every report that comes out of the DW/BI system:

- *Report name:* Create a clear, descriptive name for each report that communicates the contents of the report to the viewer.

- *Report title:* Develop standards for the information that's included in the title and how it's displayed.

- *Report description:* Every report should have a comment or description. This is what we often have appear when the users hits the help button.

- *Report body:* Establish standards for each report component, including the column and row layout of data, including data justification, data precision, column and row heading formats, background fills and colors, and formatting of totals or subtotal breakout rows.

- *Header and footer:* Create a standard layout, font, and justification scheme, and stick to it. The header and footer typically include the report name, parameters used, report location information, report notes, page numbering, report execution date and time, data sources, confidentiality statement, and of course, the DW/BI logo.

- *Report file name:* Create the report definition file name that is based on your standard file-naming convention. The file itself and any associated code should be under source control.

Figure 10-8 shows one way to lay these elements out on a page. The angle bracket signs (<>) and curly brackets ({}) indicate elements that are context sensitive. That is, they may be system variables, or parameters specific to the report that is being run.

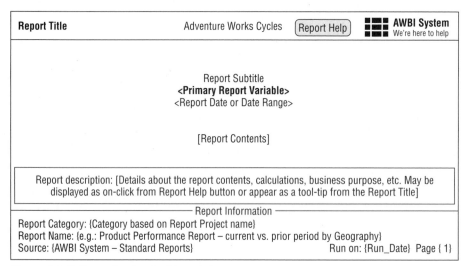

Figure 10-8: Example standard template

Not all report information is displayed on the report itself. You will also need to identify and document the following information for each report:

- All parameter values used in the execution of the report. This is often set up as an addendum to the report that prints as a separate page. It's especially useful for identifying why two reports are different.

- User entered parameters and other user interactions like drill downs and report links.

- Report metadata, including descriptions, calculations, derivations, author, the date created, and so on.

- Security requirements, including a list or description of the security groups that can see the report.

- Execution cycle, if the report is to run automatically on a periodic basis.

- Execution trigger event, if the report is to be executed in response to a system event like the completion of the nightly HR data load.

- Delivery mechanisms, like email, web site, file directory, or printer.

- Delivery list, which is generally the name of an email distribution list.

- Standard output format, like text, html, PDF, Excel, or Word.

- Page orientation, size, and margin settings.

Observe that all of these elements are essentially *report metadata*. Therefore, this information should be kept in a metadata repository at some point, so it can be used during report creation or accessed by the users on demand when they need to understand more about a given report. Meanwhile, you can use a spreadsheet or text document while you are creating the specs. Metadata structures for Reporting Services are discussed in Chapter 14.

Creating Report Specifications and Documentation

It may sound obvious, but during the application specification step in the Lifecycle, you should create a specification for each report. The report specification consists of the template information outlined previously plus a report mock-up and supporting detail. The report mock-ups are a great way to communicate the content and purpose of the reports. Beyond the mock-up itself, create two additional items to complete the spec: a user interaction list and detailed documentation. We'll go through the report mock-up first, and then discuss the user interaction list and the detailed documentation.

Report Mock-Ups

The example report mock-up shown in Figure 10-9 is based on the standard template we created earlier. The difference is we've filled in the report structure for one of the reports on our target list (you can see another report mock-up example later in this chapter).

It's helpful to indicate several user interaction functions on the mock-up. For example, the double angle bracket signs (<<>>) indicate drill-down capabilities — that is, a user can click on an entry in this column or row header and drill down to the next level of detail. We've found it useful to indicate the functions shown in the following table on the mock-up. You may have additional needs, or prefer to use other indicators.

< >	User-entered variable
<< >>	Drillable field
{ }	Application-entered variable (either from the system or metadata)
\\ \\	Link/URL — link to another report or documentation source
( )	Page or section break field
[ ]	Report template comments

| Product Performance Report | | | | Adventure Works | | Report Help | | ▦ AWBI System We're here to help |

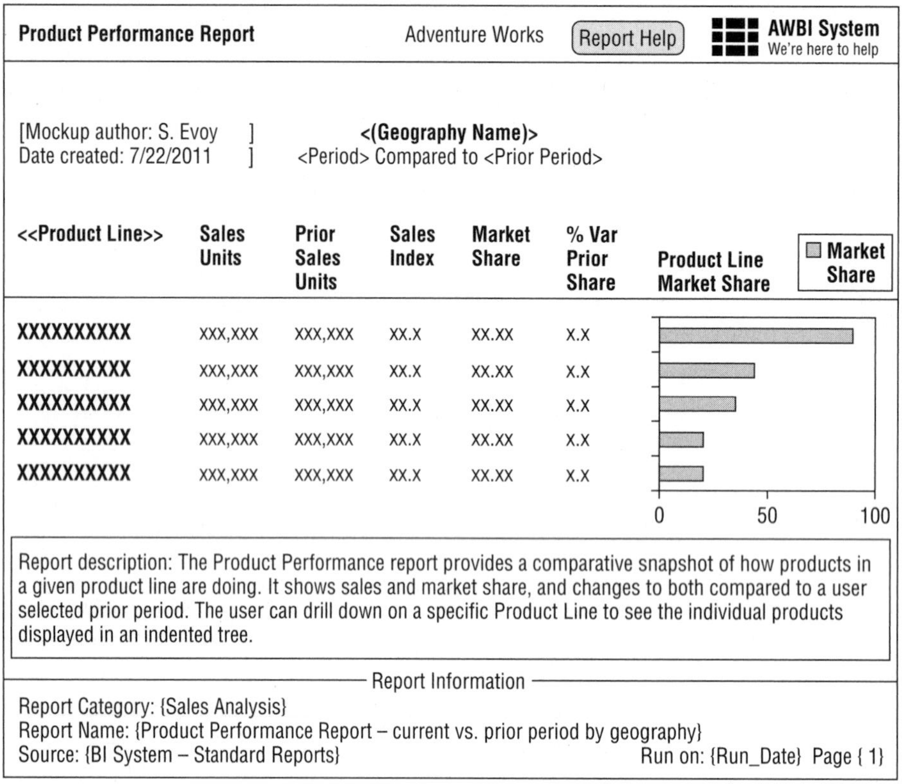

[Mockup author: S. Evoy   ]
Date created: 7/22/2011   ]

<(Geography Name)>
<Period> Compared to <Prior Period>

<<Product Line>>	Sales Units	Prior Sales Units	Sales Index	Market Share	% Var Prior Share	Product Line Market Share	☐ Market Share
XXXXXXXXXX	XXX,XXX	XXX,XXX	XX.X	XX.XX	X.X		
XXXXXXXXXX	XXX,XXX	XXX,XXX	XX.X	XX.XX	X.X		
XXXXXXXXXX	XXX,XXX	XXX,XXX	XX.X	XX.XX	X.X		
XXXXXXXXXX	XXX,XXX	XXX,XXX	XX.X	XX.XX	X.X		
XXXXXXXXXX	XXX,XXX	XXX,XXX	XX.X	XX.XX	X.X		

0   50   100

Report description: The Product Performance report provides a comparative snapshot of how products in a given product line are doing. It shows sales and market share, and changes to both compared to a user selected prior period. The user can drill down on a specific Product Line to see the individual products displayed in an indented tree.

———————— Report Information ————————
Report Category: {Sales Analysis}
Report Name: {Product Performance Report – current vs. prior period by geography}
Source: {BI System – Standard Reports}   Run on: {Run_Date} Page { 1}

Figure 10-9: Example Product Performance Report mock-up

User Interaction List

Although the function indicators on the report template tell you what kind of interaction is possible, they don't tell you what that interaction is like. The user interaction list identifies the nature and degree of interaction a user may have with a given report. This can range from None for a completely static report to an extensive list of fields and behaviors for a fully interactive report. Capture the basic interactions: variable specification (and its sub-types: user entry or user selection), drill down, and field addition/replacement. Figure 10-10 shows an example user interaction list for the Product Performance report shown in the mock-up in Figure 10-9.

Figure 10-10 shows a row on the user interaction list for each function indicator on the report mock-up. Include enough information so that someone who's building this report can use the mock-up and the user interaction list to do the job.

Detailed Documentation

Create detailed documentation to collect the information you haven't captured elsewhere. Note the report category, the sources of the data in the report, the calculations for each column and row, and any exceptions or exclusions to build into the query. Additional information about the report might include creation and modification tracking, and an expiration date, if the report has a limited useful life. A good place to keep this is at the end of the user interaction list.

Doc Title:		Project:				Prepared by:	Date Prepared:
User Interaction List		AWBI System: Orders business process				K. Berg	07/09/2011
#	Report Element	Source	Function Type	Default value(s)	Handled in:	Comments:	
1	Geography Name	Primary data query	Page/ Section break	N/A	Reporting tool	Sales wants this at the region level, but it may be helpful to have a version that allows user selection of the geography level.	
2	Product Line	Data query	Drill down	Product Line Level	Reporting tool	SELECT DISTINCT Product_Line from DimProduct	
3	Period	Initial prompt screen	Pull down menu	Current month	Reporting tool	User can determine granularity of period (e.g., week, month, quarter, year)	
4	Prior Period	Initial prompt screen	Pull down menu	Year ago month	Reporting tool	Note: Prior period must be before current period and must be at same grain as the Period entry.	
5	Report Category	Report metadata	Application entry	N/A	Hard coded	See if the tool can read this from the metadata at execution time, otherwise, hard code it in the report itself.	
6	. . .						

Figure 10-10: Example user interaction list

Designing the Navigation Framework

Once you know which reports to build, you need to categorize them so the users can find the information they're looking for as quickly as possible. We call this organizing structure the *navigation framework*, or *navigation hierarchy*. Ideally, this structure is self-explanatory. That is, anyone who knows something about the business can generally find what they want fairly quickly.

The best approach we've found, and this may sound obvious, is to organize the reports by business process. If someone knows your business, even at a cursory level, they will be able to find what they need. There are a lot of additional design principles that come into play here, but we will leave them to the SharePoint chapter when we describe a simple navigation framework for Adventure Works Cycles.

Conducting the User Review

Once you have a solid set of application specs in place, it's extremely helpful to go over them with the user community. This design review covers a lot of ground. Validate your choice of high priority applications and test the clarity of the specifications — do they make sense to the business folks? The review involves users in the process, emphasizing their central role and developing their commitment. It also can keep people engaged in the project by giving them a sense for what will be possible in just a few short months. Leave time in your project plan to make any modifications to the specs that come out of this design review.

Once the specs are complete and have been reviewed, you can put them on the shelf, so to speak. Unless you're planning to do a BI tool evaluation, in which case these specs can be invaluable, there isn't much you can do with them until you're ready to begin the report development process.

Reporting System Development

It's difficult to start the reporting system development process before a lot of the DW/BI system infrastructure is in place. You need the final dimensional model implemented in the presentation database and populated with a reasonably representative subset of the data. The BI tools must be selected and installed. And of course, you must have completed the report specifications. Typically, all of these events don't occur until sometime close to the system test process we describe in Chapter 16. As a result, we usually develop the reporting application at the same time as the system testing phase just prior to deployment. This makes sense because these reports are excellent test cases for several reasons: They represent a range of analyses, they are typically more complex than fake test reports, and they are real-world in that they are based on how users want to see the data.

The reporting system development process itself is a fairly typical development effort. We usually cover the steps listed in Table 10-2 within the Prepare-Build-Test-Rollout framework.

Table 10-2: Reporting System Development Process

PREPARE →	BUILD →	TEST →	DEPLOY
Install BI tool(s)	Build reports	Unit test	Publish to public server
Set up user data access security system	Create the BI portal	System test	Monitor and maintain
Create business metadata	Build other BI applications	User test/ acceptance	
Capture process metadata			

Let's examine each of these tasks in more detail.

Prepare

- *Install software:* Installing Reporting Services by itself isn't difficult, but integrating with SharePoint can be. We described some of these options in Chapter 4.

- *Set up security:* As we describe in Chapter 14, most standard reports and other BI applications rely on security in the BI application layer (Reporting Services and/or SharePoint). A relatively small number of reports rely on row level security implemented in the database.

- *Create business metadata:* As you begin report development, you should plan ahead for the business metadata that describes the contents of the standard reports. See Chapter 15 for more information on business metadata.

- *Create process metadata:* Process metadata for the BI applications is information about the execution of reports, and usage of other applications. As we describe in Chapter 15, Reporting Services naturally captures information about every connection and report execution. Other BI applications, such as a data mining application, may need to be explicitly designed to collect process metadata.

Build

- *Build reports:* Finally, you get to have some fun! Actually building the reports takes relatively little time compared to the rest of the process. As we mentioned earlier, it also provides a great opportunity to build relationships with your user community. Set up a temporary lab (it can be the training room) and dedicate it to report development for as long as necessary. Bring in a group of power users to help build out the initial target list of reports. Encourage lots of interaction. Keep at least two lists of issues and difficulties: one for the data and one for Reporting Services. If this is your first experience developing reports with Reporting Services, bring in an expert as a consultant toward the mid-point of the development process. Go through your list of issues and have the person show you how to solve or work around the problems you've encountered. You may have to actually pay for the consulting unless you negotiated it as part of the software purchase. Either way, get help from an expert. It's worth it.

▪ *Create the navigation portal:* At the same time you're building the initial set of reports, you need to be building them a home as well. Although Reports Services ships with a default website, called Report Manager, it doesn't provide all the functionality needed to help your users successfully navigate the DW/BI system. As we describe in Chapter 12, most Microsoft shops will implement a navigation portal in SharePoint.

▪ *Build other BI applications:* Building other BI applications follows a similar process, although with different tools. Even if you are building a .NET application, it's a great idea to get business users involved in a similar agile-style rapid iteration approach.

Test

▪ *Unit test:* Test each report. Have someone other than the developer go through the report piece by piece, testing the calculations, report layout, user inputs, and results. If possible, compare the results to those from another, independent source from outside the DW/BI system. We cover testing in Chapter 16 when we describe the deployment process.

▪ *System test:* Once the report is deemed to work on a stand-alone basis, see how it works as part of the production process. Depending on your front-end tool and the complexity of your warehouse environment, there can be a large number of elements that need to be tested, including time- or event-based scheduling, distribution, and failure notification processes. If you're supporting a large user community with these reports, plan for some stress testing as well. Include ample time in your project plan to tune these applications for large user communities.

▪ *User test:* If the users have not yet seen the reports, or you'd like to get reactions from non-technical users, include a task in your process to give them a chance to inspect and approve them. This may be a hands-on session, or it may take the form of a demo to a group of users with time for questions and answers. Or, it can be something users do from their desks with a simple web survey form or email response.

Deploy

▪ *Publish:* The initial release of a report set is primarily a public relations process. You need to notify users that the new reports are now available in the BI portal and give them a link to check it out. The users will immediately begin to think of many other reports they would like to see, so you should plan for a period of additional report development and deployment. Report deployment also includes creating a system for users to get the help they need. These issues are discussed in Chapter 16.

▪ *Maintain:* Ensure the existing report set is available and continues to perform as expected. Make sure that the existing reports are being used; prune or replace them if their usage falls below the expected level. Chapter 17 describes the activities associated with maintaining a healthy DW/BI system.

Building and Delivering Reports

At last, it's time for you to put together your standard reporting environment. This section concentrates on the process of building the environment and the reports themselves. As always, our process starts with a bit of planning and preparation. We then proceed to the creation of the initial set of standard reports based on the prioritized list created in the BI application design phase. We leave the topics of creating the BI portal, and report operations and maintenance for subsequent chapters. Although this section is not intended to be a step-by-step tutorial, we will build an example report based on the Adventure Works DW 2008 R2 Analysis Services database that is included in the SQL Server samples. You should be able to follow this walk through and create the example report once you get a little Reporting Services experience.

Planning and Preparation

The temptation to dive in and start building reports is almost irresistible at this point. Be strong. Even if you're a Reporting Services pro, it's worth taking a few days to set up your reporting environment and figure out the overall reporting process before you start creating reports. You should also have done all the application specification work described earlier in this chapter. The major setup items you need to address are setting up the development environment, creating standard templates and styles, setting up the delivery and notification metadata and processes, and setting up a usage tracking system.

Setting Up the Development Environment

We discussed setting up the development environment for Reporting Services in Chapter 4. The main challenge lies in finding the optimal combination of services and machines. There are two major components to consider: the Reporting Services server and the Reporting Services metadata database called ReportServer.

While it is possible to have a single SQL Server machine with Reporting Services, the ReportServer database, and the data warehouse database all together, it's generally not a good idea for all but the smallest implementations. Moving Reporting Services and its metadata database to its own SQL Server instance on a separate machine is the easiest way to improve Reporting Services performance. Of course, this has licensing implications.

Depending on your reporting workload, it is common to develop new reports and run production reports on the same server. You can set up folders in Report Manager that are only accessible to the developers. Once a report is finished, tested, and ready for public use, you simply move it into a publicly accessible folder.

Creating Standard Templates

Once the development environment is in place, you need to set up the standard report layout templates we described earlier. The easiest way to create a report template is to create a blank report with the standard elements you and your business partners defined, and lay it out according to your design specifications. We won't go through the step-by-step process of creating the template because it's the same process as creating a report, which we do in the next section. Figure 10-11 shows what a simple report template might look like in the Report Designer. It includes both a Table and Matrix pre-formatted with the appropriate styles (fonts, background colors, and the like) predefined, but there are no data fields in these items. Usually, the developer uses the appropriate controls for the report and deletes the controls that are not needed.

After you've defined your layout template, use your source control system to make it available to the development team. If you'd like to have it appear as a template in the dialog box when you choose Add New Item … from the Project menu in BIDS, you need to save the template to a special directory. Save the completed layout template report to its project directory and copy the resulting .rdl file to the template directory. To make the template available to Report Builder, put it on the Report Server, or put it in the file system.

There are other ways to impart a basic look and feel to all your reports. If you are handy with cascading style sheets, you might consider creating a report style sheet and referencing it in the `RSReportServer.config` file. Books Online doesn't provide much help with this, but search for the string "customizing style sheets" to get started.

> **NOTE** The location of the template directory for BIDS depends on how your system is configured. It's usually located under the Visual Studio folder inside Program Files. Search for the ReportProject directory in the Program Files directory.

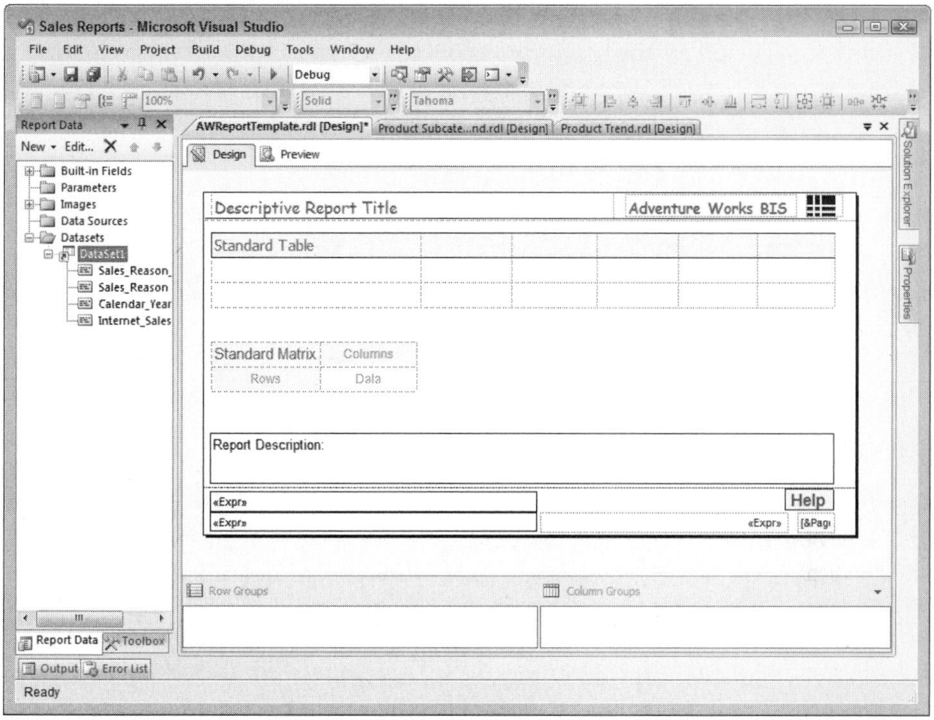

Figure 10-11: Example Adventure Works Cycles report template in the Report Designer

In most cases, experienced report designers will start each report from the standard layout template by selecting the Add New Item … choice in the Project menu, or by right-clicking on the project in the Solution Explorer pane. One of the report item choices will be your standard layout template, if you put it in the right directory.

> **NOTE** The Report Wizard is a great place to start if you are just learning Reporting Services because it provides a structured step-by-step framework for creating a report. However, you will soon move beyond its capabilities as you begin to create real-world reports. Also, the wizard does not provide the opportunity to select a layout template.

One drawback of the standard layout template in Reporting Services is that it does not include a master style sheet. The developer can define the style of each individual element in the template — bold type, font, color, and so on — but he or she cannot set default styles for any new elements that are added once the template is being used to create a specific report. New controls added to the report take on the bland styles of the generic report. This is where a cascading style sheet would be particularly useful.

Interestingly enough, while the Report Wizard does not access the layout template, it does allow the selection of a style template. You can choose from at least six predefined styles in the Report Wizard and in the wizards for the various controls: Slate, Forest, Corporate, Bold, Ocean, and Generic. If these don't work for you, you can add to the XML document that defines the available styles. This XML document is called StyleTemplates.xml.

RESOURCES Search Books Online for the "Creating a Report Using Report Wizard" topic for more information on finding and editing the StyleTemplates .xml document.

Creating Reports

Now that you're ready to build some reports, revisit the report specifications you created in the BI Application Design step of the Lifecycle described earlier to figure out where to start. These specifications list the standard reports in priority order along with mock-ups and documentation on the definitions and contents of the reports. After reviewing the specification document, work through the report creation process to build out your report set. When the set is complete, deploy them to the test server for testing. Finally, deploy them to the production server. We'll go through each of these steps in this section using the Report Designer in BIDS. You can use Report Builder 3.0 just as easily, because they share most design components.

Revisit the Report Specifications

The BI Application Design step of the Lifecycle involved creating a list of candidate reports based on the requirements interviews and then prioritizing the list with the business folks. At a smaller product-oriented company such as Adventure Works, orders data is almost always the top priority. During the requirements gathering process, it becomes clear that everyone wants to see orders data, but they all want to see it sliced differently. Because you did such a great job capturing the standard reporting needs in the design step, all you need to do at this point is pull out the prioritized list and the associated mock-ups and start at the top.

The specifications from Figure 10-7 list the Sales Rep Performance Ranking report as the top priority report. The specifications include a report mock-up for this report, illustrated in Figure 10-12. At first glance, this is a simple report, but as you'll see as you work through this section, even a straightforward report like this presents some development challenges.

REPORTING SERVICES WORKAROUNDS

Your standard template should include the layout of standard elements on the page (headers, titles, footers) and the standard formatting styles (fonts, sizes, colors). Reporting Services can use standard layout templates or custom report styles, but not both at the same time. If you're willing to go the extra mile, you can have both a layout template and a style template. Create a metadata table with the standard style entries in your database, and then create a dataset to retrieve the style information into your report. You can then use this to set style properties based on the query results. If the dataset is named StyleDataSet, and it has a column called FontFamily, then an expression to assign the FontFamily property of a Textbox might look like the following:

```
=First(Fields!FontFamily.Value,"StyleDataSet")
```

This option is probably overkill for most DW/BI projects, but it does give you the best of both worlds. You can create a standard layout template and include a dataset that reads the style information along with the code that applies it. You need to create this only once and save it out to the template directory. From then on, all reports built from this template will have the standard layout and style. An extra benefit comes from the fact that the styles are applied dynamically, every time the report is run. When you change the standard styles in the metadata table, all the standard reports will automatically change to the new style the next time they are run.

The Report Creation Process

The process of creating a report in the Reporting Services world goes through the following five basic steps, whether you are working with Report Designer or Report Builder. This list defaults to Report Designer, but we note Report Builder differences.

1. **Create or select the data source(s)**: In Report Designer you can create a data source connection that will be embedded in the report, or choose from a list of existing shared data sources in your BIDS report project, or from the report server in the case of Report Builder.

2. **Create or select the dataset(s)**: You can create a dataset based on a data source from step 1 using a query designer. The resulting dataset is a flattened table of rows and columns with repeating values as needed to fill each row. Or, in Report Builder, you may choose to use an existing, shared dataset which you select from the Report Server. In this case, if the original dataset is updated, it will update your version automatically. Note that you can create and deploy a shared dataset in BIDS, but you cannot use it in the Report Designer in SQL 2008 R2. If you are creating your own query, you will work with one of several query designers depending on the type of data source you select.

RESOURCES For a descriptions and screen captures of the major query designers, search Books Online for "Query Design Tools in Reporting Services."

3. **Define report layout on the Design tab:** You can build the structure of your report from scratch by dragging toolbox components onto the design pane and populating them with fields from your datasets. The design pane is under the Home Ribbon in Report Builder. Report Builder also allows you to drag in report parts from the Report Part Gallery. A report part is a predefined report component that will bring any needed data sources and datasets along with it. Once the report part is in place, you can change it as needed. If the original is updated, Reporting Services will ask if you want to update your copy the next time you edit the report.

4. **Preview report by selecting the Preview tab:** This is usually an iterative process. You make changes in the design pane and preview the report to see how it looks, repeating until it looks the way you want it. To preview a report in Report Builder, select Run in the Home Ribbon.

5. **Deploy report to the server:** You can deploy a single report to the report server in BIDS by right-clicking on the report name and selecting Deploy. In Report Builder, you deploy a report by simply saving it to the report server. You can also save the report locally.

This outline should help keep you from getting lost as you work your way through the creation of a standard report in BIDS or Report Builder.

TIP To get the most out of this section, you should be at your computer with SQL Server and the Adventure Works relational and Analysis Services sample databases installed. This section uses a walk-through format to describe the process of creating a report. We don't describe every mouse click, but if you've at least worked through the SQL Server Reporting Services tutorials, there should be enough information in each step for you to follow along.

Creating Your First Standard Report

Begin by creating a new Report Server Project in BIDS. Check the box labeled "Create directory for solution," rename the solution to **Sales Reports**, and rename the project to **Sales Rep Performance**. Close the Report Wizard and add a new report to the project by right-clicking the Reports directory in the Solution Explorer pane and select Add ➢ New Item from the popup menu. Be careful not to use the Add New Report choice because it will bring up the Report Wizard, and you won't be able to select your standard template.

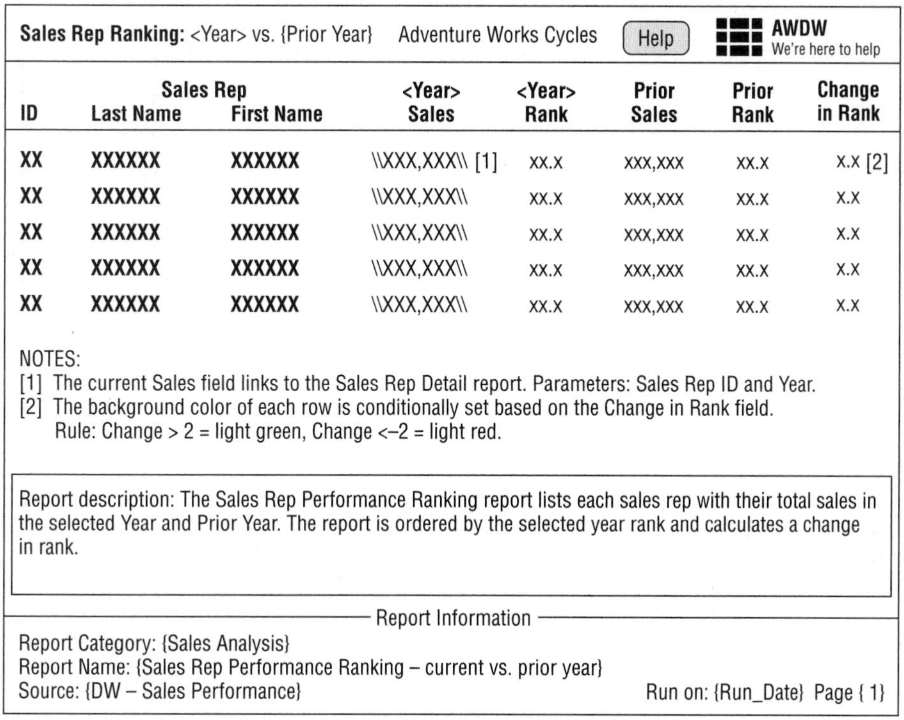

ID	Sales Rep Last Name	First Name	<Year> Sales	<Year> Rank	Prior Sales	Prior Rank	Change in Rank
XX	XXXXXX	XXXXXX	\\XXX,XXX\\ [1]	XX.X	XXX,XXX	XX.X	X.X [2]
XX	XXXXXX	XXXXXX	\\XXX,XXX\\	XX.X	XXX,XXX	XX.X	X.X
XX	XXXXXX	XXXXXX	\\XXX,XXX\\	XX.X	XXX,XXX	XX.X	X.X
XX	XXXXXX	XXXXXX	\\XXX,XXX\\	XX.X	XXX,XXX	XX.X	X.X
XX	XXXXXX	XXXXXX	\\XXX,XXX\\	XX.X	XXX,XXX	XX.X	X.X

Sales Rep Ranking: <Year> vs. {Prior Year}   Adventure Works Cycles   [Help]   ▪▪▪ AWDW
We're here to help

NOTES:
[1] The current Sales field links to the Sales Rep Detail report. Parameters: Sales Rep ID and Year.
[2] The background color of each row is conditionally set based on the Change in Rank field.
     Rule: Change > 2 = light green, Change <–2 = light red.

Report description: The Sales Rep Performance Ranking report lists each sales rep with their total sales in the selected Year and Prior Year. The report is ordered by the selected year rank and calculates a change in rank.

──────────── Report Information ────────────
Report Category: {Sales Analysis}
Report Name: {Sales Rep Performance Ranking – current vs. prior year}
Source: {DW – Sales Performance}   Run on: {Run_Date} Page { 1}

Figure 10-12: Sales Rep Performance Ranking report mock-up

Select your standard template in the Add New Item dialog window and rename it Sales Rep Performance Ranking. Click the Add button, and the new report should open up in the Report Designer design surface with the Design tab selected and all the standard report elements in place. At this point, it should look much like your version of the standard report template shown back in Figure 10-11. If you haven't defined a standard template, just add a new blank report item.

Creating the Data Source and Dataset Query

Reporting Services uses the same kind of data sources that Integration Services and Analysis Services use. Share data sources across the reports in your projects to make it easy to change connection information. Create a shared data source called AdventureWorksAS that references the Adventure Works DW 2008 R2 Analysis Services database, which you can download from the CodePlex website. Be sure to test the connection before you proceed. While you're at it, create another shared data source called AdventureWorksDW that references the AdventureWorksDW2008 R2 SQL Server relational database.

TIP In general, it makes sense to use the production data warehouse databases as the sources, even for report development (assuming the data has already been loaded into production). Report development is essentially the same as ad hoc querying and poses no significant additional risks to the database server. Using the production data warehouse server makes the development job easier because the data used for creating the report is the final data. In addition, you don't need to change the data sources when you move from development to test to production. Of course, you will need to work against dev or test databases for new data sources that are not yet in production.

Next you need to make your shared data source from the project available to the new report. You should see a Report Data pane on the far left of your BIDS window. Select Data Source… from the New dropdown menu in the Report Data pane and create a data source named AWAS using a shared data source reference to the AdventureWorksAS data source.

Now select Dataset… from the New dropdown menu in the Report Data pane and create a dataset called SalesRankData based on the AWAS data source. You typically define the dataset query by clicking the Query Designer… button in the Dataset Properties window. This will bring up the appropriate designer tool depending on the nature of the data source you are using.

If your data source was a SQL Server relational database, the query designer would allow you to enter SQL into the upper pane and view the results in the lower pane. The relational query design also has a more graphical interface mode called the query builder. It looks suspiciously like the Microsoft Access query builder. If the data source was a report model, you'd use the report model query designer to define datasets.

In this case, when you click the Query Designer… button, BIDS displays the Analysis Services query designer in a separate window. The Analysis Services query designer lets you build simple MDX queries with a drag-and-drop interface. You can view the MDX or enter it directly, by switching out of design mode in the upper-right corner of the designer.

The query design tools in the Report Designer and Report Builder are getting better as Reporting Services matures. However, in many cases, developers will end up creating the SQL or MDX in some other tool and pasting it in. Even in our simple example, the fields for the Sales Rep Performance Ranking report require the creation of calculated members in MDX.

WARNING If you enter your SQL or MDX directly, do not try to switch over to the query builder or into design mode. The designer will try to rewrite your query and may fail because of its complexity, ruining the SQL and the formatting in the process. In the MDX case, it doesn't even pay to rewrite the query. You have to start over.

According to the mock-up for the Sales Rep Performance Ranking report in Figure 10-12, the VP of Sales wants to compare current year and prior year sales by sales rep. Like many business requests, this is conceptually simple, but it turns out to be not so easy to do in MDX, SQL, or the Report Designer. For purposes of the example, this report will use an MDX query against the Analysis Services database. The Query Designer window in Figure 10-13 shows the completed dataset.

When you create a report, you need to break it down into subsets to make it easier to build. You usually need a minimum of two datasets: one for the report contents and at least one for the user input parameter prompt lists. The report in Figure 10-12 is more complex than it first appears because it has two subsets of data, current year sales and prior year sales by employee. To make matters worse, you need to rank each of those subsets independently and calculate the change in ranking from the prior year to the current year. In MDX, the easiest way to accomplish the creation of subsets within the Query Designer is to create calculated members for each of the two sales subsets (in the Calculated Members pane in the lower-left corner), then create calculated members that rank those subsets, and finally, calculate the difference of the two rank members.

NOTE By far the easiest way for the report developer to get `Prior Year Sales` is to have the Analysis Services cube developer create the measure inside the database. Then all you'd have to do is drag and drop it into the query designer. Measures that are likely to be used in many reports and analyses should be defined within the cube. Nonetheless, report developers inevitably will need to create some complex MDX snippets.

First, drag the `Employee` attribute from the `Employee Department` hierarchy in the `Employee` dimension onto the results pane. Next, the current year sales calculated member is easy because it is just the `Reseller Sales Amount` measure. To create this calculated member, right-click in the Calculated Members box and select New Calculated Member. Drag the appropriate measure from the Measures list in the Metadata box in the lower-left corner of the Calculated Member Builder window into the Expression box. For this report, the expression would be:

```
[Measures].[Reseller Sales Amount]
```

Technically, you don't need a calculated member for this measure, but it helps clarify the contents of the report and subsequent calculations. Next, recall that the mock-up identified the target year as a user-entered parameter. If you limit the calendar year to `CY 2008` in the filter pane at the upper part of the designer, you will see a check box to make this limit a parameter. When you check the box, the Analysis Services report designer creates a Reporting Services parameter along with the query needed to populate the choice list.

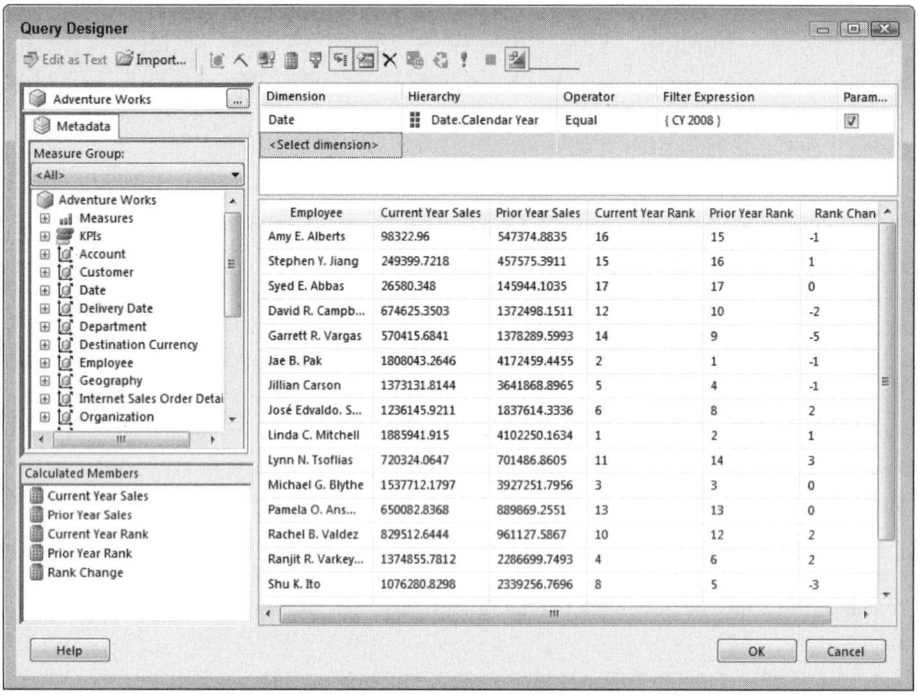

Figure 10-13: The completed data tab for the Sales Rep Performance Ranking report

The next calculated member is the prior year sales field. This is a bit more complex because it relies on the `ParallelPeriod` function:

```
SUM({ParallelPeriod([Date].[Calendar Year].LEVEL,1)},
     [Measures].[Current Year Sales])
```

This says to sum the measure for one year lagged behind the current year. Notice that it refers to the `Current Year Sales` measure you defined first.

The next calculated measure, `Current Year Rank`, does a rank on current year sales. Like so much of the MDX language, the RANK function in MDX is not like the RANK function in SQL, although it has the same name. The MDX RANK tells you the location of a member in its current set. For employees, the current set might be in alphabetical order. Therefore, a straight ranking of sales reps would rank Amy Alberts as number one, even though she's sixteenth on the list as measured by sales. When you use the RANK, you need to tell it what set it is part of, and what order the set is in, as follows:

```
IIF (ISEMPTY( [Measures].[Current Year Sales] ), NULL,
    RANK (
        [Employee].[Employee Department].CurrentMember,
        ORDER (
            [Employee].[Employee Department].[Employee].Members
```

```
        , ([Measures].[Current Year Sales])
        , BDESC
        )
    )
)
```

This MDX uses the ISEMPTY function to make sure the employee has Current Year Sales before it does the RANK. This is because only a handful of employees are sales reps, and you don't want the report to list all 296 employees. Next, the expression ranks the current employee according to where it is in a set of employees ordered by Current Year Sales, in descending order. The Prior Year Rank is the same expression ordered by Prior Year Sales.

The final column, Rank Change, is simply the difference in the two ranking calculated members:

```
[Measures].[Prior Year Rank] - [Measures].[Current Year Rank]
```

While this may seem complicated, there are two aspects to consider that might make it seem relatively easy. First, you can define commonly used calculated members, like Current Year Sales or Prior Year Sales, in the Analysis Services OLAP database once; then they become drag-and-drop fields in the query designer, just like any other measure. Second, the SQL alternative to this query is even less attractive; it goes on for almost a page to accomplish the same results. (You can get a script for the equivalent SQL query at the book's Web site: www.KimballGroup.com/html/booksMDWTtools.html.)

Even though the primary dataset is complete, you still have at least one more dataset to consider. When you select the parameter check box in the Date .Calendar Year limit, the MDX query designer automatically creates a second dataset, called DateCalendarYear, and links that dataset to a parameter also called DateCalendarYear. The dataset retrieves the distinct list of choices for the attribute selected and includes a value field and a caption field. The caption field is used to populate the choice list of a pulldown menu in the user interface, and the corresponding value field is passed to the DateCalendarYear parameter in the MDX query. If you use the SQL query designer, you have to create the dataset to populate the parameter choice list yourself.

NOTE To see the DateCalendarYear dataset, right-click the Datasets folder in the ReportData tab and toggle the Show Hidden Datasets choice. To change the parameter so the user cannot choose more than one target year, right-click the DateCalendarYear parameter in the Parameters folder and uncheck the Allow multiple values check box. See if you can figure out how to omit the All Periods choice. Even better, see if you can omit the earliest year from the list because there won't be a prior year for the earliest year.

Design the Report Layout

Once your datasets are defined, switch over to the Design tab in the Report Designer design surface and start laying out the actual report. Fortunately, the Sales Rep Performance Ranking report has a simple layout. We'll start with the core report layout, and then add a few subtle items like the DateCalendarYear parameter and some conditional formatting to highlight potential problem areas.

The design surface in the Design tab should look familiar to anyone who has created forms or reports with Access, Visual Basic, VBA, or Visual Studio. The basic process involves dragging various Report Items from the Toolbox (a tab in the same pane as the Report Data tab on the left) onto the design surface and then specifying their properties as appropriate.

The standard template shown back in Figure 10-11 already has predefined Table and Matrix items. The report mock-up looks like a good candidate for the Table control, so delete the Matrix control to clear up a little space. (If you're not using a standard template, just drag a Table from the Toolbox into the report area.) Fill in the Table control by dragging columns from the dataset in the Report Data pane onto the columns of the Table control. Once you have the columns in place, select the Preview tab to see how the initial report looks.

NOTE If the template doesn't have enough columns in the table, you can add more by right-clicking in the gray header for any column. You can also drop a data field in between two columns. Either way, the report designer will clone any pre-set formatting into the new column.

WARNING Be careful if you drop-insert a column because it may create an item with the same name as an existing item except with a difference in case. Thus, you may end up with TextBox1 and Textbox1. If you have expressions in the text boxes, the parser won't like the similar names and will give you a fairly unhelpful error message.

When you select Preview, the report should run and generate results for the default calendar year of 2008. Try changing the Date.Calendar Year parameter in the pulldown menu at the top of the report. You need to hit the View Report button to re-execute the query. If you haven't already fixed it, the pulldown menu allows you to select more than one year by default. This will break the prior year calculations, so go back and change this.

To improve the default settings, return to the Design tab and select the Parameters folder in the Report Data pane on the left. Double-click the DateCalendarYear parameter to display the Report Parameter Properties dialog box, as illustrated in Figure 10-14.

Change the prompt string to make sense to your business users, and uncheck the multi-value box in the Properties section. Now, if you select the Preview tab, you should be able to select only a single year in the pulldown menu.

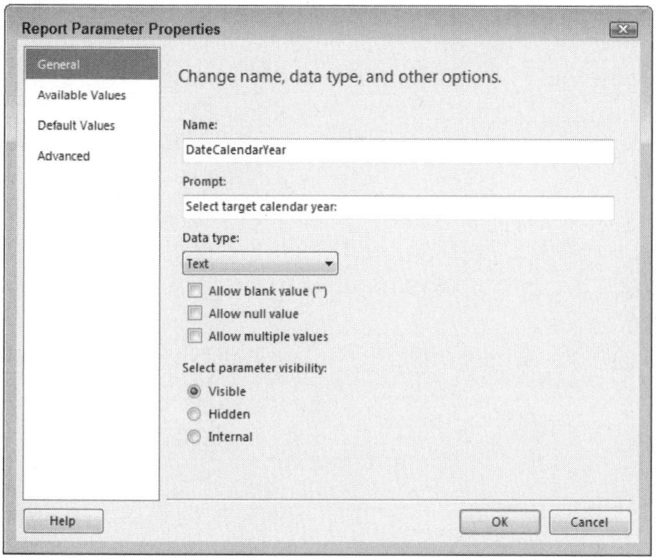

Figure 10-14: Report Parameter Properties dialog box

Creating reports is a classic 80/20 process, or even 90/10, in that it takes only 10 percent of the time to create 90 percent of the report. Most of the final 10 percent of creating a report is formatting, and it usually takes much longer than you would expect. In this case, the Sales Rep Performance report now has the key elements it will have when it's finished, but it doesn't look very professional. Go back to the Layout view and take a few minutes to clean up some of the following appearance problems:

- Change the column widths to make better use of the available space.
- Format the sales columns to get rid of all those decimal values and add some commas. Try selecting the field in the Detail row and putting an "N0" in its Format property, or try a custom format string, like "#,##0." (Search for the "Predefined Numeric Formats" topic in the Visual Basic language reference at `http://msdn.microsoft.com` for more options.)

NOTE You might think that number formatting would be easier if the data source is Analysis Services rather than SQL. One of the advantages of Analysis Services is that it contains metadata about such things as formatting for measures. Reporting Services will show the correct formatting, but it is not the default. You have to change the text box expression to `=Fields!<your field name>.FormattedValue`.

- Verify the line spacing and borders.
- Add and format appropriate totals.

Figure 10-15 shows the finished report in the Preview tab of the Report Designer environment.

The guiding philosophy for creating and formatting reports is that they should be as clear, consistent, and self-explanatory as possible. Users will not take the time to look elsewhere for report documentation, nor should they be expected to. Clarity is one of the major challenges the DW/BI team takes on when it includes standard reports as part of its responsibilities. Involve someone who has solid graphic design expertise in the design process of the layout template and the initial report set. Experiment with alternatives and get feedback from users as to which one works best. A bit of extra work at this point will pay off massively in the long run.

Design	Preview				

Select target calendar year: CY 2008 ▾   View Report

◀◀ ◀ 1 of 1 ▶ ▶◀ | ← ⊗ ⊕ | 🖨 🗔 🗔 🖅▾ | 100% ▾   Find | Next

Sales Rep Ranking: 2008 vs. 2007   Adventure Works BIS

Employee	2008 Sales	2008 Rank	2007 Sales	2007 Rank	Rank Change
Amy E. Alberts	98,323	16	547,375	15	-1
Stephen Y. Jiang	249,400	15	457,575	16	1
Syed E. Abbas	26,580	17	145,944	17	0
David R. Campbell	674,625	12	1,372,498	10	-2
Garrett R. Vargas	570,416	14	1,378,290	9	-5
Jae B. Pak	1,808,043	2	4,172,459	1	-1
Jillian Carson	1,373,132	5	3,641,869	4	-1
José Edvaldo. Saraiva	1,236,146	6	1,837,614	8	2
Linda C. Mitchell	1,885,942	1	4,102,250	2	1
Lynn N. Tsoflias	720,324	11	701,487	14	3
Michael G. Blythe	1,537,712	3	3,927,252	3	0
Pamela O. Ansman-Wolfe	650,083	13	889,869	13	0
Rachel B. Valdez	829,513	10	961,128	12	2
Ranjit R. Varkey Chudukatil	1,374,856	4	2,286,700	6	2
Shu K. Ito	1,076,281	8	2,339,257	5	-3
Tete A. Mensa-Annan	837,495	9	1,218,975	11	2
Tsvi Michael. Reiter	1,089,192	7	2,222,128	7	0
	16,038,063		32,202,669		

Report Description: The Sale Rep Ranking report ranks sales reps based on Reseller Sales attributed to each rep in the calendar year selected.

Report Name: Sales Rep Performance Ranking   Help

Report Folder: Last run date: 3/2/2010 12:17 PM   1

Figure 10-15: Final report layout for the Sales Rep Performance Ranking report

TWEAKING THE REPORT LAYOUT

To create a clear, understandable, professional-looking report, you need to go beyond these basic formatting items. Some additional improvements to consider include:

- *Add a report description to the report's metadata.* This description lives in the properties of the report itself. To access these properties, select the area outside the design surface in the Design tab and look for the description property in the properties window.

- *Add conditional formatting.* Reporting Services supports expressions written in Visual Basic .NET. You can use this powerful capability to define most of the properties in the report programmatically. Conditional formatting is a good example of this capability. (Search for the "Expression Examples" topic in Books Online for more examples.)

  For example, in the Sales Rep Performance Ranking report, the VP of Sales might want to highlight those sales reps that have risen or slipped more than two places in the rankings. You need a soothing green color for the rising stars and an ominous red color for the slackers. To accomplish this, apply conditional formatting to the entire detail group row. Select the row, and then select the pulldown menu for the BackgroundColor property in the Properties window. The last choice in the menu is <Expression ... >. Select it and the Edit Expression dialog window opens. Delete the contents of the Expression box and enter the following expression:

  ```
  =iif( Fields!Rank_Change.Value > 2, "LightGreen",
     iif(Fields!Rank_Change.Value < -2, "MistyRose", "White"))
  ```

  Select OK, and then select the Preview tab. You should see some nice highlighting at this point. Can you tell who is going to be in trouble when you publish this report?

- *Add parameterized labeling.* This is another useful application of expressions. Rather than have generic column labels that don't tell the user exactly what is in the column, you can use expressions to incorporate parameters right into the report text. This is particularly helpful for when reports are printed. Once you separate the report from the Reporting Service, it is unclear which parameters you used to generate the report. Labels can be made more descriptive by using expressions as follows:

  - Right-click the SalesAmnt header field and select Expression. In the Expression box, delete the text title and enter the following expression:

    ```
    =Left(Right(Parameters!DateCalendarYear.Value,5),4) & " Sales"
    ```

Continued

(continued)

- Select OK, and then select the Preview tab. If the `TargetYear` is still set to 2008, the `Sales` column header should now be `2008 Sales`.

- Make appropriate, similar changes to the `CurrentRank`, `PriorSalesAmnt`, and `PriorRank` header fields. Remember, the parameter is a string value, so you may need to use the `Val()` and `Str()` functions to get the prior year into the titles.

■ *Add an interactive sort.* Enable the Interactive Sorting in the Text Box Properties on the Current Ranking column header text box. This will allow your users to sort out the top or bottom performers.

■ *Verify print layout.* It is rare that a report you have created to fit on the screen will also fit on the printed page the first time. You may need to change the column widths and font sizes to squeeze things in a bit. You can change the page setup as well, adjusting margins and switching from portrait to landscape. If you can't keep all the columns on a single page, you may need to change some of the properties of certain fields and groups to cause them to repeat on subsequent printed pages.

Unit Test

Report developers should do the first round of testing right in the development environment. At the very least, the developer should test various combinations of the parameters and validate the results with existing reports if possible.

Test different parameters. For example, try the Sales Rep Performance Report with the year 2007. What happens? It looks like some of the rows are missing a few values. This makes sense in this case because you would expect some sales reps to have data in one year and not the other. Fortunately, Analysis Services does an outer join for you to make sure everyone in the target year is represented in the report. Try it again with the year 2005.

Validate the numbers. Check the numbers as carefully as possible. Compare them to any known alternative sources for the same information. If the numbers should be the same and they are not, figure out why. Research the business rules in the alternative source and compare them to your own. The problem may be in your query, or all the way back somewhere in the ETL process. If there's a problem, resolving it is serious detective work and can take a lot of time and energy.

If the numbers are supposed to be different because they have been improved or corrected in the ETL process, carefully document the reasons for the differences. If possible, show how you can get from the data warehouse numbers back to the alternative source numbers. This documentation should be available in the BI portal, and the report description should refer to it.

Before you actually deploy the report, you may want to create a few more reports and deploy an entire project all at once. In this case, you can add a Sales Rep Detail report or a report that includes quota information and set up the ranking report to drill-through to the detail.

Deploy to the Test Report Server and Test Some More

In large environments with hundreds or thousands of users pounding on the standard report set, it makes sense to deploy the reports to a test server environment that is as similar to the production environment as possible. This step allows the reporting team to stress test the new reports to ensure they perform and they don't reduce the performance of other reports before moving them into production. In medium-sized or smaller organizations where the user population is smaller, it may not be necessary for a full test server environment. The reporting team can deploy the reports to the production Report Server and test them there. You can minimize the risk of this move by limiting access to the new report directories, and by not publishing the new reports in the BI portal until you have completed testing.

This test phase typically involves several steps. The process begins with deploying the project to the target Report Server (either test or production). Once there, the reports need to be retested to ensure proper performance, display, and printing. If they are not working well enough, there are a number of tuning techniques available. These range from tuning the query to creating report snapshots to actually changing the server configurations.

Deploying the project or report to a report server is straightforward. Each project has its own configuration properties, so if you have multiple projects in a solution, you will need to set up the properties for each project. Within each project, there are several configurations and each can have its own target Report Server. The default configurations are DebugLocal, Debug, and Production. To set up the target server in the project properties, in the Project menu, select Properties. This opens a project-specific Properties pages window. To deploy the project, you need to provide a target server URL for the active configuration. In the simplest case, where the web server is on the same machine as the development environment, the target server URL can be `http://localhost/ReportServer`.

After you test the basics of appearance and performance, the next step is to integrate the new reports into the production process. If there are standard schedules these reports depend on, the reports should be linked to the appropriate schedules in the Report Manager. If there are standard distribution lists that should receive these reports, they should be set up at this point. The DW/BI team should also validate the subscription process to make sure the report is available for users to subscribe to and receive on a regular basis.

Deploy to Production

When there is an actual deployment to the production server, you will need to repeat many of the steps you went through to move the reports into test. These include schedules, snapshots, subscriptions, and email distribution lists. However, in most cases, the deployment to production has already taken place in the test step, so this step is more of an unveiling than anything else. This is especially true when the primary user interface with the reporting environment is through a web site or portal. In this case, the reports are not visible to the users until you make them available in the portal.

The BI portal is such a powerful tool for the DW/BI system that we explore it in detail in Chapter 12 when we discuss SharePoint. At this point, it is enough to say that if you are providing reports through a portal, you need to integrate this new set of reports into that portal as part of the production deployment.

An important part of deploying a report to production is setting the security for the report. Reporting Services has several options for managing security, as do the relational engine and Analysis Services. We discuss security in Chapter 14.

Reporting Operations

The report deployment process included steps to tie the new reports in with existing reporting operations processes like schedules and distribution. These operations processes will also need to be maintained on an ongoing basis, independent of the introduction of new reports.

In addition to deploying the reports to the report server, you may need to cause a set of reports to run automatically when the data load for a business process dimensional model is finished. Reporting Services isn't directly tied to the ETL system, but it does have a control structure called a *subscription* that can help. Create a set of subscriptions that the main load processes will kick off as part of the regular update process.

One way to accomplish this is to write a script that invokes the subscription from within the data load Integration Services package. The problem with this approach is it hard-codes the link between Integration Services and Reporting Services, making it difficult to maintain and enhance.

An alternative solution is to create a metadata layer between the two components. You can use a simple metadata table to drive the relationships between your ETL and reporting systems. The table-driven approach is easy for an administrator to manage once it's set up.

REFERENCE We uploaded detailed instructions on how to build this metadata-driven system, including scripts and an example Integration Services solution to the book's website: `www.kimballgroup.com/html/booksMDWTtools.html`.

As you deploy new standard reports to the Report Server, add them to the appropriate schedules and create any system subscriptions to distribute the reports as needed. The DW/BI team will also need to maintain any data-driven subscriptions that involve individual users and email lists. The team may need to add and delete users from these lists as they come and go from the organization.

The same goes for other distribution mechanisms, like file shares. Computers and networks have a tendency to change. For example, the accounting department may have requested a set of reports distributed to their file server. Then they get a new file server and turn off the old one without telling you. At this point, you have a subscription failing on a regular basis and a set of users not receiving scheduled reports.

Ad Hoc Reporting Options

There is a class of users who actually want to get their hands directly on the data. This group of power users is relatively small, but very important, so you need to make sure they have the tools they need. There are many options for providing ad hoc access to the DW/BI system. Reporting Services has Report Builder 3.0, as we've mentioned, and Office has Access and Excel. As we describe in Chapter 11, Pivot tables and PowerPivot are particularly enticing data access tools for many of the power users because these users are very comfortable with Excel. Beyond Microsoft, there are dozens of products designed to support this user community, some of which are big, multi-platform products, and some of which are targeted specifically at one platform, such as Analysis Services.

Given that Report Builder is part of Reporting Services, we will describe some of its unique capabilities. There are previous versions of Report Builder, but beginning with Report Builder 3.0, the product has progressed far enough to be considered a broadly useful query and reporting tool. As you can see in Figure 10-16, Report Builder shares most of its report controls and design panes with the Report Designer, so much of what you've seen in this chapter applies to Report Builder. Report Builder has made several efforts to simplify the report creation process. These efforts began with the metadata layer called the report model, that Report Builder can use to access relational and Analysis Services data. They also include the concepts of shared datasets and report parts.

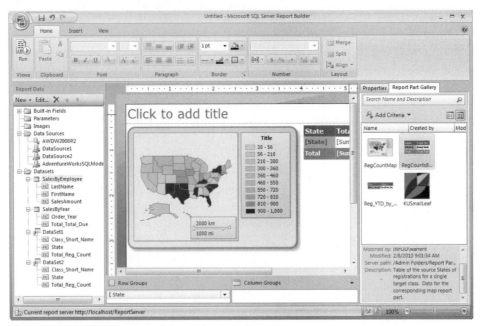

Figure 10-16: The Report Builder design interface

The Report Model

The report model is a remnant of the original reporting tool Microsoft bought in 2004 that became Report Builder 1.0. It is a metadata layer between the tool and the data that defines the tables and columns and the relationships among tables. It also defines aggregation options, such as sum and count, and allows the user to choose the appropriate option for a given query. You only work with a report model when you define a data source on a model and then build a dataset based on that data source. You can auto-generate a model for both Analysis Services and relational databases by navigating to the appropriate data source in the Report Manager and selecting Generate Model in the header bar. Relational models work best if you create them via a report model project in BIDS. You are probably better off using the Analysis Services query designer rather than creating a report model for an Analysis Services cube. The report model was originally created for relational access, and doesn't do its best work against Analysis Services.

Interacting with the model takes a bit of getting used to. The model follows the join paths, so if you have a model of the Adventure Works DW Analysis Services database, and select the `Customer` table in the Entities list as a starting point, and then select the `Location` folder, you see `Customer` location columns in the Fields list below. If you select the `Country` field and drag it to the column list, your choice of entities now shrinks to those tables that are joined to `Customer` in the model. In this case, `Customer` only joins to the `Internet Sales` fact table, so you can continue to select `Customer` columns, or select the fact table. If you select the fact table, you can now select fields from the fact table, or select any of the tables the fact table is joined to, which of course is all of the dimensions.

Shared Datasets

Rather than having to define a dataset from scratch, a Report Builder user can select a pre-existing dataset from a directory on the Report Server. This can simplify the process of defining the dataset, but it introduces its own issues. The user only sees the name of the dataset and its directory path. The description is not shown. This means the naming convention for datasets must be carefully thought out, documented, and followed. You can ease the navigation problem by keeping the number of shared datasets as low as possible. This means each shared dataset will likely have a fairly large set of data that can be filtered within the report itself. This can result in everyone building reports that run large queries to answer smaller questions. In other words, it may lead to an unnecessary increase in query workload.

Once the shared dataset is linked to Report Builder, it appears in the Datasets tree on the left of Figure 10-16. The arrow in the icon, similar to a shortcut icon, distinguishes a shared dataset from an embedded dataset. This link is fixed, which means changes to the master dataset will be reflected in all reports that use that shared dataset.

Shared datasets might be a good way to define common parameter pick lists across your standard report set.

Report Parts

Report parts are a similar attempt to reuse existing components rather than build from scratch for each report, but rather than stop at the dataset, report parts go all the way out to the finished and formatted data region or other report element. This means a user can build a report by simply dragging in report parts as needed. Report parts are on the Report Server; you can specify a default directory by clicking the Options button under the Report button at the top left of the Report Builder window. The report parts available to the user are displayed in a pane called the Report Part Gallery, seen on the right side of Figure 10-16.

The Report Part Gallery is more advanced in terms of how it displays its contents than the basic dataset selection window. The gallery allows a user to search for report parts based on the name and description. The gallery displays the results with a thumbnail of each report and displays the selected report's metadata at the foot of the gallery. It also displays the report description when you mouse-over the report.

The Report Part Gallery is a good start at providing a means to organize and access a set of report parts. Its success will be determined by how well you manage your business metadata, especially the names and descriptions of each report part.

It will be interesting to see how effective report parts are at easing the report creation task. It may be the case that report parts are too specific and users always need to make changes to someone else's work, which may be harder than starting from scratch. Or, it may be a big timesaver.

Summary

BI applications are the vehicle for delivering value to the business users. There are different kinds of BI applications you might need to create depending on the business requirements for your DW/BI system, including ad hoc access tools, standard reports, dashboards and scorecards, analytic applications, and data mining tools.

Delivering a set of high value standard reports is usually a major DW/BI team responsibility. These reports are the primary interface to the DW/BI system for a large majority of the user community. Since Reporting Services is SQL Server's standard reporting platform, we examined the Reporting Services architecture to see what functions it provides to meet the organization's reporting needs. This gave you a good sense for the components of the tool and how those components fit together. Comparing the Reporting Services architecture to the business requirements for reporting, we concluded that Reporting Services has a reasonable feature-cost ratio, especially considering its incremental cost.

With this understanding in place, the next section offered a detailed process for creating a set of standard reports. Start with some preparation steps to get the development environment set up and to create a standard template that serves as a starting point for every new standard report. Next, revisit the standard report prioritization list, specifications, and mock-ups that you captured as part of the requirements gathering process early on in the Lifecycle.

The last major section of this chapter walked through a case study that picked the top-priority report from Adventure Work's list and dove into the development process.

We ended up with a brief look at ad hoc reporting options including the Report Builder and its report model, shared datasets, and report parts.

Delivering the reports is only half of delivering the information. The DW/BI team needs to provide a navigation framework to help users find the reports they need. You can build this framework using standard web tools, a web portal system like SharePoint, or using the portal capabilities of a third-party BI tool. We explore this more in Chapter 12.

The standard reports are a critical part of the DW/BI system, but they take a fair amount of work to build and maintain. The DW/BI team must plan for that work on an ongoing basis, as we describe in Chapter 15.

CHAPTER 11

PowerPivot and Excel

"Easy" is a relative term.

Depending on how you count, Excel is arguably the most popular reporting and analysis tool on the planet today. This is not to say it is the best tool, but its broad availability, powerful expression language, programming capabilities, fine grained formatting functions, and data accessibility make it the starting point for most business analysts.

Microsoft's PowerPivot add-in for Excel 2010 takes Excel reporting and analytics to a whole new level. PowerPivot for Excel is an in-memory database add-in that allows Excel users to work with millions of rows of data at memory speeds. This evokes a high level of enthusiasm among its supporters. One of Microsoft's white papers on PowerPivot includes the line: "The ultimate goal of PowerPivot for Excel is to make data analysis really easy." It goes on to describe PowerPivot as "…a new product that provides self-service BI (Business Intelligence) functionality for users of Microsoft Office." It sounds like all you really need to do is hand out Office 2010 licenses and set free all that self-service BI. Once you've heard these kinds of statements enough times, you might start to question your efforts to create a full-scale DW/BI system. In fact, you're probably wondering why you read this far in the first place.

Of course, reality is seldom as rosy as marketing would have you believe. PowerPivot is the equivalent of pivot tables on steroids. You can load and effectively work with much larger data sets, with millions of rows of data. You can join data from multiple, disparate sources in the PowerPivot database. You can employ an expression language to create complex calculations and measures that calculate correctly in any context within the pivot table. How easy all this is depends on your background and experience level with Excel, databases, the structure and complexity of the data you are working with, and BI in general.

We start this chapter with a brief description of Excel as an analysis and reporting tool. We then take a look at PowerPivot and its product architecture. The bulk of the chapter is dedicated to working through an example to give you a sense for what it takes to apply PowerPivot to a simple, realistic problem. We'll finish up with a brief discussion of PowerPivot in the SharePoint environment and its role the overall DW/BI system.

In this chapter, you learn the following:

- Options for using Excel as a reporting and analysis tool
- The functionality and architecture of the PowerPivot add-in for Excel and the supporting components in SharePoint
- The main steps in creating a PowerPivot database and an associated PivotTable
- A basic understanding of how to create calculations and measures in a PowerPivot database
- A sense for how PowerPivot works in the SharePoint environment
- Guidance on how to include PowerPivot as part of your managed DW/BI system strategy

Using Excel for Analysis and Reporting

Excel has clearly staked its claim as one of the leading tools for business intelligence analysis and reporting. The ability it provides to create formulas, tables, and to manipulate data is the heart of many ad hoc BI style investigations. In many organizations, Excel is also the standard delivery vehicle for enterprise reports.

Excel does have basic functionality built in to support reporting and analysis. Data connections allow authorized users to access both the SQL and Analysis Services databases in the data warehouse. The relational query designer is not very sophisticated: It returns a single, flat record set rather than separate dimensions and facts. The Analysis Services connection leverages the cube metadata to group columns in the field list by the dimension or fact table they came from.

While it is possible to access this dataset using Excel commands, the Excel PivotTable control is the primary data manipulation tool for analytics. It allows the user to create basic row and column matrix reports by dragging and dropping attributes from the field list. Excel 2007 added report filter fields to the PivotTable Field List, and Excel 2010 enhanced this filtering capability with slicers. A slicer is a visual list of the available values for a given field. You can filter the PivotTable display by selecting values in the slicer control. A single slicer can control multiple PivotTables and charts. Figure 11-1 shows an Excel dashboard with three slicers in the lower-left quadrant that allow the report user to filter the report based on country, year, and customer type.

Figure 11-1: A simple Sales Summary dashboard in Excel

Creating flexible, parameter-driven reports in Excel is often much harder than it might first appear because our organizations, products, and customers are not symmetrical. For example, if you chose a country other than the United States in the report in Figure 11-1, the regional sales section falls apart because other countries have different numbers of regions. The report has to be able to expand and contract based on the user's parameter choices. While it is possible to do almost anything in Excel, these complexities often lead to programming in Excel macros — an activity that is not for everyone.

Excel, and especially the PivotTable control, is an excellent tool for ad hoc projects where the analyst needs to analyze data in a new way, potentially bringing in data from multiple sources. This ad hoc access works best against a well designed Analysis Services cube because of the nature of the PivotTable control. However, interactive pivot table browsing of Analysis Services data is not very practical against cubes with large dimensions. It's too easy to drag in the wrong column and get stuck while Excel tries to load 20 million customers into the PivotTable. As you will see later in this chapter, PowerPivot for Excel greatly expands the limits of what's possible in Excel in terms of analytic capabilities and raw data volumes.

The PowerPivot Architecture: Excel on Steroids

There are actually two major components to PowerPivot: PowerPivot for Excel 2010 and PowerPivot for SharePoint.

PowerPivot for Excel is a free add-in for Microsoft Office Excel 2010 that provides greatly enhanced data management and query capabilities to the Excel users' desktops. Users can install PowerPivot for Excel and use it on a standalone basis; it does not require a separate server component to function. As Figure 11-2 shows, the add-in includes the assembly and the database, called the VertiPaq engine. The VertiPaq database is designed to load the data into memory in a highly compressed, column-oriented format that is especially well suited to analytic slicing and dicing. This engine, known as an *in-memory, column-store database*, was developed by the Analysis Services product team.

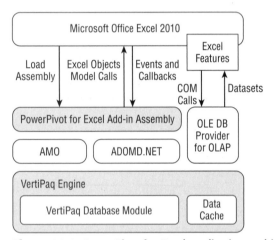

Figure 11-2: PowerPivot for Excel application architecture

The data itself is stored in a compressed form in a section of the spreadsheet file. You may see some large spreadsheets when you start using PowerPivot, but they are surprisingly small relative to the number of rows in the tables because of the compression. The PowerPivot add-in and its data are loaded into the Excel process address space. This is particularly important for 32-bit Excel because it must share the available 2GB of memory with Excel and any other add-ins.

PowerPivot for SharePoint is a SharePoint add-in that is the enterprise version of PowerPivot, allowing Excel users to publish their PowerPivot workbooks and share them with others in the organization. Users and applications can access PowerPivot workbooks via two main Service applications, shown in the middle of Figure 11.3. Users who do not have Excel and PowerPivot installed can come in through a web

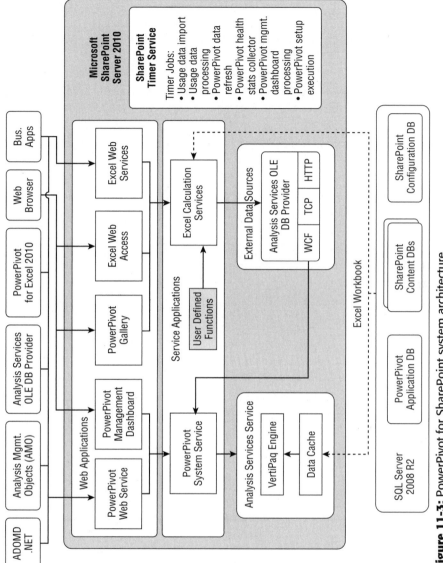

Figure 11-3: PowerPivot for SharePoint system architecture

browser via SharePoint Excel services and get most of the functionality of the desktop PowerPivot. PowerPivot for SharePoint also adds its own web service so PowerPivot for Excel and other clients can access PowerPivot for SharePoint data as a data source.

The SharePoint implementation allows IT to monitor and manage these shared PowerPivot workbooks through the PowerPivot Management Dashboard. It also supports an automated data refresh function and provides a graphical interface called a gallery that lets users view screen shots of worksheets in PowerPivot files without having to open them up. Unlike the free PowerPivot for Excel add-in, PowerPivot for SharePoint requires licensing for SharePoint and SQL Server 2008 R2.

PowerPivot is positioned as a tool that can enable business users familiar with Excel to easily create powerful analytics on their desktops, and share those analytics with other users via SharePoint. IT helps in this process by setting up the SharePoint environment to support enterprise access to PowerPivot-based reports and analyses. IT will also ensure performance by monitoring report usage and managing the PowerPivot update and maintenance process.

We agree with this positioning in theory, but it's important for you to have a good understanding of what it takes to make PowerPivot work in your environment before you decide what role it plays in your DW/BI system. Let's dive in to PowerPivot at this point and create a simple analysis.

Creating and Using PowerPivot Databases

The best way to understand PowerPivot is to work with it hands-on. We'll run through the process of creating a PowerPivot database and an associated analysis. If you haven't used PowerPivot before, you'll get the most out of this section by installing it on your computer, downloading the example files from the book's website, and following along. (If you don't have Office 2010, you can always set up a virtual machine and download a trial version.)

Our scenario is a simple one: we're going to load population and income data from an external source and join it to the customer dimension. Our goal is to explore the data for relationships between our customers and the demographics of the geographies in which they live. The initial exploration will be to see if there is a correlation between customers and per capita income. If there is a relationship, we could use it to tune our marketing campaigns. For example, if it turns out our products are more popular in higher income states, we can target our advertising toward those states, or to media channels that focus on higher income households across all states.

This kind of ad hoc integration of disparate data sources is generally known as an *analytic mashup,* a term we borrow from the web development space. In this example, we might get demographic data from the U.S. Census Bureau. It offers extensive demographic data down to the zip code level and lower in some cases. The example we'll work with in this section uses small tables of simplified data so you can see what PowerPivot is doing. We are not out to test its ability to load millions of rows here.

DOWNLOADS You can download the source files and resulting Excel workbook from the book's website at `kimballgroup.com/html/booksMSDWTtools .html`. You can also download a few other useful tables, such as a `Date` table from 2000 to 2020, and census data at the zip code level from the 2000 census.

Getting Started

If you are starting from scratch, you need to have Office 2010 and the PowerPivot for Excel add-in installed. Installation of PowerPivot is fairly straightforward. Once you have Office 2010 installed, you download and run the PowerPivot for Excel installation package from Microsoft's PowerPivot website: `http://www .powerpivot.com`. You need to install the 32-bit version if you have 32-bit Office installed, or 64-bit if you have 64-bit Office installed. They are not interchangeable. Note that the 64-bit version will allow you to access more memory, which is important to support larger data sets. If your data doesn't fit in memory, PowerPivot won't be able to load it.

Once you've installed the add-in, Excel may still ask if you want to install it when you open Excel. Once it's fully installed, you should see a message indicating that Excel is loading the add-in every time you start the program.

Start by exploring the add-in a bit to get familiar with its functions and interface. When you select the new PowerPivot Ribbon tab, you'll see around 10 buttons arranged in categories. The one you will use most often is the PowerPivot Window button on the left of the Ribbon, which launches a separate window used to design and load data into the PowerPivot database. You'll see two main ribbon tabs in the PowerPivot window: Home and Design. The Home Ribbon includes the buttons for getting external data. This is where you will typically start building your PowerPivot database.

PowerPivot Table Design

You can load data from a range of sources including relational databases, Analysis Services, flat files, and Excel spreadsheets. In our example, we load data into PowerPivot from a table already in the Excel spreadsheet and from an external flat file. These data sets are small and don't prove PowerPivot's ability to handle large data, but they do make it easier to understand what PowerPivot is doing when we start adding calculations and measures.

First let's get a sense for the analysis we want to create. Figure 11-4 shows the final layout of the report with the appropriate calculated columns.

	A	B	C	D	E	F	G	H
1								
2								
3		Row Labels	CustCount	TotalPop	CustPer100MPop	NormPenRate	TotalInc	PerCapitaInc
4		Alaska	2	4	50.00	2.86	152.4	38.1
5		Arkansas	1	6	16.67	0.95	171.0	28.5
6		California	8	36	22.22	1.27	1,425.6	39.6
7		Georgia	1	9	11.11	0.64	288.9	32.1
8		Illinois	4	13	30.77	1.76	499.2	38.4
9		Michigan	1	10	10.00	0.57	338.0	33.8
10		New Mexico		2		0.00	59.8	29.9
11		Texas	1	23	4.35	0.25	809.6	35.2
12		**Grand Total**	**18**	**103**	**17.48**	**1.00**	**3,744.5**	**36.4**

Figure 11-4: Target Analysis—Customer counts, population, and per capita income by state

This analysis brings together customer counts by state and lines them up with external income and population measures. The two data columns in the middle measure how popular we are in each state. CustPer100MPop is a relative measure of how far we've penetrated into the population of each state. We are doing relatively well in Alaska, for example. The two customers we have in a state with a population of 4 million people gives us a relative penetration rate of 50 customers per 100 million population. The math looks like this: (2/4) × 100 = 50.0.

The NormPenRate column simply normalizes the CustPer100MPop column by dividing each row's value by the overall number. For Alaska, the math looks like this: 50.0/17.5 = 2.857. This says our penetration rate is above average if the normalized penetration rate is greater than one, and below average if it is less than one. We will use this column on the chart at the end of this exploration.

The per capita income, the last column on the right, provides the values for the X axis in the final chart. Let's deal with generating the numbers since that's the hard part.

Loading the Data

If you'd like to work through this exercise, start with the spreadsheet named 1 Simple Cust and Pop Example Starting Point.xlsx and follow these steps to load the example customer data from an Excel table into a PowerPivot table:

1. Open the spreadsheet and select any cell in the Customer table. Normally you would load in customer data from a clean, trustworthy, reliable source, such as the data warehouse. In this case the Customer table is only 18 rows so you can load it into PowerPivot directly from Excel.

2. Select the PowerPivot Ribbon tab at the top of the Excel window and select the Create Linked Table button in the Excel Data section of the Ribbon.

3. This should open the PowerPivot window and copy the customer data over into a PowerPivot table called Customer. That's one table loaded — you're half way there! Examine the PowerPivot window to see what functions are available.

Next, you'll load in some data from an external source, in this case, from the U.S. Census Bureau. Again, the data set is abbreviated so you can more easily understand what PowerPivot is doing.

1. In the PowerPivot window, on the Home Ribbon, select the From Text button in the Get External Data section. This will open a Table Import Wizard to help you provide the parameters of the import.

2. Change the Friendly connection name to **PopByState**.

3. Click the Browse button next to the File Path box and navigate to the Simple Population Data.txt file. Select the file and select Open. PowerPivot will do its best to parse the file with the default settings.

4. Change the Column Separator from Comma (,) to Tab (t).

5. Finally, check the "Use first row as column headers" box. If everything looks good, click Finish. You should now have two tables in separate tabs in the PowerPivot window.

6. Notice that the new table name is Simple Population Data. Select the name by double-clicking, or right-clicking and selecting Rename. Change the name to **CensusData**. PowerPivot can handle names with spaces, but this simpler name with no spaces will make our formulas a bit easier later.

Creating the Relationships

Now that you have these two tables in place, you have the data you need to do the calculations in Figure 11-4. However, you still need to define the relationship between the two tables in order for PowerPivot to be able to join them together.

1. Select the Design Ribbon at the top of the PowerPivot window. Select Manage Relationships from the Relationships section. The Manage Relationships dialog box should open with no relationships. Sometimes PowerPivot can figure out the relationships but in this case, you need to help it.

2. Click the Create button at the top of the Manage Relationships dialog box. You should see a Create Relationship window like the one shown in Figure 11-5. The order of the tables in this dialog box is important because you are defining a one-to-many relationship. In this case, the "many" table is Customer and the join column is StateCode. The "one" table is CensusData and the join column is also StateCode. This says a single customer from a given state should only return one row from the CensusData table, but a row from the CensusData table for a single state may return many customers. Click Create to create the relationship, and then close the Manage Relationships window.

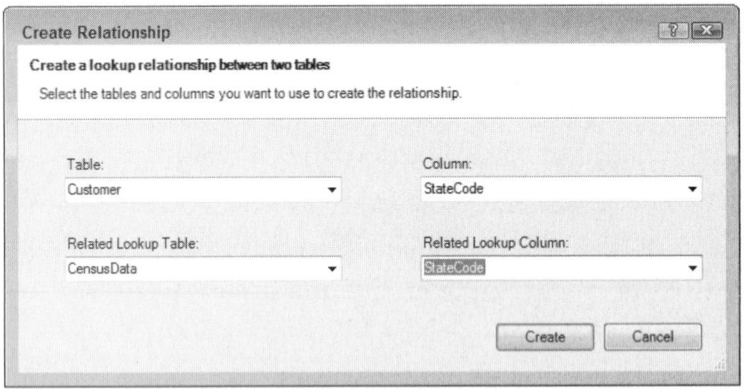

Figure 11-5: The Create Relationship window

PowerPivot will use this relationship to properly align data from the two tables in the same query. Note that the relationship definition can use only a single column from each table, and any given column can be used in only one relationship. This means you may need to create a single "key" column for some of your input tables. One way to do this is by adding a calculated column to the table that concatenates multiple fields from the table together to create a unique join field.

PowerPivot does help define these table relationships by importing existing primary key/foreign key relationships, and by recommending relationships it has auto-detected using common naming semantics, cardinality, and data patterns.

PowerPivot does not support the concept of a role-playing dimension. For example, if you have `OrderDate` and `RequestedShipDate` in your fact table, you will need to load two separate copies of your date dimension.

At this point, you've brought data from multiple sources into a single, high performance, "mashup" database.

Creating Analytics with PowerPivot

Now that the data's loaded (that was easy, wasn't it?), you can start doing some analytics in a PivotTable back in the Excel worksheet. This section goes through the steps needed to create a PivotTable and the calculations used to generate our target analysis.

Creating a PowerPivot PivotTable

First, insert a PivotTable that is tied to the PowerPivot database you just created into a new worksheet:

1. Select the Home Ribbon in the PowerPivot window and then select the PivotTable button in the Reports section. PowerPivot should shift control back to Excel and you should see a Create PivotTable window. Click OK to let the PivotTable default to a New Worksheet. You should see a PowerPivot Field List and a PivotTable results area in the new worksheet.

2. Take a look at some data. Expand the `CensusData` table in the field list and check StateName, or drag it to the Row Labels well at the bottom of the field list. Next, check the Pop field, or drag it to the Values well. Your spreadsheet should now look similar to Figure 11-6.

Explore the PivotTable a bit at this point. You can work with the `CensusData` table, but the `Customer` table doesn't add much value yet. In particular, you need a customer count as part of the calculation for several of the columns shown in Figure 11-4.

DAX – YET ANOTHER EXPRESSION LANGUAGE

PowerPivot has its own language for creating custom calculations and measures called the Data Analysis Expressions language, or DAX for short. DAX uses a syntax that was explicitly designed to be familiar to Excel formula experts, but because it works with the PowerPivot database, its arguments are columns and tables, not cells or arrays. There are more than 80 functions, operators, and constants in the initial version of DAX. Most of these functions will be familiar to Excel users; a few are unique to PowerPivot and are critical to creating correct calculations across multiple tables.

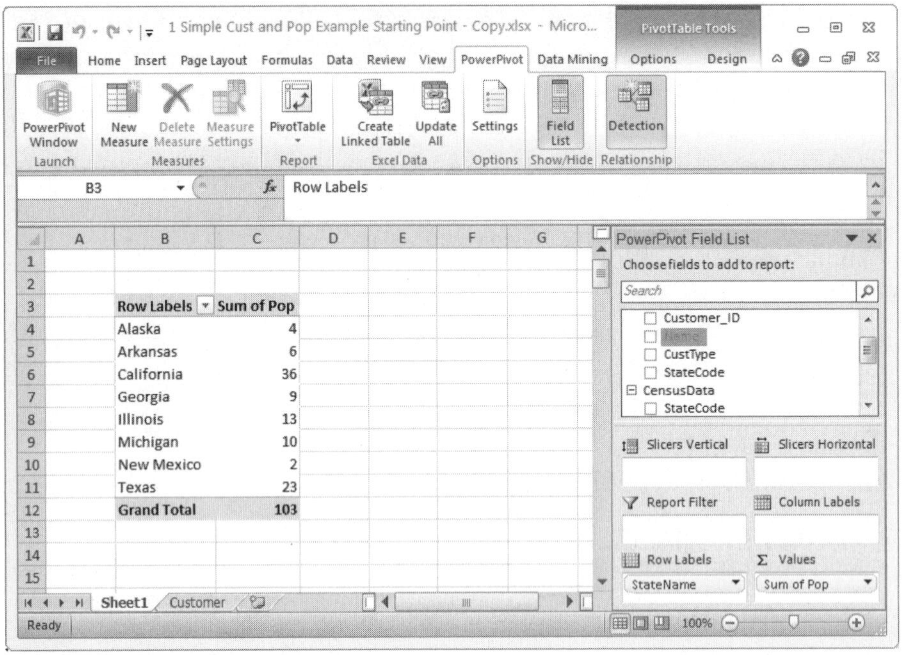

Figure 11-6: Initial PivotTable results

There are a couple of concepts that will be helpful in working with PowerPivot data. Users can define two kinds of computed columns: *measures* and *calculated columns*. Measures are computed columns that get added to the field list in the PowerPivot field list in Excel. Measures are calculated according to the row and filter context in which they appear in any given PivotTable report. Calculated columns are computed columns that get added to the base tables in the PowerPivot window. Calculated columns are populated with values when they are created, and act like any other data element in the database. When they are reported in a PivotTable, they can only be aggregated using the core aggregate functions (Sum, Count, Min, Max, and Average). Calculated columns generate row level detail data and are not as flexible or as sensitive to the row and filter context as measures.

Adding New Measures to the PivotTable

The best way to create calculations and measures in PowerPivot is to break long, complex formulas up into their component parts and build them incrementally. This allows you to experiment with the data and quickly see the results of your formulas. We'll start with the CustCount measure and build up from there.

1. Right-click on the Customer table in the PivotTable Field List in Excel and select Add New Measure (or select Customer and then select New Measure from the PowerPivot Ribbon).

2. Change the Measure Name to **CustCount**.

3. Since COUNT() seems like the right function, enter the following in the Formula box:

```
=COUNT(Customer[Customer_ID])
```

4. Click OK and you should see a new column appear in your PivotTable and at the end of the Customer field list. It should match the CustCount column in Figure 11-4: a total of 18 customers with none in New Mexico.

That was easy! But let us share a few words of warning. The COUNT() function counts cells in a column that contain numbers. Since Customer_ID is a number, this works in this case. If you needed to count cells with any values in them, you would use the COUNTA() function. The real world begins to creep in when you realize your Customer table will likely have multiple rows per customer because you have type 2 change tracking in place in your data warehouse. In that case, you could use the DISTINCT() function on the Customer_ID column to only count the distinct Customer_IDs. However, the DISTINCT() function returns a table that contains a one-column list of distinct values, and the COUNT() functions expect a column as an argument. Fortunately, there is a COUNTROWS() function that counts the number of rows in a table. As a result, the following formula is more likely to give you the count you want across a variety of data structures:

```
= COUNTROWS(DISTINCT(Customer[Customer_ID]))
```

You might want to edit the CustCount column to give this a try even though it won't make a difference in our simple example.

Explore the PivotTable a bit more at this point. Add in CustType from the Customer table. Note that the state population is repeated, independent of customer. PowerPivot does an outer join to include all values of CustType and displays the lowest grain of population it has: state population. The customer count, which is based on the Customer table, is only shown where a customer exists.

The CALCULATE() Function

Next you want a calculation that shows how many customers you have per 100 million people (CustPer100MPop); this is your penetration rate. The basic formula would be (Customer Count *100)/Population. Naively converting this to the DAX syntax you've learned thus far, you might create a formula like this:

```
=(Customer[CustCount]*100)/CensusData[Pop]
```

Unfortunately, this formula will give you an error claiming the value for Pop cannot be determined in the current context. The problem here is CustCount is a measure that creates an aggregate based on the row and filter context, but Pop is a detail level field. You need to apply some form of aggregation to the Pop column so PowerPivot can properly roll it up to the row and filter context.

We've found it to be a useful practice to create a measure that automatically applies the appropriate aggregation; we then use that measure in subsequent calculations. This is the root of our earlier recommendation to build measures incrementally. In this case you'll create a TotalPop measure, and then use it to create the CustPer100MPop measure.

1. Right-click on the CensusData table in the PivotTable field list and select Add New Measure.

2. Change the Measure Name to **TotalPop**.

3. Enter the following formula in the Formula box and click OK:

   ```
   =SUM(CensusData[Pop])
   ```

4. Add another new measure to the CensusData table called CustPer100MPop with the following formula:

   ```
   =(Customer[CustCount]*100)/CensusData[TotalPop]
   ```

At this point, your PivotTable should look something like the one shown in Figure 11-7, assuming you removed the CustType column. Note that the total under CustPer100MPop is a division of the sums, not a sum of the divisions.

	A	B	C	D	E	F
1						
2						
3		Row Labels ▾	Sum of Pop	CustCount	TotalPop	CustPer100MPop
4		Alaska	4	2	4	50
5		Arkansas	6	1	6	16.66666667
6		California	36	8	36	22.22222222
7		Georgia	9	1	9	11.11111111
8		Illinois	13	4	13	30.76923077
9		Michigan	10	1	10	10
10		New Mexico	2		2	
11		Texas	23	1	23	4.347826087
12		**Grand Total**	**103**	**18**	**103**	**17.475728155**

Figure 11-7: Intermediate PivotTable results

The formula for the CustPer100MPop measure is actually a shorthand version of a very powerful DAX function called CALCULATE(). The full syntax is

```
CALCULATE(<aggregate expression>, <filter 1>, <filter 2>,...)
```

We provided the aggregate expression, but we didn't use any filters in the formula, relying entirely on the row context to determine the appropriate inputs. (You are also allowed to leave off the word CALCULATE() as we did.)

The next computed column is the normalized penetration rate value, called NormPenRate, which will serve as the Y axis column. The challenge here is that every row must be divided by the overall average to normalize the values around 1. Fortunately, DAX offers a particularly useful filter called the All() function.

The filter list in the CALCULATE function allows you to override the existing row and filter setting in the context of the cell. The generic formula should be something like this: CustPer100MPop/Average Total CustPer100MPop. You use the All() function in the CALCULATE filter to return the total CustPer100MPop over the entire CensusData table.

1. Add a new measure to the CensusData table called NormPenRate with the following formula:

   ```
   =CensusData[CustPer100MPop]/CALCULATE(CensusData[CustPer100MPop],
   ALL(CensusData))
   ```

2. Take a look at this new column in the PivotTable. The largest penetration rate should be around 2.86 in Alaska. The Grand Total value should be 1.

So far, all your calculations have been associated with population and customer counts. As the last step in your PivotTable, bring in the per capita income numbers which will become the X axis in our chart.

1. Check the box next to the PerCapitaIncome field in the field list under the CensusData table, or drag it down to the Values well.

2. Notice the name of the new column in the PivotTable is Sum of PerCapitaIncome. This default aggregation isn't right because per capita income is not directly additive. The total number in this column of 275.6 has no useful meaning.

3. Try changing the aggregation to Average by clicking the Sum of PerCapitaIncome field in the Values well and selecting Edit Measure from the pop-up menu and then selecting Average in the Measure Settings window. Changing from sum to average is better, but it's still not right. You'll fix this next.

Adding a Computed Column to the PivotTable Database

The 34.45 total value is the sum of each state's per capita income divided by the number of states. Instead it should be the total income across all states, divided by the total number of people in all states. Since you already have a TotalPop column, all you need is a total income column to do this right. You'll create a TotalInc measure in two steps, by first creating a TotalIncome calculated column and then creating a measure on that column that uses the SUM() function. Finally, you'll finish by creating a PerCapitaInc measure that is TotalInc/TotalPop.

1. To create the TotalIncome calculated column, open the PowerPivot window and select the CensusData table tab. Remember, a calculated column is defined in the PowerPivot window and is part of the underlying table, as opposed to the measures you've been creating out in the PivotTable field list.

2. Select the first cell in the `Add Column` column (or the entire column), and enter the following formula:

   `=CensusData[Pop]*CensusData[PerCapitaIncome]`

3. Change the name of the new column from `CalculatedColumn1` to `TotalIncome`.

4. Return to the PivotTable field list in Excel and add a measure called `TotalInc` to the `CensusData` table with the following formula:

   `=SUM(CensusData[TotalIncome])`

5. Add the final measure called `PerCapitaInc` to the `CensusData` table with the following formula:

   `=CensusData[TotalInc]/CensusData[TotalPop]`

This calculation gives you an opportunity to learn the importance of verifying your calculations. Compare the `PerCapitaInc` column with the `Average of PerCapitaIncome` column. The value in the total line for `PerCapitaInc` is 36.35. The raw difference is only 1.9, but in the business context, this translates to a difference in per capita income of almost $2,000 per person compared to the Average value. Over the 103 million people in our simple data set, this is a total of $196 billion. This is not an amount you would care to lose due to an incorrect calculation.

You've created all the calculations you need. Wasn't that easy? The rest of this example is standard Excel work and is left as an exercise to the student. You might want to remove the unused columns, format the remaining columns, and add in a scatter chart. Figure 11-8 offers a completed PivotTable and chart, along with a correlation calculation.

Try adding a few slicers to the report; drag `CustType` and `StateGroup` down to the Slicers Horizontal well and see how that changes the user experience. If you add multiple pivot tables from the PowerPivot window, the slicers are automatically configured so they apply to all of the pivot tables. In other words, when you change the values selected in a slicer, all of the pivot tables change. Slicers are pretty cool, but they work best with low cardinality columns.

Note that the scatter chart control does not work directly with PivotTable data. You can trick it by choosing Select Data in scatter chart, then clicking the Add button in the Select Data Source window. Name the series in the Edit Series window that pops up, then select the numbers in the `PerCapitaInc` column for the Series X values, and the numbers in the `NormPenRate` column for the Series Y values. By the way, when you work through the chart, you'll figure out you need to go back and add an `IF(ISBLANK(),0,...)` around the `NormPenRate` formula in order to show a zero for New Mexico. This will result in data points for all eight states on the chart.

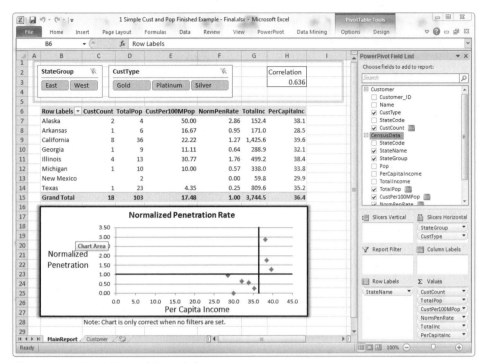

Figure 11-8: Final PivotTable and chart

To finish the business scenario, Figure 11-8 shows a clear correlation between the penetration rate and median income. You don't know cause and effect and your data set is a little small to be conclusive, but you have shown an interesting relationship that you can explore in more detail.

Observations and Guidelines on PowerPivot for Excel

The tag line for this chapter is "Easy is a relative term." Look back over the steps you just went through to create a fairly simple analysis. Our conclusion after this and several other efforts is that using PowerPivot is not easy. True, it is a very powerful tool, and it is easier to load data and query it than in earlier versions of Excel. And it's faster, and you can load much more data. However, like other BI tools, there are a lot of nuances and subtleties to master before you can fully apply the tool. Most organizations will find that the people who will be able to do self-service BI using PowerPivot are the same people who were already able to query data sources, create macros, and use complex functions in Excel.

Whatever your opinion is, our main point is, don't oversell the power of PowerPivot. It has a role in the DW/BI system, and can add significant value, but it is not a miracle tool.

Here are a few guidelines for working with PowerPivot for Excel, some of which we've already mentioned:

- *Work from a dimensional model:* PowerPivot is a dimensional engine under the covers, and it is most easily understood if you create the PowerPivot database using a dimensional model. That is, design your PowerPivot database with a fact table that joins to a set of dimension tables on a strict many-to-one basis.

- *Create incremental calculations:* As we described in the example, it's very helpful to build simple measures first, and then use those measures to create more complex calculations.

- *Check your work:* Work through any calculations you do manually to verify they are correct. Drag in attributes from all of the tables in the PivotTable to verify your calculations work across all dimensions as expected. Look for common problems like edge condition failures, such as a year-over-year calculation in the first year of data, or blanks or zeros in the denominator of a ratio.

- *Create a robust date dimension:* This is a table with one row for every date in your fact table. You can build this in Excel, download one from the book's website, or simply extract it from the data warehouse. The date dimension is important because PowerPivot has 35 functions expressly designed for working with dates. For example, there are functions for comparison, such as `PREVIOUSYEAR()` or `SAMEPERIODLASTYEAR()`, and for selecting data on specific dates, such as `STARTOFMONTH()` or `ENDOFYEAR()`.

- *Use naming conventions:* It's a good idea to establish some simple naming conventions for calculated columns and measures to help distinguish data that comes directly from the source versus data that has been manipulated locally in some way. You may also want to hide some of the underlying fields if you create measures on top of them, in order to reduce the level of complexity other users see in the PowerPivot Field List.

The goal of this section was to give you a good sense for what PowerPivot for Excel is and how it works. You can make your own assessment of how easy it is, especially after you've had a chance to get your own hands on the tool and try it out.

The other part of the PowerPivot story is the centralized SharePoint component. The next section takes a high level look at the main capabilities of PowerPivot for SharePoint.

PowerPivot for SharePoint

SharePoint is Microsoft's web portal and application platform. One of the services SharePoint can host is PowerPivot. This service is called the PowerPivot add-in for SharePoint and it provides three main functions. First it allows a PowerPivot for Excel developer to upload a PowerPivot-based spreadsheet and share it with others in the organization in conjunction with Excel Services. Second, it brings server-level resources to bear on PowerPivot applications. And third, it allows IT to monitor and manage these shared resources, including automatically refreshing PowerPivot databases.

The PowerPivot SharePoint User Experience

Users work with PowerPivot for SharePoint in three different modes: publishing, viewing, and data sourcing. We'll look at each of these in turn.

PowerPivot Publishing

PowerPivot for SharePoint is primarily a PowerPivot for Excel "viewer" application. The SharePoint user experience begins when a user publishes a PowerPivot report or analysis. It's easy for users to upload a PowerPivot workbook to the BI Portal site in one of two ways. From within the Excel workbook on the user's desktop, open the PowerPivot window and select Publish from the File menu. Enter the URL to the appropriate directory in the BI Portal and click the Save button. Figure 11-9 shows the resulting Save As window. Users can upload to any SharePoint document library with the appropriate permission. Commonly used PowerPivot workbooks will usually end up in a special type of SharePoint document library called a PowerPivot gallery.

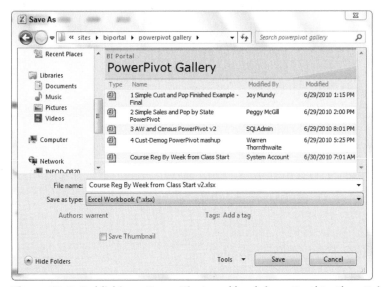

Figure 11-9: Publishing a PowerPivot workbook from Excel to SharePoint

The Excel publish capability offers two advantages. First, it is asynchronous and restartable, so a user can start a large upload and proceed with other work. Second, users can publish a subset of objects from within an Excel file, such as certain worksheets, or even selected objects within a worksheet.

Alternatively, users can upload their PowerPivot workbooks by navigating to the appropriate SharePoint directory in a web browser and selecting Upload Document from the Documents Ribbon under Library Tools. A third approach is to use the WebDAV facility, where a SharePoint site is made to look like a file share. In this case the user would navigate to the SharePoint directory in Windows Explorer, and copy in the PowerPivot file.

Once the PowerPivot workbook is in SharePoint, users can browse available workbooks using one of several list formats, known as views. The Gallery view is the default view for a PowerPivot workbook stored in a PowerPivot gallery. The Gallery view uses Silverlight to give users a more visual sense for the contents of the available PowerPivot workbooks. Figure 11-10 shows the thumbnail pictures from a PowerPivot report in the Gallery view.

The ability to visually browse through the PowerPivot workbooks and the sheets within those workbooks is particularly helpful when you don't know exactly what you are looking for. However, it may not be the best interface for infrequent users who need to look through hundreds of workbooks for a report they might not recognize visually.

Figure 11-10: SharePoint PowerPivot Gallery view

By the way, much of the SharePoint user interface, including the PowerPivot gallery, uses Silverlight to achieve its visual impact. This means PowerPivot users will need to view the SharePoint BI portal using a 32-bit browser until Microsoft releases a 64-bit version of Silverlight.

PowerPivot Viewing

Once you click a PowerPivot workbook in the gallery, SharePoint invokes the Excel Services web access control and opens up the workbook in the browser. Excel Services does not offer full Excel functionality, therefore PowerPivot for SharePoint offers a very limited set of the full featured desktop version of PowerPivot. SharePoint users can slice and dice the data using the slicer controls and can set or change filters. They cannot make changes to the report layout or format, or access the PowerPivot field list.

This server-based functionality is fine for reports and analytics that can be driven by a relatively small set of user specified parameters. This makes PowerPivot for Excel and SharePoint a good candidate for developing the enterprise set of standard reports that are often the starting point for most business inquiries.

PowerPivot as a Data Source

In addition to interacting with a PowerPivot workbook, Excel users can use the data set as a starting point for their own analyses. There are several ways this can be accomplished, each with its own capabilities. The most powerful and flexible approach is to simply download the Excel workbook and go from there. If you have permission, you can do this by selecting the workbook, and then selecting Download a Copy in the Documents Ribbon under Library Tools. Of course, this copy is now on your desktop and will no longer be automatically updated, tracked, or managed by SharePoint. You also need Excel 2010 to manipulate the workbook, and the PowerPivot for Excel add-in to edit PowerPivot.

Users can also extract data from an existing PowerPivot data set and use it to create a local PowerPivot data set by using the Get External Data from Database function in the PowerPivot window. This brings up the same Analysis Services report designer we saw in Reporting Services. The resulting data set is imported into the workbook and becomes a flattened, single table in the PowerPivot window. In other words, all the fact and dimension fields you select are joined together to create a single table in the new PowerPivot window. This can then be refreshed like any other PowerPivot data source by clicking the Refresh button in the PowerPivot window.

Finally, the PowerPivot workbook can be used as a data source for either an Excel pivot table, a Reporting Services report, or any other application that can connect to and query SQL Server Analysis Services. Users can have SharePoint set this up by selecting the new document button in the upper right of the Gallery view for each PowerPivot workbook. This creates a workbook connection in Excel, which allows the user to access a PowerPivot data set hosted in SharePoint much like accessing an Analysis Services cube (which is actually what it is doing). In this case PowerPivot for Excel does not need to be installed locally, although the SQL 2008 R2 Analysis Services OLE DB provider does need to be installed. No data is downloaded to the Excel workbook except the PowerPivot table definitions, which are fed into a pivot table control. The PowerPivot cube is re-queried for every change in the pivot table definition. Since this is not PowerPivot, you are limited to the standard pivot table functionality.

Server-Level Resources

SharePoint brings enterprise functionality to PowerPivot through its server infrastructure. This includes workload management, data caching, automated data refreshing, and security.

SharePoint can scale out PowerPivot across multiple servers in the SharePoint farm to support large numbers of users. Incoming user queries can be allocated across available servers based on a round robin or server health–based methodologies.

The PowerPivot System service also caches data on PowerPivot servers rather than re-extracting the data from content servers to speed query response times. There is also an associated caching discovery and maintenance function that unloads cached data that is no longer needed, or that may not be valid.

Keeping data in spreadsheets current is typically a manual process. Fortunately, PowerPivot for SharePoint can be set to automatically refresh PowerPivot data. Each PowerPivot workbook can be set to refresh its data on its own schedule. The data refresh facility is fairly simple. The refresh is set to run based on day and time of day, and the most frequent refresh interval available is once a day.

Security within SharePoint does not have the fine grain that can be defined in an Analysis Services database, but it is much better than a standalone Excel workbook. SharePoint security is integrated with the Windows Active Directory structures, and can be administered at the site and document level. The IT or DW/BI system security manager can monitor who is accessing which workbook.

There is a whole list of SharePoint and third party capabilities you can leverage for PowerPivot files. Since these files are SharePoint documents, you can enable version management, set up approval workflows, create email alerts for content changes, and define record retention rules.

PowerPivot Monitoring and Management

PowerPivot for SharePoint includes a usage logging function and a set of BI dashboards to allow the DW/BI team to monitor usage and system functions. There will be a set of management activities including system resource allocation, performance tuning, and security. The DW/BI team can leverage some of SharePoint's workflow functions to create a content validation and approval process to manage the submission of workbooks for publishing, rather than allow users to publish directly.

PowerPivot Monitoring

The PowerPivot Management dashboards are built using PowerPivot and provide a nice example of how the tool can be used. You can view these reports by selecting the PowerPivot Management Dashboards link under General Application Settings on the SharePoint Central Administration home page.

The PowerPivot Management dashboard includes a whole set of reports that look at several measures of user and server activity across several dimensions, including date, user, server, and workbook. The measures include CPU and memory usage, user counts, query counts and response times, workbook size, and refresh duration.

Figure 11-11 shows the Activity view of one of the sub-reports on the home page of the PowerPivot Management dashboard. This report takes advantage of Excel 2010's conditional formatting and data bars to highlight peak days across a range of measures including connections, queries, data loaded and unloaded, and user counts.

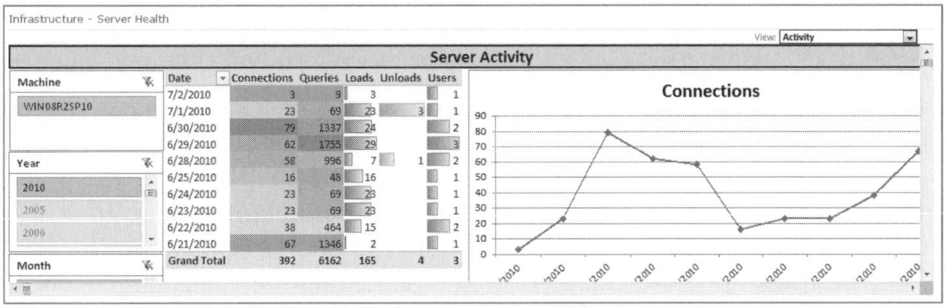

Figure 11-11: A sub-report in the SharePoint PowerPivot Management dashboard

The PowerPivot Management dashboard home page includes a report with a Silverlight slider control that gives an animated view of how usage for each workbook is changing over time. Very sexy. There are a few additional reports that can be accessed from the Reports list in the lower-right area of the management dashboard home page. Figure 11-12 shows the Workbook Activity report, which lists each workbook and shows the users, queries, and maximum load size.

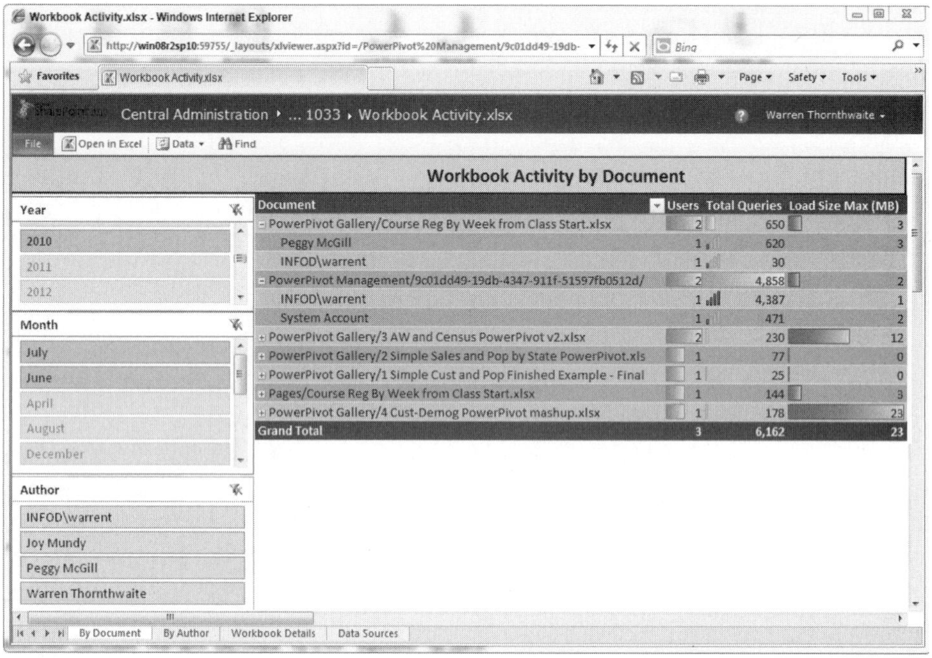

Figure 11-12: The Workbook Activity report from the SharePoint PowerPivot Management dashboard

PowerPivot Management dashboard reports can be a big help in identifying performance problems and tracking down the likely causes. SharePoint collects and aggregates the usage data every night and puts it in a PowerPivot workbook. Because the data's in PowerPivot, you can add your own reports to the dashboard, or create separate reports that do not require SharePoint Central Administration access rights.

RESOURCES Search the internet for "custom powerpivot management dashboard" to find several Microsoft and third party documents on customizing the dashboard.

PowerPivot Workbook Publishing Process

Even though it's pretty easy for a user to publish a PowerPivot workbook in SharePoint, you may want to help them do it right. This has to do with making sure the report contents and calculations are correct, verifying that there is no hidden data in the workbook, and determining the appropriate security settings.

RESOURCES Search `technet.microsoft.com` for "Secure a PowerPivot Workbook on SharePoint" to find additional guidance.

You can set up a SharePoint workflow and alerts to allow users to submit a PowerPivot workbook (or Reporting Services report). The workflow would notify the appropriate member of the DW/BI team, and guide them through the review and approval process. You can start creating an approval workflow by selecting the Library Settings button in the Library Ribbon of the PowerPivot gallery library. Then select Workflow Settings under the Permissions and Management heading. The setup forms are fairly self-explanatory.

RESOURCES Search the internet for "PowerPivot approval workflow" to find several Microsoft and third party documents on creating SharePoint workflows to manage PowerPivot publishing.

PowerPivot's Role in a Managed DW/BI Environment

Since PowerPivot for Excel is a standalone tool, Excel 2010 users can download and install it without knowledge or permission of the IT organization, for free. Regardless of what you would prefer, PowerPivot will be part of your BI environment.

While there are limits to what PowerPivot can do, and how easy it is to do it, many Excel experts will be able to use it to create useful analytics they never could have created before. Many of these, like many Excel-based BI applications, will be one-off analyses to help understand a unique situation, or explore a new idea; or they will only be of individual or departmental interest. Some of them will prove to have broader value and will rise to the top, perhaps identified through SharePoint's PowerPivot Management dashboard.

Once the broader appeal of these popular reports is known, the data sources they use that are not in the data warehouse should be brought in through your rigorous ETL process so they match the structure, quality, and availability of the rest of the DW/BI system. In a way, this is a usage-based method for identifying the business value of data. It should not be the only method you use to determine what goes into the DW/BI system, but it can play a role. The dark side of this monitoring is it can be used to police data usage and confront users with evidence of their transgressions. Do not do this. One of the fastest ways to drive your users away is to use these Big Brother tactics.

On its own, PowerPivot can offer significant value to the individual Excel advanced user. It does bring many of the same costs Excel has always had in terms of data quality, data updates, business rules, and multiple versions. PowerPivot for SharePoint helps mitigate some of those costs by bringing these reports out into the open where they can be validated, shared, and better managed. However, SharePoint itself is a big cost, both in terms of money and resources.

Summary

PowerPivot is powerful analytic tool that allows advanced users of Excel to pull together large, disparate data sets and explore them to find new relationships and insights that can add significant business value. PowerPivot can act as a platform to support the development of reports and analyses that would otherwise take too long, or would not be possible to create at all.

PowerPivot for SharePoint provides a way for creators of PowerPivot databases and analytics to share those with others in the organization who may be able to use the same analyses. PowerPivot for SharePoint also allows IT to monitor and manage these PowerPivot reports, and to automatically update the data in the underlying PowerPivot databases.

We see PowerPivot adding value to the DW/BI system in the following major ways:

- *Database prototyping*: The DW/BI team can use PowerPivot to test out dimensional model design options based on real data.

- *Data profiling*: The DW/BI team can pull data from the source systems into PowerPivot and quickly create a set of data profile reports and an issues list.

- *Report/Dashboard prototyping and delivery*: The DW/BI team can use PowerPivot to design complex reports and analyses that can be distributed across the enterprise via SharePoint. Business users may also create analytics that migrate into the DW/BI standard report set.

- *Business user analytics*: Power users can create more advanced ad hoc analyses, combining data from multiple sources with relative ease. This could include external data, or new attributes or hierarchies.

PowerPivot does not remove the need for the DW/BI system. All the work that goes into creating a robust ETL system and data warehouse, with its data cleaning, dimensionalization, and quality controls, is work that must be done to support accurate analytics, whether or not PowerPivot is part of the system. PowerPivot users will generally source their internal data, such as customer, account, product, or promotion, straight out of the data warehouse database.

PowerPivot does not replace other components in the BI layer either. You will still need Reporting Services to manage the execution and distribution of standard reports, and to provide interactive execution of those reports as needed. Users who are not Excel experts, but who want ad hoc access to the data warehouse, may prefer a query and reporting tool such as Report Builder 3.0.

PowerPivot does enable rapid data combination and exploration. For those who can use it, it will open up a whole new level of analytic possibilities. It will likely be the source of much of the unforeseen value of the DW/BI system. PowerPivot users are good for you and you need to make sure they are well supported.

CHAPTER 12

The BI Portal and SharePoint

Thinking outside the box.

Reporting Services and PowerPivot bring significant functionality to the BI user community. However, these are not the complete solution to the problem of delivering business value. As you add more and more reports and analyses to the DW/BI system, you will need to provide some means for organizing and structuring them. This is the role of the BI portal. The BI portal is the primary starting point in the information quest for a large part of the business community. It needs to be structured in a way that allows people to find what they are looking for within an ever increasing number of reports and analyses. Ideally, it will be more than just a directory structure; it will provide additional useful features such as search, customization, collaboration, metadata access, and user support.

For many smaller organizations, the Report Manager component of Reporting Services, along with basic web development skills, can be made to serve as a crude BI portal. However, DW/BI teams who want to provide rich portal experience, especially in larger organizations, will need a portal environment to serve as the BI portal platform.

SharePoint is Microsoft's offering in the portal and web-based application platform category. Microsoft has chosen SharePoint 2010 to serve as the hosting environment for several BI related components, including Reporting Services, Excel Services, PowerPivot, Office Web Applications, Visio Services, and PerformancePoint Services. SharePoint also includes a broad set of portal functions to help you create a powerful BI portal experience.

The first part of this chapter is a discussion of the BI portal concept, including design guidelines and a simple example. In the second part, we take a high level look at SharePoint as a BI portal platform and provide a summary of what it takes to get SharePoint going with a set of BI-related functionality including Reporting Services and PowerPivot for SharePoint.

In this chapter, you will learn the following:

- The major design principles and guidelines for a BI portal
- The general structure and organization of a BI portal
- What SharePoint is and how it works as a BI portal
- An approach to setting up SharePoint as a BI portal

The last section of the chapter summarizes the major steps involved in setting up a test SharePoint environment with its major BI-related components. We have provided a more detailed walk through of these steps on the book's website, but decided to spare you the pain of reading through those steps here.

The BI Portal

In Chapter 10, we introduced the concept of the navigation framework as the organizing structure for the standard report set. Any time we use the word *portal*, it invokes visions of a major enterprise effort to collect and categorize all structured and unstructured information throughout the organization and make it available through a rich user interface with intelligent search capabilities and the ability to personalize the experience. Building the enterprise information portal may be a useful and important task, but in most cases, it is someone else's task. What you need to worry about is the BI portal, not the overall enterprise portal. Think of the BI portal as the central place where people can find the analytic information they need.

The success of the DW/BI system is determined by whether or not the organization gets value out of it. For the organization to get value from the DW/BI system, people have to use it. Since the BI portal is the primary interaction most people have with the DW/BI system, the DW/BI team needs to do everything in its power to make sure the BI portal provides the best possible experience.

As you begin the design process, keep in mind that a significant component of the work a DW/BI team does is about managing organizational change (which is just another way to say "politics"). The BI portal plays a significant role in this change process, so it has to work at several levels. It must be:

- *Usable:* People have to be able to find what they need.
- *Content-rich:* It should include much more than just the reports. It should include as much support information, documentation, help, tutorials, examples, and advice as possible.

- *Clean:* It should be nicely laid out so people are not confused or overwhelmed by it.

- *Current:* It needs to be someone's job to keep the content up-to-date. No broken links or 12-month-old items labeled "New!" allowed.

- *Interactive:* It should include functions that engage the users and encourage them to return to the portal. A good search tool, a metadata browser, maybe even a support-oriented discussion group are all ways for people to interact with the portal. The ability for users to personalize their report home page, and to save reports or report links to it, makes it directly relevant to them. It also helps to have new items appear every so often. Surveys, class notices, and even data problem warnings all help keep it fresh.

- *Value-oriented:* This is the organizational change goal. We want everyone who comes to the BI portal to end up with the feeling that the DW/BI system is a valuable resource, something that helps do their jobs better. In a way, the BI portal is one of the strongest marketing tools the DW/BI team has and you need to make every impression count.

In short, the design principles that apply to any good website apply to the BI portal.

Planning the BI Portal

The process of creating the BI portal requires the careful combination of two basic design principles: density and structure.

- *Density:* The human mind can take in an incredible amount of information. The human eye is able to resolve images at a resolution of about 530 pixels per inch at a distance of 20 inches. Even though computer monitor resolutions have been improving over the years they still don't come close to this number. Typical desktop LCD monitors have a resolution of about 100 pixels per inch. Our brains have evolved to rapidly process all this information looking for the relevant elements. The browser gives us such a low-resolution platform that we have to use it as carefully and efficiently as possible. Every pixel counts.

- *Structure:* Although we need to fill the BI portal home page with information, it doesn't work if we jam it full of hundreds of unordered descriptions and links. Your brain can handle all this information only if it's well organized. For example, a typical major daily newspaper has an incredible amount of information but you can handle it because it's structured in a way that helps you find what you need. At the top level, the paper is broken up into sections. If you're looking for certain kinds of information, you know which section to start with. Some readers look at every section, but most skip a few that they deem irrelevant to their lives. At the next level down, each section may be divided into subsections and all sections use headlines as their common organizing structure. Headlines (at least non-tabloid headlines) attempt to communicate the content of the article in as few words as possible. These headlines are the "relevant elements" that allow readers to quickly parse through the newspaper to find information that is interesting to them.

RESOURCES For interesting reading about image density, see the work of R. N. Clark: *Visual Astronomy of the Deep Sky*, Cambridge University Press and Sky Publishing, 1990.

- http://www.clarkvision.com/articles/eye-resolution.html.

Edward Tufte's three-volume series provides a good general reference for structure and information display. Tufte has described the three books as being about, respectively, "pictures of numbers, pictures of nouns, and pictures of verbs.":

- *The Visual Display of Quantitative Information, Second Edition*, Graphics Press, May, 2001.

- *Envisioning Information*, Graphics Press, May, 1990.

- *Visual Explanations: Images and Quantities, Evidence and Narrative*, Graphics Press, February, 1997.

Impact on Design

The idea of density translates to the BI portal in a couple of ways. Primarily, it means we *flatten* the information hierarchy. Categories are often represented as hierarchies in the browser. You see a list of choices, each representing a topic. Click on a topic, and you're taken to a page with another list of choices, and so on until you finally reach some content. Flattening the hierarchies means bringing as much information to the top-level pages as possible. Information that was hidden in the sub-pages is now pulled up to an indented list of category and subcategory headings on a single page.

Figure 12-1 translates these concepts into the world of Adventure Works Cycles. The BI portal shown here demonstrates how two levels of report categories have been collapsed into one page. The portal is easy to navigate because you can identify major categories of information based on the headings and ignore them if they don't apply to your current needs, or examine them more closely if they seem relevant. Having the two levels on the same page actually gives the user more information because the two levels help define each other. For example, Sales helps group the sales-related subcategories together, but at the same time, the subcategory descriptions help the user understand what activities are included in Sales.

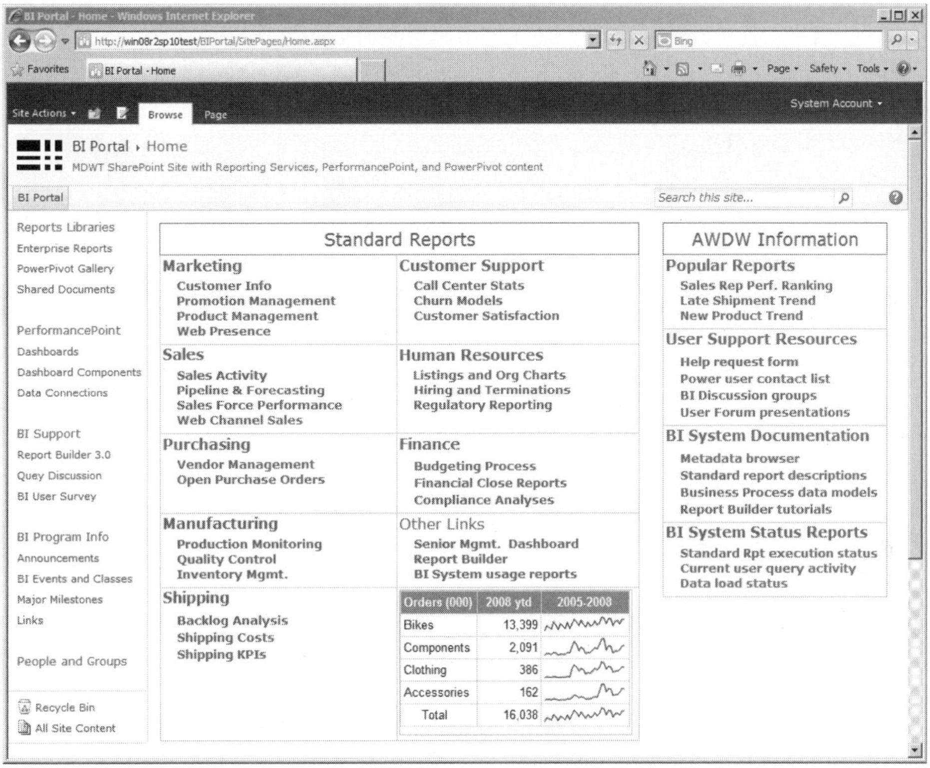

Figure 12-1: The Adventure Works Cycles BI portal home page

You can see other examples of this dense design with flattened hierarchies in the management pages in SharePoint. When you get to the SharePoint section later in this chapter, take a look at the Site Settings page on any SharePoint site. The entire SharePoint Central Administration site follows this highly dense, flattened hierarchy approach. (See Figure 12-7.) It's not so easy to use for someone who is new to SharePoint because the categories and descriptions are not obvious to the uninitiated.

Business Process Categories

Every word you include on the portal — every header, description, function, and link — all need to communicate what content people will find behind it. The categories you choose as the top level of your taxonomy will determine how understandable the BI portal is to your users. Generally, the best way to organize the portal is to use your organization's business processes as the main outline. Look at Figure 12-1 from a business process perspective. The left column under Standard Reports includes Adventure Works Cycles' major business processes. You can also think about this as the organization's value chain. In

Adventure Works Cycles' case, marketing and sales business processes come early in the value chain, working to bring in new customers and new orders. Once the company has orders, they purchase materials from their suppliers, manufacture the bikes, and ship them out to the customers. Customer support may interact with the customers at any point along the way, and even after the product has been shipped. There are also internal business processes that generate information that is useful across the organization, like headcount data from HR, or cost data from finance.

Beyond business process categories, the BI portal needs to have a standard layout so people can easily find what they're looking for. If your organization has a standard page layout that you can adapt for the BI portal, use it. Your users won't have to learn a new interface when they come to the BI portal.

Additional Functions

Although one of the main purposes of the BI portal is to provide access to the standard reports, it must offer much more than just reports. In addition to the categories and reports lists, you need to provide several common functions:

- *Search:* The search tool serves as an alternative report locator if the business process categories aren't helpful. A good search tool that indexes every report name and description, document, and page on the BI website can dramatically shorten the amount of time it takes users to find what they want.

- *Metadata browser:* A metadata browser can be as simple as a few ASP.NET pages or even Reporting Services reports that allow users to browse through the metadata's descriptions of the databases, schemas, tables, columns, business rules, load statistics, report usage, report content, and so on. You could also build this using Master Data Services and export the taxonomy into SharePoint. However you build it, interested users will learn a lot about the DW/BI system through the metadata browser.

- *Forum:* It may make sense to host a support-oriented forum or discussion on the BI portal. This can be a good way for users to find help when they need it. It can also create a record of problems and their solutions for future reference. It takes a fairly large user community to generate the critical mass of activity needed to make a forum successful. The DW/BI team should be active participants.

- *Personalization:* Users should be able to save reports or report links to their personal pages. This personalization can be a powerful incentive for people to return to the portal every day.

- *Announcements and calendars:* It helps keep things interesting to have new items appear on a regular basis. Offer a survey, have people sign up for tool training, or post a notice of an upcoming User Forum meeting.

■ *Feedback*: You need to provide a direct means for your user community to submit requests and suggestions. You should also enable social media style feedback mechanisms such as document ratings and rankings.

There is also a whole set of support and administration content the BI portal needs to provide. This includes online training/tutorials, help pages, metadata browser, example reports, data cheat sheets, help request forms, and contact info for the DW/BI team. This information all goes in the lower right corner, the least valuable real estate on the screen (at least for languages that read from left to right and top to bottom). We discuss this supporting content again in Chapters 15 and 17.

Building the BI Portal

Creating and maintaining the BI portal is much more work than most DW/BI teams expect. However, the effort is worth it because the BI portal is the farthest-reaching tool the DW/BI team has for delivering value to the organization. It is also one of your best tools for marketing the DW/BI system.

■ *Line up the resources:* You will need to have resources on the BI team, or dedicated to the BI team, who are proficient at web development and web content creation. This includes some facility with the server operating system, user authentication, and the portal software.

It's also a brilliant idea to get a good graphic designer involved; someone who has a clean, practical sense of design. Do not blindly copy our examples because they were designed to be shrunk down and printed in black and white. Besides, we are not the best graphic designers.

■ *Learn the tools:* How much learning you will need depends on what expertise you already have and what areas you will be managing. At the very least, someone on the BI team will need to know how to create and maintain the BI portal pages and the reports they reference. You may also need to know how to set up a portal site and enable the various functions you'd like to provide, such as search, help requests, and discussion forums. In the worst case, you may need to develop expertise in installing and maintaining the BI portal software itself. This can be a significant effort, as you will see in the SharePoint section later in this chapter.

If you don't have any recent experience with web development, plan to spend some time learning how to be productive and efficient in the portal development environment. There's a whole lot more to it than just writing some HTML code. Templates, cascading style sheets, scripting languages, and graphic design tools can help you create a flexible, easy to maintain website. But it takes time to figure out how they work and how to use them well.

- *Create a code management process:* Most of the portal tools have change management systems built in. After all, they are primarily web content management tools. Spend a little time learning how you put a directory or site under management, how you check a page out and in, and how you revert to a previous version.

  You will need to get the basics of your portal security in place at this point as well. From a code management perspective, you need to have security groups to determine who can see, edit, and create or delete which pages. This becomes especially important once you have users uploading their own reports to the portal.

- *Create a report submission process:* You will have a set of reports that are your organization's official BI reports. They have been tested by the BI team and bear the official DW/BI logo. BI professionals in other parts of the organization will want to add their work to the BI portal. This has pros and cons. On the pro side, the reports they create will likely be useful to many people in their groups and you want to encourage these folks to develop their skills and share their expertise. On the con side, they may not have the same attention to detail and quality control that you have. Their reports may be wrong, and ultimately undermine the DW/BI system's credibility.

  Consider having separate locations for user submitted reports in the portal. They can have a specific directory or site for their department where they keep local reports. These reports are not created, tested, or maintained by the BI team, and should not sport the DW/BI system logo. A certain percentage of these reports will prove to have value to a broader audience. Move those reports into the official reports section after you have verified their contents, structure, and calculations.

- *Create the core BI portal pages:* Design the BI portal home page and sub-pages based on the navigation framework from the BI applications design process. The BI portal home page typically corresponds to the overall bus matrix. It represents information from across the enterprise. Sub-pages usually correspond to individual business processes, such as orders or shipments, and typically include several standard report groups, including time series, time comparisons, geographic comparisons, key indicators, or KPIs.

  You will usually need to start your BI portal at the business process sub-page level because you do not have data for the rest of the bus matrix. If you start at the home page level, most of the links will be inoperative. Such a limited home page would undermine your credibility.

  Over time as you add more rows on the bus matrix and the associated BI applications your home page will gradually move toward the full BI portal shown in Figure 12-1.

- *Manage expectations:* As you learn more about your portal tools, the BI applications, and your user community, the BI portal will change. You should let people know this early on, and even enlist them in helping design new generations of the BI portal. People can deal with changes they have been a part of creating, but unexpected change will almost always generate resistance.

These principles, guidelines, and preparation steps will help you create a BI portal in any web environment. We now shift our focus to delivering a BI portal in a specific portal environment: Microsoft's SharePoint.

Using SharePoint as the BI Portal

While it is possible to create a workable BI portal using HTML editors, there are several major enterprise portal players on the market offering an extended set of web functionality (search www.wikipedia.org for "Enterprise Portal" to see a list of vendors and products). SharePoint is Microsoft's full service portal and web application platform with multi-tier, workload-balanced, distributed application support. SharePoint is an enterprise class tool. It is complex and multi-faceted, and can be a challenge to install and manage.

You can use SharePoint strictly as the website environment for the BI portal. However, SharePoint provides much more than just website hosting. It offers a range of features including connection and collaboration tools, an application platform, data capture, and workflow. Many parts of your organization could use SharePoint functionality but may have limited interest in the BI portal.

Let's be clear right from the start: SharePoint is big. Ideally, your organization already has SharePoint installed and working. If that's the case, see if the folks who have the scars of experience will help you get the incremental components needed to support BI installed and working. If your organization does not have SharePoint up and running, see if you can get some other group in IT to own SharePoint and be responsible for its broader use in the organization. This will likely be the team who already provides intranet support. This may slow things down, but it is generally a good idea because of SharePoint's complexity and broad applicability. In the worst case, if you need to install SharePoint and get it working yourself, be prepared for a few weeks of work. It may not take that long, but the probability of it taking longer than you expect is very high.

Because SharePoint is so big, we don't have the room (or the patience, or frankly, the expertise) to give you step-by-step guidance on installing all the pieces you will likely need. This section points out the major landmarks in the SharePoint ecosystem, but you still need to do a lot of work to get them going. We will list out the major BI-related components, offer general guidance on how to get those components working, and provide references on where to get more details. If you want real hands-on experience, which we strongly encourage, we have posted a guide to installing the test system we describe here on the book's website at `http://www.kimballgroup.com/html/booksMDWTtools.html`.

RESOURCES If you are going to manage SharePoint yourself, you will need more detailed instruction. One useful resource is *Professional SharePoint 2010 Administration*, by Todd Klindt, Steve Caravajal, and Shane Young (Wiley, 2010).

Architecture and Concepts

This section provides an overview of the SharePoint product, including a description of the software editions, the architecture, and key terminology.

There are three major editions of SharePoint 2010: SharePoint Foundation, SharePoint Server Standard, and SharePoint Server Enterprise. Each level includes the functionality of the previous level. Microsoft SharePoint Foundation 2010 was known as SharePoint Services. It provides the core website, service management, and document sharing features. Microsoft SharePoint Server 2010 Standard edition extends SharePoint Foundation 2010 to provide a full-featured business collaboration platform that scales from the enterprise to the Web. It provides additional collaboration, content management, and more robust search features. Microsoft SharePoint Server 2010 Enterprise edition includes many of the BI features such as Excel Services and PerformancePoint Insight. SharePoint uses Internet Information Service (IIS) as its underlying web server in all its editions.

RESOURCES You can learn more about SharePoint's features and capabilities, and the various SharePoint editions at Microsoft's main SharePoint marketing site: `http://sharepoint.microsoft.com`.

SharePoint's Three-Tier Architecture and Topology

Microsoft SharePoint Server 2010 and SharePoint Foundation Server 2010 provide the infrastructure for hosting services. SharePoint services and functions generally map to one of three roles that relate to each other in a three-tier structure. In Figure 12-2, the user-facing role is assigned to the web server tier. The primary function of the servers in this layer, also known as Web Front Ends or WFEs, is to serve web pages and process requests for services from the farm.

Server Roles	Components for Service Applications		
Web Server	• Hosts web pages, web services, and web parts • Directs requests to the appropriate application servers • Can be shared with query role in small farms		

Application Server	**Cross-farm**		**Other services**
	• Search: Query • Search: Crawl • User Profile • Managed Metadata	• Business Data Connectivity • Secure Store Service • Web Analytics	• Application Registry Service • Central Admin • Others

Single-farm

Client-related services	**Other single-farm services**	
• Excel Calculation Svcs • Access Svcs • Visio Graphics Svcs • Word Svcs and Viewing • PowerPoint	• Usage and Health Data Collection • Master Data Services • Subscription Settings • State Service	• PowerPivot SSAS Services • PowerPivot System Svcs • PerformancePoint

Database Server	**Search databases** • Search Admin • Property • Crawl **Content databases (multiple)**	**Other services databases** • State Service • Managed Metadata • Subscription Settings • Secure Store Service • Usage and Health Data Collection • Business Data Connectivity • User Profile databases

Figure 12-2: SharePoint's three-tier architecture

Most of the services are found in the application server tier in the middle of Figure 12-2. You deploy only the services you need, and a deployed service is known as a *service application*. Service applications are services that are shared across sites within a farm (for example, Search and Excel Calculation Services) or in some cases across multiple farms. You deploy service applications by starting the associated services on the desired server computers using the Services on Server page on the SharePoint Central Administration site. Service applications can be co-hosted on a single computer, deployed on a dedicated server, or activated on multiple servers across the farm, depending on the scale required.

Some services include multiple components and deployment of these components requires planning. For example, the PowerPivot for SharePoint feature mentioned in Chapter 11 includes multiple application components and multiple databases.

The third tier is the database. SharePoint sets up several databases to store technical metadata and content. The search function, for example, starts with three separate databases: administration, crawl, and property. You can create more crawl and property databases as you scale out the search function. For a list of SharePoint databases, search `technet.microsoft.com` for "using DBA-created databases."

SharePoint will automatically create the necessary databases for you as part of creating a new service application. Since the default names are based on GUIDs, you might want to override this and provide more friendly names. You can find a guide to creating SharePoint 2010 database names by searching `technet.microsoft.com` for "Introduction to the Microsoft SharePoint 2010 Database Layer."

SharePoint Terminology

Understanding all the terms used in the SharePoint world can give you a big advantage. Starting with the big picture, a SharePoint *farm* is the collection of all servers running in a SharePoint deployment and the services running on those servers. You can have a single server farm, or spread your service applications and websites across many servers. The point of the farm is to provide load balancing, scalability, and availability.

From the web perspective, a top-level domain URL is known as a *web application*, and it corresponds to an Internet Information Services (IIS) website. A web application contains one or more *site collections*, which is a set of one or more websites that have the same owner and administration settings. The top-level site collection in a web application contains the default site for the web application itself. For example, entering **http://finance/** will display the default home page from the top-level site in the `http://finance` web application.

A site collection always has a top-level site and can contain many additional sub-sites. A *site* is a coherent set of pages with a home page, libraries, lists, a common layout template and theme, all based off the same root URL. Each site can have multiple *sub-sites*. A typical company might have several web applications at the top level of its SharePoint implementation, each with a different base URL. For example, SharePoint may be supporting the organization's extranet site, and several independent intranet sites. The associated web applications in SharePoint might be as follows:

Root URL	Purpose
`http://www.adventureworks.com/`	Extranet
`http://finance`	Finance
`http://hrweb`	Human Resources
`http://AWweb`	General organization intranet

This hierarchy-based approach gives significant flexibility to the SharePoint administrator because it allows the assignment of servers, services, databases, and other resources at multiple levels. It also allows different groups and individuals to create and maintain their own section of the overall SharePoint environment. Figure 12-3 shows a hierarchy for the `http://enterprise` web application we create later in this chapter.

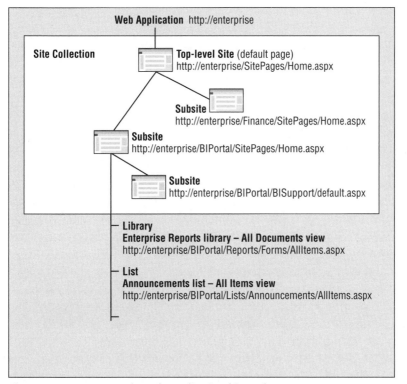

Figure 12-3: An example web application hierarchy

Note that the default URL for a web application would typically start with the name of the SharePoint server. You would need to use your Domain Name Server (DNS) to map a friendly name such as `http://enterprise` to the actual web application name which might be `http://ServerGrpShrPtProd01:59732`. If this organization only had one SharePoint server, each of the preceding web applications would map to different ports on the same server. This is known as *alternate access mapping*, and it makes the websites easier to remember.

Once you have your sites set up, you have to have some content for people to work with. When you direct your browser to a website, the web server displays a page (or invokes a program that generates the page). SharePoint has several types of content that are often displayed, entered, and edited on SharePoint pages: lists, libraries, and Web Parts.

Lists are collections of items of a single type. SharePoint lists include tasks, calendars, announcements, links, and contacts. Think of a list like a spreadsheet table with one row per entry and columns of attributes appropriate for that type of list. For example, a calendar is a list of events with attributes such as event date, event description, start time, and duration. A calendar list is displayed in a Web Part that provides the known context of a calendar: days, weeks, and months.

Views are ways to view the contents of a library or list, sort of like a report definition. They provide a display format for the list and allow you to filter it. For example, you can change the view from Calendar to the All Events view to see the individual items in the calendar list.

Libraries are a special type of list that store files as well as information about files (essentially directories). Libraries may be set to hold certain content types, such as pages, reports, or images. You can have different content types in a library, but you may have to enable this in the library's properties (via the Library Settings button in the Library Ribbon under Library Tools). You can add content types from the set of types enabled on the site. The library's property page is also where you identify what types of new documents a user can create in this library. If you want to enable a new content type on the site, you need to activate it through the Manage site features under Site Actions, or Site collection features under Site Collection Administration in Site Settings.

The kinds of lists and libraries (and sites) available to you in the Site Actions/ More Options list depend on the site features you have activated in the Site Settings menu (both under Site Actions for the BI Portal site, and under Site Collection Administration (Site collection features) for the overall set of sites). The initial template you select to create your BI Portal site will determine the initial feature set available. For example, the Business Intelligence Center template only includes a few libraries and lists, and some sample PerformancePoint pages. The PowerPivot site template includes announcements, calendar, links, and task lists; several empty document libraries; and a team discussion list. We have created a site template that includes all these features and more.

Web Parts are reusable code modules that allow you to display various types of content on your pages. You may use a Web Part to show a mini version of the calendar in the corner of the page, for example. Two of the most used Web Parts in BI are the Excel viewer and Reporting Services report viewer. These allow you to embed reports in a web page, and provide some level of interaction for the users.

Setting Up SharePoint

If you plan to use SharePoint as your BI portal, now is as good a time as any to dig in and get your hands dirty. This is one case where actually working with the product will help you understand what it is and how it works. If you don't have SharePoint 2010 already running in your company, and if the BI team will be responsible for providing its own SharePoint functionality, we strongly recommend getting started with a simple test installation of SharePoint and supporting components. Find an available 64-bit server, set up a 64-bit virtual machine, and get started. The earlier you do this the better because you have a lot to learn about how to get SharePoint working in your DW/BI system environment, and you will make a lot of mistakes.

Installing SharePoint is very much like the old example of bad documentation for shutting down a nuclear power plant where the instructions read:

1. Pull the red lever.
2. But first, push the green button.

A lot of pieces must fall neatly into place to get SharePoint working, but sometimes they step on each other. There is no perfect install order, and you often need to go back and redo some steps before you can move forward with the next step. Because of this uncertainty, we can only provide a summary of the install process for a test system here. We have posted a more detailed set of instructions on the book's website if you are inclined to actually set up a test system.

We strongly recommend using a virtual machine for your test environment. One huge advantage is that you can take snapshots at the end of each major install step, once you've verified the successful completion of that step. This will let you go back to a known good point rather than starting all over if something goes wrong.

The Installation Process

Figure 12-4 illustrates the flow of the install steps you will need to take to get a test installation of SharePoint going along with the other products, add-ins, and SharePoint services that help provide a full featured BI portal. You can install the various components in a different order, but you will have a different set of configurations needed for each install order. There are a lot of steps to this process in the initial release of SharePoint Server 2010 and SQL Server 2008 R2. We hope Microsoft will quickly make this process less cumbersome, and we suggest search `technet.microsoft.com` for "SharePoint Server installation and deployment" for more recent information.

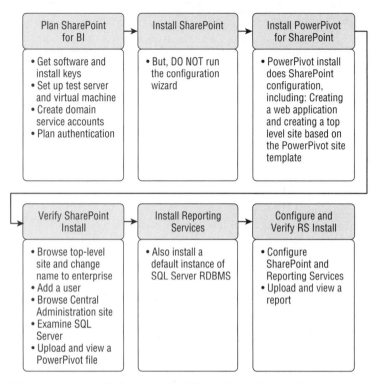

Figure 12-4: Installation steps for SharePoint and related components

Our test system install process is based on a clean version of Windows Server 2008 R2 installed on a dedicated server in an existing domain. Create a virtual machine on this server, also running Windows Server 2008 R2, and make sure you can allocate plenty of memory; 4 or more gigabytes would be good and at least two CPU cores. Note: If you need to create a true standalone installation with its own domain controller, go to `http://www.powerpivot-info.com/` and search for "single machine."

Following Figure 12-4, the remainder of this section starts with a few planning steps, and then summarizes the install steps for SharePoint and its supporting products and add-ins, including SQL Server Analysis Services in SharePoint mode and PowerPivot for SharePoint, SQL Server Reporting Services in SharePoint integrated mode for reports. We'll also mention some supporting steps around access and security and enabling various SharePoint services. Once you have the base infrastructure in place, you can do some simple experimentation with PowerPivot and Reporting Services.

In the last part of this install summary, we offer you two options to build out the rest of SharePoint's BI portal related services, both of which require a download from the book's website. The first option is to create a new site based on a special template created from the site shown in Figure 12-1. The second option is to follow a separate guide to build out the full BI portal yourself. Wait until you've had some experience with SharePoint before you decide which option to take.

Plan SharePoint for BI

Before you slip the install disks into your DVD drive, take some time to plan out your installation. Here are several prerequisites for you to think through and get in place first.

Verify software versions and editions.   Most of the features we describe here require the enterprise editions of both SharePoint 2010 and SQL Server 2008 R2, or higher. Many BI features will not work with the standard editions, and most will not work with prior versions of these two products. Some features, such as PowerPivot for SharePoint 2010, also require Windows Server 2008 SP2 or Windows Server 2008 R2.

Obtain install files and product keys.   Download all the software install files or gather the DVDs you will need ahead of time and have your product keys handy. This includes 64-bit versions of the following:

- Windows Server 2008 R2 (unless your server OS is already running)
- SQL Server 2008 R2 Enterprise edition
- SharePoint 2010 Enterprise edition

If you have an MSDN license, you can get the install files and keys online from the download section of `http://msdn.microsoft.com`. There are a few other components and add-ins you will download along the way.

Create service accounts in the domain.   SharePoint server(s) must be part of a Windows domain to manage network security and accounts. Out test system install had eight service accounts to support various SharePoint and SQL Server services. The list of accounts we used is included in the walk through guide on the book's website. Your real install should include additional accounts to support additional SharePoint services and IIS application pools, depending on which services you enable and how you want to scale out your farm. You may want to adopt your server group's account naming conventions.

Our recommendation is to set these up in Active Directory on your domain and give them appropriate permissions on your test machine right away. When you set up your official system, you should also create separate service accounts for each SQL Server service and SharePoint service application to properly isolate them. Search `technet.microsoft.com` for "service accounts required for initial SharePoint deployment" for more detail about the permissions these accounts will need.

Plan authentication and secure store.   Windows default authentication mode, called *NTLM*, does not support the pass-through of user credentials resulting in a login failure if more than two machines are involved in an interaction. This phenomenon, known as the *double-hop problem*, is common in the DW/BI system environment when the database is on a separate machine from the report access server. This is almost always the case when SharePoint is introduced into the DW/BI system environment because the SQL Server data warehouse database is usually located on a separate server from SharePoint. In this case, a user connects from client machine A to the SharePoint server B, and then selects a report from the BI portal. SharePoint then attempts to connect to SQL Server on server C, at which point the login fails because SharePoint cannot provide enough information for SQL Server to authenticate the user. To avoid this, you must switch to a different authentication method called *Kerberos* if you want to have user-level authentication. Kerberos is considered more secure than the default Windows authentication system and has been part of the Windows environment since 2000. It can be a challenge to configure, but it is getting easier as Windows improves its implementation.

Kerberos will solve the double-hop problem whether SharePoint is part of your DW/BI system or not. If the problem is limited to data access from SharePoint, you could address it with Secure Store Services, which replaces Single Sign On from SharePoint 2007. Secure Store Services provides an option to store credentials in a Secure Store database on the SharePoint server. Credentials are then mapped as user-to-user or Domain Group-to-user and can be renewed at the SharePoint server. Secure Store Services are used in SharePoint to manage PowerPivot data refreshes and other unattended account activity. They require storing a copy of user name and password information in the secure store database.

You don't need to get Kerberos working for your test SharePoint install. You can avoid the double hop problem by doing your testing on the SharePoint server, perhaps via remote desktop, rather than using a browser from a separate client machine. You will need to figure out your authentication strategy when you build out your SharePoint development and production systems. If you control all the servers you are working with, this is a manageable problem. If others are involved, you are probably facing some negotiations. You also don't need Kerberos if you are only querying PowerPivot for SharePoint databases. This is because they are hosted within the SharePoint environment and do not require additional authentication.

There are a lot of online guides to getting Kerberos working with SharePoint. This one from the SQL Server Customer Advisory Team, called "Configuring Kerberos Authentication for Microsoft SharePoint 2010 Products," is particularly helpful: `http://go.microsoft.com/fwlink/?LinkID=196600`.

Installing the Test System

This section summarizes our test installation based on the steps in Figure 12-4.

Set Up the Test Server

Once you've done the BI planning, you need to set up the test system itself. Figure 12-5 shows the topology and environment for the SharePoint test server installation we created. This is by no means a model or recommended topology for anything you might put into production. All three layers of the SharePoint architecture are on one machine. Even if you choose to access data on an existing database machine, the SharePoint test machine will still have SQL Server to host the SharePoint databases. A more robust version of this farm would have two load-balanced front end servers to host the Web Front End (WFE), two load-balanced application servers to host the services layer, a failover cluster setup for the database layer, and perhaps a separate cluster for the Reporting Services component. We set our goals a little lower to get it all working on one machine first.

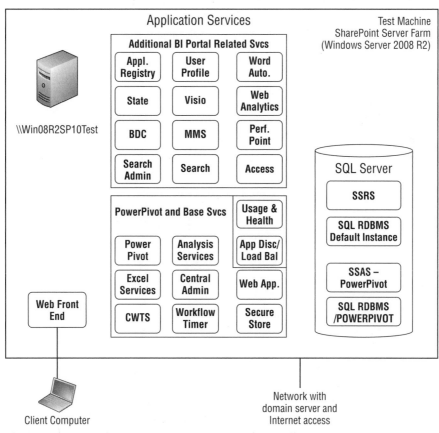

Figure 12-5: Test SharePoint environment topology and services

The test server doesn't start out with all the servers and services installed. Each of the following steps adds one or more servers and services to the environment. It's this incremental process that can cause conflicts because each new layer may reconfigure the system in a way that breaks one of the previous layers.

SQL Server in particular plays several roles in the SharePoint world. It acts as the database engine for the SharePoint admin, content, and property databases. In the case of this book, SQL Server is the data warehouse platform for the relational dimensional model and for the Analysis Services database. SQL Server also provides a separate Analysis Services engine for PowerPivot for SharePoint. Finally, SQL Server Reporting Services is commonly used in an integrated mode with SharePoint to access data kept in a SQL Server data warehouse. All of these roles are installed and configured at different points, and have the potential to cause problems for SharePoint and for the other SQL Server roles.

Install SharePoint Server 2010

SharePoint has several prerequisites that must be in place before the actual product can be installed. Install the prerequisites from the SharePoint installer, then install SharePoint itself. Because of the install order we chose for our test system, we ran the installation, but did not run the SharePoint Products Configuration Wizard. As a result, this initial install step only enables the Web Front End and a few of the service applications. You can't view a SharePoint site or the central administration site yet.

Once the SharePoint install has completed without errors, this is a good point to take a snapshot of your virtual machine.

Install PowerPivot for SharePoint

The approach we took for the test server lets the PowerPivot installer configure SharePoint server for us. This part of the installation is run from the SQL Server 2008 R2 installer. Once you get to the Setup Role step, select SQL Server PowerPivot for SharePoint, and make sure the Add PowerPivot for SharePoint To option is set to New Server.

The PowerPivot installation adds the PowerPivot service, the PowerPivot SQL database instance, and the Analysis Services engine in SharePoint mode. It also configures the top-level site.

You can find install guides for other scenarios, such as installing PowerPivot on an existing SharePoint farm, on MSDN. Search `msdn.microsoft.com` for "How to: Install PowerPivot for SharePoint."

Verify the SharePoint Install

Once you have the PowerPivot for SharePoint components installed, there are several things you can do to make sure your server is working as it should be. First, open a browser and navigate to the top-level site of your test server. Figure 12-6 shows the homepage for this site which was automatically configured using the PowerPivot site template.

At this point, you can upload a PowerPivot for Excel workbook and see how it is displayed in the PowerPivot Gallery (which we saw back in Figure 11-10 in the chapter on PowerPivot). You can also take a look at the SQL Server instance in SQL Server Management Studio and see what databases SharePoint has created.

It's a good idea to visit the SharePoint Central Administration Site to see how it works and check the status of your server. This site is command central for running your SharePoint farm. From here you can enable new service applications, manage servers and services running on those servers, monitor usage, and much more. Figure 12-7 shows the Central Administration site's homepage. To get to the Central Administration site, enter the URL with the port number in your browser. If you neglected to memorize the port number, you can always find a link to the Central Administration site in Start ≻ All Programs ≻ Microsoft SharePoint 2010 Products ≻ SharePoint 2010 Central Administration.

Note that the Central Administration site follows the portal design patterns we described in the first part of this chapter, with a dense set of links grouped into a collapsed hierarchy of categories. If you know what the categories mean in the SharePoint context, you should be able to find what you are looking for. If you're not familiar with SharePoint terminology, it's a bit mysterious.

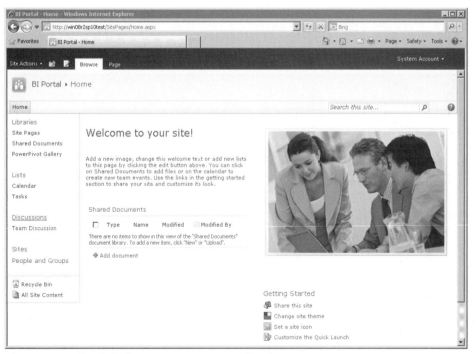

Figure 12-6: The default PowerPivot site template homepage

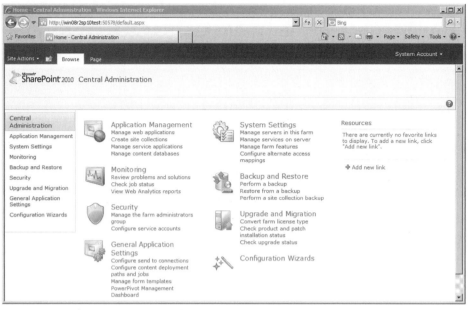

Figure 12-7: SharePoint Central Administration home page

Install, Configure, and Verify Reporting Services

The next step for the test server is to install Reporting Services along with the default instance of SQL Server to give you a chance to create some reports and display them on a SharePoint page. Remember, the relational database and Reporting Services would typically be installed on a separate machine (or machines). In fact, the SharePoint Health Analyzer will flag SQL Server on the same machine as a problem.

The final installation step is to configure Reporting Services to work in SharePoint integrated mode from SharePoint Central Administration. Verify that the integration was successful by uploading a reporting services RDL file to the Shared Documents library. Once it is in SharePoint, click on the file name to execute the report.

Completing the BI Portal

At this point, you have the core capabilities enabled in SharePoint to build a basic BI portal. You can offer Reporting Services reports and PowerPivot reports to your user community from a common interface. You can learn a lot about SharePoint by experimenting with your test server in its current state. You did good work.

However, you still have a long way to go before you have a fully functioning BI portal to unveil at the first user deployment education session. If you want to learn all the details, you can continue from this point and install PerformancePoint, enable a whole range of useful services and content types, and create your portal home page along with the site theme and layout. This is the best path to take if managing SharePoint will be one of your jobs, or if you are truly interested in understanding how SharePoint works and what you can do with it.

The individual steps for this detailed installation are in a document titled `SharePoint BI Portal Detailed Install Completion Step-by-step.doc` in the zip file you can download from the book's website. We encourage you to pull them out and work through them to get the full SharePoint experience.

Alternatively, if you don't need to learn all the portal creation details, you can still get the full experience by creating a new SharePoint site with the BIPortal template also included in the zip file, which will do most of the setup and configuration for you.

The steps for installing the template are also included in a file in the zip file called `SharePoint BI Portal Template Install Steps.doc`.

The end result of either path is a full featured BI portal site.

The Added Functionality of the BIPortal Site Template

Both the BI Portal site template and the step-by-step guide enable many features that are not grouped together in the standard templates found in SharePoint. We started with the BI Center template and added on the following features, each of which requires several steps to enable within SharePoint:

- PerformancePoint dashboard and scorecard capabilities
- Search across the portal environment
- Announcements to provide information to users
- Web-based surveys
- User support discussion groups
- User support request database
- Alerts to notify users when documents or other items of interest change
- User personalization capabilities (my reports, custom layouts, and so on)
- A workflow to manage user submission and approval of reports and PowerPivot analytics
- Group work lists including calendars and team resource scheduling tools

In addition to these features, there are examples of the actual pages that make up the portal: the home page, sub-pages for the enterprise business process reports, and supporting pages for documentation and user support, along with the navigation links on the left side of the site.

The point is, once you get the core SharePoint and SQL Server components installed, there is still a lot more work to do. By using the BIPortal site template, you will be able to experiment with all this added SharePoint functionality, but you will not gain a good understanding of how it got there. If you are going to use SharePoint as your BI portal and application delivery platform, you, or someone else on the BI team, will have to learn the details of how to make it work. That's where the detailed step-by-step approach will help.

Exploring SharePoint

Once you get the BI Portal site template loaded, or go through the steps to build it out yourself, you should spend some time playing around with it. Upload some of your own PowerPivot examples and see what they look like in SharePoint. Try to create a report in Report Builder. Try to edit a SharePoint page in SharePoint Designer. Experiment with the PerformancePoint Dashboard Designer. Work with security groups a bit to see how you tie them to Active Directory.

The best way to do this would be to create a beta version of your own BI portal. Start working on your standard page layouts, color themes, navigation bar, user documentation, and user interactions. This will likely take a couple of weeks, so make sure it is built into the project plan.

Summary

Your BI portal will provide the first impression of the DW/BI system for most users in your organization. You need to make sure it's a good impression. It needs to be usable, fast, clear, and complete. It also should look appealing to the eye. Building and maintaining an effective BI portal is a lot more work than most teams imagine. You can judge your success by the number of people who use the portal, and how often they use it. These should be part of your standard DW/BI system metrics.

The obvious choice for a BI portal platform in the Microsoft world is SharePoint. One of the main goals of this chapter was to take you far enough into SharePoint to give you a sense for the capabilities of the product and the effort involved in getting it to work. If you installed SharePoint following the guide on the book's website, and your SharePoint experience has been anything close to ours, you must be exhausted. Nonetheless, we encourage you to continue on and create a BI portal site with the site template, or build out all the features yourself following the step-by-step guide from the book's website.

Microsoft has created a flexible, distributed, web-based application platform that can be scaled out to meet the information and collaboration needs of large enterprises. But all this power and flexibility is a two-edged sword. It is a fair amount of work to install and maintain, and much of the complexity of SharePoint is overkill for most small-to-medium sized businesses.

However, Microsoft has chosen SharePoint as its application delivery vehicle for its enterprise BI offerings. Using SharePoint is appealing because of the add-on connections it has to many of Microsoft's BI products and the core portal and collaboration functions it provides.

CHAPTER 13

Incorporating Data Mining

"We dig up diamonds by the score
A thousand rubies, sometimes more."
—From *Snow White* by Walt Disney Company,
music by Frank Churchill, words by Larry Morey, ©1938

Data mining is not a single topic; it's a loosely related collection of tools, algorithms, techniques, and processes. This makes it a difficult subject area to tackle, especially in a single chapter. However, we must tackle it for two main reasons: First, data mining offers the potential of huge business impact; and second, SQL Server includes a suite of data mining tools as part of the product. In short, high value, low cost — the motivation is obvious.

The first part of this chapter sets the context for data mining. We begin with a brief definition of data mining and an overview of the business motivation for using it. We then look at the Microsoft data mining architecture and environment provided as part of SQL Server, including a brief description of the data mining service, the algorithms provided, and the kinds of problems for which they might be appropriate. We next present a high-level data mining process. The process breaks into three phases: business, mining, and operations. The business phase involves identifying business opportunities and understanding the data resources. The data mining phase is a highly iterative and exploratory process whose goal is to identify the best model possible, given the time and resource constraints. Once you identify the best model, you need to implement it in a production form where, you hope, it will provide the intended business value.

The second part of the chapter puts these concepts and processes into practice by demonstrating the application of SQL Server data mining in two examples. The first example creates clusters of cities based on economic data, and the second creates a model to recommend products for the Adventure Works Cycles website.

By the end of this chapter, you should have a good understanding of the following:

- What data mining is and how it can be applied to a range of business opportunities
- The major components of the SQL Server data mining toolset and how they work together
- A high-level process for employing data mining in your organization
- And, although this is not a tutorial, you should also end up with a basic idea of how to use the SQL Server data mining toolset

Defining Data Mining

We generally describe data mining as *a process of data exploration with the intent to find patterns or relationships that can be made useful to the organization.* Data mining takes advantage of a range of technologies and techniques for exploration and execution. From a business perspective, data mining helps you understand and predict behavior, identify relationships, or group items (customers, products, and so on) into coherent sets. These models can take the form of rules or equations that you apply to new customers, products, or transactions to make a better guess as to how you should respond to them.

The field of data mining is known more broadly as *Knowledge Discovery and Data Mining (KDD)*. Both terms shed light on the purpose and process of data mining. The word "mining" is meant to evoke a specific image. Traditional mining involves digging through vast quantities of dirt to unearth a relatively small vein of valuable metallic ore, precious stones, or other substances. Data mining is the digital equivalent of this analog process. You use automated tools to dig through vast quantities of data to identify or "discover" valuable patterns or relationships that you can leverage in your business.

Our brains are good examples of data mining tools. Throughout the course of our lives, we accumulate a large set of experiences. In some cases, we're able to identify patterns within these experiences and generate models we can use to predict the future. Those who commute to work have an easy example. Over the weeks and months, you develop a sense for the traffic patterns and adjust your behavior accordingly. The freeway will be jammed at 5:00 p.m., so you might leave at 4:30, or wait until 6:00, unless it's Friday or a holiday. Going to the movies is another example of altering behavior based on experience. Deciding when to arrive at the theater is a complex equation that includes variables like when the movie opened, whether it's a big budget film, whether it got good reviews, and what's showing that you want to see. These are personal examples of building a data mining model using the original neural network tool.

The roots of data mining can be traced back to a combination of statistical analysis tools like SAS (Statistical Analysis System) and SPSS (Statistical Package for the Social Sciences) that took form in the academic environment in the 1960s and 1970s, and the Artificial Intelligence surge back in the 1980s. Many of the techniques from these areas were combined, enhanced, and repackaged as data mining in the 1990s. One benefit of the internet bubble of the late 1990s is that it showed how data mining could be useful. Companies like Amazon began to mine the vast quantities of data generated by millions of customers browsing their websites and making purchase selections, popularizing the phrase "Customers who bought this item also bought these items."

Data mining has finally grown up and has taken on a central role in many businesses. All of us are the subject of data mining dozens of times every day — from the junk mail in our mail boxes, to the affinity cards we use in the grocery store, to the fraud detection algorithms that scrutinize our every credit card purchase. Data mining has become so widespread for one reason: it works. Using data mining techniques can measurably and significantly increase an organization's ability to reach its goals. Often those goals can be boiled down to "sell more stuff." Our goal here is to describe the technology, not judge the application; how you use it is up to you.

There are two common approaches to data mining. The first is usually a one-time project to help you gain an understanding of who your customers are and how they behave. We call this *exploratory or* undirected data mining, where the goal is to find something interesting. The second is most often a project created to work on a specific problem or opportunity. We call this more focused activity *directed data mining*. Directed data mining typically leads to an ongoing effort where models are generated on a regular basis and are applied as part of the transaction system or in the ETL application. For example, you might create a model that generates a score for each customer every time you load customer data into the BI system. Models that come from the data mining process are often applied in the transaction process itself to identify opportunities or predict problems as they are happening and guide the transaction system to an appropriate response on a real-time basis.

While exploratory data mining will often reveal useful patterns and relationships, this approach usually takes on the characteristics of a fishing expedition. You cast about, hoping to hook the big one; meanwhile, your guests, the business folks, lose interest. Directed data mining with a clear business purpose in mind is more appealing to their business-driven style.

In Chapter 10, we defined an analytic application as a BI application that's centered on a specific business process and encapsulates a certain amount of domain expertise. A data mining application fits this definition perfectly, and its place in the Kimball Lifecycle is clearly in the Application track boxes for BI Application design and development.

Basic Data Mining Terminology

Data miners use a lot of terms that sound familiar to the general public, but have specific meaning in data mining. It's helpful for us to define a few of these terms early on. This is not an exhaustive list of data mining terms, only the relevant ones for our discussion.

- *Algorithm:* The programmatic technique used to identify the relationships or patterns in the data.

- *Model:* The definition of the relationship identified by the algorithm, which generally takes the form of a set of rules, a decision tree, a set of equations, or a set of associations.

- *Case:* The collection of attributes and relationships (variables) that are associated with an individual instance of the entity being modeled, usually a customer. The case is also known as an observation.

- *Case set*: A group of cases that share the same attributes. Think of a case set as a table with one row per unique object (like *customer*). It's possible to have a nested case set when one row in the parent table, like "customer," joins to multiple rows in the nested table, like "purchases." The case set is also known as an observation set.

- *Dependent variable(s)* (or predicted attribute or predict column): The variable the algorithm will build a model to predict or classify.

- *Independent variable(s)* (or predictive attribute or input column): The variables which provide the descriptive or behavior information used to build the model. The algorithm creates a model that uses combinations of independent variables to define a grouping or predict the dependent variable.

- *Discrete or continuous variables:* Numeric columns that contain continuous or discrete values. A column in the `Employee` table called `Salary` that contains the actual salary values is a continuous variable. You can add a column to the table during data preparation called `SalaryRange`, containing integers to represent encoded salary ranges (1 = "0 to $25,000"; 2 = "between $25,000 and $50,000"; and so on). This is a discrete numeric column. Early data mining and statistical analysis tools required the conversion of strings to numeric values like the encoded salary ranges. Most tools, including most of the SQL Server data mining algorithms, allow the use of character descriptions as discrete values. The string "0 to $25,000" is easier to understand than the number 1. Discrete variables are also known as categorical. This distinction between discrete and continuous is important to the underlying algorithms in data mining, although its significance is less obvious to those of us who are not statisticians.

- *Regression:* A statistical technique that creates a best-fit formula based on a data set. The formula can be used to predict values based on new input variables. In linear regression, the formula is the equation for a line.

- *Deviation:* A measure of how well the regression formula fits the actual values in the data set from which it was created.

- *Mining structure:* A Microsoft data mining term used as a name for the definition of a case set in Analysis Services. The mining structure is essentially a metadata layer on top of a Data Source View that includes additional data mining–related flags and column properties, such as the field that identifies a column as input, predict, both, or ignore. A mining structure can be used as the basis for multiple mining models.

- *Mining model:* The specific application of an algorithm to a particular mining structure. You can build several mining models with different parameters or different algorithms from the same mining structure.

Business Uses of Data Mining

Data mining terminology has not yet become completely standardized. There are terms that describe the business task and terms that describe the data mining techniques applied to those tasks. The problem is, the same terms are used to describe both tasks and techniques, sometimes with different meanings.

The terms in this section are drawn from the book *Data Mining Techniques: For Marketing, Sales, and Customer Relationship Management* by Michael J. A. Berry and Gordon S. Linoff, Second Edition (Wiley, 2004). Berry and Linoff list six basic business tasks that are served by data mining techniques: *classification, estimation, prediction, affinity grouping, clustering,* and *description and profiling.* We've added a seventh business task to the list called *anomaly detection.* We describe each of these business task areas in the following sections, along with lists of the relevant algorithms included in SQL Server Data Mining. A word of warning: Some of these tasks overlap in what seems to be odd ways to the uninitiated because the distinctions between the areas are more mathematical than practical.

Classification

Classification is the task of assigning each item in a set to one of a predetermined set of discrete choices based on its attributes or behaviors. Consumer goods are classified in a standard hierarchy down to the SKU level. If you know the attributes of a product, you can determine its classification. You can use attributes like size, sugar content, flavor, and container type to classify a soda. Typical classes in business include *Yes and No; High, Medium, and Low; Silver, Gold, and Platinum.* What these are classes of depends on the business context; Good Credit Risk classes might be Yes and No. Classification helps organizations and people simplify their dealings with the world. If you can classify something, you then know how to deal with it. If you fly often with the same airline, you have no doubt been classified as an elite level, or Platinum, customer. Knowing this classification allows the airline employees to work with you in a way that is appropriate for top customers, even if they have never met you before. The key differentiating factors of classification are the limited (discrete) number of entries in the class set and the fact that the class set is predefined.

A common example of classification is the assignment of a socioeconomic class to customers or prospects in a marketing database. Companies like Nielsen Claritas, with its PRIZM system, have built an industry around classification. These systems identify classes of consumers who have common geographic, demographic, economic, and behavioral attributes and can be expected to respond to certain opportunities in a similar way.

Classification algorithms predict the class or category of one or more discrete variables, based on the other variables in the case set. Determining whether someone is likely to respond to a direct mail piece involves putting them in the category of Likely Responder or not. Microsoft Decision Trees, Microsoft Neural Network, and Microsoft Naïve Bayes are the first choice algorithms for classification when the predict column is a discrete variable.

Estimation (Regression)

Estimation is the continuous version of classification. That is to say, where classification returns a discrete value, estimation returns a continuous number. In practice, most classification is actually estimation. The process is essentially the same: A set of attributes is used to determine a relationship. A direct mail marketing company could estimate customers' likelihood to respond to a promotion based on past responses. Estimating a continuous variable called `Response_Likelihood` that ranges from zero to one is more useful when creating a direct marketing campaign than a discrete classification of High, Medium, or Low. The continuous value allows the marketing manager to determine the size of the campaign by changing the cutoff point of the `Response_Likelihood` estimate. For example, a promotions manager with a budget for 200,000 pieces and a list of 12 million prospects would use the predicted `Response_Likelihood` variable to limit the target subset. Including only those prospects with a `Response_Likelihood` greater than some number, say 0.80, would give the promotions manager a target list of the top 200,000 prospects. The continuous variable allows the user to more finely tune the application of the results.

Estimation algorithms estimate a continuously valued variable based on the other variables in the case set. Microsoft has built several algorithms that can be used for either discrete or continuous variables. Microsoft Decision Trees and Microsoft Neural Network are good choices for estimating a continuous variable.

Most of the estimation algorithms are based on regression analysis techniques. As a result, this category is often called *regression,* especially when the algorithm is used for prediction. Microsoft includes a separate linear regression algorithm in its list of algorithms, but it is a specially-parameterized version of the decision trees algorithm. You will also see the Microsoft Logistic Regression algorithm on the list; it is based on the neural network algorithm.

Prediction

Where classification and estimation are assignment of values that are "correct" by definition, *prediction* is the application of the same techniques to assign a value that can be validated at some future date. For example, you might use a classification algorithm to classify your customers as male or female based on their purchasing behaviors. You can use this classification as an input to designing various marketing programs.

> **TIP** Be careful not to reveal your guess to your customers because it could adversely affect your relationship with them. For example, it would be unwise to use this variable by itself to send out promotional pieces for a "For Women Only" sale. However, the variable is useful for the business even though you will never know for certain which customers are actually male or female.

Prediction, on the other hand, seeks to determine a class or estimate as accurately as possible before the value is known. This future-oriented element is what places prediction in its own category. The input variables exist or occur before the predicted variable. For example, a lending company offering mortgages might want to predict the market value of a piece of property before it's sold. This value would give them an upper limit for the amount they'd be willing to lend the property owner, regardless of the actual amount the owner has offered to pay for the given property. In order to build a predictive data mining model, the company needs a training set that includes predictive attributes that are known prior to the sale, such as total square footage, number of bathrooms, city, school district, and the actual sale price of each property in the training set. The data mining algorithm uses this training set to build a model based on the relationships between the predictive variables and the known historical sale price. The model can then be used to predict the sale price of a new property based on the known input variables about that property.

One interesting feature of predictive models is that their accuracy can be tested. At some point in the future, the actual sale amount of the property will become known and can be compared to the predicted value. In fact, the data mining process described later in this chapter recommends splitting the historical data into two sets: one to build or train the model and one to test its accuracy against known historical data that was not part of the training process.

TIP The real estate sale price predictor is a good example of how data mining models tend to go stale over time. Real estate prices in a given area can be subject to significant, rapid fluctuations. The mortgage company would want to rebuild the data mining model with recent sales transactions on a regular basis.

Microsoft Decision Trees and Microsoft Neural Network are the first choice algorithms for regression when the predict column is a continuous variable. When prediction involves time series data, it is often called *forecasting*. Microsoft Time Series is the first choice algorithm for predicting time series data, like monthly sales forecasts.

Association or Affinity Grouping

Association looks for correlations among the items in a group of sets. E-commerce systems are big users of association models in an effort to increase sales. This can take the form of an association modeling process known as *market basket analysis*. The online retailer first builds a model based on the contents of recent shopping carts and makes it available to the web server. As the shopper adds products to the cart, the system feeds the contents of the cart into the model. The model identifies items that commonly appear with the items currently in the cart. Most recommendation systems are based on association algorithms.

Microsoft Association is an association, or affinity grouping algorithm. Other algorithms, like Microsoft Decision Trees, can also be used to create association rules.

Clustering (Segmentation)

Clustering can be thought of as auto-classification. Clustering algorithms group cases into clusters that are as similar to one another, and as different from other clusters, as possible. The clusters are not predetermined, and it's up to the data miner to examine the clusters to understand what makes them unique. When applied to customers, this process is also known as *customer segmentation*. The idea is to segment the customers into smaller, homogenous groups that can be targeted with customized promotions and even customized products. Naming the clusters is a great opportunity to show your creativity. Clever names can succinctly communicate the nature and content of the clusters. They can also give the data mining team additional credibility with the business folks.

Once the clustering model has been trained, you can use it to categorize new cases. It often helps to first cluster customers based on their buying patterns and demographics, and then run predictive models on each cluster separately. This allows the unique behaviors of each cluster to show through rather than be overwhelmed by the overall average behaviors.

One form of clustering involves ordered data, usually ordered temporally or physically. The goal is to identify frequent sequences or episodes (clusters) in the data. The television industry does extensive analysis of TV viewing sequences to determine the order of programs in the lineup. Companies with significant public websites may use sequence analysis to understand how visitors move through their website. For example, a consumer electronics product manufacturer's website might identify several clusters of users based on their browsing behavior. Some users might start with the Sale Items page, then browse the rest of the e-commerce section, but rarely end with a purchase (Bargain Hunters). Others may enter through the home page, and then go straight to the support section, often ending by sending a help request e-mail (Clueless). Others may go straight to the e-commerce pages, ending with a purchase, but rarely visit the account management or support pages (Managers). Another group might go to the account management pages, checking order statuses and printing invoices (Administrators). A Sequence Clustering model like this one can be used to classify new visitors and customize content for them, and to predict future page hits for a given visitor.

Microsoft Clustering and Microsoft Sequence Clustering are segmentation algorithms. The Microsoft Sequence Clustering algorithm is primarily designed for sequence analysis (hence the clever name).

THE POWER OF NAMING

When Nielsen Claritas originally created its customer segmentation system called PRIZM, it likely used clustering techniques to identify about 60 different groups of consumers. The resulting clusters, called lifestyle types, were numbered 1 through 60+. It's clear that someone at Nielsen Claritas realized that numbers were not descriptive and would not make good marketing. So, they came up with a clever name for each cluster; a shorthand way to communicate its unique characteristics. A few of the names are: 02. Blue Blood Estates (old money, big mansions), 51. Shotguns and Pickups (working class, large families, mobile homes), and 60. Park Bench Seniors (modest income, sedentary, daytime TV watchers).

Anomaly Detection

Several business processes rely on the identification of cases that deviate from the norm in a significant way. Fraud detection in consumer credit is a common example of anomaly detection. Anomaly detection can take advantage of any of the data mining algorithms. Clustering algorithms can be tuned to create a cluster that contains data outliers, separate from the rest of the clusters in the model.

Anomaly detection involves a few extra twists in the data mining process. Often it's necessary to bias the training set in favor of the exceptional events. Otherwise, there may be too few of them in the historical data for the algorithm to detect. After all, they are anomalies. We provide an example of this in the case studies later in this chapter.

Description and Profiling

The business task Berry and Linoff call *description and profiling* is essentially the same activity we earlier called undirected data mining. The task is to use the various data mining techniques to gain a better understanding of the complexities of the data. Decision trees, clustering, and affinity grouping can reveal relationships that would otherwise be undetectable. For example, a decision tree might reveal that women purchase certain products much more than men. In some cases, like women's shoes, this would be stereotypically obvious, but in others, like hammers, the reasons are less clear and the behavior would prompt additional investigation. Data mining, like all analytic processes, often opens doors to whole new areas of investigation.

Description and profiling can also be used as an extension to the data profiling tasks we described in previous chapters. You can use data mining to identify specific data error anomalies and broader patterns of data problems that would not be obvious to the unaided eye.

Business Task Summary

The definitions of the various business tasks that are suitable for data mining and the list of which algorithms are appropriate for which tasks can be a bit confusing. Table 13-1 gives a few examples of common business tasks and the associated data mining algorithms that can help accomplish these tasks.

Table 13-1: Examples of business tasks and associated algorithms

BUSINESS TASK	EXAMPLE	MICROSOFT ALGORITHMS
Classifying customers into discrete classes	Assigning each customer to an Activity Level with discrete values of Disinterested, Casual, Recreational, Serious, or Competitor.	Decision Trees Naïve Bayes Clustering Neural Network
Predicting a discrete attribute	Predicting a variable like ServiceStatus with discrete values of Cancelled or Active might form the core of a customer retention program.	Decision Trees Naïve Bayes Clustering Neural Network
Predicting a continuous attribute	Predicting the sale price of a real estate listing or forecasting next year's sales.	Decision Trees Time Series Neural Network
Making recommendations based on a sequence	Predicting website usage behavior. The order of events is important in this case. A customer support website might use common sequences to suggest additional support pages that might be helpful based on the page path the customer has already followed.	Sequence Clustering
Making recommendations based on a set	Suggesting additional products for a customer to purchase based on items they've already selected or pages they've viewed. In this case, order is not important. ("People who bought this book also bought . . .").	Association Decision Trees
Segmenting customers	Creating groups of customers with similar behaviors, demographics, and product preferences. This allows you to create targeted products and promotions designed to appeal to specific segments.	Clustering Sequence Clustering

Roles and Responsibilities

Microsoft's Data Mining tools have been designed to be usable by just about anyone who can install BIDS. After a little data preparation, a competent user can fire up the Data Mining Wizard and start generating data mining models. Data mining is an iterative, exploratory process. In order to get the most value out of a model, the data miner must conduct extensive research and testing. The data mining person (or team) will need the following skills:

- *Good business sense and good-to-excellent working relationships with the business folks:* This skill set is used to form the foundation of the data mining model. Without it, the data miner can build a sophisticated model that is meaningless to the business.

- *Good-to-excellent knowledge of Integration Services and/or SQL:* These skills are crucial to creating the data transformations needed to build the case sets and packaging them up in repeatable modules.

- *A good understanding of statistics and probability:* This knowledge helps in understanding the functionality, parameters, and output of the various algorithms. It also helps to understand the data mining literature and documentation — most of which seems to have been written by statisticians. Microsoft has tried hard to minimize the amount of statistics you need to know, but the more you know, the better.

- *Data mining experience:* Much of what is effective data mining comes from having seen a similar problem before and knowing which approaches might work best to solve it. Obviously, you have to start somewhere. If you don't have a lot of data mining experience, it's a good idea to find a local or online data mining special interest group you can use to validate your ideas and approach.

- *Programming skills:* To incorporate the resulting data mining model into the organization's transaction systems, someone on the team or elsewhere in the organization will need to learn the appropriate APIs.

SQL Server Data Mining Architecture Overview

Microsoft SQL Server Data Mining offers a rich, well-tuned, integrated, and easy-to-use data mining environment. In this section, we give an overview of the data mining environment using the high-level architecture drawing presented in Figure 13-1 as a guide.

From a system point of view, integrating data mining into the overall SQL Server product allows the data mining service to take advantage of the functionality offered by the rest of the system. For example, point A in Figure 13-1 shows how data mining models are built using the Analysis Services dimensional engine, leveraging its ability to load data and quickly perform the base statistical calculations like sums, averages, and counts. The data mining server can easily pull case data through the Data Source View from a wide variety of data sources including relational and Analysis Services, as seen at point B in Figure 13-1.

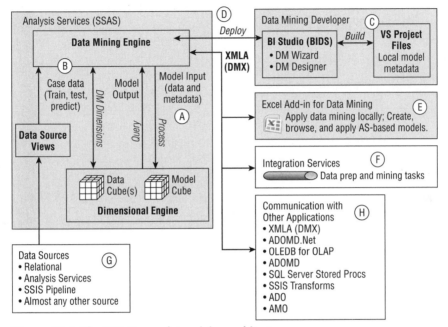

Figure 13-1: The SQL Server data mining architecture

From a system point of view, integrating data mining into the overall SQL Server product allows the data mining service to take advantage of the functionality offered by the rest of the system. For example, point A in Figure 13-1 shows how data mining models are built using the Analysis Services dimensional engine, leveraging its ability to load data and quickly perform the base statistical calculations like sums, averages, and counts. The data mining server can easily pull case data through the Data Source View from a wide variety of data sources including relational and Analysis Services, as seen at point B in Figure 13-1.

Point C in Figure 13-1 shows how the typical data miner will first experience data mining by creating an Analysis Services project in BIDS and then using the Data Mining Wizard to create a new data mining structure and an initial data mining model. The mining structure is a construct that provides a metadata layer allowing several mining models to work with the same input data. Each mining model in a mining structure can have different algorithms and parameters. The wizard provides model building guidance with auto selection and adjustment of variables based on the algorithm selected. The wizard also helps you create case sets, including complex, nested queries.

The Data Mining Design Environment

When the wizard is finished building the mining structure and the initial data mining model, it drops the developer into the data mining design environment. At this point, the mining model has not been built; the project contains only the metadata that defines the model. The Data Mining Designer is broken up into five tabs to support the data mining process. Several of these tabs work with the completed mining model as it exists on Analysis Services, so they are not available until the model has been built and deployed. The first tab shows the Mining Structure with its underlying Data Source View. The second tab is the Mining Models tab, showing the source mining structure and all the data mining models that have been defined based on this structure. The third tab is the Mining Model Viewer that lets you select a model and a viewer type, and then provides several sub-tabs, each with a different graphic or tabular representation of the contents of the model. The Mining Model Viewer tab is the primary tool the data miner uses to explore the various models. The fourth tab is the Mining Accuracy Chart. This tab provides three ways to compare the relative accuracy of certain kinds of predictive models: the Lift Chart, the Classification Matrix, and Cross Validation. Finally, the fifth tab is the Mining Model Prediction tab that allows the data miner to specify a prediction query using a rudimentary query builder interface. You will see examples of most of these tabs in the screenshots throughout this chapter.

Build, Deploy, and Process

Most of the functions in the Data Mining Designer work with the actual model as it exists in Analysis Services. This means once the wizard is complete, the developer must build and deploy the project (which includes processing the model cubes) before any more progress can be made. Building the project writes the metadata out to project files in the development environment. The actual model does not come into being until the project is deployed to an Analysis Services instance. At that point, BIDS creates a database for the project in Analysis Services. It writes out the mining structure metadata and the definition of each model. Finally, it creates a cube for each mining structure and processes the models, inserting the training data so the algorithm can calculate the rules, correlations, and other relationships. Until the project is deployed and a model is processed, it cannot be viewed in the viewers.

> **TIP** It is possible to process a single model rather than all models in a mining structure by selecting the model in the Mining Models tab, and then selecting Process Model from the Mining Model menu. This can save a lot of time if you are working with large case sets and complex models.

Accessing the Mining Models

As you see at point D in Figure 13-1, the Data Mining eXtensions to SQL language (DMX) is at the core of all the Microsoft data mining APIs. As the name suggests, DMX is an extension to SQL designed to create, train, modify, and query data mining models. DMX was introduced with SQL Server 2000 and enhanced in 2005 and 2008 as part of the OLE DB for Data Mining APIs. An easy way to begin learning about DMX is to use the Mining Model Prediction tab in the Data Mining Designer and examine the syntax it generates for DMX queries. The code can be copied to a DMX query window in SQL Studio for further exploration. There are also some data mining schema rowsets in Analysis Services that act like the predefined system views in the relational system. Although DMX is an extension to SQL, queries are submitted to the Analysis Services server — that's where the data mining services are.

The development environment works with Analysis Services mostly using Analysis Management Objects (AMO) to define and build the underlying cubes. Once the models are in place, they are available to any application as a web service by using SOAP protocols because Analysis Services is a native XMLA server. It is still possible to access the server with OLE DB APIs, ADO, ADO.NET, or ADOMD.NET.

Point E is where many analysts, and some data miners, will experience Microsoft data mining, often without even realizing it. Microsoft has created a set of add-ins for Excel and Visio. The Excel add-ins bring some of the core algorithms into the Excel analytic environment and provide an Excel friendly interface to create, access, and manage Analysis Services-based data mining models. The Excel data mining add-ins are an excellent way for many analysts to get started exploring data mining without having to first conquer the Visual Studio development environment. You'll see this Excel interface in the first data mining case study later in this chapter.

Integration Services and Data Mining

Integration Services can play a major role in the data mining process as shown in Figure 13-1. Many of the standard transforms used for data cleaning and data integration are particularly valuable for building the training and test data sets. Besides the obvious tasks, like Data Conversion and Derived Column, tasks like the Percentage Sampling, Row Sampling, Conditional Split, Lookup, and Merge Join are powerful components the data miner can use to build a set of packages to prepare the case sets for the data mining process. This is shown at point F in Figure 13-1. In addition to the standard tasks, there are two Integration Services tasks that directly interact with the data mining models, shown at point G in Figure 13-1. The Data Mining Model Training destination transformation feeds the data flow into a training command for a mining model. This capability is perfect for the ongoing re-training required to keep certain mining models current — recommendation models, for example. The Data Mining Query task is specifically designed to do prediction joins against a model in the SSIS pipeline, once the model has been trained and tested. The task passes query values to a model and receives the results, which could be used to add scores to the `Customer` table or identify significant data anomalies during the nightly ETL process. It could also be used in a low latency mode to flag transactions that were potentially fraudulent.

Additional Features

There are several additional features that will be important for certain applications. Most of these can be found at point H in Figure 13-1 and are listed briefly here:

- *Extensibility:* Microsoft has provided a set of COM APIs that allow developers to integrate additional data mining algorithms into the data mining engine. They can integrate custom viewers into the Data Mining Designer as well. Someone could even create a new viewer for an existing Microsoft algorithm.

- *Analysis Management Objects (AMO):* AMO is an API for managing the creation and maintenance of data mining objects, including creating, processing, backing up, restoring, and securing.

- *Stored procedures and user-defined functions:* A developer can create what are essentially stored procedures or user-defined functions and load them as managed assemblies into Analysis Services. This allows clients to work with large mining models through the intermediate layer of the server-based managed assembly.

- *Text mining:* It is possible to do some interesting data mining on unstructured text data, like the text in HTML files in a set of web directories, or even text fields in a database. For example, use the Integration Services Term Extraction transformation to build a dictionary of terms found in the text files. Next, use the Term Lookup transform to convert the contents of the unstructured document data into term vectors. Then use data mining to create classification rules to categorize the documents according to the terms they contain. This is essentially a data mining application, not a new data mining algorithm, but it has value in dealing with unstructured data.

RESOURCES To find more information about the text mining technique, see the Books Online topic "Term Extraction Transformation," or visit www .sqlserverdatamining.com for a text mining tutorial.

Architecture Summary

Our goal in this section is to show how data mining fits into the overall SQL Server architecture, and to show how well data mining has been integrated into the SQL Server environment. It should be clear by now that data mining is a serious component of the BI toolset, and that it leverages the capabilities of other SQL Server components. Data mining and application developers will have a lot more to learn before they are proficient with all the data mining components. Fortunately, Microsoft's documentation is heavily weighted toward the development community. Additional help should be easy to find. A good place to start is a website called www.sqlserverdatamining.com, maintained by members of the SQL Server data mining development team.

Microsoft Data Mining Algorithms

Data mining algorithms are the logic used to create the mining models. Several standard algorithms in the data mining community have been carefully tested and honed over time. One of the algorithms used to calculate decision trees uses a *Bayesian method* to determine the score used to split the branches of the tree. The roots of this method (so to speak) trace back to its namesake, Thomas Bayes, who first established a mathematical basis for probability inference in the 1700s.

The Data Mining group at Microsoft has been working diligently to expand the number of algorithms offered in SQL Server and to improve their accuracy. SQL Server Data Mining includes seven core algorithms that cover a large percentage of the common data mining application areas. The seven core algorithms are:

- Decision Trees (and Linear Regression)
- Naïve Bayes
- Clustering
- Sequence Clustering
- Time Series
- Association
- Neural Network (and Logistic Regression)

The two regression algorithms set parameters on the main algorithm to generate the regression results. Some of these higher-level algorithms include parameters the data miner can use to choose from several underlying algorithms to generate the model. If you plan to do serious data mining, you need to know what these algorithms are and how they work so you can apply them to the appropriate problems and are able to get the best performance. We briefly describe each of these algorithms in the following list. The Books Online topic "Data Mining Algorithms" is a good starting point for additional information about how each of these algorithms work.

> **RESOURCES** For more detailed information on Microsoft's algorithms, see the following resources:
>
> ▪ *Data Mining with Microsoft SQL Server 2008* (Wiley, 2008) by Jamie MacLennan, ZhaoHui Tang, and Bogdan Crivat; all current or former members of the Microsoft SQL Server Data Mining team.
>
> ▪ Search in SQL Server Books Online for "data mining algorithms" for descriptions and links to technical details, query guides, and model content.

Decision Trees

The Microsoft Decision Trees algorithm supports both classification and estimation. It works well for predictive modeling for both discrete and continuous attributes.

The process of building a decision tree starts with the dependent variable to be predicted and runs through the independent variables to see which one most effectively divides the population. The goal is to identify the variable that splits the cases into groups where the predicted variable (or class) either predominates or is faintly represented. The best starting variable for the tree is the one that creates groups that are the most different from each other — the most diverse.

For example, if you're creating a decision tree to identify couples who are likely to form a successful marriage, you'd need a training set of input attributes for both members of the couple and an assessment of whether or not the partnership is successful. The input attributes might include the age of each individual, religion, political views, gender, relationship role (husband or wife), and so on. The predictable attribute might be MarriageOutcome with the values of Success or Fail. The algorithm might determine that the first split in the decision tree — the one that creates the biggest split — is based on a variable called PoliticalViews: a discrete variable with the values of Similar and Different. Figure 13-2 shows that this initial split results in one group (PoliticalViews=Similar) that has a much higher percentage of successful marriages than the other (PoliticalViews=Different). The next split might be different for each of the two branches. In Figure 13-2, the top branch splits based on the height difference between the two (calculated as height of husband minus height of wife). The lower branch also splits on height difference, but uses different cutoff points. It seems that couples can better tolerate a greater height difference if their political views are similar.

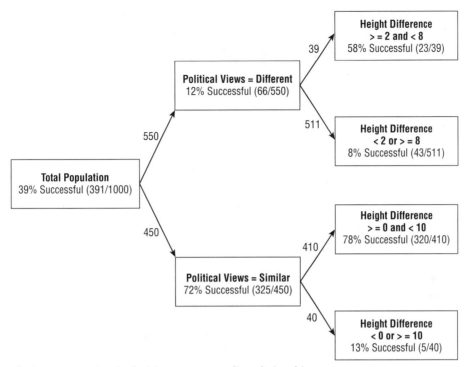

Figure 13-2: A simple decision tree to predict relationship success

The bottom branch of this tree indicates that the chances of having a successful marriage are more likely when the couple shares similar political views (.72). Following down that same branch, the chances get better when the husband is at least as tall as, but not more than 10 inches taller than the wife (.81). The group with the lowest probability of success (.08) is characterized by different political views and a height difference where the husband is either less than 2 inches taller or 8 inches or more taller than the wife. Once you build a decision tree like this, you could use it to predict the success of a given relationship by entering the appropriate attributes for both partners. At that point, you'd be well on your way to building a matching engine for a dating website.

Naïve Bayes

The Microsoft Naïve Bayes algorithm is a good starting point for many data mining projects. It is a simplified version of Decision Trees, and can be used for classification and prediction for discrete attributes. If you select the Naïve Bayes algorithm in the Data Mining Wizard, it will offer to ignore any continuous variables in the input case set. You can always use the mining structure to "discretize" these variables.

The Naïve Bayes algorithm is fairly simple, based on the relative probabilities of the different values of each attribute, given the value of the predictable attribute. For example, if you had a case set of individuals with their occupations and income ranges, you could build a Naïve Bayes model to predict Income Range given an Occupation. The decision tree in Figure 13-2 could have been generated by the Naïve Bayes algorithm because all the variables are discrete (although the Tree Viewer is not available for Naïve Bayes models). The required probability calculations are almost all done as part of the process of building the mining model cube, so the results are returned quickly.

Clustering

The clustering algorithm is designed to meet the clustering or segmentation business need described earlier. Clustering is generally considered a density estimation problem with the assumption that there are multiple populations in a set, each with its own density distribution. (Sentences like the preceding one serve to remind us that statisticians speak a different language.) It's easier to understand clustering visually: A simple spreadsheet chart of data points serves as an eyeball clustering tool — especially with only two variables. It's easy to see where the dense clusters are located. For example, a graph showing per-capita income versus per-capita national debt for each country in the world would quickly reveal several obvious clusters of countries. We explore the idea of graphically identifying clusters further in the next section. The challenge is finding these clusters when there are more than two variables, or when the variables are discrete and non-numeric rather than continuous.

NOTE The Microsoft Clustering algorithm uses what's known as an Expectation-Maximization (EM) approach to identifying clusters. An alternative, distance-based clustering mechanism called K-means is available by setting parameters on the model.

Sequence Clustering

Sequence clustering adds another level of flexibility to the clustering problem by including an ordering attribute. The algorithm can identify common sequences and use those sequences to predict the next step in a new sequence. Using the website example, sequence clustering can identify common click-paths and predict the next page (or pages) someone will visit, given the pages they have already visited.

Time Series

The Microsoft Time Series algorithms can be used to predict continuous variables, like Sales, over time. The algorithms include both ARIMA- and ARTxp-based algorithms to provide the best prediction over variable time spans. The algorithm includes time-variant factors like seasonality and can predict one or more variables from the case set. It also has the ability to generate predictions using cross-variable correlations. For example, product returns in the current period may be a function of product sales in the prior period. (It's just a guess, but we'd bet that high sales in the week leading up to December 25 may lead to high returns in the week following.)

Association

The Microsoft Association algorithm is designed to meet the business tasks described as association, affinity grouping, or market basket analysis. Association works well with the concept of nested case sets, where the parent level is the overall transaction and the child level is the individual items involved in the transaction. The algorithm looks for items that tend to occur together in the same transaction. The number of times a combination occurs is called its *support*. The MINIMUM_SUPPORT parameter allows the data miner to set a minimum number of occurrences before a given combination is considered significant. The Association algorithm goes beyond item pairs by creating rules that can involve several items. In English, the rule sounds like "When Item A and Item B exist in the item set, then the probability that Item C is also in the item set is X." The rule is displayed in this form: A, B → C (X). In the same way the data miner can specify a minimum support level, it is also possible to specify a minimum probability in order for a rule to be considered.

Neural Network

Neural network algorithms mimic our understanding of the way neurons work in the brain. The attributes of a case are the inputs to a set of interconnected nodes, each of which generates an output. The output can feed another layer of nodes (known as a hidden layer) and eventually feeds out to a result. The goal of the Microsoft Neural Network algorithm is to minimize the error of the result compared with the known value in the training set. Through some fancy footwork known as back propagation, the errors are fed back into the network, modifying the weights of the inputs. Then the algorithm makes additional passes through the training set, feeding back the results, until it converges on a solution. All this back and forth means the Neural Network algorithm is the slowest of the algorithms in terms of the time it takes to build a model. The algorithm can be used for classification or prediction on both continuous and discrete variables.

Using these seven core algorithms, separately or in combination, you can create solutions to most common data mining problems.

The Data Mining Process

There are probably as many ways to approach data mining as there are data mining practitioners. Much like dimensional modeling, starting with the goal of adding business value leads to a clear series of steps that just make sense.

You'll be shocked to hear that our data mining process begins with an understanding of the business opportunities. Figure 13-3 shows the three major phases of the data mining process — Business, Data Mining, and Operations — and the major task areas within those phases.

RESOURCES We didn't invent this process; we just stumbled on it through trial and error. Others who've spent their careers entirely on data mining have arrived at similar approaches to data mining. We're fortunate that they have documented their processes in detail in their own publications. In particular, three sources have been valuable to us. The book *Data Mining Techniques, 2nd Ed.* by Michael J. A. Berry and Gordon S. Linoff (Wiley, 2004) describes a process Berry and Linoff call the Virtuous Cycle of Data Mining. Another, similar approach comes from a special interest group that was formed in the late 1990s to define a data mining process. The result was published as *Cross Industry Standard Process for Data Mining (CRISP)*. Visit www.crisp-dm.org for more information. Also, search SQL Server Books Online for "Data Mining Concepts" to see Microsoft's version of the approach.

Like most of the processes in the DW/BI system, the data mining process is iterative. The arrows that point back to previous processes in Figure 13-3 are the most common iteration points. There are additional iteration points; for instance, it is also common to return to the business phase tasks based on what is learned in the data mining phase. In this section, we examine the three phases and their task areas in order, beginning with the business phase.

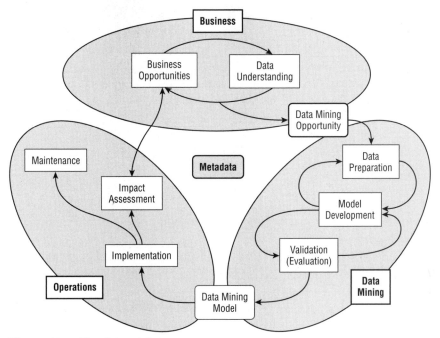

Figure 13-3: The data mining process

The Business Phase

The business phase is a much more focused version of the overall requirements gathering process. The goal is to identify an opportunity, or a list of opportunities and their relative priorities, that can have a significant impact on the business. The business opportunities and data understanding tasks in Figure 13-3 connect to each other because the process of identifying opportunities must be bounded by the realities of the data world. By the same token, the data itself may suggest business opportunities.

Identifying Business Opportunities

As always, the most important step in successful business intelligence is not about technology; it's about understanding the business. In data mining, this usually takes the form of a set of discussions between the business folks and the data miner about potential opportunities, and the associated relationships and behaviors that are captured in the data. The purpose of these meetings is to identify several high value opportunities and think through each one carefully. First, identify the overall business value goal of the data mining project. It helps to describe this in as narrow and measurable a way as possible. A goal like "increase sales" is too broad. A goal like "reduce the monthly cancellation, or churn, rate" is a bit more manageable. Next, think about what factors influence the goal. What might indicate that someone is likely to churn, or how can we tell if someone would be interested in a given product? While you're discussing these factors, try to translate them into specific attributes and behaviors that are known to exist in a usable, accessible form. The data miner may hold several of these meetings with different groups to identify a range of opportunities. At the end of these meetings, the data miner should work with the business folks to prioritize the various opportunities based on the estimated potential for business impact and the difficulty of implementation. These priorities will change as you learn more about the data, but this is an important starting point.

The data miner then takes the top-priority business opportunity and its associated list of potential variables back to the BIDS for further exploration.

Understanding the Data

The data miner typically spends a significant amount of time exploring the various data sets that might be relevant to the business opportunities discussed. At this stage, the goal is to be reasonably confident that the data needed to support the business opportunity is available and clean enough to be usable. This exploration is generally not much more complex than the data exploration and data profiling that took place during the data modeling step in Chapter 2, and in designing the ETL process in Chapter 7. Any problems identified at this point should be noted so they can be included in the data mining opportunity document.

Describing the Data Mining Opportunity

The data mining opportunity document describes the top-priority opportunity discussed with the business folks. The opportunity description should include the following sections:

- Business Opportunity Description
- Data Sources, Transformations, and Potential Data Issues
- Modeling Process Description
- Implementation Plan
- Maintenance Plan

It's important to document the opportunity, and have the business folks review it to make sure you understand their needs, and they understand how you intend to meet them. The data mining opportunity document is also a milestone in the data mining process. Once the data miner has a solid, clearly described, approved business opportunity, the data mining process enters the second phase: the data mining phase.

The Data Mining Phase

Once you understand the business opportunities and supporting data, you can move into the data mining phase of the project. The data mining phase is where the data miner works through the tasks of preparing the data, developing alternative models, comparing their accuracy, and validating the final model. As Figure 13-3 shows, this is a highly iterative process. Data preparation feeds the model development task, which often identifies the need for further data preparation. By the same token, the process of validating a model commonly indicates the need for further improvements, which loops the data miner right back to the model development task, and potentially back to data preparation. In some cases, when serious problems arise, the loop goes all the way back to the business opportunity step. We ignore all this iteration in our description and move sequentially through the tasks.

Data Preparation

The first task in the data mining phase is to build the data mining case sets. Recall that a case set includes one row per instance or event. For many data mining models, this means a data set with one row per customer. Models based on simple customer attributes, like gender and marital status, work at the one-row-per-customer level. Models that include behaviors like purchasing work at the one-row-per-event level. A case set for customer purchases would have one row for each product purchased by a customer. This is called a *nested case set* with two components — the customer case set with one row per customer and all the applicable customer attributes, and the nested product data set, which includes the customer key and the products purchased by the given customer. Building the case set involves creating SQL scripts, MDX scripts, and/or Integration Services packages to clean and transform the data, and copy it into the data sets needed to support the model building process.

Cleaning and Transforming

Ideally, the variables in the data set are fully populated with only the appropriate values and no outliers or null values. The bulk of this book describes the incredible amount of work it takes to create that cleaned, conformed information infrastructure we call the data warehouse. This is why the data warehouse is the ideal source for data mining case data. In the easiest case, many of the variables identified in the business opportunity already exist as attributes in the data warehouse database. This is often true with fields like CustomerType, or ProductColor. The data miner's world gets even better when demographics and other external data are already loaded as part of the standard ETL process. While these variables can be integrated directly into the data mining training set from their sources, it is always a good idea to verify that basic data quality rules have been appropriately applied.

Unfortunately, directly selecting variables from the data warehouse database rarely provides us with a rich enough data set to build a solid mining model. You may have to apply additional transformations to the data to make it more relevant to the business opportunity. This might include converting variables into more useful forms, such as combining fields or creating standard discrete ranges for continuous variables. Your organization or industry may already have them — audience age range in television programming and advertising is a common discrete range. If no standard ranges exist, the data mining designer can be used to automatically discretize these variables based on different methods, like a histogram of the values, or an even distribution. This can also be done by preprocessing the data in a SQL statement using the CASE function. Some attributes might need multiple conversions, like birth date might be converted to age, which could then be converted to age range.

As you work through the data mining phase, you may discover that these descriptive variables are generally not enough to build a highly predictive model, even after they have been transformed into more relevant forms. The most influential variables in a data mining model are typically behavior-based, not descriptive. Behaviors are generally captured as facts. What did customers do, how often did they do it, how much did they do it, and when did they do it are basic behavior questions. For example, knowing which web pages someone has viewed, what products they bought, what services they used, what problems they complained about, when the last time they complained was, and how many complaints they had in the last two months can help you build a clear picture of the status of your relationship with that customer.

These behavioral variables are painstakingly extracted from the detailed fact tables as part of the data preparation process. The initial choice of which behavioral variables to create is based on the business's understanding of behavior. Note that many of these behavior-based attributes require full table scans of the fact tables to create.

Integrating External Variables

Unfortunately, behavioral variables may still not be enough. Building an effective model often means bringing in additional data. These attributes, like demographics, come from various systems around the company or even from external sources. They will need to be merged together to make a single case set. When the source tables share a common key, this typically means joining them together to create a single row per case (usually per customer). However, it is not uncommon to have to map keys from the external source to the transaction system's natural keys, and then to the dimension's surrogate keys. In the worst case, the external data will not have a known key that ties to any field in the data warehouse database. When this happens, the relationship will need to be determined using matching tools such as Master Data Services or third party software. You can also use PowerPivot and the data mining add-ins for Excel to pull data together. You still need an instance of Analysis Services to process the mining models and you need to flatten the pivot tables and convert them to regular tables.

In organizations with large analytic communities, such as insurance companies or large web retailers, a tension may exist between professional data miners and the DW/BI team. Data miners sometimes reach for the raw source system data, clean it, analyze it, and then go directly to management with recommendations for decision making. The resulting models will not include all the data cleaning and conforming that goes into the data warehouse, but will contain whatever changes each data miner felt was appropriate. This results in another variety of the multiple versions of the truth problem.

WARNING Accurately tracking history is critical to successful data mining. If your DW/BI system or external sources overwrite changes in a type 1 fashion, your model will be associating current attribute values with historical behavior. This is particularly dangerous when integrating external data that might have only current attribute values. See the section "Slowly Changing Dimensions" in Chapter 2 for an example of how this might create problems.

Building the Case Sets

Build these data sets by defining data cleaning and transformation steps that build a data structure made up of individual observations or cases. Cases often contain repeating nested or child structures. These case sets are then fed into the data mining service. It's helpful to manage these tables independent of the data warehouse itself. Keep the data mining case sets in their own database, on their own server if necessary, where the data miner has permission to create tables. The process of building the case sets is typically very similar to the regular ETL process. It usually involves a set of transformations and full table scans that actually generate a resulting data set that gets loaded into the data mining database.

There are two main approaches to data preparation in the SQL Server environment. Folks who come from a SQL/relational background will be inclined to write SQL scripts, saving the results to separate case set tables that become inputs to the data mining process.

NOTE Creating case sets can also be done through views if you are creative enough with your SQL. We don't recommend this because if the underlying data changes (like when new rows are added), the mining model may change for no apparent reason.

Folks who come from an ETL background will be more comfortable using SSIS to merge, clean, and prepare the data mining case sets. The Integration Services approach has some advantages in that there are many transformation components built into the SSIS toolbox. Integration Services can also more easily pull data from external sources and in different formats and can be used to deposit the prepared case set wherever it is needed, in a variety of formats.

Depending on the business opportunity and the data mining algorithms employed, creating the initial data sets often involves creating separate subsets of the data for different purposes. Table 13-2 lists two common data sets used for data mining. The Microsoft mining structure has the ability to automatically divide its input case set into training and test subsets. The data miner's main task is to identify the appropriate source data sample to serve as the input case training set to the data mining process. In some cases, the Percentage Sampling and Row Sampling tasks are particularly well suited to creating the input case set.

Table 13-2: The primary data mining data sets

SET	PURPOSE
Training	Used as input to the algorithm to develop the initial model.
Test	Data not included in the training sets — often called *holdout data.* Used to verify the accuracy or effectiveness of the model.

One last advantage Integration Services offers is that it allows you to build a package or project that contains all of the steps needed to prepare data for a given data mining project. Put this SSIS project under source control, and re-use it to create new data sets to keep the model current. In our opinion, SSIS is the best choice for data mining data preparation. SQL plays a role in defining the initial extracts and some of the transformations, and will be part of any data preparation effort, but building the whole flow generally works best in Integration Services.

Model Development

The first step in developing the data mining model is to create the mining model structure in BIDS. The mining model structure is essentially a metadata layer that separates the data from the algorithms. The Data Mining Wizard creates the initial mining model structure, which can then be edited as needed.

Once the mining structure is defined, the data miner builds as many mining models and versions as time allows, trying different algorithms, parameters, and variables to see which combination yields the greatest impact or is most accurate. Usually this involves going back and redefining the data preparation task to add new variables or change existing transformations. These iterations are where SQL Server Data Mining shines. The flexibility, ease of use, range of algorithms, and integration with the rest of the SQL Server toolset allows the data miner to run through more variations than many other data mining environments in a given time period. Generally, the more variations tested, the better the final model.

Model Validation (Evaluation)

There are two kinds of model validation in data mining. The first involves comparing models created with different algorithms, parameters, and inputs to see which is most effective at predicting the target variable. The second is a business review of the proposed model to examine its contents and assess its value. We will look at both validation steps in this section.

Comparing Models

Creating the best data mining model is a process of triangulation. Attack the data with several algorithms like Decision Trees, Neural Network, and Naïve Bayes. You'd like to see several models point to similar results. This is especially helpful in those cases where the tool spits out an answer but doesn't provide an intuitive foundation for why the answer was chosen. Neural Network models are notorious for this kind of result. Triangulation gives all the observers (especially end users and management) confidence that the predictions mean something.

Analysis Services Data Mining provides three tools for comparing the effectiveness of certain types of data mining models — a lift chart, a classification matrix, and cross validation. These can be found under the Mining Accuracy Chart tab in the Data Mining Designer. To use the Accuracy tab tools, first select the mining structure that supports the models you want to compare and join it to your test data set. The lift chart works in a couple of different ways, depending on the models being compared. The basic idea is to run the test cases through all of the models, and compare the predicted results with the known actual results from the test data set. The lift chart then plots the percentage of correct predictions for a given percentage of the overall test population, beginning with the most accurate portions of the model (the cases with the highest predicted probability). Figure 13-4 shows a lift chart that compares two simple models used to predict Income Range based on the other non-income demographics in the AdventureWorksDW `Customer` table.

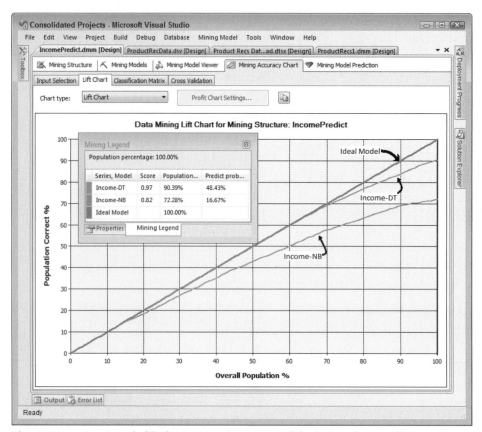

Figure 13-4: An example lift chart comparing two models designed to predict Income Range

The lines representing the two models are bounded by an upper limit that represents the best possible prediction. In the best case, the model would be 100 percent correct for whatever percent of the population it processed. The best case is represented by the heavy, straight line between 0 and 100. The worst case would be a random guess. Because this model has only six possible values of predicted income ranges, a random guess would be right 1/6 or 16.67 percent of the time. The Decision Trees model called Income-DT is clearly more predictive than the Naïve Bayes model called Income-NB. At the 100 percent point, the Decision Trees model accurately predicts 90.39 percent of the cases while the Naïve Bayes has tailed off to only 72.28 percent of the cases. The Lift Chart tab also includes the ability to add in incremental costs, fixed costs, and revenue to create a profit chart that helps determine the optimal percentage of the overall population to target.

The second tool, called the classification matrix, is a matrix with the actual values of the data set on the columns and the values predicted by the model on the rows. Ideally, you'd like to see a single vector down the diagonal of the matrix with values, and the rest of the cells should be zeros. This would represent the outcome where all of the cases the model predicted to be in a certain Income Range actually were in that range. Figure 13-5 shows the classification matrices for the Decision Trees and Naïve Bayes models from Figure 13-4.

In this example, the Naïve Bayes model clearly is incorrect more often than the Decision Trees model. For example, for cases where the actual range is 70,812.1–98,020.4 (the third data column), the Naïve Bayes model incorrectly predicts an Income Range of 39,272.8–70,812.1 for 105 cases, while the Decision Trees model makes this error only 54 times.

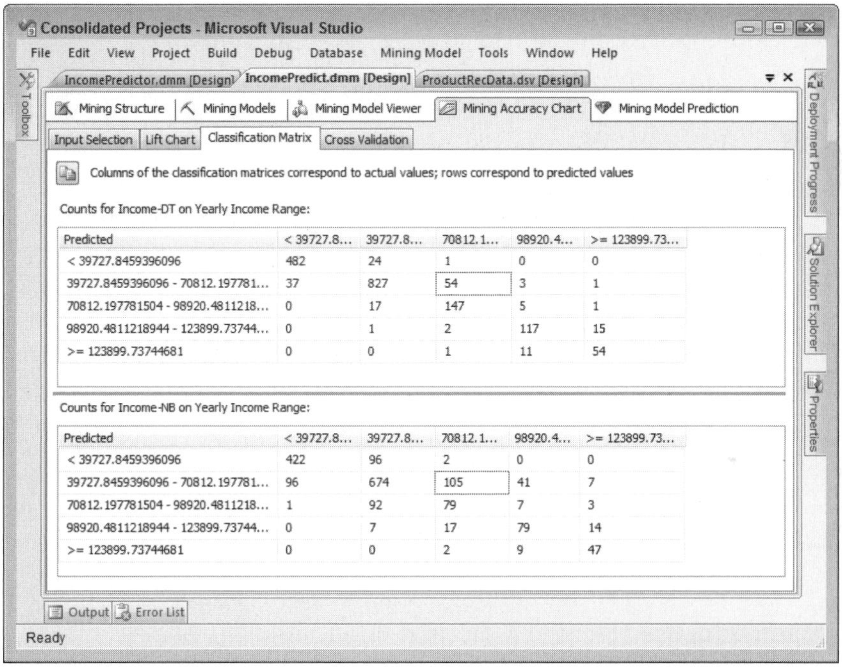

Figure 13-5: Example classification matrices for the Income Predictor models

The fourth Mining Accuracy Chart tab is called Cross Validation. It breaks up the input data set into a number of subsets and creates models based on those subsets for each of the mining models in the mining structure. It then generates a report with a set of statistics about the accuracy of each data subset within each mining model. The results are not so visually interesting to the average business person, but do have value to an experienced data miner/statistician.

Unfortunately, the mining accuracy tools work only for single-valued results at this point. They don't work for result lists, like recommendation lists. In those cases, you will need to build your own comparison tests using the Integration Services tasks or the Excel data mining add-in to query the mining model with the test data set and compare the results. We show an example of this in one of the case studies later in this chapter.

RESOURCES For more information about using lift charts, classification matrices, and cross validation, search for "Validating Data Mining Models" in SQL Server Books Online.

Business Review

The data mining phase ends with the selection of the "best" model based on its performance in the model comparison process and its implementation cost. Ultimately this is a business decision, so you need to review the contents and performance of the model with the business folks to make sure that it makes sense.

Prepare for this review by carefully combing through the selected model to understand and document the rules it uses, the relationships it defines, and the impact you expect it to have. The various tabs in the Data Mining Designer are particularly helpful in developing this understanding. Or, consider using the model rendering template for Visio, which is part of the Office Data Mining Addins. Present this documentation to the business users and carefully walk them through the logic behind the recommended model. This presentation also includes evidence of the model's performance from the Mining Accuracy Chart tab tools and other sources. This helps all participants understand the expected impact of the model. Once the business review is complete, the next step is to move the model out into the real world.

The Operations Phase

The operations phase is where the rubber meets the road. At this point, you have the best possible model (given the time, data, and technology constraints) and you have business approval to proceed. Now you get to put it into production and see what kind of impact it has. The operations phase involves three main tasks: implementation, impact assessment, and maintenance.

Implementation

After all participants have approved the final model and the implementation plan, the team can move the model into production in the implementation task. Production can range from using the model once a quarter to assess the effectiveness of various promotions, to classifying customers as part of the nightly ETL process, to interactively making product recommendations as part of the web server or customer care transaction system.

Each of these alternatives involves a different cast of characters. At one end of the spectrum, the quarterly update of the customer dimension may involve only the data miner and the ETL developer. At the other end of the spectrum, making online recommendations will clearly involve the production systems folks. And, depending on the transaction volume, they will likely want a production Analysis Services server (or cluster) dedicated to providing recommendations. Moving the data mining model into production may also involve significant changes to the transaction system applications to incorporate the data mining query and results into the business process and user interface. This is usually a big deal. You must figure out who needs to be involved in the implementation task for your data mining model and let them know as early as possible, so they can help determine the appropriate timeframes and resources. Deploy in phases, starting with a test version, to make sure the data mining server doesn't gum up the transaction process.

Assess Impact

Determining the impact of the data mining model can be high art. In some areas, like direct mail and web-based offers, the process of tuning and testing the marketing offers and collateral and the target prospect lists is often full-time work for a large team. They do test and control sets with different versions of the mailing before they do the full mass mailing. Even in the full campaign, often several phases with different versions and control sets are built in. The results of each phase help the team tweak subsequent phases for best results. One method, known as A/B testing, involves comparing the responses of people who are randomly selected into subgroups that receive different versions of an offer. A/B testing is a simple and powerful way to minimize the influence of external variables.

In general, the data miner should adopt as much of this careful assessment process as possible.

Maintain the Model

Almost all data mining models will need to be re-trained, or be completely rebuilt over some period of time. As the world changes, the behaviors that have been captured in the model become outdated. This is particularly noticeable in a fast changing industry like retail where new fashions, products, and models are announced on a daily basis. A recommendation engine that didn't include the most recent behavior and latest models would be less than useful to the customer. In a case like this, the basic model structure may still apply, but the rules and relationships must be re-generated based on new behavior data.

Metadata

In the best of all possible worlds, the final data mining model should be documented with a detailed history of how it came into being. What sources contributed to the case set? What kinds of transformations were applied to the variables, and at what points in the process were they applied? What was the initial model and what were the intermediate versions considered and discarded? What parameter values were used for which versions of the model? A professional data miner will want to know exactly what went into creating a model in order to explain its value, to avoid repeating the same errors, and to re-create it if need be. The data miner should also keep track of how and when the model is used, and when it should be maintained.

The problem with tracking the history of a mining model is that because Analysis Services makes it so easy to create additional versions of the model, it takes much more time to document each iteration than it does to actually do the work. Nonetheless, you still need to keep track of what you have and where it came from. We recommend keeping a basic set of metadata to track the contents and derivation of all the transformed data sets and resulting mining models you decide to keep around. This can get much more complex if you like, but the simplest approach is to use a spreadsheet, as pictured in Figure 13-6.

Project Information	Data Preparation SSIS Package Information
Project Name:	Package Name:
Project Owner:	Package Location:
Business Contact:	Data Mining Server Name:
Start Date:	Data Mining Database Name:
Expiration Date:	
Project Description:	

Data Mining Data Sources					
Source Name	Type	Create step	Version	Version Date	Xforms and changes
. . .					

Data Mining Data Structures			
Structure Name	Version	Version Date	Xforms and changes
. . .			

Data Mining Models									
Model Name	Parent Structure	DM Algorithm	Version	Version Date	Input Vars	Predict Vars	Parameter settings	Results
. . .								

Figure 13-6: A simple spreadsheet for tracking data mining models

NOTE The data mining process takes place across the various DW/BI system platforms and relies on their security mechanisms. The data miner needs to have enough privileges on the data source servers to create new tables and/or cubes. Additionally, to create and modify data mining models, the data miner must be a member of the Analysis Services Administrators group on the data mining computer.

Data Mining Examples

For many of us, the best way to learn something is by doing it. This is especially true for technical folks, and even more so for data mining. You really need to work through the SQL Server basic data mining tutorial before you run through the following examples. This will give you a chance to get familiar with the tools and the user interface, which will make these examples easier to understand and follow. If you haven't already done so, please take the time to work through the data mining tutorials now.

In this section, we start with a simple example to get a feel for the data mining tool environment and the data mining process. In fact, the first example is so simple that its case set of economic data can be presented on a single page. It's perfect to show the power and accessibility of the data mining add-ins for Microsoft Office Excel. Then we dig into a more detailed example based on the Adventure Works Cycles data warehouse data. Both of these examples are based on business scenarios and will follow the general flow of the data mining process presented in the previous section.

Case Study: Categorizing Cities

This first example is a small, simplified problem designed to provide a clear understanding of the process. The data set has only 48 cases total — not nearly enough to build a robust data mining model. However, the small size allows us to examine the inputs and outputs to see if the resulting model makes sense. The scenario is based on a large non-governmental organization (NGO) with a mission and operations much like that of the World Bank:

> *(T)o fight poverty and improve the living standards of people in the developing world. It is a development Bank that provides loans, policy advice, technical assistance and knowledge sharing services to low and middle income countries to reduce poverty. The Bank promotes growth to create jobs and to empower poor people to take advantage of these opportunities.*

```
http://web.worldbank.org/
```

Categorizing Cities: Business Opportunity

The data miner on the NGO's DW/BI team held meetings with key directors and managers from around the organization to identify business opportunities that are supported by available data and can be translated into data mining opportunities. During these meetings it became clear that there were not enough resources to properly customize the NGO's programs. The NGO had historically focused its efforts to provide financial aid at the country level. Several economists felt that targeting policies and programs at the city level would be more effective, allowing for the accommodation of unique regional and local considerations that are not possible at the country level.

A switch to the city level would mean the people who implemented the NGO's programs would need to deal with potentially thousands of cities rather than the 208 countries they were working with around the world. This switch would significantly expand the complexities of managing the economic programs in an organization that was already resource limited.

The group discussed the possibility of designing programs for groups of cities that have similar characteristics. If there were a relatively small number of city groups, the economic analysts felt it would be possible to design and manage much more appropriate economic programs.

Categorizing Cities: Data Understanding

During the meetings, there was discussion about what variables might be useful inputs. The analysts had a gut feel for what the city groups might be, and some initial guesses about which variables would be most important and how they could be combined. The group came up with a list of likely variables. The data miner combed through the organization's databases to see if these inputs could be found, and to see what other relevant information was available. This effort turned up 54 variables that the organization tracked, from total population to the number of fixed line and mobile phones per 1,000 people. This wealth of data seemed too good to be true, and it was. Further investigation revealed that much of this data was not tracked at the city level. In fact, there were only ten city-level variables available. The data miner reviewed this list with the business folks and the group determined that of the ten variables, only three were reliably measured. Fortunately, the group also felt these three variables were important measures of a city's economic situation. The three variables were average hourly wages (local currency), average hours worked per year, and the average price index.

At this point, the data miner wrote up a description of the data mining opportunity, its expected business impact, and an estimate of the time and effort it would take to complete. The project was described in two phases; the goal of the first phase was to develop a model that clusters cities based on the data available. If this model made sense to the business folks, phase two would use that model to assign new cities to the appropriate clusters as they contact the NGO for financial support. The data mining opportunity description was reviewed by the economists and all agreed to proceed.

Categorizing Cities: Data Preparation

The data miner reviewed the data set and realized it needed some work. First, the average hourly wages were in local currencies. After some research on exchange rates and discussion with the economists to decide on the appropriate rates and timing, the data miner created a package to load and transform the data. The package extracted the data from the source system and looked up the exchange rate for each city and applied it to the wages data. Because the consumer price data was already indexed relative to Zurich, using Zurich as 100, this package also indexed the wage data in the same fashion. Finally, the package wrote the updated data set out to a separate table. The resulting data set to be used for training the cluster model, containing three economic measures for 46 cities around the world, is shown in Figure 13-7 (split into two tables in the figure for easier viewing). Note that the total data set has 48 cities, but we held out two cities to use later as examples in the implementation section.

NOTE This data comes from the Economics Research Department of the Union Bank of Switzerland. The original set contains economic data from 48 cities around the globe in 1991. It has been used as example data for statistics classes and can be found on many websites. You can find this data set by searching for "cities prices and earnings economic (1991) globe." You can find more current versions by searching for "UBS Prices and Earnings." The current version includes 73 cities.

Observe that two of the cities do not have complete data. The data miner might opt to exclude these cities from the data set, or include them to see if the model can identify them as outliers. This would help spot any bad data that might come through in the future.

Obs.	City Name	Avg Work Hrs	Price Index	Wage Index	Obs.	City Name	Avg Work Hrs	Price Index	Wage Index
1	Amsterdam	1714	65.6	49.0	24	Madrid	1710	93.8	50.0
2	Athens	1792	53.8	30.4	25	Manila	2268	4.0	40.0
3	Bogota	2152	37.9	11.5	26	Mexico City	1944	49.8	5.7
4	Bombay	2052	30.3	5.3	27	Milan	1773	53.3	82.0
5	Brussels	1708	73.8	50.5	28	Montreal	1827	72.7	56.3
6	Buenos Aires	1971	56.1	12.5	29	Nairobi	1958	45.0	5.8
7	Cairo		37.1		30	New York	1942	83.3	65.8
8	Caracas	2041	61.0	10.9	31	Nicosia	1825	47.9	28.3
9	Chicago	1924	73.9	61.9	32	Oslo	1583	115.5	63.7
10	Copenhagen	1717	91.3	62.9	33	Panama	2078	49.2	13.8
11	Dublin	1759	76.0	41.4	34	Paris	1744	81.6	45.9
12	Dusseldorf	1693	78.5	60.2	35	Rio de Janeiro	1749	46.3	10.5
13	Frankfurt	1650	74.5	60.4	36	Sao Paolo	1856	48.9	11.1
14	Geneva	1880	95.9	90.3	37	Seoul	1842	58.3	32.7
15	Helsinki	1667	113.6	66.6	38	Singapore	2042	64.4	16.1
16	Hong Kong	2375	63.8	27.8	39	Stockholm	1805	111.3	39.2
17	Houston	1978	71.9	46.3	40	Sydney	1668	70.8	52.1
18	Jakarta		43.6		41	Taipei	2145	84.3	34.5
19	Johannesburg	1945	51.1	24.0	42	Tel Aviv	2015	67.3	27.0
20	Lagos	1786	45.2	2.7	43	Tokyo	1880	115.0	68.0
21	London	1737	84.2	46.2	44	Toronto	1888	70.2	58.2
22	Los Angeles	2068	79.8	65.2	45	Vienna	1780	78.0	51.3
23	Luxembourg	1768	71.1	71.1	46	Zurich	1868	100.0	100.0

Figure 13-7: The city economic dataset after data preparation

Categorizing Cities: Model Development

Because the goal in the first phase was to identify groups of cities that have similar characteristics, and those groupings were not predetermined, the data miner decided to use the Microsoft Clustering algorithm. Once the Data Mining Add-in for Microsoft Office was installed, the data miner copied the data into a table in a worksheet, and then selected Create Mining Structure under the Advanced button in the Data Modeling section of the Data Mining Ribbon as shown in Figure 13-8. (The Cluster button would be a more obvious choice, but the add-in assumes you want to include the city name in the clustering process. The Advanced button requires a two step process, but it is still pretty easy.)

This opened a wizard to create a new mining structure. The wizard asks for a source, defaulting to the data set in the local table. On the Select Columns screen, the data miner set the Usage of the RowID to Do Not Use, and set the usage of the CityName to Key. On the "Split data into training and testing sets" screen, the data miner set the percentage of data for testing to 0, so data from all the cities will be used to determine the clusters. The structure name was entered on the last screen, and then the data miner clicked the Finish button to write the new mining structure out to Analysis Services.

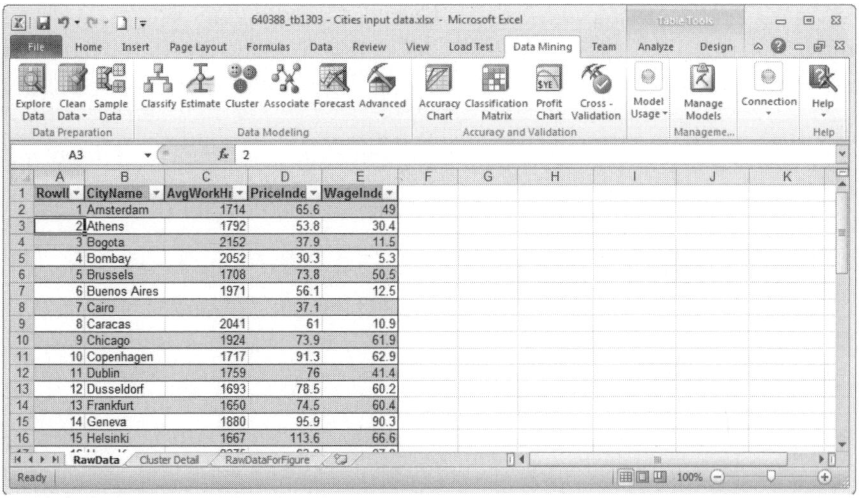

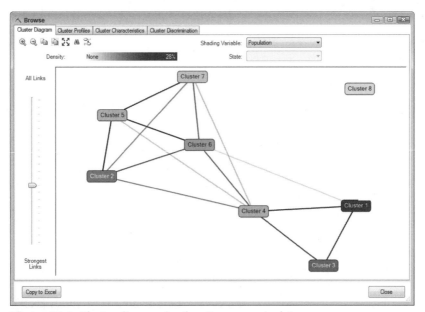

Figure 13-8: Data Mining Ribbon in Excel

With the mining structure metadata layer in place, the data miner then selected the Advanced button again, and selected "Add model to structure." A wizard asked which data mining technique should be used. The data miner chose Microsoft Clustering and specified the city name as the key and the other columns as input and changed the model name on the final wizard screen. After the wizard finished processing the model on Analysis Services, it opened up a model browser window and presented the cluster diagram shown in Figure 13-9.

Figure 13-9: Cluster diagram for the city economic data

At first glance, this diagram isn't that helpful. Without knowing anything about the problem, the Microsoft Clustering algorithm is limited to names like Cluster 1 and Cluster 2. At this point, the data miner can explore the model by using the other tabs in the model browser, and by using the drill-through feature to see which cities have been assigned to which nodes. The data miner can also use the other tabs in the model browser to examine the underlying rules and distributions. The data in Figure 13-10 is grouped by cluster and was created by right-clicking each cluster in the model browser and selecting Drill Through Model Columns.

Cases Classified to: Cluster 1

City Name	Work Hrs	Price Idx	Wage Idx
Amsterdam	1714	65.6	49.0
Brussels	1708	73.8	50.5
Chicago	1924	73.9	61.9
Dublin	1759	76.0	41.4
Dusseldorf	1693	78.5	60.2
Frankfurt	1650	74.5	60.4
Houston	1978	71.9	46.3
London	1737	84.2	46.2
Montreal	1827	72.7	56.3
Paris	1744	81.6	45.9
Sydney	1668	70.8	52.1
Toronto	1888	70.2	58.2
Vienna	1780	78.0	51.3
Cluster Avg	1775	74.7	52.3

Cases Classified to: Cluster 2

City Name	Work Hrs	Price Idx	Wage Idx
Buenos Aires	1971	56.1	12.5
Lagos	1786	45.2	2.7
Mexico City	1944	49.8	5.7
Nairobi	1958	45.0	5.8
Panama	2078	49.2	13.8
Rio de Janeiro	1749	46.3	10.5
Sao Paulo	1856	48.9	11.1
Cluster Avg	1906	48.6	8.9

Cases Classified to: Cluster 3

City Name	Work Hrs	Price Idx	Wage Idx
Copenhagen	1717	91.3	62.9
Geneva	1880	95.9	90.3
Helsinki	1667	113.6	66.6
Madrid	1710	93.8	50.0
Oslo	1583	115.5	63.7
Stockholm	1805	111.3	39.2
Tokyo	1880	115.0	68.0
Zurich	1868	100.0	100.0
Cluster Avg	1764	104.6	67.6

Cases Classified to: Cluster 4

City Name	Work Hrs	Price Idx	Wage Idx
Los Angeles	2068	79.8	65.2
Luxembourg	1768	71.1	71.1
Milan	1773	53.3	82.0
New York	1942	83.3	65.8
Cluster Avg	1888	71.9	71.0

Cases Classified to: Cluster 6

City Name	Work Hrs	Price Idx	Wage Idx
Athens	1792	53.8	30.4
Johannesburg	1945	51.1	24.0
Nicosia	1825	47.9	28.3
Seoul	1842	58.3	32.7
Tel Aviv	2015	67.3	27.0
Cluster Avg	1884	55.7	28.5

Cases Classified to: Cluster 5

City Name	Work Hrs	Price Idx	Wage Idx
Bogota	2152	37.9	11.5
Bombay	2052	30.3	5.3
Caracas	2041	61.0	10.9
Singapore	2042	64.4	16.1
Cluster Avg	2072	48.4	11.0

Cases Classified to: Cluster 8

City Name	Work Hrs	Price Idx	Wage Idx
Cairo		37.1	
Jakarta		43.6	
Cluster Avg		40.4	

Cases Classified to: Cluster 7

City Name	Work Hrs	Price Idx	Wage Idx
Hong Kong	2375	63.8	27.8
Manila	2268	4.0	40.0
Tai Pei	2145	84.3	34.5
Cluster Avg	2263	50.7	34.1

Figure 13-10: City economic data listed by cluster

The clusters in Figure 13-10 make general sense given a basic understanding of the world economic situation in 1991. Many of the poorer cities of South and Central America and Africa ended up in Cluster 2. Similar cities ended up in Cluster 5, except Cluster 5 has significantly more work hours on average. The two cities that had only price data, Cairo and Jakarta, are on their own in Cluster 8, and that cluster was not connected to the other seven in Figure 13-9. Cluster 8 seems to be the data anomalies cluster.

While you can make some sense of the raw tabular output, SQL Server also provides tools to improve your understanding. For example, the Cluster Profiles tab of the model browser shown in Figure 13-11 makes it easier to identify the characteristics of the individual clusters. The table shows the average value and range of each cluster for each of the three input variables. The clusters are listed from largest to smallest starting with the distribution for all 46 cities. Cluster 1 includes cities whose wages and prices are relatively high, and have relatively low work hours. These are the cities that make up the day-to-day workforce of their respective countries — we might call this cluster the "Heartland" cities, although Paris might not like that name. The next cluster, Cluster 3, is even more upscale, with the highest average prices, second highest average wages, and the lowest work hours. Cluster 2, on the other hand, has extremely low wages, higher work hours than most, and relatively lower prices. This is similar to Cluster 5, which has even higher work hours. These are the newly developing cities where labor is cheap and people must work long hours to survive. You might call this cluster the "Hard Knock Life" cities. The NGO would likely call it something a bit more politically correct, like the "Developing Cities" cluster. As we mentioned earlier, good names can help crystallize the defining characteristics of each cluster.

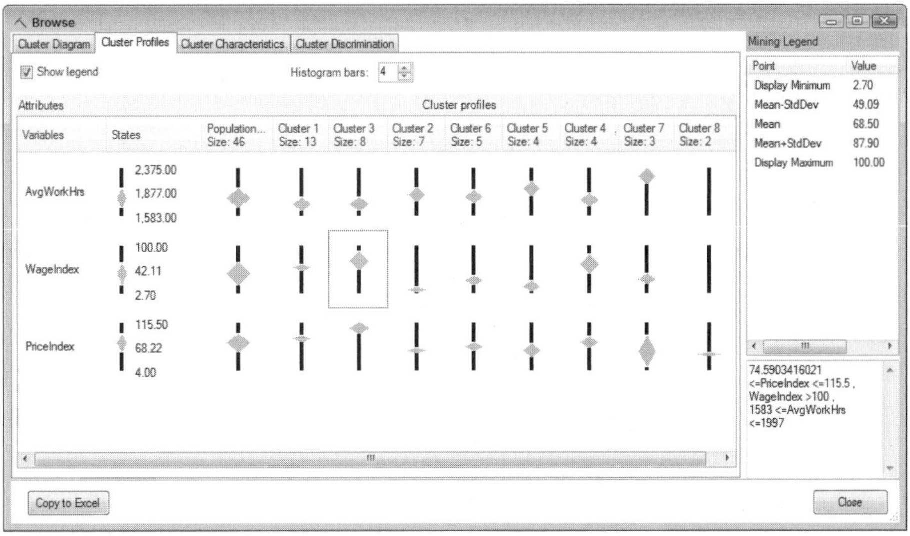

Figure 13-11: The Cluster Profiles tab of the model browser

Categorizing Cities: Model Validation

Some data mining models are easier to test than others. For example, when you're building a prediction model, you can create it based on one historical data set and test it on another. Having historical data means you already know the right answer, so you can feed the data through the model, see what value it predicts, and compare it to what actually happened.

In the City cluster example, validating the model is not so straightforward. You don't know the categorization ahead of time, so you can't compare the assigned cluster with the right cluster — there is no such thing as "right" in this case. Validation of this model came in two stages. First, the data miner went back to the economic analysts and reviewed the model and the results with them. This was a reasonableness test where the domain experts compared the model with their own understanding of the problem. The second test came when the model was applied to the original business problem. In this case, the team monitored the categorization of new cities to make sure they continued to stand up to the reasonableness test. Ultimately, the question was "Do the categorizations seem right, and do they help simplify how the organization works at the city level?" Is it easier and more effective to work with eight clusters rather than 48 (or 4,800) cities?

Categorizing Cities: Implementation

Once the team decided the model would work, or at least that it was worth testing in an operational environment, it was time to move it into production. This can mean a whole range of activities, depending on the nature of the model and the business process to which it's being applied. In this city categorization example, new economic data at the city level can arrive at any time. While is it easy to assign new cities to clusters using the Excel data mining add-in, the team decided to have this new data entered into a table in the database and assign clusters to it in a batch process once a night.

The data miner wrote a simple Integration Services package that reads in unassigned cities, submits them to the data mining model for cluster assignment, and writes the full record out to a table called CityMaster with a batch date identifying when the cluster was assigned. Figure 13-12 shows what the data flow for this simple package might look like. This flow has a data viewer inserted right after the Data Mining Query transformation showing its output. Compare the cluster assignments for Kuala Lumpur (Cluster 5), and Lisbon (Cluster 6), with the other cities in those clusters in Figure 13-10. Do these assignments pass the reasonableness test?

Implementation would also integrate this package into the rest of the nightly ETL process. The package should include the standard data and process audit functions described in Chapter 7. Ultimately, the process should be part of the package that manages the City dimension.

This nightly data mining batch process is a common one in many DW/BI systems, using a data mining model to populate a calculated field like a Default Risk score across all loan records or a Credit Rating across all customers. These scores can change depending on customer behaviors, like late payments or deposit balances. Every loan and customer may have to be re-scored every night. The same batch process can be used on a one-time basis to address opportunities like identifying customers who are likely to respond to a new product offering or who are at risk of canceling their service.

NOTE The Integration Services Data Mining Query transformation is an Enterprise Edition feature.

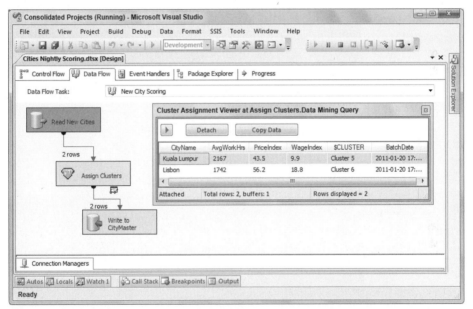

Figure 13-12: An Integration Services package to assign clusters to new cities

Categorization Cities: Maintenance and Assessment

As the data changes, the data mining model will likely change as well. In this case, the data mining model should be re-built as existing data is updated or data about additional cities is collected. The team would then review the resulting clusters to make sure they make sense from a business perspective. Given the nature of the business process and the changing data, this review should probably happen on a regularly scheduled basis — perhaps monthly to start, then quarterly as the model and data stabilize.

This example shows how clustering can be used to improve an organization's business processes. Although this data set is too small to produce reliable results, it does generate a model that makes sense and shows how that model can be applied to new incoming data.

Case Study: Product Recommendations

The ability to recommend products that might be particularly interesting to a given customer can have a huge impact on how much your customers purchase. This example follows the data mining process from identifying the business requirements through to the implementation of a product recommendation data mining model. It's based on the SQL Server Adventure Works Cycles data set. Recall from Chapter 1 that Adventure Works Cycles is a manufacturer, wholesaler, and internet retailer of bicycles and accessories.

The SQL Server data mining tutorial steps you through the process of building a model that predicts whether or not someone will be a bike buyer. While this is interesting information, it doesn't help you figure out what to display on the web page. Even if you're pretty certain someone will be a bike buyer, you don't know which bike to show them. Also, what products should you show all those folks who are not bike buyers? Our goal in this example is to create a data mining model that produces a custom list of specific products that you can show to any given website visitor based on demographic information provided by the visitor. To the extent that the custom product list is more appealing than a random list of products, the visitor is more likely to make a purchase.

In this example, we try to give you enough information to work through the model creation process yourself. It's not a complete step-by-step tutorial, but if you've already worked through the SQL Server data mining tutorial, you should be able to follow along and see how it works firsthand.

Product Recommendations: The Business Phase

Recall that the business phase of the data mining process involves identifying business opportunities, and building an understanding of the available data and its ability to support the data mining process. The Adventure Works Cycles data is not real, but it is more complete than many real-world systems we've seen, and it has more than enough customers and purchases to be interesting.

Product Recommendations: Business Opportunities

In many companies, the DW/BI team has to sell the idea of incorporating data mining into the business processes. This is usually either because the business folks don't understand the potential or because the business will have to change the transaction system, which is a big and scary task. Sometimes, the team gets lucky and data mining starts with a request from the business community. This is how it worked in the Adventure Works Cycles example. One of the folks in marketing who is responsible for e-commerce marketing came to the DW/BI team asking for ways to boost web sales. Web sales accounted for about $9,000,000 in the first half of 2008, or about one-third of Adventure Works Cycles total sales. The marketing group has created a three-part strategy for growing the online business: Bring in more visitors (Attract), turn more visitors into customers (Convert), and develop long-term relationships with customers (Retain). The marketing person who came to the DW/BI team is responsible for the Convert strategy — that is, for converting visitors to customers.

> **TIP** In a case like this, if the marketing person has a PowerPoint presentation that goes into detail on the marketing strategy, the data miner should review it. We feel sure they have such a presentation.

Because the marketing person is responsible only for conversion, the team will investigate alternatives for increasing the conversion of visitors to customers. They will check to see if the final model also increases the average dollars per sale as a beneficial side effect. After some discussion, the team decided that influencing purchasing behavior (conversion) with relevant recommendations is likely to be the best way to achieve their goals. They translated the idea of recommendations into specifics by deciding to dedicate one section of the left-hand navigation bar on the e-commerce website to hold a list of six recommended products that will be tailored to the individual visitor. While the marketing person investigated the level of effort required to make this change on the website, the data miner dug into the availability of relevant data.

Product Recommendations: Data Understanding

After some research, the data miner discovered that when visitors come to the Adventure Works Cycles website, they are asked to fill out an optional demographics form ("to better serve them"). A few queries revealed that about two-thirds of all visitors actually do fill out the form. Because the form is a required part of the purchase process, the information is also available for all customers. In either case, this demographic information is placed in a database and in cookies in the visitor or customer's browser. The DW/BI system also has all historical purchasing behavior for each customer at the individual product and line item level. Based on this investigation, the data miner felt that sufficient data was available to create a useful mining model for product recommendations.

The data miner knew from experience that demographic based models are generally not as predictive as behavior based models (like purchases or page views). However, there were several opportunities to make recommendations where no product related behavioral data was available but demographic data was available. As a result, the data miner believed that two data mining models might be appropriate: one to provide recommendations on the home page and any non-product pages, and one to provide recommendations on any product related pages. The first model would be based on demographics and would be used to predict what a visitor might be interested in given their demographic profile. The second model would be based on product interest as indicated by the product associated with each web page they visit or any products added to their cart.

At this point, the data miner wrote up a Data Mining Opportunity document to capture the goals, decisions, and approach. The overall business goal was to increase conversion rates with an ancillary goal of increasing the average dollars per sale. The strategy was to offer products that have a higher probability of being interesting to any given visitor to the website. This strategy breaks down into two separate data mining models, one based on demographics and one based on product purchases. This decision was considered a starting point with the understanding that it would likely change during the data mining phase. This example goes through the creation of the demographics-based model. The product-based model is left as an exercise for the reader.

The team also agreed on metrics to measure the impact of the program. They would compare before and after data, looking at the change in the ratio of the number of new customers (conversions) to the total unique visitor count in the same time periods. They would also examine the change in the average shopping cart value at the time of checkout. A third impact measure would be to analyze the web logs to see how often customers viewed and clicked on a recommended link. Some of these comparisons could be done by randomly assigning visitors either to a server on the web farm that offers recommendations or to other servers that are unchanged. This A/B comparison evens out the influence that any external factor, such as a big holiday, may have.

Product Recommendations: The Data Mining Phase

With the opportunity document as a guide, the data miner began with the demographics-based model. This section follows the development of the model from data preparation to model development and validation.

Product Recommendations: Data Preparation

The data miner decided the data source should be the AdventureWorksDW2008R2 relational database. The advantage of sourcing the data from the data warehouse is that it has already been through a rigorous ETL process where it was cleaned, transformed, and aligned to meet basic business needs. While this is a good starting point, it's often not enough for data mining.

The data miner's first step was to do a little data exploration. This involved running some data profiling reports and creating some queries that examined the contents of the source tables in detail. The goal is to relate customer information to product purchases based on the theory that if someone bought something, they must have had an interest in it. Customers have a one-to-many relationship with purchases, which results in two levels of granularity to the case sets. The demographic case set is generally made up of one row per observation: in this example, one row per customer. Each row has the customer key and all available demographics and other derived fields that might be useful. The product sales nested table is at a lower level of detail, involving customers and the products they bought. This is a master/detail relationship, where each row in this case set has the customer key and the product model name (`DimProduct.ModelName`) of the purchased product along with any other information that might be useful. Thus, each customer case set row has a one-to-many relationship with the product sales case set (called a nested case set). You could create a single case set by joining the demographics and sales together up front and creating a denormalized table, but we prefer to rely on the data mining structure to do that for us.

After reviewing the source data in the AdventureWorksDW database, the data miner decided to pull the demographic case data from the `DimCustomer` table and combine it with other descriptive information from the `DimGeography` and `DimSalesTerritory` tables, and to pull the product purchasing case data from the `InternetSalesFact` table along with some product description fields from `DimProduct` and related tables. The data exploration also helped the data miner identify several additional transformations that might be useful in creating the data mining model. These are shown in Table 13-3.

Table 13-3: Additional transformations used to create the example case set

TRANSFORMATION	PURPOSE
Convert BirthDate to Age	Reduce the number of distinct values by moving from day to year, and provide a more meaningful value (`Age`) versus `YearOfBirth`.
Calculate YearsAsCust	`DATEDIFF` the `DateFirstPurchase` from the `GetDate()` to determine how many years each case has been a customer. This may help as an indicator of customer loyalty.
Create bins for YearlyIncome	Create a discrete variable called `IncomeGroup` to use as input to algorithms that cannot handle continuous data. Note: This is optional when creating the case set because binning can also be accomplished in the Mining Structure tab, or through the Data Mining Wizard.

The size of the case set depends on the nature of the model. In this example, we are really building a model for each product model in the product dimension, so we need enough data to support up to 119 data mining models, not just one. After a bit of customer count experimentation, the data miner decided to build an Integration Services package to randomly select 18,000 customers from the customer dimension. As a critical part of data preparation, the data miner recognized the need to split the historical data set into two subsets: one to train the initial model, and one to test its effectiveness. SQL Server 2008's mining structure metadata layer can be set to automatically select a random subset of the input data set to use as a test set. The data flow shown in Figure 13-13 is the part of this package that selects the customers, adds the derived columns, and writes them out to a table called DMCustInput.

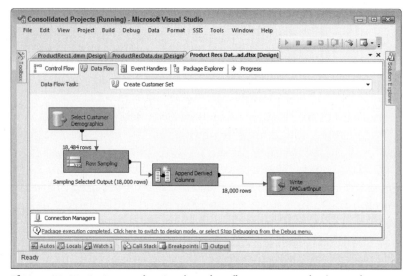

Figure 13-13: An Integration Services data flow to create the input data set

> **TIP** This approach works for the Adventure Works Cycles customer data set because there are only 18,484 customers total. If you have millions of customers, you might look for a more efficient way to extract your data mining input set. One possible approach is to use the last few digits of the customer key (as long as it is truly random). For example, a WHERE clause limiting the last two digits to "42" will return a 1 percent subset.

Another data flow later in this package joins the selected customer input set to the FactInternetSales table and writes their purchases out to a table called DMCustPurch. This is the nested product data set. Depending on how rapidly the product list changes, it might make sense to limit the data sets to only those products that have been purchased in the last year and their associated customers.

You can see the tables for the input data set and the nested product data set in the Data Source View in Figure 13-14.

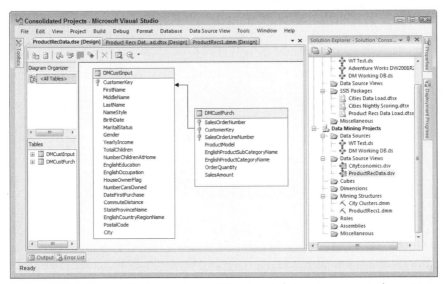

Figure 13-14: The product recommendation input data sets, presented as a Data Source View

The nested product case set has one or more rows for each customer. Just the fact that someone with a certain set of demographics bought a certain product is all the information you need. Notice from Figure 13-14 that the data miner decided to include some additional fields from the `orders` fact table that will not play a role in making recommendations but may be helpful in troubleshooting the data set.

TIP Integration Services makes it easy to create separate physical tables of the exact data sets and relationships at a point in time. You can then use these tables to build and test many different mining models over a period of time without tainting the process with changing data. It's common to set up a separate database or even a separate server to support the data mining process and keep the production databases clear of the toxic tailings of data mining debris.

The SQL Server Data Mining Tutorial uses views to define the case sets. This helps keep the proliferation of physical tables in the database to a minimum, but it's not our preferred approach. The views need to be defined carefully; otherwise their contents will change as the data in the underlying database is updated nightly. It also creates the burden of re-executing potentially complex, full table scans every time the model is re-processed.

At this point, the data miner has enough data in the proper form to move on to the data mining model development process.

Product Recommendations: Model Development

The data miner began the model development process by creating a new Analysis Services project in BIDS called Data Mining Projects. She added a data source that pointed to the DMWorkingDB relational database created to store data mining data sets. She then created a Data Source View that included the two tables created in the Integration Services package: DMCustInput and DMCustPurch. After adding the relationships between the tables, the project and Data Source View looked like the screen capture shown in Figure 13-14. The keys shown in the tables are logical primary keys assigned in the Data Source View.

Next, the data miner used the Data Mining Wizard to create a new mining structure by right-clicking the Mining Structures folder and selecting New Mining Structure. The data is coming from an existing relational data warehouse, and the data miner chose the Microsoft Decision Trees data mining technique in order to predict the probability of purchasing a given product based on a set of known attributes (the demographics from the registration process). In the Specify Table Types dialog window of the wizard, the data miner checked DMCustInput as the Case table and DMCustPurch as the Nested table.

The Specify the Training Data window can be a bit tricky because it's unclear what columns should be used in what ways. For this model, you would check the input column of all of the demographic variables because they are the independent variables — you're trying to use known demographics such as age or gender to predict an interest in products.

Also, you need to correctly specify which column or columns you'd like to predict. These are product related and can be found in the nested DMCustPurch table. First you need to specify a key for the nested data set.

In this example, ProductModel is the appropriate key for the DMCustPurch data, although it's not enforced in the creation of the table. You can now specify which column or columns to predict. ProductModel is the obvious choice because it contains the description of the products to recommend. The data miner also included EnglishProductCategoryName as a predicted column because it groups the product models and makes it easier to navigate later on in the Model Viewer. Finally, the data miner did not include the quantity and amount fields because they are not relevant to this model. Remember, these are the nested purchases for each customer case. With a new visitor, you'll know their demographics and can use that as input to the model, but you won't have any purchase information so it makes no sense to include it as available input data. The bottom section of the completed Specify the Training Data window is illustrated in Figure 13-15.

The next step in the Data Mining Wizard is meant to specify the content and data types of the columns in the mining structure. The data miner accepted the defaults at this point and went to the next screen, called Create Testing Set. By entering 10 percent, the data miner set the mining structure to automatically hold out 1,800 rows from the model training process to use as test data. On the final screen, the data miner changed the mining structure name to ProductRecs1, and the mining model name to `ProductRecs1-DT` (for Decision Trees). When the Finish button was clicked, the wizard completed the creation of the mining structure and the definition of the Decision Trees data mining model. The data miner could then view and verify the model definitions by selecting the Mining Models tab.

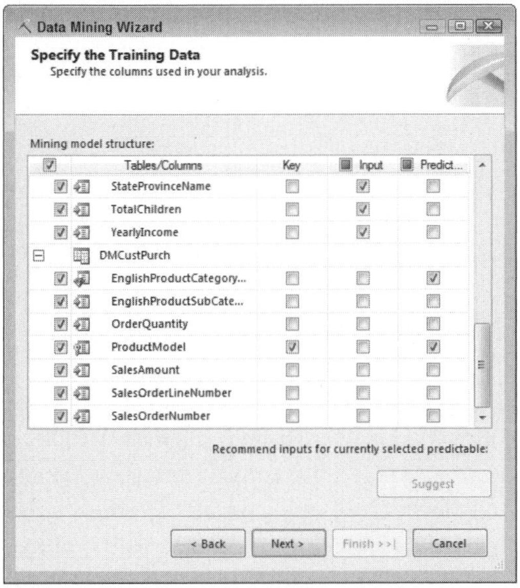

Figure 13-15: The nested table portion of the Specify the Training Data window

The next step is to deploy and process the model. Typically, a data miner works with one model at a time to avoid the overhead of processing all the models in the project (even though there is only one at this point, there will be more).

TIP To deploy and process the model, select any column in the `ProductRecs1-DT` model, right-click, and select Process Model. Select Yes to build and deploy the project, Run at the bottom of the Process Mining Model window, Close in the Process Progress window (when it's finished), and finally Close back in the Process Mining Model window. This should all look very familiar if you've built Analysis Services cubes before (since that's exactly what you are doing).

The Decision Trees algorithm generates a separate tree for each predicted value (each product model), determining which variables historically have had a relationship with the purchase of that particular product. This means it will build 40 trees, one for each distinct value of the predicted variable, `ProductModel`, found in the `DMCustPurch` table. Once the processing is complete, the data miner is finally able to explore the results. Selecting the Model Viewer tab automatically brings up the currently selected mining model in the appropriate viewer — in this case, the Decision Trees sub-tab of the Microsoft Tree Viewer. The tree that appears is for the first item alphabetically in the predicted results set: the tree for the All-Purpose Bike Stand, which seems to have a slight bias toward females (at least in our random subset). Selecting a more interesting product like the Mountain-200 mountain bike from the Tree pull-down menu at the top of the window brings up a more interesting tree — or at least one with more nodes. Figure 13-16 shows an example of the Mountain-200 decision tree later in the data mining process.

The first time you run through this example on your own machine, you will notice that the first split in the initial Mountain-200 tree is on `DateFirstPurchase`, and then several other fields come into play at each of the sub-branches. The data miner immediately recognized a problem with this model. The `DateFirstPurchase` field was included in the case set inadvertently because it is an attribute of the customer dimension. However, it's not a good choice for an input field for this model because visitors who have not been converted to customers will not have a `DateFirstPurchase` by definition. Even worse, after looking at several trees for other bicycle products, it is clear that `DateFirstPurchase` is always a strong splitter — perhaps because the longer someone has been a customer, the more products they have purchased, and the more likely they are to have purchased a bike. If you included the `YearsAsCust` field, you will notice the same problem because it is a function of `DateFirstPurchase`, and contains essentially the same information. The data miner decided to remove these fields from the model and reprocess it.

One easy way to do this is to delete the fields from the Mining Structure by right-clicking the field and selecting Delete. The more cautious way is to leave them in the structure, but remove them from the mining model by changing their type from Input to Ignore in the dropdown menu on each field. This keeps the fields in the mining structure, just in case. After changing the type to Ignore on these two fields and reprocessing the model, the decision tree for the Mountain-200 now looks something like the one shown in Figure 13-16.

After exploring the model in the Decision Tree tab for a bit, it's useful to switch over to the Dependency Network tab. This tool provides a graphical way to see which demographic variables are predictive of which product models. The dependency network shows the relationships between the input variables and the predicted variables. But the meaning of the initial view of the dependency network for this example, shown in Figure 13-17, is not immediately obvious. Each node in the network stands for one of the variables or products in the mining model. Some input variables are predictive of many product models, others only a few. Because the model contains 19 input variables and 40 individual product models and so many relationships among those variables, the dependency network looks like a spider web. In fact, the viewer automatically limits the number of nodes it will display so as not to overwhelm the user.

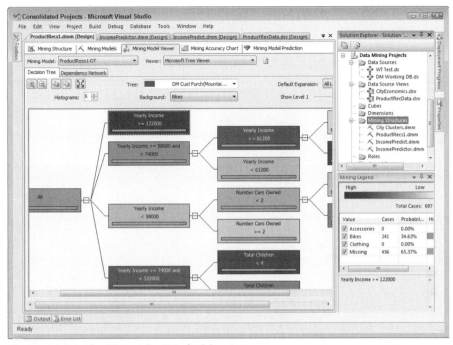

Figure 13-16: The Mountain-200 decision tree

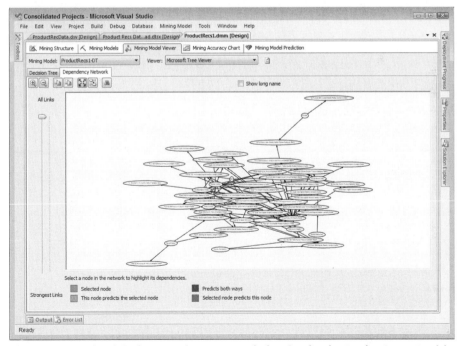

Figure 13-17: The default Dependency Network drawing for the ProductRecs1 Decision Trees model

Fortunately, there's more to the Dependency Network tab than just this view. Zooming in to see the actual names of the variables is a good way to start. Selecting a node highlights the nodes with which it has relationships. The tool uses color and arrow directions to show the nature of those relationships. Finally, the slider on the left of the pane allows the user to limit the number of relationships shown based on the strength of the relationship. The default in this viewer is to show all the relationships. Moving the slider down toward the bottom of the pane removes the weakest relationships in ascending order of strength.

WORKING WITH THE TREE VIEWER

It's worth taking a few minutes to discuss the elements of the tree viewer and how to work with it. The main pane where the picture of the tree is presented holds a lot of information. Starting with the parameter settings at the top of the Decision Tree tab in Figure 13-16, you can see the Mountain-200 is the selected tree. (Okay, you can't really see the whole description unless you select the dropdown menu. This is an argument in favor of using very short names for your case tables and columns.) The Default Expansion parameter box to the right shows that you're viewing All Levels of the tree — in this case, there are four levels but only three are visible on the screen. Some trees have too many levels to display clearly so the Default Expansion control lets you limit the number of levels shown.

The tree itself is made up of several linked boxes or nodes. Each node is essentially a class with certain rules that would determine whether someone belongs in that class. (This is how decision trees can be used for classification.) The shading of each node in Figure 13-16 is determined by the number of people who have Mountain-200s in that node divided by the total number of people who meet the rules for that node. The darker the node, the higher the probability that a person classified in that node owns a Mountain-200. You can change the shading calculation to divide by the total number of cases to show the overall distribution of cases. Then, the darkest nodes would have the most Mountain-200 bikes, regardless of the probability calculation.

Selecting a node reveals the counts and probabilities for that node along with its classification rules. In Figure 13-16, the node at the top of the second column labeled Yearly Income >= 122000 has been selected. As a result, its values and rules are displayed in the Mining Legend window in the lower right of the screen. We see that 697 cases meet the classification rules for this node. Of these 697 cases, 241 have Mountain-200 bikes, which results in a probability of 241/697 = 34.63%. In English, this reads "If you are one of our customers and your income is $122,000 or greater, the chances are about 1 out of 3 that you'll own a Mountain-200."

When the model is used for predicting, the theory is that probabilities based on existing customers can be applied to the folks who are not yet customers. That is, the chances are about 1 out of 3 that someone with an income of $122,000 or greater would purchase a Mountain-200. All you need to do to use this model is feed your web visitor's demographic input variables in and it will find the nodes that the visitor classifies into and return the trees (ProductModels) that have the nodes with the highest probabilities.

One way to get a better sense of the relationships in the Dependency Network tab is to drag the predictive (input) variables over to one corner of the screen. Figure 13-18 shows the model from Figure 13-17 after the data miner dragged the predictive variables to the upper-left corner.

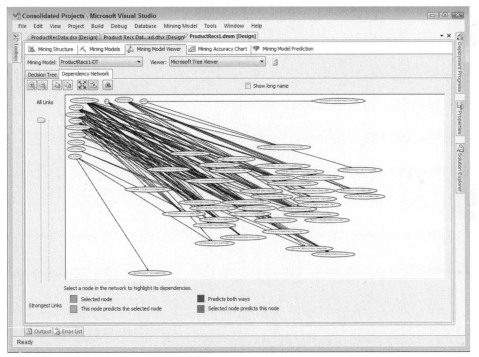

Figure 13-18: The Dependency Network with predictive variables dragged to the upper-left corner

This is still not very helpful. By zooming in on the upper-left corner, as shown in Figure 13-19, you can see that these, in fact, are some of the input variables. Note that there are only 12 shown in the dependency network. Variables such as First Name, Last Name, and StateProvinceName did not play enough of a role in the model to make it onto the graph. Figure 13-19 has had another adjustment as well: The slider on the left side was moved down to about one-third of the way up from the bottom. This shows that most of the relationships, and the strongest relationships, come from only a few variables. This comes as no surprise to an experienced data miner. Often there are only a few variables that really make a difference — it's just difficult to figure out ahead of time which ones they'll be. (Actually, it's not so difficult for certain models. When you specify the input and predicted variables in the Data Mining Wizard, there is a Suggest button at the bottom of the window that will calculate the strength of the relationship between the predictable variable and the input variables. This lets you narrow the model down right from the start.)

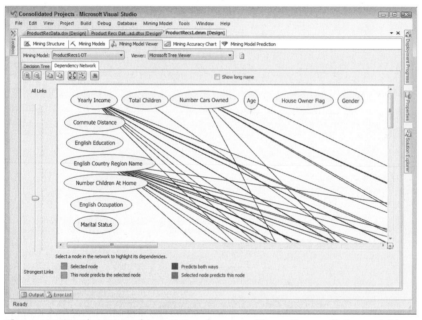

Figure 13-19: The Dependency Network zoomed in on the predictive variables

The input variables with the strongest relationships shown in Figure 13-19 are `Yearly Income`, `English Country Region Name`, `Number Cars Owned`, `Age`, and `Total Children`. True to the iterative data mining process, this brings up an opportunity. Removing some of the weaker variables will allow the model to explore more combinations among the stronger variables and to generate a more predictive model. For example, Figure 13-20 shows the decision tree for the Women's Mountain Shorts product based on the initial model.

There is clearly a variation in preference for these shorts by country. More than 15.5 percent of the Canadians bought a pair, but about one-half of one percent of the Germans bought a pair. Given this information, recommending Women's Mountain Shorts to a German website visitor is probably a waste of time.

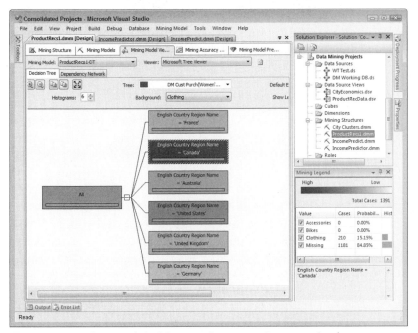

Figure 13-20: The initial decision tree for Women's Mountain Shorts

Figure 13-21 shows the decision tree for the same product after the model has been narrowed down to the five strongest input variables shown in Figure 13-19.

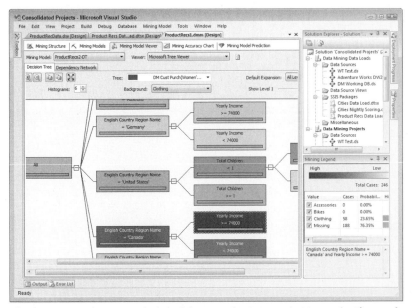

Figure 13-21: The expanded decision tree for Women's Mountain Shorts after reducing the number of input variables

The first split is still based on English Country Region Name, but now there is a second split for three of the country nodes. Canada can be split out by income, showing that Canadian customers making >= $74,000 are more likely to own a pair of Women's Mountain Shorts (probability 23.65 percent) — much higher than the 15.5 percent we saw for Canada based on the English Country Region Name split alone in Figure 13-20.

The process of building a solid data mining model involves exploring as many iterations of the model as possible. This could mean adding variables, taking them out, combining them, adjusting the parameters of the algorithm itself, or trying one of the other algorithms that is appropriate for the problem. This is one of the strengths of the SQL Server Data Mining workbench — it is relatively easy and quick to make these changes and explore the results.

Moving back to the case study, once the data miner worked through several iterations and identified the final candidate, the next step in the process would be to validate the model.

Product Recommendations: Model Validation

As we described in the data mining process section, the lift chart, classification matrix, and cross validation sub-tabs in the Mining Accuracy Chart tab are designed to help compare and validate models that predict single, discrete variables. The recommendations model in this example is difficult to validate using these tools because, rather than one value per customer, the recommendations data mining model generates a probability for each ProductModel for each customer.

Another problem with validating the model is that the data miner doesn't really have historical data to test it with. The test data available, and the data used to build the model, is actually purchasing behavior, not responses to recommendations. For many data mining models, the bottom line is you won't know if it works until you try it.

Meanwhile, the data miner wants to be a bit more comfortable that the model will have a positive impact. One way to see how well the model predicts actual buying behavior is to simulate the lift chart idea in the context of recommendations. At the very least, the data miner could generate a list of the top six recommended products for each customer in the test case set and compare that list to the list of products the person actually bought. Any time a customer has purchased a product on their recommended list, the data miner would count that as a hit. This approach provides a total number of hits for the model, but it doesn't indicate if that number is a good one. You need more information: You need a baseline indication of what sales would be without the recommendations.

In order to create a baseline number for the recommendations model, the data miner also created a list of six random products for each customer in the test case set. Table 13-4 shows the results for these two tests. As it turns out, the random list isn't a realistic baseline. You wouldn't really recommend random products; you would at least use some simple data mining in the form of a query and recommend your six top-selling products to everyone — people are more likely to want popular products. Table 13-4 includes the results for the top six list as well.

Table 13-4: Recommendations model validation data points

TEST	NUMBER OF HITS	TOTAL POSSIBLE	HIT RATE
Random Baseline	1,508	10,136	14.9%
Top Six Products	3,733	10,136	36.8%
Recommended List	4,181	10,136	41.2%

The data miner and marketing manager learn from Table 13-4 that the model is reasonably effective at predicting what customers bought — it's not great, but it's better than listing the top six products, and a lot better than nothing at all. Note that the hit rate in Table 13-4 has very little to do with the click-through rate you'd expect to see on the website. The real number will likely be significantly lower. However, based on these results, the data miner and the marketing manager decided to give the model a try and carefully assess its impact on the original goals of the project, increasing the percentage of visitors who become customers, and increasing the average sale amount.

Product Recommendations: The Operations Phase

The decision to go forward moved the project into the operations phase of the data mining process. The implementation details are well beyond the scope of this book, but the high-level steps would involve making the data mining model available to the web server, and writing the ADOMD.NET calls to submit the visitor's demographic information and to receive and post the recommendation list. Figure 13-22 shows an example of a DMX query to return the top 6 products for an individual from the ProductRecs1-DT mining model.

In this case, for a 43-year-old person from France who makes $70,000 per year, has no children, and owns one car, the model recommendations include a Mountain-200, a Road-250, and a Touring-1000. This is good — you like seeing those high-revenue bikes in the recommendations list.

Assessing the impact of the model would involve several analyses. First, the team would look at the number of unique visitors over time, and the percentage of visitors that actually become customers before and after the introduction of the recommendation list. Increasing this percentage is one of the goals of providing recommendations in the first place. This analysis would look at the average purchase amount before and after as well. It may be that the conversion rate is not significantly affected, but the average purchase amount goes up because current customers are more interested in the recommendations and end up purchasing more.

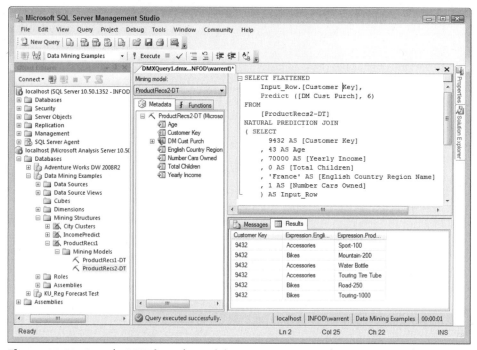

Figure 13-22: Sample DMX for a data mining query to get product recommendations based on an individual's demographics

The second analysis would look at the web browsing data to see how many people click one of the recommendation links. The analysis would follow this through to see how many people actually made a purchase. In a large enough organization, it might be worth testing the recommendation list against the top six list, or with no recommendations at all, using the random assignment process described earlier in this chapter.

The model would also have to be maintained on a regular basis because it is built on purchasing behaviors. New product offerings and changes in fashion, preference, and price can have a big impact on the purchasing behaviors — you don't want your recommendations to go stale.

Summary

Congratulations for making it this far. You should have a basic understanding of the data mining concepts and how data mining can have an impact on your organization. Data mining is not just a tool; it's a process of understanding business needs and data issues, working through various alternative models, testing and validating their viability, rolling them out into production, and making sure they address the opportunity and don't get stale.

Early in the chapter we reviewed some basic data mining concepts, describing how data mining is used for several different business tasks: classification, estimation or regression, prediction, association or affinity grouping, clustering or segmentation, anomaly detection, and description and profiling. We then discussed SQL Server's data mining architecture and toolset, reviewing the key components and showing how they fit together. Digging down into the technology, we briefly described the seven algorithms provided with the product and how they applied to the various business tasks.

Next we went into some detail on the process of data mining, outlining a step-by-step approach starting with identifying business opportunities and the associated data, moving through the actual data mining phase with its data preparation, model development, and model validation steps, and ending with the operations phase with the implementation of the model, maintenance, and an assessment of its impact.

Most of the second part of the chapter walked through this process based on two data mining scenarios: a large international lending organization that wants to cluster and classify cities, and an Adventure Works Cycles marketing person who wants to increase the number of website visitors who become customers by offering targeted product recommendations.

By this point, we hope it's clear that data mining is a powerful set of tools the DW/BI team can use to add significant, measurable business value. And that the SQL Server Data Mining toolset is effective, easy to use, and easy to incorporate into your overall system environment.

We encourage the data miner on the team or in the organization to explore SQL Server's data mining capabilities. The Excel add-in is a particularly easy way to get started. We also encourage everyone who uses the data mining tools to be careful with them. Data mining is a true power tool. As with a chainsaw, you can do amazing things, but you can also hurt yourself. It doesn't help your credibility if you roll out a model based on the clever finding that customers who have been with you longer tend to have purchased more items.

Deploying and Managing the
DW/BI System

The last part of the Lifecycle is the most exciting. Security! Deployment! Operations! As you can see in the diagram, we've placed these steps at the end of the Lifecycle. But don't wait too long to start thinking about these issues. The successful deployment and operations of your data warehouse must be built into the system from the outset.

As you're designing your plans for securing the data in the system, a good business sponsor can keep you on track. The costs of not securing the data are easily understood, but don't underestimate the costs associated with tightly securing information. The biggest cost of restrictive security is that it hinders the analyst's ability to combine data in unexpected ways, which can lead to valuable insights into your business.

A large part of deploying the fully developed and tested system is ensuring the user community is ready to use the new tools effectively. You should augment the metadata that underlies all the system components with business-oriented descriptions. These descriptions become part of the user-facing documentation and must be ready as soon as the system is launched. In production, you should rely on your operational procedures to load the DW/BI system with excellent data quality and system reliability.

Just as your system will grow as you include new business process dimensional models, so too do we expect the Microsoft toolset to continue to grow and improve. You're embarking on an exciting project with your DW/BI system, and we wish you the best of luck with it.

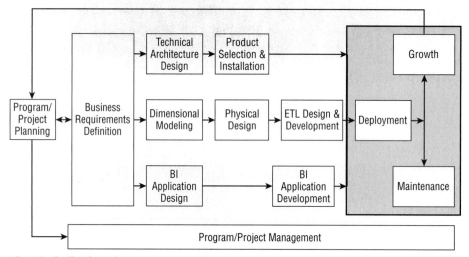

The Kimball Lifecycle steps covered in Part 4

CHAPTER 14

Designing and Implementing Security

How much security is enough?

Security is another one of those black holes of the DW/BI system. It seems straightforward at first glance, but it often ends up being more complicated and uses more resources than originally planned.

If you're serious about security, and take the necessary steps to educate yourself, keep up-to-date on security bulletins and software updates, and design your system to minimize your attack surface, you'll be in a good position to run a safe system. Microsoft throws so much information and so many security options at you that the greatest risk may be that you'll give up out of frustration and confusion. We hope this chapter helps by highlighting the most important issues for a DW/BI system.

You can minimize the cost and risk of implementing security by — yes! — writing a security plan. That plan should have a section for securing the environment, including the hardware and operating system; a section for securing the operations and administration of the system; and a section for securing data. No security plan is complete without a discussion of how to test the security. Designing and implementing tests for whether the right people have access to the right data can be as hard as any other task in developing and operating the DW/BI system.

In this chapter, we talk about the major components of DW/BI system security. These are the components that should be included in your security plan. The easy part is securing the physical environment and operating systems. A serious corporate environment will lock down the physical servers and systems. Turn on only those services and features that are necessary to run your system.

After you've slammed the security doors shut, you need to start re-opening them to allow users into the system. A DW/BI system is valuable only if people can access it. The more information that's broadly available, the more valuable your system will be. Information is an asset. If you keep it in the equivalent of a Swiss bank account with zero interest, you're doing your organization a disservice. Careful stewardship of data requires that you protect the information that's truly confidential and broadly publish the rest. Some organizations' executive teams and culture are diametrically opposed to open access, but it's worth arguing and pushing. Let's hope your executive sponsor can carry this battle forward.

You need to ensure that only authorized users can access the DW/BI system, and limit everyone's view of data as appropriate. There are as many ways to do this as there are possible configurations for your DW/BI system. This is especially true if you're using non-Microsoft software in your system. The bulk of this chapter is devoted to discussing the most common configurations. The SQL Server documentation in Books Online does a good job of discussing security for Reporting Services, the relational database engine, and Analysis Services. Figuring out how these components work together is harder, so that's where we've focused our attention.

After reading this chapter, you should be able to answer the following questions:

- How do you secure the hardware and operating systems for all the servers in your DW/BI system?

- What kinds of security will you need for different kinds of user access, from running reports to ad hoc query and analysis?

- How should you implement and test security features in the various components of your DW/BI system?

- How can you monitor your customers' usage of the DW/BI system?

Identifying the Security Manager

The first thing you must do is to explicitly identify a team member who's responsible for the security of the DW/BI system. If no one owns the problem, it won't be addressed. Define the role in the organizational context: What security is the security manager responsible for? What tasks does the security manager do, and what tasks does he or she direct others to do? The security manager has to be involved in the architecture design and in verifying the actual setup and use of the DW/BI system. Every new component, upgrade, user group, indeed any system change, needs to be examined from a security perspective to make sure it doesn't compromise the system. Many organizations require a mandatory signoff by the security manager as part of the change deployment process.

We recommend that the security manager be part of the DW/BI team. The DW/BI security manager should have a formal relationship with any enterprise security office or Internal Audit. But to be effective, the security manager must be intimately familiar with the DW/BI system. In small organizations, the DW/BI team lead may play the role of the security manager. In any case, it needs to be someone fairly senior, with a broad understanding of the end-to-end system.

Securing the Hardware and Operating System

The most direct way to steal access to the valuable information in the DW/BI system is to gain physical access to the computers on which the system is running. You absolutely must implement the following simple but essential recommendations for your production system, and should think very seriously about doing so for the development and test servers as well.

- Place the server computers in a locked room with restricted access.
- Disable the option to boot from the CD-ROM drive. Consider removing access to the USB ports.
- Consider creating a power-on password, and protect the motherboard's settings with a CMOS-access password.
- Consider using a computer case that supports intrusion detection and can be locked. Don't leave the key dangling from the computer.

Securing the Operating System

The second most direct way to access the DW/BI system is by way of the operating system. You should implement the following procedures for all the servers in your development, test, and production systems:

- *Restrict login access.* No business user needs to log on to the servers. Most DW/BI team members don't need to log in, as their tools work remotely. Only system administrators need to log in; others can access services across the network.
- *Restrict network access.* This includes preventing anonymous sessions and disabling unneeded services.

- *Ensure data folders are secure.* By default, the SQL Server relational database and Analysis Services databases store data in file structures that are appropriately protected. Other sensitive information includes backups and trace logs, and Integration Services packages. Ensure all information is appropriately protected.

- *Keep up-to-date with security patches for the operating system.* Keep up-to-date with service packs for the SQL Server components.

- *Secure backup media.* Backup files or tapes are more portable than the underlying databases; make sure these are protected as well.

Using Windows Integrated Security

Microsoft SQL Server uses Windows Integrated Security as its primary security mechanism. Set up Windows users and groups in the Windows environment — this is usually a task for system administrators rather than someone on the DW team. Then in Management Studio, create a set of roles. Grant or deny permissions to database objects for each role. Then assign the Windows groups to the appropriate roles. In a large enterprise, users will be assigned to several groups and roles. Use this same general approach for the relational database, Analysis Services, and Reporting Services.

NOTE Don't assign a Windows user directly to a SQL Server role. This creates a maintenance problem if that user leaves the organization. Use the level of indirection provided by the Windows group construct, even if you create a group with only one member.

In a Microsoft-centric enterprise, the users and some or all of the groups will be defined on the domain in Active Directory. In a heterogeneous environment, someone will need to integrate Active Directory into your environment. This is a job for a system administrator rather than a DW/BI expert, so we won't go into any details here. Buy a book or hire a consultant to help you with this project.

It's possible to connect to Reporting Services, Analysis Services, and the database engine through mechanisms other than Windows Integrated Security. These options are less secure than truly Integrated Security, so you should consider this approach only if you can't possibly make Integrated Security work in your environment. Even if you use these alternative authentication mechanisms, you'll still need to create Windows users and groups on the database servers, and grant privileges to those groups.

NOTE The SQL Server database engine supports database security, where you define users and groups within the SQL Server relational database. Those of us who've been building databases for a long time find this security model familiar and comfortable, but it's inherently less secure than Integrated Security and should be avoided.

In this chapter, when we talk about users and groups, we mean Windows Integrated Security users and groups unless we explicitly say otherwise.

Securing the Development Environment

It's quite common for development teams to have fairly loose standards — or no standards at all — for management of the development environment. The development environment and servers should be managed professionally, although usually not to the same standards as the test and production systems. The data on the development servers is often sensitive, as it's drawn from the production source systems. You certainly should secure the hardware and operating system as we've just described, within reason. You should have a policy against, or strict procedures for, granting access to development servers to anyone outside the development portion of the organization.

To ease deployment, make the development machines' security environment similar to the production systems. On the other hand, you don't want to lock down the systems so tightly that the developers will have problems getting their work done.

A common approach is to manage shared development resources fairly well, yet allow developers to create private databases. Institute a change control process for the shared resources, like the relational data warehouse data model. Once other team members depend on a data model, allow changes only weekly and require 24 hours advance notice.

Once you've instituted change control on the shared resources, you'll see private databases popping up. That's because some team members, in a sensitive part of their development cycle, really need an unchanging database, or they need to change it more frequently. Changes to the shared database can, at times, be incredibly annoying. Because the SQL Server database software is easy to install on a desktop machine, it's hard to prevent private databases from cropping up. If you can't, or don't want to, forbid private databases, make it easy for your team members to secure them. Develop a policy for private databases, including system security procedures — usually the same procedures that you implement for your shared development resources. Better yet, write a lockdown script — probably a combination of a document script and a batch file — to perform basic lockdown.

Developers should use read-only access to the source transaction systems. This is especially true for the DBAs and ETL developers, who may be creating and deleting database objects in the relational data warehouse database. It's not impossible to imagine that they could be careless and inadvertently execute a destructive statement against a transaction system. (If you've ever accidentally created a table in the Master database, you know what we're talking about.)

It's safest to use only the minimum privileges necessary to get the job done. In the case of DW/BI system development, that should mean read-only access to the source databases. In a large corporation, this is unlikely to be an issue: the DW/BI team will not have write privileges into a transaction system. In a small company where people wear many hats, it's not uncommon for a DW/BI developer to have high privileges on a production system.

Securing the Data

Now that we've done the basics, we come to the most interesting part of the security plan: securing the data while making it available for users to query.

Providing Open Access for Internal Users

We strongly encourage you to develop a data access policy that is fairly open for corporate users. The best approach is to start from the position that all data should be available to internal users; any exceptions should be justified.

We've worked with organizations that approach the problem from the other direction. Even internally, these folks' natural reaction is to make data available only on a "need to know" basis. They say that the sales manager in one region cannot see sales numbers for other regions. The problem with this mindset should be obvious: A sales manager can't assess her region's performance outside the context of the rest of the company. She may think a 10 percent growth in sales is a great number, until she realizes that all other regions saw 15 percent. The more information you hide, the less valuable your DW/BI system is going to be.

Regardless of who has permission to access the data, it's a good idea to have a written data access policy. Depending on your organization, the data access policy doesn't have to be a long statement. A reasonable statement would say something like:

> *Open access to administrative information is provided to employees for the support of corporate functions. Inappropriate use of information is a violation of your employment agreement. Default access is: Open Access to all employees, except for data elements on the Restricted Access list. Restricted Access is a designation applied to certain data elements, and limits access because of legal, ethical, or privacy issues. Access to elements so designated can be obtained with the approval of the designated data trustee. Any request to restrict employee access must be documented to Data Administration by the designated data trustee. Any employee denied access may appeal the denial to Data Administration.*

UNEXPECTED VALUE OF OPEN ACCESS

One of our clients had an enlightened data access policy — or perhaps, as a tech startup, they hadn't gotten around to drafting a more restrictive policy. At any rate, they experienced the power of open access. A Customer Care agent — a kid just out of high school — was poking around the data and uncovered a trend. A certain kind of trouble ticket was associated with a specific supplier's hardware, hardware which, as it turned out, was not manufactured to specification. Our client wrung several million dollars out of the supplier, and averted unsatisfactory user experiences for many customers. This for a startup, for whom several million dollars and customer satisfaction were tremendously important.

Many organizations would say a Customer Care agent has no business getting a global view of the data. It sounds reasonable to limit an agent's view only to specific tickets. The upside is unknowable in advance, but we've seen it happen often. The doomsday scenarios are easier to see, but many people have a tendency to overstate both the likelihood and potential financial downside of data getting out of the hands of those who "need to know."

The ideal situation is to have very little truly sensitive information, like credit card numbers or Social Security numbers, in the DW/BI system. Just don't bring it in. In most organizations, any data around employee compensation is highly sensitive. In a health care environment, details about an individual patient are extremely sensitive, and access is highly regulated as well. We're not saying that you should make such sensitive information widely available. Rather, identify the information that's sensitive and document it as an exception to the general rule of data availability.

NOTE There are cases where you can solve a data sensitivity problem by applying a hashing algorithm to the data. For example, it may be important for some business users to know that a customer's credit card number has changed, without necessarily knowing what that credit card number is. In this case the ETL system would hash the credit card number on the way into the data warehouse.

For an open access policy to work, you must:

- Gain executive sponsorship for the approach. You can't change corporate culture on your own. Many healthcare and law enforcement organizations are hopelessly — and justifiably — paranoid about data security.

- Develop a system use policy statement, which users must sign before gaining access. Set up a mechanism for ensuring users sign this document before accessing the DW/BI system. We generally require people to apply for access and include the policy on the application form.

- Confirm that executives are willing to carry out any sanctions against security violations implied in the policy statement.

- Gain executive agreement on the list of sensitive data elements.

- Review the security policy at the beginning of every training class.

- Publish (on the BI portal) the detailed security policy, including the list of sensitive data elements.

RESOURCES You can get a good starting draft for a complete data access policy from the internet. Many universities and government agencies post their policies online. Search for "data access policy."

Itemizing Sensitive Data

Whether you approach the problem from a mindset of "most data is available" or "most data is sensitive," you need to document what data is hidden (or available), and to whom. As you're developing your data sensitivity document, remember that the vast majority of system use is at aggregated levels, where sensitivity is usually less.

Our primary concern is read-only access to data. Any writing activities, like developing forecasts and budgets, should be securely managed by an application. Specify the level at which aggregated information becomes available. For example, most people can't see sales by salesperson, but anyone can see aggregated sales at the region or district level, and corporate-wide.

DOWNLOADS You can find a sample data sensitivity document on the book's website.

There is a subtlety associated with allowing data access at aggregate levels, but not at the detailed level. Returning to our discussion of sales by salesperson, what if we allow aggregate reporting at the district level, by gender? That can be an interesting question, but what if a district has only one saleswoman? Anyone in the company can infer her sales figures. There's no easy answer to the inferred data member problem, although we discuss this issue again in the upcoming sections.

Securing Various Types of Data Access

The more restricted data you have, the more difficult it is to provide ad hoc access to the DW/BI system. Look back at your data sensitivity document and think about how to implement open access at aggregate levels and restricted access at detailed levels. The easiest way to do that is through an application like a report. Define aggregate-level reports that everyone can see, and limit access to reports that contain sensitive information.

If you allow direct ad hoc access to the information, you may need to apply complex access rules in the database. This is difficult in the relational database, as we discuss in the section "Relational DW Security." This is a place where Analysis Services really shines: It's possible — and really not that difficult — to meet a wide range of access scenarios by using Analysis Services permissions. In particular, the tool addresses the difficult problem of hiding detailed data but publishing aggregated data for ad hoc access.

Reporting Services and most third-party tools like Business Objects, Cognos, and Analysis Services–specific tools like Panorama all contain security features. You should carefully examine the security features of any client tool before you decide to rely on those features. If a user has login privileges to the underlying database (Analysis Services or relational), the security must be applied to the database objects. Otherwise, users can simply use Excel or any other client tool to create an ad hoc connection, log on, and browse restricted data.

Many front-end tools, including Reporting Services, can — or even must — be configured to use a shared report execution service account for access to the database server. If your front-end tool manages user security this way, you typically don't even grant database login access to the users. This is very secure, assuming you're exceptionally careful not to compromise the password to the report execution service account.

WARNING If a user is not allowed to see certain data, then he must either be:

- **Denied logon privileges to the database containing that data, or**
- **Denied read privileges to the data table, columns, or rows.**

Security through obfuscation is not security.

External reports bring an additional layer of security issues. An external report is a report from your DW/BI system that's available to people outside your organization. For example, you may let your suppliers see your inventory of their products, or see how well their products are selling.

The easiest way to meet the security requirements for standard external reporting is to use a push model: Email reports to your partners. The data-driven subscription feature of Reporting Services (Enterprise Edition) should meet the majority of external reporting requirements. This is a preferred approach because you don't need to provide any access into your system, and you're completely controlling when the report is run and to whom it's delivered.

Data-driven subscriptions don't meet all external access requirements. You probably don't want to send a daily email to millions of customers about their account status. We're tempted to call this operational reporting, and wash our hands of the problem. Indeed, you should think seriously about whether you want external users accessing the same system that your employees are using to run the business. Most often you'll decide to spin out a data mart, and associated reporting portal, dedicated to this application. You'll need to figure out how to authenticate those external users to allow them into the portal. These users will typically access only filtered reports, using the same techniques we've already discussed.

It's unusual for a company to provide ad hoc access to external people. Those who do are generally in the Information Provider business. You can use SQL Server and other Microsoft technologies to develop a robust Information Provision system, but this topic is beyond the scope of this book.

Most implementations have a variety of security requirements. Some reports are available for anyone in the company, some have limited access to the complete report, and some filtered reports return a different result depending on who runs the report. Beyond reporting, you need to support some ad hoc access as well. You need to define some security in Reporting Services as well as the relational database and Analysis Services, to cover all these contingencies. Each component has several kinds of security options, which means you can probably figure out a way to do anything you want. But it also means that it's hard to know where to begin. We begin by looking at how you use SQL Server's components together to deliver the different levels of access.

Securing the Components of the DW/BI System

There are so many security features, and combinations of security features, that it seems overwhelming. The first items to knock off the list are predefined reports. Reporting Services handles these very well and easily, whether the report is sourced from the relational database or Analysis Services. Next, we turn our attention to describing how to implement security in the various components of the DW/BI system, including Analysis Services, the relational database, and even Integration Services.

Reporting Services Security

Reporting Services can source reports from the relational data warehouse, other relational and even non-relational sources, and from Analysis Services. Reporting Services is a client of the databases, but a special kind of client: one that is also a server, and that contains its own security features.

Administrative Roles for Reporting Services

Reporting Services is installed with a set of predefined roles for administrative and business users. You can modify these roles, or replace them with custom roles. But most organizations will simply assign these predefined roles to various people who are performing administrative tasks.

The relational database and Analysis Services have administrative roles that are clearly the purview of the DW/BI team, and only the DW/BI team. By contrast, your configuration and use of Reporting Services may distribute the administrative workload out to the business units. You may have some business users who need an administrative role.

The predefined administrative roles include:

- *System Administrator.* Set server level features and security, and manage jobs. Clearly this highly privileged role should be granted to only one or two members of the DW/BI team.

- *Content Manager.* Manage report folders and items within those folders, including security on those items. Content management permissions are not necessarily system-wide. In other words, you can have one person be the content manager for one set of reports like marketing and a different person manage sales reports.

- *Publisher.* Publish content, like a report, to a report server. Some organizations will tightly control publishing rights, linking this role with Content Manager. Others will let anyone publish a report to the enterprise. We recommend being careful about who has publishing rights.

Everyone involved with administering the reporting system should understand that securing folders is the most common way to manage user security. Security is inherited through the folder structure, so you can simplify the administrative burden by grouping reports in folders according to how confidential those reports are. When you restrict a folder, you are by default restricting all the items in the folder.

One sensible use of a highly restricted folder is a place to hold reports that are being tested. Testing report definitions and layouts straddles the line between an administrative function and a user function. Often, you want a business person to sign off on the report before it's published more broadly. Using roles and a designated test folder, you can make it easy for the testers to find the reports under development, yet hide those reports from the rest of your organization.

Remember that the security assigned to a folder is the default security setting for any item, like a report, that's created inside that folder. You can change an individual report's settings, but that's a second step that you (or the distributed Content Managers) may forget to take.

You can use either Management Studio or the Report Manager web application to manage permissions. The DW/BI team might use Management Studio; business users who are Content Managers will almost certainly use Report Manager.

User Roles for Reporting Services

When a user connects to Reporting Services, the report list shows only the reports that user is allowed to see. When a report is executed on demand, it's usually executed not with the user's credentials, but instead with a reporting service account used only to execute reports. In this scenario, users do not have login privileges to the underlying database.

Most of your reports will be *standard reports*: predefined reports that are available to some or all DW/BI system users. These reports are simply secured through Reporting Services or SharePoint Reporting Services Integrated Security. Reporting Services' security model is perfectly targeted for standard reports. It's very easy to set permissions on folders and reports. You may have a Data Administration team manage this function, or you can distribute some administration out to the departments who design and develop the reports.

Some of your reports will be *filtered reports*, which return a different result set depending on who runs the report. Filtered reports require some security infrastructure in the underlying database. You have several options, most of which require some sort of permissions table in the underlying database:

■ *Use a stored procedure as the source query for the filtered report.* This technique works if the source database is the relational database. You can pass the username as an input parameter to the stored procedure.

■ *Pass the user's credentials to the database.* This technique works with either SQL Server or Analysis Services serving the query.

NOTE If you pass the user's credentials to the underlying database, you may face the "two hop" problem. Typically, when a user connects from one computer to another, Windows credentials work for only one connection. If you need to connect to a second computer, for example to use the user's credentials to log in to a database server, you must use one of the following strategies:

■ *Enable Kerberos.* Implementing Kerberos is a project for system administrators, and is not usually a task that the DW/BI team would tackle.

■ *Use SQL Server authentication.* This technique works only for the relational database, not Analysis Services. And in general we recommend that you avoid using SQL Server authentication as it's less secure than Integrated Security.

Reporting Services in SharePoint Integrated Mode

A popular configuration for Reporting Services is integrated with SharePoint. As we describe in Chapter 12, this configuration can be a bit complicated to set up. One of those points of complication is the security model. Reporting Services and SharePoint have different security structures, which are largely but not entirely compatible with each other.

You have three choices for setting up security with SharePoint in integrated mode:

- *Windows authentication with Kerberos:* This supports passing the user's Windows credentials to the data warehouse database (such as for the filtered reports described previously).

- *Windows authentication without Kerberos:* This works with any authentication protocol, but does not support passing the user's credentials to the underlying database. The users will have to authenticate a second time in order use their own credentials to execute a filtered report.

- *Forms authentication:* This has the same advantages and disadvantages as Windows authentication without Kerberos.

Windows authentication with Kerberos is the recommended strategy, if it fits within your IT environment.

You can set permissions on report definitions, models, and connections from SharePoint. These permissions are integrated with Reporting Services. The security truly is integrated, and can be managed in either place.

Analysis Services Security

When you install Analysis Services, all members of the Administrators local group are granted access to the server and all databases and data. Until you set up roles and explicitly grant access, no other users can even connect to the Analysis Services instance, much less browse data.

Administrative Roles for Analysis Services

First, set up an administrative role for each Analysis Services database. A database administrator has full control over the database, including processing, aggregation design, and security. Analysis Services database administrator is a highly privileged role, but it doesn't require system administrative privileges on the server. If your Analysis Services server contains multiple databases, create a database administrator role for each.

The easiest way to create a role, including an administrative role, is within Management Studio. While you're logged in with server administration privileges, use the Object Browser to navigate down to a database, then to Roles within that database. Right-click to create a new role.

The person who administers security needs unrestricted access to the cube's data. That's because the security administrator will need to test the roles and permissions. With Analysis Services, the security administrator must have Full Control (Administrator) permissions to the database. This is more permission than a security administrator needs — a security administrator shouldn't be able to process the database or modify aggregations — but it's as fine grained as you can get.

> **NOTE** Management Studio is the only tool that Microsoft provides for managing Analysis Services security. This is troubling, because the person who's creating and testing roles, and mapping roles to groups, must have database administration privileges. If the security manager is careless, she can inadvertently damage the database.
>   We recommend that you limit this risk in one of two ways:
>
> - Write a tool that provides the same security management functionality as in Management Studio, but no other functionality. We're surprised that we haven't been able to find such a tool in the market or on Codeplex.
> - Develop and modify roles on the test system and script the deployment to the production system. This is always a good idea, whether or not you're worried about the security manager's administrative privileges.

User Roles for Analysis Services

Now that you understand how to administer security, it's time for the more interesting topic of how to define users' permissions. Use the Role Designer dialog box to define and test Analysis Services roles on your test server. You can find the Role Designer under the Roles node in the Object Explorer pane of Management Studio.

The Roles Designer dialog box, illustrated in Figure 14-1, contains eight pages, of which only a few are interesting:

- *General.* Use the General page to name the role.

- *Membership.* Use the Membership page to assign Active Directory groups to the role. When you first set up a role, you don't need to assign any groups to that role. Although you might think that the first step in defining a user role is to assign users to the role, that assignment is actually the last step.

- *Data Sources.* This page is seldom used. The Data Source is the source of the Analysis Services database's data, usually a SQL Server relational database. The database and cube definition place a layer between the user and that source; very few users need access to the Data Source. The exception is that if the Analysis Services database includes a data mining model, users may need access to a data source in order to perform a predictive query.

- *Cubes.* Use the Cubes page to grant user access to the cubes within the database. You must grant access to a cube; users are not automatically granted cube access. If you simply grant access to a cube and immediately save the role, you've created a role with full access to all the data in the cube. If that's not what you want to do, continue through the pages of the Role Designer to set the appropriate cell and dimension limits for the role.

- *Cell Data.* Use the Cell Data page to grant user access to a subset of numbers in the cube. Cell security acts by replacing some of the cube's numbers (facts) with #N/A. Cell security is discussed in greater detail below.

- *Dimensions.* You can use the Dimensions page to deny access to a complete dimension.

- *Dimension Data.* Use the Dimension Data page to grant or deny access to a portion of a dimension. Dimension security acts by making the cube look smaller by hiding some dimension members. Dimension security is discussed in greater detail below.

- *Mining Structures.* Use the Mining Structures page to grant access to data mining models.

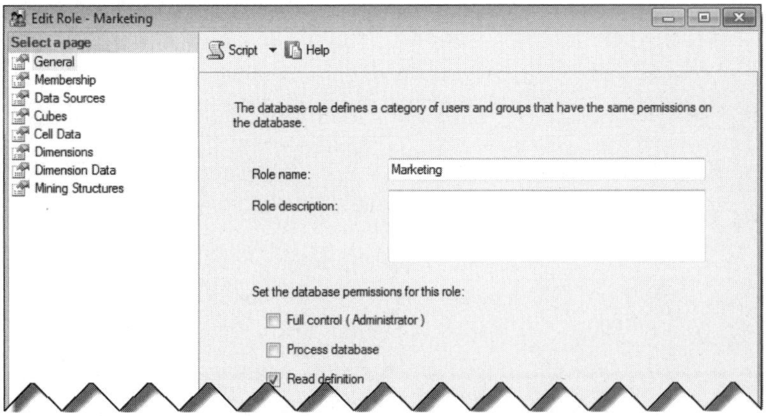

Figure 14-1: The Analysis Services Role Designer dialog box

Before you launch into the process of designing cell and dimension security rules, map out the strategy for this role. Remember that dimension security makes a report grid smaller: It limits the display of dimension attributes. Cell security doesn't change the row or column headers of a report; instead, it replaces some numbers inside the body of the report with #N/A. It's easiest to envision dimension versus cell security in the context of a tabular report, but of course the security holds no matter how you're viewing the results of a query.

If you want to hide descriptive information about an employee, like his Social Security number, you use the Dimension Data page. If you want to hide quantitative information, like a salesperson's sales quota, you use the Cell Data page. Think of cell security as security on facts.

Remember that a user or group can have multiple roles: A user can be in both the Marketing role and the Executive role. When Analysis Services combines multiple roles, it does so additively, with a union operation. If a user belongs to two roles, one forbidding access to a data element but the other allowing it, the user will have access to that data element.

There's one quasi-violation of this union rule. If a user has roles with both cell security and dimension security, the dimension security trumps the cell security. In other words, even if a role is permitted to see every fact cell in the cube, that data won't show up if the role can't see the dimension or dimension member. This is just what you'd expect to happen because the dimension security would forbid dimension members from showing up as row and column headers.

When you're testing your role definitions, you will really come to appreciate the role impersonation feature of the cube browser in Management Studio. Figure 14-2 illustrates cube browsing with a different role's credentials. Note that you can switch users (or roles) by clicking the Change Users icon in the upper left of the browser window, highlighted by the tooltip in Figure 14-2. You can test multiple roles overlaid on top of each other. When you're working on security, you'll quickly get in the habit of looking at the message near the top of the window, informing you of which role or roles you're impersonating.

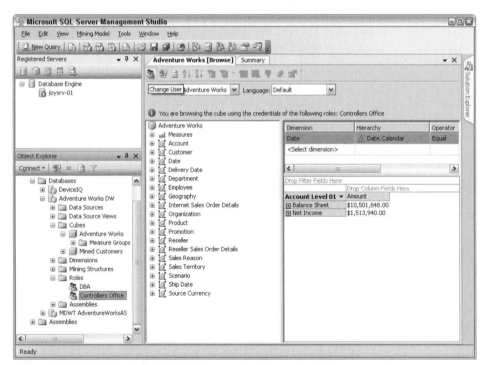

Figure 14-2: Test role definitions by impersonating credentials

Dimension Security

There are two basic approaches to defining dimension security on a dimension attribute: Specify the members that are allowed (all others are excluded), or specify the members that are denied (all others are accessible). In most cases, your choice of whether to specify the allowed set or denied set depends on the relative size of the included and excluded sets of members. There's a second order problem that can be really important: if a new member is added to the dimension, should it be accessible or excluded by default? The safest thing is to specify the members the role is allowed to see. Then when new members are added, they won't be visible to restricted roles until the role definition is explicitly changed.

Figure 14-3 illustrates a simple definition of dimension security on a dimension attribute. In this case, we're using the Deselect all members option to explicitly define the allowed set. Any new members will be excluded.

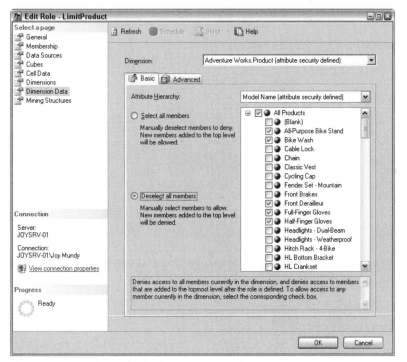

Figure 14-3: Defining basic dimension security

We've introduced the problem of new dimension members joining the dimension. If this happens rarely, it's not too big a burden to redefine the roles to account for the new member. If the dimension changes rapidly — for example a customer dimension — you'll want to take a different approach.

One of the neatest solutions is to use MDX to define the included (or excluded) set of members. Under the covers you're always using MDX: The pick list illustrated in Figure 14-3 is simply a user interface that generates an MDX expression. In this case, the expression is a list of members. You can see this expression by switching over to the Advanced tab on the Dimension Data page.

A common MDX security expression will include (or exclude) all the children of a parent. For example, imagine you want to create a role that can see all the product categories (Bikes, Clothing, Accessories, and Components), cannot see any of the subcategories under Bikes, but can see all the subcategories for the other three categories. Instead of listing the products that are in the brand today, define the MDX expression for the subcategory attribute of the product dimension as illustrated in Figure 14-4.

MDX expressions can be a lot more complicated than this, but the Exists function illustrated here, and its close friend the Except function, cover most cases. Books Online has more examples under the topic "Granting Custom Access to Dimension Data." For more complex examples, you should look at a reference book on MDX. Chapter 8 lists several MDX references.

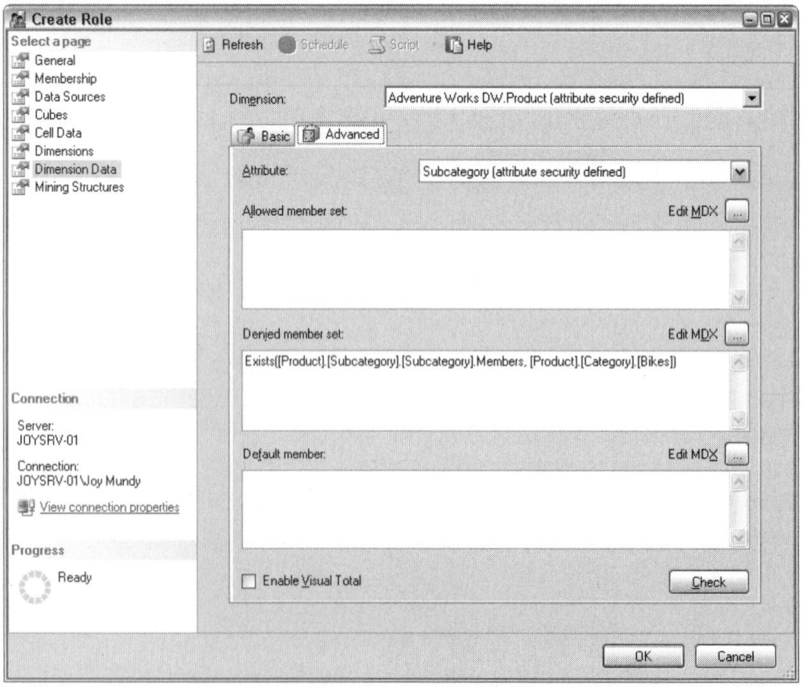

Figure 14-4: Using MDX expressions to define dimension security

There are a few wrinkles associated with dimension security. The first is the behavior of related attributes; the second issue is referred to as Visual Totals.

We introduced related attributes in Chapter 8. One of the common uses of related attributes is to define a natural hierarchy, like product category to subcategory to brand. Related attributes have an implication for the way dimension security works for denied sets. If you deny access to a specific product category, then you're also denying access to its children (subcategories and brands). This behavior doesn't come from the definition of a hierarchy between these three attributes. Instead, the behavior is driven by the definition of the relationships between the attributes — which is what makes it a natural hierarchy.

TIP It really feels like the hierarchy definition should be the thing that drives the security relationship, not the related attribute definition that users never see. To help keep it straight, think of the hierarchy merely as a drilldown path for the user interface; it's the underlying related attribute definitions that are really important. A product attribute like color that has no related attribute to the item you're securing (product category in our example) will not be affected by the security definition. Which, after all, makes perfect sense.

The second complexity with dimension security is the notion of Visual Totals, which you can see as a checkbox at bottom of the Advanced tab of the Dimension Data page in Figure 14-4. Imagine a role that grants permission only to a single product and doesn't restrict the brand level. What should be the subtotal by brand, for the brand containing the one product the role can see? Should the subtotal be the real subtotal for the brand? Or should it be the subtotal for the visible product? The answer depends on your business user requirements. The default behavior is to not use Visual Totals: Subtotals reflect both visible and invisible cells.

TIP This is a difficult concept with a mediocre name. Visual Totals refers to what you would expect the total to be if you were looking at a report, and added all the numbers you're allowed to see on the report.

We usually prefer the default behavior for several reasons. First, the server has to work harder to support Visual Totals. It makes much less use of predefined aggregates. More important, with Visual Totals turned on, you're sowing confusion among your business users. Two people running the same report would come up with different totals at the brand level. This is a situation you've built your DW/BI system to avoid.

A downside of using the default behavior is that users may be able to infer a piece of hidden information. The simplest example is if you're hiding only one product, and showing the true brand total. Any user can calculate the hidden product's sales as the difference between the brand total and the sum of the accessible products' sales.

Cell Security

Cell security affects which numbers or facts are displayed in the grid of a report, and which are blanked out (or replaced with #N/A or some other display element). Cell security, like dimension security, uses MDX expressions to define the cells that are accessible or hidden. Unlike dimension security, the Cell Data page of the Role Designer doesn't have any user interface other than entering MDX expressions. Cell security is so flexible that the best available UI is the MDX editor window.

Figure 14-5 illustrates the Cell Data page of the Role Designer. We've started by granting read privileges to one node of data in the product dimension: those data elements that roll up to the "Bikes" category. Data for other categories will display #N/A.

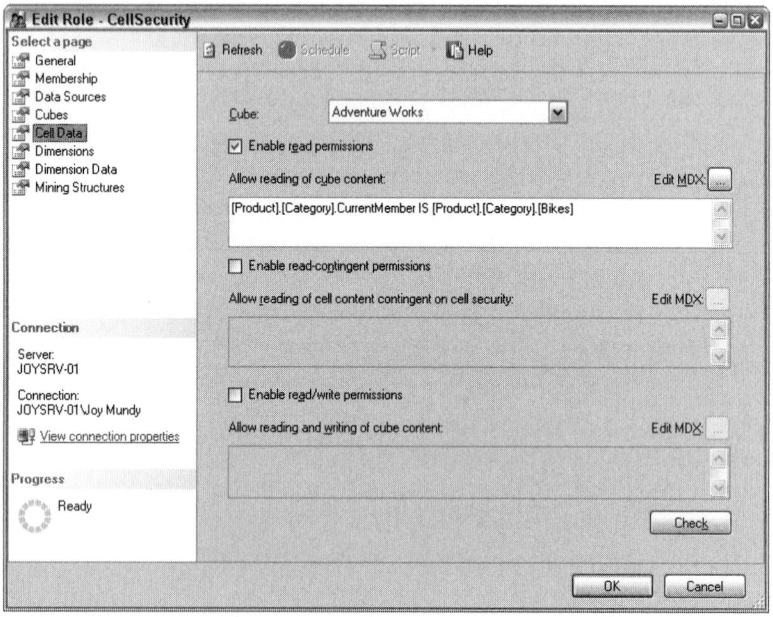

Figure 14-5: Defining cell-level security

NOTE Users in the United States are familiar with the use of #N/A to mean Not Available because that's the convention in Microsoft Excel. If you don't like #N/A, your client application may be able to translate this abbreviation for you. Or, you can specify a different value for the `Secured Cell Value` property in the user's connection string.

The expression in Figure 14-5 refers to the product dimension. Data along other dimensions in the cube is currently unrestricted. You can build up an

MDX expression that refers to multiple dimensions, with clauses connected by ANDs and ORs. We recommend you start simply and build up the expression piece by piece, testing after each addition.

RESOURCES The Books Online topic "Granting Custom Access to Cell Data" contains a nice set of increasingly complicated cell security definitions.

Look back at Figure 14-5, and notice the option to enable read-contingent permissions. This is an advanced option that most applications will not need. Read contingency is relevant for permissions on derived cells. The definition of read-contingent permissions is the same as for read permissions, but the behavior is different. Read-contingent permission will show a derived cell only if the role has access to all the data that goes into that derived cell. For example, if you have a derived measure for contribution to margin, the role can see that measure only if the underlying data to calculate contribution to margin is also accessible to that role. The rationale for this feature is similar to the Visual Totals discussion under dimension security: A smart user may be able to infer information that you don't want him to have. We advise caution with implementing read-contingent security. No doubt there are cases where this finesse is important, but it's more likely to leave everyone confused.

Return to Figure 14-5, and notice the third place to enter an MDX expression for read/write permissions. Write permissions have to do with Analysis Services databases that support data writeback. These are typically financial applications like budgeting and forecasting. This book doesn't address this kind of application, but not because it's uninteresting or because it's not part of business intelligence. Rather, it's a huge topic worthy of a paper or book of its own. Within the context of our security discussion, assigning write permission to a portion of the cell data uses exactly the same kind of MDX expression we've already discussed. Most organizations should steer clear of developing write-enabled cubes, and instead look to purchase packaged budgeting and forecasting software that is implemented on Analysis Services.

WARNING Be careful about checking the Read Contingent or Read/Write checkboxes without adding an MDX expression to focus the permission. If you check the Read/Write checkbox but don't add an expression, you're giving the role Read/Write privileges to the entire cube. Similarly for Read Contingent. This is unlikely to be what you intended.

Dynamic Security

You can use the dimension and cell security features to implement complex security rules. However, a large organization with individualized security may find that maintaining the MDX for many groups to be burdensome. Consider the scenario where you plan to deploy ad hoc Analysis Services access to a thousand users, and each user must be allowed to see a personalized part of the cube, such as their own accounts or employees. You can be in the position of creating, testing, and maintaining hundreds or thousands of roles.

An alternative approach is to use dynamic or data-driven security. This technique builds security into the structure of the cube, by creating a user dimension and a relationship fact table that describes what data elements each user is allowed to see. The UserName MDX function is your secret weapon. Creative definition of calculations can dynamically hide access to most detailed data (except your own), and still reveal aggregated data across the enterprise.

Dynamic security is more expensive at query time than standard security implementations. We'd be cautious about using the technique for terabyte-scale data volumes. The good news is that most of the dynamic security scenarios we've encountered, such as financial or personnel data, are good candidates for the technique.

RESOURCES The book *SQL Server 2008 MDX Step by Step* (Microsoft Press, 2009), by Bryan Smith and Ryan Clay has more information on how to implement dynamic security. You can also find many alternative techniques on the web by searching "Analysis Services dynamic security."

PowerPivot Security

As we describe in Chapter 11, the PowerPivot functionality that's new in SQL Server 2008 R2 is basically a reporting and analysis Excel add-in. The user who's creating a new PowerPivot model is subject to the security rules of the databases from which he's sourcing the data (usually Analysis Services and the relational data warehouse). Once a PowerPivot model is created, it can be secured at an overall level, like any other Excel document. There is no functionality for securing a portion of the data in a PowerPivot model.

Relational DW Security

If the only access to the relational data warehouse comes through Analysis Services cubes and Reporting Services, then the relational security model is simple. If you'll allow ad hoc access into the relational data warehouse, especially if you have requirements for filtering data (also known as row-level security), the relational security model grows increasingly complex.

No matter how users access the relational data warehouse, begin by thinking about the roles necessary for administering the relational database. After securing the operations, we'll discuss issues around users' security.

Administrative Roles for the Relational Database

The SQL Server database engine has predefined server and database roles. These roles work the same for a DW/BI system as for any other SQL Server database application. Compared to the administrative roles for Analysis Services, the database engine has fine-grained permissions.

There are a great many server and database roles for the SQL Server relational database. There's nothing particularly unusual about a data warehouse. You should find it easy to create server and database roles for your team members that provide exactly the permissions you want.

It's always good practice to grant people, even people on the DW/BI team, as few privileges as they need to get their jobs done. Occasionally people are malicious, but more often they're just careless.

The processing account that runs the Integration Services packages needs to have high privileges. You should always run production operations, like the ETL system, under a service account that's not associated with a person's login.

It's common for the DW/BI team members to all have high privileges on the development system. The test system should be set up the same way as production. One of the things you need to test before moving into production is whether the permissions are set correctly. This is a very common task to overlook.

SQL Server uses the ANSI-standard concept of a schema. Object names are fully qualified as *server.database.schema.object*. We usually create the data warehouse tables under a single schema, but we've seen people use schemas to segregate dimension, fact, utility, and metadata tables.

> **NOTE** For maximum database security, consider using the Enterprise Edition transparent database encryption feature. Transparent database encryption, or TDE, encrypts the entire database, much as if you encrypted the file system or drives. TDE protects the entire database, and as its name implies it's transparent to users and applications. It places a modest demand on the database (around 5 percent for most data warehouse databases). TDE is most appropriate to meet regulatory or compliance requirements, in tandem with the user-oriented security discussed in the upcoming section.

User Roles for the Relational Database

There are two main kinds of accounts that issue relational queries in a DW/BI system: reporting accounts used by Reporting Services, and business user accounts. You're likely to have one or several reporting accounts. Depending on your business requirements, you may have business user accounts for individual users that can log in to the relational database.

Reporting Account Permissions

Depending on how users access the DW/BI system, you may have only a few user roles to worry about. If you're using Reporting Services, you should expect to create and manage a reporting query account. Like the ETL processing account, the reporting query account should not be associated with a person. If you're using Analysis Services, you should create a separate Analysis Services processing account. This account may have the same privileges as the reporting account, but it's foolish to assume they'll always be the same.

We have already said several times that all users should access the relational data warehouse through views, rather than directly querying tables. There are several reasons for this:

- Views let you insulate the user experience from the physical database. It's amazing how much the view layer lets you restructure the database with minimal disruption to the user.

- Views let you hide or rename columns to suit users. You can remove the prefixes (like Dim and Fact, which we use in MDWT_AdventureWorksDW) from the view names.

- Views let you define role playing dimensions with meaningful column names, such as Ship_Year and Order_Year.

- Views let you add row-level security seamlessly.

Create a view on every user-accessible table, even if the view simply selects all columns from the table. Grant user access to the views, not to the tables. This includes the reporting account and the Analysis Services processing account. Both of these service accounts should use views rather than the underlying tables.

NOTE Create all user-oriented views and stored procedures under a single schema, and have that schema own no other objects. This makes it easier for you to find these objects when it comes time to assign permissions.

The reporting account should have read access to the appropriate views, possibly all the views. As we discussed previously in this chapter, Reporting Services secures the reports, so the reporting account will have greater read privileges than any individual user would. Some reports will use a stored procedure to deliver up the rowset. If so, the reporting account will need execution privileges on those stored procedures. The reporting account should never have write privileges on any table or view.

We can't think of a technical way for the encrypted reporting account credentials to be stolen. But the most likely way for those credentials to get out is the obvious one: Someone — presumably on the DW team — tells someone else. There's no point in tempting fate. This is especially true for any custom reporting front-end or non-Microsoft query software that might use a reporting account. Microsoft is very careful about security these days — don't laugh, they really are. You should thoroughly investigate the security mechanisms of any software on your system.

The Analysis Services processing account should have read access to the appropriate views, possibly all the views. The Analysis Services users should not need any direct privileges in the relational database.

Business User Roles

Business users will need login privileges into the relational data warehouse database if they need to perform ad hoc analyses. In this scenario, you'll need to grant them only the appropriate permissions. This means read-only permission on the appropriate views, columns, and stored procedures. You can use the Management Studio user interface to administer security, or write SQL scripts.

> **NOTE** What if you want to hide a few columns, like Social Security number, from some users but not others? One approach is to define two views on the table, one with all public information and the other with all public and private information.
>
> The best approach is to encrypt the columns containing private information and distribute decryption keys only to the appropriate users.

Create new roles that grant permissions to objects for the subset of people who can access that object. For example, say you protected the employee dimension from BIPublic, but you want everyone in human resources to have access to it. Create a new role for HR, granting access to the appropriate views. Roles are additive, so if you have a user who's a member of both BIPublic and HR, that user can see the employee view.

Row-Level or Filtering Security

You may need to build row-level or filtering security into your relational data warehouse. What we mean by row-level security is that users' views of sensitive data differ not at the column level, as we discussed in the preceding text, but by rows. One person should see a different set of rows than another person.

There's no row-level security feature of SQL Server, but the classic solution is not difficult to implement. First, create a table that lists users' IDs and the identifiers for the rows they're allowed to see. For example, secure the FactOrders table from MDWT_AdventureWorksDW to limit a user's view of the data only to a specific set of salespeople (identified by SalesRepKey).

Listing 14-1 shows some DDL for this permissions table, beginning with the code to create the table:

Listing 14-1: Data definition for the UserPermissions_SalesRep table

```
IF OBJECT_ID ('[dbo].[UserPermissions_SalesRep]', 'U') IS NOT NULL
    DROP TABLE [dbo].[UserPermissions_SalesRep];

CREATE TABLE [dbo].[UserPermissions_SalesRep](
    UserPermissions_SalesRepKey int IDENTITY NOT NULL,
    [UserName] sysname NOT NULL,
    [EmployeeKey] int NOT NULL
CONSTRAINT [PK_UserPermisssions_SalesRep]
    PRIMARY KEY CLUSTERED ([UserPermissions_SalesRepKey] ASC)
);
```

Next, insert some rows into this table. Let's say that the user Joy is allowed to see only information for employees 272 and 281. Listing 14-2 inserts two rows that identify the sales reps that Joy can see:

Listing 14-2: Insert rows that define which employees Joy can see

```
INSERT UserPermissions_SalesRep VALUES ('KIMBALLGROUP\Joy', 272);
INSERT UserPermissions_SalesRep VALUES ('KIMBALLGROUP\Joy', 281);
```

In the case of Listing 14-2, you're using Windows Integrated Security, and Joy is a user on the KimballGroup domain.

The final step is to create a view definition that joins the fact table to this new permissions table, as illustrated in Listing 14-3:

Listing 14-3: Define a view to provide row-level security

```
IF OBJECT_ID ('OrdersSecure', 'V') IS NOT NULL
DROP VIEW OrdersSecure;
GO
CREATE VIEW OrdersSecure
AS
SELECT f.* FROM FactOrders f
INNER JOIN UserPermissions_SalesRep u
ON (f.SalesRepKey = u.EmployeeKey)
WHERE u.UserName=SYSTEM_USER;
GO
```

As you can see by looking at the view definition, the trick is to limit the view to only those rows where the user name in the permissions table is the same user name as the person issuing the query. If you maintain the permissions table, many people can access this OrdersSecure table and see only the appropriate set of rows.

This solution is not as satisfactory as the dimension and cell security that you can define in Analysis Services. You've safely protected the detailed data, but no one can use this view to see company-wide sales. You need to create a second view, simply called Orders, that drops the SalesRepKey. The BIPublic role can query the Orders view and use that for most queries about sales volumes. The dual views create a usability problem for ad hoc business users, but it's the best solution the relational database offers.

Note that the row-level view is useful not just for ad hoc querying. You can also set up Reporting Services filtering reports that use the view. When you define that report, you need to pass credentials from the user into the database.

If you need to support filtering reports and row-level security, you should consider building an applet to help maintain the UserPermissions tables. For performance reasons, you want the UserPermissions tables to use the warehouse surrogate keys. But your requirements are probably phrased along the lines of granting permission to all the employees in a department or sales reps in a region. A simple applet can help the security administrator be more effective than writing INSERT statements, and can greatly reduce errors.

Testing Relational Security

Even though relational security isn't as complicated as Analysis Services security, it's still plenty complicated. You must thoroughly test all the roles and the combinations of roles.

You can impersonate a user and then run a query. Compare the results of the queries before and after impersonation to evaluate whether the security definitions are correct. Listing 14-4 shows you how. The script assumes you've created the OrdersSecure view described previously, and also that you created a role BIPublic to which you granted access to OrdersSecure. We further assume that when you run this script, you have sufficiently high privileges that you can create logins and users. Sysadmin would work just fine.

Listing 14-4: Create a temporary user to test security roles

```
--Create a temporary login and user
CREATE LOGIN LoginBIPublic WITH PASSWORD = 'J345#$)thb';
GO
CREATE USER UserBIPublic FOR LOGIN LoginBIPublic;
GO
--Display current execution context. This should come back as you.
SELECT SUSER_NAME(), USER_NAME();
--As a simple, not very accurate test, how many rows can you see?
SELECT COUNT(*) FROM OrdersSecure
--Set the execution context to LoginBIPublic.
EXECUTE AS USER = 'UserBIPublic';
--Verify the execution context is now 'UserBIPublic'.
SELECT SUSER_NAME(), USER_NAME();
```

Continued

Listing 14-4 *(continued)*

```
--Select from the view. You should get a permissions error
SELECT COUNT(*) FROM OrdersSecure
--Revert back to yourself and add the user to the BIPublic role
REVERT;
EXEC sp_addrolemember @rolename='BIPublic', @membername='UserBIPublic'
GO
--Now select from the view as UserBIPublic. We expect to see zero rows
--because UserBIPublic is not in the UserPermissions table.
EXECUTE AS USER='UserBIPublic';
SELECT COUNT(*) FROM OrdersSecure
--Revert back to yourself
REVERT;

--Remove temporary login and user
DROP LOGIN LoginBIPublic;
DROP USER UserBIPublic;
GO
```

With our security hats on, we recommend that you always run impersonation tests from a script, and bracket the script with CREATE and DROP login and user, as we illustrated here.

Integration Services Security

Integration Services is a back-room operation, so its security story is simple. First, make sure the packages are secure, so no one can mess with package contents. You don't want anyone to replace the package that performs an incremental load of the data warehouse with one that deletes all the data. This is a pretty far-fetched scenario. More likely someone on the team is careless and does something wrong.

Packages can be stored in the file system as XML, or in SQL Server. You should secure the package location. Packages stored in SQL Server are stored in the msdb database, in the table called sysssispackages. Simply use the database engine's security to grant limited permissions to msdb, and the package contents are automatically secured. If you store the package on the file system, use Windows security to limit access.

In addition to this basic security, you can sign or encrypt packages. Digitally sign the package and set the package's CheckSignatureOnLoad property to True to prevent anyone from modifying a package's contents. More accurately, what you're doing is telling the package to check for a signature before it runs. If the package has been modified unintentionally, it wouldn't have been signed. If someone maliciously modified the package, they should not be able to sign it.

Packages contain sensitive information within them, including the connection information to an account that, usually, has very high privileges in the data warehouse database. Integration Services automatically encrypts all connection information for you, but you can go farther and encrypt more of the package contents. There are several encryption options, but they come down to requiring a password before anyone can view the package.

The "Relational DW Security" section earlier in this chapter provides guidance on the kinds of relational database permissions you'll need to provide for the connections from your Integration Services packages to the data warehouse database.

Usage Monitoring

A secure DW/BI system will have usage monitoring in place. In an increasingly regulated world, it's extremely valuable to know who is connected to the system and what they're doing.

In Chapter 17 we talk about how to set up usage monitoring on Analysis Services, Reporting Services, and the relational engine. For some organizations it's sufficient simply to collect logons: who's accessing the database and when? Other organizations need to know exactly who is accessing which information.

Reporting Services collects usage information by default. In addition, Reporting Services provides an option to copy the usage logs from the Reporting Services catalog into a separate database. This option provides a target relational database, Integration Services packages to move the data, and a starter set of reports. This database should suffice for the majority of usage reporting requirements from Reporting Services.

Usage monitoring provides other valuable benefits. It's a valuable tool for performance tuning. Spending a bit of time analyzing how business users are accessing data is very valuable for understanding how to improve your DW/BI system.

If you set up a usage monitoring system — as we strongly recommend — you should inform your business users of what you're doing, why, and how the information will be used.

Summary

The goal of this chapter is to highlight the most important security issues for a DW/BI system and to help you figure out where and when to secure data. We cannot possibly cover all the security features of SQL Server or all the details of how to implement those features. We hope we have provided you with the tools to develop a security plan and security test plan.

One of the most important steps you can take for a secure DW/BI system is to identify which DW/BI team member is in charge of security. That security manager drives the development and implementation of the security plan.

The easiest pieces of the security plan have to do with physical security and operating system security. There's lots of information available about how to secure servers and the Windows operating system. You just have to commit to doing it.

The harder question, and the one to which we devoted most of this chapter, has to do with securing the data. As we described, securing predefined reports in Reporting Services is easy, painless, and effective. Securing data for ad hoc analysis is a harder problem. You'll definitely find it easier, and the user experience much better, to define security rules in Analysis Services than in the relational database. Analysis Services' security features make this a fairly straightforward task for a wide range of requirements. And because security rules are defined in MDX, even very complicated scenarios are feasible.

Finally, we struggled with how to set up the relational database security to support direct ad hoc access. It's possible — people have been doing it for years — but it's hardly as easy or satisfactory as we'd like.

The SQL Server documentation in Books Online has a strong emphasis on security features. But the security documentation is scattered across the different components, and it isn't always easy to find the information you need. You might be able to cut corners in some aspects of system development, especially if your data volumes are small, but everyone needs to be careful about security.

CHAPTER 15

Metadata Plan

The Bermuda Triangle of data warehousing.

Metadata is a vast, relatively uncharted region of the DW/BI system. Some teams sail into it full speed ahead, never to be heard from again. Most teams try to avoid the problem by sailing around it. Unfortunately, the metadata region is smack in the middle of your path to the great new world of business value, and you need to figure out how to navigate it successfully.

One of the first metadata challenges is figuring out what metadata is. We begin this chapter with a brief definition and description of the three major categories of metadata found in a DW/BI system: business, technical, and process metadata.

With a common terminology in place, your next challenge is to figure out what metadata you have and where it comes from. We explore the various sources and uses of metadata across the SQL Server toolset. Every component of the toolset is metadata-driven. The problem is the metadata is kept in different locations and different formats, so finding and managing the metadata is challenging. Finally, we describe a basic, practical approach for dealing with the most important and broadly used metadata elements.

Metadata creation and management can be a tangled topic. What we present here is a starting point. Many of you, and certainly those of you in larger organizations, will need to expand on our recommendations and customize them to your environment.

In this chapter, you will learn:

- What we mean by metadata and why you need it.
- What metadata features are included in SQL Server 2008 R2.
- How to implement an effective metadata strategy with the tools available.

Metadata Basics

One of the most common definitions of metadata is "Metadata is data about data." This is vague to the point of uselessness. It doesn't help you understand what metadata is or why you should care. We think about metadata as *all the information that defines and describes the contents, structures, and operations of the DW/BI system.* Metadata describes the contents of the warehouse and defines the structures that hold those contents and the processes that brought those contents into being. In this section, we talk about the purpose of metadata, describe the common types of metadata found in the DW/BI environment, and discuss the concept of the metadata catalog.

The Purpose of Metadata

Metadata serves two main purposes: defining and describing the objects and processes in a system.

Some metadata is used to *define* a process, object, or behavior. When you change the metadata, you change the process. A simple example is the start time of a SQL Server Agent job. Change the value of the start time element and you change the start time of the process. This idea of using metadata to define a process outside the code was an early, practical use of metadata. Separating a program's code from its parameters and definitions allows the developer (and in some cases, the user) to change the parameters and definitions without having to edit and recompile the code. This concept has been around for decades in forms like table-driven programs and configuration files.

Other metadata is used to *describe* an object or process. This kind of descriptive metadata is essentially documentation. If you change the process, but don't change the description, the process itself still works, but your understanding of the process based on its description is now incorrect. Some of the common properties of an object, like its name or description, do not affect its appearance or behavior; they simply describe it in some way. It's this idea of describing that leads to metadata as documentation.

Metadata Categories

The DW/BI industry often refers to two main categories of metadata: *technical* and *business*. We've added a third category called *process metadata*. As you'll see in the descriptions of these categories that follow, technical metadata is primarily definitional, while business and process metadata are primarily descriptive. There is some overlap between these categories.

- *Technical metadata* defines the objects and processes that make up the warehouse itself from a technical perspective. This includes the system metadata that defines the data structures, like tables, columns, data types, dimensions, measures, data mining models, and partitions in the databases. In the ETL process, technical metadata defines the sources and targets for a particular task, the transformations, and so on. This description of technical metadata is cause for some confusion, because some of this technical metadata can also be used as business metadata. For example, tables and columns, security rules, and occasionally even ETL rules are of interest to some users.

- *Business metadata* describes the contents of the data warehouse in more accessible terms. It tells us what data we have, where it comes from, what it means, and what its relationship is to other data in the warehouse. The name and description fields in Analysis Services are good examples of business metadata. Business metadata often serves as documentation for the data warehouse. As such, it may include additional layers of categorization that simplify the user's view by subsetting tables into business-oriented groups, or omitting certain columns or tables. When users browse the metadata to see what's in the warehouse, they are primarily viewing business metadata.

- *Process metadata* describes the results of various operations in the warehouse. In the ETL process, each task logs key data about its execution, like start time, end time, rows processed, and so on. Similar process metadata is generated when users query the warehouse. This data is initially valuable for troubleshooting the ETL or query process. After people begin using the system, this data is a critical input to the performance monitoring and improvement process.

The Metadata Repository

All of these metadata elements need a place to live. Ideally, each tool would keep its metadata in a shared repository where it can be easily reused by other tools and integrated for reporting and analysis purposes. This shared repository would follow standards for how metadata is stored so the repository can be easily accessed by any tool that needs metadata, and new tools can easily replace old tools by simply reading in their metadata.

For example, suppose you had a shared, centralized repository in your DW/BI system. When you use your ETL tool to design a package to load your dimensions, the ETL tool would save that package in the repository in a set of structures that at least allow inquiry into the content and structure of the package. If you wanted to know what transforms were applied to the data in a given dimension table, you could query the repository.

Unfortunately, this wonderful, integrated, shared repository is rare in the DW/BI world today, and when it does exist, it must be built and maintained with significant effort. Most DW/BI systems are like the Tower of Babel, and Microsoft SQL Server is no exception. Each component keeps its own metadata in its own structures and formats.

It may provide some comfort to know that managing metadata is a challenge that is not unique to the Microsoft platform. For decades, people in the software industry have realized that managing metadata is a problem. There have been, and continue to be, major efforts within many companies to build a central metadata repository. At best, these are unstable successes. The amount of effort it takes to build and maintain the central repository ends up being more than most companies are willing to pay. At the same time, several major software companies have tried to address the problem from a product perspective. Most of these products are large-scale, enterprise repositories that are built to handle every kind of system complexity. Implementers have a hard time navigating the product complexity, so most of the functionality remains unused. The cost and effort often bring the project stumbling to its knees. We've often seen initial success at implementation followed by a slow (or rapid) divergence from reality until the repository falls into complete disuse.

Metadata Standards

While projects to build an enterprise repository are often less than successful, the effort continues because there are at least four good reasons to have a standard, shared repository for metadata:

- When tools exchange metadata, you can reuse existing metadata to help define each new step in the implementation process. Column names and descriptions captured in the data model design step can be used to build the relational tables, reused to populate the OLAP engine, and used again to populate the front-end tool's metadata layer.

▪ If the metadata is in a standard form, your investment in defining objects and processes is protected — you are not locked in to a particular tool. For example, Reporting Services Report Definition Language (RDL) is a language standard that describes a report. If all your reports are stored in RDL, you can potentially switch to a new front-end tool and still be able to use your existing report library. (This benefit is not particularly popular with tool vendors.)

▪ A central repository gives you a single, common understanding of the contents and structure of the data warehouse — it's the best documentation you can have. To the extent that this shared repository holds the official, active metadata for each tool, you know it's the current version and not a copy that may be out of date.

▪ An integrated metadata repository allows you to more easily assess changes through impact and lineage analysis. The two concepts are essentially like looking down the same pipe from either end. In *impact analysis*, you want to know what downstream elements will be affected as a result of a potential change, like dropping a table. In *lineage analysis*, you want to know how a certain element came into being — what sources and transformations it went through to get to where it is.

You'd like to have a standard repository for metadata in the DW/BI environment. The tools would write their metadata to the repository during the design phase and read it back in during the execution phase. In theory, any tool can write to and read from the standard model.

There is a published standard framework for data warehouse metadata, called the Common Warehouse Metamodel (CWM). That standard was published in 2001, but it is not maintained and seems to be dead. At the time of this writing, there appears to be no effective, active, independent data warehouse metadata framework.

SQL Server 2008 R2 Metadata

The good news is that the SQL Server toolset is metadata driven. The relational engine has a slew of system tables and views that define and describe the data structures, activity monitoring, security, and other functions along with a set of stored procedures to manage them. Other components, like Analysis Services and Integration Services, are based on similar metadata, stored in an object-oriented structure in XML files. Much, if not all, of the property based metadata in SQL Server can be accessed through the various object models.

The bad news is that every major component of SQL Server keeps its metadata in independent structures, from database tables to XML files, which have their own access methods, from SQL Management Objects (SMO) and Analysis Management Objects (AMO) to stored procedures to APIs. Not only do the tools manage their own metadata, but the metadata they use is not integrated across the tools.

As we describe in the next section, the first step in every metadata strategy is to assess the situation. You need to conduct a detailed inventory of what metadata structures are available, which ones are actually being used, what tools you have to view the metadata, and what tools you have to manage it. Table 15-1 provides a convenient summary of the various metadata sources and stores across the SQL Server BI platform, and identifies various tools for accessing and viewing them. The remainder of this section describes the major components in Table 15-1.

Cross-Tool Components

Several metadata components in SQL Server support more than one tool in the system. We decided to list those once rather than repeating them under each heading:

- *SQL Server Agent* is the job scheduler of the SQL Server world. It contains information about jobs, job steps, and schedules. SQL Server Agent metadata can be accessed through a set of stored procedures, system tables, SQL Management Objects (SMO), and SQL Server Management Studio.

- *SQL Server Profiler* is SQL Server's activity monitoring tool. You define a trace to track the occurrences of specific events, like Audit Logon, and have those occurrences written out to a table or file. SQL Server Profiler can be used interactively from the Profiler tool, or initiated programmatically using stored procedures. Chapter 17 describes using SQL Server Profiler to create an audit log of DW/BI system usage.

- *BIDS Helper* is a nice Visual Studio.NET add-in that extends BI Development Studio (BIDS). It has functionality for Analysis Services, Integration Services, and Reporting Services, including design warnings and health checks, synchronizing descriptions, and project cleanups.

- *SQL Server Metadata Toolkit* provides a hint of what a future metadata tool might look like. The Toolkit will read your SSIS packages and Analysis Services cubes, put the information into a metadata database, and provide some tools for seeing the chain of relationships between packages and cubes.

Table 15-1: Metadata sources and stores in the SQL Server 2008 DW/BI platform

TOOL/COMPONENT	TYPE	CONTENT	ACCESS AND MAINTENANCE METHODS	RESOURCE LOCATION
SQL Server Agent	All	Job and schedule definition and execution	SQL Server Studio; stored procedures; SQL Management Objects (SMO)	BOL search: "automating administrative tasks" or "Programming SMO"
SQL Server Profiler	Process	Relational and Analysis Services engine activity	SQL Server Profiler; SQL Trace	BOL search: "Introducing SQL Server Profiler"
SQL Server Metadata Toolkit 2008	All	Various metadata from relational, SSAS, and SSIS; enables some dependency and lineage analysis	Standalone tool	CodePlex: sqlmetadata
System tables and views (relational engine)	All	Object descriptions, definitions, parameters, security, relationships, and settings	Catalog views (CVs); Information Schema views; SMO	BOL search: "catalog views;" "information schema views"
Stored procedures (relational engine)	All	Integrated system table queries, database management functions	System stored procedures (SPs); SMO	BOL search: "system stored procedures"
Extended properties (relational engine)	Biz	Business metadata	Design spreadsheet, SQL Studio, Stored Procedures, Catalog views, and SMO	BOL search: "extended properties"
Management Data Warehouse (relational engine)	Process	Relational engine activity	Predefined reports; customized reports and queries	BOL search: "management data warehouse"
Analysis Services object model	All	Object descriptions, definitions, parameters, security, relationships, hierarchies, and settings	SQL Server BI Development Studio; SQL Server Management Studio; Analysis Management Objects (AMO); SQL queries of the catalog views.	BOL search: "analysis management objects" SSAS Samples: Programming Samples

Continued

Table 15-1: Metadata sources and stores in the SQL Server 2008 DW/BI platform *(continued)*

TOOL/COMPONENT	TYPE	CONTENT	ACCESS AND MAINTENANCE METHODS	RESOURCE LOCATION
Analysis Services dynamic management views	Tech, Process	Object definitions, current activity	SQL queries executed in the DMX window of SQL Server Management Studio	Internet search for "SSAS Dynamic Management Views"
BIDS Helper	All	Add-on to BI Development Studio (BIDS), for SSAS, SSIS, and SSRS	SQL Server BI Development Studio	CodePlex: bidshelper
Analysis Services Management Data Warehouse	Process	Analysis Services engine activity	Predefined reports; customized reports and queries	CodePlex: sqlsrvanalysissrvcs
Integration Services object model	All	Object descriptions, definitions, parameters, security, relationships, hierarchies, and settings	SQL Server Management Studio; Integration Services object model; SQL Server BI Development Studio	BOL search: "integration services programming" SSIS Samples: Programming Samples
SSIS Log Analyzer	Process	Utility to analyze SSIS logs resulting from package execution; understand the sequence of events and identify bottlenecks	SSIS process logs; standalone utility	CodePlex: ssisloganalyzer
Data Warehouse audit system	Process	ETL process metrics, data quality flags, and metrics	SQL queries; Reports	See Chapters 7 and 17
Report Manager (Reporting Services)	All	Report definitions, schedules, folders, security, and so on	SQL Server Management Studio; Report Manager web page; web service (ADO.NET)	
Execution Log (Reporting Services)	All	Server, user, and report activity	SQL queries and reports	CodePlex: Reporting Services samples: Execution Log

Continued

Table 15-1: Metadata sources and stores in the SQL Server 2008 DW/BI platform (continued)

TOOL/COMPONENT	TYPE	CONTENT	ACCESS AND MAINTENANCE METHODS	RESOURCE LOCATION
SCRUBS: Log and optimization analysis (Reporting Services)	Process	Utility to report on and analyze report execution logs; understand which reports are being used, and by whom	Report execution logs; stand-alone utility	CodePlex: scrubs
Report Builder Models (Reporting Services)	Tech, Biz	Semantic layer between user interface and data sources	SQL Server BI Development Studio; Reporting Services object model	BOL search: "Reporting Services object model" (yields several topics)
Master Data Services object model	All	Model definitions, security relationships, business rules, workflow rules, usage	Master Data Manager web application; MDS stored procedures; MDS object model	BOL topics on Master Data Services PowerShell Cmdlets and Class Library
SharePoint	All	Site definitions, security rules, usage	SharePoint management pages; SQL queries and reports	
System Monitor Performance tool	Process	System level performance (reads, writes, buffers, and so on)	System Monitor, also known as perfmon	Monitor tool: Administrative Tools/ Performance BOL search: "monitoring performance" (yields several topics)
Active Directory	Tech, Biz	Security, organizational info, employee info	System.DirectoryServices namespace in .NET Framework; Query through OLE DB Provider	BOL search: "Query Active Directory," "OLE DB Directory"

Relational Engine Metadata

The SQL Server relational engine itself has system tables that can be accessed through a set of system catalog views or system stored procedures designed to report on the system table contents and, in some cases, to edit the contents. Alternatively, they can be accessed programmatically through SQL Server Management Objects (SMO).

Business metadata can be stored along with the table and column definitions by using the extended properties function. This allows the developer to append any number of additional descriptive metadata elements onto the database objects. The dimensional model design spreadsheet described in Chapter 2 makes use of extended properties to store several metadata columns like description, comments, example values, and ETL rules. The names of these extended properties must be part of your naming convention so programs and queries can find them.

Process metadata for the relational engine can be captured through the SQL Server Profiler component described earlier in this section. You can use the Management Data Warehouse feature of SQL Server to configure Profiler and other tools to collect and report on the key elements of ongoing database activity. Chapter 17 describes a performance monitoring log for the relational engine.

Analysis Services

Analysis Services' object model has all the same kinds of metadata that the relational engine has and more. From the definitions of the databases, cubes, dimensions, facts, and attributes to the KPIs, calculated columns, and hierarchy structures, not to mention the data mining models — all are available through the object model. The first and obvious access tools for the developer are the BI Development Studio and the SQL Server Management Studio. Beyond these, you can build custom .NET based applications that use Analysis Management Objects (AMO) to access the Analysis Services object model. In addition, there are Dynamic Management Views that use SQL syntax to access the Analysis Services object model. Your DBAs can use these DMVs to monitor activity and processes in the Analysis Services database, the same way they use system views to monitor the relational database.

Analysis Services process metadata can be captured through the SQL Server Profiler component described earlier in this section. Chapter 17 describes a performance monitoring log for Analysis Services.

Analysis Services PowerPivot is the Excel-based cube development and analysis functionality added in SQL Server 2008 R2. There must be metadata associated with PowerPivot, but its object model is not exposed in its initial release. We must await a future release of SQL Server to develop a coherent metadata story for a DW/BI architecture that includes PowerPivot.

Integration Services

As one might expect, SQL Server Integration Services has its own object model. Integration Services is essentially a visual programming environment, as opposed to a structured database environment like the relational engine or Analysis Services. SSIS packages can be incredibly complex and do not follow a common structure. In fact, much of what might be considered Integration Services metadata will actually be the result of defining and using standard naming conventions for packages and tasks. Another challenge with Integration Services metadata is its time-dependent nature. At any point in time, it is difficult to tell which package was used to execute which load. One day, a certain ETL process can be run from a package saved in the file system. The next day, the ETL developer changes the SQL Agent task to point to another package stored in the database that uses different logic and business rules. While the packages will have distinct GUIDs, the names will be the same. Keeping track of this obviously requires a clear set of development process rules, naming standards, discipline, and monitoring.

Regardless of where a package comes from, it can and should be set up to create its own process metadata. As we describe in Chapter 17, you should turn on logging at the package level, and select from a long list of events to log. Table 15-1 references some example Reporting Services reports on CodePlex that demonstrate how to access the log data and use it to track the execution and performance of your SSIS packages.

In addition to this base process-level logging, the data warehouse audit system described in Chapter 7 ties the process metadata back to the actual data that was loaded in a given ETL package. This metadata surfaces in the user interface in the form of an audit dimension and associated audit tables that allow the user to get a sense for where the data came from and how it was loaded.

Reporting Services

Reporting Services is entirely metadata driven. The contents, operation, usage, and security are all described in a set of metadata tables in the ReportServer database. It is possible to query these tables directly to see how Reporting Services works. However, rather than build reports on top of the production database, which can impact performance and potentially break when Microsoft changes the database, it makes sense to extract the process metadata into a separate reporting and analysis schema. Microsoft has included a couple of SQL scripts that create this schema and update it on a scheduled basis, along with a few example reports written against the schema. A similar tool, called SCRUBS, is available on CodePlex. The Reporting Services database is also surfaced through an object model that itself is accessible through a web service.

Like many front-end tools, one of the Report Builder query designers uses metadata to define the objects, attributes, join paths, and calculations that it needs to formulate a query. This metadata set is called a Report Builder model and is created using the BI Development Studio. The relational version is built on top of its own Data Source View and is kept in the Reporting Services database. Report Builder models used to access Analysis Services are built directly from the Analysis Services cube.

Master Data Services

Like the other components of SQL Server, Master Data Services is metadata driven, and its services and components are available through a rich object model. There are also stored procedures installed in each master data services database. You can use these stored procedures to interrogate the model, load data, and verify business rules.

SharePoint

SharePoint keeps its metadata in several relational databases which it sets up and manages in SQL Server. This metadata is programmatically accessible through SharePoint's object model which includes both client and server components.

SharePoint is a content management system at its heart. It supports the capture of metadata in lists and provides the ability to define shared taxonomies and terms in a managed metadata service. Most of this metadata is not relevant to the DW/BI system, but the tools can be used to keep track of your business metadata.

External Metadata Sources

Several useful metadata sources exist in the broader computing environment. Chief among these are the System Monitor tool and Active Directory. If you use a source control tool like Team Foundation Server, you may also consider that tool's data as a metadata source.

System Monitor

The Windows System Monitor performance tool is familiar to anyone who has done system performance troubleshooting in Windows. It works at the operating system level much like SQL Server Profiler does at the SQL Server level. You can define traces for a whole range of system activities and measures across the BI toolset and in the operating system itself. These traces can be defined to run in the background and to write to log files. If necessary, these logs can be tied back to SQL Profiler logs to help understand the possible causes of any problems. Chapter 17 describes which System Performance indicators are most important to log during regular operations.

Active Directory

Active Directory is Microsoft's network based user logon management facility. It is a directory structure that can hold user, group, security, and other organizational information. Depending on how your organization is using Active Directory, it can be a source for security-related information. It can also be the system of record for some of the descriptive attributes of the employee and organization dimensions. This is another example of where the line between metadata and data can get fuzzy.

Looking to the Future

Clearly the SQL Server development team understands the importance of metadata from a development point of view. However, even though SQL Server has lots of metadata, that metadata is not integrated. Careful metadata integration and active metadata management has not been a top priority for the core SQL Server product. In the past, Microsoft has been a leader on metadata issues, so we continue to hope that upcoming releases of SQL Server address the problem of metadata integration and management in a serious way.

A Practical Metadata Approach

This brings us to the question you've all been asking: What do we do about metadata to support data warehousing and business intelligence in the SQL Server 2008 R2 environment? In the long term, we expect Microsoft to tackle the metadata management problem. Meanwhile, you have to figure out what you are going to do about metadata in the short to medium term. It's easy to get trapped in the metadata morass (as the authors can certainly attest). It's a major effort to figure out what metadata to capture, where to capture it, how to integrate it, how it should be used in the warehouse processes, and how to keep it synchronized and maintained. Vendors have been building metadata repositories and maintenance utilities for decades, and companies (some companies) have been trying to use these tools, or tools of their own creation, to tame the metadata beast for just as long. Even so, there are very few examples of large-scale, robust, successful metadata systems. It's a really hard problem.

Again you ask, "So what am I supposed to do?" First you need to appoint someone on the team to the role of metadata manager. If no one owns the problem, it will not be addressed. The metadata manager is responsible for creating and implementing the metadata strategy. The ideal candidate has to know everything. No joke. If one person has to do the whole thing, he or she will need to have SQL and DBA skills. The metadata manager needs to know how to program in the Visual Studio environment and how to create and publish reports, and needs to understand the business, at a detailed level.

Creating the Metadata Strategy

We believe the following approach is a good compromise between having little or no managed metadata and building an enterprise metadata system. Our main recommendation is to concentrate on business metadata first. Make sure it is correct, complete, maintained, and accessible to the business users. Once that's done, provide a way to view the other major metadata stores. We often see a tendency to over-engineer metadata. The key to making this strategy work is to not overdo it. Here's the basic outline:

1. Survey the landscape to identify the various locations, formats, and uses of metadata in SQL Server. The previous section and Table 15-1 give you a starting point. Use the tools described to explore the system for metadata locations. Where there aren't any tools, you will need to create query or programmatic access to the rest of the sources so you can explore and track them. Create a list of the metadata elements you find, including where they are, where they came from, who owns them, how you view and change them, and where and how you might use them.

2. Identify or define metadata that needs to be captured and managed. These are the elements you'll use more broadly and therefore need to keep updated and distributed throughout the system. What you need to manage depends on a lot of factors: your organizational commitment to data stewardship and predisposition to actively manage metadata, the level of support for actively managing metadata on the DW/BI team and by the user community, and the resources available to address the problem. At the very least, you must manage a basic level of business metadata. We will describe alternative approaches to this later in this section.

3. While you're at it, decide on the definitive location for each metadata element to be managed. This is the location where the element will be stored and edited. It is the source for any copies that are needed by other parts of the system. It might be in the relational database for some elements, in Analysis Services for others, and so on. For some elements, you might decide to keep it in a third-party tool. In the Adventure Works example, we are using extended properties in the relational database to capture several useful metadata fields.

4. Create systems to capture any business or process metadata that does not have a home. Try to use all available pre-existing metadata structures, like description fields, before you add your own metadata tables. However, you will likely identify many fields that need a place to live; the comment field in the data model spreadsheet and the data warehouse usage history table are good examples of this. If the users are the owners of these elements, they should be responsible for maintaining them. Many of our clients have created a separate metadata database that holds these metadata tables along with any value-added content tables that are maintained by the business users. It's not too difficult to create a .NET front end to let users manage the contents of these tables. Or, you may consider creating a Master Data Services system just to manage business metadata.

5. Create programs or tools to share and synchronize metadata as needed. This primarily involves copying the metadata from its master location to whatever subsystem needs it. Fill in the description fields, the source fields, and the business name fields in all the tables, extended properties, and object models from the initial database all the way out to the front-end tools. If these are populated right from the start as part of the design and development process, they will be easier to maintain on an ongoing basis.

6. Educate the DW/BI team and key business users about the importance of metadata and the metadata strategy. Assign metadata creation and updating responsibilities. Your business sponsor's support is vital for elevating the importance of data governance throughout your organization.

7. Design and implement the delivery approach for getting business metadata out to the user community. Typically, this involves creating metadata access tools, like reports and browsers. Often, you need to create a simple metadata repository for business metadata and provide users with a way to browse the repository to find out what's available in the BI system. We describe a simple business metadata catalog in the next section. While you may actually use several reporting tools to provide access to the various metadata sources, this should appear as seamless as possible to the users. The different metadata access tools can all be linked to form a single page in the BI Portal.

8. Manage the metadata and monitor usage and compliance. Make sure people know the information is out there and are able to use it. Make sure the metadata is complete and current. Being able to view the metadata is the hardest part of monitoring — especially in the SQL Server environment — because there are a lot of different metadata sources. A large part of the baseline metadata effort is spent building reports and browsers to provide access to the metadata. Monitoring means you have to actually look at those reports on a regular basis.

Even though this is the balanced strategy between nothing and too much, it is still a fair amount of work. Make sure you include time in your project plan in all development tasks to capture and manage metadata, and that you include separate tasks for the preceding steps.

Business Metadata Reporting

Business metadata is the most important area to address because it supports the largest and most important segment of BI stakeholders — the users — who can't get this information any other way. In other words, the technical folks can usually dig around and find the information they need in order to understand the contents of the data warehouse. The user community, for the most part, doesn't have this skill set. You must provide them with an easy, accessible way to explore the contents of the DW/BI system if you want them to know what's available. We'll approach the task of providing business metadata to the users from the best case to the worst case.

Analysis Services as Primary Query Platform

If your organization's data and analytic needs are such that Analysis Services can meet them, and you have chosen Analysis Services as your primary user access platform, delivering basic business metadata can be relatively easy. Start with your front-end tool. See what kind of metadata layer it offers. The major front-end tool vendors offer rich metadata layers that can serve as the business metadata catalog.

Most of the major front-end tools pull directly from the metadata fields found in Analysis Services. This includes the descriptions of cubes, dimensions, and attributes, often shown to the user right in the tool's interface. Therefore, filling in the few metadata fields found in Analysis Services is a critical first step to improving users' understanding of the database contents.

Perhaps you've decided your query and reporting tool doesn't do an adequate job of publishing Analysis Services metadata. There are several approaches to bridging this gap; some are more work than others. If Analysis Services is your primary user database, the easiest approach is to build a simple browser that allows the user to navigate the Analysis Services object model. The SQL Server Product Samples available on CodePlex include a program called the AMO Browser, shown in Figure 15-1, which allows the user to browse the Analysis Services object model.

This sample program illustrates how to retrieve the properties of various Analysis Services objects. It would be fairly easy for a C# programmer to modify (or a VB programmer to replicate) this program to limit its output to strictly those objects and properties, like name and description, that are interesting to business users. Because this approach is based on the actual Analysis Services database and its contents, it has the advantage of never being out of sync with what users will see in their tools. This makes Analysis Services the system of record for these few metadata elements. However, it is limited to the metadata properties provided in Analysis Services: name, friendly name, description, display folders, and perspective.

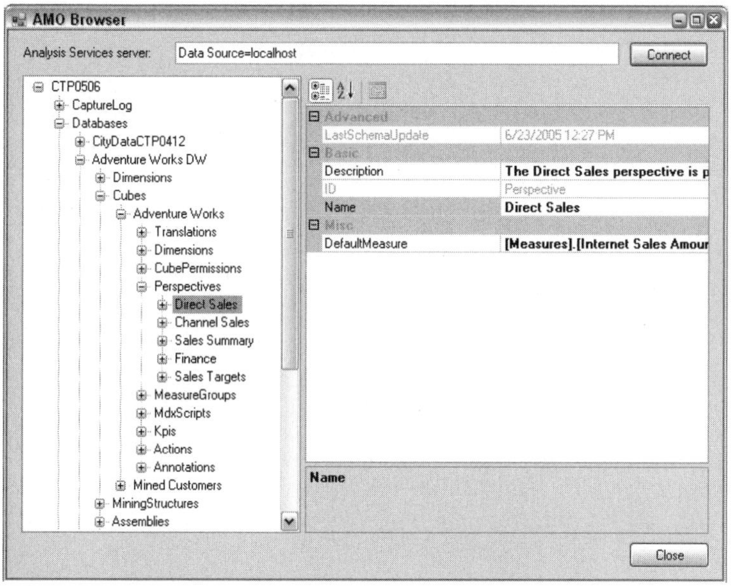

Figure 15-1: The sample Analysis Management Objects browser

Relational Engine Extended Properties

If your primary user access platform is the relational engine, or if you feel the Analysis Services properties are too limiting, you can always go back to the relational model and provide a simple set of reports that allows users to explore the metadata in the extended properties that was created from the original business process dimensional modeling spreadsheet back in Chapter 2.

The problem with this approach is that it's limited to the relational structures as defined in the relational system tables. There's no intermediate layer that lets you group subsets of tables into business process dimensional models and no display folders to group similar attributes to simplify the user view. And, it doesn't include any other user access platforms like Analysis Services.

DOWNLOADS On the book's website, we have provided a simple Reporting Services report that presents the extended properties for each column in a table. This report queries the system views in the relational database.

Business Metadata Schema

If the extended properties browser still isn't enough, you can create a simple business metadata schema that will support both relational and Analysis Services databases, accommodate multiple subject areas, and allow for additional metadata fields that may not exist elsewhere. Figure 15-2 shows a basic business metadata schema.

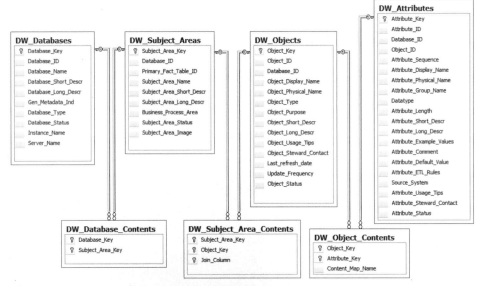

Figure 15-2: An example business metadata schema

> **NOTE** The metadata schema is essentially a transaction model meant to keep track of the relationships among the various data elements in the warehouse, and to allow maintaining and updating that data. This is not a dimensional model.

The schema is a hierarchy that starts at the database level in the upper-left corner (with servers and instances collapsed into the database table). Each database can contain zero to many subject areas, each of which contains zero to many objects, each of which contains zero to many attributes. Subject areas are groupings of objects, like business process dimensional models or Analysis Services perspectives or measure groups. The three contents tables allow you to map the same subject areas into several databases, the same objects into several subject areas, and the same attributes (or columns) into several objects. Your product dimension will probably participate in several subject areas, like sales, customer care, and returns.

Once you populate this metadata schema, it is easy to report on the subject areas in a database, the contents of a subject area, and the detailed attributes of a dimension or fact table (or cube). These reports constitute a simple analytic application: the metadata browser. Like any analytic application, creating the reports so they flow well and formatting them so they communicate well is a learned skill. Test your efforts on some of the users. Get their feedback on what works and what might be improved. A good metadata browser can help users learn faster and thus accelerate the overall acceptance of the BI system.

DOWNLOADS We have done a lot of this work for you. Look under Chapter 15 on the Tools page of the book's website to find the metadata schema scripts:

- The script to create a business metadata relational database illustrated in Figure 15-2.
- Scripts to populate the metadata database from the system tables and table and column extended properties.
- Scripts to populate the metadata database from the Analysis Services database.
- A set of linked reports for users to browse the business metadata catalog.

The business metadata schema is generally as far as we go in terms of creating, managing, and providing access to business metadata and it is meant to be a Pretty Good Practice. We believe the metadata schema is a great example of the 80-20 rule: you get 80 percent of the value of a sophisticated metadata management system with 20 percent of the effort. The four levels in this schema can be used to accommodate a range of designs, platforms, and product editions. There are plenty of enhancements that would make it more detailed and flexible. There are probably a few additional enhancements that will be important for your environment, but beyond that, the return on increased sophistication is pretty low.

Process Metadata Reporting

There is more metadata work to do beyond business metadata. You will need to create a suite of reports to provide quick, easy insight into what's going on across the BI system right now, and how it is changing over time. These process metadata reports often serve as a starting point for technical folks to assess the status of the system and investigate any problems. Savvy business users want to see if their queries are running and why the system is so slow. We've seen users use these reports to identify the culprit amongst their co-workers and call them up and request that they kill their queries. The data warehouse team and the DBAs will most likely turn to more sophisticated tools, like SQL Server Management Data Warehouse, to get a better sense of what's really happening and to be able to respond to the situation appropriately.

The process metadata reports include:

- *Reports on active processes in SQL Server:* You can report information on current user activity directly from the SQL Server system views or system stored procedures. You can also set up SQL Profiler trace logs to capture current activity and create a historical log, as described in Chapter 17.

- *Reports on active processes in Analysis Services:* You can also set up SQL Profiler trace logs to capture current activity and create a historical log. Or, use the Dynamic Management Views to report on current activity.

- *Reports on currently running and historical ETL processes:* These can be based on log files and audit tables as described in Table 15-1. You can also view current Integration Services activity in the SQL Server Management Studio.

- *Reports on Reporting Services activity:* You can view history using the Reporting Services execution log schema described in Table 15-1. You can monitor current activity by adding Reporting Services events to the Performance tool.

Publish these reports on the BI portal for all to see. This supports the idea of a single place to go for business information, even for the DW/BI team.

What's interesting in the here-and-now is even more interesting over time. Each of these "real-time" monitoring tools has a historical counterpart. The data warehouse team should set up systems to capture performance and usage data over time, as we describe in Chapter 17. These logs are the input data to warehouse management, performance tuning, long-term capacity planning, and educating management about the use and prevalence of the BI system.

Technical Metadata Reporting

Technical metadata reporting is not the first priority for the warehouse team because most of the development tools are already built with the technical user in mind. That is, they provide the developer or operations person with direct access to the technical metadata. Much of the functionality of SQL Server Management Studio is essentially creating, browsing, and managing technical metadata. The SQL Server team has also created some add-on tools that provide extended metadata browsing capabilities. These are listed in Table 15-1 and were discussed earlier in this chapter.

Ongoing Metadata Management

A metadata system is more than just a set of table or cube definitions — it is also a set of processes that allow you to manage those tables and cubes, obtain and distribute their contents, and keep them current. If you build a separate metadata repository, nightly refreshes of the metadata are typically acceptable. The safest approach would be to trigger a refresh whenever any of the metadata values is changed.

You will also need to build processes to extract key metadata values from the systems of record and copy them to wherever they are needed. These targets can be the business metadata schema, Analysis Services cubes, or even a Report Builder model.

You will need to implement ongoing data governance that includes business users in the process of maintaining business metadata. For user participation to be successful, you must create an interface for users to edit the business metadata values. This then ties in with assigning maintenance responsibility and monitoring and notification reports. Bottom line, you are building a data stewardship system, not just filling in a few columns as part of the initial data load.

Summary

Metadata is a fuzzy, complex subject. In this chapter, we defined metadata as information that defines and describes the contents, structures, and operations of the DW/BI system. We described business, technical, and process metadata. Next, we described the various sources and access methods for SQL Server metadata. The rest of the chapter was dedicated to our recommended approach for creating and managing metadata in your DW/BI system. Our approach begins with the requirement that the DW/BI team must assign the role of metadata manager to one of the team members. We then provide the metadata manager with nine steps to develop a metadata strategy. These steps are:

1. Work with the data stewards to help them learn their metadata roles and responsibilities.
2. Conduct a metadata inventory.
3. Identify key metadata elements that you will actively use and manage.
4. Identify the definitive location (system of record) for each element.
5. Create tools to capture and store any needed elements that do not exist in the SQL Server system.
6. Create tools to synchronize and share metadata as needed.

7. Educate the DW/BI team and key business users about metadata and their metadata roles and responsibilities.

8. Determine and build the metadata delivery approach, especially for business metadata.

9. Manage the metadata system and monitor usage and compliance.

The education step is critical to long-term metadata success. Everyone must view the creation and maintenance of metadata as being of equal importance as any other DW/BI task.

Keep in mind that metadata can evolve into an overwhelming enterprise project that will suck all the energy and enthusiasm out of anyone who gets trapped in its clutches. We described our approach as a Pretty Good Practice. It requires about 10 percent of the effort involved in a major metadata initiative, but returns a much greater percentage of the value. Use the business value measuring stick to determine how far you need to go down the metadata path.

CHAPTER 16

Deployment

*"Great occasions do not make heroes or cowards;
they simply unveil them to the eyes of men."*

— Brooke Foss Wescott

As you see in Figure 16-1, the deployment step in the Kimball Lifecycle is where the three parallel development tracks come back together. This is the great unveiling of the DW/BI system to the business community. The quality of this first impression will strongly influence the acceptance of the system — and you get only one shot at it. Like any big event, a lot of details must fall into place in order for the show to be successful.

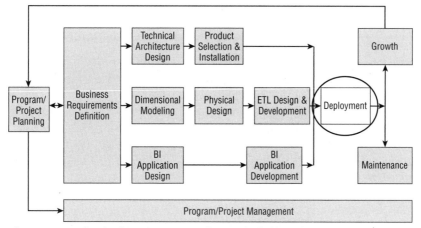

Figure 16-1: The deployment step in the Kimball Lifecycle

Most systems professionals think of deployment as moving code from development to test to production. As far as it goes, they're correct: Deploying code and data to the production servers is a fundamental part of providing end user access. But the system deployment is only part of the deployment story. The deployment step includes pre-deployment testing, as well as all the pieces needed to give the business users access to the information. To be effective, the deployment effort should begin early in the Lifecycle. While you're creating the architecture and building the data warehouse and the BI applications, you must also be defining and running tests, creating documentation, preparing training, and organizing the user support processes. All these services need to be in place before the curtain goes up for the first time.

This chapter is split into two parts: The first concentrates on the system testing and deployment process and the second spotlights all the other critical but less technical activities needed to ensure a successful deployment.

In this chapter, you will learn:

- What kinds of testing need to be performed for a new DW/BI system or changes to an existing system.
- How to effectively set up test environments to test continuously.
- How to deploy the various components of the SQL Server DW/BI system into production.
- Various strategies for deploying changes to a system already in production.
- What steps you need to take to ensure your user community is ready for the roll out of the new DW/BI system.

Setting Up the Environments

Although deployment is one of the final steps in a project's lifecycle, you must plan for deployment from the outset. Many deployment tasks are painful if you wait until the last minute. But as with most things, a bit of planning will minimize that pain.

For your initial project deployment of a brand new DW/BI system, you may be able to get by with two environments: development and test. You can have one very easy technical deployment by building out and testing in the test environment, and then simply declaring it to be production. But that technique only works once. To manage changes to a system already in production, you need multiple environments:

- *Development:* The development environment includes development server(s) and developer workstations. The development server environment *should* mimic production with respect to:

  - CPU architecture. Do yourself a favor: don't use an old 32-bit machine as your development database server. Drivers and connectivity are different in the 64-bit environment, and finding the best new drivers can be tedious. This is particularly true if you will be connecting to databases other than SQL Server.

  - Disk layout. Ideally, development will have the same number of drives and addresses as production, though of course much smaller.

  - Server topology. Ideally, have as many development servers as you plan in production. Place the various server components (relational, Integration Services, Analysis Services, Reporting Services) as you plan to do on production.

  - Virtual machines may be helpful.

  - Security. At the very least, use service accounts to administer the server components. Ideally, use the same service accounts that you'll use in production.

  - Operating system and other software versions should be identical, although it's fine to use SQL Server Developer Edition.

- *Primary Test:* The primary test environment is used to test the DW/BI system changes that are soon to go into production. The primary test system *must* mimic production in all particulars. We recommend that the primary test servers and environment be identical to production. This is particularly true if you will conduct performance tests. Of course, this is an ideal configuration, and many installations fall short of purchasing a second high powered server just for testing. However, the primary test environment must contain a complete copy of the data warehouse, or at least a complete copy of the portion of the data warehouse that's under development or change. How can you possibly test data quality unless you have all the data? Pay particular attention to:

  - Disk layout and server topology.

  - Software versions.

  - Security: the service accounts must be the same as in production, or you are guaranteed a rocky deployment.

- *User Acceptance Test (UAT):* If you are outsourcing the development of your DW/BI system, you should require a complete UAT system in addition to the vendor's internal test system.

- *Deployment Test:* As we will discuss, one of your pre-deployment tests is to confirm that the deployment scripts and processes will work. You need a copy of the production system, usually with significantly scaled down data volumes, on which you can test the deployment process. Often, the deployment test server can be a virtual machine.

- *Other test environments:* Depending on the complexity of your environment, you may need additional test systems. Multiple projects may be working on the DW/BI system, and each may need slightly different flavors of an early test environment. For example, you may be working on a project to move to a different version of SQL Server at the same time a new subject area is being added to the DW. Often, these other test environments can use a scaled down database. It may be possible to use virtual machines.

There are several additional considerations for the development environment.

- Install SQL Server Developer Edition on the development database servers.

- Install SQL Server Business Intelligence Development Studio (BIDS) on the ETL development server, which is usually the same server as the relational data warehouse database. ETL developers typically use remote desktop to access this server while working on SSIS packages. Otherwise, SSIS will run on the developers' desktops as they develop and debug packages.

- Install BIDSHelper on the ETL development server.

- Install BIDSHelper on the workstation of each Analysis Services developer.

NOTE BIDSHelper is an add-on to BI Development Studio (BIDS). It's available from CodePlex, and has been developed and maintained since the SQL Server 2005 era. Although we hate to recommend that development teams depend on third-party software, we do so in this case.

  - BIDSHelper affects the development experience, not the final database structure.

  - It is an open source Visual Studio.Net add-in, with source code available if necessary.

  - Among its many valuable features is SmartDiff, which compares two SSIS packages or Analysis Services (SSAS) databases, to identify changes. We know of no other usable tool for performing this vital action.

Your organization should already have change management processes and applications in place to help manage any development project. These include:

- Version control, also called source control
- Work item tracking, also called bug tracking
- Test case creation, scripting, and test execution tracking

Visual Studio 2010 and its companion server Team Foundation Server 2010 are the current Microsoft products to provide this functionality. They do a really nice job, and the server is far easier to install than it used to be. Older versions of Visual Studio, or other Microsoft or third-party software, are perfectly acceptable as well.

Figure 16-2 illustrates source control integration with BIDS. In Figure 16-2, an entire SSIS project has been placed under source control. In the Solution Explorer on the right, you can see the locked sign by most of the packages. You can check in a package directly from the Solution Explorer. Note that the dropdown menu has new options for checking in and checking out. There's also a new Pending Checkins window, displayed in the bottom left.

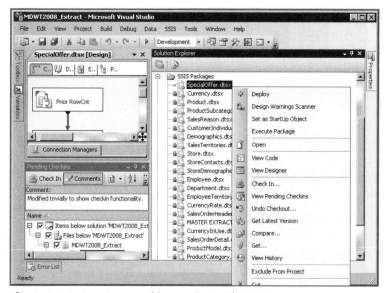

Figure 16-2: Source control integration with BIDS

NOTE Visual Studio 2010 was released at almost the same time as SQL Server 2008 R2, and as a result the two products are not fully integrated. SQL Server BIDS is based on Visual Studio 2008. It may seem that with a simultaneous release, there's a better opportunity to fully integrate the two products, but that's true only if they were originally planned to release together.

Testing

Before you start deploying your system, you should perform extensive testing. Throughout the development process, you should have been conducting unit tests to confirm that components have been written properly. As we discuss in the next section, you need to perform extensive end-to-end testing, too.

The less time you spend on testing, the harder the deployment process will be. If you don't perform end-to-end testing before you deploy to production, you're guaranteed to find problems on production. If you don't rigorously check data quality, your business users will do it for you, and lose confidence in the DW/BI system at the same time. If you don't check performance and tune the system in advance, you'll have to do it while trying to avoid disrupting business users.

If you test, tune, and adjust the system before you begin deployment, the move to production will be fairly straightforward. This is especially true if this is a new system. Moving incremental changes into production while minimizing end-user impact can be a delicate dance.

To successfully deploy a new DW/BI system, or changes to an existing system, plan ahead and test repeatedly until you've completed:

- *Development testing:* The developers test as they develop the ETL system. This is also called unit testing.

- *System testing:* The databases load and process correctly, from start to finish. Cubes are processed, automated reports are run, and downstream BI application processes are launched.

- *Data quality assurance testing:* The data is accurate and complete, both for the historical load and for ongoing incremental loads.

- *Performance testing:* The system performs well both for loads and for queries and reports, with live data rather than a smaller development data set.

- *Usability testing:* Business users can find what they need and accomplish necessary tasks.

- *Deployment testing:* Deployment scripts are solid and have been rehearsed.

The following section covers each of these testing areas in greater detail.

Development Testing

The first phase of testing is performed in concert with all development activities, especially the development of the SSIS packages for the ETL system. Development testing is almost always performed by the developer, and is often called unit testing.

Testing for a DW/BI system is no different in theory than testing for any other kind of system development. Developers need to create and run tests throughout the development process. Tests should be additive: run all old tests every night, rather than testing only new functionality. Test results should be logged and reported on.

In practice, DW/BI testing is difficult. There are plenty of methodologies and tools available to help build test cases into code, but the SSIS developer doesn't write much code. Instead, SSIS developers manipulate the user interface in BIDS to create a package. Of course, a package is a unit of code, but the developer doesn't have the same level of control over it as, say, a C# module or a stored procedure.

As a developer creates functionality in the package, he should create a test for that functionality. Developers create these unit tests as a natural part of the development process, and the tests should be documented and formalized. Expect developers to create a lot of tests; even a simple package will have dozens, and a complex package can easily have several hundred.

> **NOTE** Your organization should already have test management software and processes in place for documenting tests. The key metadata about a test is:
>
> - **Who created it, and when.**
> - **Description of what condition is being tested, for example, "Surrogate key lookup failure between orders fact and currency dimension."**
> - **Part of the system the test applies to, for example, "Data flow task of the orders_xform.dtsx package."**
> - **How to run the test.**

Testing begins from a known, unchanging test source database: a subset of the real transaction database. A realistic test source database will include all sorts of data problems, so many unit tests can work directly on that source. Other tests — the most obvious kind being a test of the incremental extract process — require that the test source database be modified. Each developer should maintain a script for modifying the test source database to "cook in" test cases.

CREATING A SOURCE TEST DATABASE

In order to develop consistent unit tests, you must start from a known, unchanging source. We recommend that you take the time to develop a source database that replicates the schema from the source transaction system. This test database will be used to test the functionality of the system, primarily the ETL system. It's not used to check data quality or performance.

The source test database should have the following characteristics:

- **Static:** Once it's developed and in use, it shouldn't be changed. Changes can invalidate existing tests, so any change should be managed and thoroughly communicated to the entire team.

- **Small:** In most cases, you want a small but not tiny set of data, on the order of 50,000 to 100,000 rows.

- **Consistent:** More accurately, as consistent as the source system allows. If the source system has referential integrity in place between two tables, maintained via foreign key relationships, so should the test database.

- **Representative:** Grab data from the entire history that will be loaded into the data warehouse, not just the most recent month.

Copy small tables in their entirety. There's usually an obvious driver table — often `Customer` — that you can use to subset the transactional data. Pull a random subset of perhaps 5,000 customers, and all the transactions associated with them.

If it's important that developers not have access to real data, you can transform the data in the test database. There are programs that will generate test data for you, but they're not very useful for testing ETL, because real data is never so well behaved.

If your development project spans multiple source systems, you should develop consistent test databases for each.

Each developer should also maintain a script for performing the tests. Most often, these scripts involve counting rows in the test source and the test target (the data warehouse or staging database). Sums and hashes are also used to confirm that data was not corrupted or modified. Of course, each test should log its results.

We have found it effective to execute many unit tests together in a single test group. Begin with a script to modify the test source database; run the package or packages; and then run a script to test the results. You may be able to group hundreds of unit tests together; remember that many test cases will be covered by the data in the static test database, without need for modification.

NOTE The recommendation of grouping unit tests runs counter to most testing methodology best practices, which would have you make a small change, run the test, clean up, and run the next test. We prefer to group tests to avoid running the packages hundreds of times.

An alternative, and arguably better, approach would be to bind the source database changes and the SSIS package execution into a single transaction. The script would make (but not commit) modifications in the test source database, run the package and record the results, then rollback the transaction.

You will need to invest in a little infrastructure to make consistent, ongoing unit testing be effective. It has to be easy for the developers, or they'll constantly put off writing formal tests.

Today, many ETL developers keep their own data sets, containing the malformed data used in unit tests. Instead, have developers keep the script to make those modifications to the test source database, rather than keep the data itself.

The execution of a group of tests consists of the following steps:

- *Test initialization:* Set up the test environment by restoring a copy of the static test source database and target relational DW. The restored database is uniquely named (auto-name it by adding a timestamp to the name, or tag it with the developer's name). Alternatively, clone a virtual machine with the test environment.

- *Test setup:* Run a script or SSIS package to modify the test environment, for example to apply inserts, updates, and deletes to data in the test source systems. This step can include multiple data modifications to cover multiple unit tests.

- *Test execution:* Run the SSIS package(s).

- *Test result verification:* Evaluate whether the test passed or failed. Many tests are verified simply, by counting rows in the source and target. Other tests look for the existence of an error file. Results should be logged to a tracking table, which is probably the same test results tracking table you use elsewhere in your test environment.

- *Test cleanup:* Drop the test databases and clean up any operating system artifacts. If you're using a virtual machine, simply delete it.

Every time a developer checks in a package, he should annotate the checkin with a reference to the unit test run results. Alternatively, the check-in process can automatically launch the test runs. All unit tests should run every night on all checked in code. If a new failure pops up, it will be much easier for the developers to diagnose and fix it.

USING INTEGRATION SERVICES CONFIGURATIONS

In order to test SSIS packages, you'll need to modify some characteristics of the package, including:

- Connection information for both source and target systems.

- Extract date range.

- Data quality limits built into the package, such as a minimum number of rows to extract, below which threshold processing is halted. Generally you'd want to lower this threshold if you are testing with smaller data sets.

These characteristics can easily be modified at runtime by using SSIS package configurations.

Integration Services configurations are a powerful tool for modifying the way a package behaves at runtime, without editing the package. This capability is very important for controlling package contents and quality: Once a package's quality has been assured, it should be locked down and not edited again. But some things about a package may have to change. This is particularly true of connectivity information, which almost always changes as you move a package from development to test to production.

You can pull out almost any characteristic of a task or connection into a configuration file. At the time the package is executed, SSIS reads the configuration files, overwriting the default value of a parameter or variable with its value from the configuration file. You can have many configuration files, and even overwrite the same parameter multiple times. The last configuration file in order will "win."

Some applications, especially those built as shrink-wrapped systems, will make extensive use of configurations. Even the simplest application will probably use them at least twice:

- To pass parameter values from a master package to its child packages

- To modify package connection information as packages move from development to test and production

When you create a package configuration in BIDS, the product will create a template XML file structure for you containing the elements you've chosen to configure. You should script the modification of the configuration files. For example, the nightly load process would automatically set the extract date range variables to yesterday's date.

There is nothing magic about SSIS configurations. If you're more comfortable keeping parameter values and connection information in a database table, and reading them into your packages via an Execute SQL task, that's perfectly fine.

System Testing

System testing ensures the system is complete, and the requirements (as documented) have been met. These are not only functional requirements, but also quality requirements like performance and security. Data quality can be considered part of system testing, but it's so central to the data warehouse that we discuss it separately.

The system tester must not be a developer. Even if you're a tiny organization with a one-person development "team," you should recruit someone else to evaluate the operation of the system. A developer is simply too tied in to the way things are. You need a second set of eyes.

The system tester should design her tests from the system specifications. In the all too common absence of a formal specification document, work with the DW/BI team lead to understand detailed requirements.

The goal of system testing is to ensure the periodic (usually nightly) load process works smoothly and completely. It takes place on the test server, beginning with a copy of the source and target databases. The last system tests, just before the system goes into production, should use live feeds if possible. Typically, the one-time historical load is not subject to rigorous system tests. The one-time historical load is subject to extensive data quality tests, as we discuss in the next section.

The system testing will test the following major categories:

- Job environment setup
  - Setting up variables and connection strings.
  - Creating a clean copy of the source environments if necessary.
- Job startup
  - Waiting for any startup conditions, such as files showing up in a directory or another signal that a source process has finished.
  - Launching the master package with the correct configuration file.
  - Handling correctly any startup problems (it's 4 a.m. and the source system process still hasn't completed).
- ETL job execution
  - With correctly formed input data, the ETL job runs to completion.
  - Error rows are handled appropriately.
  - If the input data violates any conditions built into the ETL job stream (such as a minimum number of extracted rows), the ETL job terminates smoothly.
- Automated data quality checking
  - Rowcounts, sums, and hashes that are built into the ETL process are checked and errors reported appropriately.

- Analysis Services cube processing

  - Completed without error.

  - Provides accurate data (run the same query in SSAS and the relational database).

- Automatic report execution and distribution.

- Data mining and other BI application execution.

- Job environment clean-up, including copying, deleting, or renaming files or other objects as needed.

If you've followed our advice in the preceding section, to set up development unit tests to run automatically, continuously, even obsessively, then you'll find most of system testing to be straightforward. Setting up the system tests requires little new testing infrastructure beyond what you set up for the development tests.

Ideally, system testing begins as soon as there is even a single SSIS package checked in. More precisely: two packages, a master package and a child package. Implement tests for all components of the final system, even if you know those tests will fail now. For example, you can add a test for the accurate incremental processing of the SSAS database even before that database is created.

Start running system tests as soon as possible. The test process will mature in tandem with development. Long before you're really interested in the results of the system tests, the details of *how* to test should have been worked out. The system tester should start testing against the test data, rather than waiting for the live data to come online. This will mean that the system tester will need to generate some transaction data. They can talk to the developers and look at their unit tests, but should create their own scripts for inserting, updating, and deleting data in the test source system. One of the many advantages of starting system testing against test data is that you can cook in data problems, such as a referential integrity violation, that might not surface in the real data during the period on which you're performing live testing.

While there are potentially dozens of infrastructure-related problems that surface during system testing, you'll almost inevitably stumble over security issues. As we described in Chapter 14, system operations should use system accounts that are independent of any individual user ID. System testing must use the same security roles and accounts as production.

SYSTEM TESTING FOR SQL SERVER STANDARD EDITION

Most organizations use Developer Edition for their development and testing environments. The best practice is to use the same edition as production for your final system testing on live data. This is especially true if you're deploying to Standard Edition, because Developer Edition contains all the functionality in Enterprise Edition.

Data Quality Assurance Testing

We can't overemphasize the importance of testing the quality of the data in your DW/BI system. The data needs to be checked very carefully before the system goes live. Develop subsystems and procedures for continuing to check data accuracy after deployment. Delivering bad data is much worse than delivering no data at all.

Data quality testing, at its heart, consists of running a query or report from the source system or systems, running the corresponding query or report from the DW/BI system, and comparing results. The magic comes in knowing the corresponding query or report. You may need significant business knowledge to match up the multiple systems, applied transformations, and business rules. For this reason and for buy-in from the business community, you must include the business users in the data quality assurance process. Hopefully, you already have some data stewards from the user community identified as subject area data quality experts.

NOTE Even in the unusual case in which you're completely outsourcing your DW/BI system design development, your organization — and your business user community — must take ownership of data quality test definition. Your vendor should provide a framework for running those tests and folding them into the ETL process, but only those with deep business knowledge can confirm that the data is accurate.

The vendor user acceptance testing (UAT) process is far too late for you to start testing data quality. By the time you're in UAT, there's going to be huge political pressure, from both your management and the vendor, to accept the system and move into production. This is especially true if the DW/BI system is an add-on to a new source system that's also part of the UAT. Any significant data quality problem can easily require large re-work, leading to delays of weeks or months.

Make sure you can reproduce existing reports to the penny. Sometimes we find during DW/BI system development that existing reports have long been in error. This makes it harder to verify the new reports, but you absolutely must audit them and document any discrepancies. If you have an Internal Audit group, enlist their assistance in this process.

We've often been asked to recommend tools to help test data quality. We don't know of any tools that help with the hard part of testing: determining what data needs to be tested and how to do so. At the very least, the data quality testing reports should include row counts, grand totals, and subtotals along major dimensions, hierarchies, and by time.

Your Analysis Services database may include some complex calculations and KPIs. You should have someone test the calculations externally — usually in Excel — to confirm that the MDX expressions are correct.

Report definitions sometimes include calculations as well. Check everything: in a budget variance report that displays budgets, actuals, and variance, confirm that the variance is truly the difference between the other columns. Even in this trivial case you may see a penny difference due to rounding. Discuss that rounding with your business users and get a decision from them on how to handle it.

As with other kinds of tests, automate data quality tests as much as possible. During testing and deployment, you'll typically run the data quality tests at least three times:

- *Test the outcome of running the primary test data set:* This static data set is small, and is easy to check thoroughly.

- *Test the historical load:* Perform extensive data quality checks on the one-time historical load. Get a handful of business users involved. Not only are they the ones who know the data, but you can leverage their reputation among the user community.

- *Test the live data:* Once you start running live data through your test system, continue testing the validity of that data. Often the data stewards are granted permissions into the system while it's still in test.

Any automated data quality tests that you developed for the deployment phase should eventually be folded into the ETL process. Develop processes for logging the results of the ongoing data quality tests, and publish data quality reports to the business community.

RESOURCES The management of data quality is a whole topic unto itself and beyond the scope of this book. Beginning with a data profiling tool, data anomalies need to be identified, and checks or filters need to be built to catch those data problems that cannot be fixed in the source transaction-processing system. The Kimball Group's recommended architecture includes many *data quality screens* inserted into the data flows coming from the source systems and leading to the final presentation schemas used by the BI tools. Each time one of these screens detects a data quality problem, a record is written to an *error event schema.* This back room dimensional structure is the primary source for managing data quality issues. This architecture is discussed in detail in a Kimball Group white paper, "An Architecture for Data Quality," published in 2007, which can be found in the Kimball Group article archive at http://www.kimballgroup.com/html/articles.html.

Performance Testing

The larger and more complex your system is, and the more users — especially ad hoc users — you have, the more important it is for you to conduct rigorous performance testing before you go into production. You want to launch your system with the best performance possible, and you certainly want to be confident that you can perform all processing within the necessary load windows.

You may have several goals for conducting performance tests. The most common are:

- *System tuning:* How can you tweak the system to deliver the best possible performance?

- *Confirmation of service levels:* Will you meet your uptime and query performance requirements?

- *Headroom analysis:* How long will today's system and hardware meet your requirements, as the DW/BI system continues to grow?

As with everything else associated with systems, the performance testing process is best begun with some planning. Specify the goals from your testing process, and develop tests to address those goals.

Rather than thinking about performance testing as associated with each of the components of SQL Server (RDBMS, Analysis Services, and so on), we prefer a more integrated approach. Test processing performance as a whole: ETL to cube processing to standard report generation. Test query performance as a whole, including ad hoc queries being executed at the same time as standard reports are being run.

Service Level Confirmation

Increasingly, DW/BI teams are entering into Service Level Agreements with the user community. These agreements cover data latency, and system availability often user query performance.

If you have such an agreement in place, then you surely must test that your system is likely to conform to the agreement. This is often a first step that leads to more extensive performance testing for tuning work, or even alternative system sizing and configuration efforts. But if you've cleverly made an agreement with pretty low minimum standards, you may simply need to confirm that you're above those standards.

> **NOTE** Service Level Agreements (SLAs) are a valuable tool for focusing management attention on important issues. But don't let your SLA drive you to deliver mediocrity by striving only to meet the stated requirements. Under-promise and over-deliver. Never promise more than your clients are requesting, but always try to deliver more than they've imagined possible.
>
> Be very careful in negotiating Service Level Agreements that include metrics for ad hoc query performance. Don't let yourself agree to an absolute ceiling for ad hoc query times, like all queries complete in 10 seconds. You'd be much better off agreeing that 90 percent of queries would complete in 5 seconds. In a system of any size and complexity, it's always possible to write an ad hoc query that exceeds any reasonable maximum.
>
> Clearly specify in the SLA what you mean by important terms, like query completion. Does this mean on the server side, or does it also include the transport (over a potentially low bandwidth WAN) to the client? The SLA is, basically, a contract between you and your users. You probably don't need to include Legal on this contract, but you should take it seriously. Your management will take it seriously if you don't maintain service levels.

Processing Performance: Getting Data In

Performance testing for the data processing side of the problem is fairly straight-forward. The live testing that we described earlier in this chapter is the basis for the processing performance tests.

The simplest approach to building a processing system is to serialize the major components. All ETL work to the RDBMS finishes before you begin cube processing, and that completes before you start generating reports. Such a serialized system is easy to performance test and diagnose, because the units of work are isolated. You can test and tune each unit separately. Unless your load window is very small or your latency requirements approach real time, you'll probably start off with serialized processing.

You may be able to design your processing system so that work is parallel-ized. You need to process shared dimensions first, but you should be able to start the work on one fact table while a second fact table is still loading. You can make significant improvements in the overall loading time by parallelizing some activities, but this is a much harder system to design and tune. Your performance tests must run on the integrated processing system. All parts of the DW/BI system compete for resources. You can't test each component separately and sum their processing times. This is true even if the different components are distributed across multiple servers because there's always some burden placed on the upstream servers.

Another issue to consider is confirming that changes made to improve the performance of one part of the system don't negatively impact another part of the system. The classic problem is index and aggregation design. You may want lots of indexes and aggregations for queries to run quickly. But these structures must be maintained, which can place an intolerable burden on the processing performance. Every time a change is considered, evaluate the effects on a complete test system before deploying to production.

Query Performance: Getting Data Out

Testing query performance, especially ad hoc query performance, is much harder than testing processing performance. The fundamental problem is that you don't know what your users are going to want to do. You can ask them and get some ideas, but those ideas are going to bear, at best, only a resemblance to reality.

Standard reports are either pre-run and cached, or run on demand. Pre-run reports are executed at the end of the ETL processing. You can set up Reporting Services to email the results of a pre-run report to the users; doing so shifts the entire burden of report generation to a scheduled time. Alternatively, users might access the pre-run report from the BI portal, in which case there's a modest on-demand element associated with displaying the report. A solid performance test of pre-run standard reports uses estimated usage patterns for accessing the pre-run reports. For example, 500 people will access the report at random times between 8 a.m. and 9:30 a.m. The relational database where the Reporting Services catalog is stored, the Reporting Services engine, and the web servers are all involved with serving pre-stored reports.

A standard report that's executed on demand involves more work. The first demand is on the database upon which the report is defined, to serve up the basic data for the report. Then, Reporting Services works on that result set to render the report. Finally, the report is distributed, usually across the web to the user's browser window. On-demand reports are often used for parameterized reports, for infrequently accessed reports that don't warrant pre-executing and storing the results, and for reports with low latency. A good performance test for on-demand reports includes a realistic estimate of who is running the reports, when, and with what parameters. Reports can be cached in memory, which is great for performance. In the absence of real-world data about how users are running reports, it's very difficult to accurately estimate the use of the report cache.

Finally, laboratory testing of the performance of ad hoc queries is fiendishly difficult. The first problem is to know what users are going to want to do. You know your predefined reports and other BI applications, but ad hoc is, well, ad hoc. You have to return to your business requirements document to extract information about analyses. Watch (by collecting query text) what the early business users and testers are doing with the system. Of course, if you're testing a system that's already in production, you should collect a broad range of queries from the system logs that we discuss in Chapter 17.

Usability Testing

Unless you've developed custom user-oriented software as part of your DW/BI solution, usability testing will not be a huge burden. In large part this is because, with shrink-wrapped front-end tools, there are relatively few things you can change. You can typically change the names of things (columns, tables, and reports) and the way they are organized.

Nonetheless, perform some usability testing with actual business users. As with all usability tests, you need to find fresh minds: people who have not been intimately associated with the project. Walk a few people through the BI portal and the reports, and see what trips them up.

Earlier in the system development process, when you start working on the Analysis Services database and defining reports, you should show a draft of the object names to business users. Rely on them to tell you what objects should be called in the interfaces they see. You tried to get object names correct when you were designing the dimensional model. But often business users change their minds about names when the system gets closer to reality. We let business user names diverge from the physical names, if it helps the business users understand the system. Because there's always at least one layer between the physical relational database and the business user — be it relational views, Analysis Services cubes, Reporting Services Report Models, or all of these layers — you can change names that business users see without messing up your ETL system development. But you do need to get the names right for Analysis Services and the reporting metadata layers.

> **NOTE** Another issue to think about early on is the hierarchies within dimensions. Dimension hierarchies become dropdown lists for ad hoc queries and parameterized reports. During the database design sessions you should think about the user experience associated with large, flat hierarchies. What will the user experience be if they are trying to navigate a dropdown list and you populate a list with 100,000 items? This is a common problem, and not one that's easily fixed at the last minute, just before rollout.

Before your new system goes live, you must have implemented and tested security at the user, role, report, and database levels, as we described in Chapter 14. If users don't have the correct security permissions, the system is — from their point of view — completely unusable.

Testing Summary

Our main advice with respect to testing your DW/BI system is to test early, often, and thoroughly. Visual Studio or other testing tools can help by providing a central environment in which to define tests and log their results. Write reports on test logs so that they highlight changes, especially tests that worked yesterday but not today.

NOTE Visual Studio Team Foundation Server comes with a project data warehouse, which includes an Analysis Services cube and Reporting Services reports on work items, bugs, and so on. It is really fun to use.

The biggest challenge of DW/BI testing is that the project is, by its nature, about integration. So standard test methodologies and tools aren't a perfect fit for our world. Begin by investing in some infrastructure:

- A static test source database
- A development testing environment that begins from that known source, and makes it trivially easy for developers to run automated tests every night

Throughout the development cycle, developers must maintain a script to modify the test source databases, and a second script to execute the tests. This isn't fundamentally different from what most developers do anyway, you're just asking them to manage the process, and commit to running tests repeatedly.

Fairly early in the development cycle, after the kinks have been ironed out of the daily development testing process, begin system testing. The system tester, who should not be a developer, defines tests that cover the entire DW/BI process, from data extract, transformation, and loading to cube processing, report delivery, and downstream BI applications. Begin system testing on the test databases. There are several reasons for this recommendation:

- Iron out problems with the system testing process early before you're pressured to go live in two weeks.
- Some system tests of unusual data conditions might not be encountered during normal live testing.
- In the absence of perfect specifications, the system tester(s) will have more time to identify and develop tests.
- The developers will have more time to respond to faults found in the system testing process.

Once the testing infrastructure is in place, the system tester will need to devote a significant amount of time developing tests. The time required ranges from a few weeks of full-time effort to significantly more than that, depending on the quality of the system specifications. After the tests are defined, the system tester can spend perhaps a day a week on system testing, until it's time to move to live testing and the run up to deployment.

Data quality testing primarily consists of tests of rowcounts, sums, and hashes. A key component of data quality testing is to match reports from the source system. Some of this work can begin early in the development cycle as well, but the first big milestone for data quality testing is the one-time load of historical data. This data set should be extensively tested. It some cases it's possible to match old reports exactly. If not, write an audit report that describes exactly why the new reports are different. A small number of highly regarded business users must participate in data quality testing. These business users should be the subject area data stewards, who are part of the overall data governance program.

Finally, once development is largely complete, you'll hook up the ETL process to live data. At this point, the real system testing is under way. You can also perform performance tests, both of the processing steps, and the queries. If you've been running all tests nightly, you should be in great shape for getting through the testing period with minimal pain. The next big step: deployment!

Deploying to Production

Once your system is fully tested and accepted by the data stewards, it's time actually to deploy. Whether you're a tiny team or a large organization with deployment specialists on staff, you need to think through all of the issues before the actual day arrives.

If you're implementing a new system on new hardware, your deployment procedures can be somewhat casual. It's common to use the production system for testing and even user training, before the new system goes live. You can think of the deployment process in this simple case as via email — send a message when the system has passed all tests and is ready to go live.

After that first free deployment, it gets a lot harder. Any modifications to the system — and there are always modifications — should be accomplished with minimal disruption to the business user community. The only way to do this is to:

- Perform testing on a test system that's as identical to the production system as possible.
- Use scripts rather than clicking through a user interface. Any time you need to open a tool and especially to click through a wizard, you open the possibility of doing the wrong thing.

- Develop a deployment process playbook that describes exactly what to do and in what order. This is especially vital if you can't run a script but instead must do something within a tool. It's tempting during development to think you can remember all the little steps of deployment, but after you have been away from the system for a few weeks or months, you will be *very* glad you made a detailed playbook. If you create a really awesome playbook, you will be surprised that it contains a hundred steps or more.

- Test the playbook on a test system before trying it on production.

Relational Database Deployment

Perhaps the simplest way to deploy changes in the relational database is to back up and restore the test database to the production environment. The standard data warehouse environment, with nightly loads, enables this technique on a moderately large data warehouse. You just need to bring the DW/BI system down for several hours or a day, back up the database(s) from the test system, and restore them on production.

Backup and restore is a relatively uncommon approach to deploying changes. In many projects, the database is either too large for this approach to be comfortable, or the test system includes only the portion of the DW/BI system currently under modification. Instead, most deployment projects script the changes to conform the test and production databases.

In the old days, it was the job of the development DBA to keep track of schema and data changes, and maintain scripts for modifying the production database. That's still true, but the job is much easier now that there are tools available to automate the comparison of two schemas. Visual Studio 2010 includes this schema comparison functionality in both its Premium and Ultimate versions.

In Figure 16-3 we illustrate the results of running a SchemaCompare on two versions of a database. The schema on the left is the new database. We've added a new column (NewColumn) to the StageSpecialOffer table. In the top panel of the window is the list of tables in the schema. The schema compare process has correctly identified the table and column that are different. In the bottom panel is a small snippet of the deployment script that Visual Studio has generated.

When you run the schema compare process, you have fine control over the details to compare, including security, extended properties, filespaces, and so on.

> **NOTE** The schema compare feature is part of Visual Studio 2010. It's also available in several earlier versions of Visual Studio. It's not a feature of BIDS. There are third-party tools that perform the same function.

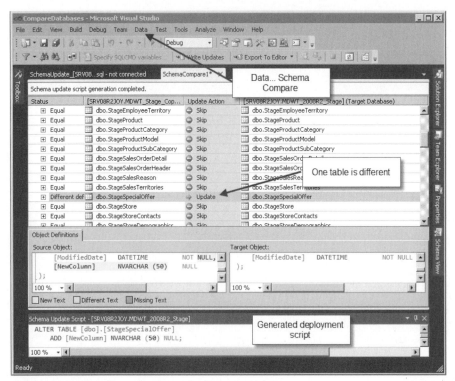

Figure 16-3: Creating a database deployment script

Visual Studio contains a second, related feature to compare data between two identically structured tables. Visual Studio will generate a script to insert, update, or delete rows in the target. This functionality is very useful for most dimension tables, and other reasonably sized tables in the environment. Fact tables and extremely large dimension tables should be excluded, as you'll want to update their data in bulk. For large tables, build a simple Integration Services package to copy the data from test to production.

All deployment scripts should be tested before being applied to the real production system.

NOTE The Deployment Playbook for deploying a new relational database or modifications to an existing database should include the following:

■ If your test database structure doesn't mirror production, include any edits to make to SQL scripts (like editing file locations or database names). It's far safer to parameterize these changes, but writing the scripts is a lot more complicated if you do so.

- **A mechanism for verifying that any necessary edits were done correctly. At the very least, advise the operator to search for specific phrases that should have been changed during the editing process.**

- **DML scripts to insert and update data in the new database. This data can include small dimension tables, configuration data, metadata, SSIS configurations, or global variables. And don't forget to populate any new static dimensions.**

- **Integration Services packages to run that will load data into the fact tables.**

- **The run command for any scripts, like SQL scripts, including any parameters used in the script execution.**

- **A script or instructions to verify that all completed correctly.**

Integration Services Package Deployment

The process of deploying a package from development to test to production is straightforward. Fundamentally, you copy the packages into the production environment. Production packages should be locked down in source control.

There are tools to help with package deployment. The first tool is Integration Services configurations, which we discussed earlier in this chapter. Configurations let you change at runtime the characteristics of an Integration Services package, like the connection string to sources, the location of file folders, a parameter, or a variable value. Changing values at runtime is valuable because it lets you modify the way a package executes without opening and editing the package.

The second feature of Integration Services that simplifies deployment is the aptly named deployment utility. Launch the deployment utility by choosing Deploy from the Solution Explorer in BIDS. The deployment utility bundles into a deployment folder all the components associated with a set of packages, including any configuration files, code libraries, or other files that you included in your project. You can copy the deployment folder from one server to another, and then open the deployment folder to launch a simple wizard to install the packages.

> **NOTE** During the development process, you probably discovered that you don't need the Deployment Wizard and Installation Wizard. You can easily copy SSIS package and configuration files, and they work just fine on the new server. The deployment and Package Installation Wizards are a convenience.

Some organizations are deeply opposed to using a wizard for deploying to production. Scripts can be fully tested and automated in advance. If you use a wizard with a user interface, like the Package Installation Wizard, you run the risk of someone clicking the wrong box or making a typo during the deployment process. If your organization is adamant about not using wizards, you can write a batch script that calls dtexec. Dtexec is a command-line utility that is used mainly to execute packages in test and production. But with different parameters, dtexec will copy, delete, encrypt, or deploy a package into SQL Server or a file folder. If your deployment folder includes multiple packages, you'd need to call dtexec multiple times to install them one by one. In addition, if your deployment folder contains configuration or other files, your script would also need to move them to the appropriate places.

As part of the pre-deployment testing and code review process, it's extremely helpful to be able to identify the changes between two versions of an SSIS package. SSIS packages are XML documents, but simply comparing the two versions isn't very effective. A minor change in the physical layout of objects in the package can have a large effect on the XML document. However, the recommended add-on BIDSHelper has a SmartDiff SSIS utility, which you can execute from BIDS. It strips out formatting information and regularizes the layout of the SSIS package, to highlight real changes. It's a valuable addition to your change management procedures.

NOTE The Deployment Playbook for deploying a package should include the following:

- **The location of the deployment folder to be copied to the production server.**
- **Where to copy the deployment folder to.**
- **Instructions for running the Package Installation Wizard, including all choices to make in the dialog boxes. Alternatively, the command script to run that calls dtexec to install the packages, and which copies other necessary files to the appropriate destinations. Don't forget the configuration files and code libraries.**
- **Instructions for creating any Windows global variables that the package uses.**
- **A script or instructions to verify that all completed correctly.**

Analysis Services Database Deployment

As with the other software components of the Microsoft DW/BI solution, there are several ways to deploy a new Analysis Services database or to make modifications to an existing database. These are included in Table 16-1.

Table 16-1: Methods for deploying changes to an SSAS database

METHOD	COMMENTS	GOOD CHOICE FOR...
Backup/ restore	If the full SSAS database exists on your test system, fully processed with all data, then you can back it up and restore it on the production server. SSAS backup and restore work at the database level only, and can be fully scripted.	Initial deployment or a significant structural change. Scenarios where you don't need to minimize downtime.
Deployment Wizard	The Deployment Wizard is a standalone utility. It creates a script to deploy the metadata of the entire SSAS database. Then, either now or at a future time, you kick off processing of the entire SSAS database on the production server.	Moving from development to test.
Synchronize Database	Synchronize Database also works at the database level. It copies the metadata of the entire SSAS database. It also copies the data files from source to target. Synchronization's data copy is a much less expensive operation than full processing of the database. Synchronization creates a shadow copy of the existing database on the target server, so users can continue to access the database during the synchronization. Users are automatically shifted to the new version when the synchronization is complete. Note that this means you'll need twice the disk space on your production server. Synchronization is launched from Management Studio and can be scripted.	Moving from test (staging) to production. Scenarios where you must minimize downtime.
XMLA script	An XMLA (XML for Analysis) script is the closest thing to DDL constructs familiar from the relational database. But they are in the form of XML syntax rather than something like TSQL. You can write or generate an XMLA script to create the new structure of an SSAS database. Most often, it's used to make relatively minor changes to an existing structure. You can write and execute XMLA scripts in Management Studio.	Changing calculations. Making minor changes to an existing system.
AMO code	You can write to the AMO (Analysis Management Objects) object model to create or modify SSAS databases.	Packaged BI solution vendor.

The biggest problem with SSAS system deployments is that the easiest methods work at the database level: backup/restore, deployment, and synchronization. This is fine if your SSAS database is of modest size, but can be quite problematic at the terabyte scale.

The only way to deploy incremental changes is to write some code: XMLA code, which is analogous to T-SQL in the relational database, or AMO code. Most organizations use XMLA rather than AMO.

Incremental deployment of changes is a good choice for modifications that don't affect data storage. These include:

- The MDX script for all cube calculations such as calculated measures
- Definitions of Actions and KPIs
- Security definitions

The XMLA specification is complete, and you can write an XMLA script to implement any modification in the production database. However, you must understand that many modifications will result in significant database reprocessing. Some changes to a core conformed dimension that's used throughout the database will effectively result in the need to reprocess much of that database — all the fact tables that subscribe to the dimension. For this reason, many organizations use XMLA scripts only for the calculated information described earlier. Any more significant change is made by one of the other methods, usually database synchronization.

If your SSAS database is extremely large, you may want to invest in the XMLA skills to perform more incremental modifications.

> **NOTE** The easiest way to generate the XMLA script for changes in calculations is to use the Deploy MDX Script feature of BIDSHelper. You should never deploy an MDX script from BIDS directly into production, but you can do so into a test server. Use SQL Server Profiler to monitor the test server; it will pick up the text of the XMLA script. You can copy that script and move it into your deployment script library. Chapter 17 describes Profiler in more detail.

As part of your change management and deployment procedures, you should thoroughly document the changes to a system in production. There's no built-in tool to help with that, but BIDSHelper provides the same kind of assistance described previously. The BIDSHelper feature SmartDiff for Analysis Services lets you compare the full database definitions for two SSAS databases, highlighting the differences in a reasonably useful way.

> **NOTE** We certainly look forward to the day when Microsoft provides the same kinds of management and tools for Analysis Services as exist for the relational database.

Reporting Services Report Deployment

Deploying a new report is generally a lot easier and less exciting than deploying or changing a database or package. When you launch a new DW/BI system or add a business process dimensional model, you will probably begin the development of the initial suite of reports on a test server, ideally against a complete set of data. As soon as the production server is populated, migrate any existing reports, and continue report development on the production server. If you use shared data sources for Reporting Services reports, it's a simple task to point the reports to the production databases.

You will modify and create reports far more often than you'll modify the underlying databases. All reports should be tested before they're released to the user community. The most important tests are to ensure the report definitions are accurate. Complex reports that access a lot of data, especially if the reports are run by a lot of people, should be tested for performance. You may find that you need to write a stored procedure to generate the report's data set as efficiently as possible.

REPORT DEPLOYMENT PROCESS

Complete the following steps to safely deploy a new or changed report on the production system:

- Identify the business users who will test and verify the new or changed report.

- Create a Reporting Services role named ReportTest that includes the DW/BI team and the business users who'll test the report. You may need several report testing roles, if there are a lot of report development projects going on at once.

- Set up a TestFolder folder structure in the BI portal that's accessible only to the ReportTest role.

- Develop the new report in BI Studio or Report Builder and deploy it to TestFolder.

- Notify the testers that the report's available, and when you expect to hear back from them about it. Your organization may have formal user acceptance procedures for you to rely on here. If you are using SharePoint, you can set up the TestFolder to automatically generate an approval workflow.

- When the relevant people have signed off on the report, redeploy it to its appropriate place in the BI portal with the appropriate security.

Most companies will develop and test new reports in a private area of the production report server, rather than set up a completely separate test instance of Reporting Services. Standard reports don't change data, so you don't need to worry about damaging the databases. All you need is to insulate most users from the test area, which is easy to do with the Reporting Services security settings discussed in Chapter 14.

As you may expect, the hardest part of deploying reports isn't technical but political. The greatest challenge is to create policies and procedures that enable your business community to contribute new reports and analyses, while maintaining the appropriate level of control over published reports. You should develop a quality assurance process, and procedures for publishing reports to a broad audience. This is particularly important for highly regulated companies.

> **NOTE** Sometimes, changes to the underlying databases require existing reports to be modified. Earlier in this chapter, we stressed the importance of end-to-end testing for any significant modifications to the DW/BI system. The standard report suite must be tested before database changes are moved into production. It's usually easy to fix reports in response to a schema change, but if you forget this step, the user experience is the same as if you messed up the underlying data. From their point of view, the DW/BI system is broken. Also, any change that breaks a standard report will likely break user reports, too. If you're implementing these kinds of changes, notify your users early on and discuss what they'll need to do to deal with the changes. You may want to set up a user report migration project to help rewrite some of the key user reports.

Master Data Services Deployment

Master Data Services applications are easy to deploy. The main characteristic that simplifies their deployment is that they typically include small volumes of data — dimension data — rather than the large fact tables in the full DW/BI system.

MDS has two features that you can use for deployment. Within any one MDS implementation, an MDS model (for example, for the customer dimension) can have multiple versions. You can theoretically have a single server, and a single implementation of MDS, supporting a production version of the model at the same time as a development and/or test version. A version cannot be validated and committed unless all the data conforms to the structure and business rules that have been defined.

We don't want to suggest that maintaining development and test versions on the same server as production is a best practice; we always want to isolate production systems. However, it's a matter of just a few mouse clicks in the management console to package up a model, including the structure, the business rules, and all existing data. Copy the deployment package to the production environment, launch the management console, and deploy.

Data Warehouse and BI Documentation

We all seem to skimp on documentation in the run up to system deployment. It seems as though the business should be able to use the system without a ton of documentation. After all, we spent a lot of time and trouble organizing and naming things in a sensible way. The bad news here is that the team needs to do a lot of documentation of the system in order to offer a complete solution to the users. The good news is most of the documentation is really metadata dressed up in presentable clothes. If you've been capturing metadata all along, much of the job now is to create a nice front end for users to access that metadata. If you've been ignoring the metadata issue, you've got a lot of work ahead of you.

As we detail in Chapter 12, the BI portal is the organization's single source for reporting and analysis and associated information. The main content of the BI portal will be the navigation hierarchy and the standard reports contained therein. Around the edges of the main BI portal page, users should find links to all the documentation and tools described here.

Core Descriptions

The first things to document are the data: the business process subject areas including facts and dimensions, and the tables, columns, calculations, and other rules that make up those subject areas. Standard reports and other BI applications should also be documented, though their documentation is often integrated with the reports themselves.

Business Process Dimensional Model Descriptions

The BI documentation begins with the dimensional model. The DW/BI team must write a clear, succinct description of each dimensional model in the warehouse. This document will be the starting point for anyone who wants to understand what's in the DW/BI system. If orders was the initial row selected on the bus matrix, write a document that describes the orders dimensional model. Recall that a business process dimensional model usually consists of a small number of related fact tables (1–3), and their associated dimension tables. The document answers such questions as:

- What's the nature of the business process captured in this data?
- What are the salient business rules?
- What's the grain of each fact table?
- What date range is included in each fact table?

- What data has been left out (and why)?

- What dimensions participate in this business process? Many of the dimensions will need their own descriptive documents that this document can link to.

This document should have a few screen captures that show the target dimensional model in a graphical form, some example values, and a few reports to demonstrate the kinds of business questions it can address. The graphic of the dimensional model can be derived directly from a data model, or it can be a simple drawing as illustrated in Figure 16-4. Remember that the purpose of the picture is to communicate to the user community. It helps to start at a high level as illustrated here, and then to drill down to greater levels of detail. Don't overwhelm users with the details of a 200-table data model without providing context.

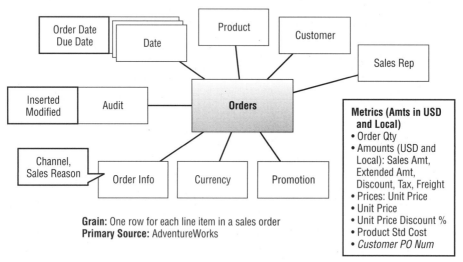

Figure 16-4: High level graphic of a dimensional model

Table and Column Descriptions

Once people have a general understanding of a particular schema, they need to be able to drill down into the details table by table and column by column. This is where the descriptive metadata you captured when you were building the initial target model comes back into service. Refer back to Chapter 15 for the details of this metadata.

DOWNLOADS As you may recall from Chapter 15, we have provided tools to populate a metadata database with much of the descriptive information that you captured when you created the data model. On the book's website you will find the metadata schema scripts:

■ The script to create a business metadata relational database.

■ Scripts to populate the metadata database from the system tables and table and column extended properties.

■ A set of linked reports for users to browse the business metadata catalog.

Report Descriptions

Each report must have a base set of descriptive information as part of the standard template described in Chapter 10. Some of this information, like the report title and description, can be written out to the Reporting Services metadata structures when the reports are built or updated. Other information will need to be captured in the metadata repository described in Chapter 15. The navigation framework described in Chapter 10, and the assignment of individual reports to categories and groups, help people understand what information is available. These category assignments should follow the same organizing framework used to present the reports in the BI portal. In fact, this metadata can be used to dynamically create the portal interface.

Additional Documentation

Data and report documentation are certainly the most commonly used, but other documentation is also important. The most valuable additional documentation comes in the form of online tutorials, support guides, and a list of colleagues who use the system and may be able to help.

As we discuss later in this chapter, you should develop and deliver training to the business users. This training should be mandatory for business users who'll be creating ad hoc queries, but it's useful for everyone. Realistically, not all users will come to a class. Even if you do have 100 percent attendance, users can benefit from online tutorials and class materials. These may be as simple as an annotated version of the classroom materials made available on the website.

A support guide will help your business users know whom to call when they have a problem. You should list the escalation hierarchy with contact names, emails, and phone numbers. You may get significant leverage out of publishing a list of frequently asked questions and answers. We discuss user support issues later in this chapter.

Cheat sheets are brief summaries of common commands, processes, terminology, constraint lists, and so on — whatever people use or do on a regular basis that might be hard to remember. A cheat sheet is a single-page document, often meant to be folded into a tri-fold format for easy access and storage. In some ways, these cheat sheets are marketing brochures for the DW/BI system. They will be prominently displayed in your users' offices, so make them look professional. The cheat sheets should also be part of the BI portal content.

Publish a current list of users on the BI portal, with an indicator showing which users are designated analytic support people and which users have at least had ad hoc tool training. Include a simple report showing query activity by user in the last month or so, sorted from most to least active.

Your BI portal should incorporate additional functionality, including:

- *Metadata browser:* The metadata browser is the reporting and navigation front end for the metadata repository. Chapter 15 describes a metadata schema that should be accessible from the BI portal.

- *Search function:* The BI portal should include the ability to search the contents of the warehouse, and especially the report descriptions. Chapter 12 describes how to set up your SharePoint BI portal to include search (which is not as trivial as it sounds).

- *Warehouse activity monitors:* Power users and the DW/BI team always want to know what's going on in the DW/BI system right now. You might hear this question in slightly different forms, like "Who's on the system?" or "Why is the report so slow?" Develop a few reports that execute against the SQL Server system tables or Analysis Services database. We discuss activity monitoring in greater detail in Chapter 17.

User Training

One of the main purposes of the BI applications is to provide information for the 80 percent of the organization who'll never learn to access the data directly. Unfortunately, the remaining 20 percent will never learn either, unless you teach them. Offer classes that will help ad hoc users climb the learning curve to master both the ad hoc tool and the underlying data.

It's hard to know when to start developing user training. You need to start after the database is stable and the front-end ad hoc tool has been selected, but long enough before the actual rollout begins to be able to create and test a solid set of course materials. Training development breaks down into two primary tasks: design and development of the course materials. Beyond these, the DW/BI educator might also need to create supporting materials and a training database.

After the system has been in use for a few months, you may add an advanced techniques class for ad hoc users. You may also provide a separate, data-centric class for each new business process dimensional model added to the DW/BI system.

Part of the design process includes outlining each class. The sidebar titled "Introductory One-Day Ad Hoc Query Course Outline" shows a typical outline. The outline will evolve during development, testing, and delivery of the class based on the reality of what it takes to teach people, and how long it takes them to learn.

INTRODUCTORY ONE-DAY AD HOC QUERY COURSE OUTLINE

Introduction (gain attention) [30min]
- **DW/BI system overview (goals, data, status, and players)**
- **Goals of the class**
- **Student expectations for the class**

Tool Overview (Demo) [15]
- **Basic elements and user interface**
- **The query building process**

Exercise 1 — Simple query [45]

Break [15]

Querying orders from the orders fact table (Demo) [15]

Exercise 2 — Simple multi-table query [45]

Review and questions [15]

Lunch [60]

Working with query templates (Demo) [15]

Exercise 3 — Sales over time [60]

Exercise 3 review (Demo) [15]

Break [15]

Saving, scheduling, and sharing reports (Demo) [15]

Exercise 4 — Saving and scheduling reports [30]

Overall review and next steps [15]

Exercise 5 — Self-paced problem set [75]

Creating the course materials for hands-on training requires a good sense for computer-based education. Many of the classic communications principles apply. Each module should be short enough to finish within the average adult attention span of 45 minutes to an hour. Each module should follow the same structure, beginning with a summary of the lesson and the key points the student should learn from the module. The body of the module should use a relevant business problem as the motivation for working through the material. Learning how to count the number of customers who responded to a new promotion would be more interesting than learning how to count the number of rows in the TABLES system table, even if the two exercises teach exactly the same concept. The exercises should be well illustrated with screen captures that look exactly like what the students will see on their computers.

RESOURCES Much of the instructional design approach we follow is based on the work of Robert Gagné. His influential books, *The Conditions of Learning and Theory of Instruction* (Harcourt Brace College Publishers; 4th edition, 1985), and his more practical *Principles of Instructional Design* (Gagné, et.al., Wadsworth Publishing; 5th edition, June 15, 2004), take an approach based on cognitive psychology and information-processing theory. These theories posit that there are internal mental processes involved in learning that are influenced by external events.

Gagné uses this relationship by viewing instruction as the arrangement of external events to activate and support the internal processes of learning. There is a lot more to creating effective training materials than just writing down a list of "click here" steps.

The modules should become progressively more complex, with the early ones providing step-by-step instructions and the later ones offering higher-level guidance. Include bonus exercises at the end of each module to keep the quick learners occupied.

Include time to test the training materials as part of the course development plan. Test each module on a few people from your team, and then test the whole package on a few of your friendly end users.

THE TRAINING DATABASE

Most organizations that create ad hoc training materials also create a training database. The training database contains the same schema as the real DW/BI system, but it is scaled down and doesn't require security. It's typically derived from the static test database used in the development process.

Although it's nice to have real, up-to-the-minute data in training, you also need users to be able to see on their screens the exact image that's in the training book. A static database that doesn't require security filters is the easiest way to make that happen.

Creating a good class takes a lot of work. Count on at least eight hours of work to create an hour of class materials. A one-day class will take about a week and a half to two weeks of hard work for someone with experience developing course materials. If this is your first time, double the estimate to give you more time to research other examples of good materials, and to test the materials you create.

Keep hands-on classes for ad hoc users relatively small — 10 to 20 people at a time. Have an assistant in the classroom to help answer individual questions during the exercises. Plan to have one assistant for every 10 students.

User Support

A well-designed and well-implemented DW/BI system is much easier to use than any alternative, but it's still not that easy. The DW/BI team will need to provide ongoing support to its user community. We recommend a three-tiered approach to providing user support. The first tier is the website and self-service support, the second tier is your power users in business units, and the third tier is the front-end people on DW/BI team (the BI part of the group).

- *Tier 1, the Website:* We've already discussed the support-related contents of the website in the documentation section. Having great content and the tools to find it (navigation, search, and metadata browser) is fundamental to providing support through the website.

- *Tier 2, the Expert Users:* If someone needs help creating an ad hoc query, or needs a specific report that doesn't already exist, they need to talk to someone with the skills to help. Set the expectation that this initial contact should be with someone who is based in the business, preferably in the person's department.

- *Tier 3, the DW/BI Team:* When the website and local experts are unable to solve the problem, the DW/BI team must offer a support resource of last resort. This front-end team actually has responsibilities across all support tiers. They own the BI portal site and must maintain and enhance its content including the BI applications. They own the relationships with and the training of the expert users. And, they provide direct support to the users when needed. This list of responsibilities represents a significant amount of work. Plan to have more people on the DW/BI team dedicated to these front-room tasks than to the back room — in an eight-person DW/BI team, for example, at least four people will be dedicated to front-room responsibilities.

> **NOTE** In some organizations, the BI portion of the DW/BI team gets split off to become its own entity. While there are probably good reasons to do this, we believe the DW/BI system is so closely tied to the business that splitting the two is like what happens when a cartoon character gets cut in half. The bottom half can't see where it's going, and the top half has lost its mobility. It's important to dedicate people to the front-end responsibilities, but separating them into their own organization is generally not productive in the long run.

The BI applications should be self-supporting, with pulldown menus, pick lists, and help screens. The DW/BI team will need to monitor their usage, maintain them as the data and data structures change, and extend and enhance them as additional data becomes available. Provide a means for users to give feedback on existing BI applications and request new ones.

Many IT organizations began building their DW/BI systems with the goal of letting users create their own reports. The real goal was a bit more self-serving — the IT folks wanted to get off the report generation treadmill. Unfortunately, while this treadmill may slow down a bit, it never goes away. Even though accessing data is easier, the majority of knowledge workers don't have the time or interest to learn how to meet their own information needs from scratch. Often, these people can be found at senior levels in the organization, so meeting their needs is particularly important. The DW/BI team will need to include creating custom reports in its responsibilities list, and to make sure there are resources available to meet the most important requests. The good news is that these custom reports can almost always be turned into (parameterized) standard reports and integrated into the existing BI application set.

Desktop Readiness and Configuration

The initial deployment must consider issues across the entire information chain, from the source systems to the user's computer screen. Most PCs can handle the rigors of querying, reporting, and analysis. They already support large spreadsheets and Access databases. In some ways, the DW/BI system should reduce the strain on the user's PC by moving most of the data management back to the servers. Don't assume that everything will work fine at the user desktop. Test this assumption well before users attend training.

Before you inspect the situation, decide how much capability a user's desktop machine will need to have. Create a minimum configuration based on the front-end tools, the amount of data typically returned, and the complexity of the BI applications. This minimum configuration includes CPU speed, memory, disk space, and monitor size. It should also indicate the base computer type and operating system supported, and browser version requirements. We've been in organizations that insist on supporting multiple operating systems on users' desktops: Windows, Apple, Linux, and UNIX. Obviously, this diversity has a big impact on the architecture and tool selection steps, long before you get to deployment. Let's hope those who are implementing a Microsoft DW/BI system are less interested in supporting multiple types of operating systems, but there are still many flavors of Windows.

When you go out into the user community, consider the following issues.

▪ *Connectivity:* Connectivity is not usually an issue in today's workplaces, but there can be a problem getting from one part of the organization to another. For example, a remote field office may not have the appropriate network configuration to get to the DW/BI server. Bandwidth to the desktop is usually not an issue either, but it's worth verifying, especially for a mobile workforce.

NOTE Windows Remote Desktop can be a good, inexpensive solution for bandwidth problems. It works very well across even fairly slow connections. We use it all the time over a virtual private network to shared servers. Many of our clients have reported great success in increasing user satisfaction — especially for salespeople and others who are often on the road.

▪ *Installation:* Some front-end tools are desktop-based and need to have software installed on the user's machine. PowerPivot, for example, requires Excel 2010 plus the actual PowerPivot add-in for Excel. Even browser-based tools may require a later version of Internet Explorer than your organization supports. Test the installation process from a selection of user machines and document any problems. If the installation process is anything more than clicking a button on the BI portal, make sure you document it clearly and use it to create a set of installation instructions.

Summary

The goal of this chapter is to highlight the most important issues to think about when deploying a DW/BI system. Deploying a system safely and successfully requires a lot of work and planning. You need the entire DW/BI team and help from business experts.

The DW/BI team has to focus on developing solid operations and performance tests. Equally important, these back-room folks should concentrate on building and testing a playbook for the actual deployment process. The deployment playbook is vitally important when you're adding new functionality to an existing system, while minimizing end user impact. The goal for the playbook should be to write instructions so clear and simple that anyone can follow them. System deployment is no time to be thinking!

The front-room team focuses on queries, reports, and user interactions. During the deployment process, this team concentrates on running quality assurance tests on the data and reports. You have to rely heavily on the business experts for this testing work too. They're the ones who will confirm the data's accuracy. The front-room team also needs to develop system documentation, tools for searching and viewing that documentation, and training for the business users. Unless you've done documentation and training development before, you'll be surprised at how much time it takes to do this "soft" stuff well.

In our experience, problems with deploying a system almost always derive from incomplete testing. Test early and often. Test everything: your procedures, operations, and performance. Test the upgrade scripts. Check the results. Don't approach the actual rollout date with an attitude that says, "This should work." The right attitude is "We've tested this every way we can think of, and it *will* work."

When you do finally roll out the system, with no wrinkles at all, take a break. You've earned it! Then turn on your usage-monitoring tools, sit back, and watch what the business users are doing with their great new system.

CHAPTER 17

Operations and Maintenance

"To administer is to govern: to govern is to reign."

— Honor Gabriel Riquet

We've seen too many DW/BI teams postpone thinking about how to operate their new system until it's nearly in production. When deadlines are looming and users are clamoring for data and reports, it's too late to start designing your operating procedures. You'll be making stuff up as you go along, and you'll make mistakes.

There are two major sets of issues to think about with respect to the ongoing operations of your system. The first set of issues revolves around communicating with, training, and supporting the users. Of course you'll be publishing reports to them about the business, but you also need to communicate with them about the DW/BI system itself.

The second set of issues focuses on technical systems management. You need to think, long before you go into production, about a host of issues. Your decisions about these operational issues will affect your system configuration and design. These issues include monitoring performance and usage, automating operations, and managing resources for ad hoc use.

At launch your system's performance might be great, but with increased data volumes and user load, performance might degrade. A solid monitoring plan, implemented from the start, is your best weapon for identifying and solving bottlenecks. With the right information you can continuously tune the system so bottlenecks are solved before users even notice them.

Finally — but very important — you need to plan for, implement, and test your backup and recovery strategy.

The now-familiar Business Dimensional Lifecycle diagram (see Figure 17-1) places operational issues at the end of the Lifecycle where you loop back around on the next iteration. Operationally that's accurate, but as we discuss throughout this chapter, you need to be planning for safe operations from the outset.

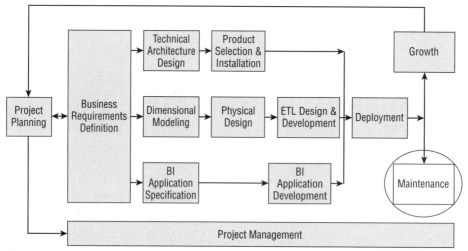

Figure 17-1: The Business Dimensional Lifecycle

In this chapter, you'll find answers to the following questions:

▪ What do you need to worry about with respect to maintaining and extending the BI portal and BI applications?

▪ How do you monitor the system? What kinds of counters and events should you track? How can you see what users are doing right now, and kill bad queries?

▪ How do you conduct performance tuning of a DW/BI system?

▪ What data do you need to back up and how often? How should you perform backup and recovery?

▪ How do you execute Integration Services packages in production?

Providing User Support

The design and development of your DW/BI system has focused on building a system that's easy to use, intuitive, and performs well. You've built BI applications, be they canned reports, a dashboard portal, a closed loop data mining application, or a combination of all. You've trained the users on the data and applications. What's left to do? A lot.

The business user community will grow and change. Some users will learn the new tools immediately. Others will require some hand-holding and retraining. Even if your system is perfect and the business users catch on immediately, you'll need to train new employees. On an ongoing basis, it's common to have the same number of people involved with supporting the business users as initially developed the system.

The user-facing part of the DW/BI team engages in the following activities:

- BI portal maintenance and enhancement
- BI application specification and development
- BI Help Desk support and training, discussed in Chapter 16

We've seen the user-facing side of the DW/BI team range in size from dozens of people for large companies with a centralized DW/BI system, to a single person. The smallest organizations often have a single-person shop, but it's really hard for that person to handle the back-room maintenance while communicating effectively with the business users. Ongoing, it's hard to see how you can get by with fewer than two people: one for the back room, and one for the front room.

> **NOTE** Many CIOs and IT managers imagine that the DW is like a normal project: heavily staffed during development, but requiring only 1–2 people once it's in operation. Not so! The front room team, often called the BI team, requires a lot of resources. So often we see technically sound DW/BI systems that are underutilized because the ongoing BI team is too small to be effective. A good rule of thumb is to expect the overall DW/BI team to be as large in production as in development, but resources shift from back room development (DW) to front room user support (BI).
>
> Although we refer to an integrated DW/BI team throughout this book, the BI team sometimes reports in to the business. We generally prefer a single team, because the simpler organizational structure ensures better communication between the front room and the back room. There are, however, advantages to having the BI team report to the business. Their presence embedded in the user community increases user buy-in and improves DW credibility, as long as the two teams communicate as if they were a single virtual team.

Maintaining the BI Portal

Even the smallest DW/BI team should maintain an intranet site where users get information about the system. In Chapter 12 we discussed how to create a portal to host the reports from Chapter 10; in Chapter 15 we described the metadata that should be published on the portal; and in Chapter 16 we talked about documentation and training materials that should be hosted on the site.

Here we briefly present an additional set of information that should go on the portal, having to do with operations and maintenance:

- System status — what is the most recent day of data in each business process dimensional model

- Schedules of planned outages

- Honest and complete status of any unplanned outages or data quality problems

- The system's current operational status, including:

  - How many queries have been answered in the last hour or day

  - How many reports were generated

  - Current number of active users

  - On-demand report of active queries, how long they've been running, and who's running them

- Proof points about the system's capacity, to foster user confidence in the system:

  - How long the last data load took

  - How big the largest data load was, and how long it took

  - Maximum count of simultaneous users

Every 12 to 18 months, you should review the entire DW/BI system. Evaluate what's working well for the users, and what should change. Remember, change is inevitable, and is a sign of a healthy system. As part of this periodic evaluation, consider refreshing the look, layout, and content of the BI portal.

Extending the BI Applications

The initial reports and BI applications for a new business process dimensional model will soon be modified and augmented. Users don't always know what reports and analyses they want until you show them something fairly close. Then they'll tell you what they *don't* want — the report you just created — and, let's hope, give you clearer information about what they now think they need.

The cycle repeats as business imperatives change.

Data mining applications, and other kinds of closed loop systems, are seldom implemented in the first phase of a DW/BI system. First, the basic data is brought online. Then, business users and DW/BI team members build ad hoc models and analyses. This analytic work has tremendous value to the business, for example by improving their understanding of customers, or providing mechanisms for reducing costs. The next step, beyond improving understanding, is to systematize the knowledge gained from ad hoc analysis by building a closed loop system.

In our experience, ad hoc analyses are usually valuable enough to provide a positive ROI on the DW/BI investment, and many implementations stop there. Those DW/BI teams that go on to build data mining applications and other kinds of closed loop systems usually reap greatly increased ROI.

The process of developing a closed loop BI system requires close partnership between the business people, who can effectively develop the business rules and analytic models, and the DW/BI team, who will write the system specifications and formalize the models. The majority of the application development effort requires a fairly standard development skill set, which is often met by the same developers who work on the operational systems. The developer needs a relatively small amount of specialized knowledge — for example, of the Analysis Services object models — in order to implement the calls into the databases or data mining model.

System Management

Most of this chapter focuses on the back-room requirements for managing your DW/BI system in production. Although we've separated these operational issues into this chapter, you need to think ahead during design and development to ensure you build a maintainable system.

There are several components of the back-room system management:

- Monitoring resources and usage
- Managing data growth and disk space
- Performance tuning
- Managing partitioning
- Data quality monitoring
- Backup and recovery
- Generating statistics for the BI portal
- Executing and monitoring the ETL system

The more automated you can make your systems management, the better. At the very least, automate backups and launching the ETL packages. SQL Server provides enough tools that the basics are easy, and there's no excuse for not implementing some system automation.

Unlike many issues where we've talked about how small teams might cut corners, organizations of any size benefit from system automation. Indeed, the smallest organizations are perhaps least equipped to apply human resources to a problem that can be automated. It's hard to imagine how a DW/BI team of one to three people could possibly operate without significant automation.

The ideal management system requires no human intervention except for the occasional troubleshooting. Such a system automatically adds and drops partitions, checks for disk space, reports on performance problems or unusual usage, and corrects the vast majority of data oddities during the ETL process.

No matter how automated your operations are, you must have a plan. Like all plans, your operations plan should be written down.

Governing the DW/BI System

How does the DW/BI system administrator know what's going on in the DW/BI system right now? What tools are available to manage and maintain the DW/BI system on a day-to-day basis?

As you might expect, Microsoft and SQL Server provide a wide range of tools, solutions, and approaches. Some of the technologies, notably the relational engine, are richly instrumented and easy to manage. Others are not as well instrumented, but can be fairly well managed by using a combination of third-party software, free downloads, and custom scripting.

Identifying and Terminating User Sessions

The most basic question for ongoing administration of a DW/BI system is who's logged in and issuing queries right now. The immediate second question is how to kill a query. No matter how well we design the DW/BI system to support ad hoc use, and train our user community, there's inevitably a need to kill the occasional query that's using too many system resources.

Relational Database

The relational engine has very nice tools for real-time analysis and management of server activity. As you might expect, there are several alternative methods for identifying and terminating user sessions. The main two are T-SQL and Activity Monitor.

For decades, DBAs have used T-SQL commands such as `sp_who` to identify user sessions, and the `kill` command to terminate those sessions. Activity Monitor is a tool hosted within SQL Server Management Studio (SSMS) to provide information about user sessions, queries, and other processes. As you can see in Figure 17-2, Activity Monitor presents a summary display and detailed information about active processes, resource usage, I/O, and recent queries. The Processes section is used most frequently, and you can right-click a process to terminate it. Activity Monitor runs for the entire instance of SQL Server, although you can filter down the view to focus on a single database.

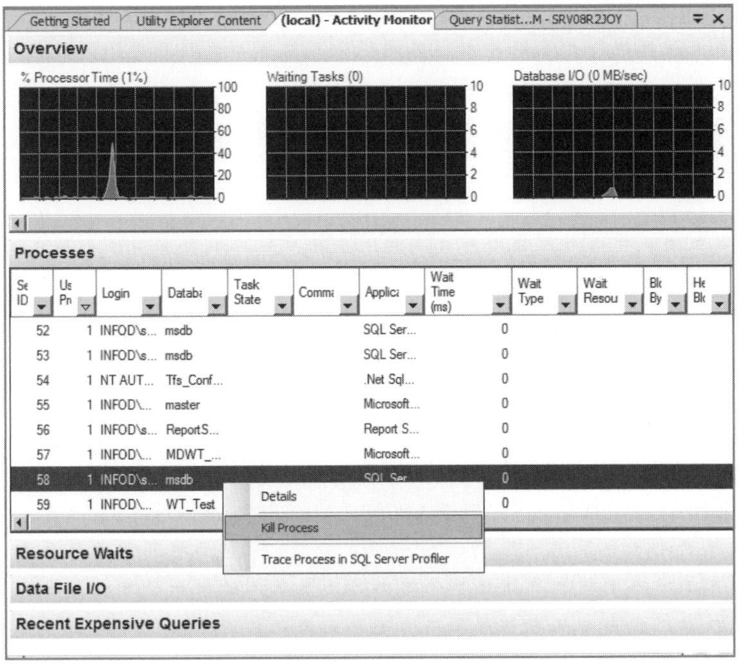

Figure 17-2: Relational database Activity Monitor

Alternatively you could use SQL Server Profiler to see all the activity on the server. Profiler is launched from the Tools menu in SSMS, and captures a broad and configurable set of information about user processes. But since Profiler is read only, you'd need to switch over to Activity Monitor or a query window to actually kill a query.

Analysis Services Database

There are similar tools for Analysis Services to identify active sessions and queries, but these tools are not as nice as for the relational engine. The "old fashioned" way to identify users is to execute a DMX statement with familiar SQL syntax, such as:

```
select * from $system.discover_connections
```

We call this old fashioned because it's similar to the old-fashioned way to view activity in the relational database. But this functionality, called Dynamic Management Views, was new in SSAS 2008.

To list currently executing queries, you can type:

```
select * from $system.discover_commands
```

Within SSMS, you do *not* execute these statements in a normal SQL query window. Instead, you open a DMX or MDX window, as illustrated in Figure 17-3.

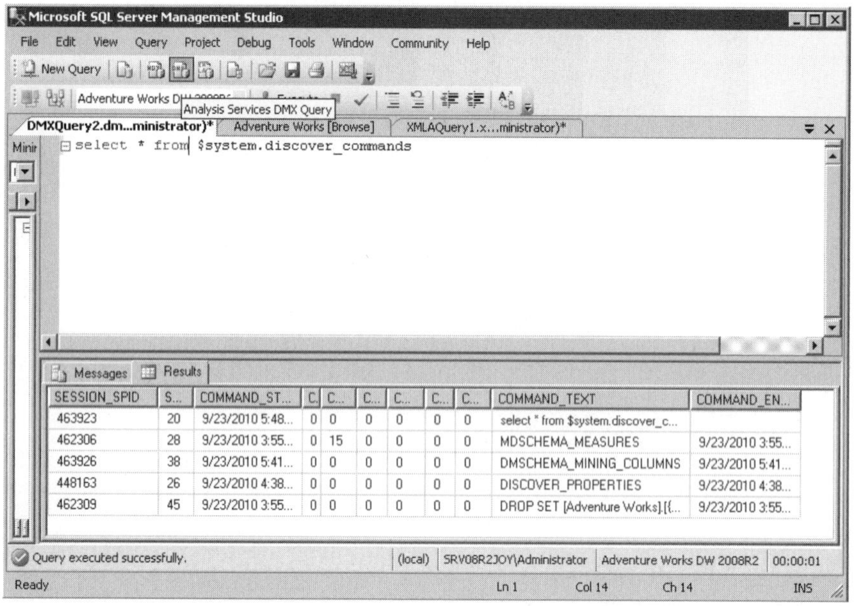

Figure 17-3: Executing a command to see active SSAS queries

NOTE The DMX window was originally designed for executing data mining commands. When you open a DMX window, a browser pops up that lets you choose the data mining model you want. This is perplexing the first time you try to execute a Dynamic Management View command for Analysis Services. To be honest, it continues to be perplexing, but you'll ignore it after a while.

Alternatively, you can use the MDX window to execute Dynamic Management View commands. This doesn't make sense either (since the DMX language is not the same as MDX, despite containing the same letters in its name).

Unfortunately, you can use the Dynamic Management Views only to identify problem queries. There's no kill command that you can execute from the same DMX window. In order to kill a query from within SSMS, you must execute an XMLA script.

The best solution is to download the Analysis Services Activity Viewer tool from CodePlex. This tool, illustrated in Figure 17-4, shows active sessions and queries. You can use it to kill a specific query by clicking the button in the lower right. Most systems use the Activity Viewer rather than DMX and XMLA.

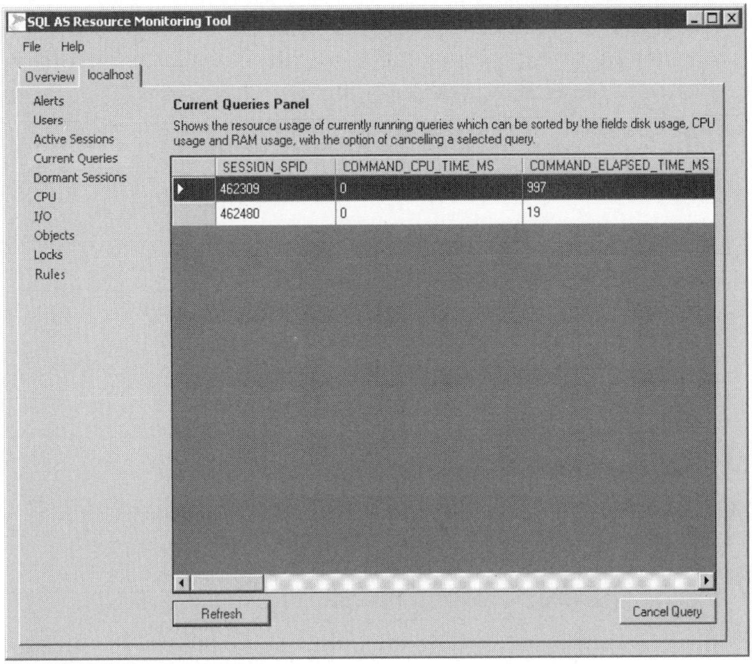

Figure 17-4: Using the SSAS Activity Viewer to kill a query

Reporting Services

You may occasionally want to cancel a specific report execution in Reporting Services. In SSMS, you can view currently executing reports in the Jobs folder of a Reporting Services instance. Right-click the offending report to find the option to cancel it.

Canceling a Reporting Services job cancels only the Reporting Services activity, notably the work involved in rendering output into the display format. If the problem report is spending all its time in the database query, you'll need to go to the underlying database (relational or Analysis Services) to cancel the query as a separate step.

Resource Governance

The ability to find and kill a specific user query is useful, but no one wants to sit at a monitor all day, zapping the occasional query. Instead, the DBA would like to automate the ongoing allocation of resources to users and other processes. He may even want to set up a process to automatically kill extremely long-running queries.

Relational Database

The SQL Server relational engine has a nice feature called Resource Governor. As you might expect from the name, Resource Governor is the right tool for the job of ongoing management of CPU and memory resources. Resource Governor doesn't help you manage I/O.

First, you can define multiple workload groups. You may want to create separate groups for:

- Integration Services jobs
- Reporting Services report execution
- DW/BI team members
- Most ad hoc users
- Vice presidents
- That guy in accounting who keeps trying to download half the data warehouse into Excel

You can define resource pools and policies for each workgroup, as illustrated in Figure 17-5.

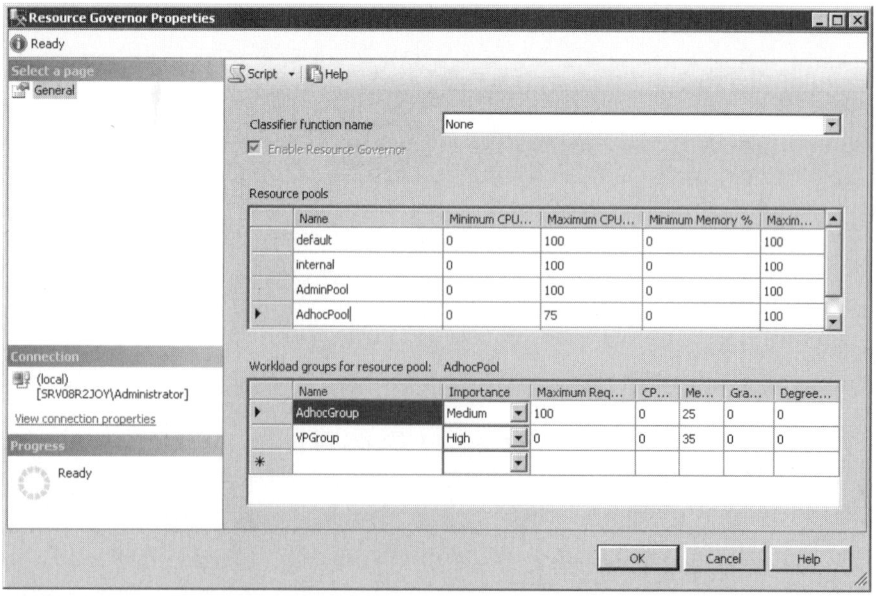

Figure 17-5: Defining pools and groups in Resource Governor

You must write a T-SQL function to classify requests into groups. The classification is typically based on usernames and the name of the application (such as Excel) that's submitting the request. Any request that's not explicitly classified into a workload group will fall into the default group.

Resource Governor will limit the resources for a query only if there's resource contention. In other words, if a user with low priority kicks off a query in the middle of the night, she may use all the server's resources if there's no other activity on the server at that time.

> **REFERENCE** Books Online has adequate documentation for the Resource Governor, starting with the topic "Managing SQL Server Workloads with Resource Governor." The topic "Considerations for Writing a Classifier Function" is also useful.

If a query exceeds the maximum CPU defined for its workload group, Resource Governor will throw a CPU Threshold Exceeded event. You can use SQL Server Profiler to monitor for this event. Usually it's sufficient for the DBA simply to view the logs generated by Profiler, in order to determine if the maximum CPU level is set appropriately.

Whether or not you're using Resource Governor, you can set up an alert in SQL Server Agent to notify the DBA of long running queries. Although it's possible to set up a response in SQL Server Agent to automatically kill queries, we recommend keeping a person in the loop, at least during the work day.

Analysis Services Database

The SSAS Activity Viewer can define alerts and actions. You can easily set up Activity Viewer to alert you when a query has been running for more than 30 minutes, or even to kill that query. You can even eliminate special people (such as yourself!) from the rule.

Performance Monitoring

You need to implement and understand two types of monitoring. First, what's going on in your system? What system resources like memory are being used, when, and by what processes? If you can't monitor system events and resource usage, you'll never be able to troubleshoot and tune your system. The other kind of monitoring focuses on the users: Who's accessing the system, and when? What queries are they running and how much time are those queries taking? If you don't know what your users are doing, you'll never be able to satisfy them.

The good news: this is all easy to set up. There are a handful of underlying tools, including:

- System Monitor is an operating system tool to collect and view real-time performance data in the form of counters, for server resources such as processor and memory use. The usage of many SQL Server resources is exposed as System Monitor counters.

- SQL Server Profiler tracks an instance of the relational engine or Analysis Services. Profiler is a tool with a simple user interface for defining a trace to track activities of interest, such as user logins or query executions. Profiler can be set up to capture query text for both Analysis Services and the relational engine.

- Event Viewer is an operating system tool that collects information about system events, such as Analysis Services shutting down unexpectedly.

It's useful to know about these underlying tools, and you certainly could use them directly to monitor your DW/BI system. However, most organizations can rely on a packaged monitoring configuration supplied by Microsoft, known as Management Data Warehouse. As we discuss next, Management Data Warehouse is useful out of the box for monitoring the relational database. And you can extend it to capture information about Analysis Services as well.

Relational Database

The easiest way to set up comprehensive monitoring for the relational data warehouse is to install Management Data Warehouse (MDW). You can do this by right-clicking on Data Collection in the Management folder in SSMS. MDW sets up monitoring on a wide range of counters and SQL Server events, including:

- CPU usage
- Memory usage
- Disk I/O usage
- Logins, logouts, and connections
- Queries, including query SQL

In addition, the MDW configuration performs the following tasks:

- Sets up the SQL Profiler traces as needed (for example, to capture query SQL)
- Sets up the System Monitor logging to capture information from the operating system (for example, CPU usage)
- Creates a database to store the collected information

- Sets up SQL Agent jobs to collect and upload logged information, including a few SSIS packages
- Installs and schedules stored procedures to periodically purge aged logs
- Installs a starter set of reports on the collected data

Each set of information has a schedule for collection and upload into the MDW. For example, server usage statistics are collected every minute, and uploaded every 15 minutes. The information about queries is logged first to a file, then scheduled to be moved into the MDW daily. These schedules are easy to modify.

NOTE Although you can install Management Data Warehouse on the same server that it's monitoring, it's generally recommended to host it on a separate server. You can monitor multiple servers from a central MDW location.

Figure 17-6 illustrates one of the sample MDW reports, on server activity. You can execute the report from SQL Server Management Studio. The reports are associated with the MDW database and also in the Management section of SSMS, under the Data Collection heading. As you can see, it's a dashboard-style report that presents a rich set of information on the operations of your database server. The underlying tables and views are available for you to query, should you want to develop a custom report.

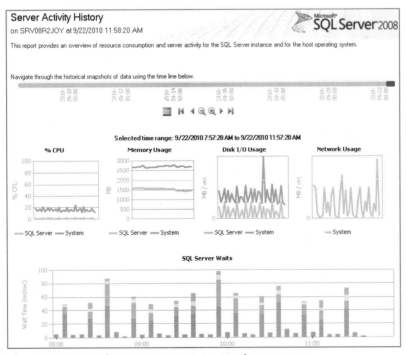

Figure 17-6: Sample Management Data Warehouse report

The MDW logic does not store the SQL for every query executed against the system. Instead, during each snapshot (default is 15 minutes), the system chooses the top three most expensive queries by each of six metrics (elapsed time, execution count, and so on). After eliminating parameters and literals, the logic identifies unique queries within that set, and then adds them to the list of "notable" queries in the MDW. It's a good practice to minimize the number of queries for which you're capturing and storing the SQL, as that one piece of information alone is larger than the rest of the logging combined. It's possible, but not advised, to modify that logic.

The collection, upload, and purge schedules are easy to modify. By default, SQL for notable queries is retained for 14 days, but we recommend extending that to 30 or 60 days. Note that by so doing, your MDW database will grow substantially larger! But a data warehouse that supports ad hoc queries should have a long time series of query text available for performance testing purposes. Figure 17-7 illustrates how to change the schedule for the query statistics information. You manage this information in SSMS, under Management ⇨ Data Collection.

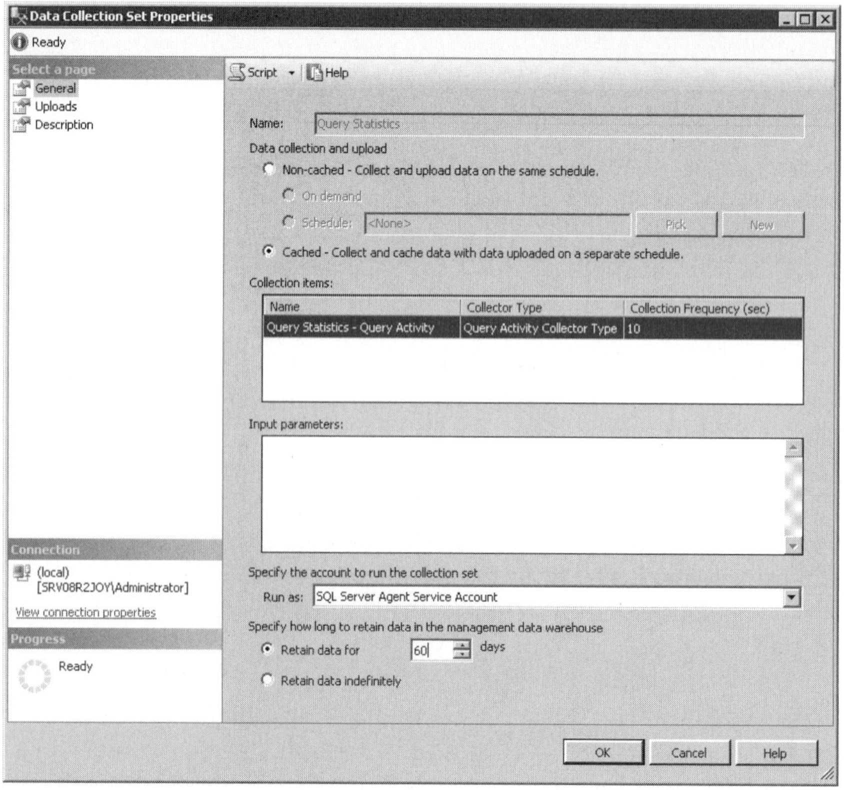

Figure 17-7: Changing the retention policy for query statistics and the text of SQL queries

Analysis Services Database

The kinds of things that we want to monitor for the core Analysis Services database are the same as for the relational database. We want to know what resources are being used (CPU, disk, memory); we want to know who's logging in and what queries they're issuing. The underlying tools — System Monitor counters and Profiler traces — work for Analysis Services, and can be configured to monitor similar information as for the relational database.

In theory, Analysis Services monitoring should be as simple to set up as for the relational database. That's not entirely true in practice: although similar components exist, the installation procedure is not as smooth as for the relational engine.

The Analysis Services Management Data Warehouse components are not included with the installation media. Instead, you can find them on CodePlex. To be honest, it looks like these components were supposed to be a feature of SQL Server 2008 or 2008 R2 but just didn't get finished in time. Although they're not as polished as the relational system components, they get the job done.

> **DOWNLOADS** You can find the CodePlex project for Analysis Services monitoring at `http://sqlsrvanalysissrvcs.codeplex.com/`. It's called "A Solution for Collecting Analysis Services Performance Data for Performance Analysis." In addition to the scripts to set up MDW to collect information from Analysis Services, the CodePlex project includes two white papers, one eponymously titled "A Solution for Collecting Analysis Services Performance Data for Performance Analysis," and the other is the "Analysis Services Performance Guide." Both documents are highly recommended.

Once you've successfully completed the installation as described in the "Solution" document, you'll have extended MDW to collect performance information from Analysis Services as well as the relational database. However, the Analysis Services solution does not automatically purge old performance data, so you'll have to manage that process yourself.

On the plus side, the solution does come with a dozen predefined reports for examining the performance of your core Analysis Services database.

The MDW solution collects the MDX text of queries, which is tremendously valuable for the performance tuning process. The query text will become the script for testing any proposed changes in the Analysis Services physical design. There is a second related reason to collect information about the queries: to feed the process that designs usage-based performance aggregations. Usage based aggregations are one of your most effective weapons for improving query performance of your Analysis Services database.

If you do not use the MDW monitoring solution, you should nonetheless capture the information needed to feed the usage-based aggregation design wizard. Turn on the query log for usage-based aggregations within SSMS, by changing the Query Log property of the server.

If you do use the MDW monitoring solution, you should turn *off* the query log for usage-based optimization. That's because the MDW solution includes a process for converting the normal query logs, which are stored in human-readable MDX, into the proprietary format of the usage-based optimization logs. This way, you only need to log usage one time, then periodically convert the information to the other format.

Analysis Services aggregation design and the usage-based optimization wizard were discussed in Chapter 8.

Reporting Services

During the course of its operation, Reporting Services stores most of the information useful for performance and operations monitoring in its ReportServer database. However, you shouldn't report directly from ReportServer. These tables are part of the Reporting Services operational system, and reporting directly from them is analogous to reporting directly from any other transaction system.

The ReportServer catalog is just like any other transaction system. It will lose history when its transaction logs are truncated. It will lose referential integrity when reports are deleted that have been run in the past, or when users are removed who have used the system in the past. Definitions of the tables and columns may change over time, breaking the existing library of usage reports. It is not easy to query directly because it uses codes instead of descriptions for most of the attributes. Most important, even a simple interactive query could place read locks on the running system, dramatically reducing system performance. For all these reasons, it makes sense to build a simple database that tracks the process of generating reports. As you can probably guess, the solution to these problems is in a CodePlex project.

> **REFERENCE** The relevant files are part of the SQL Server product code samples found at `sqlserversamples.codeplex.com`. Once you install the samples, look for the Execution Log Sample Reports directory. It contains a database definition for a simple star schema built from the ReportServer catalog, plus an Integration Services package for moving data from one database to the other. Of course, sample reports are also provided.

Integration Services

The primary goal for monitoring Integration Services package execution on the production system is to help you evaluate whether and how to improve processing performance. You also want to be able to tie the audit dimension, discussed in Chapter 7, to information about the package's execution.

The most important tools for monitoring Integration Services are System Monitor and Integration Services Logging. The SSIS System Monitor counters are not as useful as you'd hope because they track information at a high level. What you really want to see is how much memory each step of a data flow is using; instead, you can see how much memory Integration Services is using.

Nonetheless, the following SQL Server: SSIS Pipeline counters are somewhat useful:

- *Buffer Memory:* How much memory is Integration Services using? If this number is larger than the physical memory available to Integration Services, some data is being spooled to disk during processing.

- *Rows Read:* The total number of rows read from source adapters.

- *Rows Written:* The total number of rows written to destination adapters.

The logging that's generated by Integration Services packages is akin to the SQL Server tracing and profiling functionality that we discussed previously. Like Profiler, it tracks events. The kind of events that can be tracked and logged will be familiar to anyone who's run an Integration Services package: It's exactly the same kind of information that you can see in the Execution Results tab every time you execute a package in BIDS.

You seldom want to store all those package execution results permanently. Define package logging so that you store information about interesting events only. Most often, you'd set up the packages on your production system so they log to a SQL Server database, though you have several choices.

For every task, and for the overall package, you can track many events, of which the most useful are:

- *OnPreExecute:* Logs a row when execution begins

- *OnPostExecute:* Logs a row when execution ends

- *OnWarning:* Logs a row when the task issues a warning

- *OnError:* Logs a row when the task issues an error

Unfortunately, the data flow task is like a black box to the logging system. There are multiple steps and transformations within a data flow task, and ideally you'd like to know how long each step takes. This is simply impossible with the logging framework as it exists. In order to get this kind of information, you need to hand craft logging into your packages, by writing row counts and timestamps at various points within the data flow task of the package.

Set up logging by editing the package in BIDS. Choose SSIS ➢ Logging, and specify where the logs will be stored. Note that SQL Profiler is one of the options. Logging to Profiler makes it easier to interleave package events with database events, and is especially useful during testing. However, most people log to a SQL Server table in production. You can direct SSIS logs to the MDW database, but you should create a separate schema for your own logged information. Integration Services will automatically create its logging table.

As we described in Chapter 7, you should build your packages to collect information about package execution times, rows inserted into target tables, and possibly other information like the sum of amounts. This metadata is stored in the audit dimension and, at your discretion, is available to business users for querying. You may choose to pick up additional information from logging, to include with the audit system.

Finally, you may want to set up package logging to log errors to the application event log, accessible from the Event Viewer. This application event may still be written even if Something Really Bad happens on the database server, which would prevent the standard logging from working properly.

PowerPivot

A PowerPivot workbook by itself presents no monitoring challenges, because it's unmanaged and there's really nothing we can monitor. However, if your organization has implemented PowerPivot for SharePoint, your power users will be uploading their PowerPivot workbooks to SharePoint. The rest of the user community will access these analytic workbooks via SharePoint.

Once you've set up PowerPivot to work with SharePoint, the two products work together to collect useful information. The basic performance monitoring information is collected for you, and is available within the PowerPivot Management Dashboard as we saw in Chapter 11. You can access the dashboard from the SharePoint Central Administration site. Performance information includes CPU and memory usage on the PowerPivot SharePoint server, as well as counts and timings of queries.

The dashboard contains some useful reports, and you can always write your own. Logged information is stored in SQL Server, in the PowerPivot database with a name that begins DefaultPowerPivotServiceApplication. There are about a dozen tables in the Usage schema, which hold the logged information. For performance monitoring, the most useful table is Usage.Health. By default, the usage logging information is moved into the PowerPivot database every night. The management dashboard is a web part page, so you can customize it with additional web parts showing the reports that you have created.

Usage Monitoring

The usage of your DW/BI system has a huge impact on its performance. Our discussion of performance monitoring suggested that you collect information about usage, including the text of notable queries. You should always be collecting counts of queries run and rows returned, by type of application.

You should also log information about user logins and attempted connections. For the relational database, set up a trace in Profiler, capturing the following events:

- Audit Security: Audit Login
- Audit Security: Audit Logout

Take a look through the many additional Audit Security events to see if any strikes your fancy.

Similarly, set up an Analysis Services trace for logins and logouts.

You can send the results of both traces either to a file or directly to a table. For a DW/BI system, we usually have a relatively modest number of logins so you can log them directly to a database table. It's appealing to use the MDW database for this purpose, but you should separate out your trace tables into their own schema.

Reporting System usage is captured in the ReportServer database. If you've implemented the reporting management solution described in the previous section, that information will be moved nightly to a separate database appropriate for reporting. Every report execution is logged, along with the chosen parameters.

PowerPivot for SharePoint usage is captured by SharePoint and moved nightly to the PowerPivot SQL database, as described in the previous section. Usage logging is an extremely valuable feature of PowerPivot for SharePoint. The collected information and predefined reports make it easy to see who's using the system, which PowerPivot workbooks they're accessing, and which PowerPivot workbooks are most popular overall. By monitoring the changing popularity of PowerPivot workbooks, you can proactively manage your system.

An example of the PowerPivot Management Dashboard activity report is illustrated in Figure 17-8.

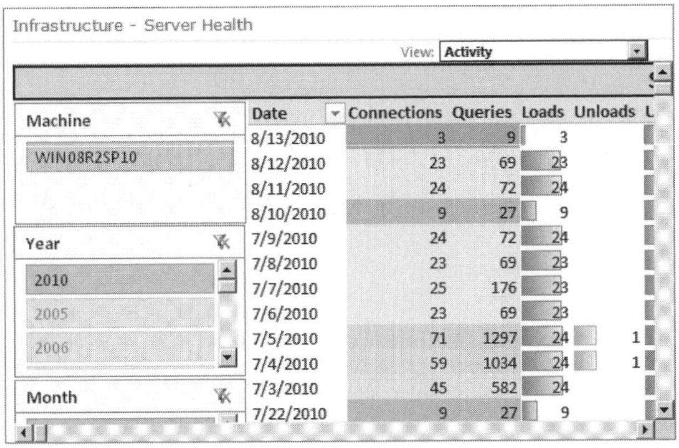

Figure 17-8: PowerPivot activity report

Your BI portal website should devote a small amount of screen real estate to reporting on system usage. VPs and Directors are often very interested in how much their staff members are using your system. They tend to be competitive people, and simply seeing another department using the DW/BI system has been known to spur a VP to encourage his or her staff to use the system more. A time series of reporting and ad hoc use by department is a really good report to publish.

Managing Disk Space

One of the most common reasons for ETL job failure is one of the easiest to prevent: running out of disk space.

At the very minimum, set up a System Monitor counter and alert to warn when free space on each disk falls below a certain threshold. The relevant counter is Logical Disk: Free Megabytes. Set up two alerts: one to warn when you're within a month of running out of disk space, and one to blare stridently when you're about a week away. Anyone — even someone who's never seen System Monitor before — should be able to set up a simple alert on disk space. An alternative, equally effective approach is to set up an alert in SQL Agent.

The Management Data Warehouse for the relational database includes a very nice sparkline report that shows how your database's disk usage has been changing. This disk usage report is illustrated in Figure 17-9.

The incremental disk space you'll be using each month goes to fact data storage, whether in the file system, relational database, or Analysis Services database. Most dimensions are relatively small and static in size, at least compared to fact tables.

Disk Usage Collection Set

on SRV08R2JOY at 9/24/2010 2:06:24 PM

This report provides an overview of the disk space used for all databases on the server and g
for the last 85 collection points between 9/3/2010 12:00:17 PM and 9/24/2010 12:00:12 PM.

Database Name ↕	Start ↕ Size (MB)	Trend	Current ↕ Size (MB)	Average Growth (MB/Day)
AdventureWorks2008R2	194.81		194.81	0
AdventureWorksDW2008 R2	88.31		88.31	0
KU_Reg_Copy	4.25		4.25	0
master	4.00		4.00	0
mdw	100.00		3,750.00	182.5
MDWT_2008R2	2.25		2.25	0
MDWT_2008R2_Stage	22.00		22.00	0
MDWT_Stage_Copy	22.00		22.00	0
model	2.25		2.25	0
msdb	17.88		147.06	6.459

Figure 17-9: Disk Usage sparkline report

When you set up a relational database, you can specify an initial size, an automatic growth factor like 10 percent, and a maximum file size. We recommend that you enable automatic growth as a failsafe, but monitor free space so that you extend database space on your own schedule. This is classic relational database management. There are tons of books available on the subject, and there's nothing particularly unusual for the data warehouse environment — except the overall size of the system and the (usually) batch nature of inserts and updates.

You could get a lot fancier than the simple mechanism we've described here. If your data volumes are accelerating, you should write a little program to look at the sizes of your staging files and Analysis Services databases. Forecast next month's disk requirements based on the recent trend. You could write this program as a Script Task from within Integration Services, and schedule it using SQL Agent. You could go so far as to automatically allocate more disk space for the RDBMS, staging area, or Analysis Services. But do the basics at least: You should be embarrassed if you actually run out of disk space on your production system.

Service and Availability Management

The DW/BI team is responsible for ensuring that the system, including data, reports, and other applications, is available to end users. The level of availability required, measured as the amount of acceptable down time, depends on the business impact of the system's unavailability. You should work with the business users to develop a service level agreement (SLA), and build a plan for meeting that specified service level.

When you develop your availability plan, consider the components of the DW/BI system within the context of your entire IT infrastructure. Let's hope your IT team already has plans and procedures for managing hardware, software, software installation media and product keys, and usernames and passwords — all necessary for rebuilding or restoring a system as quickly as possible. Assess the following issues:

- Do any parts of the DW/BI system need continuous, 24-hour-a-day query access? Analysis Services? The relational data warehouse? If so, how do you process new data without compromising availability?

- If continuous query access is not required, how do you ensure that processing fits within the nightly processing window?

- How do you handle situations that require an entire Analysis Services cube to be reprocessed? As discussed in Chapter 8, this can happen if an attribute declared to be unchanging does in fact change, among other reasons.

- How do you recover from a system failure during Integration Services processing? How do you restart a process mid-stream?

- How is the DW/BI system protected against failure of one or more components on the server(s)?

- How is the DW/BI system and data protected against failure within the enterprise, like source system outages, or serious problems with the Active Directory servers?

Develop a plan for addressing these issues to achieve the necessary availability. Test each element of the plan. A well-trained staff that is prepared to handle any contingency is an essential part of any disaster recovery plan.

Your availability plan must explicitly state how you'll detect a problem with a service. Maybe you want to wait for the VP of Marketing to call, but you probably want to be a bit more proactive.

Your Windows system administrators should already have procedures in place for identifying service outages. These procedures probably use System Monitor, Windows Events, or both. Use those same techniques to identify whether the components of your DW/BI system are currently available. If your organization doesn't already use Service Center Operations Manager, you should consider purchasing it or a third-party operations manager like Tivoli. Any operations management product will be looking at standard Windows logs like System Monitor and Windows Events, and SQL Server Profiler.

The SLA should be explicit about the availability that's required for each component of the DW/BI system. For Analysis Services, it's particularly important to distinguish between the SLA for unavailability and the SLA for query performance. In many cases, Analysis Services incremental processing can occur in the background, with user access to the cubes undisturbed. During this period, however, query performance may degrade significantly. You need to help your business users understand these tradeoffs, so they can help make the case for a different architecture if needed to meet their availability and performance requirements.

The same issues of availability versus query performance are relevant for the relational data warehouse. Many organizations simply close access to the DW/BI system during ETL processing. Others, with higher availability requirements, will perform the bulk of processing in the background or on a remote server. User query performance on the relational data warehouse usually suffers during ETL processing on the same server, perhaps intolerably so. A careful consideration of these issues, and good communication with the users, will help you design a cost-effective architecture that meets your requirements.

Performance Tuning the DW/BI System

The system operations plan should include strategies for periodic performance tuning of all system components. The performance monitoring that we described earlier in the chapter provides the base information you'll need to determine how to improve system performance. If performance is degrading, you need to identify which operations are causing the problem, and whether the primary bottleneck is in memory, disk, or processing power. All the BI components love memory, so it's a good bet to check memory usage first.

The best way to solve resource contention may be to distribute your DW/BI system across multiple servers. A lot of DW/BI teams will try to build an all-in-one system, with the four major BI components (relational database, Integration Services, Analysis Services, and Reporting Services) on a single server. As we discussed in Chapter 4, it's often sensible to distribute across multiple servers. There's no hard and fast rule about which components to group together, although most often we see the relational database and Integration Services on the same box.

Look to see if your system is memory-bound. Although there are circumstances where you can redesign your DW/BI system components to use less memory, it's usually far cheaper simply to buy more memory. It feels intellectually lazy to recommend a hardware upgrade to solve performance problems, but if you've done a good job on your system design it's often the easiest — if not the only — degree of freedom.

The query performance of your relational data warehouse database may be improved by adding or changing:

- Fact table partitioning
- Indexes and indexed views
- Filtered indexes, especially for the common scenario where many queries are limited to the most recent data (filter on date)
- Statistics, including filtered statistics. Everyone knows that statistics are associated with each index you build. But you can also create standalone statistics, which at times can greatly assist the query optimizer in determining the correct query plan. Statistics aren't free to build, but they are much cheaper to build and store than the corresponding index.

For Analysis Services, your two big weapons for improving query performance are:

- Adding or increasing partitioning. Especially helpful is to partition by multiple dimensions.
- Adding or changing your aggregation design. Use the usage based aggregation wizard.

REFERENCE There is a very nice performance guide available for download from http://download.microsoft.com, called "SQL Server 2008 White Paper: Analysis Services Performance Guide." Though written for Analysis Services 2008, it remains relevant for 2008 R2.

No matter what you're doing to improve performance, it's really important to follow good change management and tuning techniques:

- Work on the test system, and script any changes to production.
- Document baseline performance.
- Change one thing at a time.
- Document changes to performance.
- Test all the changes together before moving to production.

Backup and Recovery

No matter what the availability requirements are on your system, you need a backup and recovery plan. This seems like an intuitively obvious statement, but we've seen any number of DW/BI systems that purported to be in production, but which had no backup plan.

It's as important to have a recovery plan as it is to have a backup plan. And it's equally important to test these procedures. When the inevitable emergency happens, you want to be ready, practiced, and calm. Your test system is an ideal platform for testing these procedures. If you haven't fully tested your recovery procedures, you're lying to yourself and your management that you have a real backup and recovery plan.

In the DW/BI world, you can experience the same kinds of emergencies as transaction systems, from server outages and disk failures to earthquakes and floods. Plan for your daily or monthly load cycle to break down occasionally. Develop your ETL system so that failure is fairly unlikely. But let's face it: The DW/BI system is at the end of a long train of data flows over which you have no control. Only a foolish manager would neglect to plan for backing out a bad load. The auditing system described in Chapter 7 lays the foundation for identifying the rows that were changed during a specific load process.

Relational Databases

The relational databases are usually the most vital sets of information to back up regularly. Ideally, back up the following databases after each load:

- Relational data warehouse databases
- Staging databases and files
- Metadata databases
- ReportServer

Other databases should be backed up on a regular schedule, though perhaps not daily. These include:

- Msdb, which contains SQL Agent job definitions and any SSIS packages that are stored in SQL Server.
- Logging databases, including MDW and the Reporting Services logging database.

Your backup and recovery strategies are intertwined with each database's recovery model. The Simple recovery model lets you restore only to the point of a backup. The transaction log is not backed up. This works fine for many relational data warehouses, where data flows in nightly, weekly, or monthly. The Simple recovery model is appropriately named; it's faster and simpler to manage than the Full recovery model. Nonetheless, as your DW/BI system moves closer to real time, the Full recovery model becomes increasingly appropriate.

REFERENCE See the Books Online topics "Overview of the Recovery Models," "Restore and Recovery Overview," and "Selecting a Recovery Model" for more information.

Most systems use the standard SQL Server backup facilities for relational backup and recovery. The relational data warehouse database is usually quite large, and so it's often challenging to run a backup at the end of each (nightly) load cycle. There are several alternatives:

- Store the database on a Storage Area Network (SAN), and use the SAN software to perform the backup. The SAN backup techniques are high performance, and this approach has been a common practice for very large databases with SQL Server 2000.
- Partition the large fact tables, and set aged partitions to be read-only. Perform occasional full backups, but rely primarily on a strategy of filegroup and partial differential backups. Under the Simple recovery model, partial backups back up the primary filegroup and all the read-write filegroups. Read-only partitions are backed up when they're filled and converted to read-only status. The innovation of read-only partitions greatly improves your ability to quickly back up the changed portions of the relational data warehouse. However, if you have late-arriving fact data, you'll need to partition by load date in order to take greatest advantage of fast partition table backups. If instead you are partitioning a very large fact table by transaction date and have late-arriving fact data, you'll need to plan for SAN backups.

REFERENCE See the Books Online topics "Partial Backups" and "Differential Partial Backups" for more details.

The logging database is written to constantly. Some DW/BI teams think the logging data is vitally important, and implement a very strong backup strategy. Other teams are sanguine about the notion of losing a week's worth of logging data, and manage the database far more loosely. Obviously, if your logging data contains usage data necessary for regulatory compliance, you need to develop a serious backup and recovery strategy. Use Full recovery mode and a backup strategy appropriate for a transaction database. Books Online, and any number of SQL Server books, are filled with information about backup strategies for transaction databases.

Approaches differ on backup and recovery strategies for the staging databases. Many DW/BI teams think of the data in the staging tables as ephemeral, and back up only the table CREATE scripts. On the other hand, most staging databases contain only data for the most recent loads — for example, the last seven days — so a full database backup is really fast.

You may have built a simple application for business users to manipulate custom hierarchies or other attributes of a dimension. Such an application is a transaction system, however small scale. Typically you want the application to write directly to a different database than the data warehouse, one with Full recovery mode and log backups. Similarly, the metadata database should also be treated more like a transactional database than the large data warehouse database.

The msdb system database may include your Integration Services packages. It will certainly include any SQL Agent job definitions and schedules, and other information used by Management Studio, including information about which databases were backed up. For that reason, the msdb database should always be backed up immediately after any other backup operation. Use Full recovery mode for msdb.

Integration Services

The most important information to back up for Integration Services is the package definitions themselves. Packages can be stored in SQL Server, in the file system, or in a managed mode in the file system called the Package Store.

If the package definitions are stored in SQL Server, they're located in the msdb system database, which as we've already discussed should be backed up religiously.

If the packages are stored in the file system or the Package Store, simply use a file system backup utility like Windows Backup to back up the package definitions, configuration files, and associated information. Of course, package definitions should be under source control, and that source control database should be backed up too.

As we discussed in Chapter 7, you may be staging or storing data in the file system. Use Windows Backup or another copy utility to back up staged data.

This is especially vital if you're relying on re-running staged extracts to bring your data warehouse database up-to-date.

Analysis Services

Throughout this book we've encouraged you to think of the Analysis Services database as ephemeral — a database that may need to be fully reprocessed at some point. That's necessary because Analysis Services doesn't support the full level of data manageability, notably updates and deletes, as the relational database. The great benefits provided by Analysis Services in query performance, complex security, a calculation engine, and easy user navigation come at a cost. You need a plan for being able to fully reprocess the dimensional database; never throw away the relational data.

You absolutely must back up the definition of the Analysis Services database: the information that enables you to fully process the database. You might think that, because you have the database definition on your development server and checked into source control, you're safe. You could always re-deploy and re-process the Analysis Services database. That's largely true, but you've probably modified aggregation design and partition strategy on the production database; these changes are not reflected in the version on the development server.

You won't find a formal command or utility for backing up the database's definition. The most straightforward approach is to generate a complete CREATE script for the database, and back up that script.

The recommended method for backing up the Analysis Services database is to use the Analysis Services backup and restore facility in Management Studio. The greatest drawback of Analysis Services backup is that it works only at the database level. On the plus side, you can launch the Backup and Restore wizards from Management Studio. From within the wizard, you can script the commands for automated operations. Schedule the backup from SQL Agent or launch it from an Integration Services package.

The Analysis Services Backup facility backs up all metadata, but only data that's stored in MOLAP format. This includes all data and aggregations for MOLAP partitions, and aggregations only for HOLAP partitions. Data stored in the relational data warehouse should be backed up using relational backup techniques. Plan for your Analysis Services backups to take about as much space as the database itself. Analysis Services databases are stored so efficiently that we see very little additional compression upon backup.

If your Analysis Services database is small, in the tens of gigabytes, the simplest approach is to perform a full backup every load cycle, or whenever you make a metadata change. No matter how efficient the backup utility might be, if your Analysis Services database is multiple terabytes, it might not be practical to perform daily full backups.

> **NOTE** If you have a Storage Area Network (SAN), frequent full backups are more practical, with very limited downtime and minimal pressure on server resources. You can circumvent the backup utility and create a static copy of the files directly:
>
> - Create a mirror set and wait for it to fully synchronize.
> - Stop Analysis Services; break the mirror; restart Analysis Services.
> - Mount the mirrored image as a separate drive and perform a file level backup of the entire data folder (`Program Files\Microsoft SQL Server\MSSQL\OLAP\Data`).

Our recommended practice is to back up the database whenever the metadata changes. Metadata changes include redesigning aggregations, adding a partition, or changing security groups and permissions. If you just can't do a full backup every time the metadata changes, you *must* capture the complete database definition scripts.

Reporting Services

All of your Reporting Services report definitions and schedules are in the ReportServer database. This database should use Full recovery mode, and be backed up like any transactional database.

Recovery

It is as important to document and test your recovery plan as it is to perform backups. During an emergency is not the time to test out your recovery procedures. We could regale you with sad tales of daily backups to corrupt media that were never tested until too late. Despite the fact that this is kindergarten-level system administration, we are past being astonished at finding people who don't know if their recovery procedures will work.

> **NOTE** We've said it several times already, but once more: Backup without verification is meaningless and a waste of time. You're better off not even doing the backup, and not kidding yourself that you're protected. Good intentions don't count.
>
> Verification doesn't mean checking the checkbox in the utility, which verifies the physical media. That's a good thing to do; it's just not what we're talking about. We're talking about testing the full recovery process, including the BI applications, to make sure everything really works. And it's not just that the scripts work. You need to confirm, by testing, that your staff knows what steps to take to successfully restore the system.

Executing the ETL Packages

During development, you design and execute Integration Services packages within BI Development Studio (BIDS). In the development environment, you can set breakpoints, examine variables' values and status, watch the movement of data through a data flow task, and explore the data with data viewers. All of these tools are valuable during development, but are of no interest in production. You want the ETL system to execute, upon a schedule, with no human intervention.

Integration Services packages are easy to schedule. SQL Server ships the tools you need: `dtexec` and SQL Server Agent. You should already be familiar with dtexec and its friend `dtexecui`, from the process of testing the Integration Services packages. `Dtexec` and `dtexecui` execute a package from the command line. They are basically the same, except that dtexecui brings up a user interface that helps you construct the command by choosing which package to run and picking various options like logging levels and connection information.

Once you've set up the package execution options, you can create a SQL Agent job to run the package, and then schedule that job. SQL Agent is a standard feature of the SQL Server database.

REFERENCE The `dtexec` utility is well documented in the Books Online topics "dtexec Utility" and "How to: Run a Package Using the DTExec Utility."

Once you've set up your SQL Agent job step, schedule it to run on the appropriate schedule. In most cases, you'll define one or a small number of SQL Agent jobs for your ETL system. Each job calls a master Integration Services package, which in turn calls subpackages in the correct order. Build logic flow and dependencies into the master package, and use SQL Agent only to kick off the main job.

Some organizations have standardized on enterprise-wide job management software like Autosys. SQL Agent is nothing special; if your organization uses such software, by all means conform to the corporate standard. The job management software simply calls `dtexec` on the computer running Integration Services.

Summary

Most of us find it more fun to think about designing and developing, than operating and maintaining. But there's no point in undertaking the design activities if you're not confident your system can operate smoothly, efficiently, and with good performance. And it's important to think about these issues early, during the design and development phases of the system. Good operating procedures are cooked into the system, not tacked on at the end.

This chapter talked about two kinds of operational procedures: front-room operations and back-room operations. Front-room operations, from maintaining the BI portal to extending BI applications and educating users, requires a continuing commitment to meeting the needs of the business. It requires a significant number of ongoing staff, usually as many, if not more, as were involved with the initial development of the DW/BI system.

Most of the chapter was devoted to a discussion of back-room operations. We described the tools available to easily monitor your system and usage. We introduced some of the issues you will need to consider in order to meet availability and performance SLAs. And we discussed the most important factors to consider when tuning your DW/BI system for excellent performance.

The last section of this chapter discussed issues around backing up and restoring your databases and other components of your system. We'll take one last opportunity to remind you to take backup and recovery seriously, or don't do it at all.

CHAPTER 18

Present Imperatives and Future Outlook

The endless loop.

This final chapter is a mix of topics. We begin with a brief guide to growing your DW/BI system after you have completed your first Lifecycle iteration. Next, we review the overall Lifecycle process, including some of the most common problems of each phase. Finally, we conclude with some of our likes and dislikes of the Microsoft DW/BI toolset and a brief wish list of how we hope to see the Microsoft BI product strategy and toolset evolve over the next few years.

Growing the DW/BI System

The DW/BI system is not a single one-time project; it is an ongoing, never-ending program. Once you complete an iteration of the Lifecycle, it's time to go back and do it again with the next top priority set of data on the bus matrix. If you've done the first pass right, you will have some happy users and evidence that you have provided real business value. It's always a good idea to verify the opportunity priority list with senior management before you start in on the next row of the bus matrix. It has probably been six to nine months or more, especially if this was your first round, and priorities may have changed.

Checking in again helps ensure you're working on the most valuable data set, and it also reminds the business folks how focused you are on business value. They will be impressed!

At the same time you are focused on building the second and subsequent iterations, you need to be outwardly focused on the connections between the data warehouse and the rest of the organization. *Marketing* is probably the wrong term to use for this task because marketing has a bad reputation with most technical folks; although not as bad as its evil twin, sales. (Just kidding — some of our best friends are in sales.) It may be more appealing to view the activities in this section as educational efforts. But call it what you will — in this "what have you done for me lately" world, you must actively and constantly market the BI system.

From an educational perspective, your goal is to make sure everyone knows what they need to know about the BI system. Management needs to know how their investment is going. Specifically, they need to know how it is being used to generate value for the organization. It also helps them to see how it is being used in different parts of the company. Analysts and other knowledge workers need to know how they can use the DW/BI system more effectively and why it's important to them. The IT organization needs to know what's going on with the DW/BI system. You need close working relationships with the source system managers on the input side of the data warehouse, and with other information-driven systems on the output side of the DW/BI system.

Fortunately, you have some quantitative and qualitative tools to help educate all these groups. On the quantitative side, you can turn to your report and query usage monitoring systems. You should be able to generate some reports from these systems that show how DW/BI system usage is growing over time, in terms of the number of users you support, the number of departments they come from, and the number of queries they generate on a daily basis.

Qualitative measures are a bit harder to come by. You need to go out and talk to your users to find out what kinds of analyses they've done and what impact it has had on the organization. We like to describe impact in specific terms, such as a dollar increase in revenue, or dollars of expense reduction.

At the risk of sounding like a scratched CD, your long-term success will largely be determined by how well you identify specific, high-value business opportunities and then deliver them.

RESOURCES For additional guidance on marketing your DW/BI system, search the KimballGroup.com website for the following: "Educate management."

Lifecycle Review with Common Problems

We can't resist showing you the Kimball Lifecycle drawing one last time. This time, we've grouped the Lifecycle task boxes into phases that are slightly different from the major sections of the book. These phases are:

- Requirements, realities, architecture, and design
- Setting up the hardware and software, and developing the databases
- Developing the BI applications and portal environment
- Deploying and managing the DW/BI system

These phases (see Figure 18-1) are essentially linear, with each phase building on the previous one. As we review each phase, we'll list the most common errors made by DW/BI teams.

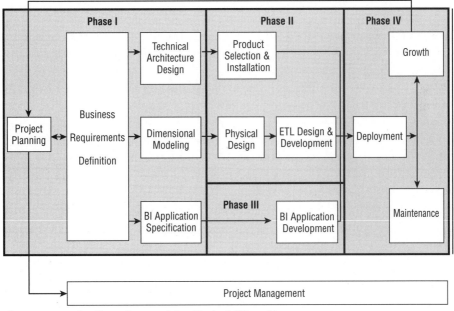

Figure 18-1: The four phases of the Kimball Lifecycle

Phase I — Requirements, Realities, Plans, and Designs

Phase I involves understanding and prioritizing the business requirements, creating the system architecture, and designing the business process dimensional model needed to meet the top-priority requirements. The BI applications specification step is also part of this design phase, although we didn't actually describe it until Chapter 10.

The biggest problem we see in the projects we get called into is that the DW/BI team essentially skipped Phase I. Other than doing some project planning around system development tasks, they dove right into developing the databases. This haste leads to unnecessary pain and suffering and is often fatal to the project. A good way to tell if you're headed in the wrong direction is that the technology involved in Phase I should be limited to a project management tool, a word processor, a presentation tool, a modeling tool, and a spreadsheet. If you're installing server machines or SQL Server at this point, you're getting ahead of yourself. The only reason to do this is if you need to work through the tutorials.

After skipping the requirements step, the next most common problems in Phase I are failing to secure business sponsorship, and failing to take responsibility for the full solution, including the BI applications and portal. We hope that a business sponsor has been a member of your team from the very beginning. Ideally this sponsor should be a sophisticated observer of the development process along with you and should appreciate the need to do midcourse corrections and frequent recalibrations of how well the system addresses critical business issues.

Other oversights that will raise their ugly heads later, during the ETL development task, are the failure to identify and investigate data quality issues, and the related failure to set up a data governance program to work with the source system organizations and deal with any problems early on.

Finally, a problem that arises when implementing the second and subsequent data sources in the DW/BI system is the need to provide integration, especially in the form of conformed dimensions.

Phase II — Developing the Databases

Phase II is the hard, systems-oriented work of designing and developing the ETL systems, the DW/BI relational databases, and the Analysis Services databases. This is the comfort zone for most DW/BI teams. It's where you wrestle with the tough technical issues, such as how to handle changes in various attributes, or how to re-create historical facts. Every decision, every design tradeoff in Phase II, must weigh the development effort against the business requirements identified in Phase I. Without those requirements, the design decisions are based on technical expediency. Statements like "The eight-character Product description is fine — it's always worked in the source system and it will save a lot of space," and "We'll save a lot of time if we include only the base numbers; the users can create any calculations they like on the fly" are warning flags that your developers are making decisions that will undermine the ultimate acceptance and success of the system. These statements are much harder to make when the primary goal of the DW/BI team is to meet a set of clearly defined user requirements.

The most common problem we see in Phase II involves underestimating the effort required to extract, clean, transform, and load the required data. This is typically the result of not identifying a high priority business opportunity that narrowly bounds the Lifecycle iteration. Another common cause is doing a poor job of digging into the dimensional model design, and not uncovering data quality problems early on. If your requirements and design phase is light, the development phase will always be worse than it initially appeared.

It's also not unusual for a DW/BI team to think of Phase II as the complete project. These teams are doomed to fail because they don't do the upfront planning and design work in Phase I, or provide the user access tools in Phase III. Although Phase II is where the hard technical challenges are met and overcome, these technical challenges are seldom the point of failure. Missing the underlying business requirements, and therefore not delivering real value to the organization, is the root cause of almost every DW/BI system failure.

Phase III — Developing the BI Applications and Portal Environment

Building the BI applications is the fun part of the Lifecycle (well, for some of us, it's all fun). You get to play with the data, building reports and other applications that you can show to the business users and get immediate feedback on. The technology is pretty easy and straightforward — although not without its frustrations — and the development process usually goes quite swiftly *if* you did a good job in Phase I. Even if you need to develop complex analytic applications, perhaps including data mining technology, this is generally easier and more fun than slogging through the mountains of bad data that you uncover when building the ETL system.

It's also common for a team to omit the BI applications from its project. This is a bad idea. First of all, why cut out the fun and rewarding piece of the project? Second and most important, if you don't pave the path to the door of the data warehouse, only a few hardy souls will make the trek. The other risk is to start designing the BI applications too late, or without involving the business users. Getting early user input on the BI applications will help you validate your design and allow you to make relatively minor adjustments to the DW/BI system that can really please the business users.

Phase IV — Deploying and Managing the DW/BI System

The efforts in Phase IV revolve around the testing, training, and support needed to reach an all-systems-are-go state. This involves making sure the system works as promised, the data is correct, the users are properly trained and prepared, the system is documented, the standard reports are working and are correct, support is available, and deployment and maintenance procedures and scripts are in place and tested.

The biggest problem in Phase IV comes when the team views its primary goal as delivering technology rather than a solution. In this case, most of the user-oriented work in Phase IV is seen as "not our job" or unnecessary. The team defines success as making the database available. But if the goal is to meet the business requirements, all of the pieces in Phase IV are crucial links in the chain. Omit any piece and the chain will break. The team must view success as delivering real, measurable, substantial business value.

Another common problem in Phase IV is associated with underestimating the effort required to fully test and maintain the DW/BI system, and to start the planning for ongoing operations too late in the development cycle. For example, your strategy for backing up each day's extract is inextricably linked to the ETL system. If you don't think about this issue until the system is developed and ready for deployment, your maintenance plan may be awkward or weak.

One of the challenges in Phase IV is correctly estimating the effort required to build out a full solution, including the documentation, support, and delivery portal. Quality-assuring the data in the DW/BI system is often another issue, and it takes a lot of time to do right. If you haven't already gotten the business users involved with this data governance process, you need to do it now. They need to have full confidence in the data, and what better way than to have helped with the testing? Besides, sometimes deep business knowledge is needed to determine what the business rules should be, and whether the data truly is accurate.

Iteration and Growth

Extending the DW/BI system is about adding new business process dimensional models to the databases, adding new users, and adding new BI applications. In short, it's about going back through the Lifecycle again and again, incrementally filling in the bus matrix to build a solid, robust enterprise information infrastructure. One or more of these new business process dimensional models may require data that's near real-time. As we discussed in Chapter 9, including real-time data in the DW/BI system presents some interesting technical and design challenges.

The two main challenges in growing the DW/BI system present an interesting paradox. Often, the success of the first round leads to too much demand and the DW/BI team must carefully balance these demands and maintain an achievable scope based on prioritized business requirements. This may also involve securing additional resources and revisiting priorities with senior management.

At the same time, the DW/BI team must begin an ongoing education program to make sure the organization understands and takes advantage of the incredible asset that is the DW/BI system. In the age of what have you done for me lately, the DW/BI team needs to have a detailed, compelling, ongoing answer.

What We Like in the Microsoft BI Toolset

The appeal of a single source technology provider, like Microsoft with SQL Server, is that it makes the process of building a DW/BI system easier in several ways. First, many elements of the architecture are predefined. The major technology issues you need to tackle involve data sizing, server configurations, and performance, rather than which products to buy and whether they work well together. Some organizations may need to develop or buy functionality to meet specific business requirements, such as large-scale consumer name and address matching. Many organizations will also want to add one or more third-party, user-oriented query and reporting tools to the mix.

The Microsoft toolset includes credible versions of all the tools you need to build and deliver a solid, viable data warehouse and business intelligence system. Some components of the SQL Server architecture are more than credible: Analysis Services, for example, is one of the top OLAP engines available.

Many of the tools are designed specifically to support dimensional data warehouses. For example, Integration Services has the Slowly Changing Dimension transform, and Analysis Services is built with dimensional constructs from the ground up. Even the relational database offers star join optimization as an Enterprise Edition feature.

The tools are open and programmable. If you want to build a heterogeneous DW/BI solution, you can swap out any component. If you want to build a fully automated DW/BI management system, you can script any operation in practically any programming language you wish.

The overall Microsoft BI toolset includes software beyond SQL Server. This book focuses mostly on SQL Server because it provides the core DW/BI components. But BI functionality is spreading rapidly across the Microsoft product line. At the desktop level, Excel is extremely popular for accessing, manipulating, and presenting data. This popularity continues to grow with each release of Office, and with additional tools such as PowerPivot for Excel. Business users love Excel, and that's where they want their data to end up. Even Reporting Services makes it easy for a business user to save a report to Excel.

Beyond Office, SharePoint has its roots in the web portal space, but is becoming the applications delivery platform for the Microsoft-based enterprise. This adds a new layer of functionality and complexity to the Microsoft BI story.

Future Directions: Room for Improvement

There are organizations dedicated to trying to figure out what Microsoft is going to do next. We have no interest in playing that game, so rather than trying to predict the future, we'll highlight a few of the areas we'd like to see Microsoft improve on, starting with tools and functionality, and ending with direction and strategy.

Query Tools

Excel, despite being the most popular data tool on the market, is not the ideal query and reporting tool. There are several problems, the most troubling of which is that Excel is fundamentally a two-dimensional grid. It's hard for us to imagine how the Excel team will address this issue without creating a whole new product, or breaking the existing (hugely valuable) product. Lucky for us, this isn't our problem.

The existing query interfaces for Excel are imperfect, too. Queries from Excel into the Analysis Services database are limited. The mechanism for specifying a relational query within Excel is archaic. We detested it in the early 1990s when we first saw it, and it hasn't improved since then. PowerPivot's use of the PivotTable construct with the added ability to define calculated fields is a leap forward in terms of creating reports with flexible content in the Excel environment. Unfortunately, it brings with it the need to create a PowerPivot database along with the report.

Report Builder 3.0 is a big step forward in terms of ad hoc query capabilities for the relational engine. It has reasonable display functionality, including mapping, and a crude but manageable interface for defining data sets. It's still a rudimentary query tool in terms of defining more real-world queries and reports. Many relatively simple questions require you to drop out of the GUI and write your own SQL statements; this is what we did 25 years ago. It feels like we should be able to expect a bit more at this point.

We were disappointed with Microsoft's treatment of the ProClarity query tool for Analysis Services. Some components, such as the decomposition tree, have found their way into other tools, but the desktop query tool is dying a slow, painful death. Analysis Services needs a strong desktop query and report definition tool that allows users to build ad hoc queries directly against an Analysis Services database. It needs to offer a decent user interface, good flexibility, and generate well-formed MDX. And, it needs to be part of the core SQL Server toolset. Customers should not have to go buy the equivalent of a steering wheel from a third-party company after they bought the rest of the DW/BI car from Microsoft.

Metadata

Microsoft's SQL Server metadata management story hasn't changed since the first edition of this book came out with SQL Server 2005. The Microsoft toolset is full of metadata, as we discussed in Chapter 15. But the metadata systems don't talk to each other: It's a bunch of metadata islands with a few tenuous bridges thrown across between them. At the time of this writing, it's your job to build or buy a coherent metadata bridge.

The lack of integrated metadata hasn't prevented Microsoft's past customers from successfully implementing a DW/BI system — or else they'd have demanded a solution in this version of the toolset. Indeed, through the years we've seen very few good metadata implementations on any platform. But because Microsoft owns the entire toolset, they should find it easier to provide an innovative, interesting, and valuable solution for managing and integrating metadata than is possible with a heterogeneous architecture. We hope they decide to leverage this opportunity soon. We hear the next release is going to be great.

Relational Database Engine

The relational database engine is primarily designed to support a transaction load. We can't comment on its advantages and disadvantages in that role. From a DW/BI point of view, we find several things puzzling or frustrating.

Ad hoc query optimization is inconsistent. Mostly, the query optimizer does a good job with ad hoc queries against a dimensional model, and the relational database engine performs extremely well. But its performance is variable. For some queries, the optimizer takes a path that is clearly suboptimal. And the nature of ad hoc queries makes adding optimizer hints a nonviable solution. There are times, for example, when you will get better performance by directly constraining the date field in the fact table rather than constraining the date dimension. The Analysis Services query optimizer does a much more consistent job of resolving dimensional queries, even if you strip away its advantage of pre-computed aggregations. Why can't the relational database engine perform at the same level?

We're thrilled to have true partitioning in the relational engine, so we don't want to seem like complainers, but managing relational partitions is a headache, especially when you have a rolling set of partitions to maintain over time. In

Chapter 5 we walked through the periodic process of managing partitions. All the tools are there, but it should be an order of magnitude easier to manage partitions than it is.

Analysis Services

Analysis Services can be a bit overwhelming. The wizards are helpful, but they still leave you with a lot of hand work to do in an environment that's necessarily complex. We certainly wouldn't expect any but the most intrepid power users to succeed at developing their own cubes from scratch. Granted, Analysis Services is targeted not at this market but at the enterprise DW/BI system. PowerPivot is an implicit acknowledgement of this cube building complexity. PowerPivot does allow analysts to throw together a cube in order to explore a specific analytic problem, but those cubes are too simple to capture the data complexities found in most organizations. Plus, the resulting PowerPivot cubes are not standard Analysis Services cubes, and cannot be directly queried from across the DW/BI environment except in a crude way through SharePoint.

The other big flaw we see in Analysis Services is its inability to respond to SQL queries. It can handle only the very simplest SQL — syntax too simple to be useful. Although MDX is superior to SQL for analytics, people with expertise and investment in SQL and SQL-based tools are reluctant to move to Analysis Services. It seems unrealistic to expect the world to move to MDX-based tools in order to take advantage of even the most basic Analysis Services functionality.

Master Data Services

Master Data Services, described in Chapter 6, is an interesting addition to the SQL Server toolset. Its focus and use cases are a bit fuzzy in SQL Server 2008 R2, which is its first release. Is it a grown-up master data management toolset, designed to integrate and inter-operate with your transaction systems? Or is it a tool to help you build a system to help your data stewards implement good data governance procedures? Currently, the tool appears to be trying to meet both needs, without complete success.

The master data management scenario seems to get most of the focus of the documentation and white papers. But so much is missing from the documentation that it's hard to imagine anyone attempting to use the tool in that way without significant participation from Microsoft.

The data governance tack is a much simpler problem, and it seems to be well addressed by the structure and features of MDS. Of course, the user interface in this first version is awkward, but we can be reasonably confident that Microsoft knows how to fix that problem. The documentation is probably the greatest barrier to the success of MDS. It really is very difficult for someone to walk up to the tool and figure out what to do with it.

Integration

The greatest problem with the Microsoft BI toolset, underlying the criticisms we've already discussed, is *integration* — or, more accurately, the lack of integration. The various components of even the SQL Server BI tools — the relational database, Analysis Services, Integration Services, and Reporting Services — are clearly built by different groups. And other Microsoft technologies outside that core set, like Office and SharePoint, appear to be developed by different companies. This results in the same class of functionality being developed with different paradigms and interfaces to solve the same problem in multiple places. The various versions of a query interface are a good example of this. The six or more different ways you can define a data model in SQL Studio, Visual Studio, Analysis Services, Report Builder, Visio, Access, and PowerPivot are another good example.

We understand why this situation occurs; it is essentially a political and organizational problem. However, we believe it is past time for a more holistic view of business intelligence at Microsoft. We're not holding our breath on its resolution.

Customer Focus

Microsoft has brought DW/BI to the small to medium sized businesses that have long been its primary customer base. In order to grow, Microsoft has worked to gain credibility with larger organizations by focusing on key features that are important to scale up the system and play with the big players. Microsoft is caught between a rock and a hard place on this issue. This fundamental shift in the nature of the product is making it more complex, and more expensive. This may be acceptable to the major corporations, but it's tough for the small to medium sized organizations out there. Deciding how to allocate features and limitations to editions, and how to price those editions, must be a difficult task. We encourage Microsoft to make sure it does not squeeze out the smaller organizations that may need these capabilities, but cannot afford enterprise edition prices. After all, it's these organizations that helped make Microsoft successful.

Conclusion

There you have it. We've done our best to teach you how to build a *successful* business intelligence system and its underlying data warehouse using the Microsoft SQL Server product set. Now it's up to you to get out there and do the work of actually making it happen.

As fun as it is to criticize Microsoft, its SQL Server DW/BI toolset contains the features necessary to build a complete DW/BI system. The tools are relatively easy to use, and will scale from small operations like the hypothetical Adventure Works Cycles to large enterprises with significant data volumes. The smaller implementations can rely heavily on wizards, and not worry too much about all the technical details. Large systems may use the wizards to get started, but will need to dig far deeper into the products.

Microsoft is delivering the technology you need, but you are the ones who will put that technology to use. If you can maintain your focus on the needs of the business users and on adding business value, you should be able to build a great DW/BI system.

Good luck!

Index